The Blackwell Guide to the
Philosophy of Language

Blackwell Philosophy Guides

Series Editor: Steven M. Cahn, City University of New York Graduate School

Written by an international assembly of distinguished philosophers, the *Blackwell Philosophy Guides* create a groundbreaking student resource - a complete critical survey of the central themes and issues of philosophy today. Focusing and advancing key arguments throughout, each essay incorporates essential background material serving to clarify the history and logic of the relevant topic. Accordingly, these volumes will be a valuable resource for a broad range of students and readers, including professional philosophers.

The Blackwell Guide to the
Philosophy of
Language

Edited by

Michael Devitt and Richard Hanley

Blackwell
Publishing

2006

© 2006 by Blackwell Publishing Ltd

BLACKWELL PUBLISHING
350 Main Street, Malden, MA 02148-5020, USA
9600 Garsington Road, Oxford OX4 2DQ, UK
550 Swanston Street, Carlton, Victoria 3053, Australia

The right of Michael Devitt and Richard Hanley to be identified as the Authors of the
Editorial Material in this Work has been asserted in accordance with the
UK Copyright, Designs, and Patents Act 1988.

First published 2006 by Blackwell Publishing Ltd

1   2006

Library of Congress Cataloging-in-Publication Data

The Blackwell guide to the philosophy of language /
edited by Michael Devitt and Richard Hanley.
p.cm.—(Blackwell philosophy guides ; 19)
Includes bibliographical references and index.
ISBN-13: 978-0-631-23141-7 (hardback : alk.paper)
ISBN-10: 0-631-23141-2 (hardback : alk.paper)
ISBN-13: 978-0-631-23142-4 (pbk. : alk. paper)
ISBN-10: 0-631-23142-0 (pbk. : alk.paper)
1. Language and languages—Philosophy. I. Devitt, Michael,
1938– II. Hanley, Richard. III. Series.
P107.B582006
401—dc22
2005028555

A catalogue record for this title is available from the British Library.

Set in 10/13 Galliard
by SPI Publisher Services, Pondicherry, India
Printed and bound in the United Kingdom
by TJ International Ltd, Padstow, Cornwall

The publisher's policy is to use permanent paper from mills that operate a sustainable forestry
policy, and which has been manufactured from pulp processed using acid-free and elementary
chlorine-free practices. Furthermore, the publisher ensures that the text paper and cover board
used have met acceptable environmental accreditation standards.

For further information on
Blackwell Publishing, visit our website:
www.blackwellpublishing.com

Contents

Contents

Contents

Contributors

Kent Bach is Professor of Philosophy at San Francisco State University.

Simon Blackburn is Professor of Philosophy at the University of Cambridge.

Max Cresswell is Professor of Philosophy at the University of Auckland and Texas A&M University.

Martin Davies is Professor of Philosophy in the Research School of Social Sciences, Australian National University.

Jerry Fodor is State of New Jersey Professor of Philosophy at Rutgers University.

James Higginbotham is Linda Hilf Chair in Philosophy, and Professor of Philosophy and Linguistics, at the University of Southern California.

Paul Horwich is Professor of Philosophy at New York University.

Frank Jackson is Distinguished Professor of Philosophy and Director, Research School of Social Sciences, the Australian National University.

Ernie Lepore is Professor of Philosophy and Director of the Center for Cognitive Science at Rutgers University.

Brian Loar is Professor of Philosophy at Rutgers University.

Peter Ludlow is Professor of Philosophy and of Linguistics at the University of Michigan.

William G. Lycan is William Rand Kenan, Jr. Professor of Philosophy at the University of North Carolina.

Vann McGee is Professor of Philosophy at the Massachusetts Institute of Technology.

Alexander Miller is Professor of Philosophy at the University of Birmingham.

Stephen Neale is Professor of Philosophy at Rutgers University.

Karen Neander is Professor of Philosophy at the University of California, Davis.

John Perry is Henry Waldgrave Stuart Professor of Philosophy at Stanford University.

Mark Richard is Professor of Philosophy at Tufts University.

Stephen Schiffer is Professor of Philosophy at New York University.

Stephen P. Schwartz is Professor of Philosophy and Religion at Ithaca College.

Josef Stern is Professor of philosophy and of Jewish studies at the University of Chicago.

Acknowledgments

Editorial assistance was provided by Sophia Bishop, James Dow, and Scott Jones. Thanks to Timothy Czech for compiling the index. Richard Hanley's work on this volume was supported in part by the University of Delaware General Research Fund. Thanks also to Jeff Dean, Danielle Descoteaux, Graeme Leonard, and Nirit Simon.

Introduction

Michael Devitt and Richard Hanley

Foundational Issues

The philosophy of language is both fascinating and difficult. One reason for this is that hardly any issue in this area is uncontroversial. Controversy begins with some foundational and methodological questions. Consider, for example, this very basic question: What are the tasks of the philosophy of language? One obvious task is: the study of linguistic *meanings*. But this immediately raises two questions.

First, what are these "meanings"? Linguistic expressions have the function of communicating messages, conveying information about the world. Clearly, the meanings of expressions play a crucial role here. Yet, as Martin Davies notes in chapter 1, we cannot simply identify meanings with messages because the one sentence can be used to communicate different messages on different occasions; it can imply things that it does not literally say. We need to distinguish its literal meaning, studied by *semantics*, from other properties it may have that are studied by *pragmatics*. But there is much controversy about where and how to draw the line between semantics and pragmatics; see discussion in chapter 8.

Second, what sort of "study" do we have in mind? Is semantics empirical or is it a priori? Is it a science? In what way is it philosophical? These questions dominate Davies' discussion. Someone who supposes, as many do, that philosophy is entirely a priori, will think that semantic theorizing can go on independent of any science. This antireductionist view is what Davies nicely calls "philosophical isolationism." At the other extreme, naturalistically inclined philosophers will think that semantics reduces to empirical cognitive science. Davies calls this "cognitive scientism." He would like to find an intermediate position, as most philosophers probably would. But finding it is difficult. Paul Horwich discusses reductionism and anti-reductionism in chapter 2.

There is a related issue. The dominant method in semantics is to consult "intuitions" about what an expression means, refers to, and so on, intuitions that are usually elicited in "thought experiments." What are we to make of this practice? The isolationist will think of this as the characteristic method of "armchair philosophy," yielding intuitions based on a priori knowledge of concepts. And she is likely to think that it is *the* task of semantics to account for these intuitions. The naturalist must see the intuitions as having the same empirical status that intuitions generally have in science and as serving at best as fallible evidence for a semantic theory.

Other foundational issues press in. What is the relation of language to *thought* (discussed in detail in chapter 4)? The folk idea that "language expresses thought" leads to the view, developed by Paul Grice (1989), that thought is explanatorily prior to language. Another influential view, developed by Donald Davidson (1984), is that thought and language are interdependent with the result that their explanations proceed together. In contrast to both these views, Michael Dummett (1993) gives priority to language. This approach is, as Davies remarks, "apt to sound rather behaviouristic." Even Davidson's approach starts from the behavioristic assumption that "meaning is entirely determined by observable behavior, even readily observable behavior" (1990: 314).

How does the obvious fact that competent speakers of a language "know," in some ordinary sense, the meanings of its expressions bear on our theory of the meanings known? Our answer to this will depend on what we make of the knowledge. It is mostly not explicit propositional knowledge but it is common to think of it, as Davies does, as "implicit" or "tacit" knowledge. This can lead to the view that the semantic task simply is the study of this state of knowledge: as Dummett puts it, "a theory of meaning is a theory of understanding" (1975: 99). Or it can lead to Davidson's view, noted by Davies, that a theory of meaning *suffices* for understanding. But perhaps we should think of the speaker's knowledge as mere knowhow, a cognitive *skill*, that need not involve any propositional knowledge, whether explicit or tacit. This view leads to a sharp distinction between the theory of meaning and the theory of the competent person's knowledge of meanings.

Davies sympathetically contrasts the Davidsonian and Gricean approaches to meaning. We note that each has been subject to criticisms of a foundational sort. Thus, the Gricean approach aims to explain linguistic meaning in terms of thought content but leaves the latter unexplained, as Brian Loar notes in chapter 4. This can seem unsatisfactory given that thought content is rather similar to linguistic meaning. Davidsonians have the idea that the semantic task is to spell out the conditions on axiomatic theories that correctly specify the meanings of expressions in particular languages, conditions on the "radical interpretation" of those languages. This interesting idea is rather taken for granted by Davidsonians and yet it is not obviously right. If we suppose that the task is to *explain* meanings in general, why suppose that we can accomplish this by studying the constraints on meaning *specifications* for languages?

For more on some of these foundational questions, see Devitt (1996: ch. 2).

Part II: Meaning

Theories of meaning

Moving from foundational to more substantive matters, we note the very important principle of *compositionality*: the meaning of a sentence is determined by the
meanings of the words that constitute it and by the way those words are put
together, by the syntactic structure of the sentence. This is a fairly uncontroversial
fact about language, although, as Horwich points out (chapter 2), there is controversy about how to take account of it theoretically.

Compositionality enables us to explain an obvious fact about linguistic competence, as Davies notes. A competent speaker of a language is able to understand an
indefinitely large number of sentences that are entirely novel to her. How? She
understands the words in the sentences and has mastery of the syntactic rules that
govern the structures of sentences.

An idea that seems to strike everyone when they first think about meaning is that
the meaning of an expression is tied closely to the way in which we would *tell*
whether the expression applies to something. The idea was captured in the logical
positivists' slogan, "Meaning is method of verification." This verificationism was
very popular in philosophy in the 1930s and 1940s, the heyday of positivism, but
has since fallen from favor. However, a form of verificationism had a brief revival
under the influence of Dummett (1993).

The most popular idea in philosophy for explaining meaning has been the idea
that it is largely, if not entirely, a matter of explaining truth conditions. The idea is
that the meaning of a sentence is to be explained by relating it to the circumstances
under which it would be true, an explanation that will involve the referential
relations of its words. Gottlob Frege, whose theory is described by James Higginbotham in chapter 3, is usually regarded as the father of the truth-referential
approach to semantics. Bertrand Russell also had a truth-referential theory.
There have been many different theories of this sort since, but an influential one
in recent times has been Davidson's, inspired by Tarski's famous theory of truth
(which is discussed in chapter 20). Davidson's basic idea is for specifying the
meanings of the sentences of a language in that very language. We construct a
theory with referential axioms like ' "Socrates" refers to "Socrates" ' and axioms
for combining words into sentences, a theory which enables us to derive as
theorems ' "*s*" is true if and only if "*p*" ' whenever '*s*' is replaced by a canonical
description of a sentence, and '*p*' by that very sentence. The basic idea then has to
be extended to specifications of the meanings of one language in another language, and to cope with ambiguities and other complications, as Higginbotham
brings out; see also Loar in chapter 4.

Compositionality leads us to expect that a truth-referential explanation of
meaning will proceed in two steps. First, the truth conditions of sentences will

be explained in terms of their syntactic structures and the references of the words that fit into those structures. Second, the references of the words will be explained by theories of reference (of the sort discussed in part III of this book). So we expect theories of reference to be a central part of explaining meaning. A controversial consequence of Davidson's holistic interpretative approach is that there is no need for, nor possibility of, theories of reference.

There has been a problem from the beginning with supposing that the truth-referential properties of a sentence exhaust its meaning. For, as Frege pointed out, the meaning of 'Hesperus = Phosphorus' surely differs from the meaning of 'Hesperus = Hesperus.' Yet, according to the supposition, they should have the same meaning because 'Hesperus' and 'Phosphorus' have the same referent (the planet Venus) and hence the same meaning. This led Frege to introduce his famous notion of *sense*: although 'Hesperus' and 'Phosphorus' have the same referent – the planet Venus – they differ in sense or "mode of presentation," the former meaning, say, "the heavenly body seen in the evening" and the latter, say, "the heavenly body seen in the morning." This matter comes up often; see particularly chapters 10 and 14.

It is obvious that the meaning of an expression depends somehow on its use: if we had used the word 'cat' to refer to dogs instead of cats it would have had a different meaning. Inspired by this fact, and his "deflationist" view of truth and reference (see chapter 20), Horwich (1998) has proposed a "use theory" of meaning. The guiding idea is that the meaning of a word is engendered by its "basic acceptance property," the fact that specified sentences containing it are accepted underived. See section 10 of chapter 2 for a brief discussion.

Thoughts and meaning

We have already mentioned one issue that arises in thinking about the relation of thought to language. This is an issue of explanatory priority. Thus Grice thinks that thought content is explanatorily prior to linguistic meaning. Davidson, on the other hand, sees no priority, taking the two concepts to be coordinate. Davidson's view rests, as Loar notes in chapter 4, on "the principle of charity." According to this rather surprising principle, we should interpret another's sentences, and ascribe beliefs to another, so as to make the sentences and beliefs come out, so far as possible, *true*. The principle reflects the influence of Quine's meaning skepticism (see chapter 5) and Davidson's basically antirealist view of mind and meaning: meanings are not for the most part objective properties with natures awaiting our discovery; interpretation is more a matter of *imposing* a reality than discovering it. Loar discusses the views of Grice and Davidson, as well as the earlier views of Frege and Russell; see also Horwich in chapter 2, section 4.

As Loar points out, Russell's discussion (1989) of "internal speech" raises another issue about the relation of thought to language: Do we think in a language? And if we do, what language do we think in? These have been controversial issues. Jerry Fodor (1975) has argued for "the language-of-thought hypothesis" according to which we think in a language-like system of representation. He rejects the idea, endorsed by Gilbert Harman (1973), that this system is the natural language of the thinker. For Fodor the language of thought is not the language of talk but rather an innate universal internal language, often called "Mentalese."

Meaning skepticism

Meaning skepticism is not simply the view that we cannot find out the facts about meanings. It is the view that there are no facts to be found out: there is no fact of the matter about what expressions mean. Clearly if it *were* a factual matter then it would also be a factual matter whether two expressions mean the same and hence whether one translates the other. So an argument that it is not a factual matter whether one expression correctly translates another is an argument for meaning skepticism. Quine's famous argument for the indeterminacy of translation is such an argument (1960). In fact, he had two arguments for indeterminacy, "the argument from below" and "the argument from above" (1970). Alex Miller discusses the two arguments and some responses to them in chapter 5. Whatever one makes of the arguments, it is important to note, as Miller does, that the terms of the debate are Quine's. Quine has a very restrictive behavioristic view of the sort of facts that *could* determine meaning.

The second argument for meaning skepticism discussed by Miller is one that Saul Kripke (1982) extracts from Wittgenstein. This argument has a much broader view of possible meaning-determining facts, allowing in mental facts. The argument is that no facts determine that a person using an expression is following one rule for its use rather than many others; hence that no facts determine that it means one thing rather than many others. Kripke's skeptic has a number of arguments for this view but the main one, briefly discussed by Miller, concerns normativity. The argument is that the dispositional facts alleged to determine the meaning of a term fail to do so because they do not tell us how we *ought to* apply the term. This argument has much exercised commentators.

The analytic–synthetic ("a–s") distinction

It has been common to believe that some true sentences are "analytic" in that they are true solely in virtue of meaning, whereas those that are not so true are "synthetic." Thus it was held that (U), 'All bachelors are unmarried', is analytic because 'bachelor' just means the same as 'unmarried man.' In contrast, (F), 'All bachelors are frustrated' is synthetic, depending for its truth on extralinguistic facts about bachelors. As Jerry Fodor and Ernie Lepore point out in chapter 6, the hope was that this would explain why a sentence like (U) is *necessary* whereas one like (F) is contingent; and, on the assumption that we *know* the meanings of the terms in (U) and (F), why (U) is a priori whereas (F) is a posteriori. Aside from all this hoped for work, the a/s distinction seemed intuitively plausible. But there is a problem: surely, (U) is not true *solely* in virtue of meaning. The fact about the meaning of 'bachelor' shows that (U) is synonymous with 'All unmarried men are unmarried' but it is hard to see how that "logical truth" could be true solely in virtue of meaning. So how could (U) be? The definition of "analytic" had to be modified: a true sentence is analytic if it can be reduced to a logical truth by substituting synonyms for synonyms. (This modification dashes the hope of explaining apriority by analyticity: knowledge of the truth of (U) rests on knowledge of a logical truth and analyticity is no help in explaining that.)

Even the modified a/s distinction seemed to fail in the face of Quine's sweeping criticisms. Recently, however, Paul Boghossian (1996, 1997) has argued that someone who is a realist about meanings, hence the opposite of a meaning skeptic, must accept the a/s distinction. This argument is the main target of Fodor and Lepore. Their case starts from the premise that analyticity requires not simply concept synonymy but concept *identity*: for (U) to be analytic, the concept expressed by 'bachelor' must be identical to that expressed by 'unmarried male.' They argue that this is not the case: the former concept, BACHELOR, is simple, the latter, UNMARRIED MALE, is complex. They note that their starting premise might be challenged but they offer several considerations in its defense.

Formal semantics

Formal semantics uses the techniques of formal logic to throw light on the meanings of natural language sentences. The expressions of a formal language have a clear and transparent semantics: the relation between the syntactic forms of these expressions and the situations that would make them true is well understood. So if we can find a formal expression that "means the same as" a natural language sentence, then we can learn a lot about the meaning of the sentence. The formal paraphrase of a sentence is often called its "logical form." The key to finding these paraphrases is the earlier-mentioned principle of compositionality: the meaning of the whole is a function of the meaning of the parts and their mode of combination. This principle is central to formal semantics.

As Max Cresswell points out in chapter 7, compositionality can be nicely illustrated by definitions of 'not', 'or', and 'and'; for example, "not α is true if α is false and false if α is true." Things are not mostly that simple, of course. To take account of tensed sentences we need to consider truth at a time; to take account of modal sentences we need to consider truth at a possible world. In general we need to consider truth *at indices*. Cresswell demonstrates the success of these formal techniques in handling tensed sentences, quantifiers, and other features of language.

Speech acts and pragmatics

As already noted, we need to distinguish what a sentence means from what a speaker means when using that sentence. Thus, as Kent Bach points out in chapter 8, in a performative utterance one performs an act by uttering a sentence. For example, one can apologize by saying "I apologize." Some performative utterances are institution-bound conventions, such as a judge's "Overruled!" J.L. Austin identifies three distinct levels of action beyond the act of utterance itself. He distinguishes the act of saying something, what one does in saying it, and what one does by saying, and dubs these the "locutionary," the "illocutionary," and the "perlocutionary" act, respectively. An illocutionary act succeeds if the speaker's audience recognizes the speaker's intentions. As a perlocutionary act it succeeds only if the audience actually fulfills the speaker's request.

Grice's theory of conversational implicature aims to explain how a speaker can mean just what he says or can mean something more or something else entirely. His notion can be applied to illocutionary acts. When an utterance is performed indirectly, it is performed by way of performing some other one directly. When an utterance is nonliteral, what the words mean is not at all what the speaker means. However, Bach argues, Grice overlooks conversational "implicature," where what the speaker means is implicitly conveyed rather than implicated, by way of expansion or completion.

Historically, the semantic–pragmatic distinction falls into three types: linguistic meaning vs. use, truth-conditional vs. non-truth-conditional meaning, and context independent vs. context dependence. Bach argues that the proper distinction can be drawn with respect to various things, such as ambiguities, implications, presuppositions, interpretations, knowledge, process, rules, and principles. The distinction applies fundamentally to types of information. Semantic information is information encoded in what is uttered together with any extralinguistic information that provides values to context-sensitive expressions in what is uttered. Pragmatic information is the information the hearer relies on to figure out what the speaker is communicating. This distinction is particularly useful in providing a simple account of how people can often communicate efficiently and effectively without the need to make explicit what they are trying to convey.

Figurative language

The oldest conception of metaphor characterizes it as improper or deviant use of the literal. This idea is undermined by the observation that some metaphors are equally true in the same contexts, whether interpreted literally or metaphorically. A second claim is that a sentence used metaphorically might have a different truth-value from what it would have were it interpreted literally. This entails that the same sentence must have a different meaning when used metaphorically than when used literally. However, the meaning of a metaphor often cannot be understood without knowing the literal meaning of its utterance. This metaphorical-literal dependence is best understood by a theory of pragmatics. The literal can be identified as what a sentence 'S is P' means, whereas the metaphorical meaning is what a speaker can use it to mean, say, that S is R. Searle proposes that R is the metaphorical meaning of the predicate P on a particular occasion, and the fact that P conveys R according to some pragmatic principle is the sense in which the metaphorical depends on the literal. Josef Stern argues in chapter 9 that although Searle's account correctly demonstrates that there is no single "ground" that generates all metaphorical contents, it insufficiently explains why something is or is not a metaphorical meaning. Others, like Richard Rorty, claim that "metaphor belongs exclusively to the domain of use." Similarly, Donald Davidson claims that "a metaphor doesn't say anything beyond its literal meaning." But, Stern points out, if a sentence used metaphorically does not have a literal meaning its metaphorical effect cannot depend on it or be explained by its means; and if literal meaning is anything like truth-conditions, it is not at all clear that we know under what conditions many classical metaphors like 'Juliet is the sun' would be true.

Metaphorical meaning is context dependent. First, metaphorical interpretations of utterances of the same expression may vary widely from one occasion, or context, to another. Second, the interpretation of a metaphor is typically a function of all sorts of extralinguistic presuppositions, skills, and abilities such as the perception of similarity or salience. However, Stern argues, metaphorical interpretation does not come simply from looking at the content of each metaphor. Rather, only at a level that relates each content of the same expression used metaphorically to a relevant feature of its respective context of use, namely, the shared presuppositions, will metaphorical interpretations follow regularities. The presuppositions here are the sets of propositions to which a speaker, in making an utterance, commits himself, in the absence of which his assertion would be inappropriate or uninterpretable. Following this method, we see that a metaphorical interpretation or content is always fixed or constrained by its actual context of utterance.

Propositional attitude ascription

People often say things of the following sort: 'X believes that p', 'X said that p', 'X hopes that p, 'X wonders whether p', and so on. Since these seem to ascribe attitudes to the proposition p they are called "propositional attitude ascriptions." These ascriptions are very important in our relations with X – they help us explain and predict X's behavior – and with the world in general – if X believes that p and is reliable then probably p. The meaning of such an ascription is unusual in two interesting ways. First, it is not extensional (on one reading, at least). Thus, suppose that (T), 'Mary believes that Twain is witty', is true. Still (C), 'Mary believes that Clemens is witty', might be false. For, even though 'Clemens' and

'Twain' are coextensional – they both refer to the one person – Mary may not know this. Substituting a coextensional term in the 'that' clause is not guaranteed to preserve truth. Second, these ascriptions give rise to what Brentano called "intentional inexistence." 'Octavia believes that Zeus destroyed Pompeii' might be true even though Zeus does not exist. These ascriptions can be true even though a term in the 'that' clause fails to refer. Attempts to explain propositional attitude ascriptions have played a major role in the philosophy of language.

As Mark Richard points out in chapter 10 the key issue in recent times has been how modes of presenting, ways of thinking about, an object enter into the truth conditions of attitude ascriptions. As we have already noted, Frege argued that a proper name like 'Hesperus' has a sense which is a mode of presenting the referent, say, "the heavenly body seen in the evening." Russell thought that the meaning of a "logically proper name" would be its referent but thought that all ordinary proper names were truncated descriptions. So, in effect, his view of ordinary names was similar to Frege's. This view became known as the description theory of names. This theory provides 'Twain' and 'Clemens' with different modes of presentation which can then be used to explain the different truth values of (T) and (C). But, under the influence particularly of Kripke (1980), many came to think that the description theory was false: a name does not have a descriptive sense (see chapter 14). Where to go from there? One, sadly unpopular, response was to suppose that names have a nondescriptive *causal* sense or mode of presentation which can then be used to handle attitude ascriptions (Devitt 1981, 1996). A more popular response was that of "direct reference": there is no more to the meaning of a name than its referent. How then are we to explain the difference between (T) and (C)? Typically, appeal is made to the distinction between what (T) and (C) strictly say, which is alleged to be the same, and the other information that they convey, which is different. This is a distinction between semantics and pragmatics of the sort that we have just been discussing. But, as Richard argues, it is hard to make a solution along these lines persuasive. In particular, it is hard to make it compatible with the role of attitude ascriptions in commonsense psychological explanations. Richard's own explanation of attitude ascriptions is that ascribing an attitude to a person involves a sort of translation of the person's mental representation.

Conditionals

Conditionals are sentences of the form 'If A then B': in symbols $(A \rightarrow B)$. It is widely agreed that '~', '&' and 'v' ('not', 'and' and 'or', respectively) are truth functions: the truth values of a compound sentence formed using them is fully determined by the truth values of the component sentences. The simplest and oldest theory of the conditional holds that '$\rightarrow$' is also a truth function, known as material implication, and in particular that $(A \rightarrow B)$ is equivalent to both of: $(\sim A \lor B)$, and $\sim(A \& \sim B)$. This implies that the falsity of A and the truth of B are separately sufficient for the truth of (A → B). Many find these results very implausible and they are known as the paradoxes of material implication.

David Lewis (1973) and Robert Stalnaker (1968) responded, as Frank Jackson points out in chapter 11, by proposing that (A → B) is true if and only if the closest A-world, the possible world most like the actual world at which A is true, is a B-world, a possible world at which B is also true. This account is attractive because it avoids the paradoxes of material implication, while making Modus Ponens and Modus Tollens valid, as is intuitively correct, and explaining why Strengthening the Antecedent, Transitivity, and Contraposition are invalid. A different response to the paradoxes is the no-truth theory, which states that conditionals have justified assertion or acceptability conditions but not truth conditions.

Vagueness

There is a philosophical *problem* of vagueness because of the sorites paradox, an instance of which is the following inference: (1) A person with $50 million is rich. (2) For any n, if a person with $n is rich, then so is a person with $n − 1¢. (3) Therefore, a person with only 37¢ is rich. This inference constitutes a *paradox* because it appears to be valid, each of its two premises appears to be true (at least when considered on its own), and the conclusion certainly appears to be false. All theorists recognize that the weak link in the inference is the "sorites premise," (2), but they disagree as to what exactly is wrong with that premise and the intuitively compelling argument for it.

In chapter 12, Stephen Schiffer reviews the best known attempts to account for vagueness, and thereby to solve the sorites, and finds them all problematic. He argues that vagueness is neither an epistemic nor a semantic notion, but rather a *psychological* notion, one explicable in terms of a previously unnoticed kind of partial belief he calls vagueness-related partial belief, and which he contrasts with the familiar kind of partial belief, which he calls standard partial belief, that is generally assumed to be normatively governed by the axioms of probability theory. Bringing his psychological account of vagueness to bear on the sorites, Schiffer argues that the paradox doesn't have the sort of neat solution theorists of vagueness typically seek, but instead admits of no determinate resolution.

The semantics of non-factualism, non-cognitivism, and quasi-realism

Non-factualism in some particular area of speech is the claim that the sentences in that area do not function purely representatively, expressing beliefs, but rather express some other mental states that a speaker is voicing. Simon Blackburn lists three motivations for this non-factualism in chapter 13. The metaphysical motivation may be the most important: the apparent queerness of any facts that would be represented. Thus, the apparent queerness of moral facts has led many to non-factualism, or "non-cognitivism," about moral discourse. Non-factualism has been proposed in many areas including causation and religion.

Peter Geach (1962, 1965) raised a severe problem for non-factualism. How can it account for 'indirect' contexts, ones where a sentence is used, but not asserted or put forward as true. Consider, for example, the role of 'lying is wrong' in the statement 'If lying is wrong, then getting your little brother to lie is wrong.' That role is surely not the expression of an attitude. This problem leads to another: preserving the validity of an argument from that conditional statement together with 'Lying is wrong' to the conclusion 'Getting your little brother to lie is wrong.' Both Blackburn himself (1984) and Alan Gibbard (1990) have proposed solutions that have been the subject of considerable controversy, as Blackburn brings out.

A debate has arisen about whether non-factualism is compatible with a deflationist view of truth (see chapter 20). That view of truth appears to be an example of non-factualism although some think that it takes away the terms in which non-factualism can be formulated. Blackburn's "quasi-realism" which attempts to mirror everything a realist wants to say whilst not having any realist commitment is one way of responding to this apparent conflict.

Part III: Reference

The revolution in the theory of reference

Reference, in ordinary parlance, is aboutness. "What are you referring to?" is more or less equivalent to "What are you talking about?" If the utterance was an ordinary declarative sentence, it's usually a question of what the *subject* of that sentence is, and investigation into reference has understandably focused on terms in subject position.

Many different terms can occur in subject position – chapters 14–18 examine various ones in turn – so an important question is whether or not one theory of reference fits all. The short answer seems to be no. For instance, J. S. Mill (1843) argued that a proper name like 'Dartmouth' does not depend for its reference on any descriptive associations it may have, but he thought general names like 'horse' had their reference determined by an associated description. Frege (1892), as we have already noted, thought all names were descriptive, and indeed that proper names were equivalent to definite descriptions, a view espoused and defended by Russell (1905, 1919). Their views were orthodox until overturned, largely by Kripke (1980), who argued that Mill was right about proper names and wrong about general names. In the last forty-plus years, philosophers of language have continued this lively exchange, and turned the same critical focus upon other referring expressions, including descriptions themselves, all the while attending to developments in – with the hope of reciprocal illumination – logic and linguistics.

Two main questions arise concerning reference: (1) what is the mechanism by means of which reference is secured? (2) what is the meaning of a referring expression? The discussion of these issues invokes three different distinctions that we have already mentioned in discussing chapter 6. The first is metaphysical: a *necessary* true proposition could not have been false, and a *contingent* true proposition might have been false. The next is epistemic: an *a priori* true proposition is knowable independent of experience, and an *a posteriori* true proposition is not. The third is semantic: an *analytic* true proposition is true in virtue of meaning, and a *synthetic* true proposition is not.

Kripkean arguments show to the satisfaction of most that a pure description theory of names is inadequate to answer either the mechanism question or the meaning question. As for mechanism, the view that speakers succeed in referring in virtue of knowing a uniquely identifying – yet non-circular – set of descriptions is beset by ignorance and error problems, as William Lycan notes in chapter 14. As for meaning, archetypal descriptions and archetypal names just seem too different. For example, let 'the F' be the description alleged to constitute the meaning of the name 'Aristotle' for speaker S. Then, according to the description theory, 'Aristotle is F' should be analytic, known a priori and necessary (provided Aristotle exists). Intuitively, however, the sentence seems as synthetic, a posteriori, and contingent as they come.

It's just implausible that competent speakers must have essential properties of an individual in mind in order to refer to it, and similar considerations apply to natural kinds, as Stephen Schwartz notes in chapter 15, drawing on Kripke and Hilary Putnam (1975). For instance, reference to gold and water succeeded long before the a posteriori discovery of the molecular structures that are their essential properties. And the essential properties of biological kinds are even now far from settled.

The works of Kripke and Putnam offer an important competitor to the description theory – one that is capable of explaining the relative ease of referring despite ignorance and error – the causal or historical theory. As to mechanism, the theory distinguishes reference *grounding* from reference *borrowing*. Grounders of a name are relative experts, in more or less direct contact with the thing named, but others borrow the reference successfully when their tokenings are appropriately causally related to those of grounders.

As to meaning, many have combined the causal theory of mechanism with a Millian theory of meaning, called "the direct reference theory," according to which there is no content to a name over and above its reference. There is another option, however; the one mentioned in discussing propositional attitude ascriptions: one might take the meaning of a name to be its particular causal mode of referring to its bearer; the causal network underlying the name determines its meaning (Devitt and Sterelny 1999).

A pure causal theory is anyway inadequate as a theory of mechanism, thanks to the *qua* problem. In the case of natural kind terms, a grounder is in contact with an individual that is a token of several different kinds. In order to secure reference to just one kind, the grounder's intentions matter, and so the description theory turns out to contain a grain of truth after all. This suggests a third account, a hybrid descriptive/causal theory. Lycan sets out problems for all three accounts and the varieties of associated theories of meaning. Schwartz argues that even if a hybrid account succeeds for natural kind terms, other general terms are less amenable; think particularly of "artifactual" kind terms like 'chair' and social kind terms like 'philosopher.'

Schwartz brings out an important legacy of the "causal revolution" in the theory of reference. This is semantic externalism: a person's relations to the world, including her social world, have a big role in determining the meanings of her terms. A remark of Putnam is the slogan for this externalism: "meanings just ain't in the *head*" (1975: 227). We shall have more to say about this below.

Descriptions

Descriptions come in two basic surface forms: definite and indefinite. Russell's 1905 account of definite descriptions analyses them as object-independent, non-referring terms. In chapter 16, Peter Ludlow and Stephen Neale canvass the many challenges to the Russellian view from referentialists, who argue that at least some definite descriptions – those appearing in what Donnellan (1966) called referential uses – are indeed referring terms. Some referentialists extend the claim to indefinite descriptions as well. Russellians respond by leaning heavily on the distinction between what is literally said, and what is pragmatically communicated, in order to preserve a semantic unity in definites. Ludlow and Neale make the case for Russellianism, and consider the view that there is no semantic distinction between definites and indefinites, either. Whatever the outcome of these debates, Russell's Theory of Descriptions remains an outstanding contribution to philosophy of language. In particular, it has provided a productive framework for philosophers to think about the role of quantification in language.

Indexicals

Pragmatic considerations also weigh heavily in chapter 17, in John Perry's discussion of indexical terms such as "I," "here," and the demonstrative "this." These terms vary their reference according to the context of use, but how do they do this, and why? Perry argues that the meaning of an indexical term is a property of the expression type, which together with the relevant particular context determines the content of an utterance. So "This is Tuesday" has the same meaning whenever it is uttered, but varies in content depending upon what day it is uttered. In considering such variations, Perry makes two distinctions. Is the designation automatic as with 'I' or does it vary according to the intentions of the speaker as with 'now'? Does the reference depend only on the speaker, time, or place of utterance as with 'now' or 'here,' or does it depend on other facts as with 'this'? Why do we use indexicals? In Perry's view, "to help the audience find supplementary, utterance-independent, channels of information about" the object referred to.

Anaphora

As Perry notes, a pronoun can function like a demonstrative; for example, 'he' in "He loves Sheila," said with a gesture toward Ralph. But pronouns have important other uses brought out in Neale's chapter 18. They can function as bound variables; for example, 'he' in "Every man loves Sheila but he is always disappointed." And they can be anaphoric; for example, 'he', 'she', and 'him' in "Ralph loves Sheila, and he thinks she loves him back." Anaphoric pronouns are the focus of Stephen Neale's discussion in chapter 18.

Neale shows first that pronouns exhibit a variety of behaviors that appear to distinguish them from the bound variables of formal logic. One response to these phenomena is to posit a systematic ambiguity between bound and indexical uses. Another (a methodology paralleling that of the Russellians discussed in chapter 16), is to sweep them up in a pragmatic theory. A third is to regard anaphoric pronouns as standing proxy for descriptions. Neale proposes speaking neutrally of the *binding* of anaphoric pronouns without commitment to one or other of these approaches.

Neale discusses these options in historical context, in which Chomsky's Binding Theory has played a central role. The theory aims to provide syntactic constraints on interpretation, but binding cannot, argues Neale, be purely syntactic. After examining a welter of examples from linguistics, Neale concludes that pronouns do not function as bound variables, but rather *contain* variables that may be bound, a version of the descriptive approach.

Naturalistic theories of reference

The final two chapters concern what might be called metasemantic issues concerning reference, and so dovetail with the concerns of parts I and II. In chapter 19, Karen Neander examines a methodological program for thinking about reference: naturalism. An obvious first step in a naturalistic program is to explain linguistic phenomena such as reference in terms of mental phenomena. Hence naturalistic theories of reference have focused on mental representations.

Causal theories of mental content gain impetus from thought experiments like Putnam's (1975) about Twin-Earth, a planet where all the waterish stimuli consist of XYZ rather than H_2O. Earthling "water" thoughts seem to be about H_2O and not XYZ, even though (a couple of centuries back, at least) nothing strictly in the mind/brain of Earthlings determines that this is so: no images, associated descriptions, or whatever, determine that we refer to H_2O rather than XYZ. This suggests that reference is at least partly determined by causal relations to things external to the thinker; it suggests semantic externalism. These causal relations to particular environmental features make nice naturalistic candidates for reference determination. But a "crude" causal theory faces insurmountable difficulties, many involving a failure to distinguish the "right" causings of mental tokens from the "wrong" ones. Attempts to supplement the causal account to overcome these difficulties include Fodor's asymmetric dependence theory, in which the wrong depend on the right, but not vice versa; teleosemantic theories, which postulates *functions*, understood as what items were selected for, as the arbiter of right and wrong causings; and information theories, according to which representations carry information in virtue of the causal regularities they participate in. Even though none of these approaches seems to solve all the difficulties, they present promising ideas for naturalizing reference.

Truth

Some common notions can appear very mysterious upon inspection. Truth seems obvious and familiar, but what is it? The central issue is whether or not " 'p' is true" says anything more than "p." If so, what kind of property is the property of being true? Will it comport with naturalistic theories of meaning and reference? Vann McGee centers the discussion in Chapter 20 upon a theory that attempts to define truth in non-semantic terms. The theory in question is Tarski's, which enables us to derive, for each sentence s of a language L, a "T-sentence" of the form:

s is a true sentence of L iff _____,

where what fills the _____ is the translation into English of s. The famous paradigm is " 'Snow is white' is true in English iff snow is white." Tarski's theory supplies no general definition of truth, but rather only of truth in a language. Furthermore it applies only to a range of formal languages (despite the paradigm). Within these limits, the theory is "an undoubted triumph," says McGee, but the fact that its methods are inapplicable to natural languages – the Liar paradox and its variations led Tarski to conclude that no consistent account of truth in a natural language is possible – raises the threat "that substantial aspects of human life lie forever beyond the reach of our human understanding."

A range of responses to Tarski's restrictions have been contemplated, most notably one by Kripke (1975), motivated by the idea that the Liar Sentence, and others, are neither true nor false. Aside from this problem, Hartry Field (1972) argued that the theory needs to be supplemented by theories of reference (like those just mentioned) if it is to provide a physicalistically respectable *explanation* of truth; the list-like definitions of reference on which Tarski's theory rests are insufficient. The theory as it stands does not capture the idea that truth consists in a robust correspondence to the facts. McGee concludes with a discussion of an alternative to the correspondence conception. This is the "deflationary" view that the truth term is a logical device for disquotation; the term does not refer to a robust property that plays an explanatory role in science. The idea goes back at least to Frege (1892), who wrote,

> One can, indeed, say: 'The thought, that 5 is a prime number, is true.' But closer examination shows that nothing more has been said than in the simple sentence '5 is a prime number.'

On this view, the addition of the words "is true" to a sentence adds no further content. One battleground between correspondence and deflationary theories is over vagueness (cf. chapter 12).

As we remarked at the outset, hardly anything in the philosophy of language is settled. There is plenty of work to be done, but that does not mean that no progress has been made. Modern analytic philosophy of language has made a substantial contribution to our overall understanding of the world we occupy, and the language we use to talk about it.

Note

Our thanks to Panu Raatikainen for helpful comments on a draft of this introduction

Part I

Foundational Issues

Chapter 1

Foundational Issues in the Philosophy of Language

Martin Davies

Linguistic expressions are meaningful. Sentences, built from words and phrases, are used to communicate information about objects, properties, and events in the world. In philosophy of language, the study of linguistic meaning is central.

1 Meaning and Communication: Semantics and Pragmatics

Just connecting meaning with communication does not yet tell us which properties of expressions and their uses are to be brought under the umbrella of linguistic meaning. For there is often an intuitive distinction to be drawn between the message that a speaker communicates and the meaning of the sentence that the speaker uses. Offered coffee after dinner, Nigel may utter the sentence, 'Coffee keeps me awake,' and thereby decline the offer. But declining an offer is no part of the linguistic meaning of the sentence. In a different context – imagine that there is an after-dinner speaker who is known to be boring but that the occasion demands that people not doze off – the very same sentence could be used to accept an offer of coffee. In yet another context, the sentence might be used in a simple factual report about factors that exacerbate insomnia.

It is usual, in philosophy of language, to distinguish between properties that are strictly aspects of an expression's literal linguistic meaning and other properties of the expression or its use that may contribute to the message that is communicated. The study of literal linguistic meaning is *semantics*. The study of the use of language to communicate messages – very often, messages that go far beyond the literal meanings of the expressions used – is *pragmatics*.

As a rough guide to the semantics–pragmatics distinction, we can say that semantics is concerned with the properties of expressions that help to determine the conditions under which an utterance would be literally true, rather than false. In contrast, pragmatics focuses on the conditions under which an utterance would be helpful, rather than misleading, or more generally appropriate, rather than inappropriate. The semantic properties of the English words 'coffee' and so on, and the way that the words are put together, determine that an utterance of the sentence 'Coffee keeps me awake' is true under the conditions that coffee keeps the speaker awake, and false otherwise. So if coffee keeps Nigel awake then his utterance is true. But an utterance that is true may be misleading. Late in the evening, with no after-dinner speaker scheduled, Nigel's utterance may give the impression that he is declining the offer of coffee, so that his next remark, 'I'd like some,' comes as a surprise. The fact that the utterance has the truth conditions that it does is explained by semantics. The fact that the utterance gives the misleading impression that it does is explained by pragmatics.

However, it is important to recognize that equating semantics with the study of literal linguistic meaning does not quite guarantee that semantics is concerned with truth conditions while pragmatics deals with appropriateness conditions. One kind of example that helps to make this point is provided by pairs of expressions that apply to the same things but differ in literal meaning because one word is a polite or neutral form while the other is an impolite or derogatory form. Thus, for example, the English word 'cur' applies to the same things as the word 'dog'; but, while 'dog' is the neutral form, it is part of the literal meaning of 'cur' that its use expresses contempt. Suppose that Rover is a dog of mixed, or even indeterminate, breed. Some people might feel contempt towards Rover, but suppose that Fiona's attitude is one of admiration and affection. Then an utterance by Fiona, pointing at Rover, of 'This cur slept all night' would be seriously misleading as to her attitude. But if Rover did sleep all night then Fiona's utterance would not be false. It would be true but misleading. In that respect, Fiona's utterance would be similar to Nigel's. But there is also an important difference between the cases. Someone who hears Nigel's utterance and grasps the literal meaning of what he says may very well fail to draw the misleading inference that he is declining the offer of coffee. The hearer might know that Nigel wants to stay awake to write a philosophy essay, for example. But someone who has no tendency to draw the misleading inference that Fiona is contemptuous of Rover has failed to grasp the literal meaning of the word 'cur.'

It appears, then, that two words may differ in their literal meaning even though they make the same contribution to truth conditions. Here we can make use of a distinction drawn by Frege (1892) between *sense*, on the one hand, and illumination, coloring or *tone*, on the other (Dummett 1973: ch. 1). Many complex issues surround Frege's notion of sense. But for present purposes, the only aspects of meaning that belong to the sense of an expression are those that help to determine the truth conditions of sentences in which the expression occurs. Frege's notion of tone is more heterogeneous, including even the various ideas that may be evoked in individual readers by the eloquence of a poet. But Frege also mentions that conjunctions such as 'but,' 'although,' and 'yet' *illuminate* the sense of the following clause 'in a peculiar fashion.' This is the point, familiar to every student of logic, that 'but' differs from 'and' in some aspect of meaning but not in the contribution that it makes to truth conditions. The use of 'but' in 'Bruce is Australian but he is cultured' carries the implication that there is some kind of contrast between being Australian and being cultured. If there is, in reality, no such contrast, then this is a misleading thing to say. But that does not make it false. The truth value of the sentence with 'but' is the same as the truth value of the more neutral 'Bruce is Australian and he is cultured.' In Fregean terminology, 'but' differs from 'and,' not in sense, but in tone.

We have distinguished between two distinctions. There is the distinction between literal linguistic meaning and communicated messages or implications that go beyond literal meaning. And there is the distinction between aspects of meaning that contribute to the determination of truth conditions and factors that generate implications that are not directly relevant to questions of truth or falsity. We have introduced the terms 'semantics' and 'pragmatics' to mark the first distinction. But we should note that some theorists might prefer to use these terms for the second distinction, restricting semantics to the study of sense rather than tone, and correspondingly expanding the domain of pragmatics. These theorists must, of course, recognize a difference, within the domain of pragmatics, between implications that are generated by aspects of literal meaning (as in Fiona's utterance) and those that result from some kind of interaction between literal meaning and contextual factors (as in Nigel's). Whether or not anything of substance turns on this terminological decision, it is important to be clear about the difference between the two distinctions. In some writings on philosophy of language the difference is apt to be obscured because the phenomenon of tone is set aside, virtually without comment.

2 Meaning, Science, and Philosophy: Semantics and Metasemantics

We have taken some time to describe the domain of semantics. But it may seem that, whatever the details of the demarcation, there is a puzzle as to how semantics could be of central interest for philosophy of language. Facts about what expressions a language contains, how those expressions are used in utterances, and what those expressions refer to or mean are empirical facts about the natural order. It is an empirical fact about the language spoken in Italy that there is a word 'prosciutto,' pronounced with the stress on 'u' and with 'sci' sounding much like English 'sh,' that refers to a particular kind of ham. It is an empirical fact that this Italian word has been incorporated into our language just as the ham has been incorporated into our diet. It is an empirical fact that the Italian word can be used in the sentence 'Prosciutto è buono con melon' to mean that this kind of ham is good with melon. These facts are surely of limited philosophical interest. It is difficult to regard them as belonging alongside facts about the nature of free agency or about the conditions for a conception of objects as existing independently of our perception of them, for example. So, how could the study of meaning and reference be a distinctively philosophical project rather than simply a part of natural science?

To this question, put in this way, an answer immediately suggests itself. If there is a science of meaning and reference then, presumably, the philosophy of science includes a division that offers philosophical commentary on the key concepts deployed by that science. So philosophy of language can concern itself with meaning and reference just as philosophy of biology concerns itself with species and selection. Now, in fact, there are reasons to hesitate over this assimilation of the philosophy of language to philosophy of science. There is indeed a science of language, namely linguistics, and philosophy of linguistics is a division of philosophy of science. But we are not obliged to hold that philosophy of linguistics is all there is to philosophy of language. For philosophy of language also includes questions that arise from our ordinary, everyday conceptions of language and meaning. (In a similar way, we should not hold that philosophy of mind is exhausted by philosophy of cognitive science.) However, we do not need to embrace a gratuitous scientism in order to respond to the apparent puzzle about how semantics could be of importance to philosophy.

There is a familiar distinction between questions of first-order ethics ('How should I behave?') and questions of metaethics ('What is the nature of ethical judgments?'). Similarly, there is a distinction between aesthetic questions about works of art ('Is this a beautiful painting?') and questions in aesthetics ('What is the nature of beauty?'). So also there is a distinction to be drawn between questions about the meanings of particular linguistic expressions and questions about the nature of linguistic meaning itself. Questions of the first kind belong to *semantics*; questions of the second kind belong to *metasemantics*.

There are three general points to be made about this kind of distinction between ground-level questions and meta-level questions. First, it is the meta-level questions that are most clearly philosophical in character. Questions about the nature of ethical judgments or about the nature of beauty do belong with questions about free will or about the conditions for a non-solipsistic consciousness. Second, the philosophical character of these meta-level questions does not depend on the scientific credentials of the corresponding ground-level questions. There is no science of how one should behave and there are no scientific laws about beauty as such. Third, while it is the meta-level questions that are most clearly philosophical, ground-level questions may also be philosophical questions. Moral philosophy includes, not only metaethics, but also first-order or applied ethics and arguments about the aesthetic properties of particular works of art or music are advanced within philosophical aesthetics.

In the case of semantics and philosophy of language, the three points are these. First, metasemantic questions about the nature of linguistic meaning are central for philosophy of language. Second, philosophy of language need not start from the assumption that ground-level questions about the semantic properties of expressions are scientific questions. Indeed, whether semantics is a science is a meta-level question that is debated in contemporary philosophy of language. Third, it is not to be ruled out that engagement with ground-level questions about the semantic properties of expressions may also be a philosophical project. In the remainder of this section, we shall briefly develop the first two of these points. The third point has a section of its own.

2.1 Metasemantic questions: metaphysics and epistemology

Metasemantic questions about the nature of linguistic meaning include meta-physical questions. For example, are meanings entities; and, if so, what kinds of entities are they? Intuitively, utterances of sentences are used to express thoughts, and so the meaning of a complete sentence seems to be something like the content of a complete thought. This idea might lead to the proposal that the meanings of complete sentences are *propositions* and that proposal would lead, in turn, to questions about the nature of propositions themselves. There may be other proposals about what kinds of entities meanings are, assuming that they are entities at all. But an alternative view would have it that we do not need to include meanings as entities in our ontology. Earlier, we gave an example of an Italian sentence with a particular meaning property. The sentence 'Prosciutto è buono con melon' means that prosciutto is good with melon. If meanings are entities then this sentence stands in the meaning relation to such an entity, perhaps the proposition that prosciutto is good with melon. But, on the alternative view, the meaning property of the Italian sentence is not to be conceived as a relation to an abstract entity, though it may involve relations to worldly entities like ham and melons (Devitt 1996). Consider an analogy. Suppose that Nigel has a sharp hairstyle. On a 'hairstyles as entities' view, this is a matter of Nigel standing in a particular relation to a particular abstract entity, a hairstyle. But it might be said, with some plausibility, that we do not need to include hairstyles in our ontology. Having a sharp hairstyle is not really a relational property; it is just a matter of having one's hair styled in a particular way. Similarly in the case of meaning, it might be said that for a sentence to mean that prosciutto is good with melon is just a matter of the sentence being used in a particular way.

Metaphysical questions always go hand-in-hand with epistemological questions. So, in this case, any metaphysical view as to the nature of facts about meaning must be compatible with an answer to the epistemological question how knowledge about meanings is achieved. Competent speakers of a language know, or can come to know, the meanings of indefinitely many sentences. They *understand* the sentences of their own language. Philosophy of language addresses questions about the nature of this understanding and, indeed, the question how understanding a language – with potentially infinitely many sentences – is even possible for finite creatures like us.

2.2 Is semantics a science?

Questions as to whether semantics is, or can be, a science arise from at least two sources (Chomsky 2000). One concerns our ordinary notion of a language; the other concerns the role in semantics of worldly objects, properties, and events.

Our ordinary notion of language is of a shared language, a public language, a language that is used for communication amongst several people, typically amongst thousands or millions of people. Our ordinary notion of linguistic meaning is thus meaning in a public language and semantics is conceived, at least initially, as the study of the meanings of expressions in a public language such as English or Italian. But there are reasons to doubt whether the meaning properties of a public language as such constitute a proper domain for investigation by the natural sciences. One such reason is that there may be, within what we describe as a single language, considerable dialect variation. But whether dialects are considered as variations of a single language or as languages in their own right may owe nothing to the natural order and everything to social, political, or even military factors. So the notion of a public language is the notion of an artifactual, rather than a natural, kind and the same goes for public language meaning.

A further reason to doubt the scientific credentials of public language meaning arises from the idea that the meaning of an expression is closely linked with the use of that expression in interpersonal communication. For in real-life communication, the hearer draws on information about all kinds of things in order to discern the message that the speaker is trying to communicate. And the speaker has expectations about the information available to the hearer, expectations that are themselves grounded in information about a variety of topics. It is not clear that this essential background to communication, a heterogeneous collection of pieces of information, could fit into a scientific theory. So, if meaning really is closely linked with communication, this casts doubt on the prospect of a scientific theory of public language meaning.

In order to avoid the worry that a public language is a socio-political construction rather than a natural object, we could focus on the language of an individual speaker – an idiolect, the limiting case of a dialect. However, if we do this then it becomes even clearer that interpersonal communication depends on all manner of information, assumptions, hunches, wisdom, and wit (Davidson 1986). For speaker and hearer must be ready to make adjustments for differences in the meaning properties of their idiolects. So a science of literal idiolectal meaning would need to abstract away from the use of language in interpersonal communication. We would need to conceive of communication as a massive interaction between literal meaning and other factors, perhaps not itself susceptible of scientific description.

Suppose that idiolectal meaning could be separated from communication in this way, so that questions from the first source were set aside. There would remain questions from the second source concerning the role in semantics of worldly objects, properties, and events. To see how the worry arises, suppose that we set out to describe the meaning properties of the idiolect of Maria, an Italian speaker. Her idiolect may, of course, be idiosyncratic in various ways. Perhaps she uses the word 'melon' to refer only to watermelon and not to other kinds of melon. But suppose that, in her idiolect, the word 'prosciutto' refers to that particular kind of ham, also called 'prosciutto' in English. Then our account (in English, of course) of the semantics of her idiolect will include the principle:

> The word 'prosciutto' refers to prosciutto (a particular kind of ham).

If this is a scientific principle then the various notions that figure in it should be scientific notions; that is, notions of natural kinds or categories. Given the existence of the science of linguistics, the notion of a word, and of the particular word 'prosciutto,' is not especially problematic. We might hesitate rather more over the scientific credentials of the notion of reference. But the most immediate problem is that there is no guarantee that there is or will be a natural science of prosciutto as such (cf. Fodor 1980). And the problem becomes even more vivid when we consider that, in Maria's idiolect, the word 'Roma' refers to Rome, 'la giustizia' refers to justice, and 'la bellezza' refers to beauty. For there is no natural science of cities, nor of justice or beauty.

Just indicating this worry about the scientific status of semantics does not, of course, settle the issue. But imagine for a moment that it were to be shown compellingly that semantics is not, and cannot be, a science. What would follow from that? If the domain of science were to be equated with the domain of rational inquiry concerning the natural world then it would seem to follow that doing semantics is not engaging in such rational inquiry. Perhaps, on this view, it is more like reading a novel or undergoing therapy. But we are not bound to accept that consequence because the equation really does constitute a gratuitous scientism. Whether or not semantics is science, the aim of semantics is to give a systematic description, with some theoretical depth, of the meaning properties of some objects and events in the natural world, including utterances, idiolects, and even public languages conceived as social objects (Wiggins 1997).

3   Semantics as a Philosophical Project

Metasemantic questions about the metaphysics and epistemology of meaning are clearly philosophical in character. In contrast, semantic questions about the meanings of expressions in a public language like Italian or an idiolect like Maria's seem to be straightforwardly empirical and of limited philosophical interest. So it may seem puzzling that philosophy of language should include substantial contributions to semantics as well as to metasemantics. How could the construction of semantic descriptions of languages or idiolects be a philosophical project?

One reason for philosophical interest in semantics is that spelling out the conditions for a putative semantic description to be *correct* is a way of approaching metasemantic questions of undoubted philosophical importance. Any elucidation of the concept of literal linguistic meaning furnishes a correctness condition on semantic descriptions. And conversely, correctness conditions on semantic descriptions can be transposed into elucidations of, or constraints on, the concept of meaning. A philosopher of language who adopts this approach to metasemantic questions obviously needs to know something about the semantic descriptions for which correctness conditions are to be formulated.

However, the possibility of this approach to metasemantic questions does not really explain why detailed and substantive engagement with the construction of semantic descriptions could be a philosophical project. For the formulation of correctness conditions on semantic descriptions requires only very general knowledge about the form that the descriptions are to take. In order to go further, we must take account of the compositionality of linguistic meaning.

3.1 Compositionality and finitely axiomatized semantic theories

The meaning of a sentence is determined by the meanings of its constituent words and the ways in which they are put together. It is part of our everyday conception of knowing a language that, because of this compositionality, it is possible to understand a completely novel sentence on first hearing if it is built out of familiar words put together in familiar ways. So the compositionality of meaning promises an answer to the epistemological question of how understanding a language with potentially infinitely many sentences is so much as possible. The general form of the answer must be that the meanings of finitely many words and finitely many ways of putting words together determine the meanings of infinitely many sentences. But it is not a trivial matter to give substance to this answer.

The most convincing way to develop the idea of the compositionality of meaning is to provide, for the language or idiolect under investigation, not just a semantic description, but a certain kind of formal, axiomatized semantic theory. The axioms of this theory should specify the meaning properties of words and of ways of putting words together. The background logic of the theory should then permit the derivation, from these axioms, of theorems that specify the meaning properties of complete sentences. For any particular sentence, the derivation of a meaning-specifying theorem should draw specifically on the axioms for the words and ways of putting words together that are involved in the construction of that sentence. Furthermore, the derivation should follow a natural and direct kind of route that can be specified by a canonical proof procedure. In a formal, axiomatized semantic theory of this kind, the canonical derivation of a meaning-specifying theorem for a sentence displays how the meaning of the sentence is determined by the meanings of its constituent words and the ways in which they are put together. Such a semantic theory could itself be called *compositional*.

Suppose that we could provide a compositional semantic theory in which meaning-specifying theorems for the infinitely many sentences of some language could be derived from finitely many axioms specifying the meaning properties of words and of ways of putting words together. This would constitute a relatively precise answer to the question how understanding an infinite language is *possible*. For knowledge of the finitely many facts stated by the axioms of the theory *would suffice*, given an ability to carry out logical derivations, for knowledge of the meaning of any sentence of the language. It is for this reason that philosophers of language engage in the construction of formal semantic theories subject to a *finite axiomatization constraint* (Davidson 1984).

3.2   A structural constraint on semantic theories

It is not clear, however, that finite axiomatization really goes to the heart of the notion of compositionality. In a finitely axiomatized semantic theory for an infinite language, a single axiom may be involved in the canonical derivations of meaning-specifying theorems for many sentences. Indeed, in general, an axiom will figure in the derivations for infinitely many sentences. This gives clear content to the idea that a word makes a repeatable contribution to the meanings of sentences in which it occurs. It is because the constituents of sentences make repeatable contributions to the meanings of sentences that it is possible to understand a sentence that one has never heard before provided that it is built from familiar words in familiar ways. The problem with the finite axiomatization constraint is that these features of the compositionality of meaning may be present in a finite language, no less than in an infinite language.

Imagine a toy language with one hundred sentences built from ten names ('a,' 'b,' 'c,' ...) and ten predicate terms ('F,' 'G,' 'H,' ...). A particular name makes a repeatable contribution to the meanings of the ten sentences in which it occurs; and the same goes for a particular predicate term. Someone who is familiar with the name 'a' as it is used in several sentences (to talk about Harry) and with the predicate 'F' as it is used in several sentences (to mean that various people are bald) may understand the sentence 'Fa' on first hearing as meaning that Harry is bald. But the finite axiomatization constraint does not require that a semantic theory should display the way in which the meaning of 'Fa' is determined by the meanings of 'F' and of 'a' and the way in which they are put together. It does not require that a semantic theory should be compositional. For a semantic description that simply lists the meanings of all the sentences:

'Fa' means that Harry is bald
'Fb' means that Bruce is bald

and so on, counts as a finitely axiomatized semantic theory. The one hundred axioms simply coincide with the one hundred meaning-specifying theorems for complete sentences.

It appears that we need some further constraint on formal, axiomatized semantic theories if they are to explain how it is possible to proceed from understanding of some sentences (of even a finite language) to understanding of other sentences built from the same constituents. In the case of the toy language with just one hundred sentences, the compositionality of meaning would allow someone who understood several sentences containing 'a' and several sentences containing 'F' to proceed, by intuitively rational means of inductive, abductive, and deductive inference, to knowledge of the meaning of 'Fa.' What we want of a semantic theory is that, in such a case, the axioms (and other deductive resources) that are used in the derivations of meaning-specifying theorems for the initially understood sentences should suffice for the derivation of a meaning-specifying theorem for the consequently understood sentence. A theory meeting this condition would display how a name, such as 'a,' and a predicate, such as 'F,' make repeatable contributions to the meanings of sentences in which they occur. Given such a theory, we could see how someone might proceed, by rational inductive or abductive means, from knowledge about the meanings of several sentences containing 'a' and several sentences containing 'F' to knowledge of the facts stated by the axioms that describe the meaning properties of 'a' and 'F.' And we could see how someone with knowledge of those facts might proceed by deductive means to knowledge of the meaning of the sentence 'Fa.'

Considerations of this kind motivate a *structural constraint* on semantic theories that goes well beyond the finite axiomatization constraint. The idea of this constraint is that a formal, axiomatized semantic theory for a language should display the compositional semantic structure that is present in the language, and should display it as structure that could be used by an idealized rational subject. A semantic theory meeting this constraint shows how systematic mastery of a language, a mastery marked by the ability to move from understanding of some sentences to understanding of others – and, in principle, of infinitely many others – could be a rational achievement (Davies 1981: ch. 3; Wright 1987).

3.3   Theories of meaning from the armchair

The construction of compositional semantic theories is thus a philosophical project. It makes a contribution to answering the epistemological question how knowledge of language – in particular, knowledge of meaning – is possible.

Devising an axiomatization that is finite and that satisfies the structural constraint is a fairly technical task for which largely a priori methods, similar to those of logic and mathematics, are appropriate. But it may seem that there must still be a substantial empirical, rather than philosophical, component in the project since it is an empirical question whether the meaning-specifying theorems that are derived from the axioms are correct. It is, for example, an empirical fact about Italian that 'Harry è calvo' means that Harry is bald. So the construction of an axiomatized semantic theory even for a toy version of Italian seems to be partly an empirical project.

In practice, there are two ways in which this empirical component can be factored out. On the one hand, a semantic theorist might focus on abstract, formal languages for which the meanings of sentences can be stipulated from the armchair. The theorist could address the epistemological question about natural languages indirectly by devising axiomatized semantic theories for progressively more complex formal languages that contain the same kinds of terms and constructions as natural languages do. On the other hand, a semantic theorist might focus directly on progressively more complex fragments of his or her own natural language. It is an empirical fact about English that 'Harry is bald' means that Harry is bald. But the theorist can still avoid the need to rise from the armchair and to conduct substantive empirical investigations. This is because the language for which the semantic theory is to be provided is the same as the language in which the theory is to be cast. There is no more accurate way of specifying, in English, the meaning of the English sentence 'Harry is bald' than to use that very sentence, so as to provide a *homophonic* meaning-specification. Thus philosophical work in semantics is often concerned with providing axiomatizations from which homophonic meaning-specifying theorems can be derived.

An axiomatized semantic theory in which the theorems specify meanings surely deserves to be called a *theory of meaning*. But there is another use of this term, by analogy with 'theory of knowledge' or 'theory of justice.' In this second use, a theory of meaning is a philosophical theory about the nature of meaning; it is a metasemantic theory. In this section, we have seen how the study of theories of meaning in the first sense, semantic theories, can contribute to the theory of meaning in the second sense, the metasemantic theory about the metaphysics and epistemology of meaning.

4   Approaches to Questions in Philosophy of Language

Foundational questions in philosophy of language concern the nature of meaning, understanding, and communication. But approaches to these questions vary along several dimensions. In this section, we shall briefly consider some factors that may condition choices between these various approaches. First, there are views about the proper order of explanatory priority as between philosophy of language and philosophy of mind. Second, there are conceptions of the relationship between the philosophical study and the scientific study of language and mind.

4.1   *Orders of priority*

When we use language to communicate information about the world we express our thoughts, and these are also about the world. Just as, in philosophy of language, foundational issues concern the notion of meaning, so also, in philosophy of mind, foundational issues concern the notion of *intentionality*, the way in which our thoughts are about, or represent, worldly states of affairs. It is natural to suppose that issues concerning linguistic meaning and the intentionality of thoughts are closely connected. But it is not obvious which should take priority.

We are concerned here with priority in the order of philosophical explanation, analysis, or elucidation. Let us say that the notion of X is *analytically prior* to the notion of Y if Y can be philosophically explained, analyzed, or elucidated in terms of X, while the explanation, analysis or elucidation of X itself does not have to advert to Y. This kind of priority is to be distinguished from several others including ontological priority, where X is *ontologically prior* to Y if X can exist without Y, although Y cannot exist without X. It is, for example, one thing to ask whether thought can exist without language and quite another thing to ask whether thought can be philosophically explained without adverting to language. On the question of the order of analytical priority as between language (linguistic meaning) and mind (the intentionality of thoughts) four views seem to be possible: mind first, language first, interdependence, and independence.

According to the *mind-first* option, it is possible to give a philosophical account of the intentionality of thoughts without essentially adverting to language, and the notion of linguistic meaning can then be analyzed or elucidated in terms of the thoughts that language is used to express. The mind-first view finds its boldest and most sophisticated development in the work of Paul Grice (1989; see also Schiffer 1972). One way of denying the mind-first view is to say that the philosophical explanations of language and mind are *interdependent*. There is no way of elucidating the notion of linguistic meaning without bringing in the intentionality of thoughts, nor the other way around. This *no-priority* view is characteristic of the work of Donald Davidson (1984). We shall describe the contrasting programs of Davidson and Grice in the next section.

According to the *language-first* option, an account of the nature of linguistic meaning can be given without bringing in the intentionality of thoughts, and what a person's thoughts are about can then be philosophically explained in terms of the use of language. This option finds expression in the writings of Michael Dummett (1993). Indeed, Dummett holds the view, not only that philosophy of language takes priority over philosophy of mind, but also that it is 'the foundation of the rest of the subject' (1978: 441). A philosophical account of the nature of linguistic meaning in accordance with the language-first view cannot, of course, be overtly mentalistic. So it would be unsurprising to find that, once this view is adopted, attempts to explain meaning in other terms are apt to sound rather behavioristic.

The fourth possible view is that philosophical explanations of language and of mind are quite *independent* of each other. Language is one thing and thought is another unrelated thing. This second kind of no-priority view is not plausible at all so long as we regard the objects of study in philosophy of language as being communication systems in use. But the view might be adopted by a semantic theorist whose objects of study are purely formal, abstract languages (Katz 1984).

4.2 Philosophy and science

We have been considering possible views of the relationship between philosophy of language and philosophy of mind. Now we turn to the relationship between philosophy of language and mind, on the one hand, and the sciences of language and mind, on the other. For conceptions of this relationship also condition approaches to foundational issues in philosophy of language.

Towards one end of a spectrum of possible views is a position that says that the only questions about language and mind that are susceptible of rational investigation are questions that belong to the sciences of language and mind. According to this position the business of the philosophy of language and mind is simply to hand all the substantive questions over to cognitive science. We might call this first position *cognitive scientism*. (We mentioned and rejected this kind of view at the end of section 2.2.)

Towards the opposite end of the spectrum is a position that maintains that the philosophy of language and mind offers a distinctive methodology for investigating a class of substantive questions about the notions that figure in our everyday thinking about linguistic and mental matters. The occupants of this position say that cognitive science has little or nothing to contribute to the philosopher's project of plotting the contours of our conceptual scheme. Let us call this second position *philosophical isolationism*.

These opposed conceptions of the interdisciplinary relationship go naturally with similarly opposed views about our everyday descriptions of ourselves as talking, thinking, acting, feeling, conscious and self-conscious persons. Cognitive scientism goes naturally with a *reductionist* view of these personal-level descriptions. Philosophical isolationism goes naturally with the view that these descriptions, particularly the ones that are of primary interest to philosophy, are *autonomous* in the sense that their correctness is not answerable to empirical discoveries about cognitive structures and processes.

But there are positions that are intermediate between cognitive scientism and philosophical isolationism, and there are views of our everyday personal-level descriptions that are intermediate between reductionism and autonomy. According to one kind of intermediate position, philosophy, with its distinctive methodology, reveals that some personal-level descriptions of great importance for philosophical theory carry a commitment to the existence of particular kinds of cognitive structures and processes. Yet, we cannot fully reconstruct the personal-level descriptions in cognitive scientific terms. In the case of philosophy of language, an occupant of this intermediate position could maintain that our personal-level descriptions of ourselves as having knowledge of linguistic meaning are neither reducible to, nor independent from, descriptions of the structures and processes investigated by cognitive science.

5   Two Programs in Philosophy of Language: Davidson and Grice

Grice approaches the metasemantic question about the nature of linguistic meaning head on. He aims to provide an analysis of literal linguistic meaning in terms of
conventional practices of communicating messages, and to define the notions of
conventional practice and communicating a message in terms of familiar mental
notions such as belief and intention. Davidson, in contrast, does not attempt to
provide an analysis of the concept of meaning in other terms, but approaches
questions about the nature of linguistic meaning indirectly, by way of conditions of
adequacy on semantic theories. One key feature of Davidson's program is that the
semantic theories to be considered are theories of *truth conditions*. Another is that
the conditions of adequacy on these theories are formulated in terms of the use of a
semantic theory in an imagined project of overall *interpretation*.

5.1   Davidson's program: truth conditions and interpretation

The basic idea of an axiomatized semantic theory is that the theorems of the theory
should specify the meaning properties of complete sentences. A theorem might do
this by stating that a sentence stands in the meaning relation to some entity:

The meaning of sentence S is entity m.

Alternatively, without any commitment to meanings as entities, a theorem might
adopt the format:

Sentence S means that *p*.

Davidson rejects the 'meanings as entities' view; but he also rejects the 'S means
that *p*' format.
    The problem that he finds with explicit use of the notion of meaning is that the
'means that *p*' construction presents logical difficulties with the result that formal
derivations of meaning-specifying theorems would be problematic. Now, in fact, it
is a matter of dispute whether insuperable technical obstacles stand in the way of
axiomatized semantic theories that adopt the 'S means that *p*' format. But, however that dispute may turn out, the format that Davidson favors, and the format
adopted for most philosophical work in semantics, is:

Sentence S is true iff *p*.

The logical properties of this truth-conditional format are certainly well understood. First, 'is true' is a predicate and 'iff' is the material biconditional of
propositional and predicate logic. And second, the way in which theorems

specifying truth conditions for complete sentences can be derived from axioms assigning semantic properties to words and ways of putting words together can, to a considerable extent, be carried over from the work of Alfred Tarski (1944, 1956) on certain formal languages.

Davidson imposes both formal and empirical conditions of adequacy on truth-conditional semantic theories. The formal conditions of adequacy include the finite axiomatization constraint (section 3.1). But our concern in this section is with the empirical constraint of *interpretational adequacy*. This says, roughly, that a semantic theory, θ, for a language in use is adequate to the extent that its theorems contribute to the best overall interpretation of speakers – their utterances, thoughts, and behavior:

> If θ delivers (by a canonical proof) a theorem saying that sentence S is true iff *p* then it should be the case that interpreting utterances of S as expressions of the proposition that *p* contributes to the best overall interpretation of speakers.

There are three things to notice about this interpretational adequacy constraint on semantic theories. The first is that, strictly speaking, it is not formulated as a correctness condition on the semantic descriptions that are provided by theorems. The constraint does not treat a specification of truth conditions as a surrogate for a specification of meaning. This is just as well since the logical properties of 'iff' guarantee that there is a massive gap between:

$$\text{Sentence S } \textit{is true iff } p$$

and
$$\text{Sentence S } \textit{means that } p.$$

The closest that we come to a surrogate for 'Sentence S means that *p*' in the Davidsonian framework is, perhaps, 'A semantic theory, θ, meeting such-and-such formal and empirical constraints, has a canonical theorem stating that S is true iff *p*.' (This idea of a near-surrogate for 'Sentence S means that *p*' within the framework of truth-conditional semantics could be inspired by what Frege says in a famous passage in *Grundgesetze* (1893: I:32) about the sense and truth conditions of sentences.)

The second thing to notice is that the imagined project of overall interpretation involves simultaneously assigning meanings to utterances and contents to thoughts. The aim of the interpretation is to make the best possible sense of the totality of a person's linguistic and non-linguistic behavior given the person's circumstances. The interpretational adequacy constraint can be transposed into a partial elucidation of the concept of meaning for sentences of a public language:

> If sentence S means (in the public language L) that *p* then interpreting utterances of S as expressions of the proposition that *p* should contribute to the best overall interpretation of L-speakers.

But the same notion of overall interpretation would figure in an elucidation of the intentionality of thoughts. There is no analytical priority of thought over language; nor the other way around. Linguistic meaning and the intentionality of thoughts have to be elucidated together.

The third thing to notice about the empirical constraint of interpretational adequacy is that it provides only a thin elucidation of the concept of meaning. It does not tell us what makes an interpretation of speakers a good interpretation. An interpretation will involve the description of speakers as engaging in certain speech acts (saying and asserting things, for example) and as having certain propositional attitudes (believing and intending things, for example). The constraint requires that these attributions of speech acts and attributions of propositional attitudes should fit together to make best sense of the speakers. But it does not tell us, for example, which combined attributions of speech acts and propositional attitudes make good sense, and which do not.

What seems to be missing from the Davidsonian framework is an account of which combinations of speech act attributions and propositional attitude attributions are coherent. On the face of it, this would be provided by articulating the analytical connections between the concepts of various speech acts like saying and asserting and the concepts of propositional attitudes like believing and intending. There might, for example, be conceptual connections that require that anyone who asserts that p intends an audience to take him or her (the speaker) to believe that p. There might also be conceptual connections between concepts of speech acts and the notion of literal meaning or some surrogate notion.

5.2   Grice's program: analyzing the concept of meaning

The bold proposal of Grice's program is that there are conceptual connections that actually permit the analysis of the concept of literal meaning in a public language (and the concepts of the various speech acts) in terms of propositional attitudes.

If we are aiming at an analysis of the notion:

Sentence S means that p in the language of group G

then a first suggestion might be this:

Members of G use the sentence S to *communicate the message* that p.

This suggestion is in accordance with the mind-first view. There seems to be a reasonable prospect of explaining the notion of communicating (or getting across) a message in terms of propositional attitudes, without having to re-introduce the concept of literal meaning. Certainly, someone can get across a message even though the sounds used have no literal meaning at all. For example, the perpetrator of a sound that has no literal meaning might get across the message that he or she is angry by relying on some resemblance between the sound produced and the sound made by an angry dog.

However, there is a problem with the suggestion. Suppose that, not just one member, but every member, of the group uses this same kind of sound to get across the message that he or she is angry. According to the putative analysis, this should be sufficient for the sound to have the literal meaning that the perpetrator is angry. But, intuitively, it is not sufficient. Indeed, the intuition that this is not a case of literal meaning is strong if each person who uses a sound like an angry dog to communicate anger takes himself or herself to be making an innovative use of a resemblance between sounds (Schiffer 1972: ch. 5).

When we have a case of literal meaning, in contrast, it seems that the reason why we use a particular sound is just that it does have the appropriate literal meaning. However, if the aim is to provide an analysis of the concept of literal linguistic meaning in other terms then we cannot appeal directly to this reason why the sound is used. For the resulting analysis would be clearly circular:

> Members of G use the sentence S to communicate the message that p and do so *because S means that p*.

We can do better by appealing to the idea of a convention as a *rationally self-perpetuating* regularity in the practices of a group of people (Lewis 1969). In an analysis of the concept of convention there is a clause saying that the fact of past conformity to the regularity provides members of the group with a reason to conform to the regularity in the future. The clause does not say that the reason why members of the group conform to the regularity is that there is such a convention, for such a clause would make the analysis circular. But, once the analysis has been provided, we can say, harmlessly enough, that members of the group conform to the regularity 'as a matter of convention' or 'because it is a convention.'

We can combine the concept of convention with the concept of communicating a message to provide an analysis of literal linguistic meaning along the following lines:

> In the practices of G there is a regularity of using the sentence S to communicate the message that p and this regularity is a convention.

So, when a member of G communicates the message that he or she is angry by using an expression that literally means just that, the speaker does not rely on any resemblance between the sound produced and the sound of an angry dog. Rather, the speaker relies on the fact, known to both speaker and hearer, that the expression has regularly been used to communicate that message. There is no evident circularity in such an analysis. (Once the analysis has been provided, we can say, harmlessly enough, that members of the group use the expression to communicate that message 'because there is such a convention' or, indeed, 'because that is what the expression literally means.')

This, in barest outline, is how the Gricean analytical project is supposed to go. But it will be clear, even from this sketchy account, that such an ambitious project faces many challenges. Indeed, one of the most authoritative exponents of Grice's program, Stephen Schiffer (1972, 1987), has reached the conclusion that the project of analyzing literal meaning in terms of beliefs and intentions cannot be carried through. In the next section, we present one problem for the project, the problem of *meaning without use*.

6   The Problem of Meaning without Use

The general idea that literal meaning is a matter of there being conventions to use expressions in certain ways confronts a dilemma. Either the link between meaning and convention is to be made only at the level of complete sentences or else the link is to be made at the level of words and ways of putting words together.

If we opt for the first alternative, then literal meaning will be grounded in rationally self-perpetuating regularities in the use of complete sentences. The problem is that there are many sentences that are never used at all. These unused sentences, built from familiar words in familiar ways, are perfectly meaningful. But the analysis of literal meaning for sentences in terms of conventional regularities of communicative use has nothing to say about them.

If we shift to the second alternative, then literal meaning will be grounded in rationally self-perpetuating regularities in the use of words and ways of putting words together. This alternative seems to promise a solution to the problem of meaning without use. Words and ways of putting words together have literal meanings in virtue of their use in complete sentences. And then, because of the compositionality of meaning, these literal meanings for the constituents of sentences determine literal meanings even for sentences that are never used. However, there is a price to be paid for adopting this second alternative.

If the regularities in the use of words and ways of putting words together are to be rationally self-perpetuating then we must credit members of the group (that is, users of the language) with knowledge that they and others participate in these regularities. But it is not really plausible that ordinary speakers know what these regularities of use are. It is more plausible to say that ordinary speakers just *know how* to use words and ways of putting words together in the context of complete sentences.

It seems that the problem of meaning without use cannot be solved within Grice's program. But equally, our everyday conception of literal meaning seems to require that the problem must have a solution. Suppose that S is a sentence of my language, built from familiar words in familiar ways, and that I understand it on first hearing. It is part of our conception of literal meaning that S does not come to have a determinate meaning only when I first hear or use it. If S means that p in my language then this is what it does and did and would mean whether or not I ever heard or used it.

6.1   Two solutions: tacit knowledge and compositionality

One kind of solution to the problem of meaning without use involves ideas that go beyond Grice's program in the direction of cognitive science. According to the mind-first view, as we introduced it (section 4.1), the notion of linguistic meaning is to be analyzed in terms of mental notions that figure in our everyday personal-level descriptions of ourselves. But, according to this first kind of solution, we need to mention, not only beliefs and intentions, but also cognitive structures and processes.

The envisaged solution would proceed in three steps. First, we would make the Gricean link between meaning and convention only at the level of complete sentences. This would avoid attributing to ordinary speakers knowledge of regularities in the use of words and ways of putting words together. Then, second, we would appeal to the cognitive structures and processes that underpin speakers' assignments of meanings to sentences that are actually used. We would assume that these cognitive structures and processes correspond closely to axioms of a semantic theory and to deductive resources used in (canonical) derivations of meaning-specifying theorems from those axioms. Finally, third, we would appeal to these same axioms and deductive resources to fix the literal meanings of sentences that are unused but are built from the same words, and in the same ways, as sentences that are used.

A natural way of developing this first solution would be to make use of the cognitive scientific notion of tacit knowledge (Chomsky 1965; Evans 1981; Davies 1987). Instead of saying, rather vaguely, that there are cognitive structures and processes that correspond to axioms of a semantic theory and to rules of inference used in derivations, we could say that the axioms and rules are tacitly known.

The possibility of an alternative solution becomes clear if we consider how the problem of meaning without use would arise within Davidson's program. If a sentence, S, is never used then a theorem saying that S is true iff p cannot make any contribution to an overall interpretation of speakers. So the empirical constraint of interpretational adequacy provides us with no clue as to what S means. But a solution to the problem is available within Davidson's program because semantic theories are subject to formal constraints as well as empirical constraints.

The formal constraints are intended to ensure that a semantic theory is compositional. In a compositional semantic theory, the canonical theorems specifying the truth conditions of used sentences will be derived from axioms that specify the semantic properties of the constituents of those sentences. From those axioms, canonical derivations will lead to theorems specifying the truth conditions of other sentences built from the same constituents, whether those sentences are used or unused.

Although this second solution is suggested by Davidson's program, it can be applied to the problem of meaning without use that arises for Grice's program. It avoids the attribution to ordinary speakers of any knowledge, explicit or tacit, about the meaning or use of words and ways of putting words together. Someone who adopts this solution follows the first solution in its first step, by making the Gricean link between meaning and convention only at the level of complete sentences. But the projection of meaning from used sentences to unused sentences is not achieved by following the contours of a semantic theory that is embodied in cognitive structures and processes. Rather, the projection of meaning follows the inductive, abductive, and deductive reasoning of a hypothetical idealized rational subject (section 3.2).

6.2   Comparing the two solutions

The construction of compositional semantic theories contributes to the epistemological project of explaining how knowledge of meaning is possible and how mastery of a language could be a rational achievement. But construction of a compositional semantic theory for a language does not involve any commitment to the idea that ordinary speakers of the language actually know the facts stated by the axioms of the theory. Indeed, attributing this knowledge to ordinary speakers would seem as implausible as attributing to them knowledge of the regularities in the use of words and ways of putting words together. It would over-intellectualize ordinary language use.

Suppose that the problem of meaning without use is solved in the second way, by appeal to the compositionality of meaning. Then we have an account of how it would be possible for someone – a hypothetical idealized rational subject – to come to know the meaning of a hitherto unused sentence. But this does not bring with it any account of how ordinary speakers actually arrive at such knowledge. If, however, the problem is solved in the first way, by appeal to cognitive structures and processes, then an account of the epistemology of understanding is naturally suggested. When a hitherto unused sentence is heard for the first time, the same cognitive structures and processes whose presence has provided the sentence with its meaning come into play to underpin the speaker's assignment to the sentence of that very meaning.

This epistemological difference between the two solutions might count in favour of the first solution. It might also persuade someone who starts with Davidson's program to add some cognitive scientific commitments so that ordinary speakers are credited with tacit knowledge of the axioms of a semantic theory. Indeed, there is a program in philosophy of language that combines Davidsonian truth-conditional semantics with the idea of tacit knowledge of rules and principles that is characteristic of Chomskyan theoretical linguistics (Higginbotham 1986, 1989).

There is a second difference between the two solutions that is metaphysical rather than epistemological. The two accounts offer different answers to questions about the meanings of unused sentences. Imagine that both Charlene and Bruce have used just fifty – the same fifty – of the one hundred sentences in the toy language considered earlier, and that each name and each predicate term occurs several times in this corpus. Charlene has a structured mastery of these fifty sentences, which is naturally glossed in terms of cognitive structures and processes that embody tacit knowledge of a compositional semantic theory for the language. In contrast, Bruce has an unstructured mastery of these sentences, acquired sentence-by-sentence from a phrasebook.

The first solution, which appeals to cognitive structures and processes, says that each of the one hundred sentences has a determinate meaning in Charlene's language, even though fifty of them have not been used and perhaps never will be used. But the situation with Bruce is quite different. If he has tacit knowledge of a semantic theory, it is a theory with fifty separate axioms, one specifying the meaning of each sentence. So appeal to cognitive structures and processes does not determine a meaning for any sentence beyond the fifty that Bruce actually uses.

While the first solution treats the cases of Charlene and Bruce differently, the second solution groups them together, for it takes no account of actual cognitive structures and processes. Meaning for sentences that are not used is determined by a semantic theory. But it is not a theory that is tacitly known by speakers. Rather, it is a theory that displays the semantic structure that could be used by a hypothetical idealized rational subject; the structure to which Charlene is sensitive, but to which Bruce is blind. So, as in the first solution's treatment of Charlene's case, all fifty unused sentences have determinate meanings.

There are philosophers of language who think that it is definitely wrong to attribute to Bruce, with his phrasebook knowledge of fifty sentences, a language in which a further fifty sentences, of which he knows nothing, have determinate meanings (Schiffer 1993). If we agree, then we shall prefer the first solution to the problem of meaning without use over the second solution. If we think that the case for the first solution is compelling, then we shall agree with Brian Loar when he says that 'the Chomskyan idea of the internalization [tacit knowledge] of the generative procedures of a grammar has got to be invoked to . . . make sense of literal meaning' (1981: 259).

We cannot settle this issue here. But the attractions of the first solution are also attractions of a more general position, encompassing a conception of the relationship between philosophy and science and a view about our everyday personal-level descriptions of ourselves. According to this position, intermediate between cognitive scientism and philosophical isolationism, the philosophically foundational description of ourselves as understanding a language is not reducible to, but is also not independent from, descriptions of the structures and processes that cognitive science investigates.

Further Reading

Chomsky, N. (2000). *New horizons in the study of language and mind*. Cambridge: Cambridge University Press. This is a collection of Chomsky's recent papers engaging with philosophy of language and particularly with the limits of a scientific investigation of language.

Davidson, D. [1984] (2001). *Inquiries into truth and interpretation*. Oxford: Oxford University Press. For Davidson's program in philosophy of language, this collection of his essays is essential reading. 'Truth and meaning' is a good place to start, and is also widely reprinted in anthologies including the two edited by Ludlow and by Martinich.

Davis, S. (ed.) (1991). *Pragmatics: A reader*. Oxford: Oxford University Press. This anthology covers the key topics in pragmatic theory and includes classic papers by Grice and several papers by Sperber and Wilson.

Dummett, M. (1993). *The seas of language*. Oxford: Oxford University Press. Dummett's papers on philosophy of language, beginning with his two essays addressing the question 'What is a theory of meaning?' are challenging, rewarding, and influential.

Grice, H.P. (1989). *Studies in the way of words*. Cambridge MA: Harvard University Press. This book is a rich resource, both for Grice's work on pragmatics and for his attempts to analyze the concept of literal meaning. On the first theme, 'Logic and conversation' is the place to start; on the second, 'Utterer's meaning and intentions' covers many of the essential points.

Hale, B. and Wright, C. (eds) (1997). *A companion to the philosophy of language*. Oxford: Blackwell. Pitched at a higher level of difficulty than this Blackwell *Guide*, the *Companion* offers authoritative and sophisticated surveys of many of the topics touched on in this chapter. The first chapter, by David Wiggins, plots a line of thought linking meaning and truth conditions from Frege, through Tarski, to Davidson.

Larson, R. and Segal, G. (1995). *Knowledge of meaning: An introduction to semantic theory*. Cambridge, MA: MIT Press. This accessible book offers a very thorough grounding in the approach to semantic theory that combines elements from Davidson's and Chomsky's work, as proposed by James Higginbotham.

Ludlow, P. (ed.) (1997). *Readings in the philosophy of language*. Cambridge, MA: MIT Press. Philosophy of language is an area where most of the reading that is recommended to students is in the form of articles. Ludlow's excellent anthology offers forty-two papers that include good coverage of the foundational issues in this chapter.

Martinich, A.P. (ed.) (2001). *The philosophy of language* (fourth edition). Oxford: Oxford University Press. Like Ludlow's, this anthology offers good coverage of the main topics in this chapter and of central issues in the theory of reference.

Schiffer, S. (1987). *The remnants of meaning*. Cambridge, MA: MIT Press. Schiffer's book has been massively influential in persuading most philosophers of language that Grice's analytical program cannot be carried through. It is not, however, a book for beginners in this area.

Sperber, D. and Wilson, D. (1995). *Relevance: Communication and cognition* (second edition). Oxford: Blackwell. This is the original and authoritative account of a dominant approach in contemporary pragmatic theory.

Strawson, P.F. 1971: *Logico-Linguistic Papers*. London: Methuen; (revised edition, Aldershot, UK: Ashgate, 2004). Strawson's seminal essays on philosophy of language include 'Meaning and truth,' in which he offers an important comparison of Davidson's and Grice's programs.

Part II

Meaning

2

The Nature of Meaning

Paul Horwich

1 Introduction

Each expression of a language surely *means* something – there is some fact as to what it means; but the nature of such facts is notoriously obscure and controversial. Consider the term "dog." It possesses a distinctive literal meaning in English, and this feature is closely associated with various others, for example, that we use the word to help articulate certain thoughts; that it is appropriately translated into the Italian "cane" and the German "Hund"; and that we should try to apply it to dogs and only to dogs. But such characteristics range from the puzzling to the downright mysterious. Does thought itself take place in language? How might 'little' meanings (like that of "dog") combine into 'bigger' ones (like that of "dogs bark")? What is it about that word's meaning that enables it to reach out through space and time, and latch on to a particular hairy animal in ancient China? And there is a ramified profusion of further questions, as we shall see. So it isn't surprising that philosophy abounds with theories that aim to demystify these matters, to say what it is for a word or a sentence to have a meaning.

The present review aims to map the terrain of alternative suggestions. To that end I will mention the central issues that must be confronted in developing an adequate account of meaning, the various positions that might be taken with respect to them, and some of the arguments that can be given for and against these positions.

2 Meaning Skepticism

It is sometimes maintained that the expressions of a language really do not, as we might naively think, possess meanings. But accounts of this sort may be more or less radical. At the most extreme there is a theory that, as far as I know, has never been seriously proposed: namely, that there are no semantic phenomena at all, that no word stands for anything, and that no sentence is true or false. This view is hardly credible: for no one who understands the word "dog" could doubt that it picks out dogs (if there are any dogs); and no one who understands the sentence "dogs bark" could doubt that it expresses a truth if and only if dogs bark; and so on. However, there are less radical forms of meaning-skepticism that *do* have adherents.

For example, one might deny (with Quine 1962, 1990) that there are any facts concerning the meanings or referents of *foreign* expressions (including the expressions of compatriots, who *seem* to be speaking the same language as oneself). This is not as chauvinistic as it may initially sound; for it amounts to a general and unbiased skepticism about the objectivity of translation. Quine's position is based on his 'indeterminacy thesis': namely, that linguistic behaviour at home and abroad – which he takes to provide the only facts with the *potential* to establish the correctness of any proposed translation manual – will in fact be consistent with many such proposals; so we can rarely fix what a foreigner (or any other person) means by his words. But a number of counters to this argument have appeared in the literature. One response (pioneered by Chomsky 1975, 1987) is that the failure of the phenomena of word usage to settle how an expression should be translated would not result in there being *no fact of the matter*, but merely in a familiar *under-determination of theory by data* (i.e. in a difficulty of discovering what the facts of translation are). Another common strategy of reply (e.g. Horwich 1998) is to argue that Quine has adopted too narrow a view – too behavioristic – of what the non-semantic meaning-constituting features of word use may be; that they actually include, not merely assent/dissent dispositions, but also (for example) causal relations amongst such dispositions; and that once such further evidence is taken into account, the alleged indeterminacy disappears. To illustrate using Quine's famous case: although we may be prepared to assent and dissent, in the same environmental circumstances, to "There's a rabbit" and "There's an undetached rabbit-part," we tend to assent to the second as a consequence of having assented to the first, not vice versa; and that causal fact can be a ground for deciding which of two co-assertible foreign sentences should be translated into one and which into the other.

A different and relatively mild form of semantic skepticism would countenance facts about what refers to what and about the truth conditions of sentences, but would renounce any finer-grained notion of meaning, such as Fregean 'sense.' Thus there would be no respect in which co-referential terms (such as "Hesperus" and "Phosphorus") would differ in meaning. One source of this skepticism might be a Millian/Russellian rejection (Salmon 1986; Donnellan 1989; Crimmins and Perry 1989; Lycan 1990; Soames 2002) of the argument typically offered in support of fine-grained meanings:– namely, Frege's (1952) argument that they are needed in order to accommodate our intuition that (for example) 'believing Hesperus is Phosphorus' is not the same thing as 'believing Hesperus is Hesperus.' But it remains hard to see much wrong with that reasoning (see Schiffer 2003).

Another widespread motivation for embracing the mild form of skepticism is the Davidsonian (1984) view that *compositionality* (the dependence of our understanding of sentences on our understanding of their component words) requires that fine-grained meanings be abandoned in favor of mere truth conditions and their coarse-grained determinants. But again one might well prefer a Fregean point of view: one might suppose (Horwich 1998, 2003) that the state of understanding a complex expression is *identical* to the state of understanding its various parts and appreciating how they are combined with one another. In that case compositionality will have a trivial explanation, and there will be no pressure to adopt Davidson's truth conditional account of it.

Finally, there is the so-called 'non-factualist' form of meaning-skepticism, which Kripke (1982) takes Wittgenstein (1953) to be urging. The idea is that although we may properly and usefully attribute meanings to someone's words, we should not think of these attributions as reporting *genuine* ('robust') facts about that person, but rather as implementing some quite different speech act – something along the lines of 'expressing our recommendation that his words be taken at face value.' Of course, there is a perfectly legitimate *deflationary* sense of "fact" in which "p" is trivially equivalent to "It is a fact that p"; and when we attribute a meaning we obviously suppose there to be a 'fact,' in *that* sense, as to what is meant. Thus 'non-factualism' faces the problem of specifying what makes certain facts 'genuine' or 'robust' ones; and this has not so far been satisfactorily resolved. For example, it might be tempting to identify them as those facts that enter into causal/explanatory relations. But then – since it is pretty clear that a word's meaning helps to explain the circumstances in which sentences containing it are accepted – the Kripkensteinian position would be pretty clearly false. Alternatively, it might be said that the 'genuine'/'robust' facts are those that are constituted by physical facts. But in that case, non-factualism would boil down to a familiar form of antireductionism, and one would be hard pressed to see anything skeptical about it.

3 Reductionism

Amongst *non*-skeptical accounts of meaning, some are reductionist, others are not – some aim to identify underlying non-semantic facts in virtue of which an expression possesses its meaning; others take this to be impossible and aim for no more than an *epistemological* story – a specification of which non-semantic data would tend to justify the tentative ascription of a given meaning.

Reductionist theories are typically motivated by a general sentiment to the effect that, since we humans are fundamentally physical beings (i.e. made of atoms), all our characteristics – including our understanding of languages – must somehow be constituted out of physical facts about us. However, many philosophers are unconvinced by this line of thought – arguing that the majority of familiar properties (e.g. 'red,' 'chair,' 'democracy,' etc.) resist strict analysis in physical terms, and therefore that the way in which empirical facts are admittedly somehow grounded in the physical need not meet the severe constraints of a reductive account.

In response to this point, it may be observed that although some weak form of physical grounding might suffice for *certain* empirical properties, others – those with a rich and regular array of physical effects – call for strict reduction. Otherwise, given the causal autonomy of the physical, those effects would be mysteriously over-determined. In particular, the fact that the meaning of each word is the core-cause of its overall use – i.e. of all the non-semantic facts concerning the acceptance of sentences containing it – would be explanatorily anomalous unless meaning-facts were themselves reducible to non-semantic phenomena. However, as plausible as these considerations might be, the only solid argument for semantic reductionism would be an articulation and defense of some specific theory of that form. Conversely, the best antireductionist argument is that no such account has been found, despite strenuous attempts to construct one.

Reductionist approaches of various stripes will be the focus in what follows; so I won't dwell on them now. As for *anti*reductionist proposals, amongst the most prominent in contemporary analytic philosophy are those due to McGinn, McDowell, Davidson, and Kripke. McGinn (1984) argues that our not having managed to devise a plausible reductive account of 'understanding' should be no more surprising or embarrassing than our inability to devise such an account of other psychological features, like bravery or kindness. McDowell (1984, 1994) gives this perspective a Wittgensteinian gloss: since our puzzlement about meaning is merely an artifact of self-inflicted devitrification, the illumination we need will have to come from a rooting out of confusions rather than from the development of a reductive theory, and so there is not the slightest reason to expect there to be such a thing. Davidson (1984) combines that antireductionist metaphysics with a neo-Quinean epistemology of interpretation: the most plausible translation manual for a foreign speaker's language is the one that optimizes overlap between the circumstances in which her sentences are held true and the circumstances in which we hold true the sentences into which hers are to be translated. And Kripke (1982) sketches a superficially similar idea (on behalf of Wittgenstein): it is reasonable to tentatively suppose that someone means PLUS by a symbol of hers when she deploys it more or less as we deploy the word "plus." But note that in Kripke's view, unlike Davidson's, such norms are not to be regarded as specifying the evidence for a species of 'genuine' fact.

4 Language and Thought

A further bone of contention is the relationship between overt, public languages, such as English and Chinese, and the psychological states of belief, desire, intention, and other forms of thought, which these languages are used to articulate and communicate. The central issue here is whether or not thinking itself invariably takes place within a language (or language-like symbol-system). Is it the case, for example, that the state of 'believing that dogs bark' consists in accepting (perhaps unconsciously) some mental sentence whose meaning is DOGS BARK? The overall shape of any account of meaning will depend on how this question is answered.

Consider, to begin with, the philosophers who would *deny* that thinking is inevitably linguistic. Within that group there are those (such as Grice 1967, 1969a) who maintain that the meanings of public-language sentences derive (in virtue of our intentions and conventions) from the propositional contents of the beliefs, etc., that they are typically used to express. Thus "dogs bark" means what it does because of our practice of uttering it in order to convey the belief that dogs bark. But this approach fails to address the problem of how certain configurations of the mind/brain come to instantiate the intentions and beliefs they do. Then we find those – arguably Wittgenstein (1953) and Quine (1962) – who would solve this problem by supposing that public language meanings are 'prior' (in a certain sense) to the contents of thoughts – i.e. that one can see how a given state of the mind/brain comes to possess the conceptual content it does by reference to the meaning (independently explained) of the public expression with which it is correlated.

Alternatively, there are theorists who maintain that all human thinking takes place within a mental language – either a universal 'Mentalese' or else a mental form of English, Italian, etc. (depending on the speaker). Of these theorists, many (e.g. Fodor 1975, 1987, 2001; Schiffer 1972, 1987, 2003; Loar 1981; Sperber and Wilson 1995; Neale 2004) advocate a two-stage theory: first, an account of how the terms of this mental language come to mean what they do; and, second, a neo-Gricean account of how the meanings of overt public language derive from those contents.

However, it might be argued that the agreements and explicit intentions invoked by Grice *rely* on public language meaning, and so cannot constitute it; that the link between a sound and its mental associate is fixed at an early age; and that their common meaning derives from the joint possession of the same meaning-constituting property – e.g. the same basic use, or the same causal correlations with external properties. Therefore, it is best to suppose that there is a *single* way in which meaning is constituted, applying equally well to both mental and overt languages. Such an approach would of course be non-Gricean. And it would be especially compelling if each of us thinks largely in our own *public* language. From this point of view (Harman 1982, 1987) it seems especially clear that there can be no substantial difference between an account of the contents of thoughts and an account of the meanings of the sentences that express them.

5   Compositionality

It is uncontroversial that, apart from idioms, the meaning of any complex expression-type (such as a sentence) depends on the meanings of its component words and on how those words have been combined with one another. But there is little consensus on how this obvious fact should be incorporated within a full story about meaning.

A common assumption is that compositionality puts a *severe* constraint on an adequate account of how an expression's meaning is engendered. For it requires that the facts in virtue of which a given sentence means what it does be implied by the structure of the sentence together with the facts in virtue of which the words mean what they do. And, given certain further commitments that one could well have, this condition may be difficult to satisfy.

For example, verificationists (e.g. Schlick 1959) maintain that the meaning of each sentence consists in the way in which we would go about establishing whether or not it is true (from which it follows that no untestable hypothesis could be meaningful). And they go on to say (in light of compositionality) that the meaning of each *word* must consist in the constant 'contribution' it makes to the various 'methods of verification' of the various sentences in which it appears. But this point of view suffers from the fact that no one has ever been able to spell out what these contributing characteristics are. In addition, it is hard to see why one should not be able to construct sentences that, despite being neither verifiable nor falsifiable, nonetheless possess meanings in virtue of their familiar structures and the familiar meanings of their parts. Thus compositionality and verificationism do not sit well together.

Davidson's (1984) influential view (mentioned in section 2) is that compositionality may be accommodated only by identifying the meanings of sentences with truth conditions and the meanings of words with reference conditions; for one will then be in a position to derive the former meanings from the latter by exploiting the methods deployed in Tarski's definitions of truth. And this idea sparked energetic research programs aimed towards extending the types of linguistic construction (e.g. to those involving adverbs, indexicals, modalities, etc.) for which this treatment may be given, and towards finding a notion of 'truth condition' that is strong enough to determine (or replace) meaning. Doubts about whether such problems can be solved tended to be dismissed with the response that since natural languages are evidently compositional, and since there is no alternative to the truth-conditional way of accommodating that characteristic, there *must* be solutions, and so our failing to find them can only be due to a lack of ingenuity.

In a similar vein, Fodor and Lepore (1991, 1996) also brandish a 'substantive compositionality constraint.' In their case, the aim is to knock out various accounts of word meaning. For example, they argue that the meaning of a term cannot be an associated *stereotype*, since the stereotypes associated with words (e.g. with "pet" and "fish") do not determine the stereotypes associated with the complexes (e.g. "pet fish") in which those words appear. Clearly this argument presupposes that there is a certain *uniformity* in how the meanings of expressions are constituted – i.e. that whatever sort of thing (e.g. an associated stereotype, or a reference/truth condition) provides the meanings of *words* must also provide the meanings of the *complexes* formed from them.

An alternative picture (Horwich 1998, 2005) would oppose this uniformity assumption (including the Davidsonian implementation of it). Indeed, it would oppose giving any *general* account – covering the meanings of complexes as well as words – of the sort that could leave open the question of whether the former could be determined by the latter. Instead, its account of complexes would *presuppose* compositionality; for it would say that the meaning of a complex expression is *constituted* by the facts concerning its structure and the meanings of its words. For example, the property, 'x means THEATETUS FLIES,' would be constituted by the property, 'x is an expression that results from applying a function-term that means FLIES to an argument-term that means THEATETUS.' In that case, *any* reductive account of word-meanings – no matter how poor it is – will induce a reductive account of complex-meanings that trivially complies with the principle of compositionality. Thus, that principle cannot help us to discover how the meanings of words are constituted.

6 Normativity

Focussing now on what *does* engender the meaning of a word (including suffixes, prefixes, etc.), we find a much debated division between those that favor analyses in *evaluative* terms and those that do not. There is an intimate relation (emphasized by Kripke 1982) between what a word means and how it *should* be used:– for example, if a word means DOG then one ought to aim to apply it only to dogs; therefore one should not apply it to something observed swinging from tree to tree. And many philosophers (e.g. Gibbard 1994; Brandom 1994; Lance and Hawthorne 1997) have drawn the conclusion that meaning must somehow be explicated in terms of what one ought and ought not to say – hence, that meaning is *constitutionally* evaluative. Thus it could be, for example, that the meaning of "not" is partially engendered by the fact that one ought not to accept instances of "p and not p."

In opposition to this conclusion it can be argued that the 'factual' effects of a word's meaning (namely, someone's disposition to accept certain sentences containing it) would be difficult to explain if meaning were evaluative rather than 'factual.' And in opposition to the *reasoning* behind that conclusion, it can be argued that the evaluative *import* of a meaning-property does not automatically render it *constitutionally* evaluative. Killing, for example, has evaluative import; one ought not to do it. And this could well be a *basic* evaluative fact – not explicable on the basis of more fundamental ones. But we may nevertheless give an account of killing in wholly non-evaluative language. So why not take the same view of meaning?

The answer, perhaps, is that, unlike killing, meaning is a matter of *implicitly following rules* (Wittgenstein 1953; Brandom 1994); for the patterns of word-use that a speaker displays are the result of corrective molding by his community. But even if one concedes that meaning is constitutionally *regulative* (i.e. a matter of rule following), this is not to say that attributions of meaning are *evaluative*. No doubt, the notion of 'its being *right* to follow a certain rule' is evaluative. But the notion of 'a person's *actually* following that rule' surely lies on the other side of the 'fact'/value divide.

Moreover, it would remain to be seen whether meaning is *fundamentally* regulative – for one might aspire to analyze rule-following in entirely non-normative, naturalistic terms. Some philosophers (e.g. Kripke and Brandom, in the works just cited) contend that this is impossible. They argue that any analysis of 'implicitly following rule R' would have to depend on an a priori specification of the naturalistic conditions in which an action would qualify as *mistaken*, and that such an account cannot be supplied. But there are others (e.g. Blackburn 1984) who maintain that the required account *can* be supplied. And yet others (Horwich 2005) who reject the requirement – claiming that the relevant notion of 'mistake' is defined in terms of 'following rule R,' rather than vice versa, and proposing analyses that do not satisfy it. Thus one might suppose that S implicitly follows R when, as a result of corrective reinforcement, it is an 'ideal law' that S conforms with that rule – where the notion of 'ideal' is the non-normative, naturalistic one that is often deployed in scientific models (e.g. the ideal gas laws).

7 Individualism

According to some philosophers (again following Kripke) a consequence of these *normativity* considerations is that meaning is an essentially *social* phenomenon; so a 'private language' is impossible. For the implicit rule-following which must be involved in a person's meaning something allegedly depends on activities of correction displayed within his linguistic community. And this conclusion is independently supported by the observation (Kripke 1980; Evans 1973; Putnam 1975; Burge 1979) that we in fact do interpret people, not merely on the basis of their own idiosyncratic usage of words, but also on the basis of what their community means. Thus if a boy, reporting what he has learned at school, says "Kripke discovered other worlds," we take him to be referring *not* to whichever individual satisfies some definite description that the boy happens to associate with the name – there may be no such description, or it may pick out the wrong guy – but rather to *Kripke*, i.e. the person his teacher was referring to, who was in turn referring to the same person as *her* source of the name was referring to, and so on. And when Putnam – a self-confessed incompetent with tree-names – says, pointing to a big shrub, "Is that an elm?," we take him to have asked whether it's an *elm*, i.e. whether it's what the experts would call "an elm." His own defective way of using the word does not fix what he means by it.

Opposed to this conception, however, there are a number of philosophers (e.g. Chomsky 1986; Crane 1991; Segal 2000) who maintain that there *is* a kind of meaning, better suited to psychological explanation, whereby what each person means is constituted by facts about that person and is conceptually (though not causally) *in*dependent of what other people do. These theorists could either deny that this individualistic brand of meaning is constitutionally regulative; or they could accept that it is, but regard the rules as sustained by *self*-correction. They may allow that we *also* have a notion of communal meaning, and that this is the notion that is typically deployed in ordinary language when we speak of what someone means. But, if so, they will contend that it is derived (e.g. by a sort of *averaging*) from the more fundamental notion of idiolectal meaning – so that communal meaning is not appropriate for explaining a particular person's thoughts and actions.

8 Externalism

Alongside the distinction between 'communal' and 'individualistic' accounts, there is a distinction between those theories according to which what we mean by our words (at least *certain* words) depends on the physical environment of their deployment, and those according to which meanings are wholly 'in the head.'

The former ('externalist') perspective came to prominence with Putnam's (1975) famous thought experiment. Since Oscar's physical duplicate on Twin Earth is surrounded by a liquid that, despite its superficial appearance, isn't really water, we are reluctant to say that the doppelganger's word "water" refers to the same thing as our word does – even though, since he and Oscar are intrinsically identical, their internal uses of it are exactly the same. Thus it would seem that the facts that provide certain terms with their meanings must include aspects of the outside world.

On the other hand, it has been argued (Fodor 1987; White 1991; Jackson and Pettit 1993; Chalmers 2002) that words like "water" have a certain *indexical* character – that their reference depends (as in the case of "I," "our," and "here"), not merely on their fixed meanings in English, but also on the *context* of their use. One method of implementing this idea would be to suppose that the meaning of "water" is constituted by an underived acceptance of

$$x \text{ is water} \leftrightarrow x \text{ has the underlying nature, if any,}$$
$$\text{of the stuff in } our \text{ seas, rivers, lakes and rain}$$

In this way (as Putnam himself appreciated) the usual Twin-Earth intuitions may be somewhat reconciled with internalism. Twin-Oscar would *mean* the same as Oscar, but would *refer* to something different.

9   Deflationism

An especially prominent form of externalist view is one that explains the meaning of a word in terms of its reference, which is then explained in terms of one or another naturalistic relation between the word and some aspect of the world (Devitt 1996). More specifically, Stampe (1977) and Fodor (1987) have developed (each in their own way) the idea that

$$w \text{ means } F \equiv w \text{ is causally correlated with fs}$$

where the lower-case "f" is to be replaced by a predicate (e.g. "dog") and the capital "F" is to be replaced by a name of the concept that the predicate expresses (e.g. "DOG"). Alternatively, Millikan (1984), Dretske (1986), Papineau (1987), Neander (1995), and Jacob (1997) have offered versions of the idea that

$$w \text{ means } F \equiv \text{the (evolutionary) function of } w$$
$$\text{is to indicate the presence of fs}$$

However, a good case can be made that the relational form exemplified by all such accounts – viz.

$$w \text{ means } F \equiv R(w, f)$$

is incorrect, and that the motivation for implicitly insisting on it is defective. For the reason one might be drawn to such an account is that meaning has truth-theoretic import; if a word means DOG, then it is true of *dogs*, so sentences containing it are about *dogs*; and, in general,

$$w \text{ means } F \rightarrow (x)(w \text{ is true of } x \leftrightarrow fx)$$

But this implies – assuming some reductive analysis of 'w is true of x' as 'wCx' – that whatever constitutes the meaning-fact must entail '$(x)(wCx \leftrightarrow fx)$,' and so must be indeed be an instance of the form, '$R(w, f)$.' However, as emphasized by Horwich (1995, 1998, 2005), this line of thought is undermined by the plausibility of *deflationism* with respect to truth and reference: namely, the idea that these are non-naturalistic, logical notions – mere devices of generalization. For, if this is correct, then the presumption that 'w is true of x' has some reductive analysis would be mistaken.

Thus the import of deflationism is that we should not require a reductive theory of meaning to have the *relational* form

$$w \text{ means } F \equiv R(w, f)$$

Nor – which comes to the same thing – should we expect, given some proposed reductive analysis of a specific meaning-property, to be able to *explain* why it holds (e.g. why a word with *this* particular use must mean DOG, and must be true of *that* set of objects). And nor – again equivalently – should we require an account that will enable us to *read off* what each word means from information about its use. Consequently, our inability to devise a theory that does satisfy such constraints – an inability which has been convincingly demonstrated by Kripke (1982), Boghossian (1989), and Loewer (1997) – should not tempt us to doubt (as they do) the prospects for a reductionist account. It should rather confirm what we might well have already recognized – that these constraints should never have been imposed in the first place.

The legitimate basic requirement on an adequate analysis of a meaning-property is exactly what one would expect from consideration of reductions elsewhere – i.e. in biology, physics, etc. – namely, that the alleged underlying property must contribute to explanations of the *symptoms* of the superficial property. Thus 'being magnetic' reduces to having a certain micro-structure in virtue of the fact that something's possession of that micro-structure explains why it exhibits the attraction/repulsion behavior that is symptomatic of being magnetic. Similarly, 'U(w)' provides a good analysis of 'w means F' if and only if 'U(w)' contributes to explanations of the symptoms of meaning F. But the symptoms of a word's meaning F are its having a certain overall use (– that of the word "f"). Therefore, 'U(w)' constitutes the meaning of "f" just in case it explains (in conjunction with extraneous factors) the differing circumstances in which all the various sentences containing "f" are accepted. And there is no reason why the satisfaction of this adequacy condition should dictate analyses that take the relational form.

10   Promising Directions

The preceding survey of alternative views of meaning suggests that there are reasonable prospects for an account that is (1) non-skeptical, (2) reductive, (3) applicable to both overt and mental languages, (4) focused in the first instance on word-meaning and trivially extendable to sentence-meaning, (5) not evaluative or fundamentally regulative, (6) applicable to both communal languages and idiolects, (7) internalist, and (8) deflationist, in the sense of not having to take the form of a relational account, 'w means F $\equiv$ R(w, f),' which would incorporate a naturalistic analysis of truth.

These features are characteristic of so-called *use* theories of meaning, deriving from the work of Wittgenstein (1953) and Sellars (1969), and also known as 'conceptual (or functional) role semantics' (see Field 1977; Block 1986; Harman 1982, 1987; Peacocke 1992; and Wright 2001). According to one such account (Horwich 1998, 2005), the meaning of each word, w, is engendered by its 'basic acceptance property' – that is, by the fact that w's overall use stems from the acceptance (in certain circumstances) of specified sentences containing it. A singular virtue of this proposal is that we have a plausible model – namely inference – of how such a property might, in conjunction with other factors, explain a word's *overall* use (i.e. the acceptance-facts regarding every sentence containing the word). Consequently, we can see how the just-mentioned condition on an adequate account of meaning constitution might be met.

Given the enormous variety of things that are done with language, we should not expect there to be much similarity between the basic acceptance-properties of different predicates. Perhaps those of color words resemble each other to a fair degree; and similarly there could well be resemblances within species names, numerical predicates, evaluations, mental terms, etc.; but as we move from one such type to another there is likely to be a considerable divergence of structure. In particular, there is no reason to anticipate that the basic acceptance-property of predicate "f" will generally have the form, 'R(w, f).' Indeed, one might question whether it *ever* will.

Nonetheless it will not be hard to account for a word's referential and normative character. We have the pair of fundamental schemata:

$$\text{w means F} \rightarrow (x)(\text{w is true of x} \leftrightarrow fx)$$

where F is what, in the present context, we mean by our predicate "f"; and

$(x)(\text{w is true of x} \leftrightarrow fx)$
$\rightarrow$ one's goal should be that of *accepting the application of w to x only if fx*

Therefore, once we have established (on the basis of the above-mentioned adequacy condition) that a word's meaning F is constituted by its having a certain basic acceptance property, then its principal referential and normative characteristics are trivially accommodated.

Two further features of this proposal are worth emphasizing. First, it is 'non-holistic' in the sense that it incorporates an objective separation between those sentences that are held true as a matter of meaning and those sentences whose acceptance is not required by meaning alone. This anti-Quinean (1953) distinction is drawn on the basis of explanatory priority: the meaning-constituting uses are those that are responsible for the others. Thus one may rebut the claim that 'use' theories inevitably lead, for better (Block 1994/5: Harman 1993) or for worse (Fodor and Lepore 1991), to holism. Second, the theory is 'non-atomistic' in the following sense: it implies that the existence of words with certain meanings requires the existence of further words with certain different meanings. After all, the meaning of a word can be engendered by the acceptance of some particular sentence containing it only if the *other* words in that sentence are understood appropriately. This is not the extreme view (rightly condemned by Dummett 1991) that the meaning of every word depends on the meanings of every other word in the language. What is required, rather, is that there be a limited stock of interrelated basic meanings on which all others asymmetrically depend.

11   Further Problems

This introductory survey provides no more than the briefest of discussions of some of the many important issues and options confronting a theorist of the nature of meaning. And those dimensions of controversy that I have mentioned are merely the most central ones; there are others that have not yet been considered, but which any satisfactory account must come to grips with. Let me end by listing four of them. (See Horwich 2005 for further discussion.)

(1)   It is not unnatural to think that whenever a word is used the speaker invests it with a certain meaning, and that if he uses the same word (i.e. sound-type) on another occasion, then he may or may not decide to invest it with the same meaning. It may seem, therefore, that the meaning of an unambiguous word-*type* should be explained in terms of the uniform meaning given to its various *tokens*; similarly the meanings of *ambiguous* word-types should be explained in terms of the several meanings distributed amongst its tokens. But this tempting picture is at odds with the various accounts we have been considering. For example, according to Fodor's theory, the meaning of a type is engendered by a causal correlation between its tokens and exemplifications of a certain property. And the other accounts also attribute meaning, in the first instance, to word-types. Thus we must address the following couple of questions. Can there be a reductive account (perhaps a modification of one of those discussed above) that applies initially to word-*tokens*? And if, on the contrary, *type*-meaning is indeed primary, then how – given the phenomenon of *ambiguity* – are we to account for the meanings of specific *tokens*?

(2)   We have been concentrating on our notion of 'the meaning of a word in a given language.' But there are other meanings of "meaning" that also stand in need of explication – especially:

(a)   '*what the speaker means* on a given occasion by some word,' where this is some temporary modification or refinement of its meaning in the language as a whole:– the notion of meaning in which "The President" may be used, in virtue of the speaker's local intentions, to mean "The current President of France."

(b)   '*what is said*, in a given context, by the utterance of some sentence,' '*the proposition expressed* by a sentence-token': the notion of meaning in which "I am hungry" means different things depending, *not* on the speaker's intentions, but on *who* is speaking, and on *when* the utterance is performed.

(c)   '*the conventional pragmatic content* of a term,' 'its *illocutionary force*' (going beyond the *de dicto* propositional constituent that is expressed by it): the respect of meaning in which "but" differs from "and," and in which "I promise to go" engenders a specific obligation.

(d)   '*the full information conveyed* by the making of a given utterance' (i.e. its 'conversational implicature'), that which the hearer may infer from the speaker's deciding, in the circumstances, to say what he does: the respect of meaning in which "There's no milk left" can mean "Would you buy some?."

(e) '*the non-literal meanings* of an expression' – including metaphorical and ironic meanings.

It is not implausible that the kind of meaning on which we have been focusing here is fundamental – i.e. that the other kinds are best explained in terms of it. But this assumption may be justified only on the basis of defensible concrete proposals (Grice 1989; Sperber and Wilson 1995; Neale 2003, 2004; Recanati 2004).

(3)   On the face of it, an expression's having a certain meaning consists in its standing in the relation, 'x means y,' to an entity of a special kind – a meaning-entity. Consequently, one would expect a reductive theory of any particular meaning-fact to be the product of two more basic theories: first, an analysis of the general meaning-relation; and second, an analysis of the particular meaning-entity involved. But it is not obvious how to square this expectation with any of the reductive proposals discussed above, since they do not appear to be divisible into components of this sort. In light of this tension, it would seem that at least one of the following theses must be defended: (1) that meaning-facts do not in fact have the just-mentioned structure; or (2) that their reduction does not in fact require analyses of their constituents; or (3) that some form of non-semantic 'grounding,' weaker than reduction, is the most that can be expected; or (4) that certain analysantia of the sort considered above (e.g. basic acceptance properties) can in fact be factored into one part that analyses the meaning-relation and another that analyses a particular meaning-entity.

(4)   According to Quine's thesis of radical indeterminacy there are few foreign expressions whose correct translation into English are grounded in objective facts. But even if Quine is 99 percent wrong (for the reasons mentioned in section 2), it may be that the correct translations of *some* expressions are nonetheless indeterminate. For example, Brandom (1996) and Field (1998) have argued that a language's words for the two square-roots of minus one may be used so similarly that there will be no properties that might constitute the distinctive meaning of one of them (and thereby constitute its inter-translatability with "i" rather than "–i") that are not also possessed by the other. But any such prospect is a threat to semantic reductionism. For it is not easy to see how that doctrine – in any of its specific forms – can be reconciled with the concession that there is even a *single* term whose meaning is not constituted by non-semantic facts.

What is plain from this review is that research into the nature of meaning presents interlocking problems of formidable breadth and difficulty. But for this reason it remains one of the most lively and fruitful areas of philosophical investigation.

Note

I would like to thank Ned Block, Tim Crane, Michael Devitt, and Barry C. Smith for their valuable comments on a draft of this essay. It also appears (slightly expanded) as the first chapter of my *Reflections on Meaning*.

3

Truth and Reference as the Basis of Meaning

James Higginbotham

1 Beginning with Frege

In this chapter we will expound some of the reasons for holding that the concepts of truth and reference (or the family of *referential* concepts, as we shall shortly explain) are essential to understanding the phenomenon of meaning in language, both in respect of the nature of this phenomenon, and in respect of the accurate description of the semantic properties of human languages, and the relations that hold between a language, considered as an abstract mechanism for the expression of meaning, and the speakers whose language it is. In a number of respects, this view of language may be traced to Gottlob Frege, who however also had other purposes in mind. Nevertheless, it may be well to begin with a version of Frege's views, which traditionally constitute an introduction, both historically and for the student, to the contemporary view of the subject.

Frege (1892) proposed that in complete sentences that are naturally broken down into subject and predicate, and expressed something that one could use to make a judgment; e.g., sentences like '[The cat] is out,' or 'It is raining in [Albequerque],' where the square brackets indicate the subject position (which may not correspond to the grammatical subject), the truth or falsehood of the judgment depended upon whether the *reference* of the subject *fell under the concept* given by the predicate. The notion of the reference of the subject is thus used in explaining what makes for the truth or falsehood of judgements, and if we ask what this notion is, then Frege replies that the reference, for example, of 'the cat' is a certain furry animal (and not, therefore, anyone's idea of such an animal), that of 'Albequerque' is a certain city in New Mexico with several thousand inhabitants (and not, therefore, something that varies with an individual's knowledge of this city), etc. The reference of the subject is, therefore, something that different people (or the same person at different times) with different know-ledge and beliefs but with the same language will have in common.

Frege's view of predicates is similar. The predicate, at which we arrive by stripping away the subject, and replacing it for bookkeeping purposes with a variable, as in 'x is out,' or 'It is raining in y,' is said to refer to a *concept* (in a technical sense): given any thing α of the appropriate sort, the concept will be such that either α falls under it, or does not. If the former, then if NN is any subject referring to α, and '... x ...' refers to a concept, the complete sentence '... NN ...' will be true; if the latter, it will be false. The concept that is the reference of a predicate, like the object that is the reference of a subject term, is neither an idea, nor idiosyncratically variable depending upon one's knowledge or beliefs. It follows that the truth value of '... NN ...' will not depend upon one's knowledge or beliefs either; and indeed it is this intersubjectivity of the notion of truth, its freedom from individual variation amongst speakers of the same language, that in part drives the thesis that the relevant parts of a complete sentence that may be appraised for its truth value must themselves be invariant across speakers.

The intersubjectivity of reference does not imply that the referents (any more than, say, the pronunciation) of expressions as used by speakers of what in ordinary parlance would be called "the same language" invariably coincide. In most of the United States, what is called a "milkshake" is made with ice cream; not so in Boston, where it cannot contain ice cream, and the drink made with ice cream is a "frappe." But it does imply that reference is to hold constant even as beliefs, or emotional or other associations with words, vary across speakers.

What I have above loosely called a "subject" would be in Frege's official termin-ology a *proper name* (*Eigennahme*). This terminology is awkward in English, and henceforth we follow Quine (1960) in calling the expressions in question *singular terms*. Further, we may replace Frege's notion of an object's falling under or not falling under a concept by the simpler nominalistic formulation, that the relevant property of a predicate is that it is *true of*, or else *false of* an object (or, equivalently, that the object either *satisfies* or does not satisfy the predicate). Frege's thesis then is that elementary sentences '... NN ...,' where NN is a singular term, are true or false depending upon whether the predicate '... x ...' is true or false of the reference α of NN. The thesis immediately extends to sentences with more than one occurrence of the same or different singular terms: so 'The cat is on the mat' will be true or false depending upon whether the objects referred to by 'the cat' and 'the mat' (taken in that order) satisfy the binary predicate 'x is on y.'

One of Frege's distinctive and original contributions was to show how the role of expressions of generality, 'every,' 'some,' 'most' and the like, could be brought within the referential scheme. Thus 'Everything is clean' (talking, say, of the dishes) will be true if the predicate 'x is clean' is true of every dish α. In Frege's terminology, an expression of generality referred to a concept under which *concepts* (not objects) either fell or did not. So in a sentence 'Most of them are clean' the question would be whether the things that fell under the relevant concept did or did not exceed in number those that did not fall under it; i.e., whether more things satisfy 'x is clean' than not.

The family of referential notions includes, then, that of the reference of a singular term; the reference of a grammatical predicate (which objects, or pairs, etc. of objects satisfy it); the reference of an expression of generality; and that of truth and falsehood themselves. Further logical extensions are not only possible but even, in Frege's view, inevitable, as one can introduce, for instance, expressions of generality that generalize over predicate positions (an example might be the generality in 'John is everything we expected him to be: honest, straightforward, etc.'). However, we turn now to the question what the system of referential notions and their interaction may have to do with what is most intuitive about meaning.

Let us say that two expressions, of any sort, are *referentially coincident* if the account of reference just given assigns them the same reference. If NN and MM are two singular terms such that NN = MM, then they are referentially coincident; likewise, if '... x ...' and '___x___' are two predicates such that, for all x, ... x... if and only if ___x___, then they are referentially coincident. Then expressions that are by no means equivalent in meaning will be referentially coincident. Objects can be referred to in countless different ways; and it does not take much ingenuity to fabricate, for any predicate '... x ...,' a predicate that is referentially coincident but conspicuously differs from it in meaning. Frege (1892) gave a famous example of the first case, which we repeat here for concreteness. It is a theorem of plane Euclidean geometry that the straight lines from the vertices of a triangle to the midpoint of their opposite sides meet in a point. If the lines are a, b, and c, then the intersection of a and b = the intersection of b and c. But the singular terms 'the intersection of a and b' and 'the intersection of b and c' do not mean the same. Similar examples can be repeated ad infinitum, and for predicate expressions as well as singular terms.

The same point can be put another way (a modern source for the argument is found in Church (1956: 24–5)): if indeed it is to be assumed that the replacement of a singular term NN in a sentence '... NN ...' by another MM with which it is referentially coincident does not alter the referential properties of the sentence, then, as it appears that the only thing that *must* be preserved under the replacement is the truth value of the sentence, it follows that sentences are referentially coincident when they have the same truth value. Therefore, referential coincidence can by no stretch be a proper account of sameness, or even closeness, of meaning.

Frege's view, in light of the above considerations, was that in languages set down for the purpose of expounding a science (but also in colloquial language, where a number of constructions and extensions of the basic apparatus are examined), a complete account of language should distinguish systematically, and for all categories of expressions, their *reference* (*Bedeutung*) and what he called their *sense* (*Sinn*). The sense of an expression cuts finer than its reference, so that, to use his example 'the point of intersection of a and b' and 'the point of intersection of b and c' would have different senses, but the same reference. Similarly for at least most cases of the referential coincidence of predicates, and of sentences themselves. It is to be noted, however, that the sense of a sentence is given in a manner parallel to that of its reference; that is, just as the reference (the truth value) of '... NN ...' is determined by the reference of its parts, NN and '... x...,' so the sense of '... NN ...' is given by the senses of the same parts. An expression is said to *express* its sense, and the reference is given through that sense.

We are now ready to bring the notion of sense into a sort of alignment with that of meaning (without maintaining that sense *is* linguistic meaning: see below). The critical parts of Frege's theses about sense are these:

1   The sense of an expression *determines* its reference.
2   The sense is a "mode of presentation" (*Art des Gegebenseins*) of the reference.
3   Sense is *indirect reference* (explained below).

These theses, and their interaction, constitute one way of connecting the referential notions with that of meaning in language, insofar as the notion of sense itself interacts with meaning.

We begin with thesis (2), that sense is a mode of presentation of reference. In one intuitive sense, the mode of presentation suggests a procedure for laying one's hands on the reference, as one might associate a sense with an expression like 'the Emperor's assassin,' or 'the table in the next room.' More abstractly, the sense constitutes one of the ways the reference may be given to cognition, as a certain irrational number is given by the expression 'the square root of two.' In his writing, Frege takes the sense as constituting a perspective on the reference, analogous to the image of the moon as through a telescope. As the image of the moon is available to many observers, so is sense: it is essentially intersubjective. Moreover, sense is understood as a *cognitive* notion, thus abstracting from other features of expressions that, while intersubjective, and arguably affecting the way in which they present their reference, do not bear upon the question what that reference may be. Examples include epithets, as 'La-La-Land' for 'Los Angeles,' or euphemisms, as 'pass away' for 'die.' Frege's view, which we assume in what follows, is that epithets and euphemisms have the same sense as the expressions that they are epithets or euphemisms for, but that they differ in another, separate feature, which he called *Faerbung*, and which we follow usual English practice in translating as *tone* or *coloration*. We comment briefly below on how to interpret this notion in a referentially based account of meaning.

Thesis (1) we shall understand, anachronistically, as the thesis that the sense of an expression fixes a reference for it given a possible world; or, that a way the world could have been being given, the reference of the expression in that world falls out of its sense. The thesis is thus much stronger (and vaguer) than the thesis that expressions with the same sense have the same reference. A logically exact, but incomplete, rendition would be that the sense of an expression just *is* the function that, for each possible world, has for its value the reference of the expression in that world; the *intension* of the expression, in contemporary terminology. This latter gloss, or perhaps reinterpretation, of the notion of sense is due to Carnap (1956), and is explicitly advanced as an interpretation of the notion of sense for instance in Montague (1970). It is incomplete both in the sense of leaving open what status possible worlds may have, and in leaving it open just how (beyond saying that it does that) sense delivers reference.

Thesis (1) is, then, a metaphysical thesis about the relation of sense and reference. It enunciates the way in which reference is determined, and not how anybody might go about finding out what it is. Thesis (2), however, is fundamentally epistemic, concerning the way in which a thing is presented to a thinking subject. The distinction between the two is encapsulated in the remark of Kripke (1980: 59), that "Frege should be criticized for using 'sense' in two senses." That the two may come apart – that is, that the "mode of presentation," construed as the speaker's means of identifying what the reference of an expression is (whatever the notion of *identifying the reference* exactly signifies), should diverge from what in point of fact or linguistic practice determines the reference of an expression – may form a part of considerations against a unified notion. It does not, however, immediately militate against the implication of truth and reference as fundamental to the theory of meaning. Further complications come from the interaction with thesis (3), that sense is indirect reference, to which we now turn.

It is an intrinsic feature of Frege's conception that reference should be the crucial notion in the interpretation of clauses that are appraised, not for their truth value, but for their sense, clauses that express a *thought* (*Gedanke*) in Frege's terms (we will use *proposition* interchangeably in what follows). Complete sentences, as 'The cat is on the mat,' or 'It is raining in Albequerque,' express thoughts. These same thoughts, Frege proposed, were objects of reference in the same clauses when they occurred as arguments in other sentences, as in 'I see [that the cat is on the mat],' or '[That it is raining in Albequerque] implies [that it is raining somewhere in New Mexico],' where as above we have put in square brackets expressions that are singular terms within the context of the whole sentence. But then it must be that the reference of these singular terms is determined in the way already advanced, through the reference of their constituent words and phrases. And, finally, these constituents are (apart from the introductory 'that,' anyway) just the same as the constituents of those sentences when they are used to make assertions, or ask questions, or be entertained as hypotheses.

Frege's conclusion, then, is that what is *expressed* in 'The cat is on the mat' is the object of *reference* in 'I see [that the cat is on the mat],' all the way down to the constituents 'the cat,' 'on,' and 'the mat.' The expressions themselves are said, in these latter occurrences, to have their *indirect reference*. And if we assume that the indirect reference of a sentence is its sense, then that must be true also of the constituents of a sentence; for it is the senses of those constituents that combine to produce the sense of the sentence, which is its indirect reference.

The notion of meaning, or anyway cognitive meaning, is, we have seen, to be interpreted in terms of sense; and, because sense determines reference, as well as providing a cognitive window on reference, the referential concepts have a central place in a Fregean account of how language, from ordinary speech to a one self-consciously designed for the exposition of a science, functions. However, the status of senses themselves is obscure: construed as "modes of presentation," they are nevertheless not immediately related to any particular human activity; we do not yet know what it is for expressions to have the same or different senses; how sense operates so as to determine reference has yet to be described (beyond the formal statement that it does this somehow); and the basis for the deployment of senses by speakers is unclear. Because of these obscurities, Frege's account can appear not so much mistaken as bloodless. To put the matter another way, and with reference to other articles in this volume: the life of a language (including a deliberately designed language, which must after all be explained in more ordinary terms) would seem to consist in how it is employed, in all manner of human activities; but sense has not yet been brought into contact with actual speech, or perceptual experience. Conversely, it remains to be seen whether an account that did do so would implicate reference and truth in the way that Frege's does.

There are further problems, of a somewhat more technical nature. Frege's account does succeed in explaining how predication works, provided at least that we take on board the notion of a predicate expression's being true or false of an object. But it does not appear to provide a treatment of the combination of senses, say of subject and predicate, to give the sense of a sentence. To take an example from Davidson (1967): if all we know is that the sense of 'Theaetetus flies' is that it is what you get when you apply the sense of 'x flies' to the sense of 'Theaetetus,' then we know only a mock-semantics. Below we examine a couple of ways of responding to this problem, including one that may with some justice be attributed to Frege.

As for the apparent distinction between sense construed as mode of presentation, and sense construed as the metaphysical determinant of reference, there are any number of logical and mathematical pairs of expressions that appear to illustrate that modes of presentation may diverge, where reference is infallibly determined to be the same: '3^3' and '27,' for example. More striking are empirical examples of the sort due to Kripke (1978). The words 'heat' and 'molecular motion' are, it would appear, different modes of presentation of the same physical phenomenon. But, Kripke suggests, there is no way of pulling these expressions apart, metaphysically speaking. Insofar as sense is identified with indirect reference, it is the notion of sense as mode of presentation that would survive, the thesis that "sense determines reference" (or, in some cases, that sense together with context determines reference) being left as an elementary necessary condition, that expressions with different reference also have different senses. This step, however, would leave the connection between sense and reference, and therefore the basis for implicating reference in the theory of meaning, far more tenuous than before.

2 Davidson's Program

Donald Davidson's influential article "Truth and meaning" (Davidson 1967) formulated a link between meaning and reference, but starting from a different viewpoint from Frege's, and arriving at the implication of truth in meaning from a different direction. One of the distinctive features of the approach is that Davidson asks about meaning by inquiring what would be the desiderata for a fully explicit theory of meaning for a normal human language. We summarize briefly the argument that leads to the proposal that the characterization of truth in that language is the way to do the job.

The syntax of a human language is built from a *lexicon*, or inventory of primitive parts, and a *syntax*, or a way of combining these parts so as to build expressions of various categories, these together being the *formal grammar* of the language. The essential category is the (well-formed) *sentence*, comprising those elements that can be used to say things with some force or other. What exactly constitutes the lexicon, how the syntax is given, and how, given the syntax, one goes about enumerating the sentences of the language are all of them complex matters. Waiving the issues here, we assume that the language in question is unbounded; i.e., it has infinitely many sentences. But the lexicon and the syntax of a language are both of them bounded (human beings cannot deploy infinite primitive vocabularies, nor manipulate any of infinitely many independent syntactic principles). The formal grammar is therefore a finitely characterizable object (and not too big either: surely human beings can't have millions upon millions of independent vocabulary items, or independent syntactic rules), the repeated application of whose rules derives sentences, and expressions of other categories, of arbitrary length. The *theorems* of the formal grammar are the provable statements that something is, or is not, a sentence (or well-formed sentence) of the language in question; naturally, there will be similar theorems for expressions of other categories.

What has been said of the formal grammar carries over, point by point, to the *formal semantics* of the language. Suppose that the items in the lexicon have whatever meanings they have; perhaps they are simply stipulated in a long list. To derive the meanings, no less than the syntax, of the sentences now requires a specification of how, in the construction of a sentence, one constructs also its meaning. This task, however, is not at all accomplished on the basis of what we have said thus far: we may know, for example, all there is to know about the meanings of 'the,' 'cat,' 'is,' and 'out,' and about its syntactic structure, without knowing that it means that the cat is out. (We can easily construct a formal semantics for a language in which both the meanings of the words, and the syntax, were exactly as they are in English, but the words 'The cat is out' meant that no dog is in.) We must, therefore, state the principles of combination according to which the meanings of sentences are given in terms of the meanings of their ultimate parts, and their syntactic arrangement. The formal semantics of a language will then comprise two parts: the *lexical semantics*, giving the meanings of the ultimate parts, and the *combinatorics*, stating how the meanings of the parts may or must combine to give the meanings of other expressions, and especially of the sentences. As the lexicon and the syntax were finite, so will be the lexical semantics and the combinatorics, and for the same reasons. The *theorems* of the formal semantics are the provable statements to the effect that some syntactic object means (or does not mean) so-and-so.

Amongst the theorems of an adequate formal semantics for a human language, some will hold a particular pride of place. The formal syntax will have given each sentence σ a canonical description, or standard name. The formal semantics will be adequate only if it proves, for every meaningful sentence σ something

s means that p

where '*s*' is replaced by the canonical description of σ, and 'p' by a sentence of the language in which the formal semantics is being given (presumed here to be English); and moreover that something is itself true. (Of course, for any given σ there may be more than one choice of 'p.') The formal semantics will have to do more than this, because there are unbounded categories other than sentences,[1] and because there may be sentences that are not meaningful at all, and if there are then the formal semantics should say so. However, we may regard the crucial true statements '*s* means that *p*' as the targets of the semantics, the elements against whose provability the theory, once advanced, is tested.

But now, Davidson urged, there is a difficulty: what is the system of theory construction and proof within which we are to carry out a formal semantics, so conceived? Is there an account of the workings of the construction 'means that p' in *our own* conception that will admit the systematic account just held up as an ideal? Davidson wrote:

> it is reasonable to expect that in wrestling with the logic of the apparently nonextensional 'means that' we will encounter problems as hard as, or perhaps identical with, the problems our theory is out to solve. (Davidson 1967: 22)

The difficulty is not tied to any particular conception of the logical makeup of our statements 'the expression so-and-so means such-and-such'; that is, it applies equally whether we take the expressions 'that p' as referring to meanings (or senses, as in Frege), or regard 'means that' as an expression that builds a predicate 'means that *p*' when in construction with a sentence 'p.' It applies also to other formulations of the goal of formal semantics, as 'the sentence s expresses the proposition that p,' and – notably – to 'the truth condition of the sentence s is that p,' at least where substitution under identity for singular terms is said to fail to preserve truth conditions.

At this point, Davidson suggests, for the special case in which the language of the theorist herself (the *metalanguage* in the terminology of Tarski (1956), carried over to the present case) is the *object language*, whose formal semantics is to be given, a "simple, and radical" revision of the goals of the theory. Let it be proposed that a formal semantics for this case is charged with proving every instance of

$$s \text{ is } T \text{ if and only if } p$$

whenever '*s*' is replaced by a canonical description of a sentence, and '*p*' by that very sentence. All of these will of course be true. Moreover, the predicate 'T' will be coextensive with the predicate 'true,' as applied to sentences of the language under study. Call this case, where the object language and the metalanguage are the same, the *intramural* case. The thesis, then, is that an intramural formal semantics will constitute a full theory of meaning for the language: for, for every instance of the schema above, the sentence replacing '*p*' will give the meaning of whatever canonical description is put for '*s*.'

Well, the last is not quite true, chiefly because of ambiguities of various kinds. The English expression 'Visiting relatives can be boring' is ambiguous, having one canonical description in which 'visiting relatives' is an ordinary modified noun, referring to relatives who are visiting, and another according to which it is a clause with an understood subject, referring to the activity of visiting one's relatives (which is then said to be boring to the one who is doing the visiting). We discuss some other examples below, by way of an introduction to the contemporary conception of logical form in language. But we may take it that, as the formal syntax and the formal semantics are bound to be articulated together, we shall be cleaning up the metalanguage in various respects so as to resolve these issues.

How is the theory extended to the *intermural* case, where object language and metalanguage do not coincide, and may in fact be arbitrarily distant the one from the other? In Tarski's account of truth in formalized languages, it was assumed that what replaced '*p*' in the schema was a *translation* of the sentence whose canonical description replaced '*s*.' A translation is assumed to preserve reference, and therefore in particular to preserve truth (a point that follows even if truth values are not themselves the reference of sentences, because the account of predication, for instance, makes truth depend only upon reference). To halt at this point, however, would be to leave matters nearly as bloodless as the Fregean account left them; for nothing is said about how the translations are to be arrived at, or upon what human behavior correlations between languages may depend.

It may seem, indeed, that interpretation via translation (into a language one understands) would serve as well as interpretation via a theory of truth. But this is not so: besides the (rather pedantic) point that translation is a relation between two languages, expounded in a metalanguage, whereas interpretation is just of one language, expounded in another, the same or different, we may observe that a theory of truth, breaking down sentences into their component parts, and explaining how the interpretation of these parts determines the interpretation of the whole, gives more information than does a translation; for we may know that a sentence *s* of one language is to be translated by a sentence *s'* of another, and so can be presumed to combine equivalent, or roughly equivalent, parts in the same way to reach the same result, without knowing how exactly either one manages to do this.

Davidson's own suggestion is that what replaces '*p*,' in the intermural case, is, for each *s*, something that *interprets s*, within some general account of interpretation for the language. Moreover, the theory is to be justified as a whole in virtue of observations of, and adjustment to, the apparent acts of the speakers of the language, including the empirical circumstances in which they subscribe to the truth, or the desirability of truth, of the sentences therein. In the last formulation, there is already a departure from the kinds of evidence that would be permitted on the basis just of observations of behavior: subscribing to the truth of a sentence is not the same as being willing to assert it, as we must factor out self-deception and other interferences. It is a nice question just how far down the path of attribution of mental states to speakers we must go in the name of evidence for interpretation (rather than outcome of interpretation). We turn here to some points, mostly stemming from an article by J. A. Foster (1976) that help to formulate this question more precisely.

The points in question bring into sharp focus the distinction between the original desideratum – a theory that proves statements '*s* means that *p*,' using a non-extensional construction – and Davidson's extensional replacement, '*s* is T if and only if *p*.' Because the replacement is extensional, and because in the meta-language the theorist will be able to prove all sorts of identities between singular terms, equivalences between predicates, and so forth, there will, if there is one, be any number of equivalent replacements for '*p*.'

There will also, and for the same reason, be any number of equivalent formulations of the principles governing the lexicon, and the axioms of the combinatorial part of the theory. There must, therefore, be some way of distinguishing, amongst theories of truth, all of whose consequences are true, between those that do, and those that do not, properly interpret the sentences in question.

To fix ideas, consider an elementary example. In the intramural case, speaking of and in English, we must certainly establish the truth conditions of simple sentences such as 'The sun is hot,' and specifically to say that it is true if and only if the sun is hot; and we expect the theory to proceed in the same way for all such sentences, consisting of a subject singular term and a present-tensed verbal complex (the copula plus the adjective). The following axioms will do the job:

> 'the sun' refers to the sun;
> 'is hot' is true of x if and only if x is hot.

If the sentence *S* is an instance of a singular term *a* in construction

> with a present-tensed verbal complex V, then
> S is true if and only if V is true of the reference of a.

(The last is the crucial combinatorial axiom.) Knowledge of these facts, together with the fact that 'the sun' is indeed a singular term, and 'is hot' is a present-tensed verbal complex, is sufficient to derive the desired theorem:

> 'The sun is hot' is true if and only if the sun is hot.

Our axioms were, of course, carefully chosen so as to reveal, one might say, the minimal information wanted. But other axioms would work as well. So, for example, suppose we added to the combinatorial axiom above some innocent true remark, say that $7 + 5 = 12$. Then the revised theory will prove in the first instance

> 'The sun is hot' is true if and only if the sun is hot and $7 + 5 = 12$.

Since '$7 + 5 = 12$' is known to be true, the theory with the original combinatorial axiom and that with the revised axiom prove exactly the same theorems. But surely it is the *first* and not the second, that interprets the English sentence 'The sun is hot.' How can we make the desired distinctions here?

One way to distinguish amongst truth theories, or so it has been suggested, by Davidson (1976), is that we concentrate on the empirical issues that arise in inter-pretation itself (perhaps extended as suggested in Lewis (1974) to include the interpretation of the *person*, not just her language). For instance, we may require that a theory of truth respect relations of implication that the speaker takes to hold, or not to hold, between sentences (Davidson 1999). Another possibility is that we posit, and then try to determine, what it is about an expression that a speaker is expected, as a speaker, to know about its reference (Higginbotham 1991), which would yield certain *targets* for the ascription of reference, and so of truth value. In our example, nothing about numbers would figure in the target for the combinatorial axiom. Others may suggest that the notion of *information* conveyed by a sentence is crucial, "information" here being understood as discrimination amongst open possibilities (see for instance remarks in a number of articles in Stalnaker 1999).

To put the problem swiftly: even within relatively unproblematic, extensional parts of our language, we shall want to come back to the point that the "condi-tions under which S is true" are multiple, whereas the interpretation of S, if not unique, at any rate does not wander in arbitrary ways through irrelevant facts. The case may be highlighted from another angle, by considering the problem of characterizing truth conditions in *any* perspicuous way for statements ascribing propositional attitude (those for which Frege invoked indirect reference); see the chapter (10) on propositional attitude ascriptions for further discussion. We shall briefly consider a more tractable extension, that involving the metaphysical mo-dalities.

The introduction and development of the modalities, necessity, and possibility, within logic and semantic accounts of language and thought, has exercised a considerable influence on debates about meaning in language. On the one hand, it may appear, and indeed be, that some interpretations of these notions collide with at least the general views of Frege, Davidson, and others, and are not easily reconciled with them; on the other, that their proper interpretation provides an even stronger link between truth and meaning than emerges from semantic inquiries that do not take these notions into account. We shall not attempt to survey this history here; and for the sake of concreteness we shall assume a (model-theoretic) understanding of the modalities best known through the work of Kripke (1963), and developed in various higher-order systems in the articles collected in Montague (1974).

In the works cited, an interpretation of a language goes through the parameter of possible worlds, and what answers to the interpretation of a singular term is a function that, for each possible world i, assigns that term a reference in i; what answers to the interpretation of a one-place predicate is a function that, for each possible world i, and each object o, assigns a truth value to (i,o); and so forth. Thus every expression, of every category, comes to have its ultimate semantic value only relative to a possible world. Following the terminology of Carnap (1956), its *intension*, given a family I of possible worlds i, is a function with domain i. Its *extension*, for each i in I, is a value of the appropriate and familiar sort: an object, in the case of a singular term, a determination for each object whether it is true of that object, in the case of a one-place predicate; and so on. A (one-place) *modality* is an expression with the syntax of negation (i.e., it attaches to a formula to make a formula). It is interpreted as a function from intensions to intensions. We illustrate with a few simple examples.

Suppose we introduce the symbol '$\square$' with the intention that it represent absolute necessity, i.e., truth in all possible worlds. The relevant clause for model-theoretic interpretation will then be:

$$\square\varphi \text{ is true}(i) \text{ if and only if for every } j, \varphi \text{ is true}(j)$$

If ι is an intension appropriate to a sentence; that is, a function from possible worlds to truth values, or alternatively a set of possible worlds, then '$\square$' answers to the function F given by:

$$F(\iota) = \text{True if } \iota = I; F(\iota) = \text{False otherwise.}$$

The box '$\square$' thus amounts to absolutely universal quantification over the possible worlds. The diamond '$\diamond$' of absolute possibility, truth in some possible world or other, is described according to the same formula, and is left to the reader. A modality may be relative to a structure placed on the possible worlds, the best known example being that of an *accessibility* relation R. If '$\square^*$' is a modality of necessity that is sensitive to this structure, then we would put:

$$\Box^*\varphi \text{ is true}(i) \text{ if and only if for every } j \text{ such that } R(i,j), \varphi \text{ is true}(j)$$

and this interpretation is likewise described by a function from intensions to intensions.

Far more elaborate systems are possible, and have been suggested. But even what has been given up to this point will suffice to focus the philosophical questions. The theorist applying this logical development of the modalities to our language is bound to make truth (and other semantic values) relative to the parameter of possible worlds (and when something is said to be true *simpliciter*, that will amount to truth relative to this world, whatever it may be). What goes for truth and the category of sentences goes for the semantic values of expressions of every category, and so the theorems of a formal semantics, on this construal of our language, will take the form of:

$$\text{For all } i, s \text{ is true}(i) \text{ if and only if } p(i)$$

where '$p(i)$' represents the relativization of every constituent of p to the parameter of possible worlds, so that, for instance, it will be a theorem that the sentence 'snow is white,' as referred to by its canonical description, is true(i) if and only if snow(i) is white(i).

Actually carrying out a recursive definition of truth, when modality is incorporated along the lines given above, is a technical matter (see Gupta 1980: ch. 5 for the basic construction). More to the point for our purposes are the questions: (1) whether the introduction of modality is damaging to the thesis that truth and reference are the concepts basic to cognitive meaning; and (2) whether, after all, they turn out to vindicate those concepts as fully characterizing cognitive meaning. We comment on these in turn. For question (1), we shall want to consider the question of *realism* in the theory of meaning, insofar as meaning is intertwined with truth conditions. To this point in the exposition, our examples have been of the most humdrum sort, 'the cat is out,' for example. But these examples, and in fact anything in the language, will interact with the modalities, as well as with those locutions that have been examined on the basis of the modalities as we are understanding them here, including particularly conditionals and counterfactuals. That the cat might have been out, or must have been out, or would have been out had the door been open, are all of them statements whose meaning was to be clarified through their truth-conditional content, which we grasp as part of our understanding of our language, or anyway a person who did grasp would be able to deploy so as to understand us. And, as we have seen, grasp of the truth conditions of these modal statements is held to involve the relativization of their constituents to the parameter of possible worlds. Insofar as we exploit this account, we seem at least committed to a form of realism about metaphysical possibility.

Another point under (1) above: since the aim is to give the semantics for a whole language, we must consider those parts of language that have figured, early and late in philosophy, in debates about realism, relativism, subjectivism, and so forth; ethical and aesthetic statements, for example. These are not marked in any special syntactic way, and their target truth conditions, or meaning conditions, are as blandly stateable as any others. An account of truth, supposed a basis for an account of meaning, should not foreclose these debates in the interest of realism, so it would appear.

The force of the objection under (1) would be mitigated, however, if it could be shown that the relativization of truth and reference to possible worlds (possibly amongst other parameters) could serve to interpret cognitive meaning, as suggested in (2) above; we turn, therefore, to a brief examination of what has been said in this arena.

As noted above, there is a trivial link between truth and the meaning of sentences, in that sentences cannot have the same meaning if they differ in truth value. The observation is naturally extended to modality, in that sentences cannot have the same meaning if one could have been true while the other was false; or, in the interpretation we are considering, there is a possible world in which they have opposite truth values. We may therefore ask, conversely, whether sentences have the same truth value in all possible worlds are alike in cognitive meaning. The intuitive answer would be, "No"; for if that were the case then any two logically equivalent sentences would be synonymous, an apparently absurd result.

There is more. It is the business of a theory of meaning to trace conditions on meaning through constituents up to the top, that is to the whole expression under consideration, through a recursive theory. It would be remarkable indeed if any such procedure did not allow notationally different expressions to end up in the same place.[2] Such is the case with truth itself, with truth relative to possible worlds and other parameters, and so on. Of course, and *ex post facto* as it were, one could paste different labels on the elements; but, barring a principled way of doing so, and one moreover that had something to do with meaning, that would be no advance. Thus cognitive synonymy would have to be combined with an account of how sentences that get at the same truths (are true in the same possible worlds) are discriminated in practice.

3   The Constitution of Meaning

We may distinguish two kinds of questions about meaning. The first, which has exclusively occupied us until now, is: what are the notions in terms of which the facts about meaning are to be articulated? In fact, we have been sectarian about this question, as we have been expounding the thesis that the notion of reference is essential to meaning; if this is correct, then reference is the central concept of semantics. The second question, which has given rise to a variety of investigations and views under the name of semantics, is: what are the non-semantic (perhaps physical, perhaps intentional) phenomena that give rise to meaning such as we find it in language, and how do they do so? These are the questions that constitute what may be called *metasemantics*, not semantics proper, but rather the questions raised by asking what sort of phenomenon meaning is. They may, but need not be, raised with a reductive intent. If they are, then much depends upon whether psychological states are admitted as primitives. We noted above, for instance, that Davidson was willing to constrain truth-theoretic interpretations of alien speech by requiring that interpretation honor the relation of implication, as conceived by the interpreted; but that a subject holds that some set S of sentences implies a sentence s, though it is of course conjectured on the basis of language use or behavior, is hardly revealed in use or behavior, however broadly these notions are interpreted.

It is not part of the current essay to investigate conceptions of metasemantics. We may, however, note that if the meanings of expressions are to have properties that they are at least very plausibly said to have, then reference (parameterized to possible worlds, and perhaps other elements) is implicated. We are all of us psychologically different, and different and at different times within ourselves. A natural view, however, is that the meanings of our words, being intersubjective, do not vary with variance in our beliefs over time, or our differences of opinion one with another. Meaning is something that is stable at least through a wide variety of psychological differences. The concept of reference fills this bill nicely, and it satisfies the obvious desideratum that there are genuine disagreements, cases where one person holds S true, and another holds it false, but where the thing in question is the same for both. Furthermore, the notion of reference has the virtue that it is applicable to all categories of expressions, as we illustrated through the examples of names, predicates, and quantifiers above—the list could be extended. Finally, the reference of an expression would appear to be suitably context-independent, as the meaning of an expression should be if it accompanies that expression wherever it goes.

To all of the above points at least hypothetical rejoinders are possible, and must be considered seriously. For the last, which has attracted considerable recent discussion, we might ask, for example, whether there is a stable meaning (conditions on reference) even to words like 'red' or 'hot,' applying as they do depending upon circumstances, and the point of saying that something (John's hair, or the sunset) is red, or that something else (the stove, the sun) is hot. (A source of many examples and discussion here is Travis (2001).) Furthermore, it is clear that fully understanding what a person is saying requires a filling-in of purposes and intentions, together with unstated matters—one does not know, for example, what is meant by an assertion of 'Everyone was happy' until one knows the intended range of the quantifier. These complexities, if intractable, do not dethrone reference from its signal place in the theory of meaning. But they might imply that a proper theory of communication should not rigidly separate reference as determined by linguistic forms from reference in context.

4 Theoretical Prospects

What are the prospects for a theory of truth and reference for a fully developed, historically given human language? Davidson (1967) concludes his essay by noting a number of areas in which the fundamental combinatorics of language was, at the time of writing, in his opinion not well understood; and even a casual survey of the literature will reveal a number of areas where, to use Michael Faraday's expression, we are anyway far closer to the "particular go" of the semantic design of human language than we were even a few years ago. Overwhelmingly, these areas concern truth and reference. Naturally, some involve truth and reference because it is part of their semantics precisely to affect truth and reference: so the modals, quantifiers, and so forth. But there are, for example, matters of relative scope; structural ambiguity; the interpretation of mood; the ordering and semantic effects of modification; and a host of others. The inquiries in this area can be classified under the broad heading of inquiries into logical form; i.e., the combinatorial structure, as opposed to the meanings of words, characteristic of human language. We close this chapter by indicating some of the points where research activity, more or less up to its ears in the referential concepts, goes forward.

The notion of logical form is resonant within philosophy, as it may be concerned with uncovering the "true structure of the proposition," as in the point of view toward definite descriptions taken by Russell. The aim in many concrete investigations is more modest. In any general inquiry into the workings of language, it is crucial to generalize over whole families of sentences or other expressions, alike in their structure, in order to determine what the combinatorics of that structure is.

A simple but significant example of the last point is provided by the semantics of the tenses. If we concentrate merely upon simple sentences, as in (i):

(i)(a)   The cat is on the mat (now)
(i)(b)   The cat was on the mat
(i)(c)   The cat will be on the mat

then a natural proposal is that they represent operations upon a tenseless radical, 'the cat be on the mat,' whose truth value is relative to time; and that 'now' in (i)(a) is pleonastic. We would thus derive logical forms as in (ii):

(ii)(a)   Present[the cat be on the mat (now)]
(ii)(b)   Past[the cat be on the mat]
(ii)(c)   Future[the cat be on the mat]

The effect of the Past operator would be summed up in a general statement, as

Past[φ] is true at time t iff for some $t'<t$, φ is true at t'

and similarly for the others. The picture changes at one, however, when we note that in tensed sentences containing other tensed sentences as parts there are relations between the tenses. Thus consider (iii):

(iii)   Mary said that John was sick.

This is ambiguous, as Mary (speaking English) could have said, "John is sick," or "John was sick." Furthermore, we can see that in these complex cases the word 'now' is not always pleonastic. Suppose that I am standing (now), and consider (iv):

(iv)   It will always be the case that I am standing.

Certainly false. But (v) is intuitively true!

(v)   It will always be the case that I am standing now.

A similar example, due to Kamp (1971), is provided by the pair (vi)–(vii):

(vi)   A child was born that would be king of the world.
(vii)   A child was born that will be king of the world.

The interpretation of (vii) must bring out the fact that, unlike (vi), if it is true, then the kinghood of the child in question must follow, not only the time of birth, but also the time of speech, or evaluation. In these and similar cases, the elementary operator-treatment of the tenses will not suffice, and more sophisticated machinery is wanted.[3]

Whatever the difficulties in providing a full compositional theory of truth conditions for the whole of a human language, we should note that even those aspects of meaning or usage that do not have to do with the truth value of what is strictly speaking said (that is, belongs to cognitive significance or sense), seem to depend upon referential concepts to get launched into language. We may approach the point first of all by considering that, when people speak with definite intentions, they perform actions of various kinds: asserting, asking, commanding (or exhorting), warning, and so forth. The nature of these actions, at least when they involve declarative sentences, is independent of the interpretation of the sentences themselves.[4] Thus the content of 'The ice is thin' is the same (in a given context) independently of whether one is asserting it, warning that it is so, or asking whether it is so. Assuming the hearer's sound uptake on this content (together with her appreciation of the action being performed), it is natural to conclude that what is exchanged between people is information about what possibilities there are in the world: assertion rules some things in and others out; warning does the same, but with the implication that the things that are in may be harmful; and asking puts forth the possibilities themselves, perhaps because the speaker wants to know, and perhaps because (as in test questions) the speaker knows perfectly well and wants to know whether her audience knows. The act of assertion implicates belief (the liar simply represents himself as believing what he does not believe). Warning implicates belief, and more; and so on. Whatever content Mary intended to convey in saying to John, as a warning, "The ice is thin" is presumably the same as the content of the complement clause in the true report, "Mary warned John that the ice was thin."

Now, much is implicated by a speaker that is not said (see the chapter (8) on speech acts and pragmatics), and among things implicated some actually hold by virtue of the language employed; i.e., they do not depend upon context. Such would appear to be the case with epithets, as 'La-La-Land' for Los Angeles, where the speaker (not speaking ironically) implicates something like: Los Angeles is a frivolous city. Euphemisms fall in here as well, as 'pass away' for 'die,' where the speaker may implicate that the use of 'die' is offensive. Still more stringently, there may be a taboo against pronouncing some name of God. But all of these acts presuppose something about reference. You have to know that 'La-La-Land' refers to Los Angeles to grasp the speaker's implication; and in the case of the taboo, you must know that the forbidden name is a name of God. If this is right, then at least these phenomena of tone or coloration in the sense of Frege, understood as linguistically controlled implications that speakers make in their choices of expression, rely on the notion of reference to get started.

In this chapter, we have concentrated upon considerations in favor of, and some skeptical of, the thesis that systematic characterizations of reference and truth for a language are essential to an account of how it works. But how does that characterization interact, if at all, with the familiar thesis that meaning is use? We should take care to distinguish the thesis (1) that patterns of use, or the intentions of speakers as revealed therein, constitute the genesis of a reductive account of the phenomenon of meaning from the thesis (2) that the concepts of reference and truth should not, or need not, be seen as the basis of meaning. Even if (1) should be true, (2) does not follow. A particularly clear statement of the distinctions here is to be found in Lewis (1975). Lewis regards a *language* as, on the one hand, and abstract object, characterized by a syntax to which is adjoined and account of reference and truth (for him, this includes truth in a possible world, and other parameters to which truth may be relative), and, on the other hand, a social practice in which people engage, for deliberate purposes and with the usual intentions and mutual understandings that mark the practice. Any appearance of conflict between these conceptions, Lewis argued, is illusory. An abstract language L is the language of a certain population P just in case certain social conventions with respect to the expressions of L are in effect. These conventions include asserting only those things, as evaluated by the semantics of L, that you believe to be true; believing that others do so; and believing that all this is common knowledge. We will not attempt further examination of Lewis's view here; but we note that it is an example of how, for instance, the dry statement that our word 'snow' refers to certain cold stuff that typically falls from the sky in winter (part of the lexical semantics of an idealized and abstract English language) is consistent with the view that this language is our language because of various psychological states that we are in, and expect others to be in, with respect to the use of this word.

Notes

1   For example, the category of Noun Phrases is infinite, as relative clauses of arbitrary length can be embedded in them. If 'John ...' is a sentence, then the expression 'the man who ...' is a Noun Phrase. Since the sentences are unbounded, so are the Noun Phrases.

2   This point is made forcefully in Soames (1989: 577–8 and n. 2); see also Higginbotham (1993). The issue has a long history, going back at least to Carnap's (1956) view that some contexts are "neither extensional nor intensional," and so resist a straightforward recursive treatment of the truth conditions of the sentences in which they occur.

3   For further discussion, see Higginbotham (1999) and references cited there.

4   That is, there must be *some* notion of content that is neutral as amongst the various uses of the sentences. When that content is expressed with a certain force, then the characteristics of that force must be considered. Thus consider commands, for instance "Do not go out without your coat," and what it is for the person to whom it is addressed to *comply with* the command. It is not sufficient for that person merely to have not gone out without her coat; rather, it must be that even if tempting circumstances should have arisen, she would not have done so (if she were all ready to go out without her coat should her friend have happened by, but the friend didn't happen by, she did not comply, although she did not disobey either). Note that the compliance conditions for a command will include, though not be restricted to, the truth conditions of the declarative: You do not both go out and not wear your coat.

4

Language, Thought, and Meaning

Brian Loar

In English the noun "thought" is ambiguous. It can mean what a person thinks or believes, that is, the *contents* of acts of thinking or states of beliefs etc., a proposition. But it can also mean an act of thinking or (in a perhaps slightly stretched sense) a state of belief. In this sense, thoughts are psychological. The central question in the literature concerns thought in the latter sense. But Frege is an exception.

Gottlob Frege

A classical starting place in discussing the relation among language, thought, and meaning is the philosophy of Gottlob Frege. When we speak of "thoughts" in connection with Frege we mean *Gedanken*, thoughts in the first sense. They are what are asserted and judged; they are abstract entities. Frege is not concerned with thoughts as psychological states. Michael Dummett (1996) speaks of "the extrusion of thoughts from the mind" in the writings of Bolzano, Frege, and the later Husserl, that is, the disengagement of thoughts from psychological factors, not only perceptions and "ideas" but also from thoughts in the second sense above, however non-empiricist an account of them we may fashion.

Frege does not say what constitutes *having* a thought, as Dummett (1993) notes. This is not surprising if the motivation of Frege's engagement in the logical study of language is not primarily to explain either the psychological basis of linguistic meaning or of having a thought. His central concern is the structure of thoughts considered as abstract, non-psychological entities. He appears not to be concerned *primarily* about how language works in use; but this is countered by the careful and sophisticated theory of linguistic meaning he presents in "On Sense and Reference" (1952) and in other places. Thoughts (Gedanken) are central in

Frege's philosophy in at least two ways. They comprise the claims of mathematics, logic, and science, for whose concepts no empiricist psychology, according to Frege, can properly account. And thoughts are what are communicated, in the sciences and also as the contents of ordinary beliefs and other propositional attitudes.

In Frege's theory of language, thoughts are the senses of statements. We might be tempted to say that senses are the meanings of linguistic statements and their components. But it is not correct to identify senses in general with literal meanings. For, as Tyler Burge points out (1979], uses of indexicals and demonstratives have senses, but not as their literal meanings; better to say that senses are their modes of presentation. For Frege the same holds for proper names; ordinary proper names typically have different modes of presentation for different users.

Modes of presentation, or senses, play three roles. The first is this: a sense is what we grasp when we understand a given statement, and how it interacts with other sentences or statements in reasoning.

The second role of senses is to determine the reference of a term, of a proper name, say. The sense of "Phosphorus" is the condition *the heavenly body visible at a certain time of the morning and at a certain location*. And the reference of "Phosphorus" is whatever object satisfies that condition, as it happens, the planet Venus. Another name, "Hesperus" say, can have the same reference while having a different sense (*being visible at a certain time in the evening* etc.) "Reference" has been one way in which philosophers have translated Frege's technical term "Bedeutung."

The sentence "Alice believes that Mars is a planet," asserts a relation between Alice and something she believes, namely, the sense of that embedded statement. So, in their third Fregean role, senses are what *that-clauses* refer to.

Many philosophers are skeptical of Frege's idea that the standard or conventional meanings of words and sentences include in general anything like "senses," even apart from indexicals and proper names. A natural accompaniment of that view is that there are non-literal "psychological" modes of presentation that play a cognitive role in thinking and reasoning. A discussion of this topic would take us into the realm of non-linguistic *concepts*, which is not among the topics in this entry.

Bertrand Russell

Russell's theory of meaning is identical with his theory of reference: there is no distinction between sense and reference. The basic terms of language are "genuine proper names" and basic predicates. Genuine proper names are somewhat like demonstratives in thought; what they directly refer to are individual sense data. Basic predicates refer to universals (properties) and relations of sense data, and to properties and relations of physical objects (those objects being as inferential for Russell as electrons are for us.)

He achieves the effect of the Fregean reference of an ordinary proper name, say "Aristotle," by holding such a name to be an abbreviation for a definite description. In a Fregean framework, "Aristotle" refers to ("bedeutet") that ancient philosopher by virtue of his being satisfied by the sense of "Aristotle," and a sense is not a linguistic entity. On Russell's theory that name abbreviates a definite description and *denotes* whatever person satisfies that description. For him, only genuine proper names and basic predicates refer, and denotation is not a form of reference. So ordinary proper names and other expressions that denote do not refer in his sense. We denote by description either genuine physical objects or "physical objects" that are merely logical constructions, depending on the stage of his metaphysics. (See *Russell's The philosophy of logical atomism.*)

Russell's distinction between reference and denotation is well motivated; reference is a semantic primitive while denotation is not. A definite description is, according to him, only a superficially unified term. For, according to Russell's theory of definite descriptions, "the F is G" is equivalent to "There is a unique F and whatever is F is G." The impression that "the F" is a referring term is undercut, for it then lacks the semantic unity it has on Frege's theory.

Russell can seem to suppose that language is the medium of thought, that thought is, at least in part, *in* language. In his early to middle writings, he regarded language as the quantificational language of formal logic. But if he were asked whether *thought* is in the language of formal logic, you might think he would say that this must be so if thought is to be treated systematically. But he does not seem to say this. There is a gap between his preferred conception of language and whatever it is he supposes we think in.

Empiricist elements of thought are central in Russell's philosophy. His "genuine proper names" refer to sense data by virtue of sensory acquaintance with them; and something similar holds of perceptually accessed universals expressed by basic predicates. So names and predicates are devices for connoting perceptually based ideas, and it seems that we think with those ideas. But they are of course idle unless they work within some sort of structure. It is natural to equate that with the structure of language, but Russell does not do so fully. He is somewhat vague about the role of language in thought in a useful passage in chapter 10 of *The analysis of mind*. There he writes, "we must pay more attention ... to the private as opposed to the social use of language. Language profoundly affects our thoughts, and it is this aspect of language that is of most importance to us in our present inquiring. We are almost more concerned with the internal speech that is never uttered than we are with the things said out loud to other people." That language affects our thoughts does not of course imply that we think in language. But the idea of inner speech gets rather closer. Why does Russell here not say directly that our thoughts are in language, or at least that the structure of thought is non-accidentally identical with the structure of (ordinary) language? Attention to perceptual elements in thought should not explain the hesitation; for those elements can be represented in linguistic structure by the use of demonstratives in thought.

H.P. Grice

In 1957, Paul Grice's paper "Meaning" appeared in the *Philosophical Review*. Its principal point is that *meaning* is grounded in certain communicative *intentions*. Someone produces a string of sounds or a hand-wave or something written, and thereby intends to communicate something to another person, a "hearer." Grice's initial project was to explain the structure of communicative intentions of that kind. One might think that a meaning-intention can be explained, in central cases of speaking or writing literally, as a person's intending to mean what her words mean. But that would not explain non-literal meaning, for instance pointing, or saying *grrr* as a sign of anger; and so it would not be fully general. But this is not just fairness to non-linguistic communication. According to Grice every intended communication, as linguistically complex as you like, will be an instance of meaning by virtue of its being produced with a certain special intention. The point is a unified theory of meaning, for both literal and non-literal utterances, a theory that rests on the fundamental concept of *speaker's meaning*. We'll explain this concept, and then say how speaker's meaning is related to linguistic meaning and its complexities.

Suppose a speaker S performs some act *u*, intending a certain person *A* to believe that S intended *A* to understand that S *means* thereby that *p* (say that the sky is clear). A *first* approximation to explaining what this amounts to is as follows:

> *S* produces *u* intending that *A* believe that *S* uttered *u* with the intention that *A* believe that *p* – e.g. that the sky is clear.

The speaker's intention will of course be realistic only if there is a salient relation between *u* and *p* such that in the circumstances S can plausibly expect *A* thereby to recognize that intention. To this end, conventional linguistic meaning may or may not be required; hand-waves, pointing, and a host of other signals often do the job.

This first approximation captures a person's openly conveying something to another person. But is it meaning? Grice's intuition was that it is not. Suppose S shows *A* a photograph in which a certain person is "showing undue familiarity" to *A*'s wife. S intends *A* to believe that that is what *A* is seeing, and S intends *A* to recognize that S intends A to recognize S's intention. Grice's intuition is that this is not a genuine case of meaning for, roughly speaking, S does not intend *A* to (as it were) take his word for it. The photograph speaks for itself. Grice's intuition was that, in central cases of meaning that p, the speaker intends the hearer to believe that p by virtue of the hearer's *recognition* that the speaker intends him to believe that p. If you ask for the time and are told it is 3:00 you believe it is 3:00 because you take the speaker's word for it. That is to say, you believe that it is 3:00 because the speaker intends you to believe that it is 3:00. Now Grice adds the further condition that the speaker intends the hearer to recognize that the speaker has that intention. This set of intentions has come to be called "the Gricean mechanism," and is in its way the ground of Grice's theory of communication.

Quite a few objections were raised against the theory and its revisions.

P.F. Strawson (1964] pointed out that Grice's theory does not yield a *sufficient* condition, describing cases in which a person has those intentions but does not mean that p because those intentions are not out in the open. As Strawson and Stephen Schiffer pointed out, adding further ordinary intentions do not block further counterexamples. And Schiffer (1972) noted that intending the Gricean mechanism is not a *necessary* condition of meaning. For, if you *remind* someone that p you mean that p; the hearer's belief that p is intended to be activated, but not because the hearer takes the speaker's word for it.

Grice proposed that meaning, in his sense, bifurcates, that the Gricean mechanism (see above) is the central factor in one fundamental concept of meaning, while it is absent in other related phenomena (Grice 1969). Schiffer proposed a unified Gricean theory of a certain complexity, as well as a rich account of how speaker's meaning grounds linguistic meaning (1972). Schiffer later rejected his earlier theory, and indeed the whole project of explicating the notion of speaker's meaning in more basic terms. For a detailed account of that rejection see his *Remnants of meaning*, chapter 9.

Despite the difficulty of explaining speaker's meaning in terms of more basic concepts, it persists in the literature as a general and *unanalyzed* concept. A number of philosophers presently take for granted the idea of "meaning in the Gricean sense." Such a notion of speaker's meaning, it is often supposed, can be understood independently of the semantics of natural language, as a psychological concept that belongs, in a broad sense, to the family of propositional attitudes and thoughts.

It could seem a mistake to give the concept of speaker's meaning such a central and basic role in the theory of meaning. A vast amount of our communications are conveyed with language, and it may seem reasonable to regard this as placing a strong constraint on what meaning in general consists in. But this is not an overwhelming argument. It is true that, in a vast proportion of communications, a speaker cannot expect another person to discern what she means unless she is communicating linguistically. One cannot hope to communicate in most cases by shrugging or running up a flag. It does not follow that the concept of communication or speaker's meaning must itself incorporate the concept of language. Nor does it follow that the concept of speaker's meaning cannot play a fundamental role in explaining linguistic meaning. And a fundamental point to keep in mind is that, when a person speaks literally and linguistically, she has certain communicative, perhaps Gricean, intentions.

We should emphasize that Grice's basic theory of communicative meaning, that is as he envisaged it, *presupposes* the concepts of belief and intention, without any attempt to explicate the latter. With that said, we must keep in mind that not every theoretical invoking of language is about communication.

Suppose we *think* in a language, so that thoughts (including beliefs and intentions) are in that language. It is then natural to regard the contents of those thoughts as meanings. Such a language of thought may be understood in two ways. First, a natural language may be used not only for communication but also to think with. And, second, it has been supposed that there is a universal language of thought, which is of course not a "natural" language (see Fodor, below). If one is inclined to either of these ideas, then Gricean meaning will of course not be the foundational semantic concept.

All of this is compatible, of course, with holding that Gricean meaning is the foundational concept of meaning in the theory of interpersonal communication, and holding that what makes a language the language of a certain population can be explained by taking Gricean meaning as the grounding idea.

The Gricean enterprise seemed, to some, to be out of sync with the general thrust of twentieth-century analytic philosophy of language. Analytic philosophy was on its way to replacing concepts and thoughts with language. But if speaker's intentions and beliefs are more basic than linguistic meaning, they bring in their wake a framework – or frameworks – of concepts and thoughts. But during the 1950s and 1960s the *pragmatics* of language, which takes thoughts and psychological states as basic, became a flourishing enterprise and the Gricean enterprise fitted in nicely. The circle had turned, at least in some precincts.

A more recent twist is the idea that beliefs and desires are themselves linguistic states – not of the public language, but of the language of thought. It has seemed to a number of philosophers that the Gricean theory fits in, not as a theory of language overall, but as a component of a theory of language as used in communication.

Donald Davidson

Linguistic meaning, according to Davidson, is not based in what a person means (say in the Gricean sense), or in any other combinations of propositional attitudes. The bearer of meaning is a language: sentences have meanings or, better, truth conditions, by virtue of their belonging to a language. A *truth theory* of a language entails, for each sentence S of that language, something of the form "S is true if and only if p." We understand the language of another person by knowing such overall assignments of truth conditions. The semantic interpretation of a language is individualist. The language of a given person is not determined by the language used by others in the same community. As a pragmatic matter, of course an interpreter will put her money on S's language being the same as that of other members of S's community. But that is not the criterion of correctness of interpretation.

The correct interpretation of a person's language obeys a *principle of charity*: the right truth theory of a person's language makes the sentences she endorses come out true. This leaves room for falsehood: some uttered sentences can be false, but that will not make sense in a general way. You cannot have a meaningful language without widespread truth among the sentences that people endorse or "hold true."

A fundamental question posed by Davidson is how the meaning of a whole expression, a sentence, is determined by the meanings of its parts. That this is not a trivial question can be seen by whether Frege or Russell give satisfactory answers.

The primary conception of meaning in Frege's theory is that of sense. As Davidson first pointed out in 'Truth and Meaning' (1984), it is not obvious that there is a positive answer to the question how the Fregean senses of terms yield the sense of a sentence. Nor can compositionality of a sort that counts as meaning be found at the level of "reference" ("Bedeutung.") The Bedeutung of a sentence is a truth value according to Frege, and that is hardly a candidate for a sentence's meaning. So semantic compositionality is not evidently accountable for in Frege's theory.

Nothing in Russell appears to answer the question. True sentences, according to him, determine *facts*. These are complex entities constructed from objects, properties and relations; but they do not give us meanings, for they do not give us meanings for false statements. In any case, the compositionality of facts themselves is not clear. You can line up the words and say "this ordered pair – <killed, <Brutus, Caesar>> – represents the fact that Brutus killed Caesar." But that does not tell us how those entities (that those words stand for) compose to constitute that fact. And it is not clear that "propositions" help. Counting them as meanings requires an understanding of how the constituents of propositions determine truth conditions for both true and false propositions. You can say that propositions *are* truth conditions; but how do the components constitute the propositions, and what do the latter as it were look like?

Davidson's solution is to adopt Tarski's technical conception of a theory of truth for a logical language and to transform it into a theory of meaning for natural languages. But Davidson reverses the status of truth and meaning. Tarski's defines truth language by language. Davidson takes "true" to be univocal and unexplicated, and the basis of meaning, which is to say truth conditions, in the form "S is true iff p."

A well known prima facie difficulty for a truth-based theory of meaning is as follows. Suppose a theory T entails, for every sentence of a language, a theorem "S is true iff p" such that "S means that p" is intuitively correct. It will then be possible to formulate a theory T^* that is extensionally equivalent to T and that entails a theorem "S is true iff q, such that "S means q" is intuitively incorrect. Meaning is apparently not an extensional concept; meanings may be extensionally equivalent without being the same. This was well known to Davidson, who then gives up the usual notion of meaning, and puts the extensional concept ("meaning") in its place.

Natural languages do not appear to have the form of a first order logical language. How Tarski's model then applies to natural languages is a part of

Davidson's work in the theory of meaning, and also of many philosophers and linguists who work within the Davidsonian paradigm. The idea, roughly, is to find ways of taking ordinary constructions as, so to speak, hidden quantified constructions, which then allows Tarski techniques to apply. Davidson's own contribution to this endeavor can be found in his elegant treatment of action sentences, which rests on the metaphysics of events. (Davidson 1980.)

Davidson's theory, "meaning" is one-dimensional. Now our knowledge of the truth-conditions of sentences is a function of our mastery of a language as a whole. In this sense that Davidson's theory of meaning is "holistic" (there are other uses of that term in theories of meaning.) No semantic properties of meaning or reference can be assigned to words independently of their roles in the language to which they belong, as a whole. That is a quite different picture of meaning and reference that emerges from the semantic theories of Putnam and Kripke.

Unlike Frege's theory there is no distinction between sense and reference. Unlike Russell's theory, the basic units of meanings are not the references of primitive proper nouns and property-terms or relation-terms. Like Frege, Davidson does not give properties a central role in linguistic meaning. In Davidson's theory, what corresponds to predicates are not properties or relations, but Tarski-type satisfaction conditions.

Davidson rejects the Gricean idea that linguistic meaning is grounded in propositional attitudes, that is to say, in a certain sort of thought. Beliefs or intentions cannot be more basic than linguistic meaning according to Davidson; ascribing beliefs and ascribing meanings must be understood as on a par. In his view, what a person believes depends on what sentences that person "holds true." This does not tell us what content such a state has; for that depends on the meaning of what is held true. And we cannot determine what language a person speaks without making assumptions about what sentences the person holds true. For without that the principle of charity cannot get a grip. This may appeal to leave room for the construction's bottoming out in "holding true," "intending true" – that is, sentential attitudes. It may be objected that there is no real psychology that operates only with sentential attitudes, that is, without thoughts of the more usual propositional sort, for psychological theories will in general be independent of what language a person speaks. (See the two-factor theory below, and the language of thought hypothesis.) The foundation of Davidson's theory of meaning is the principle of charity; it is what anchors language to reality. This is quite different from the various semantic anchors than we find in Frege's and Russell's theories of reference, and in the rather different more recent causal theories of Kripke and Putnam.

Truth theories of meaning

It is useful to think of theories of meaning as those for which meaning is a matter of truth conditions, and, roughly speaking, those theories on which meaning is a matter of how sentences interact with each other. In Frege's theory, a statement has a sense, and that determines under what condition it is true or is false. Putting aside the above complexity of Frege's theory, we might say that the core of Frege's account is a certain theory of meaning. Russell's "propositions" are the bearers of truth and falsity. They are what we think with, and so in their way are thoughts. Russell did not endorse truth conditions over and above propositions – nothing like senses. A given proposition will be true under such and such conditions and false under so and so conditions; there is nothing else to meaning for Russell.

With the former two theories as exemplars, it should be clear that Grice, Davidson, Kripke, Putnam, and Fodor, among those we are discussing, count as endorsing truth theories of meaning.

Use Theories of Meaning

Twentieth-century theory of meaning is divided into two: *truth* theories, and *use* theories. Use theories hold that the meaning of a term is determined by how it is used, for example, how to verify an instance, or how to use it in inferences. According to verificationism, the meaning of "cat" is not the set of cats or the kind *cat*, or any sense that determines such references. It is rather the perception that prompts one to assert "there is a cat," or more generally a sentence's 'verification conditions' or 'assertibility conditions.' Here we have an epistemic property determining a semantic property. Verificationism is most closely associated with the Vienna Circle and logical positivism. A clear and straightforward account of verificationism is to be found in A.J.Ayer's *Language, truth and logic*.

Another somewhat different sort meaning-as-use is found in a certain way of understanding scientific theories. To understand a theory, one has, typically, to learn a set of theoretical terms and how they function together. A toy example is the layperson's understanding of the concepts electron, proton, neutron, quark (of various kinds), charge etc. Knowing the meaning of each term requires knowing what the others mean and knowing how to use them in internal and external inferences. We may say that the meanings of those terms consist in their interactive conceptual roles. (But there are truth-theorical way of accounting for that sort of theoretical structure. See Lewis 1972.)

A yet more comprehensive meaning-as-use is to be found in radical semantic holism. W. V. Quine held that we cannot verify an empirical proposition by confirming it directly in experience. The confirmation of propositions must be global: our beliefs must face "the tribunal of sense experience" as a whole. According to Quine, this epistemic doctrine has a semantic upshot. The meanings of terms and statements are determined by the interconnections of all other terms. But that does not allow for the network's determining as a whole an isolable meaning for each term or statement. On the face of it, the sentences we hold true would then not have meanings we may share with others, for each pair of us will differ in at least something we hold true. Similarly, holism seems to imply that when a person changes a belief, all her meanings shift; and that casts doubt on what we could mean by changing a belief. For a defense of holism see Block (1995), and for an argument against see Devitt (1996).

A proponent of conceptual role semantics may escape these difficulties by espousing a non-holistic conceptual role semantics. For a recent novel theory that should be counted as a use meaning, see Horwich (1998a.) We have not mentioned *concepts*, but that topic arises centrally in discussions of holism and anti-holism. For an anti-holist theory of concepts, see Peacocke (1992).

Thinking in Language

The idea that thoughts are *in* language began to be taken seriously among analytic philosophers in the 1970s. Gilbert Harman (1973) argued that we think in the language we speak. This would directly explain the structure of propositional attitudes. The propositional structure of a belief that grass is green and apples are red is explained by an underlying mental sentence of the form "grass is green and apples are red" for English speakers, and similarly for speakers of other languages.

Hartry Field proposed that propositional attitudes are grounded in "sentential attitudes," certain internal states. So "x believes that p" is to be understood as having the deeper structure *"x believes* * *sentence s"* and *"s means p."* Here *"believes* *"* designates a sentential attitude, as does *"wants* *"* etc. These are relations between a thinker and an internal sentence. What defines the relevant sentential attitude (e.g. *"believes* * sentence s") is its functional role, that is, its role in the processes of thought and decision making. On Field's understanding, as on Harman's, these internal sentences are sentences of a natural language. These internal sentences have references and semantic structures, and those semantic properties would be explained by familiar theories of reference, such as those proposed by Kripke, Putnam, and Fodor. How syntactic structure determines semantic structure is an interesting question that is not widely discussed. The argument then is that cognitive capacities are as systematic as our mastery of a natural language. And the best explanation of this is that thoughts have constituent structure. But if thoughts have constituent structure, then there must be a language of thought.

Jerry Fodor has proposed a more radical theory of the nature of internal language (1975, 1981). According to him, we do think in language, but not in the language we speak. There is a *language of thought*, often called Mentalese, which is independent of and more basic than natural language. We all think in that language however our ordinary languages differ. Fodor argues for this as follows. Consider a person's mastery of her natural language; she will not understand the form of words 'John loves Mary' unless she also understand the form of words 'Mary loves John.' This general phenomenon in a natural language attests to a "systematicity" of one's ordinary language. Now the point is, the same holds for thoughts. Cognitive capacities are as systematic as our mastery of a natural language. And the best explanation of this is that thoughts have constituent structure. But if thoughts have constituent structure, there is a language of thought. (This phenomenon is an argument for a language of thought, but not in itself an argument for an innate mentalese.)

To return to natural language, why might our cognitive capacities not be grounded in a natural language? Carruthers (1996) has argued that this is in fact our situation, more specifically, that our conscious thoughts are in a natural language. His principal reason for the thesis is the evidence of introspection, i.e. people's reporting that they think in ordinary language, together with other empirical facts. In his review of Carruthers, Fodor (1998) expresses skepticism about whether what we introspect is adequate to explain what we think. A central problem is the ambiguity of the sentences we encounter in our conscious thinking, especially their syntactic ambiguity. Consider "Everyone loves someone," which has two meanings, depending on how one understands the scope of the quantifiers. As Fodor points out, "thought needs to be ambiguity free," and so must a language of thought be. The linguistic events we introspect do not meet this condition. But it is a jump from that observation to Mentalese, the universal language of thought. As Fodor himself points out, one might regard the objection as met by the supposition that we think "in some ambiguity-free regimentation of English." For proposals of this sort, see Harman 1973 and Field 1978. Another point should be noted. As Fodor indicates, some thoughts can be expressed by either of a pair of complex synonymous sentences, while it is implausible to suppose that in a given thought one has used one rather than the other. The identity of the structure of that thought is then not available to introspection.

There could be another explanation of the systematicity of thought, namely that thought is language-like but does not involve a language in the foregoing sense. Suppose some concepts are perceptually based. Or suppose we can make sense of internal concept-like components of thought that are intrinsically intentional, that is, not purely syntactical. Thoughts that incorporate such concepts would still be systematic and have constituent structure. Such concepts would not involve a language in Fodor's sense, or an internal natural language; they would not be purely syntactic or formal entities.

This would allow of course that some elements of thought are purely syntactic in the strict sense, viz. connectives. There might be an argument to the effect that purely linguistic entities must involve language-like structures of Fodor's sort. But that would be a separate point.

Two-level Theories of Reference

The externalist theories of reference mentioned above determine truth conditions. But they may not easily explain what is sometimes called "Frege's problem."

A person may believe that Hesperus is a planet and also believe that Phosphorus is not a planet, without being irrational. Yet the *fact* that Hesperus is a planet is the same as the fact that Phosphorus is a planet. Philosophers have explained this in different ways. The majority has supposed that, despite the sameness of their truth conditions (that single fact), there are two beliefs here, individuated by different conceptual roles, or at least different concepts. The former seems to lead to holism, as we have seen. Many suppose that there must be ways in which sense-like concepts are individuated in ways that do not lead to holism. If there is a viable theory of this sort, the general idea of a two level theory of thoughts will be found attractive.

The Social Construction of Meaning

A number of philosophers have proposed that thoughts, concepts, and linguistic meaning are constituted socially. This of course does not mean merely that our concepts and thoughts depend on learning from others. Many abilities depend on having learned them from others. Yoga is an example. But it does not follow that yoga is an essentially social activity. Examples of the latter would be marrying, and voting. Some theories hold that meaning is quite like these latter examples, and we will see extreme views of them. But there is, to begin with, a less radical pair of views that introduce a social element into fixing reference and determining belief contents, without implying that all meaning and content are socially constituted.

Hilary Putnam pointed out that the references of one's words are often determined by what others refer to by them. We use certain words, possibly without knowing more than vaguely what they mean or refer to, and thereby mean or refer to whatever certain other people mean or refer to. Putnam professed not to be able to distinguish elms and beeches, even though by "elm" he referred to elms and by "beech" beeches. The idea is that we implicitly intend certain words to refer to what the established users of that word refer to. They are sometimes called "experts," when they have unusual or specialized knowledge.

Tyler Burge's "Individualism and the mental" (1979) has been an extremely influential argument for a social construction of thought. Consider the ascription "Albert believes that he has arthritis in his thigh." Suppose Albert is mistaken about the nature of arthritis, which is a disease of the joints but which he supposes can strike in other places. If he is like most speakers, when he is corrected he will *defer* to the experts, and regard his belief as being false. On the face of it, this shows that the content of beliefs is not in general determined by individualist considerations, that is, by a person's conceptual roles and non-social causal reference relations. These phenomena, Burge argues, show that many beliefs cannot be constituted by individualist factors, e.g. functional roles, personal ways of conceiving things, and individualist reference relations.

Some philosophers have proposed that an individualist interpretation can be achieved by translating say "arthritis" into a definite description of the form "the ailment that the experts call 'arthritis' or the like. That assumes that the references of the predicates in the description are themselves constituted either by non-social causal relations or by non-causal relations of reference. Burge argues effectively against this reply, and a large numbers of philosophers have been persuaded.

Burge's anti-individualist argument generalizes. Whether we suppose that the concept "arthritis" is a word in Mentalese or in internalized English, or in any other way that concepts or bits of thinking are constructed, those internal states, those thoughts, will be determined in part by social factors.

Kripke's Wittgenstein

In his *Wittgenstein on rules and private language*, Saul Kripke offers an interpretation of Wittgenstein's well known passages on rules in the *Philosophical investigations*. There is a dispute among aficionados about whether the interpretation is correct. But interpretation is not why Kripke's book has been so philosophical challenging. The argument that Kripke lays out would undercut the determinacy of semantic facts. It goes like this. We are normally confident that the arithmetical "plus" is determinate in its meaning. Now think of a person who has satisfactorily added numbers less than 57. Suppose we then ask him to calculate $57 + 68$, and suppose he answers 125. What makes that answer correct? The commonsense answer is the fact that he has been using "+" to mean plus, something about his past thoughts and dispositions. But what makes it the case that those past thoughts and dispositions do not establish that "+" means *quus*, where 57 quus 68 = 5? The previous answers on their own do not rule that out. Merely repeating that our subject's dispositions rule it out won't do the trick. Our subject has not done that piece of "addition." He hasn't thought about it. He could now stipulate that 57 "+" 68 = 125. But we think that his prior performance, knowledge, understanding already establishes that his "+" means plus and not quus, and that such a stipulation would be beside the point. Kripke suggests that we have here a skeptical problem. A lot of ink has been spilled answering and dismissing the problem. Some philosophers have thought that nothing needs to be done at all, that, in the circumstances we have described, it is a bare fact that we mean "plus," and nothing constructive is needed. Needless to say not everyone accepts this.

For Kripke's Wittgenstein we must bring in the social background. At the same time we cannot give a "straight solution," an objective grounding for the truth of that person's "$57 + 68 = 125$." All that is socially established are "assertion conditions" for the favored answer. Nothing makes it objectively right. This is meant to be not merely about arithmetic, but also about "swallow" and "epidemic." The argument would undercut the very idea of ordinary concepts not only of meaning but also about whether thoughts of every sort can be genuinely about things. There would be no objective grounding that makes it a fact that one means that such and such or thinks that so and so.

5

Meaning Scepticism

Alexander Miller

1   Introduction

"Jones means *addition* by '+'," "Smith means *rabbit*, and not *undetached rabbit part*, by 'rabbit'," "Murphy understands 'green' to mean *green*." Ordinarily we consider assertions like these capable of truth and falsity, and, in many cases, true. *Meaning-scepticism* is the view that *there are no facts of the matter* as to whether Jones means *addition* by '+' or whether Smith means *rabbit* and not *undetached rabbit part* by 'rabbit' or whether Murphy understands 'green' to mean *green*. In general, meaning-scepticism is the view that ascriptions of meaning to symbols, or linguistic understanding to speakers, are literally neither true nor false.[1] Meaning-scepticism has been an almost constant preoccupation of philosophers of language since the middle of the twentieth century. We will consider the views of two major philosophers whose work has shaped the debates on meaning-scepticism: W. V. O. Quine and Ludwig Wittgenstein. In sections 2 and 3 we look at Quine's arguments for the indeterminacy of translation, and in section 4 we consider the argument developed in Saul Kripke's interpretation of Wittgenstein's writings on rule-following. Before proceeding, some clarificatory remarks are in order.

1.1   Epistemological and constitutive scepticism

Epistemological scepticism concedes that there are facts about a subject matter, but questions whether we are entitled to the knowledge claims we make with respect to it. For example, Descartes' sceptic concedes that there is a fact of the matter as to whether I'm currently dreaming – the statement that I'm currently dreaming is determinately either true or false – but questions whether I am ever entitled to claim that I *know* that I'm not currently dreaming. Meaning-scepticism is more radical than epistemological scepticism. The meaning-sceptic doesn't argue that there are facts about meaning that we have no genuine entitlement to claim to know, but rather that there are no facts about meaning at all. Thus, meaning-scepticism is a form of *constitutive*, as opposed to merely epistemological scepticism. Of course, if there is no fact of the matter as to whether P there can be no plausible claim to know that P: constitutive scepticism leads to a form of epistemological scepticism. But it is important to keep the two notions separate, since the most interesting arguments for constitutive scepticism about meaning proceed via an epistemological route. The generic form of these arguments is as follows. First, it is assumed that if there are meaning-facts, they must be found within some distinctive set of facts: call this the *base set*. Second, we are assumed to have *unlimited access* to the facts in that set. Third, it is argued that even with this unlimited access to the facts in the base set we cannot find the sought-for facts about meaning. Finally, it is concluded that there simply are no facts about meaning (since if there were, unlimited access to the base set would have uncovered them).

1.2   Linguistic meaning and mental content

Just as linguistic symbols are ordinarily taken to possess meaning, mental states like beliefs, desires, intentions, and wishes – the propositional attitudes – are ordinarily taken to possess mental content. Just as the sentence "The Manly ferry leaves from Circular Quay" means *that the Manly ferry leaves from Circular Quay*, Jordana can have a belief with the content *that the Manly ferry leaves from Circular Quay*. Is the notion of linguistic meaning to be explained in terms of the notion of mental content, or vice versa, or is there no relation of priority (so that linguistic meaning and mental content have to be explained together or not at all)? Paul Grice argues that linguistic meaning is to be explained in terms of prior facts about the contents of propositional attitudes (Grice 1989), Michael Dummett argues that linguistic meaning is explanatorily prior to propositional attitude content (Dummett 1993), while Donald Davidson defends a "no priority" view of the relationship between the two notions (Davidson 1984). Which of these views is the most plausible is outwith the scope of this essay, but we can ask: what is the relationship between meaning-scepticism and scepticism about mental content? Paul Boghossian answers:

> There would appear to be no plausible way to promote a *language-specific* meaning scepticism. On the Gricean picture, one cannot threaten linguistic meaning without threatening thought content, since it is from thought that linguistic meaning is held to derive; and on the [Dummettian] picture, one cannot threaten linguistic meaning without *thereby* threatening thought content, since it is from linguistic meaning that thought content is held to derive. Either way, [mental] content and [linguistic] meaning must stand or fall together. (1989: 144)

The same holds on the Davidsonian view: if linguistic meaning and mental content have to be explained together or not at all, a cogent argument for constitutive scepticism about one will straightforwardly yield an argument for constitutive scepticism about the other. Thus, if the arguments for meaning-scepticism are cogent, it follows that there are no facts about the contents of propositional attitudes. The role that propositional attitudes play in the explanation of human action is essentially tied up with the contents that they possess: Martin opened the humidor because he believed that it contained a *Bolivar No. 1*, and desired that he smoke a *Bolivar No. 1*. So the stakes are high: if the meaning-sceptical arguments are successful they will undermine our folk-psychological practice of explaining our actions in terms of mental states.

2 Quine on Indeterminacy of Translation: The Argument from Below

2.1 Introduction

Rosa, an English speaker, sets out to translate German into English. Her aim is to invent a translation manual that correlates the terms and sentences of English with the terms and sentences of German. Intuitively, we would want to say that there is a fact of the matter as to whether the translation manual Rosa invents is correct or not. Thus, if Rosa comes up with a translation manual that pairs "Das ist ein Kaninchen" with "There is a rabbit" her manual correctly captures the fact of the matter, while this is not the case if her manual pairs "Das ist ein Kaninchen" with "There is an undetached rabbit part" or "There is a time-slice of a four-dimensional rabbit-whole." Facts about correct translation have to be capable of discriminating between translation manuals like these: if there are no facts about which of these manuals are correct, it would appear to follow that there are no facts at all about correct translation. According to Quine, there is no fact of the matter as to whether "Das ist ein Kaninchen" is correctly translated as "There is a rabbit," "There is an undetached rabbit part," or "There is a time-slice of a four dimensional rabbit-whole." So, for Quine, there are no facts at all to be captured by the process of inventing translation manuals. Although some manuals may be simpler, more elegant, natural, or useful than others, these are purely pragmatic considerations: the simpler or more elegant manual does not capture any fact missed by its less simple competitor. This is Quine's thesis of *the indeterminacy of translation*.

What does this have to do with meaning-scepticism? Rosa's translation manual has the job of pairing the sentences of German with the sentences of English, and her manual will be correct if and only if the sentences that it pairs together have the same meaning. So, if there is no fact as to which translation manual is correct there will be no fact as to the meanings of the German sentences. Since the same would hold of Clara's attempt to construct a translation manual from English into

German, the same would hold of English: there are no facts of the matter as to the meanings of sentences of English. Thus, the indeterminacy of translation appears to lead straightforwardly to meaning-scepticism.

Quine has two main arguments for the indeterminacy thesis. The first is the "argument from below," featuring Quine's famous "gavagai" example (Quine 1960). This argument is the topic of this section. Quine's second "argument from above," based on the underdetermination of scientific theory by observational evidence (Quine 1970), is discussed in section 3.[2]

Central to Quine's arguments is the notion of *radical translation*. Radical translation is the project of constructing a translation manual for a language – Native – spoken by a tribe of whose language, culture, history, and so on, we are hitherto completely ignorant (1960: 28). In radical translation the only evidence available is evidence we can obtain from observation of the natives' behavior. The motivation for looking at translation in this austere setting stems from Quine's conception of the base class mentioned in 1.1. According to Quine, the only facts to which we can legitimately appeal in our search for the facts constitutive of correct translation are facts about the natives' observable behaviour. Quine restricts the facts in the base class to facts about *stimulus meaning* (1960: 33). The stimulus meaning of a sentence is an ordered pair consisting, first, of the sensory stimulations that typically elicit native assent to the sentence (its affirmative stimulus meaning) and, second, of the sensory stimulations that typically elicit native dissent from the sentence (its negative stimulus meaning). Quine argues that even given unlimited access to all of the facts about stimulus meaning, there will still be no fact of the matter about which translation manual is correct.

2.2   The argument from below

Radical translation begins with the radical translator attempting to identify the signs in Native for assent and dissent. He can form working hypotheses about these by e.g. seeing which expression is elicited by echoing natives' volunteered pronouncements, and so on (1960: 29–30). The radical translator now observes that the Native sentence "Yo gavagai" has the same stimulus meaning as the English sentence "There is a rabbit": the natives are prepared to assent to "Yo gavagai" when there is a rabbit present, and are prepared to dissent from "Yo gavagai" when no rabbit is present. The translator now goes on to propose that the Native expression "gavagai" be paired with the English expression "rabbit" in his translation manual. In Quine's terminology, he proposes an "analytical hypothesis" (1960: 68). However, the Native sentence "Yo gavagai" also has the same stimulus meaning as the English sentence "There is an undetached rabbit part": after all, whenever a rabbit is present so is an undetached rabbit part, and vice versa. So as far as the facts about stimulus meaning are concerned, an analytical hypothesis that pairs "gavagai" with "undetached rabbit part" is just as good as the original (henceforth "favored") hypothesis that "gavagai" should be paired with "rabbit." And there are plenty of other analytical hypothesis that respect the facts about stimulus meaning in the same way (1960: 51–2). For example, the Native sentence "Yo gavagai" also has the same stimulus meaning as the English sentence "There is a time-slice of a four-dimensional rabbit-whole": like before, whenever a rabbit is present so is a time-slice of a four-dimensional rabbit-whole, and vice versa. So as far as the facts about stimulus meaning are concerned, an analytical hypothesis that pairs "gavagai" with "time-slice of a four-dimensional rabbit-whole" is just as good as the favored hypothesis.

However, suppose the translator has identified the expression in Native for numerical identity (paired with the English equivalent "is the same as"), and also some of the demonstratives in Native (paired with the English equivalents "this" and "that"). The next time a rabbit is present, the translator can ask the native, pointing to the rabbit's foot and then its nose, "Si siht gavagai eht emas taht gavagai?" ("Is this gavagai the same as that gavagai?"). If the native responds with the already-identified Native sign that expresses assent, then the translator can rule out the analytical hypothesis that pairs "gavagai" with "undetached rabbit part" and take this as confirming the favored hypothesis; and if the native responds with the sign that expresses dissent, then the translator can take this as refuting the favoured hypothesis and as evidence in favour of the pairing of "gavagai" with "undetached rabbit part." Quine replies (1960: 53) that this maneuver presupposes that "emas" is to be translated as "same rabbit." If "emas" is to be translated rather as "is an undetached part of the same rabbit as this" the fact that the native responds with the sign expressing assent will not rule out the translation of "gavagai" as "undetached rabbit part." So, the facts about stimulus meaning are unable to distinguish between the translation manual that pairs "gavagai" with "rabbit" and the manual that pairs "gavagai" with "undetached rabbit part." But these possess different intuitive meanings. So if there were such things as meaning-facts, they would discriminate between them. Since nothing in the base class – the sum total of all facts about stimulus meaning – does so discriminate, the conclusion is that there is no fact as to whether "gavagai" means the same as "rabbit" or means the same as "undetached rabbit part."

Quine suggests that this example generalizes (1960: 27). The facts in the base class don't discriminate between any two expressions that are intuitively different in meaning. If there were facts about meaning they would so discriminate. So there is no fact of the matter about the meaning of any expression.

2.3 Evans on the argument from below

The most sustained discussion of the argument from below is Gareth Evans's (1975). Although Quine discusses radical *translation*, his real interest is in the idea of *meaning*. Evans notes that the project of constructing a translation manual differs significantly from the project of constructing a theory that attributes meanings to the expressions of Native (1975: 25). Whereas a translation manual merely pairs expressions of Native with English expressions, an account of what a Native expression means has to *use* rather than merely *mention* the English expression. So we might as well consider the argument from below as it applies to a theory of meaning rather than translation manuals. So rather than considering analytical hypothesis that pair Native expressions with English expressions, we consider analytical hypotheses that use English expressions to give the meanings – the application conditions – of expressions of Native. Suppose, then, that the translator (or "meaning-theorist"), includes the following clause in her theory of meaning for Native:

(1) For any x: "gavagai" applies to x iff x is a rabbit.

Suppose that the meaning-theorist observes that the natives are prepared to assent "Yo etihw" if and only if something white is present. On this basis she proposes to add the following clause to her theory:

(2) For any x: "etihw" applies to x iff x is white.

Quine claims that there is nothing in the base class of facts concerning stimulus meanings that discriminates between a meaning-theory containing (1) and a meaning-theory containing (3):

(3) For any x: "gavagai" applies to x iff x is an undetached rabbit part.

Evans suggests that we can rule out the meaning-theory that contains (3) by attending to facts about the stimulus meanings of sentences in which expressions like "gavagai" and "etihw" appear *in combination*.[3] Suppose, to keep the natives as much like us as possible, that they assent to "etihw gavagai" only when a wholly white rabbit is present and dissent from "etihw gavagai" in the presence of a brown rabbit with a white foot. Evans suggests that this data corresponds to what we would expect if (1) and (2) accurately captured the meanings of the relevant Native expressions, and diverges from what we would expect if (2) and (3) captured the relevant meaning-facts. Putting (1) and (2) together gives us:

(4) "Yo etihw gavagai" is true iff a white rabbit is visible.

This fits with the relevant facts about stimulus meaning: the natives are prepared to assent to "Yo etihw gavagai" if and only if a wholly white rabbit is visible, and so on. What would happen if (3) accurately captured the application-conditions of "gavagai"? Coupled with (2) it would give us:

(5) "Yo etihw gavagai" is true iff a white undetached rabbit part is visible.

We would then expect speakers of Native to assent when a brown rabbit with a white foot was present: but *ex hypothesi* they dissent from "Yo etihw gavagai" in those circumstances. So the facts about stimulus meaning discriminate between (1) and (3), and hence between (4) and (5).

How might Quine respond? Perhaps we can retain (3) by altering the clause that gives the application conditions of "etihw." We could replace (2) with:

(6)   For any x: "etihw" applies to x iff x is a part of a white thing.

When combined with (3) this would give us:

(7)   "Yo etihw gavagai" is true iff an undetached rabbit part that is a part of a white thing is visible.

This might appear to respect the facts about stimulus meaning, but it doesn't. After all, an undetached rabbit part that is part of a white thing is indeed visible, namely, the rabbit's big toe, which is after all part of a white thing, its foot. But what if we adjust (6) to get:

(8)   For any x: "etihw" applies to x iff x is a part of a white animal.

This, together with (3), yields:

(9)   "Yo etihw gavagai" is true iff an undetached rabbit part that is a part of a white animal is visible.

This now appears to accord with the facts about stimulus meanings: natives assent to "Yo etihw gavagai" when a white rabbit is visible because then an undetached rabbit part that is part of a white animal is visible, and they dissent to "Yo etihw gavagai" in the presence of a brown rabbit with a white foot because although an undetached rabbit part is then visible it is not part of a white animal.

However, another problem emerges. The natives, recall, assent to "Yo etihw" in the presence of something white. In particular, they are prepared to assent to "Yo etihw" if a white piece of paper or a white cloud is visible. But if (8) were correct, we would expect natives to dissent from "Yo etihw" in the presence of a white piece of paper or a white cloud. No matter how Quine tampers with the application conditions of "etihw," he won't be able to respect the facts about the stimulus meaning of "Yo etihw gavagai." Somewhere along the line, a conflict with the facts about stimulus meaning will in this way emerge, so that the argument from below fails. Evans also attempts to undermine alternative-meaning theories containing

(10)   For any x: "gavagai" applies to x iff x is a time-slice of a four-dimensional rabbit-whole.

and

(11) For any x: "gavagai" applies to x iff x is an instantiation of the universal *rabbithood*.

We'll concentrate on Evans's discussion of the simple alternative (3) to allow the philosophical issues to emerge more clearly.

Can Quine defend himself against the claim that the theory containing (8) is unacceptable on his own terms because it fails to respect certain facts about the stimulus meaning of "etihw"? Christopher Hookway (1988: 155) has suggested that Quine can perhaps avoid this problem by replacing (8) with

(12) For any x: "etihw" applies to x iff either (a) "etihw" occurs conjoined with "gavagai" and x is part of a white animal or (b) "etihw" occurs in a "gavagai" free sentential context and x is white.

This would allow Quine to hold on to (3) and also respect the facts about stimulus meaning: natives assent to "Yo etihw" in the presence of white bits of paper and white clouds (covered by (b)) but they dissent from "Yo etihw gavagai" in the presence of a brown rabbit with a white foot (covered by (a)).

2.4   Wright on the argument from below

Crispin Wright has developed an argument against the suggestion that Quine can hold on to the interpretation of "gavagai" as *undetached rabbit part* etc. by invoking the likes of (12).[4] First:

> Suppose that alternative schemes along Quinean lines can indeed be constructed which can survive any envisageable addition to our pool of linguistic data, but that whereas the Quinean schemes survive by the postulation of ambiguities of various kinds, the favoured scheme has, by and large, no need for such recourse. Then the latter would be, in a clear sense, *simpler* than the Quinean alternatives. Now, the point is well taken that simplicity cannot be assumed, without further ado, to be an *alethic* - truth-conducive - virtue in empirical theory generally. There is prima facie sense in the idea that of two empirically adequate theories, it might be the more complex that is actually faithful to the reality which each seeks to circumscribe. But the thought that, when it comes to radical interpretation, there is an ulterior psychologico-semantical reality which an empirically adequate translation scheme might misrepresent is, of course, exactly what Quine rejects - exactly what he stigmatises as the myth of the semantic museum. And with that rejection in place, methodological virtues that are not, in realistically conceived theorising, straightforwardly alethic can now become so. In such cases, the methodologically best theory ought to be reckoned true just on that account. It is therefore not enough for a defender of Quine to seek to save the alternative schemes by postulations which, though still principled and general, are comparatively expensive in terms of ambiguity and other forms of complication. If a simpler scheme is available, that fact is enough to determine that these alternatives are

untrue, by the lights of the only notion of truth that, in Quine's own view, can engage the translational enterprise. (Wright 1997: 411)

Grant Wright the claim that the theory containing (1) is indeed simpler than the theory that contains (12): in the latter theory, "etihw" is ambiguous, with its meaning varying depending on whether it appears in a linguistic context that also includes "gavagai," while in the former no such ambiguity is postulated. How plausible is Wright's argument that this fact about simplicity is enough to rule out the theory containing (12) as false? Quine admits that in practice we would be justified in adopting a theory containing (1) and (2) as opposed to a theory containing (3) and (12), but argues that this preference would be justified for purely pragmatic reasons: since the two theories both respect the facts about stimulus meaning, a preference between them cannot be grounded in the idea that only one of them captures the facts about correct translation. So does Quine have any response to Wright's argument? Wright's argument turns on the idea that in the case of empirical theories about some robustly factual subject matter, the fact that one empirically adequate theory is simpler than another more complex empirically adequate theory does not entail that it is the simpler theory that captures the facts.[5] In other words, where we are concerned with a robustly factual subject matter, simplicity is not alethic. Quine can accept this conditional:

(I)   If theories deal with a robustly factual subject matter, simplicity is not an alethic virtue.

But in order to get from this to Wright's desired conclusion about the case of theorising about translation and meaning this is not sufficient. If Wright attempts to get from (I) and

(II)   Theories of meaning do not deal with a robustly factual subject matter.

to

(III)   Simplicity is an alethic virtue for theories of meaning.

he will commit the fallacy of *denying the antecedent*. What Wright requires is rather

(IV)   If theories deal with a non-robustly factual subject matter, then simplicity is an alethic virtue of those theories.

But in order to infer validly the desired conclusion from (IV) Wright would need:

(V)   Theories of meaning deal with a non-robustly factual subject matter.

And Quine will claim that Wright is not entitled to (V). In order to be entitled to (V) Wright would need to have established that the facts about stimulus meaning are capable of justifying the selection of the favoured theory of meaning in preference to one of its Quinean competitors: only so could the claim that theories of meaning deal with a non-robustly *factual* subject matter be justified. Thus, in assuming that the appeal to simplicity considerations is *by itself* capable of effecting such a selection, Wright is simply begging the question against Quine.[6] To make the point another way, Wright has not yet justified the idea that the facts the simplicity considerations select between are *facts about meaning*: since the meaning-facts, if such there be, would discriminate between two theories of meaning that respect all of the facts about stimulus meaning, there is as yet no content to the claim that the facts recorded by the simplest of the empirically adequate theories of meaning are facts about meaning. On the assumption that theories of meaning deal with a non-robustly factual subject matter, simplicity considerations may indeed be invoked: but that assumption is one to which Wright, as yet, has no genuine entitlement. Again, the appeal to simplicity considerations simply begs the question against Quine.[7]

However, Wright has a second argument that concerns not simplicity in the theory of meaning but simplicity in the "associated psychological theory." Wright points out that the clauses in theories of meaning "are presumed to correspond to the conceptual repertoire of speakers of the language in question"(1997: 412). Wright then enunciates a methodological constraint on the ascription of concepts to speakers:

> the conceptual repertoire which radical interpretation may permissibly ascribe to speakers should exceed what is actually expressible in their language, as so interpreted, only if its ascription them is necessary in other ways in order to account for their linguistic competence. (1997: 412)

You can only have the concept *undetached rabbit part* if you have the concept *rabbit*, so the theory of meaning containing (3) would not only ascribe to speakers conceptual resources "strictly unnecessary to explain their linguistic performance" it would also view the resources in question – in particular their possession of the concept *rabbit* – as "lurking behind, but inexpressible in, the actual vocabulary of the natives' language"(1997: 412). So the theory containing (3) violates the methodological constraint on the ascription of concepts.

But does it? The Quinean can retort that the ascription of the concept *rabbit* to speakers is indeed necessary in order to account for their linguistic competence, specifically, their competence with the term "gavagai" *on his interpretation of that term*: after all, they can't have the concept *undetached rabbit part* unless they also have the concept *rabbit*. Can Wright reply that Quine is not entitled to the theory of meaning that interprets "gavagai" as *undetached rabbit part*? Well, only if he has shown that this interpretation of "gavagai" does not respect the relevant facts about stimulus meaning. And, as yet, there is no compelling reason for thinking that that is the case. So Wright's argument faces the following dilemma. If we have not been given a reason for the claim that the interpretation of "gavagai" as *undetached rabbit part* fails to respect some fact about stimulus meaning, the methodological constraint will be toothless: Quine can simply cite speakers' mastery of "gavagai" as the piece of linguistic competence for whose explanation the ascription of the concept *rabbit* is necessary. On the other hand, if we *have* been given a reason for the claim that the interpretation of "gavagai" as *undetached rabbit part* fails to respect some fact about stimulus meaning, we already have a reason for rejecting the theory of meaning containing (3). In effect, Wright's argument is either toothless or superfluous.

3   Quine on Indeterminacy of Translation: The Argument from Above

3.1   Introduction

In his later paper (1970), Quine writes that the "real ground" of the indeterminacy doctrine is not the construction of an alternative set of analytical hypotheses consistent with the facts about stimulus meaning, but the idea that physical theory is underdetermined by all possible observational evidence:

> Theory can still vary though all possible observations be fixed. Physical theories can be at odds with each other and yet compatible with all possible data even in the broadest sense. In a word they can be logically incompatible and empirically equivalent. This is a point on which I expect wide agreement, if only because the observational criteria of theoretical terms are commonly so flexible and so fragmentary.   (1970: 179)

This is a consequence of the *epistemological holism* that Quine espoused in his (1953). Significant statements face the tribunal of experience not *individually*, but *en masse*: "our statements about the external world face the tribunal of sense experience not individually, but only as a corporate body" (1953: 41). Suppose we are faced with a *recalcitrant* experience - an experience which conflicts with our currently held physical theory in conjunction with a set of hypotheses ("auxiliary hypotheses") describing experimental set-up, laboratory conditions, state of the experimenter, etc.. According to epistemological holism we have the choice – at least in principle – of giving up some part of our physical theory, revising our auxiliary hypotheses, or perhaps even giving up the claim that a recalcitrant experience has occurred. Likewise, if we decide to give up some part of our physical theory, *which* part we give up will be underdetermined by all actual and possible observations: we can hold on to any part of our physical theory, provided we are prepared to make the necessary adjustments elsewhere, among the auxiliary hypotheses or wherever. And this amounts to the claim that given any set of actual or possible observations, we will have – at least in principle – a choice between a range of competing theories, all of which can be chosen consistently with the observational data subject to appropriate revisions elsewhere in the set of our empirical (or even logical) beliefs.

Quine aims to show only that the indeterminacy of translation extends *as far as* the underdetermination of physical theory: although he believes that underdetermination extends even to "ordinary traits of ordinary bodies" (1970: 180), he does not want the argument from above to turn on that assumption. His stated aim is to establish only that:

> What degree of indeterminacy of translation you must ... recognise ... will depend on the amount of empirical slack that you are willing to acknowledge in physics. If you were one of those who saw physics as underdetermined only in its highest theoretical reaches, then ... I can claim your concurrence in the indeterminacy of translation only of highly theoretical physics   (1970: 181)

3.2   The argument from above

How do we get from the claim of underdetermination of physical theory by all actual and possible observational evidence to the conclusion that translation is indeterminate to the same extent? The entire argument is to be found in a single paragraph (1970: 179–80), where Quine imagines us engaged on the project of radical translation of a foreigner's physical theory. Following Robert Kirk's (1986), we can break the argument down as follows:

1   The starting point of the process of radical translation is the equating of observation sentences of our language with observation sentences of the foreigner's language, via an inductive equating of stimulus meanings.
2   In order afterward to construe the foreigner's theoretical sentences we have to project analytical hypotheses.
3   The ultimate justification for the analytical hypotheses is just that the implied observation sentences match up.
4   Insofar as the truth of a physical theory is underdetermined by observables, the translation of the foreigner's physical theory is underdetermined by translation of his observation sentences.

Therefore:

(T)   To the extent that the truth of a physical theory is underdetermined by observables, the translation of the foreigner's physical theory is underdetermined by the totality of Quine-acceptable facts.

By way of clarification, consider a pre-1970 objection by Noam Chomsky against Quine's indeterminacy thesis:

It is quite certain that serious hypotheses concerning a native speaker's knowledge of English ... will "go beyond the evidence." Since they go beyond mere summary of data, it will be the case that there are competing assumptions consistent with the data. But why should all of this occasion any surprise or concern? (Chomsky 1969: 67)

Chomsky is objecting that Quine's indeterminacy thesis is simply an *instance* of the underdetermination of empirical theory: a translation manual, like any other empirical theory, is underdetermined by all actual and possible observational evidence. But, asks Chomsky, so what? Physical theory is likewise underdetermined by all actual and possible observational data, but Quine does not want to conclude that there are no facts capturable by physical theory. Likewise, chemistry is underdetermined by all actual and possible observational data, but Quine does not want to conclude that there are no facts capturable by chemical theory. Why should it be any different for the empirical theorist engaged on the task of constructing a translation manual?

Quine is highly sensitive to Chomsky's criticism:

The indeterminacy of translation is not just an instance of the empirically underdetermined character of physics. The point is not just that linguistics, being a part of behavioral science and hence ultimately of physics, shares the empirically underdetermined character of physics. On the contrary, the indeterminacy of translation is additional. (1970: 180)

The additional content of the indeterminacy doctrine derives from Quine's physicalism, his belief that "the physical facts are all the facts"(Hookway 1988: 212). Quine argues not just that translation manuals are underdetermined by all actual and possible observational evidence, but in addition, *that incompatible translation manuals are consistent with the totality of physical facts*. Thus, on the assumption that we are settling for a physics of elementary particles:

When I say there is no fact of the matter as regards, say, two rival manuals of translation, what I mean is that both manuals are compatible with all the same distributions of states and relations over elementary particles. In a word, they are physically equivalent. (Quine 1981: 23)

Given his physicalism, the indeterminacy thesis follows swiftly: incompatible translation manuals are consistent with the totality of physical facts, so there *is* no fact of the matter as to which of them is correct (see also Kirk 1986: 136; Hookway 1988: 137). There is an obvious contrast here with a discipline like chemistry: even though chemical theory is underdetermined by all actual and possible observational evidence, it is not the case that competing chemical theories are physically equivalent. Given a choice of physical theory, we still have incompatible translations to choose between: but given a choice of physical theory, the truth about chemistry is fixed.[8]

3.3   Kirk's objection to the argument from above

Kirk (1986: 143–4) argues that we must not assume that (1)–(3) by themselves entail the conclusion (T), since that would amount to assuming the success of the argument from below, an assumption that is officially off-limits to Quine in the context of the argument from above. But, Kirk argues, unless Quine *already* assumes that (1)–(3) generate the indeterminacy thesis, there is a non-sequitur in the move from (4) to (T). Thus, Quine faces the following dilemma. Either he assumes the argument from below or he doesn't. If he does, he can reach (T), but only by conceding that the argument from above is not "broader and deeper" than the argument from below. If he doesn't, the argument from above fails to establish its desired conclusion anyway.

Kirk illustrates his objection via an example of a physicist, Fred, who is trying to translate Chinese physics. Fred believes that (1) physics is underdetermined by observational evidence only at the level of quark theory and above and that (2) physics is not so underdetermined at levels below that of quark theory (e.g. at the level of protons, electrons, etc). Quine's aim is to convince Fred that the translation of Chinese physics *at the level of quarks and above* is indeterminate. For dramatic effect, suppose that Fred believes that the translation of Chinese physics at the level of quark theory and above is determinate. Given the official modus vivendi of the argument from above, in attempting to change Fred's mind about this latter claim Quine must concede, for the sake of argument, that Chinese physics is determinately translatable at the lower levels of electron and proton theory. Kirk now argues that for all that Quine has shown, there is nothing to prevent Fred from maintaining that he can determinately translate Chinese quark theory on the basis of his determinate translation of Chinese physics at the lower levels:

> Fred maintains that there is a large class C of theoretical sentences of Chinese physics [those dealing with levels lower than quark theory] which (a) are not observation sentences, yet (b) are determinately translatable; and that his supposedly determinate translations of all members of C supply him with a sufficiently solid basis to ensure that his translations of Chinese high-level particle physics [quark theory and beyond] are determinate too.   (Kirk 1986: 145)

The crux of Kirk's argument is that unless Quine takes the indeterminacy of translation to have been established already at step [3], he has nothing to say in response to Fred's claim about how he can translate Chinese physics at the level of quark theory and above:

> To close the gap between [4] and [T] it would be necessary to show that translations of observation sentences are the only facts on which the translation of underdetermined theories could possibly be based. Of course step [3] appears to imply just that; but we have seen that Quine cannot sensibly intend to appeal to it. Step [3] certainly

prevents the non-sequitur from becoming apparent; but once [3]'s inadmissibility is acknowledged, the gap in the argument is plain. And as the story of Fred illustrates, there is at least a plausible case for thinking the gap cannot be filled. (Kirk 1986: 145–6)

So Quine has failed to provide an argument for the indeterminacy thesis that is "broader and deeper" than the argument from below.

We'll now argue that Kirk's objection to the argument from above is unsuccessful.

Let's call 4 the principle *that translation preserves degree of "empirical slack,"* and recall that Fred (a) agrees that physics is underdetermined only at the level of quark theory and above, (b) that physics is not underdetermined below this, and (c) that the translation of Chinese physics is determinate below the level of quark theory. Suppose, for reductio, that Fred can determinately translate Chinese quark theory on the basis of his determinate translation of Chinese physics at levels below those of quark theory. Then, since translation preserves degree of "empirical slack," it follows that since Chinese physics isn't underdetermined at levels lower than that of quark theory, it isn't underdetermined at the level of quark theory either. But this contradicts (a) above. Hence translation of Chinese quark theory cannot be determinately translated on the basis of the determinate translation of Chinese physics at levels lower than quark theory. Thus, Kirk's example fails to undermine the argument from above.

Recall that Kirk writes that "To close the gap between 4 and (T) it would be necessary to show that translations of observation sentences are the only facts on which the translation of underdetermined theories could possibly be based" (1986: 145) and claims that this is not available to Quine in the present context as it would amount to assuming the argument from below as a premise in the argument from above. While it appears to be true that in order to get to (T) Quine requires the assumption that "translations of observation sentences are the only facts on which the translation of underdetermined theories could possibly be based" it can be questioned whether this amounts to assuming the *cogency* of the argument from below. In order to reach (T) from 3 via 4 we need only the assumption that the base class for facts about determinate translation consists in facts about stimulus meanings (hence facts about pairings of foreign observation sentences with observation sentences of the translator's language). This methodological assumption ensures that given 4 the indeterminacy thesis follows, since underdetermination of translation manuals by translations of observation sentences amounts to underdetermination by the facts the base class identifies as the only facts potentially constitutive of determinate translation. Crucially, in arguing in this way we are assuming only that the *methodology* of the argument from below is correct, *not that the application of that methodology yields the indeterminacy thesis.* In other words, all that is assumed is a *premise* of the argument from below: the conclusion of the argument from below is not assumed, nor is the claim that the conclusion of the argument from below follows from that premise. So *no questions are begged*, nor is the argument from below assumed in any way that would endanger Quine's claim to be providing a "broader and deeper" case for indeterminacy.

We can make this even clearer if we consider a line of argument which, if pursued by Quine, would render the argument from above problematic in the way that Kirk suggests. Imagine that Quine argued that we can get to (T) from 3 via 4 only if the following two assumptions are made. (A) The only facts relevant to correct translation of theoretical sentences are facts about the translations of observation sentences, and, (B) the facts about the translation of observation sentences do not serve to determine a unique translation manual for the theoretical sentences. Then, Kirk could fairly claim that in making assumptions (A) and (B) Quine is in effect assuming the conclusion of the argument from below. But in the argument from above, only (A) – *and not (B)* – is assumed. The role played by (B) is played by the principle that translation preserves degree of empirical slack. Since this principle is in effect 4 Kirk is mistaken in claiming that the argument from above "makes no essential use of the doctrine of the underdetermination by theory, and step 4 is redundant"(1986: 143).[9]

We have argued that the objections of Wright and Kirk do not succeed in undermining Quine's arguments. Both Wright and Kirk – at least so far as these objections are concerned – attempt to respond to Quine's arguments on Quine's own terms. That is to say, Wright and Kirk – again, at least in this context – accept Quine's conception of the base class within which facts about meaning are to be found (if anywhere), and attempt to respond to the challenge to find meaning-facts within that base class. Perhaps, though, a better strategy would be to challenge Quine's restricted conception of the base. The only facts allowed by Quine as possible candidates for constituting correct translation are observable facts about the behavioural dispositions of speakers in observable circumstances, where that behaviour is to be characterised in strictly non-semantic and non-intentional terms. As Kripke puts it:

> Quine bases his argument on the outset on behaviouristic premises ... Since Quine sees the philosophy of language within a hypothetical framework of behaviouristic psychology, he thinks of problems about meaning as problems of disposition to behaviour. (1982: 56)

And Quine himself puts it even more emphatically:

> There is nothing in linguistic meaning beyond what is to be gleaned from overt behaviour in observable circumstances. (Quine 1990: 37–8)

Perhaps a better tack would be to question the behavioristic assumptions that lie in the background of Quine's arguments. We cannot even begin to pursue that line of enquiry here. We can note, however, that it throws into sharp relief the interest of arguments for meaning-scepticism that do not depend on behavioristic presuppositions. This leads to the next figure in our introduction to meaning-scepticism, Kripke's Wittgenstein.[10]

4 Kripke's Wittgenstein's Attack on Meaning

4.1 Introduction

Kripke's Wittgenstein's (KW's) sceptic, drawing mainly on materials from Wittgenstein's *Philosophical investigations* and *Remarks on the foundations of mathematics*, argues for a "sceptical paradox": there is no fact of the matter in virtue of which an ascription of meaning, such as "Smith means *addition* by '+'," is true or false; and so, since nothing turns on the nature of Smith or of the '+' sign in particular, there is no fact of the matter as to whether any speaker means one thing rather than another by the expressions of his language.[11]

KW's sceptic outlines his argument with an example from simple arithmetic, and asks "In virtue of what fact did I mean, in the past, the addition function by my use of the '+' sign?." Suppose that "68+57" is a computation that you have never performed before. Since you've performed at most finitely many computations in the past, you can be sure that such an example exists (even if you have performed this computation before, the argument would work just as well for any other computation which you haven't actually performed). Also, the finitude of your previous computations guarantees that there is an example where both of the arguments (in this case 68, 57) are larger than any other numbers you've dealt with in the past (again, even if this is not the case in the present example, you can easily imagine one for which it is the case).

Now suppose that you do the computation and obtain "125" as your answer. After checking your working out, you can be confident that "125" is the correct answer. It is the correct answer in two senses: first, it is correct in the *arithmetical* sense, since 125 is indeed, as a matter of *arithmetical* fact, the sum of 68 and 57; and it is correct in the *metalinguistic* sense, since the "+" sign really does mean the addition function. (You can imagine how these two senses of correctness might come apart: if the "+" sign really stood for the multiplication function, 125 would still be the sum of 68 and 57, but the correct answer to the question "68 + 57 = ?" would now be "3876"). Is your confidence that you have given the correct answer justified? KW's "bizarre sceptic" argues that it is not:

> This sceptic questions my certainty about my answer, in ... the "metalinguistic" sense. Perhaps, he suggests, as I used the term "plus" in the past, the answer I intended for "68 + 57" should have been "5"! Of course the sceptic's suggestion is obviously insane. My initial response to such a suggestion might be that the challenger should go back to school and learn to add. Let the challenger, however, continue. After all, he says, if I am now so confident that, as I used the symbol "+,"

my intention was that "68 + 57" should turn out to denote 125, this cannot be because I explicitly gave myself instructions that 125 is the result of performing the addition in this particular instance. By hypothesis, I did no such thing. But of course the idea is that, in this new instance, I should apply the very same function or rule that I applied so many times in the past. But who is to say what function this was? In the past I gave myself only a finite number of examples instantiating this function. All, we have supposed, involved numbers smaller than 57. So perhaps in the past I used "plus" and "+" to denote a function which I will call "quus" and symbolize by "⊕." It is defined by

$$x \oplus y = x + y, \text{if } x, y < 57$$
$$= 5 \qquad \text{otherwise.}$$

Who is to say that this is not the function I previously meant by "+"? (1982: 8–9)

So the challenge is: cite some fact about yourself which constitutes your meaning *addition* rather than *quaddition* by the "+" sign. Any response to this challenge has to satisfy two conditions (1982: 11, 26). First, it has to provide an account of the type of fact that is constitutive of the meaning of "+." Second, it has to be possible to *read off* from this fact what constitutes *correct* and *incorrect* use of the "+" sign - it must show why the answer to the problem "68+57=?" is *justified*.

In accordance with the general strategy adumbrated in 1.1, KW's sceptic begins by allowing you unlimited access to two kinds of fact, and invites you to find a suitable meaning-constituting fact from within either of those two kinds. The kinds in question are (1) *facts about your previous behaviour and behavioural dispositions; and* (2) *facts about your mental history or "inner life."* This displays the way in which KW's sceptic's argument is potentially much stronger than Quine's arguments for the indeterminacy of translation: KW's sceptic allows us access to a much wider range of facts in our search for the facts constitutive of meaning. Quine rules out an appeal to facts of the sort mentioned in (2) from the outset, whereas KW's sceptic's argument is that even if we suppose ourselves to have ideal access to these sorts of fact, we will *still* be unable to find a fact which can constitute our meaning one thing rather than another. Moreover, in addition to countenancing meaning-constituting facts in class (2), KW works with a characterisation of class (1) that is significantly broader than Quine's. For Quine, the relevant behavioural dispositions must be observable to a third party, a linguist, for example. In contrast, KW is willing to include in class (1) behavioural dispositions whose manifestations are not observable by a third party.[12]

In short, KW's sceptic rejects the following as meaning-constituting facts; facts about: your *previous behaviour* (1982: 7–15); *general thoughts or instructions* that you gave yourself (1982: 15–17); how you are *disposed to use* the expression (1982: 22–38); the relative *simplicity* of hypotheses about what you mean (1982: 38–40); your *qualitative, introspectible, irreducibly mental states* (including *mental images*) (1982: 41–51); *sui generis and irreducible mental states* "not to be assimilated to sensations or headaches or any 'qualitative' states"(1982: 51–3); your relation to *objective, Fregean senses* (1982: 53–4). It seems, then, that facts about meaning have as Kripke puts it, "vanished into thin air" (1982: 22). Here we'll consider only the issue of semantic normativity of meaning and its impact on dispositional theories of meaning.[13]

4.2 Meaning and normativity

KW is standardly credited with the idea that the *normativity of meaning* can provide an argument against reductive dispositionalist realism about meaning. The *normativity* of morals has long been held to be problematic for moral realism (see Miller 2003b: 9.10). But one thing that is clear is that the standard route from a naturalistic conception of reasons to the rejection of moral realism, however plausible or implausible it may be in that particular case, simply has no application in the case of meaning. In the moral case, the pressure on realism stems from a *Humean* or *Instrumentalist* conception of reason coupled with the observation that moral reasons, if such there be, must be categorical reasons. Suppose that moral facts are facts about reasons for action. One can release oneself from the scope of the "ought" in "You ought to catch the 10 a.m. 518 bus at the Macquarie Centre" simply by pointing out that you have no desire to get to Gladesville by 10.40 a.m. But one cannot release oneself from the scope of a moral "ought" by citing some contingent fact about one's desires: you cannot free yourself from the obligation to help the child lying hurt in the street by citing the fact that you have no desire to help or that you have a more powerful desire to get to the bottle shop before it closes. Moral reasons, if they exist, are *categorical* reasons for action: reasons that are binding on you no matter what desires you happen to have. But according to the Humean or Instrumentalist conception of reasons there are no categorical reasons for action. So it would appear to follow that, if moral facts are facts about reasons for action, there are no moral facts. An error-theory of moral judgement looms. Clearly, this line of argument *cannot even get started* in the semantic case. It would be utterly implausible to claim that if facts about the meaning of "magpie" are facts about reasons for action, then they must be facts about categorical reasons for action. The most that can be said is that if Neil means magpie by "magpie" then *given that he has a desire to communicate, or perhaps a desire to think the truth, or a desire to conform to his prior semantic intentions,* he has a reason to apply "magpie" to an object if and only if it is a magpie. Semantic reasons are at most only *hypothetical* reasons for action. This is clearly stated, albeit *sotto voce*, by both Kripke and Boghossian:

> The point is *not* that, if I meant addition by "+," I *will* answer "125," but rather that, **if I intend to accord with my past meaning of "+,"** I *should* answer "125." (Kripke 1982: 37, emphasis added)

The point is that, if I mean something by an expression, then the potential infinity of truths that are generated as a result are *normative* truths: they are truths about how I *ought* to apply the expression, **if I am to apply it in accord with its meaning**, not truths about how I *will* apply it (Boghossian 1989: 143, emphasis added)

So the standard route from the Humean theory of reasons to the rejection of moral realism is simply not available for an argument against realism in the case of meaning.[14]

So what could the normativity argument be? Perhaps, for ease of exposition suppressing the reference to a background semantic desire, the argument against dispositionalism mooted in passages like the two quoted immediately above is just:

1   The judgment that Jones means *magpie* by "magpie" implies a judgment about how Jones *ought* to apply the term "magpie."
2   The judgment that Jones is disposed in conditions C to apply "magpie" to magpies does not imply a judgment about how Jones ought to apply the term "magpie."
3   So the judgment that that Jones means *magpie* by "magpie" is not equivalent to the judgment that Jones is disposed in conditions C to apply "magpie" to magpies.

How is premise (2) to be justified? Perhaps by something like an "open-question" argument of the sort that Moore famously directed against ethical naturalism. That is, for any selection of conditions C, it is always an open question whether Jones ought to apply "magpie" to an object that he is disposed to apply it to in C.

The shortcomings of such arguments as directed against ethical naturalism are well known.[15] But the crucial point for our present purposes is that they *cannot even get started* in the case of contemporary forms of the dispositionalist theory of meaning. This is because, as one commentator put it:

[T]he proponents of naturalistic reductions of semantic notions see their task as on a par with other theoretic reductions, such as the identification of water with H_2O or of heat to kinetic energy. The proponents of [reductive dispositionalism about meaning] aim at revealing the nature of [meaning], and of the attending normative facts, precisely in the sense in which the nature of water is revealed by its identification with a certain molecular structure.   (Zalabardo 1997: 282–3)

Just as one cannot undermine the theoretical identification of water with H_2O by showing that judgements about water are not analytically equivalent to judgements about H_2O, the versions of reductive dispositionalism currently on offer cannot be undermined via an argument to the effect that semantic judgements are not analytically equivalent to judgements about optimal dispositions (see Fodor 1990: 136).[16]

5 Conclusion

We have been able only to give a sketch of some of the most influential meaning-sceptical arguments in twentieth-century and contemporary philosophy of language. We've seen that, although commentators on Quine's arguments for the indeterminacy of translation have had some difficulty in pinpointing flaws in his arguments that facts about stimulus meaning fail to fix facts about correct translation, most philosophers these days would take Quine's arguments – if successful – as a reductio of the behaviouristic conception of the base class as containing only facts about stimulus meaning. And, as even our brief discussion of the normativity of meaning suggests, KW's sceptic has a lot more work to do if his "sceptical paradox" is to be a really serious threat. However, even though no compelling argument for meaning-scepticism has been provided by either Quine or Kripke's Wittgenstein, it is fair to say that there is little consensus in contemporary philosophy of language as to what meaning-facts are, or even as to the constraints that an account of the meaning-facts ought to satisfy. It is perhaps in their highlighting of this that the true value of meaning-sceptical arguments resides.

Notes

1 An alternative sort of meaning-scepticism, not discussed here, would claim that ascriptions of meaning are rather *uniformly and systematically false*. See Churchland 1981.

2 Considerations of space dictate that we restrict ourselves to considering only these two classic sources for the indeterminacy arguments. For Quine's more recent thoughts, see Quine 1990.

3 Evans's arguments against some of Quine's proposed alternative meaning-theories turn on facts about how sentences containing those expressions behave under negation. In the interests of clarity and conciseness we concentrate on the simplest of Quine's proposed alternatives.

4 For Hookway's own response on behalf of Quine to his suggestion, see Hookway (1988: 155–7).

5 A subject matter is robustly factual if an empirically adequate theory describing that subject matter may be false. Thus, Quine's rejection of the "ulterior psychologico-semantic reality" that an empirically adequate translation scheme may miss is in effect a repudiation of the idea that the theory of meaning concerns a robustly factual subject matter. See Quine (1969: 1–90). As we'll see, Wright erroneously assumes that Quine's denial that semantics is robustly factual constitutes an acceptance of the claim that it is non-robustly factual.

6 Note that Wright cannot rejoin by claiming that it is *Quine* who is begging the question against the appeal to simplicity considerations by *assuming* the non-factuality of meaning: all that Quine needs is the weaker claim that as yet we have no way – prior to the appeal to simplicity considerations – of distinguishing between

incompatible theories of meaning that both respect all of the facts about stimulus meaning.

7   It may be that Wright intends his "minimalism about truth-aptitude" to pick up the slack in this argument, but discussion of that would take us too far afield. See chapters 1 and 2 of Wright (1992).

8   Which is of course not to claim that the *concepts* of chemical theory simply *are* concepts of physics.

9   Kirk could raise some questions about the plausibility of the principle that translation preserves degree of empirical slack, but this principle seems relatively uncontentious, in the way that the principle that translation preserves vagueness is uncontentious. At any rate, our aim here is simply to rebut the objections that in the argument from above [4] is redundant and that the argument from above assumes the argument from below in a problematic way. Note, too, that it is hardly surprising that the behaviourist premise about the scope of the base class figures in both the argument from below and the argument from above. The claim that facts about meaning have to be constituted by facts about stimulus meaning is, in the context of the issue about meaning, simply the expression of Quine's physicalism (see Hookway (1988): 178). We shouldn't be surprised at the appearance of so fundamental a commitment among the premises of different arguments for the same conclusion.

10 Quine writes that "The gavagai example was at best an example only of the inscrutability of terms, not of the indeterminacy of translation of sentences"(1970: 182). According to the inscrutability of reference thesis, we can have translation manuals that respect all of the facts about stimulus meaning but differ over the assignments of referents to the subsentential expressions in the relevant language. These translation manuals needn't diverge with respect to truth-value: in Quine's "gavagai" example, "There is a rabbit" and "There is an undetached rabbit part," though inequivalent, are both true. According to the indeterminacy of translation thesis proper, we can have translation manuals that respect all of the facts about stimulus meaning but which are inequivalent in the sense of *differing in truth-value*. We've ignored the distinction between inscrutability and indeterminacy proper in the text in the service of bringing out the intuitive relevance of Quine's arguments for the issue of meaning-scepticism. For some reflections on the relevance of the distinction, see Orenstein (2002: ch. 6). Donald Davidson's writings on "radical interpretation" offer a distinct perspective on the issues surrounding indeterminacy and inscrutability. See the papers on radical interpretation in Davidson (1984). For a useful survey, see Heal (1997).

11 KW attempts to neutralize the sceptical paradox, by arguing that even though there are no facts in virtue of which ascriptions of meaning are true or false, we can avoid the "insane and intolerable" (1982: 60) conclusion that "all language is meaningless" (1982: 71) via a "sceptical solution" to the sceptical paradox. The main idea of the sceptical solution is that ascriptions of meaning can be viewed as possessing some *non fact-stating* role, so that our meaning-ascribing practices needn't be threatened by the sceptical paradox. It turns out that the sceptical solution is available only for languages spoken by linguistic *communities*, so that there can be no such thing as a "solitary" language. This is Kripke's spin on Wittgenstein's famous "private language argument." See Blackburn (1984) and Boghossian (1989), sections II, III, and IV.

12 For Kripke's own remarks on the relationship between Quine and KW, see Kripke 1982, 14–15, 55–8. For useful remarks on the relationship between behaviourism and reductive dispositional theories of meaning, see Fodor (1990: 53–7).

13 Of the other solutions considered by KW, the most widely-discussed after the dispositionalist theory has been the view that understanding is to be construed as some kind of sui generis, irreducible, non-qualitative state of mind. For some key papers in this non-reductionist vein, see the articles by McGinn, Wright, McDowell, and Pettit, reprinted in Miller and Wright (2002).

14 Perhaps we are under a *moral* obligation to think and tell the truth? That's debatable (at least as stated), but in any event it won't give us a route from a claim about the nature of putative *semantic* reasons to a form of irrealism about meaning. For interesting discussion, see Hattiangadi (forthcoming) and Kusch, M. (forthcoming).

15 See Miller (2003b: ch. 2).

16 In addition to the normativity argument, KW argues that the finitude of our linguistic dispositions poses an insuperable problem for dispositional theories of meaning. This is related to what is known as "the disjunction problem." See Fodor (1990). Boghossian (1989) argues that although KW's arguments fail, holism about the fixation of belief rules out any form of dispositionalism. For a reply, see Miller (2003a).

Analyticity Again[1]

Jerry Fodor and Ernie Lepore

1 Introduction

It would be ever so nice if there were a viable analytic/synthetic distinction. Though nobody knows for sure, there would seem to be several major philosophical projects that having one would advance. For example: analytic sentences[2] are supposed to have their truth values solely in virtue of the meanings (together with the syntactic arrangement) of their constituents; i.e., their truth values are supposed to supervene on their linguistic properties alone.[3] So they are true in every possible world where they mean what they mean here.[4] So they are necessarily true. So if there were a viable analytic/synthetic distinction ('a/s distinction' often hereafter), we would understand the necessity of at least some necessary truths. If, in particular, it were to turn out that the logical and/or the mathematical truths are analytic, we would understand why *they* are necessary. It would be ever so nice to understand why the logical and/or mathematical truths are necessary (cf. Gibson 1998; Quine 1998).

Any account of necessity would be welcome, but one according to which necessary truths are analytic has special virtues. Necessity isn't, of course, an epistemic property. Still, suppose that the necessity of a sentence arises from the meanings of its parts. It's natural to assume that one of the things one knows in virtue of knowing one's language is what the expressions of the language mean (cf., e.g., Boghossian 1994). A treatment of modality in terms of analyticity therefore connects the concept of necessity with the concept of knowledge; and knowledge *is*, of course, an epistemic property. So maybe if there is an a/s distinction, we could explain why the necessary truths, or at least some of the necessary truths, are knowable *a priori* by anybody who knows a language that can express them (cf. Quine 1991). It bears emphasis that not every theory of necessity yields a corresponding treatment of apriority; doing so is a special virtue of connecting modality with meaning. It would be ever so nice to understand how *a priori* knowledge is possible.

And that's not all. Lots of philosophers who are interested in the metaphysics of semantical properties find attractive the idea that the meaning of an expression supervenes on its conceptual/inferential role ('CR'; cf., Sellars 1954, Harman 1987, and Block 1986 and references therein). It is, however, a plausible objection to CR semantics that it courts a ruinous holism unless there is some way to distinguish meaning-constitutive inferences from the rest (Fodor and Lepore 1991, 1992). A tenable a/s distinction might resolve this tension; perhaps, the meaning constitutive-inferences could be identified with the analytic ones. In practice, it's pretty widely agreed that saving a/s is a condition for saving CR (cf., e.g., Block 1986; Peacocke 1992).

And, finally, there are those who just find it intuitively plausible that there are analytic truths. For many linguists, it's a main goal of 'lexical semantics' to predict which sentences express them; typically, by 'decomposing' the meanings of some words into their definitions. On this sort of view, intuitions of analyticity play much the role vis-à-vis theories of meaning that intuitions of grammaticality do vis-à-vis theories of syntax (cf. Katz 1972).

But, for all that, a lot of philosophers have been persuaded (largely by considerations that Quine raised) that there is no unquestion-begging way to formulate a serious a/s distinction (cf., e.g., Gibson 1988: ch. 4; Harman 1999; Lepore 1995). Perhaps, the moral is that we will have to learn to do philosophy without it. If, in consequence, notions like necessity, apriority, and definition seem deeply mysterious, so be it.

But now comes Paul Boghossian, who in several places (1996, 1997) offers, if not actually to delineate the a/s distinction, then at least to deduce its existence from mere Meaning Realism (MR), a doctrine which, he rightly says, is common ground to many who reject a/s itself (including, by the way, the present authors). In the course of setting out his argument, Boghossian also has much to say about CR semantics and about the logical constants; he's got a lot of irons in the fire, and his discussion illuminates a variety of issues. But, on balance, we think he has his irons by the wrong end. So, anyhow, we will try to convince you.

But first a digression: Gil Harman (following Quine) has famously offered an across-the-board argument that the notion of analyticity is untenable; namely, that the truth of analytic sentences is supposed somehow to be independent of 'how the world is,' but that it's puzzling how the truth of anything *could* be independent of how the world is. How, for example, could a stipulation, or a linguistic convention (implicit or otherwise) make a proposition *true*? How could our undertaking to respect the inference from 'bachelor' to 'unmarried' make it true that bachelors are unmarried?

> There is an obvious problem in understanding how the truth of a statement can be independent of the way the world is and depend entirely on the meaning of the statement. Why is it not a fact about the world that copper is a metal such that, if this were not a fact, the statement 'copper is a metal' would not express a truth? And why

doesn't the truth expressed by 'copper is copper' depend in part on the general fact that everything is self-identical?   (Harman 1999: 119)

We don't wish to take a stand on whether Harman's point is decisive; but we do want to remark on what Boghossian says by way of reply; which, if we are reading him correctly, is something like this: It *is* a mystery how stipulations, implicit definitions, conventions, and the like could, all by themselves, make propositions true. And, in fact, they don't even purport to.

> All that is involved in the thesis of Implicit Definition is the claim that the conventional assignment of truth to a sentence determines what proposition that sentence expresses (if any); such a view is entirely silent about what (if anything) determines the truth of the claim that is thereby expressed – *a fortiori*, it is silent about whether our conventions determine it.   (Boghossian 1997: 351)

Actually, we don't understand this, and we doubt that Harman would find it moving (cf. Harman 1996: 144–7, for his response). It's Boghossian's view that you can make a sentence true by stipulation; and that that very stipulation determines which proposition the sentences expresses. Call the sentence S and the proposition P. Surely, if S is true, then P is true, since it's a truism (assuming sentences have truth values at all) that each sentence has the same truth value as the proposition it expresses. It's thus unclear to us why making a sentence true by stipulation (which Boghossian agrees is something one can do) isn't *thereby* making the corresponding proposition true by stipulation (which, we take it, Boghossian denies is something that one can do).

However, there is perhaps an exegetical way out of this. It may be that, given what Boghossian means by 'what makes a proposition true,' not every sufficient condition for a proposition to be true is *ipso facto* what *makes* it true. Perhaps, in the usage Boghosian intends, only (what is sometimes called) its 'truth maker' can make a proposition true. So, for example, the truth maker for the proposition expressed by 'The cat is on the mat' is presumably a certain state of affairs 'in the world'; viz., that the cat is on the mat. Accordingly, not everything that entails this proposition counts as its truth maker. If the cat is on the mat or in the tub, and the cat is not in the tub, then the cat is on the mat. But, presumably, the state of affairs that (the cat is either on the mat or in the tub, and that it's not in the tub) isn't the truth maker for 'The cat is on the mat.' The truth maker for 'The cat is on the mat' is that the cat is on the mat, as previously remarked. This idea is, clearly, not without its difficulties, but perhaps it's the sort of thing Boghossian has in mind. Let's suppose so for the sake of the discussion.

So, then, Boghossian is saying that, although stipulating that a sentence is true does entail that the corresponding proposition is true, *that* the sentence is true by stipulation isn't (typically) the truth maker of the proposition that it expresses. On this reading, Boghossian doesn't, in fact, tell us what the truth maker of a proposition that is expressed by a sentence that's true by stipulation might be. Which, of course, he has every right not to do.

But we're still puzzled about how he could answer the kind of question that we take Harman to be raising. Let's say: whatever the truth maker for a proposition is, the proposition is true just in case its truth maker is 'in place.' Now consider the proposition expressed by a sentence that is true by stipulation. Presumably, the truth maker for that proposition *must be* in place since the sentence that expresses it is true. If so, then, Harman can object as follows: 'It's not obvious how a stipulation could make the world such that a certain sentence is true of it. But it's also, and equally, not obvious how a stipulation could guarantee that the truth maker of the proposition that a sentence expresses is 'in place.' ' In fact, the second question is plausibly just the first one all over again. We think this complaint would be justified were Harman to make it; so, we think, if Harman's worry about the possibility of truth by stipulation is legitimate, Boghossian has done nothing to make it go away.

End of digression.

The following discussion has two parts: First, we consider the main question Boghossian raises: what's the relation between analyticity and Meaning Realism? Second, we discuss Boghossian's views about the viability of CR semanticists as a treatment of the logical particles.

2   Analyticity and Meaning Realism

The main argument of Boghossian's paper is starkly simple. A Meaning Realist is, by stipulation, somebody who thinks that there are facts about the meaning of expressions. But, Boghossian says, if there are facts about the meaning of expressions, then it must be at least possible that the very same facts about meaning could hold of two *different* expressions. But if the same meaning facts hold of two different expressions, then those expressions are synonymous. Suppose two sentences differ only in respect of synonymous expressions. Then a hypothetical that has either sentence as antecedent and the other as consequent is *ipso facto* analytic. So, *a fortiori*, if Meaning Realism is assumed, it must be at least possible that there should be forms of words that express analytic truths. So, *a fortiori*, there *couldn't* be a principled argument against a/s that a Meaning Realist can accept. So, *a fortiori*, Quine didn't have a principled argument against a/s that a Meaning Realist could accept. QED.[5]

We think that this argument is fallacious; in particular, it relies on a crucial conflation of *analyticity* with *synonymy* (a conflation which, by the way, Quine's own usage encourages (1953: 23)). While the inference from Meaning Realism to the possibility of synonymy is sound, the inference from the possibility of synonymy to the possibility of analyticity fails; so we claim. On our view, synonymy is necessary but not sufficient for analyticity; and the further conditions that must be assumed to get to the latter from the former are highly substantive.

We'll set out the argument for this in just a moment, but first we want to be explicit about the intuition that it turns on: the traditional understanding is that " 'Fa iff Ga' is analytic" is true iff 'F' and 'G' *express the same concept.*[6] Correspondingly, our argument will be that if this is what you mean by analyticity, then the analyticity of 'Fa iff Ga' does *not* follow from the assumption that the same meaning facts hold of 'F' and 'G' (i.e., from the fact that 'F' and 'G' are synonyms). That's because it's prima facie plausible that synonyms needn't express the same concept; they may only express concepts that are synonymous.[7] So far, then, it's perfectly OK to assume that there could be distinct expressions of which the same meaning facts hold, while denying that, if there were, there would ipso facto be analytic inferences. Precisely contrary to Boghossian.

One reason why it's prima facie plausible that (e.g.) 'bachelor' and 'unmarried man' correspond to concepts that are synonymous but distinct is that it's *prima facie* plausible that the concepts that they correspond to (viz., BACHELOR and UNMARRIED MAN) have different possession conditions.[8] What makes this plausible is that one of the English locutions that expresses the concept UNMARRIED MAN is, of course, 'unmarried man'; and it's clear on the face of it that that locution contains, as a constituent, a word that expresses the concept UNMARRIED MAN. It may be, of course, that the word 'bachelor' also expresses the complex concept UNMARRIED MAN (as opposed to expressing a synonymous but primitive concept BACHELOR). But that would need arguing for in a way that the complexity of the concept that 'unmarried man' expresses does not. Well, since it's self-evident that UNMARRIED and MAN are constituents of UNMARRIED MAN, it's likewise self-evident that having UNMARRIED and MAN is a possession condition for having the concept that 'UNMARRIED MAN' names; you can't have a whole unless you have all of its parts. But the corresponding claim about the possession conditions for BACHELOR would be highly tendentious; the assumption that either UNMARRIED or MAN is a part of BACHELOR is not to be taken for granted in the course of a discussion of the analyticity (or otherwise) of 'Bachelors are unmarried men.' Indeed, the claim that BACHELOR has any constituents at all is tendentious and not to be assumed in this context. Notice, for example, that it wouldn't follow from the mere necessity of 'bachelors are unmarried men' that the concept BACHELOR is complex. For (we suppose) not all necessary truths are analytic. In fact, the usual way to argue that UNMARRIED and MAN are constituents of BACHELOR, is to take for granted that 'Bachelors are unmarried men' is analytic (and not just necessary); a dialectic which would, of course, be question-begging in the present context.

So, then, one way to see that it's tendentious to claim that BACHELOR and UNMARRIED MAN are the same concept is to note the prima facie difference between their possession conditions. Another way is to note that to take their identity for granted would beg the question against Conceptual Atomism.[9] For, suppose that Conceptual Atomism is true; then it's in principle possible to have BACHELOR without having *any* other concepts. A fortiori, it's possible to have BACHELOR but not MAN or UNMARRIED.

Perhaps, for example, you are into informational semantics (Dretske 1981). In that case, you may well hold that the only condition that is required for a mind to possess the concept BACHELOR is that it is causally connected ("in the right way") to actual or possible instantiations of *bachelorhood*. But if, as may be supposed, *bachelorhood* and *unmarriedmanhood* are the same property, then all that's required to have the concept BACHELOR is being causally connected (in the right way) to *unmarriedmanhood*. *A fortiori*, it's not required that one have the concept UNMARRIED or the concept MAN. *A fortiori*, if atomism is true, BACHELOR and UNMARRIED must be different concepts since, clearly, you can't have UNMARRIED MAN unless you have UNMARRIED and MAN.

Notice, in passing, that the question whether BACHELOR and UNMARRIED MAN are identical concepts (which would be required to make 'Bachelors are unmarried men' analytic according to our understanding) interacts not only with issues about their respective possession conditions, but also with questions about concept acquisition. This is hardly surprising since, of course, learning a concept is one way of coming to have it. So, just as it's not self-evident that you can't *have* BACHELOR unless you already have UNMARRIED MAN, it's also not self-evident that you can't *learn* BACHELOR unless you've already learned UNMAR-RIED. In fact, as it turns out, there are lots of cases where the order of concept acquisition appears not to be what you would expect on the assumption that synonymy implies identity of concepts. For example, it's said that 'dog' and 'domestic canine' correspond to the same concept, so that 'Dogs are domestic canines' is analytic. It is, however, pretty clear that, in the order of acquisition, DOG comes before either DOMESTIC or CANINE (sometimes it comes a lot before). Such considerations suggest that there's a point to insisting that the concepts DOG and DOMESTIC CANINE are *different* (though synonymous); that would explain why you can learn the former without learning the latter. This sort of issue is live in the empirical study of concept acquisition, so philosophers are not allowed to preempt it (cf., Leslie 2000).

Here's yet another way to see why inferences from synonymy to analyticity are moot (e.g., that it's moot whether BACHELOR and UNMARRIED MAN are the same concepts). The usual way of running the claim that they are the same concept is to suppose, in effect, that they are both the concept UNMARRIED MAN. That is, it's to assume that the concepts that correspond to definable words are their definitions, where definitions are assumed to be *ipso facto* syntactically complex. But it seems perfectly plausible, first blush at least, that there should be a mind in which the property of *being an unmarried man* is mentally represented by a syntactically primitive expression; for example, by the expression 'BACHELOR.'[10] Our point is that this sort of issue cannot be settled by fiat; specifically, it can't be settled by taking for granted that synonymous formulas *ipso facto* express the same concept.

Here's yet a fourth way to see that if you require conceptual identity for analyticity, then it's by no means clear that 'Bachelors are unmarried men' and the like are analytic. There's a considerable issue as to whether concepts are to be individuated by their content alone, or by their content together with their structure. Suppose that concepts that express the same property have the same content, and suppose that *water* and H_2O are the same property; so then the expressions 'water' and 'H_2O' are synonymous. Someone who accepts all that might want to claim that WATER and H_2O are nevertheless different concepts, the evidence being that it's possible to believe that a certain liquid is water without believing that it's H_2O. This would seem to be a fact over and above the apparent difference in the *possession conditions* of the concepts, since it's perfectly possible for someone who has the concept WATER to have the concept H_2O as well (e.g., he knows that there is an actual or possible chemical compound that has that structure but not that H_2O and water are the same stuff).

So if (as we claim) analyticity requires concept identity, then, *a fortiori*, merely synonymous concepts don't support analyticities. Why is it, then, that so many philosophers take for granted that if 'bachelor' and 'unmarried man' are synonyms, the corresponding concepts must be identical (and that if Conceptual Atomism would entail that synonymous concepts can have different possession conditions, then so much the worse for Conceptual Atomism)? We think they're persuaded less by an argument than by a rhetorical question: namely, 'But how could you know that someone is a bachelor and not know that he's unmarried?' Our answer is: 'It's easy.' Imagine a mind that has a concept that applies to bachelors as such, (*viz.*, it has the concept BACHELOR) but no concept that applies to unmarried persons as such (*viz.*, it lacks the concept UNMARRIED). For the owner of that mind, it's perfectly possible to know that bachelorhood is instantiated but not to know that unmarriedness is instantiated too. Indeed, that mind couldn't even frame the hypothesis that if either concept applies, so too does the other.

Notice that, if there's a distinction between synonymous concepts in this kind of case, it's because one is primitive and the other is structurally (*viz.*, syntactically) complex. In fact, all our cases of candidates for conceptual synonymy without concept identity are of this sort. They are what we are relying on to make our case that identity of conceptual contents isn't sufficient for identity of concepts. It may be that that there are no pairs of synonymous but distinct concepts both of which are primitive; if so, then the concepts expressed by 'perhaps' and 'maybe,' for example, are maybe identical. This turns out to be quite a complicated issue, and for present purposes we take no stand on it.

So far we have argued for the following hypothetical: *if* analyticities derive from concept identities (as opposed to mere concept synonymies) *then* the inference from Meaning Realism to the possibility of analyticity doesn't go through *sans* premises about the identity conditions for concepts (or for properties, or both); and that no such premises are available without charge. But we haven't argued at all for the antecedent of this hypothetical. That is, we've given no reason, so far, for assuming that only formulas that express identical concepts (and, presumably, some of their logical consequences)[11] are analytically related. In effect, we're accepting the conventional wisdom that, if there are analyticities, they are the sentences that can be turned into logical truths by substituting synonyms for synonyms. But we are denying that substitutions of synonyms for synonyms *ipso facto* preserve analyticity.

But what's the argument for denying this?

Our first point is sort of etymological; *analyticity* is after all supposed to be about *analysis*. The classic understanding of the notion required that concepts have constituent structure and that analytic sentences are true in virtue of the relation between complex concepts and their less complex parts. To enumerate the set of analytic truths in which an expression occurs is therefore tantamount to analyzing its structure. (See n. 6.) Thus there's a quite standard way of understanding analyticity according to which 'Bachelors are unmarried men' is analytic because it analyzes BACHELOR into its parts. Conversely, it's because the going theory of analyticity is that it arises from the constituent analysis of complex concepts, that so many people have wanted to deny that it could be analytic that whatever is red is colored. (We'll return to this case presently.)

Our second point is sort of historical. The view that constituency relations among concepts are the source of analyticities has been practically universal among philosophers who have endorsed any notion of analyticity (or of 'relations of ideas') whatever. If you look at what Kant says, for example, the story is that 'All bodies are extended' qualifies as analytic because EXTENDED is part of BODY, but '7 + 5 =12' is *not* analytic, presumably because there is no unique way of analyzing the concept 12 into its parts (see Kant 1781: Introduction, sec. 5, pp. 52–3).

> In all judgments in which the relation of a subject to the predicate is thought . . . , this relation is possible in two different ways. Either the predicate B belongs to the subject A, as something which is (covertly) contained in this concept A; or B lies outside the concept A . . . In the one case I entitle the judgment analytic, in the other synthetic . . . . The former, as adding nothing to the concept of the subject, but merely breaking it up into those constituent concepts that have all along been thought in it. (Kant 1781: Introduction, sec. 4, p. 48)

In a similar spirit, Hume thinks that primitive concepts must be independent; presumably that's because he too thinks that conceptual entailment comes from, and only from, the analysis of complex concepts.[12] The moral is pretty much the one we drew above: there's a historical connection between the idea that there are analytic truths at all and the idea that analyticities arise from structural relations between complex concepts and their parts. But to hold that sort of view is to acknowledge the possibility of synonymy between concepts both of which are primitive; hence, of synonymy without analyticity.

For all that, philosophers have occasionally denied that analyticities derive from conceptual analyses. Carnap (1952), for example, suggests that a concept may enter into analytic inferences even where it doesn't have constituents (in effect, even if the concept doesn't have a definition). So, for example, this account would allow 'Whatever is red is colored' to be analytic even though 'red' doesn't mean *colored and X*. In such cases, the principles invoked are called 'meaning postulates.' But there's a good (essentially Quinean) reason why this sort of proposal never became popular; namely, that it's unclear what the truth maker for a meaning postulate could be. Consider the contrast between 'red → colored' and 'bachelor → unmarried.' Someone who thinks the latter is analytic can offer an explanation of its being so; *viz.*, that it follows from the conceptual structure of BACHELOR. To be sure, this explanation requires support from arguments that the concept BACHELOR *is* complex; but at least *if* BACHELOR is complex, one can see why 'bachelor → unmarried' might be analytic. What, however, is the corresponding story about 'red → colored'? Clearly not that it follows from the decomposition of 'red.' But if not that, then what? If you can't answer this question, then the claim that 'red → colored' is a meaning postulate *just is* the claim that 'red → colored' is analytic (see Quine 1953); so what looked like an explanation of the analyticity turns out to be just a truism.

We're inclined to take this sort of point very seriously, so we pause to rub it in. We saw, earlier in the chapter, that Boghossian doesn't wish to claim that stipulations, implicit definitions, conventions or the like could be what make analyticities true. We're sympathetic with his not wishing to claim this since, even if stipulation could make *sentences* true, it seems quite hopeless as an account of the truth of analytic *thoughts*. Presumably nobody stipulated the connection between the concept BACHELOR and the concept UNMARRIED MAN; nor is it easy to see how such conceptual relations could hold by linguistic convention. As we read him, Boghossian leaves questions about the truth makers for analyticities moot; which, as we remarked, he surely has every right to do. On the other hand, such questions do have to be faced sooner or later, and the options seem a bit sparse. De facto, as far as we can tell, they're down to one. If you follow the Kantian tradition, it's constituency relations among concepts that make analyticities true. Bachelors have to be unmarried because the concept UNMARRIED is part of the concept BACHELOR. If, however, you don't follow the Kantian line, then you have much the same problem that Carnap did. It's all very well to *say* that some or other P is analytic; but such claims aren't convincing lacking an account of what it is that makes them so. If, as we suppose, Kant's story is the only one on offer, then it seems to us that a philosopher who insists on there being analytic truths, would be wise to sign up for conceptual containment at his earliest possible convenience.

We've been reviewing reasons why it's not wise to conflate synonymy with analyticity. Our third point is sort of semantical. It's supposed to be a mark of analytic inferences that they are valid in opaque contexts. The argument is that, for example, the inference from ' … thinks John is a bachelor' to ' … thinks John is an unmarried man' goes through because, since BACHELOR and UNMARRIED MAN are the same concept, you can't think the one without *thereby* thinking the other. This argument wouldn't, of course, be available on the assumption that BACHELOR and UNMARRIED MAN are distinct concepts; no more than the synonymy of 'bachelor' and 'unmarried man' entails that you can't *say* the one without thereby saying the other. Hence the general consensus that identity of content isn't per se sufficient for substitutivity; you need something more (like, maybe, that the concepts involved are identical or maybe that they are 'structurally isomorphic'). So the standard way of explaining why substitutivity co-varies with analyticity depends on assuming that only conceptual identity yields analyticity; mere conceptual synonymy isn't good enough. To be sure, we're taking for granted that concepts that are structurally distinct (e.g., BACHELOR and UN-MARRIED MAN, according to the story about them we prefer) can nevertheless be the same in content. We think this is pretty untendentious given that concepts are supposed to have structure at all. If concepts have structure and content, then why shouldn't two concepts with the same content have different structures?

To sum up: For good and sufficient reasons, analyticity is traditionally connected with concept *identity;* the latter is viewed as both necessary and sufficient for the former. If that's right, you can't hold that *synonymy* is sufficient for analyticity unless you're prepared to claim that *content*-identical concepts are identical *tout court.* But, just as Frege taught us not to identify concepts with their extensions (because there are different ways in which an *extension* may be 'grasped'), it is likewise plausible that you can't identify a concept with its *content* (because there are different ways in which a *content* can be grasped; i.e., identical contents can be grasped via structurally distinct modes of presentation.) Prima facie, you can think the content *unmarried-manhood* either via the concept BACHELOR or via the concept UNMARRIED MAN; and, as we've seen, all sorts of (broadly psycho-logical) questions about concept possession, concept acquisition, and so on, turn on which of these ways you do think it; that's because it's the structure of a concept that determines the psychological consequences of entertaining it (at least it is according to computational accounts of psychological processes). The price you pay for not allowing merely structural differences to distinguish between concepts is that you thereby abstract concepts from their psychological roles.

There is, to repeat the point one last time, a serious question whether analyticity follows from synonymy (viz., from what we all agree that Meaning Realism entails). Boghossian's argument that Meaning Realists have to accept analyticity begs this serious question.

Perhaps, however, you don't find the arguments we've offered convincing; maybe, you think that there must, after all, be *some* way of getting to analyticity from identity of 'meaning properties'; viz., from synonymy. So be it. We claim only that the inference won't go through without considerable elaboration of its premises; and that, for all anybody knows, some of the premises that the elabor-ation requires may not be true. If we've convinced you of that much, then, prima facie at least, there's no reason why you can't affirm Meaning Realism and still deny a/s.

But suppose you're *still* not convinced. Suppose you say: 'Look, guys, analyticity just is truth in virtue of meaning. If you allow synonymy (and logic), then *of course* you allow analyticity; and, by stipulation, Meaning Realists do allow synonymy. So, isn't this stuff about making analyticity contingent on concept identity much ado about nothing?'[13] Answer, 'no.' Not, at least, if you want analyticity to explain apriority in the usual Kantian way; viz., that when 'F → G' is analytic, thinking G is part of thinking F.[14]

According to the Kantian treatment, what makes a predication a priori is a certain relation between states of mind; viz., that a mind that thinks the subject thereby thinks the predicate. But this line of explanation requires more than that that 'F → G' is true in virtue of meaning; it requires also that the concept that 'G' expresses is part of the concept that 'F' expresses. You can, if you like, just hold that meaning identity engenders apriority, punkt; but, we claim, you need the stuff about identity conditions on states of mind to explain *why* meaning identity engenders apriority; and, to repeat, the stuff about states of mind assumes that some concepts are constituents of others. Why should meaning identity entail apriority if the concepts involved *aren't* structurally related?[15]

3 Logical Truths

Like many others, Boghossian makes the point that CR semantics is plausibly viewed as a generalization of one of the standard ways of treating the logical particles (Dummett 1977). The idea is that primitive logical terms can be given a role in a language(/theory) by specifying rules of introduction and elimination. Thus, the meaning of 'and' (as it is used in formalizations of propositional logic) is determined (at least up to logical equivalence) by specifying that the substitution instances of the following inference schema are valid:

'and' introduction: P,Q ∴ P and Q
'and' elimination: P and Q ∴ P,Q

Insofar as this sort of thing strikes you as a promising account of the meanings of the logical vocabulary, a parallel treatment of the rest of the lexicon might seem promising too. Some such idea is frequently cited as grounds for optimism about CR (Sellars 1954; Harman 1986, 1987; Peacocke 1992). On this view, the job of the lexicon of a language is to specify valid introduction ('entrance') and elimination ('exit') rules for *all* of its primitive expressions.

We think it's a prima facie objection to this project that 'and' and (as it might be) 'tree' seem to be such different *kinds* of words that it would be sort of surprising if their meanings were constituted in essentially the same way. (For one thing, it's plausible that 'and' doesn't refer to anything; but 'tree' clearly does.[16]) Given the prima facie magnitude of such differences, it seems CR semantics might do well enough for the logical expressions but not work at all for non-logical primitives. One of the present authors (JF) has flirted with this sort of hybrid theory, and continues to find it attractive on alternate Tuesdays.[17]

We don't propose to defend the viability of a CR treatment of the logical constants. But we do want to consider a charge that Boghossian levels; namely, that a Meaning Realist who adopts a CR semantics for the logical constants, can't reasonably deny that conceptual roles might likewise determine the meanings of nonlogical terms. As far as we can see, however, his argument for claiming this is unconvincing.

Here's what he says:

> if the only view available about how the logical constants acquire their meaning is in terms of the inferences and/or sentences that they participate in, then any indeterminacy in what those meaning-constituting sentences and inferences are will translate into an indeterminacy about the meanings of the expressions themselves. This realization should give pause to any philosopher who thinks he can buy in on Quine's critique of implicit definition without following him all the way to the rejection to the headier doctrine of meaning-indeterminacy. ... Fodor seems a particularly puzzling case; for he holds all three of the following views. (1) he rejects indeterminacy ... (2) he follows Quine in rejecting a notion of meaning-constituting inference. (3) he holds a conceptual role view of the meanings of the logical constants. As far as I am able to judge, however, this combination of views is not consistent.   (Boghossian 1997: 354-5)

Now, we agree that you can't coherently endorse {CR, MR, and no a/s} while denying indeterminacy; for MS and CR jointly imply that some part of a concept's inferential role is meaning constitutive, but (*sans* a/s) it's indeterminate which part that is. But so what? In particular, why shouldn't indeterminacy and MR be compatible? Boghossian must think that if the meaning of an expression is indeterminate, it follows that there is no fact of the matter about what the expression means. Thus:

> if there is no fact of the matter as to which of the various inferences involving a [logical] constant are meaning-constitutive, then there is also no fact of the matter as to what the logical constants themselves mean.   (Boghossian 1997: 354)

We're not prepared to concede anything of this sort. We think all sorts of indeterminacy can infect an expression which is, nevertheless, perfectly meaningful. Vagueness is a classic case; there are approximately indefinitely many shades of color that are neither determinately red nor determinately not red. Name one of these shades 'F.' This means that the inference from 'is F' to 'is red' is indeterminate; and, presumably, if some of the inferences that turn on a predicate are indeterminate, then the meaning of the predicate must be indeterminate too. But it doesn't follow that the predicate *has* no meaning; 'red' isn't meaningless; 'red' means *red*.

We don't, of course, claim that if the connectives are indeterminate, that's because they're vague. Our point is just that the inference from indeterminacy to irrealism isn't valid in the general case. As a matter of fact, though we're pretty sure that 'and' has a meaning, we also think that there are several respects in which its meaning (and *mutatis mutandis* that of the other logic constants) *is* indeterminate; just as you would expect if, on the one hand, the semantics of the logical particles is CR and, on the other hand, that there is no a/s distinction. So, our diagnosis is that Boghossian is trying to run a *reductio ad absurdum* of which the conclusion is true.

Here are three respects in which, according to views that are often endorsed in the literature, the meanings of the logical constants are indeterminate. Our point is that, whether or not these views are true, none of them would seem to be incompatible with the logical constants having meanings.

1 It's unclear, perhaps in principle, which words *are* logical constants. Are, for example, 'temporally prior to,' 'ought' and 'possible' among them? This is a way of asking whether tense logic, deontic logic, and modal logic really are species of logic. If they are, then (according to the hybrid theory) 'ought,' 'possible' and 'temporally prior to' have CR semantics; if not, then not.

Well, suppose there's no definite fact of the matter about which expressions are logical constants (i.e., that it's *indeterminate* which expressions are logical constants) hence that there are expressions for which the viability of CR semantics is also indeterminate. We doubt that anything like Meaning *Irrealism* would follow. Even if there's no fact about *which* words are logical constants, it may be true that *some* words are, and that CR semantics is true of them.

2 There are certain well-known indeterminacies about what some of the logical expressions mean. Is English 'not' Classical or is it Intuitionistic? Does English 'if/then' express the material conditional? Is the correct interpretation of English quantifiers (like 'some') objectual or substitutional? Does 'all' have existential import? And so forth. Perhaps some of these questions will turn out to be resolvable on empirical (or other) grounds. But, surely, whether the connectives are meaningful doesn't depend on their doing so.

3 There are indefinitely many ways of formulating introduction and elimination rules for, as it might be, 'and.' How, then, do you choose the ones that generate analyticities; i.e., the ones that are true in virtue of the *meaning* of 'and'? Suppose (as Boghossian is inclined to do) that there's no matter of fact here. Then, presumably, it follows that the possession conditions for AND are indeterminate. But it surely doesn't follow from *that* that the *identity* conditions for AND are indeterminate (or, still less) that there are *no* identity conditions for AND.) Notice that the satisfaction of a possession condition for a concept C is, *ipso facto, sufficient* for having C. This is so even if, by assumption, it's indeterminate which of the (logically equivalent) formulations of the possession conditions for having C is the one that determines its meaning. But, surely, you can't *have* the concept C unless there *is* the concept C.

Since these sorts of points are all pretty familiar, we're worried that maybe we've misunderstood what Boghossian means by 'indeterminacy.' Perhaps he wants 'indeterminacy' to mean whatever it does in chapter 2 of *Word and Object*; that, presumably, would be indeterminacy of translation.

> In Chapter 2 of *Word and Object* Quine argued that, for any language, it is possible to find two incompatible translation manuals that nevertheless perfectly conform to the totality of the evidence that constrains translation. This is the famous doctrine of the indeterminacy of translation. Since Quine was, furthermore, prepared to assume that there could not be facts about meaning that are not captured in the constraints on best translation, he concluded that meaning-facts themselves are indeterminate ... This is the doctrine that I have called the indeterminacy of meaning. (Boghossian 1997: 333)

Actually, we don't know of any place in Quine where he speaks of indeterminacy of *meaning*; though, of course, talk about indeterminacy of translation is ubiquitous. But suppose that the translation of the logical particles is indeterminate and that indeterminacy of meaning follows from indeterminacy of translation. To get Meaning Irrealism you need the further premise that *indeterminacy* of meaning entails *no meaning facts*; and, we're claiming, it's quite unclear whether that's true. There are lots of kinds of meaning indeterminacy, and nobody knows which, if any of them, precludes MR.[18]

Conclusion

As we understand him, Boghossian claims (1) that a consistent Meaning Realist must admit that the a/s distinction is viable; (2) that meaning indeterminacy is incompatible with Meaning Realism; (3) that you can't be a CR theorist about words like 'and' unless you are also a CR theorist about words like 'tree'; and (4) that you can't hold that implicit definitions determine meanings without also holding that there are analytic truths. Boghossian also thinks (5) that you can't be a CR theorist about words like 'and' unless you tolerate the meaning indeterminacy of some of the expressions that contain them. But he's wrong about (1)–(4) and, though he's right about (5), it's plausible that expressions containing the logical terms *are* meaning indeterminate in several different respects, just as you would expect if their meanings supervene on their conceptual roles. That's independent of whether MR holds for the logical terms, at least for anything that has been argued so far.

So, as far as we can see, everything is fine: you can hold *MR* and *no a/s* and you can hold *CR for logical constants* but not for 'tree.' Or, anyhow, you can lacking premises that Boghossian hasn't supplied and that Meaning Realists may coherently refuse to grant. So, where does this leave us vis-à-vis the question whether there could be a principled a/s distinction? Well, if it's assumed (*contra* Quine) that there is such a thing as identity of meaning facts (hence, of conceptual content) *and* it's assumed that syntactically simple expressions (e.g., 'bachelor') sometimes express complex concepts (e.g., UNMARRIED MAN),[19] then some sentences (e.g., 'Bachelors are unmarried') are indeed analytic. Our point against Boghossian has been that though a Meaning Realist must accept the first assumption, he is quite free to reject the second. So, once again, analyticity doesn't follow from Meaning Realism alone.

Addendum

And so, in the course of events, we have gone from place to place, reading the aforesaid to such as were prepared to listen.[20] Such is the custom of our tribe. We find, in the course of doing so, that the following objection is often raised: 'But, surely, one could just *stipulate* that 'bachelor' means *unmarried man*. Wouldn't it *then* follow that 'Bachelors are unmarried men' is analytic? And (given logic) that 'Bachelors are unmarried' and 'Bachelors are men' are analytic too?'

To which we make the following three replies.

- (*Ad hominum*). Maybe so; but Boghossian explicitly rejects this possibility, and it's Boghossian whom we're arguing with.
- (As *per* above). We can't see how the stipulation story could apply to relations among *concepts*; not even if it's supposed to apply to relations among words.
- (The important one). Suppose, however, you *can* stipulate that two concepts have the same content. It doesn't follow that you can stipulate they have the same *structure* or, *a fortiori*, that they have the same *constituent* structure. What would it mean to claim that UNMARRIED is a constituent of BACHELOR *by stipulation* (or, *mutatis mutandis*, that, by stipulation, 'unmarried' is *not* a constituent of 'unmarried man')? But, according to the mainline philosophical tradition, analyticity requires concept identity; *a fortiori*, it requires identity of conceptual structure. If that's right, then what analyticity requires isn't a thing that you *can* stipulate.

'So much the worse for the mainline philosophical tradition,' you may wish to say. Ok; but, (to repeat) as far as we know, it's the only theory there is that offers even a remotely plausible account of *what makes* a proposition analytic; i.e., about what the truth makers for analyticity claims could be. And it's likewise what links, on the one hand, analyticity with modality and, on the other hand, analyticity with psychology. Give up the connection with the constituent structure of concepts, and what's left of the thesis that there are consequential analytic truths is that there are philosophically interesting we-know-not-whats. The track record of such claims isn't encouraging.

Notes

1 We would like to thank Emma Borg, Ray Elugardo, Roger Gibson, Lou Goble, John Hawthorne, Paul Pietroski, Jason Stanley, Zoltan Szabo and especially, Gil Harman for discussion on earlier drafts.

2 For convenience of exposition, we'll use 'analytic' to mean *analytically true* unless notice is given to the contrary. We suppose the points we'll make to apply to analytically false sentences *mutatis mutandis*.

3 "a statement is analytic when it is true by virtue of meanings and independently of fact" (Quine 1953: 21). We will ignore complexities introduced by token reflexives and the like (cf., Kaplan 1989: 509).

4 Where, roughly, a 'possible world' is one in which all the logical truths hold. Different possible worlds are specified by different assignments of truth-values to the contingent propositions.

5 Quine isn't himself a Meaning Realist of course (see, e.g., Quine 1990: sec. 21, p. 52); so he doesn't have to care whether MR would entail the possibility of a/s.

6 We're not, of course, suggesting that analyticities have to be biconditional; the sentence 'Bachelors are unmarried' would be a counterexample. But this sentence's analyticity is usually thought to depend on its being derivable, by logic alone, from the biconditional analyticity of 'Bachelors are unmarried men.' More on this presently.

7 It's hard to find a terminology that doesn't beg the questions at issue here. We'll say that concepts are synonymous just in case they have the same content. We mean this formulation to leave it open whether concepts with the same content are identical. See n. 14 below.

8 We use formulas in quotes as names of expressions and (for the most part) italics as names of meanings (as in 'bachelor' means *unmarried man*). Sometimes, however, we'll say of one quoted formula that it means another ('bachelor' means 'unmarried man'). This is short for saying that the two formulas mean the same, *viz.*, that they are synonymous. Expressions in caps (e.g., 'BACHELOR') are names of concepts. NB: *names* of concepts rather than structural descriptions. Thus the notation is neutral as to whether the concept that 'BACHELOR' names is complex.

   It follows, of course, that the complexity of the *name* of the concept UNMARRIED MAN proves nothing one way or the other about the complexity of the concept that it names.

9 I.e., the view that there are no cases in which satisfying the possession conditions for one concept entails satisfying the possession conditions for some other concept. For discussion, see Fodor and Lepore (1992).

10 It's mostly a verbal issue whether providing a synonym for an expression counts as defining it; if it does, then one syntactically primitive expression can define another. It simplifies the exposition not to count synonyms as definitions. For what it is worth, it's our intuition that 'is synonymous with' is symmetrical but 'defines' is not.

11 It's notoriously moot which of the logical consequences of an analytic truth are themselves *ipso facto* analytic. Since we doubt that there are any analytic truths, we don't propose to take a stand on this.

12 "Every quality being a distinct thing from another, may be conciev'd to exist apart, and may exist apart from every other quality" (Hume 1739/1969: Bk. I, pt. 4, sec. 3, p. 271).

13 This line of thought ignores the Harman objection, which is, in effect, that meaning alone *couldn't* determine truth, since what a symbol means is among its intrinsic properties, whereas truth depends on how the world is. (See above.)

14 This doesn't, of course, include (putative) analyticities that depend on indexicals, like 'I am here now.' (See Kaplan.) We care about cases where philosophers say things like 'you can't have knowledge without belief because *believes P* is *part of the meaning* (our emphasis) of 'knows P.'" We think this claim is paradigmatic of the way that appeals to analyticity are typically exploited in philosophical arguments; and we take seriously its prima facie implication that (some) meanings have parts.

15 As far as we can make out, Boghossian thinks it's because the meaning facts about a language are *ipso facto* "transparent" to its speakers; so in particular, if F and G are synonymous (i.e., if the same meaning facts are true of them), then speakers would *ipso facto* know that they are synonymous. However, this claim is highly tendentious, and (as usual), that is all we require for present purposes.

16 Even theorists who think of CR semantics as a generalization of the semantics of logical particles generally think that there's more to the meaning of 'tree' than its role in inference. There's also something that reconstructs notions like denotation; perhaps it's something epistemological like a procedure for recognizing things that fall in the term's extension. (See, for example, Peacocke 1992.) Off hand, the only philosopher we can think of who approximates endorsing a *pure* CR semantics for the whole lexicon is Brandom; see his (2000). However, a fair number of linguists seem to harbor some such view too, usually in conjunction with a profound distrust of reference, truth, and the external world. Cf., Chomsky 2000, etc.).

17 He wishes to point out, however, that to hold that the meaning of a logical constant is constituted by its conceptual roles is not the same as holding that they are 'introduced' by implicit definitions. It is also not the same as holding that to formulate the entrance/exit rules for such an expression, is ipso facto a formulation of its possession conditions (see Fodor 2004).

18 Harman (1999: 149–50) has likewise suggested that Boghossian's arguments may depend on conflating various sense of 'indeterminacy.'

19 The standard formulation of this second assumption is that many words have definitions. We very much doubt that's true. See Fodor and Lepore (2002).

20 Including the CUNY Graduate Center, the University of Wisconsin at Madison, the University of Uppsala, the University of Umea, the University of Gottenburg, and the Australian National University. We want to express our gratitude for their hospitality

Chapter 7

Formal Semantics

Max Cresswell

1 Why 'Formal' Semantics

In the early part of Wittgenstein's *Philosophical Investigations* (Wittgenstein 1953) we find a discussion of a very simple language. It consists of the four words *block*, *slab*, *beam* and *pillar*. A builder calls out these words, and the assistant brings a block, slab, beam or pillar, as the case may be. Suppose an extension of this language which contains the word *not*. When *not block* is called the assistant brings a pillar. So does *not block* mean the same as *pillar*? Well maybe, until we see that the next time the builder calls *not block* the assistant brings a beam, and the third time a slab. So how can we specify the meaning of *not*? The clue is to use the notion of *truth*. Say that the *truth conditions* of an occurrence of the word *slab* are that it is *true* in conditions where the assistant brings a slab and *false* if the assistant does not.

This does not give a direct link with behavior. Suppose that the builder calls *slab* and the assistant brings a pillar. What do we say? There seems nothing about the behaviour of the builder and assistant to establish whether the assistant is disobedient, or whether the builder and assistant are playing a different language game. This is not to say that evidence may not be forthcoming. If the builder becomes angry with the assistant, and if next day there is a new assistant, that may provide evidence of disobedience; but only evidence. Although semantic facts depend on behavioural facts about language users, the nature of the dependence may be too complicated to form part of semantic theory. One response is to point out that, whether or not we can give an *analysis* of what behavioural facts constitute the facts that sentences have the truth conditions they do, it is undeniable that there are such facts.[1] Consider how to tell the difference between someone who knows English and someone who does not. You point to a table and utter the sentence:

(1)   There is a pen on that table.

First you utter it when the pen *is* on the table, and then you utter it when the pen has been taken away. You don't need to know English to know the difference between the situation in which there is a pen, and the situation in which there is not, but you *do* need to know English to know that that difference is correlated with the truth or falsity of (1) as a sentence of English.[2]

In discussing the Wittgenstein language I have spoken of words and sentences as if they were equivalent, and I have not distinguished them from utterances. Formal semantics, like formal grammar, is a discipline which looks at language using a large amount of abstraction. Even the language Wittgenstein describes involves abstraction. For we have to know when the sound that a builder makes counts as an utterance of the word **slab** rather than **pillar**, and that already involves a particular classification of linguistic acts. The other abstraction is in the notion of truth. Many philosophers would object to calling **slab** *true* when the assistant brings a slab. They might say that *true* only has a use when language is used to impart information. Many consider all non-declarative sentences to lack a truth value. But the fact remains that a sentence like

(2)   You will be here tomorrow

can be uttered as a prediction or a question or an order or...At the level of abstraction at which I will be presenting truth-conditional semantics (2) will be true, when addressed to a given person at a given place and time, if and only if (iff) that person is at that place on the day following the occasion of utterance.[3]

Suppose that each sentence in the language has a meaning by being associated with a set of truth conditions. It is then a simple matter to specify the meaning of the word **not**.

(3)   **not** α is true if α is false and false if α is true.

Notice that (3) satisfies an important principle which is often held to be a defining requirement of semantics. That is the principle of *compositionality*. The meaning of **not** specified in (3) entails that the truth conditions of **not** α are determined given the truth conditions of α. There are a number of other words which are susceptible of the same treatment. α **and** β is true iff both α and β are true, and false otherwise, α **or** β (for at least some uses of **or**) is true iff at least one of α and β is true and false otherwise, and so on. But it cannot be quite as straightforward as that. Before it can be said that (1) is true or false it must be specified what time is referred to and what pen and table are involved. Further, to know whether a sentence like

(4)   There was a pen on the table yesterday

is true we need to know, not just whether the given pen *is* on the given table at the given time, i.e. not just about whether (1) is true *at the present time*, but whether

(1) is true at some other time – to be specific at a time on the day previous to the time at which (4) is claimed to be true. And in a sentence like

(5)   There might have been a pen on the table

we need to know, not whether (1) is true *as things actually stand,* i.e. true in the actual world, but whether (1) would have been true if the world had been different in certain ways, i.e. true in this or that other possible world. Call i a *semantical index* iff it is sufficient to give a sentence a truth value. For (1) i would specify a value for a pen, a table, a time and a possible world.[4] The semantics for *not, and,* and *or* can be generalised in the obvious way. Given that sentences are true or false *at indices, not* α will be true at i iff α is false at i, α *and* β will be true at i iff α and β are both true at i, α *or* β will be true at i iff at least one of α and β is true at i, and so on.

Instead of saying that α is true or false at an index we may say more simply that the meaning or *semantic value* of a sentence α (call it $V(\alpha)$) is a *set of indices.* So α is true at i if $i \in V(\alpha)$ and α is false at i if $i \notin V(\alpha)$. The reference to V is simply to indicate that a syntactic item can be given infinitely many different semantic interpretations. I shall suppress this relativity from here on. The introduction of possible worlds in particular solves another problem. It might seem from what I have said that you cannot know what a sentence means without knowing whether it is true, and that is clearly wrong. If the way the world is is construed as the actual world, then other ways the world could be may be thought of as alternative possible but non-actual worlds. If I know the meaning of 'Massey University is in Hamilton' I do not have to know whether in fact it *is* there – in fact it is not – but I do have to know *what it would be like* for it to be there, In possible-worlds terms I have to know of any given world w, whether w is a world in which the sentence is true or whether w is a world in which it is false, but I do not have to know whether w is the actual world. To know which world is actual would be to be omniscient.

2   A Simple Fragment

To shew how to apply truth-conditional semantics to a natural language it is customary to use formally presented *fragments* which illustrate various features of a natural language. I shall use fragments of English. This chapter is not about syntax, nor indeed is it an exposition of any particular semantic proposal, except by way of illustration. Consider the sentence:

(6)   Every author shouts.

A formal syntactical theory is often based on a set of *phrase-structure rules.* These rules depend on splitting all expressions up into *syntactic categories.* For our purposes there will be five: S (sentence), NP (noun phrase), VP (verb phrase), CN (common noun) and Det (determiner). Based on these categories is a set of *phrase structure rules*, which specify how complex expressions in each category are to be built up. These rules will then be given a semantic interpretation which will show how a meaning may be attached to an item in each syntactic category in such a way as to determine the truth conditions of every sentence. The rules are:

PSR1   S → NP VP
PSR2   NP → Det CN
PSR3   Det → {*every, most, some*,... }
PSR4   CN → {*author*,... }
PSR5   VP → {*shouts*,... }

Some comments are in order here. PSR3-5 are called *lexical rules*, since they associate syntactic categories with particular lexical items. The ...indicates that they are open ended, so that the language can contain more items than just those listed. Categories like CN and VP can be further split up in a more realistic syntax, since you can have complex VPs like **walk a mile** and complex CNs like **large European butterfly**. For verbs, tense and aspect will be important. These issues will be discussed in their turn, but there is enough now to be going on with. In an obvious way the rules show the structure of (6) by means of the following 'labeled bracketing':

(7)   [[[*every*]$_{Det}$[*author*]$_{CN}$]$_{NP}$[*shouts*]$_{VP}$]$_S$

[*every*]$_{Det}$ indicates that *every* is in category Det, as it is according to the rules. [*author*]$_{CN}$ indicates that *author* is in category CN. [*shouts*]$_{VP}$ shews that *shouts* is in category VP. [[*every*]$_{Det}$[*author*]$_{CN}$]$_{NP}$ shews that this Det and this CN combine according to PSR2 to form an NP, and finally (7) indicates that the NP and VP combine according to PSR1 to form an S. (7) corresponds in an obvious way with the 'syntactic tree':

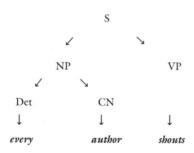

The semantic interpretation works as follows.[5] We require that the meaning of a sentence is to be a set of indices. Consider PSR1. It should tell you how to combine the meaning of a NP and a VP to get an S. At this stage the meaning of a VP is easy. The meaning of *shouts* is the function ζ such that $\zeta(a)$ is the set of indices at which a is shouting. (Some prefer to think of the set of individuals who are shouting at i, for any index i. This set is $\{a : i \in \omega(a)\}$, the set of those as for which $\omega(a)$ is true at i). The meaning of the NP $[[\textit{every}]_{\text{Det}}[\textit{author}]$ $_{\text{CN}}]_{\text{NP}}$ may be considered to be a function which associates with ζ the set of indices for which every a who is an author at i is such that $i \in \zeta(a)$, and the interpretation of PSR1 will say that the meaning of the S (i.e., (6)) is to be obtained by letting this function apply to ζ. We may consider the meaning of *author* to be the function ω such that, for any individual a, $\omega(a)$ is the set of indices at which a is an author. The meaning of $[\textit{every}]_{\text{Det}}$ may be considered to be the function θ such that for any index i, $i \in (\theta(\omega))(\zeta)$ iff every individual a such that $i \in \omega(a)$, $i \in \zeta(a)$ and the interpretation of PSR2 tells us that the meaning of $[[\textit{every}]_{\text{Det}}[\textit{author}]_{\text{CN}}]_{\text{NP}}$ is obtained by letting θ apply to ω, i.e. it is $\theta(\omega)$. With ω as the meaning of *author* and ζ as the meaning of *shouts* that makes (6) true at i iff every author shouts at i, exactly as it should be. In this process it is the lexical rules which provide the interpretation of the particular items. Thus if the quantifier were *most* instead of *every* its meaning would be (perhaps) the function θ' such that for any index i, $i \in (\theta'(\omega))(\zeta)$ iff there are more individuals a such that $i \in \omega(a)$ and $i \in \zeta(a)$ than there are such that $i \in \omega(a)$ and $i \notin \zeta(a)$, and so on.

Example (3) assumes that *not* is a sentential operator. But many linguists have observed that negation in English is not typically, perhaps not ever, expressed by a sentential operator. There are in fact two ways of negating (6). One is

(8)   Every author doesn't shout

and the other is

(9)   Not every author shouts.

Example (8) uses *doesn't* to negate a verb phrase, while the *not* in (9) appears to attach to the determiner. Because I don't want to get involved in the syntactical minutiae of negation in English I shall simply use an operator Neg introduced by the two syntactic rules:

PSR6   VP → Neg VP.
PSR7   Det → Neg Det

Then (8) and (9) become, respectively,

(10) $[[[\textit{every}]_{\text{Det}}[\textit{author}]_{\text{CN}}]_{\text{NP}}[\text{Neg}[\textit{shouts}]_{\text{VP}}]_{\text{VP}}]_{\text{S}}$

and

(11)   [[[Neg[*every*]$_{Det}$]$_{Det}$[*author*]$_{CN}$]$_{NP}$[*shouts*]$_{VP}$]s

The semantic interpretation of both rules is simple. For PSR6, where the VP is assigned ζ the semantic value of the complex Neg VP is the function $\zeta_\sim$ such that for any individual a and index i, $i \in \zeta_\sim(a)$ iff $i \notin \zeta(a)$. It should be clear that (10) will be true at i iff everyone who is an author at i fails to shout at i. For (11) the value of the complex determiner formed by Neg is the function $\theta_\sim$ such that, where θ is the value of the determiner that Neg operates on, $\theta_\sim$ is the function such that $i \in ((\theta_\sim)(\omega))(\zeta)$ iff $i \notin (\theta(\omega))(\zeta)$. It might be thought that this makes Neg ambiguous, but that is not so, because we are here talking about the semantics of a *syntactic rule*, and the meaning of any syntactically well-formed expression involving Neg is uniquely determined.

3   Categorial Languages

The approach presented in the previous section is tailored to natural language syntactic rules, but there is another approach in which the syntactic structure looks more like the languages of predicate logic. In logic *shouts* is part of a well formed formula (wff) of the form *shouts x*. This makes the syntax of *shouts* reflect its semantics as something which turns an individual into a sentence. The quantifier *every* (or $\forall$) has attached to it an 'individual' variable x, and this enables it to *bind* the xs in the formula so that it says that every value of x is such that if it is an author then it shouts. This enables Neg to be an actual unambiguous symbol, for there is an easy representation of both (8) and (9) in the standard predicate calculus notation using $\sim$ for negation, $\supset$ for material implication, and F and G for *author* and *shouts*:

(12) $\forall x(Fx \supset\sim Gx)$

(13) $\sim \forall x(Fx \supset Gx)$

Although the decomposition of *every* into $\forall$ and $\supset$ may indeed work for *that* quantifier it is not clear how, for instance, to decompose a word like *most* in a sentence like

(14)   Most authors shout

in any analogous fashion. Natural language determiners are better understood as two-place operators.[6] This can be combined with a more general approach to variable binding using what is called λ-*abstraction*. Where α is a formula read $\lambda x\alpha$ as 'is an x such that α.' Then (8) may be represented as

(15)   *every* (*author*, λx(*not shoutsx*))

and (9) as

(16)   *not every*(*author*, λx(*shouts x*))

In (16) λx(*shouts x*) is semantically equivalent to the simple *shouts*. Treating *every* as a two-place quantifier allows an easy generalization to quantifiers like *most*, which cannot be decomposed into a one-place quantifier and a two place connect- ive.

The formal languages in which (15) and (16) are expressed are sometimes called *categorial* languages. Assume that an individual variable like *x* has the category of *name* (n). Then *shouts x* will be a *sentence* (s), and nouns like *author* and verbs like *shouts* will make a sentence out of a name – they will be in category (s/n). *not* will be in category (s/s) since it makes a sentence out of a sentence, and so on. The abstraction operator turns a sentence back into a (one-place) predicate, i.e. into a (s/n). A determiner can be thought of as in category ((s/(s/n))/(s/n)), i.e. it takes a predicate (a noun) and turns it into a one-place operator which makes a sentence out of a predicate (a verb). Operators like *possibly* and *yesterday* might also be in category (s/s), while adverbs and adjectives like *carefully* or *competent* might be predicate modifiers in category ((s/n)/(s/n)) – i.e. they make one-place predicates out of one-place predicates. In getting to the syntax of ordinary English some mechanism must be introduced to ensure that adjectives only modify nouns, and adverbs only modify verbs. Prepositions are in category (((s/n)/(s/n))/n) since they make adverbial phrases out of names and so on. The advantage of presenting a language in this way is that its semantics is obvious. Items in category n denote 'things' (whatever they are) while items in category s denote sets of indices, and the meaning of an item in category (σ/τ) will be a function which operates on a thing which is the meaning of an item in category τ and gives as value something which is the meaning of an item in category σ. A language would then need syntactical rules which transform the 'surface' structure of that language into an expression at this level.[7]

The difference between the approach in the previous section and the approach in this section represents a view about the level of what is sometimes called *logical form* (see chapter 3). That is a level of structure which is apt for the determination of truth conditions, and which may not be the same as the surface grammatical structure. Examples (15) and (16) represent a level somewhat removed from surface grammar. Examples (10) and (11), by contrast, represent an attempt to assign meaning at a level much closer to the surface, and there is some debate in linguistic theory about just how close to the surface a level of logical form should be. In the remainder of the chapter I shall illustrate some developments in several areas, and where a formal framework is required I shall assume the 'categorial' framework just described. It must be continually borne in mind, however, that the complexity of natural langauge means that *no* simple semantic proposal can do justice to all the phenomena, and the remarks that follow can do no more than give hints at adequate treatments.

3 Tense and Aspect

One area of semantics particularly suited to an indexical treatment is tense. In tense logic a key operator is the past tense operator. For any sentence α whose truth or falsity requires only an index of the form $\langle w,t \rangle$ where w is a world and t a time:

(17) *Past* α is true at $\langle w,t \rangle$ iff α is true at some $\langle w,t' \rangle$, where t' precedes t.

Then

(18) Basil shouted

can be expressed, assuming **Basil** is in category n, as

(19) *Past **shouts** **Basil***

in which **shouts** is the present tense. While that may have some semantic merit it is more likely that what *Past* operates on is a pre-tense form – something like **shout Basil** where **shout** is the infinitival form. Despite the simplicity of classical tense logic natural language, as to be expected, needs refinements. Here is one. Look at *yesterday.*

(20) ***yesterday*** α is true at $\langle w,t \rangle$ iff, where t' is a moment in the day preceding the day in which t is a moment, α is true at $\langle w,t' \rangle$

But then it would seem that

(21) Basil shouted yesterday

would have the form

(22) ***yesterday*** *Past **shout Basil***

and of course (22) has to be wrong since it has the consequence that (22) is true at $\langle w,t \rangle$ iff Basil shouts at some t'' which precedes some t' where t' is on the day preceding the day in which t occurs. The past tense form of (21) might then simply be a surface agreement marker.

Here is another complexity. In formulating (20) little was said about t. Early tense logic[8] assumed that t would be a moment or instant, but there seems strong evidence that t should be an *interval* rather than a moment. For consider the sentence:

(23) Basil shouted twice yesterday.

If t in (20) is taken as an instant it would seem that there has to be a moment yesterday at which Basil shouted twice. But (23) would allow that Basil may have shouted once in the morning and once in the afternoon. This suggests that the temporal indices involved in natural language semantics should be intervals rather than indices. Intervals go some way to giving an account of *aspect*. It has been observed that while

(24)   Einstein lived in Princeton

is true, yet

(25)   Einstein has lived in Princeton

is false (on the ground that Einstein no longer exists).[9] One way in which those could be accounted for is to assume that the straight past tense in English, as in (24), uses an operator as in (17) but with the requirement that t and t' be intervals in which the last moment in t' occurs *before* the first moment in t, while for the present perfect, as in (25), all of t' must be included in t and the last moment in t' must be the same as t. (t' may extend as far back into the past as you like but must come all the way up to the present.) Whether this device, and others like it work or not is a matter for controversy, but it shows the options available within interval semantics. The world index comes into play in the analysis of (5). Take **possibly** as a sentential operator:

(26)   **possibly** α is true at $\langle w,t \rangle$ iff, where w' is a world which is possible relative to w at t, α is true at $\langle w',t \rangle$

(where what counts as 'possible relative to' depends on the precise sense of possibility involved.) Note that modifiers like **possibly** and **yesterday** are like **not** in that they can either modify the whole sentence or just the predicate. This may cause a difference if Basil is an author today but was not one yesterday and did not shout yesterday, but every other author did. Then it is true today that yesterday every author shouted, but it is not true today of every author that they shouted yesterday. Such problems about the 'scope' of operators and quantifiers are discussed in more detail in chapter 16.

Some tensed phenomena also involve the world index. While

(27)   Gaylene walked to work

entails that she arrived at work

(28)   Gaylene was walking to work

does not, since any number of calamities, or pleasant surprises, may have prevented her. Example (28) involves what is called the *imperfective* aspect, and, on at least one account of things,[10] (28) will be true at $\langle w,t \rangle$ iff Gaylene actually walks to work in some $\langle w',t' \rangle$ which starts off like $\langle w,t \rangle$ but then diverges. The idea is that w' is what is called the 'inertial world,' the world in which things go on as they appeared set to. So that (28) is true if Gaylene walks to work in the world as it appeared to be before the unforseen event occurred. A difficulty with this approach is that it seems difficult if not impossible to specify just what counts as an 'inertial world.' Further, if the calamity killed Gaylene, it seems that

(29)   Gaylene was walking to her death

is also true, but in (29) the inertial world is one in which she dies, while in (28) it is one in which she does not, so that there *can* be no appropriate notion of inertial world.

5   Indices or Variables?

Some authors[11] would put the time index into the syntax, so that *yesterday* becomes a quantifier, and (21) would be represented as

(30)   *yesterday t* (*shout Basil t*)

where *t* is a variable and *shout* becomes a two-place predicate in which the second argument place is filled by a time variable. In general, there is a two-way trade between expressing this kind of dependence by a semantical index or by means of explicit variables.[12]

Many nouns also shew a relativity which is usually not revealed in surface syntax. Consider the sentence

(31)   Every equation has a solution.[13]

On at least one reading (31) entails that the solution is a solution of the equation in question. If this relativity is expressed explicitly you would get something like

$\forall x$(*equation x* $\supset$ $\exists y$*solution yx*)

where *solution* has an extra argument place to indicate that y is a solution of x. (32) does not contain any free variables but in

(33)   That is the solution

the representation, using explicit variables, might be something like

(34) *solution xy.*

If (33) is interpreted as (34) the index i would include an assignment μ to the variables, and (34) will be true at i iff $\mu(x)$ is $\mu(y)$'s solution.

Concealed relativity might also help in the analysis of adjectives and adverbs. Adjectives come in degrees. Gwendolen may be a competent electrician, but may be a far more competent nurse. If so the basic form of an adjective like *competent* might be something like

(35) x is a y-much competent α

where y is the degree of competence applied to things of kind α. Then words like *more* and *most* can be operators which bind this degree variable.[14] Here too such relativity is not usually syntactically indicated.

It is easy to see that some adverbs, like *possibly* as in (26) can be treated as sentential modifiers, and many if not most adverbs have the syntactic form of predicate (VP) modifiers (in category $((s/n)/(s/n))$). A preposition like *in* can be put into category $((s/s)/n)$ so that a prepositional phrase like *in Palmerston* emerges as a sentential modifier, and could presumably be given a semantics if a spatial index is included in i. An adverb like *loudly* might have a causal aspect to its meaning, in that someone sings loudly if they sing in a way which has certain effects on those nearby. If so an account of causation in terms of possible worlds might enable a semantics for such adverbs.[15] An alternative account of adverbial modification[16] treats 'events' as things, and would analyze, say

(36) Alice sings competently

as

(37) $\exists x$ (x is a singing by Alice & x is competent)

If the 'event' variable is concealed in the semantics this account might be able to be incorporated in the modifier account.

There is debate in semantic circles about how much of such dependence should be brought in to the syntax and how much left as semantical indices. From a purely formal point of view things can be handled either way. One way of marking both contextual dependence and bound variables is by the use of pronouns, and a particularly significant class of sentences are what, following Geach (1962: 128), are called 'donkey sentences':

(38) If a farmer owns a donkey he beats it.

It is not hard to see that this sentence refers to all farmers and (perhaps) all the donkeys they own, even when the quantificational phrases are made as explicitly 'existential' as possible:

(39)   If at least one farmer owns at least one donkey he beats it.

One development in semantics since the last 1980s has involved the claim that semantics should be 'dynamic.' By this is meant that the meaning of a sentence should be thought of not so much in terms of its truth conditions as in terms of the 'potential to change truth conditions.'[17] Advocates of dynamic semantics tackle this by thinking of the utterance of a sentence as like a computer program. Instead of a sentence being true or false at an index, think of the first index as being how things are *before* the sentence is uttered and a second index as being how things are *after* the sentence has been uttered. This means that the meaning of a sentence is a *pair* of indices. The job of the second index in an existentially quantified sentence is to 'remember' the individual which made the existential sentence true. In English this is often done by the word 'namely,' as when we say

(40)   A mouse (namely Murgatroyd) pounced.

We can represent (40) semi-formally in the ordinary predicate calculus as

(41) $\exists x \, (x = y \, \& \, \textbf{\textit{mouse }} x \, \& \, \textbf{\textit{pounced }} x)$

and think of x as the 'before' value in a dynamic interpretation and y (i.e. Murgatroyd) as the 'after' value. (38) might then be represented in some such way as

(42) $\forall y_1 \forall y_2 (((\exists x (\textbf{\textit{farmer}} x \, \& \, x = y_1) \, \& \, \exists x (\textbf{\textit{donkey }} x \textbf{\textit{ and }} x = y_2)) \supset \textbf{\textit{beats }} y_1 \, y_2)$

In (42) the existential quantifiers respect the syntax of (38) and (39) in respect of the x variables but universals cover the 'namely' y variables.[18]

This is not the only way of dealing with such phenomena. Another way is to recall that quantification in natural language is heavily restricted. An example is a sentence like:

(43)   Whenever we have a party everyone brings something

The idea in (43) is that context supplies a function which associates with every party a domain of people and a domain of things, and that *whenever* is a universal quantifier over these domains, so that the quantifiers *a* and *everyone* are evaluated with respect to these domains. (38) might then be interpreted by letting its existential quantifiers have small domains containing just one farmer and just one donkey, where the *if* contains a concealed universal quantifier over these domains.

6   Propositional Attitudes and Situation Semantics

This chapter has concentrated on the truth-conditional account of semantics. If the meaning of a sentence is the set of indices at which it is true we have the consequence that all sentences which are true at the same set of indices have the same meaning. So for instance, since all mathematical truths are true in all possible worlds, mathematical knowledge would be trivial. However, although the entities used in formal semantics have the job of delivering a set of indices as the final result, any interpreted sentence generates a semantic structure made up from the semantic values of its simple parts.[19] This structure can then provide the input to propositional attitude operators. That and other matters are discussed more fully in chapter 10.

The kind of indices that have been used in classical truth-conditional semantics are *complete* in the sense of deciding every sentence – or at least of every sentence which might be said to have a truth value at all. In the 1980s an alternative semantic framework grew up based on the view that the entities used in semantics should not be complete. The meaning of a sentence like

(44)   Sebastian shouts

would not be the set of indices at which Sebastian shouts, but would be something like a *situation*

(45) $\langle\langle$SHOUT, Sebastian, l, YES$\rangle\rangle$

in which SHOUT is the relation of shouting which holds between Sebastian and the location at which he shouts. (45) has the appearance of being an expression at the level of logical form, and that may be a good way to view it provided that we realise that the connection between SHOUT and shouting is not conventional and in some sense SHOUT *is* shouting. If so there may be no serious incompatibility between situation semantics and truth-conditional semantics after all. But to take that further would go well beyond the bounds of this chapter.[20]

Further Reading

The most comprehensive account of formal semantics is probably van Benthem and ter Meulen 1997. Its 1247 pages contain introductions to almost every area in which work is currently being done. A more approachable collection is Lappin 1996. The first chapter of each of these volumes contains an excellent history of the development of formal semantics. Some good recent introductory works include Chierchia and McConnell-Ginet 1990, Gamut 1991, Cann 1993, and Heim and Kratzer 1998. A particularly approachable slightly earlier little book is Bach 1989. The principal figure in the early history of formal semantics for natural language is Richard Montague, whose papers from the late 1960s and early 1970s are collected in Montague 1974. An

introduction to Montague's work is Dowty, Wall and Peters 1981. Other early collections of articles are Steinberg and Jakobovits 1971, Davidson and Harman 1972, and
Keenan 1975. The subsequent history of formal semantics is well chronicled in
Linguistics and Philosophy, and readers of that journal will find that the extensive
reference lists of the various articles it contains will provide a guide through the ever
increasing literature.

Notes

1 This was the basic claim of Cresswell 1978. It is discussed in more detail in Cresswell
   1994. One of the few attempts to correlate truth conditions with linguistic behavior is
   found in Lewis 1975. The idea that meaning be understood in terms of truth
   conditions appears in Wittgenstein 1921.
2 At this point one must say something about language and metalanguage. One way of
   describing the truth-conditional meaning of (1) is to say that (1) is true iff there is a
   pen on the table, and that has an air of circularity. This apparent circularity is even
   more blatant if the goal of semantics in terms of 'T-sentences' advocated in Davidson
   1967a (following Tarski 1956) is adopted. What is happening is that the meaning of
   the English sentence (1) is being explained in English. English is the language being
   described, sometimes called the *object* language. But English is *also* the language in
   which the description is taking place. It is the *metalanguage*. But what the metalanguage is describing is not the trivial fact that (1) is true iff it is true, but the non-trivial
   fact that the sentence (1) is true under certain conditions. That these conditions
   obtain is not a fact about English. Pens could be or not be on tables whether or not
   there are English speakers around, though we could not then describe the situation in
   English. Maybe you need to be a speaker of some or other language to be able to
   know what a pen is and when one is or is not on a table, but non-English speakers can
   know this without knowing that they are called 'pens.' Semantics is about the
   connection between language and the world, it is not about recipes for translating
   one language into another. Translation presupposes semantics, not vice versa.
3 A brief discussion of how to incorporate mood into a truth-conditional semantics is
   found on pp. 163–5 of Chierchia and McConnell-Ginet 1990. An earlier attempt at
   relating mood and truth-conditions is in Lewis 1975. Interrogatives have been more
   extensively studied than imperatives. For some approaches see chapter 15 of Lappin
   1996 and chapter 19 of van Benthem and ter Meulen 1997. Common to most of this
   work is that truth-conditions form at least a central part of giving an account of the
   content of sentences in non-declarative moods. In addition to non-declaratives one
   source of truth-valuelessness is often held to occur in 'presupposition failure.'
   Another source is semantic anomaly. In a sentence like **twenty seven shouts** there
   may be no value since the function which is the meaning of **shouts** may not accept
   the number 27 as one of its arguments.
4 Early discussions of contextual indices are found in Lewis 1972 and Montague 1974.
5 The idea of giving a syntactic rule a semantic interpretation within an indexical version
   of truth-conditional semantics is found on p, 201 of Montague 1974, in a chapter first
   published in 1970 based on work done in 1966. In later work (see for instance

pp. 241ff and 256ff) Montague preferred to interpret fragments by translation into a 'logical' language like, though not identical with, the kind of language discussed here in sec. 3.

6 The need for two-place quantifiers is argued in Cresswell 1973. They are called 'generalised quantifiers' in Barwise and Cooper 1981.

7 The 'generative semantics' movement of the seventies (see the articles by McCawley and Lakoff in Steinberg and Jakobovits 1971 and Davidson and Harman 1972) represents a version of this approach. Alternatively, one may regard such a language as a way of codifying meanings, so that semantics is done in a 'two-stage' process in which a sentence of the natural language is 'translated' into a formula of this underlying 'logical' language, which is then given an indexical interpretation. As mentioned in n. 5 Montague in some places uses the language he calls 'intensional logic' (IL) as a way of representing meanings, though he is explicit that it is theoretically dispensable. Its advantage is that it often enables semantic discussion to take place without commitment to how the phenomenon is represented in a particular natural language. Categorial languages are used in Lewis 1972 and Cresswell 1973, and are discussed in a number of places. A collection of articles is found in Buzkowski, Marciszewski and van Benthem 1988 and Oehrle, Bach and Wheeler 1988.

8 See Prior 1957 and 1967. The whole indexical approach to semantics might be said to develop from Prior's work in tense logic, together with contemporary developments in modal logic, which were generalised by Montague and others. Interval semantics appear in Taylor 1977 and Dowty 1977. Adverbial modification using intervals as indices forms the principal theme of Cresswell 1985. A detailed survey of tense and aspect appears in Chapter 16 of van Benthem and ter Meulen 1997.

9 See van Benthem and ter Meulen 1997, p. 899 and the references listed there.

10 This is the analysis found in Dowty 1977. It has been criticised in Parsons 1990, p. 176ff.

11 Taylor 1977

12 In Cresswell 1996 I tried to articulate the indexical approach and that view has been advocated by others for syntactical reasons. See especially Jacobsen 1999, Steedman, 1988 and Szabolcsi, 1987. Montague 1974, p. 228, notes that assignments to free variables are a form of context dependence, though he assimilates them to demonstratives. Lewis 1972 speaks of an index as a 'coordinate' and on p. 175 explicitly includes an 'assignment coordinate' as one of the contextual coordinates.

13 Such sentences are discussed in Partee 1989.

14 This is the analysis found in Cresswell 1976. The analysis of the comparative has attracted a lot of work, some of which is summarized in von Stechow 1983. The point made in the text of course is not about the particular analysis but about the possibility of coding the relativity as a semantical index rather than as a syntactic variable.

15 A causal treatment of adverbs based on the analysis of counterfactual dependence found in Lewis 1973a and 1973b and Stalnaker 1968 is presented in Chapter 6 of Cresswell 1985.

16 Such an account is proposed (at least for prepositions) in Davidson 1967b, and elaborated and defended in Parsons 1990

17 The particular proposal I have in mind here is that found in Groenendijk and Stokhof 1991, but their work is part of a varied tradition, some of which will be referred to in

other chapters. Important 'dynamic' frameworks include those based on 'Discourse Representation Theory' as propounded in Kamp 1983 and Kamp and Reyle 1993 (or in the more or less equivalent 'file-change semantics' of Heim 1983). A rather different version of a 'dynamic' approach is found in the 'game-theoretical semantics' developed by Jakko Hintikka. (See for instance Hintikka and Kulas 1983 and 1985.

18 This account of dynamic predicate logic is developed in Cresswell 2002b.

19 An example of such structures within an indexical approach is given in Lewis's 'meanings' in Lewis 1972. The matter is discussed in detail in Cresswell 2002a.

20 The 'locus classicus' of situation semantics is still probably Barwise and Perry 1983. See also Devlin 1991, and an up to date survey in Chapter 6 of van Benthem and ter Muelen. A book which makes extensive use of situations in semantic theory is Recanati 2000. Items in the CSLI Publications series provide an ongoing survey of work in this framework.

Chapter 8

Speech Acts and Pragmatics

Kent Bach

At the beginning of *How to Do Things with Words*, J. L. Austin bemoaned the common philosophical pretense that "the business of a [sentence] can only be to 'describe' some state of affairs, or to 'state some fact,' which it must do either truly or falsely" (1962: 1). He observed that there are many uses of language which have the linguistic appearance of fact-stating but are really quite different. Explicit performatives like "You're fired" and "I quit" are not used to make mere statements. And the Wittgenstein of the *Philosophical Investigations*, rebelling against his former self, swapped the picture metaphor for the tool metaphor and came to think of language not as a system of representation but as a system of devices for engaging in various sorts of social activity; hence, "the meaning of a word is its use in the language" (1953: sec. 43, p. 20).

Here Wittgenstein went too far, for there is good reason to separate the theory of linguistic meaning (semantics) from the theory of language use (pragmatics), not that they are unconnected. We can distinguish sentences, considered in abstraction from their use, and the acts that speakers (or writers) perform in using them. We can distinguish what sentences mean from what speakers mean in using them. Whereas Wittgenstein adopted a decidedly anti-theoretical stance toward the whole subject, Austin developed a systematic, though largely taxonomic, theory of language use. And Paul Grice developed a conception of meaning which, though tied to use, enforced a distinction between what linguistic expressions mean and what speakers mean in using them.

A early but excellent illustration of the importance of this distinction is provided by Moore's paradox (so-called by Wittgenstein 1953: 190). If you say, "Tomatoes are fruits but I don't believe it," you are denying that you believe what you are asserting. This contradiction is puzzling because it is not an outright logical inconsistency. That tomatoes are fruits does not entail your believing it, nor vice versa, and there's no contradiction in *my* saying, "Tomatoes are fruits but you don't believe it." Your inconsistency arises not from what you are claiming but from the fact that *you* are claiming it. That's what makes it a *pragmatic* contradiction.

Like pragmatic contradictions, pragmatic phenomena in general involve information that is generated by, or at least made relevant by, acts of using language. It is not to be confused with semantic information, which is carried by linguistic items themselves. This distinction should be kept in mind as we examine the nature of speech acts (including Austin's explicit performatives), the intentions involved in communicating, and the ways in which what a speaker means can differ from what his words mean. Later we will return to the semantic–pragmatic distinction and survey its philosophical applications.

Performative Utterances

Paradoxical though it may seem, there are certain things one can do just by saying that one is doing them. One can apologize by saying "I apologize," promise by saying "I promise," and thank someone by saying "Thank you." These are examples of *explicit performative* utterances, statements in form but not in fact. Or so thought Austin (1962) when he contrasted them with *constatives.* Performatives are utterances whereby we make explicit what we are doing.[1] Austin challenged the common philosophical assumption (or at least pretense) that indicative sentences are necessarily devices for making statements. He maintained that, for example, an explicit promise is not, and does not involve, the statement that one is promising. It is an act of a distinctive sort, the very sort (promising) named by the performative verb. Of course one can promise without doing so explicitly, without using the performative verb 'promise,' but if one does use it, one is, according to Austin, making explicit what one is doing but not stating that one is doing it.[2]

Austin eventually realized that explicit constatives function in essentially the same way. After all, a statement can be made by uttering "I assert … " or "I predict … ," just as a promise or a request can be made with "I promise … " or "I request … ." So Austin let the distinction between constative and performative utterances be superseded by one between *locutionary* and *illocutionary* acts. He included assertions, predictions, etc. (he retained the term 'constative' for them) along with promises, requests, etc., among illocutionary acts. His later nomenclature recognized that illocutionary acts need not be performed explicitly – you don't have to use "I suggest … " to make a suggestion or "I apologize … " to apologize.

Even so, it might seem that because of their distinctive self-referential character, the force of explicit performatives requires special explanation. Indeed, Austin supposed that illocutionary acts in general should be understood on the model of explicit performatives, as when he made the notoriously mysterious remark that the use of a sentence with a certain illocutionary force is "conventional in the sense that at least it could be made explicit by the performative formula" (1962: 91). Presumably he thought that explicit performative utterances are conventional in some more straightforward sense. Since it is not part of the meaning of the word "apologize" that an utterance of "I apologize … " count as an apology rather than a statement, perhaps there is some convention to that effect. If there is, presumably it is part of a general convention that covers all performative verbs. But is there such a convention, and is it needed to explain performativity?[3]

P.F. Strawson (1964) argued that Austin was overly impressed with institution-bound cases. In these cases there do seem to be conventions that utterances of certain forms (an umpire's "Out!," a legislator's "Nay!," or a judge's "Overruled!") count as the performance of acts of certain sorts. Likewise with certain explicit performatives, as when under suitable circumstances a judge or clergyman says, "I pronounce you husband and wife," which counts as joining a couple in marriage. In such cases there are specific, socially recognized circumstances in which a person with specific, socially recognized authority may perform an act of a certain sort by uttering words of a certain form.[4] Strawson argued, though, that most illocutionary acts involve not an intention to conform to an institutional convention but an intention to communicate something to an audience. Indeed, as he pointed out, there is no sense of the word 'conventional' in which the use of a given sentence with a certain illocutionary force is necessarily conventional, much less a sense having to do with the fact that this force can be "made explicit by the performative formula." In the relevant sense, an act is conventional just in case it counts as an act of a certain sort because, and only because, of a special kind of institutional rule to that effect. However, unlike the special cases Austin focused on, utterances can count as requests, apologies, or predictions, as the case may be, without the benefit of such a rule. It is perfectly possible to apologize, for example, without doing so explicitly, without using the performative phrase "I apologize ... " That is the trouble with Austin's view of speech acts – and for that matter John Searle's (1969), which attempts to explain illocutionary forces by means of "constitutive rules" for using "force-indicating devices," such as performatives. These theories can't explain the fact that, e.g., an apology can be made without using such a device.[5] There is a superficial difference between apologizing explicitly (by saying, "I apologize") and doing it inexplicitly, but there is no theoretically important difference.[6] Except for institution-bound cases like those illustrated above, performativity requires no special explanation, much less a special sort of convention.[7]

Locutionary, Illocutionary, and Perlocutionary Acts

Austin dubbed "illocutionary" those sorts of speech acts that can (but need not) be performed by means of the performative formula. The illocutionary act is but one level of the total speech act that one performs in uttering a sentence. Consider that in general when one acts intentionally, one has a set of nested intentions. For instance, having arrived home without your keys, you might move your finger in a certain way with the intention not just of moving your finger in that way but with the further intentions of pushing a certain button, ringing the doorbell, arousing your spouse ... and ultimately getting into your house. The single bodily movement involved in moving your finger comprises a multiplicity of actions, each corresponding to a different one of the nested intentions. Similarly, speech acts are not just acts of producing certain sounds.

Austin identifies three distinct levels of action beyond the act of utterance itself. He distinguishes the act of saying something, what one does *in* saying it, and what one does *by* saying it, and dubs these the *locutionary,* the *illocutionary,* and the *perlocutionary* act, respectively. Suppose, for example, that a bartender utters the words, "The bar will be closed in five minutes," reportable with direct quotation. He is thereby performing the locutionary act of saying that the bar (i.e., the one he is tending) will be closed in five minutes (from the time of utterance), where what is said is reported by indirect quotation (notice that what the bartender is saying, the content of his locutionary act, is not fully determined by the words he is using, for they do not specify the bar in question or the time of the utterance). In saying this, the bartender is performing the illocutionary act of informing the patrons of the bar's imminent closing and perhaps also the act of urging them to order a last drink. Whereas the upshot of these illocutionary acts is understanding on the part of the audience, perlocutionary acts are performed with the intention of producing a further effect. The bartender intends to be performing the perlocutionary acts of causing the patrons to believe that the bar is about to close and of getting them to order one last drink. He is performing all these speech acts, at all three levels, just by uttering certain words.

We need the level of locutionary acts, acts of saying something, in order to characterize such common situations as these: where the speaker says one thing but, not speaking literally, means (in the sense of trying to convey) something else instead,[8] where the speaker means what he says and indirectly means something else as well, and where the speaker says something but doesn't mean anything at all.[9] Moreover, the same sentence can be used to perform illocutionary acts of various types or with various contents. Just as in shaking hands we can, depending on the circumstances, do any one of several different things (introduce ourselves, greet each other, seal a deal, congratulate, or bid farewell), so we can use a sentence with a given locutionary content in a variety of ways. For example, we could utter 'I will call a lawyer' to make a promise or a warning, or just a prediction. Austin defines a locutionary act as the act of using words, "as belonging to a certain vocabulary... and as conforming to a certain grammar,... with a certain more or less definite sense and reference" (1962: 92–3). And what is said, according to Grice, is "closely related to the conventional meaning of the ... sentence ... uttered" and must correspond to "the elements of [the sentence], their order, and their syntactic character" (1989: 87). Although what is said is limited by this *syntactic correlation* constraint, because of ambiguity and indexicality it is not identical to what the sentence means. If the sentence is ambiguous, usually only one of its conventional (linguistic) meanings is operative in a given utterance (double entendre is a special case). And linguistic meaning does not determine what, on a given occasion, indexicals like 'she' and 'this' are used to refer to. If someone utters "She wants this book," he is saying that a certain woman wants a certain book, even though the words do not specify which woman and which book. So, along with linguistic information, the speaker's semantic (disambiguating and referential) intentions are often needed to determine what is said.

We need the distinction between illocutionary and perlocutionary acts because utterances are generally more than just acts of communication. They have two levels of success: considered merely as an illocutionary act, a request (for example) succeeds if your audience recognizes your desire that they do a certain thing, but as a perlocutionary act it succeeds only if they actually do it. You can express your desire without getting compliance, but your one utterance is the performance of an act of both types.

Classifying Illocutionary Acts

Speech acts may be conveniently classified by their illocutionary type, such as asserting, requesting, promising, and apologizing, for which we have familiar verbs. These different types may in turn be distinguished by the type of attitude the speaker expresses. Corresponding to each such attitude is a certain attitude on the part of the hearer (getting the hearer to form this correlative attitude is essential to the success of the perlocutionary act). Here are some typical examples:

Illocutionary act	Attitude expressed	Intended hearer attitude
statement	belief that p	belief that p
request	desire for H to D	intention to D
promise	firm intention to D	belief that S will D
apology	regret for D-ing	forgiveness of S for D-ing

These are examples of the four major categories of communicative illocutionary acts, which may be called *constatives, directives, commissives,* and *acknowledgments.*[10] Here are some further examples of each type:

* **Constatives**: affirming, alleging, announcing, answering, attributing, claiming, classifying, concurring, confirming, conjecturing, denying, disagreeing, disclosing, disputing, identifying, informing, insisting, predicting, ranking, reporting, stating, stipulating
* **Directives**: advising, admonishing, asking, begging, dismissing, excusing, forbidding, instructing, ordering, permitting, requesting, requiring, suggesting, urging, warning
* **Commissives**: agreeing, betting, guaranteeing, inviting, offering, promising, swearing, volunteering
* **Acknowledgments**: apologizing, condoling, congratulating, greeting, thanking, accepting (acknowledging an acknowledgment)

If each type of illocutionary act is distinguishable by the type of attitude expressed, there is no need to invoke the notion of convention to explain how a particular act can succeed. An illocutionary act succeeds if the hearer recognizes the attitude being expressed, such as a belief in the case of a statement and a desire in the case of a request. As a perlocutionary act, a statement or an apology is successful if the audience accepts it, but illocutionary success does not require that. It requires only what is necessary for the statement or the apology to be *made*. As Strawson explains, the effect relevant to communicative success is *understanding* or what Austin called "uptake," rather than a further (perlocutionary) effect, such as belief, desire, or even action on the part of the hearer. Indeed, an utterance can succeed as an act of communication even if the speaker doesn't possess the attitude he is expressing, and even if the hearer doesn't take him to possess it.[11] Communication is one thing, sincerity another. Sincerity is actually possessing the attitude one is expressing.[12]

Conventional illocutionary acts, the model for Austin's theory, succeed not by recognition of intention, but by conformity to convention. That is, an utterance counts as an act of a certain sort by virtue of meeting certain socially or institutionally recognized conditions for being an act of that sort. They fall into two categories, *effectives* and *verdictives*, depending on whether they effect an institutional state of affairs or merely make an official judgment as to an institutionally relevant state of affairs.[13] Here are some examples of each:

- **Effectives**: banning, bidding, censuring, dubbing, enjoining, firing, indicting, moving, nominating, pardoning, penalizing, promoting, seconding, sentencing, suspending, vetoing, voting
- **Verdictives**: acquitting, assessing, calling (by an umpire or referee), certifying, convicting, grading, judging, ranking, rating, ruling

To appreciate the difference, compare what a judge does when he convicts someone and when he sentences them. Convicting is the verdictive act of officially judging that the defendant is guilty. Whether or not the defendant actually committed the crime, the judge's determination that he did means that the justice system treat this as being the case. However, in performing the effective act of sentencing him to a week in the county jail, the judge is not ascertaining that this is his sentence but is actually making it the case.

Communicative Speech Acts and Intentions

Our taxonomy accepts Strawson's observation that most illocutionary acts are performed not with an intention to conform to a convention but with an audience-directed communicative intention. But what exactly is a communicative intention, and why are illocutionary acts generally communicative?

People commonly think of communicating, linguistically or otherwise, as acts of expressing oneself. This rather vague idea can be made more precise if we get more specific about what is expressed. Take the case of an apology. If you say, "[I'm] sorry I forgot your birthday" and intend this as an apology, you are expressing regret for something, in this case for forgetting the person's birthday. An apology just *is* the act of (verbally) expressing regret for, and thereby acknowledging, something one did that might have harmed or at least bothered the hearer. It is communicative because it is intended to be taken as expressing a certain attitude, in this case regret. It succeeds as such if it is so taken, in which case one has made oneself understood. Using a special device such as the performative "I apologize" may of course facilitate understanding – understanding is correlative with communicating – but in general this is unnecessary. Communicative success is achieved if the speaker chooses his words in such a way that the hearer will, under the circumstances of utterance, recognize his communicative intention. So, for example, if you spill some beer on someone and say "Oops" in the right way, your utterance will be taken as an apology.

Grice discovered that there is something highly distinctive about communicative intentions: they are *reflexive* in character. In communicating a speaker intends his utterance "to produce some effect in an audience by means of the recognition of this intention" (1957/1989: 220).[14] Consider that, in general, the success of an act has nothing to do with anyone's recognizing the intention with which it is performed. You won't succeed in standing on your head because someone recognizes your intention to do so. But an act of communication is special in this respect. It is successful if the intention with which it is performed is recognized by the audience, partly on the basis that it is intended to be recognized. The intention includes, as part of its content, that the audience recognize this very intention by taking into account the fact that they are intended to recognize it. A communicative intention is thus self-referential, or reflexive. An act of communication is successful if whoever it is directed to recognizes the intention with which it is performed. In short, its fulfillment consists in its recognition.

To appreciate the idea of reflexive intentions and what their fulfillment involves, consider the following games, which involve something like linguistic communication. In the game of Charades, one player uses gestures and other bodily movements to help the other guess what she has in mind. Something like the reflexive intention involved in communication operates here, for part of what the first player intends the second player to take into account is the very fact that the first player intends her gestures etc. to enable him to guess what she has in mind (nothing like this goes on in the game of Twenty Questions, where the second player uses answers to yes-or-no questions to narrow down the possibilities of what the first player has in mind). Or consider the following game of tacit coordination: the first player selects and records an item in a certain specified category, such as a letter of the alphabet, a liquid, or a city; the second player has one chance to guess what it is. Each player wins if and only if the second player guesses right without any help. Now what counts as guessing right depends entirely on what the first player has in mind, and that depends entirely on what she thinks the second player, taking into account that she wants him to guess right, will think she wants him to think. The second player guesses whatever he thinks she wants him to think. Experience has shown that when players use the above categories, they almost always both pick the letter *A*, water, and the city in which they are located. It is not obvious what all these "correct" choices have in common: each one stands out in a certain way from other members of the same category, but not in the same way. For example, being first (among letters of the alphabet), being the most common (among liquids), and being local are quite different ways of standing out. It is still not clear, in the many years since the question was first raised, just what makes something uniquely salient in such situations.[15] One suggestion is that it is the first item in the category that comes to mind, but this won't always be right, since what first comes to the mind of one player may not be what first comes to the mind of the other.

Whatever the correct explanation of the meeting of the minds in successful communication, the basic insight underlying Grice's idea of reflexive intentions is that communication is like a game of tacit coordination: the speaker intends the hearer to reason in a certain way partly on the basis of being so intended. That is, the hearer is to take into account that he is intended to figure out the speaker's communicative intention. The meaning of the words uttered provides the input to this inference, but what they mean does not determine what the speaker means (even if he means precisely what his words means, they don't determine *that* he is speaking literally). What is loosely called 'context,' i.e., a set of *mutual contextual beliefs* (Bach and Harnish, 1979: 5), encompasses whatever other considerations the hearer is to take into account in ascertaining the speaker's intention, partly on the basis that he is intended to do so.

When Grice characterized meaning something as intending one's utterance "to produce some effect in an audience by means of the recognition of this intention," he wasn't very specific about the kind of effect to be produced. But since meaning something (in Grice's sense) is communicating, the relevant effect is, as both Strawson (1964) and Searle (1969) recognized, understanding on the part of the audience. Moreover, an act of communication, as an essentially overt act, just *is* the act of expressing an attitude, which the speaker may or may not actually possess. Since the condition on its success is that one's audience infer the attitude from the utterance, it is clear why the intention to be performing such an act should have the reflexive character pinpointed by Grice. Considered as an act of communication rather than anything more, it is an attempt simply to get one's audience to recognize, partly on the basis of being so intended, that a certain attitude is being expressed. One is, as it were, putting a certain attitude on the table. The success of any further act has as its prerequisite that the audience recognize this attitude. Communication aims at a meeting of the minds not in the sense that the audience is to think what the speaker thinks but only in the sense that a certain attitude toward a certain proposition is to be recognized as being put forward for consideration. What happens beyond that is more than communication.[16]

Conversational Implicature and Impliciture

A speaker can mean just what he says, or he can mean something more or something else entirely. Grice's (1975) theory of *conversational implicature* aims to explain how.[17] A few of his examples illustrate nonliterality, e.g., "He was a little intoxicated," but most of them are cases of stating one thing by way of stating another, e.g., "There is a garage around the corner," used to tell someone where to get gas, and "Mr. X's command of English is excellent, and his attendance has been regular," used to state (indirectly) that Mr. X is not well qualified. These are all examples in which what is meant is not determined by what is said. Grice proposed a Cooperative Principle[18] and several maxims which he named, in homage to Kant, Quantity, Quality, Relation, and Manner (Kant's Modality). As he formulates them, they enjoin one to speak truthfully, informatively, relevantly, perspicuously, and otherwise appropriately.[19] His account of implicature explains how ostensible violations of them can still lead to communicative success.

Although Grice presents them as guidelines for how to communicate success-fully, I think they are better construed as presumptions made in the course of the strategic inference involved in communication (they should not be construed, as they often are, as sociological generalizations). The listener presumes that the speaker is being cooperative and is speaking truthfully, informatively, relevantly, perspicuously, and otherwise appropriately. If an utterance superficially appears not to conform to this presumption, the listener looks for a way of taking the utterance so that it does conform. He does so partly on the supposition that he is intended to. The speaker takes advantage of this in choosing his words to make evident his communicative intention. Because of their potential clashes, these maxims or presumptions should not be viewed as comprising a decision procedure. Rather, they provide different dimensions of considerations that the speaker may reasonably be taken as intending the hearer to take into account in figuring out the speaker's communicative intention. Exploiting these presumptions, a speaker can say one thing and manage to mean something else, as with "Nature abhors a vacuum," or means something more, as with "Is there a doctor in the house?" The listener relies on these presumptions to make a contextually driven inference from what the speaker says to what he means.

. These maxims or presumptions do not concern what to convey at a given stage of a conversation (unless information of a very specific sort is required, say in answer to a question, there will always be many good ways to contribute a conversation). Rather, they frame how as a listener you are to figure out what the speaker is trying to convey, *given* the sentence he is uttering and what he is saying in uttering it. Your job is to determine, given that, what he could have been trying to convey. Why did he say 'believe' rather than 'know,' 'is' rather than 'seems,' 'soon' rather than 'in an hour,' 'warm' rather than 'hot,' 'has the ability to' rather than 'can'?

Grice's notion of implicature can be extended to illocutionary acts. With *indirection* a single utterance is the performance of one illocutionary act by way of performing another. For example, we can make a request or give permission by way of making a statement, say by uttering "It's getting cold in here" or "I don't mind," and we can make a statement or give an order by way of asking a question, such as "Is the Pope Catholic?" or "Can you open the door?" When an illocutionary act is performed indirectly, it is performed by way of performing some other one directly.[20] When an utterance is *nonliteral*, as with likely utterances of "My mind got derailed" or "You can stick that in your ear," we do not mean what our words mean but mean something else instead. the force or the content of the illocutionary act being performed is not the one that would be predicted just from the meanings of the words being used, Occasionally, utterances are both nonliteral and indirect. For example, one might utter "I love the sound of your voice" to tell someone nonliterally (ironically) that she can't stand the sound of his voice and thereby indirectly to ask him to stop singing.

Grice gives the impression that the distinction between what is said and what is implicated is exhaustive (he counted irony, metaphor, and other kinds of figurative utterances as cases of implicature), but there is a common phenomenon that Grice seems to have overlooked. Consider that there are many sentences whose standard uses are not strictly determined by their meanings but are not oblique (implicature-producing) or figurative uses either. For example, if one's spouse says "I will be home later" she is likely to mean that she will be home later that night, not merely at some time in the future. Or suppose your child comes crying to you with a minor injury and you say to him assuringly, "You're not going to die." You don't mean that he will never die but merely that he won't die from that injury. In both cases you do not mean precisely what you are saying but something more specific. In such cases what one means is what may be called an *expansion* of what one says, in that adding more words ('tonight' or 'from that injury,' in the examples) would have made what was meant fully explicit.[21] In other cases, such as 'Jack is ready' and 'Jill is late,' the sentence does not express a complete proposition. There must be something which Jack is being claimed to be ready for and something which Jill is being claimed to be late to. In these cases what one means is a *completion* of what one says. In both sorts of case, no particular word or phrase is being used nonliterally and there is no indirection. Both exemplify conversational *impliciture*, since part of what is meant is communicated not explicitly but implicitly, by way of expansion or completion.[22] In impliciture the speaker means something that goes beyond sentence meaning (ambiguity and indexicality aside) without necessarily implicating anything or using any expressions figuratively.[23]

Conventional Implicature

Grice is usually credited with the discovery of conventional implicature, but it was originally Frege's (1892) idea – Grice merely labeled it. They both claimed that the conventional meanings of certain terms, such as 'but' and 'still,' make contributions to the total import of a sentence without bearing on its truth or falsity. In "She is poor *but* she is honest," for example, the contrast between being poor and being honest due to the presence of 'but,' according to Grice "implied as distinct from being stated" (1961: 127). Frege and Grice merely appeal to intuition in suggesting that the conventional contributions of such terms do not affect what is said in utterances of sentences in which they occur.

In my opinion (Bach 1999b), the category of conventional implicature needlessly complicates Grice's distinction between what is said and what is implicated. Indeed, apparent cases of conventional implicature are really instances of something else. There are two kinds of case to consider. The first involves expressions like 'but' and 'still.' If we abandon the common assumption that indicative sentences express at most one proposition, we can see that such expressions do contribute to what is said. With "She is poor but she is honest," the main proposition is that she is poor and she is honest, and the additional proposition is that being poor precludes being honest. The intuition that the utterance can be true even if this secondary proposition is false is explained by the fact that the intuition is sensitive only to the main proposition. But what is said includes both.

The other kind of case is connected to Grice's suggestion that conventional implicature involves the performance of "noncentral" speech acts (1989: 122). He had in mind the use of such expressions as these:[24]

> after all, anyway, at any rate, besides, be that as it may, by the way, first of all, finally, frankly, furthermore, however, if you want my opinion, in conclusion, indeed, in other words, moreover, now that you mention it, on the other hand, otherwise, speaking for myself, strictly speaking, to begin with, to digress, to oversimplify, to put it mildly.

These are used to comment on the very utterance in which they occur – its force, point, character, or the role in the discourse. I see no reason to call these second-order speech acts 'implicatures.' In uttering "Frankly, the dean is a moron," for example, you are not *implying* that you are speaking frankly, you are *saying* something about (providing a gloss or commentary on) your utterance. As a result, the contribution of an utterance modifier does not readily figure in an indirect report of what someone said, e.g., "He said that (*frankly) the dean is a moron." Utterance modifiers are in construction syntactically but not semantically with the clauses they introduce.

The Semantic–Pragmatic Distinction

Historically, the semantic–pragmatic distinction has been formulated in various ways.[25] These formulations have fallen into three main types, depending on which other distinction the semantic–pragmatic distinction was thought most to correspond to:

- linguistic (conventional) meaning vs. use;
- truth-conditional vs. non-truth-conditional meaning;
- context independence vs. context dependence.

In my view, none of these distinctions quite corresponds to the semantic–pragmatic distinction. The trouble with the first is that there are expressions whose literal meanings are related to use, such as the utterance modifiers mentioned above. It seems that the only way to specify their semantic contribution (when they occur initially or are otherwise set off) is to specify how they are to be used. The second distinction is inadequate because some expressions have meanings that do not contribute to truth-conditional contents. Paradigmatic are expressions like 'Alas!,' 'Good-bye,' and 'Wow!,' but utterance modifiers also illustrate this, as do such linguistic devices as it-clefts and wh-clefts, which pertain to information structure, not information content. The third distinction neglects the fact that some expressions, notably indexicals, are context-sensitive as a matter of their meaning.

A further source of confusion is the clash between two common but different conceptions of semantics. One takes semantics to be concerned with the linguistic meanings of expressions (words, phrases, sentences). On this conception, sentence semantics is a component of grammar. It assigns meanings to sentences as a function of the meanings of their semantically simple constituents, as supplied by lexical semantics, and their constituent structure, as provided by their syntax. The other conception takes semantics to be concerned with the truth-conditional contents of sentences (or, alternatively, of utterances of sentences) and with the contributions that expressions make to the truth-conditional contents of sentences in which they occur. The idea underlying this conception is that the meaning of a sentence, the information it carries, imposes a condition on what the world must be like in order for the sentence to be true.

Now the linguistic and the truth-conditional conceptions of semantics would come to the same thing if, in general, the linguistic meanings of sentences determined their truth conditions, and they all had truth conditions. Many sentences, though, are imperative or interrogative rather than declarative. These do not have truth conditions but compliance or answerhood conditions instead. Even if only declarative sentences are considered, in a great many cases the linguistic meaning of a sentence does not uniquely determine a truth condition. One reason for this is ambiguity, lexical or structural. The sentence may contain one or more ambiguous words, or it may be structurally ambiguous. Or the sentence may contain indexical elements. Ambiguity makes it necessary to relativize the truth condition of a declarative sentence to one or another of its senses, and indexicality requires relativization to a context. Moreover, it is plausible to suppose that some sentences, such as 'Jack was ready' and 'Jill had enough,' though syntactically well formed, are semantically incomplete. In these cases, as observed earlier, the meaning of such a sentence does not fully determine a truth condition, even after ambiguities are resolved and references are fixed. Syntactic completeness does not guarantee semantic completeness.

In order to make sense of the semantic–pragmatic distinction, we need to take several other distinctions into account. The first involves context. It is a platitude that what a sentence means generally doesn't determine what a speaker means in uttering it. The gap between linguistic meaning and speaker meaning is said to be filled by "context": we say that what the speaker means somehow "depends on context," or that "context makes it clear" what the speaker means. But there are two quite different sorts of context – call them *wide* and *narrow* context – and they play quite different roles. Wide context concerns any contextual information that is relevant to determining, in the sense of *ascertaining*, the speaker's intention. Narrow context concerns information specifically relevant to determining, in the sense of *providing*, the semantic values of context-sensitive expressions (and morphemes of tense and aspect). Wide context does not literally determine anything.[26] It is the body of mutually evident information that the speaker and the hearer exploit, the speaker to make his communicative intention evident and the hearer, taking himself to be intended to, to identify that intention.

There are also distinctions to be drawn with respect to the terms 'utterance' and 'interpretation.' An utterance can either be the act of uttering a sentence or the sentence uttered. Strictly speaking, it is the sentence that is uttered (the type, not the token) that has semantic properties. The act of uttering the sentence has pragmatic properties. The notion of the content of an utterance of a sentence has no independent theoretical significance. There is just the content of the sentence the speaker is uttering, which, being semantic, is independent of the speaker's communicative intention, and the content of the speaker's communicative intention. As for the term 'interpretation,' it can mean either the formal, compositional determination by the grammar of a language of the meaning of a sentence or the psychological process whereby a person understands a sentence or an utterance of a sentence. Using the phrase 'utterance interpretation' indiscriminately, as often happens, can only confound the issues. For example, talking about the interpretation of an utterance in a context rather than of a sentence with respect to a context leads to paradox. An oral utterance of "I am not speaking" or a waking utterance of "I am asleep" cannot fail to be false, and yet the sentences themselves are not necessarily false. Relative to me, the first is true whenever I am not speaking, and the second is true whenever I am asleep.

As for the semantic–pragmatic distinction, it can be drawn with respect to various things, such as ambiguities, implications, presuppositions, interpretations, knowledge, processes, rules, and principles. I take it to apply fundamentally to types of information. Semantic information is information encoded in what is uttered – these are stable linguistic features of the sentence – together with any extralinguistic information that provides (semantic) values to context-sensitive expressions in what is uttered. Pragmatic information is the (extralinguistic) information the hearer relies on to figure out what the speaker is communicating. It is generated by, or at least made relevant by, the act of uttering it.[27] This way of characterizing pragmatic information generalizes Grice's point that what a speaker implicates in saying what he says is carried not by what he says but by his saying it and perhaps by his saying it in a certain way (1989: 39).

Applications of the Semantic–Pragmatic Distinction

Philosophers have long found it convenient to attribute multiple senses to problematic words like 'and,' 'know,' 'appear,' and 'good.' Grice deplores this tendency and recommends adoption of his "Modified Occam's Razor: Senses are not to be multiplied beyond necessity" (1989: 47). Wielding it on the many philosophically significant expressions and constructions that would otherwise seem give rise to ambiguities and other semantic complications illustrates the value of enforcing the semantic–pragmatic distinction. Taking pragmatic considerations into account acknowledges that in everyday speech not just what a sentence means but the fact that someone utters it plays a role in determining what its utterance conveys. They explain how the things we mean can go beyond the things we say and still be understood.

The words 'and' and 'or' provide good illustrations. In logic 'and' is standardly represented as conjunction ('&'), where the order of conjuncts doesn't matter. Consider, for example, the difference between what is likely to be conveyed by utterances of (1) and (2).

(1)   Hal got pneumonia and went to the hospital.
(2)   Hal went to the hospital and got pneumonia.

Despite the difference in what utterances of (1) and (2) are likely to convey, it is arguable that the sentences themselves have the same semantic content: it is not the meaning of 'and' but the fact that the speaker *utters* the conjuncts in one order rather than the other that explains the difference in how each utterance is likely to be taken. If so, then any suggestion of temporal order, or even causal connection, is not a part of the semantic content of the sentence but is merely implicit in its utterance (Levinson 2000: 122–7). One piece of evidence for this is that such a suggestion may be explicitly canceled (Grice 1989: 39). One could utter (1) or (2) and continue, "but not in that order" without contradicting what one has just said. One would be merely canceling any suggestion, due to the order of presentation, that the two events occurred in that order.

Now it has been argued that passing Grice's cancelability test does not suffice to show that the differences between the two sentences above is not a matter of linguistic meaning. Cohen (1971) and Carston (1988) have appealed to the fact that the difference is preserved when the conjunctions are embedded in the antecedent of a conditional, as here:

(3) a. If Hal got pneumonia and went to the hospital, he needed a doctor.

      b. If Hal went to the hospital and got pneumonia, he needed a lawyer.

Also, the difference is apparent when the two conjunctions are combined:

(4) It's worse to go to the hospital and get pneumonia than to get pneumonia and go to the hospital.

However, these examples do not show that the relevant differences are a matter of linguistic meaning. A simpler hypothesis, one that does not ascribe a temporal much less a causal meaning to 'and,' is that these examples, like the simpler (1) and (2), involve conversational impliciture, in which what the speaker means is an implicitly qualified version of what he says. Likely utterances of (1) and (2) are made as if they included an implicit 'then' after 'and,' and are likely to be taken accordingly (with (1) there is also likely to be an implicit 'as a result'). The speaker is exploiting Grice's maxim of manner in describing events in their order of occurrence, and the hearer relies on the order of presentation to infer the speaker's intention in that regard. On the pragmatic approach, 'and' is treated as unambiguously truth-functional, without having additional temporal or causal senses.

Even though in logic 'or' is usually represented only as inclusive disjunction ('∨'), it is often thought that in English there is also an exclusive 'or.' Also, it has been thought that the presence of 'or' entails that the speaker does not know which of the disjuncts obtains. So consider (5) and (6), for example.

(5) You can have coffee, tea, or milk.
(6) Phaedo is in the den or the kitchen.

An utterance of (5) is likely to be taken as exclusive. This might seem to be a consequence of the presence of an exclusive 'or,' but a better explanation is that if the speaker meant that you could have more than one beverage he would have said so and that if he meant that you could have all three he would have used 'and.' As Levinson explains cases like this and a wide variety of others, "What isn't said, isn't" (2000: 31). As for (6), the exclusivity of the disjunction is explained by the fact that something can't be in two places at once. Also, there is no reason to attribute an epistemic aspect to 'or,' for in uttering (6), the speaker is conversationally implicating that he doesn't know which room the dog is in. This implication is not due to the meaning of the word 'or' but rather to the presumption that the speaker is supplying as much relevant and reliable information as he has.[28]

The distinction between what an expression means and how it is used had a direct impact on many of claims formerly made by so-called ordinary-language philosophers. In ethics, for example, it was (and sometimes still is) supposed that because sentences containing words like 'good' and 'right' are used to express affective attitudes, such as approval or disapproval, such sentences are not used to make statements (and even that questions of value and morals are therefore not genuine matters of fact). This line of argument is fallacious. As G. E. Moore pointed out, although one expresses approval (or disapproval) by making a value judgment, it is the act of making the judgment, not the content of the judgment, that implies that one approves (1942: 540–5). Sentences used for ethical evaluation, such as 'Loyalty is good' and 'Cruelty is wrong,' are no different in form from other indicative sentences, which, whatever the status of their contents, are standardly used to make statements. This leaves open the possibility that there is something fundamentally problematic about their contents. Perhaps such statements are factually defective and, despite syntactic appearances, are neither true nor false. However, this is a metaphysical issue about the status of the properties to which ethical predicates purport to refer. It is not the business of the philosophy of language to determine whether goodness and wrongness are real properties (or whether the goodness of loyalty and the wrongness of cruelty are genuine matters of fact).

The fallacious line of argument exposed by Moore commits what Searle calls the "speech act fallacy." Searle gives further examples, each involving a speech act analysis of a philosophically important word (1969: 136–41). These analyses claim that because 'true' is used to endorse or concede statements (Strawson), 'know' to give guarantees (Austin), and 'probably' to qualify commitments (Toulmin), those uses constitute the meaning of these words. In each case the mistake is the same: identifying what the word is typically used to do with its semantic content.

Searle also exposes the "assertion fallacy," which confuses conditions of making an assertion with what is asserted. Here are two examples: because you would not assert that you believe something if you were prepared to assert that you know it, knowing does not entail believing; similarly, because one would not be described as trying to do something that involves no effort or difficulty, trying entails effort or difficulty. Grice (1961) identified the same fallacy in a similar argument, due to Austin, about words like 'seems,' 'appears,' and 'looks': since you would not say that a table looks old unless you (or your audience) doubted or were even prepared to deny that it was old, the statement that the table looks old entails that its being old is doubted or denied. This argument is clearly fallacious, since it draws a conclusion about entailment from a premise about conditions on appropriate assertion. Similarly, you wouldn't *say* that someone tried to stand up if doing it involved no effort or difficulty, but this doesn't show that trying to do something entails that there was effort or difficulty in doing it. You can misleadingly imply something without its being entailed by what you say.

As illustrated by many of the examples above, the semantic–pragmatic distinction helps explain why what Grice called "generalized" conversational implicature is a pragmatic phenomenon, even though it involves linguistic regularities of sorts. They are cancelable, hence not part of what is said, and otherwise have all the features of "particularized" implicatures, except that they are characteristically associated with certain forms of words. That is, special features of the context of utterance are not needed to generate them and make them identifiable. As a result, they do not have to be worked out step by step in the way that particularized implicatures have to be. Nevertheless, they can be worked out. A listener unfamiliar with the pattern of use could still figure out what the speaker meant. This makes them standardized but not conventionalized.[29]

Finally, the semantic – pragmatic distinction seems to undermine any theoretical role for the notion of presupposition, whether construed as semantic or pragmatic. A *semantic* presupposition is a precondition for truth or falsity. But, as argued long ago by Stalnaker (1974) and by Boër and Lycan (1976), there is no such thing: it is either entailment or pragmatic. And so-called *pragmatic* presuppositions come to nothing more than preconditions for performing a speech act successfully and felicitously, together with mutual contextual beliefs taken into account by speakers in forming communicative intentions and by hearers in recognizing them. In some cases they may seem to be conventionally tied to particular expressions or constructions, e.g., to definite descriptions or to clefts, but they are not really. Rather, given the semantic function of a certain expression or construction, there are certain constraints on its reasonable or appropriate use. As Stalnaker puts it, a "pragmatic account makes it possible to explain some particular facts about presuppositions in terms of general maxims of rational communication rather than in terms of complicated and ad hoc hypotheses about the semantics of particular words and particular kinds of constructions" (1974/1999: 48).

The examples we have considered illustrate the significance of the semantic–pragmatic distinction and the rationale of trying to explain linguistic phenomena in as general a way as possible. The explanatory strategy is to appeal to independently motivated principles and processes of rational communication rather than to special features of particular expressions and constructions. It is applicable to certain important topics in the philosophy of language taken up elsewhere in this volume, including conditionals, the referential–attributive distinction, and propositional attitude ascriptions. Needless to say, the issues are more complex and contentious than our discussion has indicated, but at least our examples illustrate how to implement what Stalnaker has aptly described as "the classic Gricean strategy: to try to use simple truisms about conversation or discourse to explain regularities that seem complex and unmotivated when they are assumed to be facts about the semantics of the relevant expressions" (1999: 8). Economy and plausibility of explanation are afforded by heeding the semantic – pragmatic distinction. Rather than attribute dubious ambiguities or needlessly complex properties to specific linguistic items, we proceed on the default assumption that uses of language can be explained by means of simpler semantic hypotheses together with general facts about rational communication. In this way, we can make sense of the fact that to communicate efficiently and effectively people rarely need to make fully explicit what they are trying to convey. Most sentences short enough to use in everyday conversation do not literally express things we are likely ever to mean, and most things we are likely ever to mean are not expressible by sentences we are likely ever to utter. That's something to think about.

Notes

1 We generally do this by using a performative verb like 'promise,' 'pronounce,' 'apologize,' or 'request' in a sentence beginning with 'I' followed by a performative verb in present tense and active voice. The first-person plural is possible too ("We promise ... "), as is the second-person passive ("Smoking is prohibited"). The word 'hereby' may be inserted before the performative verb to indicate that the utterance in which it occurs is the vehicle of the performance of the act in question.

2 However, it does seem that in uttering, say, "I promise you a rose garden," a speaker is at least *saying* that he is promising the hearer a rose garden. And what he is saying is true just in case he is making that promise.

3 Of course, every utterance is conventional insofar it is made with linguistic means. The question here, though, is whether special conventions are needed to explain the performativity of certain utterances.

4 Austin's focus on such cases led him to develop an account of what it takes for these formalized utterances to be performed successfully and a classification of the various things that can go wrong ("flaws," "hitches," and other sorts of "infelicities").

5 It follows that an account of explicit performatives should not appeal, as Searle's (1989) elaborate account does, to any special features of the performative formula. Bach and Harnish (1992) argue that Searle's account is based on a spurious distinction between having a communicative intention and being committed to having one and on a confusion between performativity and communicative success.

6 There numerous other forms of words which are standardly used to perform speech acts of certain types without making explicit the type of act of being performed, e.g. "It would be nice if you ... " to request, "Why don't you ... ?" to advise, "Do you know ... ?" to ask for information, "I'm sorry" to apologize, and "I wouldn't do that" to warn. Even in the case of hedged and embedded performatives, such as "I can assure you ... ," "I must inform you ... ," "I would like to invite you ... ," and "I am pleased to be able to offer you ... ," in which the type of act is made explicit, the alleged conventions for simple performative forms would not apply. For discussion of hedged and embedded performatives, see Fraser (1975) and Bach and Harnish (1979: 209–19).

7 The variety of linguistic forms that can be used to perform a given sort of speech act is too open-ended to be plausibly explained by a special convention that specifies just those linguistic forms whose utterance counts as the performance of an act of that sort. Their standardization does not show that they are governed by special conventions. Rather, it provides a precedent that serves to streamline the inference required for their successful performance (see Bach, 1995).

8   In fact, Grice oddly claimed that in speaking nonliterally, as in irony and metaphor, one is not saying anything but merely "making as if to say" (1989, p. 30). This was because he understood saying something to entail meaning it. He seems to have conflated the locutionary act of saying with the illocutionary act of stating (to be sure, we often use the word 'say' for both).

9   These are three reasons why the notion of locutionary acts is indispensable, as Bach & Harnish (1979, pp. 288–9) argue in reply to Searle (1968).

10 A detailed taxonomy is presented in Bach and Harnish (1979, ch. 3), where each type of illocutionary act is individuated by the type of attitude expressed. In some cases there are constraints on the content as well. We borrow the terms 'constative' and 'commissive' from Austin and 'directive' from Searle. We adopt the term 'acknow-ledgment' rather than Austin's 'behabitive' or Searle's 'expressive' for apologies, greetings, thanks, congratulations, condolences, etc., which express an attitude to the hearer that is occasioned by some event that is thereby being acknowledged, often in satisfaction of a social expectation.

11 The difference between expressing an attitude and actually possessing it is clear from the following definition: to express an attitude in uttering something is reflexively (see the next section) to intend the hearer to take one's utterance as reason to think one has that attitude. This reason need not be conclusive and if in the context it is overridden, the hearer will, in order to identify the attitude being expressed, search for an alternative and perhaps nonliteral interpretation of the utterance. For discus-sion see Bach and Harnish (1979, pp. 57–9 and 289–91).

12 Correlatively, the hearer can understand the utterance without regarding it as sincere, e.g., take it as expressing regret without believing that the speaker regrets having done the deed in question. Getting one's audience to believe that one actually possesses the attitude one is expressing is not an illocutionary but a perlocutionary act.

13 This distinction and the following examples are drawn from Bach & Harnish (1979, ch. 6).

14 Partly because of certain alternative wordings and perhaps indecision (compare his 1969 with his 1957 article), Grice's analysis is sometimes interpreted as defining communicative intentions iteratively rather than reflexively, but this not only miscon-strues Grice's idea but leads to endless complications (see Strawson, 1964, and especially Schiffer, 1972, for good illustrations). Recanati (1986) has pointed to certain problems with the iterative approach, but in reply I have argued (Bach, 1987) that these problems do not arise on the reflexive analysis.

15 This question was raised by Schelling, who was the first to discuss games of tacit coordination (1960, pp. 54–8).

16 If the hearer thinks the speaker actually possesses the attitude he is expressing, in effect she is taking him to be sincere in what he is communicating. But there is no question about his being sincere in the communicative intention itself, for this intention must be identified before the question of his sincerity (in having that attitude) can even arise. In other words, deceiving your audience about your real attitude presupposes successfully expressing some other attitude. You can be unsuc-cessful in conveying your communicative intention – by being too vague, ambiguous, or metaphorical, or even by being wrongly taken literally – but not insincere about *it*.

17 For a review of earlier approaches, to what used to be called "contextual implication," see Hungerland (1960).

18 In Bach and Harnish (1979, p. 7), we replace Grice's Cooperative Principle with our own CP, the "Communicative Presumption." This is the mutual belief when one person says something to another, he does so with a recognizable communicative intention.

19 For discussion of Grice's maxims, their weaknesses, and their conflicts, see Harnish (1976: 330–40), and see Levinson (2000) for extensive discussion and adaptation of them to various types of generalized conversational implicature.

20 Two Gricean approaches to indirect speech acts are presented in Searle (1975) and Bach and Harnish (1979, chs. 4 and 9).

21 These ideas are presented in Bach (1994). Sperber and Wilson speak of implicitures as the 'explicit' content of an utterance, but their neologism 'explicature' (1986, p. 182) for this in-between category is rather misleading. It is a cognate of 'explicate,' not 'explicit,' and explicating, making something explicit that isn't, is not the same thing as making it explicit in the first place. That's why I prefer the neologism 'impliciture,' since in these cases part of what is meant is communicated only implicitly.

22 Recanati (1989) suggests that on intuitive grounds the notion of what is said should be extended to cover such cases, but clearly he is going beyond Grice's understanding of what is said as corresponding to the constituents of the sentence and their syntactic arrangement. The syntactic correlation constraint entails that if any element of what the speaker intends to convey does not correspond to any element of the sentence he is uttering, it is not part of what he is *saying*. Of course it may correspond to part of what he is asserting, but I am not using 'say' to mean 'assert.' In the jargon of speech act theory, saying is locutionary, not illocutionary. Recanati and I have renewed our debate on whether intuition or syntax constrains what is said in Recanati (2001) and Bach (2001).

23 Utterances like "You're not going to die" may be described as cases of *sentence* non-literality, because the words are being used literally but the sentence as a whole is being used loosely. Compare the sentence mentioned in the text with sentence, "Everybody is going to die," which would likely to be used in a strictly literal way.

24 A classification of these and many other utterance modifiers is given in Bach (1999b, sec. 5).

25 For a collection of sample formulations, see the Appendix to Bach (1999a).

26 For this reason, I do not accept Stalnaker's contention that "we need a single concept of context that is both what determines the contents of context-dependent expressions, and also what speech acts act upon" (1999a, p. 4).

27 This conception of the distinction is defended and contrasted with alternatives in Bach (1999a). To the extent that the debate about the semantic-pragmatic distinction isn't entirely terminological, perhaps the main substantive matter of dispute is whether there is such a thing as "pragmatic intrusion," whereby pragmatic factors allegedly contribute to semantic interpretation. Various linguistic phenomena have been thought to provide evidence for pragmatic intrusion, hence against the viability of the semantic-pragmatic distinction, but in each case, in my opinion (Bach, 1999a), this is an illusion, based on some misconception about the distinction. When it and the related distinctions enumerated above are observed, there is no issue of pragmatic intrusion. Levinson (2000) argues that many alleged cases of pragmatic intrusion are really instances of generalized conversational implicature, which he thinks is often misconstrued as a purely semantic phenomenon.

28 This sounds like a combination of Grice's Quantity and Quality maxims, or what Harnish proposed as the "Maxim of Quantity-Quality: Make the strongest relevant claim justifiable by your evidence" (1976: 340; see also p. 361, n. 46).

29 Levinson describes them as "default meanings," but he does not mean sentence meanings. He thinks of them as comprising an "intermediate layer" of meaning, of "systematic pragmatic inference based not on direct computations about speaker-intentions but rather on general expectations about how language is normally used, [... which] give rise to presumptions, default inferences, about both content and force" (2000: 22). In my view, this does not demonstrate an intermediate layer of meaning – there is still only linguistic meaning and speaker meaning – but rather the fact that speakers' communicative intentions and hearers' inference are subject to certain systematic constraints based on practice and precedent (see Bach, 1995).

Further Reading

Austin, J.L. (1962). *How to do things with words.* Oxford: Oxford University Press. The classic lectures on performatives and speech acts.

Bach, K. (1994). Conversational impliciture. *Mind & Language*, 9, 124–62. Not to be confused with Grice's implicature, impliciture marks the middle ground between what is said and what is implicated.

Bach, K. and R.M. Harnish (1979). *Linguistic communication and speech acts.* Cambridge, MA: MIT Press. Integrates ideas of Austin, Strawson, and Grice into a systematic theory of speech acts and of communicative intention and inference.

Davis, S. (ed). (1991). *Pragmatics: A reader.* Oxford: Oxford University Press. This collection includes Carston (1988), Grice (1969 and 1975), Harnish (1976) Recanati (1989), Stalnaker (1974), Strawson (1964), and excerpts from Bach and Harnish (1979).

Grice, H.P. (1989). *Studies in the way of words.* Cambridge, MA: Harvard University Press. This collection includes all of Grice's papers cited here, as well as a "retrospective epilogue."

Levinson, S.C. (2000). *Presumptive meanings: The theory of generalized conversational implicature.* Cambridge, MA: MIT Press. This monumental work reformulates Grice's maxims, examines a huge range of linguistic data, and presents an account of the systematic ways in which we mean more than we say.

Neale, Stephen (1992). Paul Grice and the philosophy of language. *Linguistics and Philosophy*, 15, 509–59. A clear and comprehensive presentation of Grice's main views and their philosophical significance.

Searle, J.R. (1969). *Speech acts: An essay in the philosophy of language.* Cambridge, UK: Cambridge University Press. A theory of speech acts in terms of constitutive rules, with applications to specific problems in the philosophy of language.

Searle, J.R. (1979). *Expression and meaning.* Cambridge, UK: Cambridge University Press. A collection of Searle's important papers on topics relevant to speech acts and pragmatics.

Stalnaker, R. (1999). *Context and content.* Oxford: Oxford University Press. Contains essays on the role of context in accounting for how language is used to express thought.

Szabó, Z. (ed.) (2005). *Semantics vs. pragmatics.* Oxford: Oxford University Press. A collection of new articles on the semantics/pragmatics distinction and its applications.

Chapter 9

Figurative Language

Josef Stern

For much of the last century the philosophy of language would have been more accurately called 'the philosophy of literal language.' The study of figurative language – the range of tropes including metaphor, synechdoche, metonymy, simile, irony, over- and under-statement, etc. – was largely confined to the peripheries of aesthetics and rhetoric.[1] Logical positivists denied figures of speech "cognitive" or "empirical" content, consigning them to the grunts and wows of emotive or affective significance. Semantics and formally oriented theories of meaning, whose native language was that of science, mathematics, and logic, took as its model the eternal, the non-vague, the assertive, and the extensional. The figurative was either neglected, dismissed, or deposited in the wastebasket of pragmatics.

Matters began to change in the mid-1950s, and from the start contemporary investigation of the figurative has largely centered on metaphor. Max Black's essay "Metaphor" (Black 1962) first put the figure on the agenda of Anglo-American philosophy by presenting it, in the Oxford vocabulary of his day, as a subject of "logical grammar" and by arguing, against the prevailing current, that metaphors are cognitively significant in ways that distinguish them from the literal. A second landmark was the central place Nelson Goodman assigned to metaphor in his *Languages of art* (Goodman 1976) as part of his program to show that there are common modes of symbolization that cut across natural languages and non-linguistic representational systems. But the greatest changes have occurred since the 1980s as increasing attention has been paid to what were previously considered imperfections of natural language – especially context-dependent expressions like indexicals, vagueness, and non-extensional constructions. Philosophers have come to acknowledge the ubiquity of metaphor, in scientific discourse as well as ordinary language, making it impossible to dismiss as poetry or literature. An additional impetus has been the emergence of the cognitive sciences, for which metaphor has furnished one of the most fertile grounds for interdisciplinary research. Some of these investigators find in metaphor the key to deep truths about the human conceptual system (Johnson 1981; Lakoff 1993); for others (e.g., Stern 2000), its interest is more like that of exotic phenomena in physics: its indirect, often remote, but potentially significant implications for the general explanatory principles that are the primary interest of the field – for our notions of meaning, truth, appropriateness. In short, metaphor is now a live topic in the field.

In this chapter I shall concentrate on implications of figurative language and specifically metaphor for the philosophy of language. In particular I shall focus on the relation between the metaphorical and the literal. By singling out the particular trope of metaphor, I do not mean to suggest that all the figures constitute one natural semantic kind of which metaphor is the paradigm. Toward the end of the chapter I'll mention some considerations against this presumption, but we shall also question the degree to which all metaphors constitute a single cohesive trope.

I

Since metaphor is both contrasted with and said to depend on the literal, the appropriate place to begin ought to be with a precise, explicit definition of the literal. Unfortunately, we do not yet possess any such thing. As an opening working hypothesis, I shall assume that the literal meaning of a simple expression is whatever, according to our best linguistic theory, turns out to be its semantic interpretation and that the literal meaning of a sentence is the rule-by-rule composition of the literal meanings of its simple constituents.[2] Now, given this rough characterization of the literal, one of the oldest and most deeply entrenched conceptions of metaphor characterizes it as improper or deviant use of the literal. (For a careful history of this idea, see White 2001). With the linguistic turn in the twentieth century, philosophers and linguists resurrected this view, cashing out the relevant impropriety in (sometimes formal) terms of semantic anomaly, grammatical or sortal violations, conceptual absurdity, or category mistakes (Beardsley 1962, 1978; Matthews 1971; Levin 1977; Kittay 1987). One attractive feature of this proposal was its simple explanation of how we identify or recognize an utterance as a metaphor. On the presumption that utterances should always be taken literally unless proven "impossible" to be so understood, the deviance thesis provides semantic or syntactic conditions within the very sentence by which one can explain why, when violated, the utterance is literally uninterpretable; and from this it is immediately concluded (invalidly, however, since there are always alternative kinds of nonliteral interpretation) that it is identified as a metaphor. The same deviance is used to explain how the metaphorical interpretation is fixed. The literal semantic deviance of the utterance forces the interpreter to delete or re-weigh those lexical features in the literal meaning of the expression in virtue of which it is deviant. This in turn results in a new metaphorical meaning constructed from the residual components of the literal meaning – which also neatly explains how the metaphorical depends on the literal: the former is contained in the latter (Cohen and Margalit 1972).

The doctrine that all or typical metaphors, if they were interpreted literally, are grammatically deviant or semantically anomalous or "wildly false" (Cavell 1967), was one of the most widely held dogmas about metaphor in its day. In the mid-seventies, however, this dogma was decisively challenged. Various philosophers and linguists observed that there exist 'twice-true metaphors' that would be perfectly fine and equally true in the very same contexts, whether they are interpreted literally or metaphorically (Reddy 1969; T. Cohen 1975, 1976; Binkley 1976). For example:

(1) A revolution is not a matter of inviting people to dinner. (Mao Tsetung)
(2) Japan, the land of Hiroshima and Nagasaki, feels it has no alternative. (*Time* Magazine caption on a post-Chernobyl photo of Japanese nuclear power plants)
(3) Two roads diverged in a wood, and I –
I took the one less traveled by,
And that has made all the difference. (Robert Frost)
(4) Man, after all, is not a tree, and humanity is not a forest. (Emmanuel Levinas)

These examples demonstrated, simply on descriptive grounds, that literal deviance cannot be a necessary condition for metaphor. But there are also deeper explanatory difficulties for this view.

First, it assumes a literal-first serial model of processing on which the speaker-hearer turns to a metaphorical interpretation *only after* the literal interpretation has been eliminated. But there is good evidence that literal and nonliteral interpretations are simultaneously processed, in parallel, and that we select one over another kind of interpretation because it is the *best* rather than the *only possible* candidate interpretation (Stern 1983; Gibbs 1994; Recanati 1995). It should also be added that the factors that bear on our identification of an interpretation type are not necessarily the actual syntactic and semantic properties of the sentence, but our beliefs and presuppositions about those features as well as about the speaker's intentions, his expectations about his interpreter, and its setting – a rough set of factors that we 'compute' using Grice-like maxims to determine the *relative* plausibility and accessibility of the appropriate interpretation. In short, recognition that an utterance is of a certain interpretive kind depends on its context.

Second, the very idea that metaphorical use or meaning is literally deviant assumes that the literal is itself normative: "that there are standard meanings for words fixed by conventions normative for our use of words" (White 2001). But if it should turn out that the literal use of language is not governed by such conventions, if instead it is moved by the pressures and expectations of effective communication in context, and if the same pressures and expectations move communication by metaphor, that would leave no sharp distinction by which the latter ought to be regarded as deviant relative to the former, hence without a clear contrast between the two.

In response to these objections, diehard defenders of deviance have retreated to various brands of pragmatic inappropriateness or unacceptability, including the blatant truth of metaphors like 'Boys will be boys' that it would be pointless for anyone to assert (Beardsley 1978; Grice 1989; Kittay 1987). But this rejoinder misses the real import of the critique of the literal deviance account: there need be *nothing* irregular or unacceptable – syntactically, semantically, or pragmatically – about the literal meaning of a sentence used metaphorically. Like certain art works, metaphors are often *found* in their context rather than designed according to a manufacturer's specification (T. Cohen forthcoming). Although there is surely *some* reason why we take an utterance to be metaphorical (or of any particular kind), deviance as an explanation of the relation between the metaphorical and the literal has turned out to be a red herring.

II

A second classic claim about the metaphorical-literal relation begins from the observation that a sentence used metaphorically, e.g.,

(5)   Juliet is the sun

uttered by Romeo in the context of Shakespeare's play, might (and in that context does) have a different truth value from what it would have were it interpreted literally. But different truth *values* for the same sentence used in the same context twice-over, literally and metaphorically, entail that the different uses have different truth *conditions* and, if truth conditions are either identical with or determined by their meanings, then the same sentence used literally and used metaphorically must have different meanings on the two uses. On the one hand, then, the sentence must have a metaphorical as well as a literal meaning. On the other, the metaphorical meaning of an expression is not independent of its literal meaning in the way in which the multiple meanings of ambiguous expressions like 'bank' are independent of each other or the meaning of an idiom like 'red herring' is independent of those of its constituents 'red' and 'herring.' These other meanings are independent in that I can know one without knowing the other: I can know that 'bank' means the place to deposit my paycheck without knowing that it can refer to the side of a river, and I can know that 'red herring' means a misleading clue without having any idea what that has to do with being red or being a herring.[3] But I cannot know, or understand, what is metaphorically meant or said when Romeo utters (5) without knowing the literal meaning of 'the sun' (and without holding a variety of beliefs about the literal referent of the expression). Thus the metaphorical meaning of an utterance *depends* on its literal meaning in a way that distinguishes their relation from these other meaning relations. A main desideratum for an account of metaphor is to make sense of these two semantic facts: that expressions used metaphorically can have meanings different from their literal meanings but that the metaphorical meaning none the less depends on the literal one.

Probably the most natural way to work out this metaphorical-literal dependence would be by a theory of use or pragmatics. If we distinguish between what a *sentence* 'S is P' means and what a *speaker* can *use* it to mean, say, that S is R, we might identify the literal with the former and take the metaphorical meaning to be a special case of the latter. While R is not the semantic meaning of P, there nonetheless seems to be something systematic about their relation, hence, some principle that explains how the latter is conveyed by the former. The principle might be either a conversational maxim that generates implicatures (Grice 1989), or an interpretive rule that depends on mutual recognition of intentions (Fogelin 1988), or a special illocution or perlocution of the speech act (T. Cohen 1975), or a principle in virtue of which R is "called to mind" given an utterance of P (Searle 1993).[4] As Searle puts it, R is the metaphorical meaning of the predicate P on a particular occasion, and the fact that P conveys R according to one or the other of these principles is the sense in which the metaphorical (speaker's meaning) depends on the literal (sentence meaning).

Searle's account is an especially good example of the strengths and weaknesses of pragmatic theories of metaphor. What it correctly demonstrates is that there is no single "ground" (e.g., resemblance, salience), as it was traditionally called, that generates all metaphorical contents. For Searle, the Rs may be features definitionally or accidentally true of Ps, or only culturally or naturally "associated with P in our minds" even if they are not true or even *believed* to be true of Ps. The Rs (such as being the center of the speaker's world, in (5)) that serve as metaphorical interpretations of expressions P ('is the sun') are as heterogeneous as can be. Therefore, in order to *describe* the range of Rs, Searle's principles provide us with a helpful catalogue of *what* can serve as a metaphorical interpretation. However, the same descriptive ecumenicalism of his principles is the cause of their explanatory failure. Because a feature that one principle rules out can be ruled back in by another principle, the principles place no constraints on the class of possible features that can enter into a given metaphorical interpretation. Furthermore, what it is for *X to call Y to mind* is no better understood than the phenomenon of metaphor it is meant to explain, and even were we able to furnish an explanation of this psychological phenomenon, not everything that something calls to mind, or reminds us of, is something it *means*. Hence, such an account is hardly sufficient to explain why something is or is not a metaphorical *meaning*.

Similar difficulties arise for those who take metaphor to be, in Goodman's (1979) memorable phrase, any "moonlighting" use of language: any secondary, temporary, nonstandard use of language that is spontaneously, without special instruction or learning, derived from our mastery of a primary use. Such a view casts the net too widely; what we need is either a distinctive mechanism for metaphor (e.g., Aristotle's notion of transfer, whatever its effect) or a set of distinctive effects (e.g., bringing us to notice similarities, by whatever means) (Hills 1997).

In light of the failure of pragmatic *theories* of metaphorical meaning, it is tempting to draw a more radical moral that takes metaphor to be a matter of use as *opposed* to meaning. This is the sense in which Richard Rorty claims that "metaphor belongs exclusively to the domain of use": it follows no regular, predictable, law-like linguistic behavior like that whose "limits mark off (temporarily) the literal use of language," where "semantical notions like 'meaning' have a role" and outside of which, in the "jungle of use" (Rorty 1987: 285), there is no place for meaning, let alone metaphorical meaning. Although his own view is not as extreme as Rorty's, the most influential exponent of this general position is Donald Davidson (1984; cf. his 1986); who claims (1) that neither the individual words nor the sentence in a metaphorical utterance have a metaphorical meaning in addition to or in place of their literal meaning; (2) that what a metaphor 'conveys' is instead just an unpredictable causal effect of its utterance-event, the product of a non-rule-governed imaginative use of the sentence exclusively with its ordinary literal meaning, whose intended effect is to make us notice a likeness; and (3) that what the metaphor conveys is non-propositional: there is no "definite cognitive content that its author wishes to convey and that the interpreter must grasp if he is to get the message" (Davidson 1984: 262).

Davidson's provocative claim that "a metaphor doesn't say anything beyond its literal meaning (nor does its maker say anything, in using the metaphor, beyond the literal)" (1984: 247) has confounded many of his readers. After all, we ordinarily make and deny assertions with metaphors, give reasons using them, and either understand or fail to understand the contents of metaphors whose truth conditions are different from their literal interpretations. But on Davidson's view, there is no metaphorical content to be asserted, nothing to understand or fail to understand about a metaphor. The objection, it should be added, does not hang specifically on the notion of metaphorical meaning or taking meaning to be content or truth conditions. We ordinarily take some metaphors to be correct, or apt, others not. Whether or not one endorses metaphorical meaning, some explanation is necessary of what about an utterance leads us to judge one correct or apt, another not. Davidson's own positive story that what the metaphor conveys is simply a causal effect of the utterance is also insufficient to explain these linguistic phenomena. He compares metaphors to jokes, dreams, bumps on the head. Just as jokes make/cause us (to) laugh, so metaphors make/cause us (to) see likenesses. And just as no one would posit a "joker meaning" to explain why jokes make us laugh, so, he argues, the explanatory force of metaphorical meanings are no better than dormative powers. Instead, what causes the metaphorically distinctive effect of making us see a likeness "depends entirely on the ordinary meanings of those *words* and *hence* on the ordinary meanings of the *sentences* they comprise" (p. 247, my emphasis). Davidson nowhere explains the causal *explanation* he has in mind that appeals to semantic facts like meanings, but his shift from the ordinary, or literal, meanings of *words* to that of the *sentence* raises problems for his claim of causal dependence (White 1996, 2001; Levinson 2001; Stern 2000). If the metaphorical effect causally depends just on the component individual words, say, 'Juliet' and 'the sun' in (5) and on their co-occurrence in the linear concrete string, then syntax (which may differ not at the surface but at a deeper abstract structural level) should be irrelevant – and indeed Davidson compares the way a metaphor works to the brute juxtaposition of the alternating stanzas in T. S. Eliot's "The Hippopotamus" that refer respectively to hippopotamuses and the church. But even simple metaphors that differ only in their superficial subject-predicate structure have systematically and predictably different metaphorical effects, e.g., 'A man is a tree' and 'A tree is a man.' This suggests that not only the literal meanings of the constituent *words* but also some aspect of the literal meaning at the unit of the *sentence*, determined by or corresponding to its syntax, must be taken into account (Stern 2000) On the other hand, if we take the metaphorical effect to depend on the literal meaning of the sentence uttered, it is not clear that the sentence used metaphorically has or retains its literal meaning, i.e., that its literal meaning is what its speaker understands by the utterance on the occasion. For if we identify the literal meaning of a sentence with its truth conditions, as does Davidson, it is doubtful that we *understand* what must be the case for, say, (5) taken literally to be true, namely, the conditions in which Juliet, a human being, is the sun, a star. We know that and why the literal sentence is *false*, but knowledge of truth conditions requires that we also know what the world would have to be like for the sentence to *obtain* – which, in this case, we do not. And if the *sentence* used metaphorically does not *have* its literal meaning, if it cannot be so understood, its metaphorical effect clearly cannot depend on it or be explained by its means (White 1996; Margalit and Goldblum 1994; for additional arguments against Davidson's non-cognitivist, causal theory, see White 1996; Moran 1989, 1996; Stern 2000; Riemer 2001.)

III

Since Davidson's causal account seems no more promising than pragmatic theories like Searle's, let's turn back to the idea that it is metaphorical *meaning* that depends on the literal. Recall that according to accounts like Searle's, the metaphorical meaning of P in a metaphorical use of 'S is P' is the feature R, the feature based on resemblance or another ground, metaphorically expressed by P on the particular occasion; R (e.g., being the center of Romeo's world) is the meaning of P (e.g., 'is the sun,' used metaphorically in (5) in the context of Shakespeare's play) because it would be the constituent corresponding to P in the truth-conditions for the utterance.[5] Against this position, Davidson argues, rightly, that (1) R is not a feature of P that it "has prior to and independent of the context of use" and (2) unlike literal meaning that has explanatory power insofar as it enables us to explain why all utterances of the sentence of which it is the meaning have the same truth conditions, there are no analogous cross-contextual regularities to explain for metaphor: each metaphorical utterance in its context appears to express a different truth-conditional feature in that context.

The not insignificant grain of truth in Davidson's critique is that accounts like Searle's that employ metaphorical meanings play fast and loose with the notion of meaning. However, his criticism suggests a rejoinder that points us in the right direction to discover what metaphorical meaning really is: If we could find regularities in the behavior of metaphors that call for an explanation *and* if we could propose a candidate other than specific features like R that explain those regularities, we would be on our way toward a defensible notion of metaphorical meaning. In order to meet Davidson's two conditions, let's focus on his observation that metaphorical interpretation is context-dependent. That is to say two things. First, metaphorical interpretations of utterances of the same expression (type) may vary widely from one occasion, or context, to another. Second, the interpretation of a metaphor is typically a function of all sorts of extralinguistic presuppositions, skills, and abilities such as the perception of similarity or salience. Now, these two ways in which a metaphor is context dependent entail that a metaphorical interpretation cannot be known by a speaker *solely* or *exclusively* in virtue of his semantic competence; hence, if metaphorical meaning must be an object of semantic competence, specific features like R cannot be metaphorical meanings. However, this does not show that metaphor lies outside semantics entirely, or that nothing could be metaphorical meaning. Its context variation also does not show that metaphor is unpredictable and idiosyncratic; on the contrary, *if* we survey how metaphorical interpretations vary from context to context, we see that they are relatively systematic and regular. To illustrate this point, contrast the different interpretations of 'is the sun' in (5), first, uttered in the context depicted in Shakespeare's play –

> (6) But soft, what *light* through yonder window breaks?
> It is the East, and Juliet *is the sun*.
> Arise fair *sun* and kill the envious *moon*,
> Who is already sick and pale with grief,
> That thou her maid art far more fair than she . . .
> Two of the fairest *stars* in all the heaven,
> Having some business, do entreat her *eyes*.
> To *twinkle* in their spheres till they return.
> What if her *eyes* were there, they in her head?
> The *brightness* of her cheek would shame those *stars*,
> As *daylight* doth a *lamp*; her *eyes in heaven*
> Would through the airy region stream so *bright*,
> That birds would sing, and think it were not *night*.
>
> (*Romeo and Juliet* II, ii, 2–23; my italics)

where it means, say, that Juliet is unequaled by her peers, worshipped by her lover, and the center of his life – with its interpretation in a context in which Juliet is presupposed to be the kind of woman who consumes anyone who gets too closely involved with her, whom she simply burns up; or in yet a third context where she is presupposed to be someone utterly (and boringly) reliable, predictable, and regular in her movements, someone you can always count on to rise and set, who never surprises or even inspires. Or consider the interpretation of the 'sun' metaphor in Salisbury's description of the end of Richard II's reign to the Welsh Captain:

(7) Ah, Richard, with the eyes of heavy mind
     I see thy glory like *a shooting star*
     Fall to the base *earth* from the *firmament*.
     Thy sun sets weeping in the lowly *west*,
     Witness *storms* to come, woe and unrest;
     Thy friends are fled to wait upon thy foes,
     And crossly to thy good all fortune goes.   (*Richard II*, II, iv; my emphasis)

where the (setting) sun exemplifies and thereby expresses (declining) glory, (lost) authority, and insecurity. Or the interpretation of 'is the sun' in

(8) Achilles is the sun.

in a context where it expresses Achilles' devastating anger or brute force, or in the Spanish Hebrew poet Judah Halevi's love poem:

(9) The *night* the girl gazelle displayed to me
     Her cheek – *the sun* – beneath its *veil* of hair,
     Red as a ruby, and beneath, a *brow*
     Of moistened *marble* (color wondrous fair!)
     I fancied her *the sun*, which *rising reddens*
     Clouds of morning with its *crimson* flare.   (Scheindlin 1986: 119)

where it expresses the beloved girl's radiant but (together with the 'marble' metaphor) cold personality and character.

Looking one by one at the contents of the metaphorical interpretations of '(is) the sun' in each of these examples, there is little they share. But if we look at the triples of contents, common expression type, and their respective contexts, the different contents correspond to some difference related to their respective contexts, whether the latter differences are verbally articulated in their (literary) context or, as we see from the different contexts of (5), constituted by unarticulated beliefs or presuppositions. The moral is that there may be little that is systematic or predictable so long as we look only at the particular contents of different metaphorical interpretations in each context one by one, but at one 'level' of interpretation more abstract – at a level that relates each content of the same expression used metaphorically to a relevant feature of its respective context of use, namely, the shared presuppositions – metaphorical interpretation does follow regularities and supports predictions. Same expression, same context – i.e., same presuppositions – same interpretation; same expression, different contexts – i.e., different presuppositions – different interpretations. The structure of these variations – which I would conjecture is the "transfer" of which Aristotle (1984) spoke – is essential to understand both the productivity of metaphor and speakers' mastery of the mechanism of metaphorical interpretation.

In order to explain these variations, I have argued elsewhere (Stern 2000) that we should take the context-dependence of metaphor literally: by treating metaphors on the model of paradigmatic context-dependent expressions – demonstratives and indexicals (e.g., 'this,' 'thus,' 'I,' 'now'). The *contents* (truth-conditional factors) and referents of these words also vary across contexts, but the variation is systematic – and it is the meaning or, in David Kaplan's semantic terminology for demonstratives (1989a, 1989b), the *character* of the word, e.g., for 'I,' the rule that each of its utterances refers to its speaker, that spells out the systematic dependence of the interpretation, or content (its direct referent), of the indexical on the relevant parameter of its context. Likewise, we can identify a rule, or function, for a metaphor that spells out the way its interpretation – a set of features like R that belong to its truth conditions or content – on an occasion depends on and varies with a specific parameter of its context, namely, a particular set of presuppositions. That rule for the interpretation of a metaphor – like the rule for the first-person 'I' – is its *meaning* (character), *not* the set of features R which are instead its content. Together with its context, the meaning (character) of the metaphor – what the speaker knows in virtue of her linguistic competence when she is able to produce and comprehend a metaphor – fixes the content of its interpretation, the features R, although it is not itself part of that content. (For other accounts of the context-dependence of metaphor, see Berg 1988; Bergmann 1982; Bezuidenhout 2001; Kittay 1987; Nogales 1999; Scheffler 1979.)

Despite this analogy, there are, to be sure, significant differences between the context-dependence of metaphors and demonstratives/indexicals. In the case of singular demonstratives/indexicals, the contextual parameters are familiar and relatively well-defined: the speaker for 'I,' the time of utterance for 'now,' the demonstratum for 'that,' and so on. The contextual parameter for metaphors, whose basic syntactic unit is the predicate, is rather less defined: a set of presuppositions.[6] Presupposition here is the pragmatic notion, a species of propositional attitude (Stalnaker 1972, 1973), a set of propositions to which a speaker, in making an utterance, commits himself, in the absence of which his assertion would be inappropriate or (as with metaphor) his utterance uninterpretable as it is. These presuppositions constitute the context of a metaphor insofar as they define its range of possible interpretations on the occasion. They can also be characterized as "common knowledge" about features or properties associated with the metaphorical expression so long as we bear in mind that they need not be true or even be believed to be true. For as Black (1962) first observed, what is relevant to the metaphorical interpretation of an expression Ø are its "system of associated commonplaces," rather than its definition or the features actually true of Ø's; as we saw earlier, the contents of these presuppositions – which do the work performed by the traditional "grounds" – are as varied as can be. Indeed all the presupposed features have in common is that they are presupposed in the context to be "associated" with the expression being interpreted metaphorically. Furthermore, the full set of relevant presuppositions include not only those associated with the metaphorical expression (e.g., 'is the sun' in (5)) but also those associated with other elements in its linguistic and extra-linguistic environment (e.g., 'Juliet'). The main difference between these different sets of presuppositions is that the former serve to generate potential features of content, while the latter filter out those that cannot be appropriately taken to be the content of the metaphor in the context (Reinhart 1970; Stern 2000).[7]

What makes something a metaphor according to this account is both narrower and wider than the received view. There is no one kind of associated property (e.g., such as a feature of resemblance) that serves as the ground for all metaphors; rather, interpretations that draw on all sorts of properties count as metaphors. But what is essential is that the feature be presupposed to be associated with the metaphorical vehicle in the context, such that were a different feature presupposed in the context, then the interpretation of the metaphor would correspondingly differ. What distinguishes a metaphor is not the kind of feature that enters into its interpretation, but its context-sensitive meaning (character) that yields different features in different contexts.

The complex poetic metaphors (6), (7), and (9) illustrate another important characteristic of the metaphorically relevant presuppositions. Each of the individual metaphors in these passages is interpreted relative to a schema, network, or family of expressions, sometimes explicitly spelled out in the context (as in the poems), but often merely suggested in the context. This systemic dimension of metaphorical interpretation was first pointed out by Nelson Goodman (1976) but in recent years it has become a leitmotif in the literature, due in large measure to the research on 'conventional metaphors' of the linguist George Lakoff and his school (Lakoff 1993; Lakoff and Johnson 1980; Lakoff and Turner 1989; Gibbs 1994; for alternative systemic accounts, see Kittay 1987; Thompson and Thompson 1987; Tirrell 1989; White 1996).[8] In the complex metaphors of (6), (7), and (9), the interpretations of 'the sun' vary according to the schema of objects (marked by the italicized expressions) with which the (literal) referent or extension of the metaphorical vehicle is classified in the context. For the features associated with any one expression that are exemplified, sampled, or drawn to salient attention by its extension depend both on the other members in the schema and on the range of features sampled by the schema as a whole. Thus the underlying unit for the interpretation of an individual metaphor is its whole schema, network, or family, whether or not the latter are made explicit in the context. Moreover, such an exemplification schema is not the only kind of system or network that contributes to the metaphorical interpretation. The set of expressions (or kinds of expressions) that fill the thematic roles for predicate metaphors are implicated in its interpretation, as are the many ways in which we extend metaphors by drawing out their various, more or less strong inductive consequences. For example, in T. S. Eliot's "The Love Song of J. Alfred Prufrock," the yellow fog is a cat that rubs its back on the window, licks its tongue, makes sudden leaps, curls about the house, and sleeps. Closer attention to these roles of systematic networks in metaphorical interpretation, and their interaction, promises to explain how complex metaphors in poetry function. (The best philosophical analysis of complex metaphors in poetry and literature is now White 1996.)

IV

Let's suppose now that a speaker's semantic competence in metaphor, like the semantic competence that underlies her ability to use demonstratives, consists in knowledge of its meaning, or character, namely, a function from the metaphorically relevant associated properties in the context set of presuppositions to the particular subset of properties that constitute the content of the metaphor in that context. Still, there remains a disanalogy between demonstratives and metaphors. Meanings (or characters) are of expressions but metaphor is a kind of use or interpretation; what expression, then, is a metaphorical meaning a meaning of? In order to lexically realize metaphorical interpretation, I coin an expression 'Mthat' which is modeled after David Kaplan's 'Dthat,' an operator which, prefixed to a definite description Ø, lexically represents the demonstrative interpretation or use of Ø. Just as 'Dthat' takes the description 'the man in black' and produces the demonstrative 'Dthat['the man in black']' that directly (and rigidly) refers to the individual in the context who fits the description, so 'Mthat' takes a literal expression like 'is the sun' and produces the "metaphorical expression" 'Mthat['is the sun']' that expresses a particular subset of presupposed properties associated with the embedded expression in the context. Of course, 'Mthat' no more than 'Dthat' is an actual expression of English; but it is intended to capture the linguistic competence that underlies our ability to use or interpret expressions metaphorically. With these "metaphorical expressions" in hand, we are also now in a position to explicate how the metaphorical depends on the literal. Although neither the meaning/character nor the content/truth condition of the metaphorical expression is a compositional function of the meaning or content of its constituents, we can *individuate* the metaphorical expression 'Mthat[Ø]' by the linguistic type of Ø: If Ø and ψ are of different types, then Mthat[Ø] and Mthat[ψ] are of different types.

The notion of meaning at work in metaphor is not, then, the content or truth-conditional factor corresponding to the utterance in a context. Rather, the meaning of a metaphor is what fixes its content or truth conditions without itself being part of it. This notion of metaphorical meaning also serves a second function that linguistic meaning in general serves: to capture linguistic *constraints* that determine which of a speaker's intentions can be (literally) communicated by which expressions. Similarly, metaphorical meaning constrains the content a speaker can use an expression to express metaphorically. Let me give one example, beginning with a similar constraint that governs the interpretation of indexicals. Suppose I utter

(10)   I live in Jerusalem.

In order for Susan to report what I have said, she must say

(11)   Stern says that he lives in Jerusalem,

not

(12)   Stern says that I live in Jerusalem

because the referent and content of the indexical 'I' is *always* fixed by its actual context of utterance, the context of its actual speaker, not that of, say, the belief-worlds of the subject of the sentence expressed in (12). Therefore Susan *must* shift from 'I' to 'he' (or to another word that captures the original content of the indexical, if she wants to express that content in words). I shall call this way in which the interpretation of the indexical always cleaves to its actual context of utterance the Actual Context Constraint (ACC). Similarly, suppose I say:

(13)   He [points at a person who in c is Al] might have been president (uttered in a context c, which includes a world w).

Because (13) contains the modal 'might,' uttered in the context c (including the world w), it is true just in case

(14)   There is some possible world w^* (accessible to w) in which Al *is* president.

It is not enough for (13) to be true at w^* that there be someone in w^*, say, George, who is pointed at in w^* and who is president. Although the truth value of the sentence (13) is determined by the *facts* at the counterfactual world w^*; according to the ACC, its *interpretation* or *content* is always fixed by its actual context of utterance c.

A similar story holds for metaphor. Suppose Count Paris in Shakespeare's play denies (5) but concedes:

(15)   Well, Juliet might have been the sun (uttered in c which includes w)

where 'the sun' is again interpreted metaphorically to express the proposition that Juliet is peer-less. Since (15) is a modal sentence, it is true in w, the world of its context of utterance, just in case

(16)   There is some possible world w^* (accessible to w) in which Juliet *is* the sun.

where 'is the sun' is interpreted metaphorically. Here, again, the relevant interpretation of 'is the sun' is its interpretation in its context c – that she is peer-less – not the interpretation it would be given in w* had it been uttered there. Suppose, for example, that in w* 'the sun' is the paradigm example of boring regularity; it is not sufficient for (or relevant to) the truth of Paris's utterance of (15) in c, interpreted metaphorically, that Juliet in w* be tediously predictable in her actions. She must possess in w* the property expressed by the metaphor in c. That is, like demonstratives, metaphorical interpretation obeys the ACC. As with 'I,' it does not determine what the metaphor *must* say, or under what conditions it is true; it only specifies what the interpretation *cannot* be, and this constraint calls for a kind of meaning, common to indexicals and metaphors.[9]

Apart from expressing constraints on metaphorical interpretation, the idea of metaphorical meaning can also answer classical questions about the semantic status of metaphorical interpretations. Traditionally, it has been assumed that either (1) the metaphorical mode of expression of an utterance is merely stylistic, carrying no additional cognitive content beyond that of its literally meant words; or (2) the metaphor expresses content specific to its metaphorical interpretation but of the same type as the kind of content expressed by literal language; or (3) the content of the metaphor is entirely sui generis, completely unlike the information conveyed by the literal. And to solve this problem, philosophers have traditionally turned to a literal paraphrasability test (Black 1962; Cavell 1967). But until recently progress has been hampered by the inherently unclear criteria for success in this test. (See, however, Davidson 1984; Bergmann 1982; Levinson 2001). In recent years philosophers have turned the inquiry in new, more promising directions: looking at the cognitive functioning of metaphors in scientific theories, religious language, and art criticism (Boyd 1993; Alston 1964; Denham 1998), at ways in which a metaphor can make us *see* something *as* something else that cannot be captured by a simple belief attitude (Black 1979; Davies 1982; Davidson 1986; Moran 1989), and at the role of metaphors in creating a sense of intimacy or community and their relation to jokes and riddles, an approach that promises to illuminate other cognitive aspects of metaphor such as their sense of surprise (T. Cohen 1978; Stern 2000).

To illustrate how a metaphorical mode of expression may carry a kind of information in addition to its truth-conditional content expressed in its context, here is one example involving the explanatory power of metaphor in belief-ascriptions. Marie, a young woman in her teens, suffered from the eating disorder of *anorexia nervosa*. In treatment, she explained to her therapist that her mother had forbade her to continue seeing her boyfriend. Angrily, she reported, she had said to herself:

(17)   I won't swallow that[referring to her mother's interdiction].

Let's assume that in the context in which she uttered (17) Marie's use of the word 'swallow' was metaphorical (Merleau-Ponty, cited in Danto 1978). Let's also suppose that *what* Marie *said* by (17) interpreted metaphorically, is expressed by

(18)   Marie won't obey her mother's interdiction.

Does (18) adequately express everything said by Marie's utterance of (17)? Yes and No. Yes, insofar as (17) is true, spoken by Marie referring to her mother's interdiction, just in case Marie does not obey her mother's interdiction, i.e., (18). No, insofar as her utterance of (17) is meant to contribute to an *explanation* of her anorexic behavior, albeit as an irrational way of resisting her mother's command. For in order to explain why Marie stopped *eating* in terms of a belief we would ascribe to her on the evidence of her utterance of (17), we must somehow include as part of the representation of her belief the fact that what she said, namely, that she would not obey her mother, was expressed metaphorically using the verb 'swallow.' Only under that metaphorical mode of expression of what she said – only if we include *how* she metaphorically believed, or expressed, *what* she believed – can we see any connection, conscious or unconscious, between her belief and her subsequent anorexic behavior. To be sure, Marie's behavior and the connection she made are not rational, and no explanation should make it so. But only by acknowledging the cognitive and explanatory significance of the metaphorical meaning in which she expressed her belief can we explain her behavior at all. The metaphorical mode in which Marie expressed her belief is essential, not to determine whether what she said is true or false, but for our folk-psychological purposes of explaining her behavior.[10]

V

To conclude this chapter, I shall briefly raise three questions for future research. First, what is the relation between metaphor and other types of figurative language? Since I have now argued that there is no one ground for all metaphors, instead all that is common to different metaphors is their context-dependent meaning (character) which is sensitive to various presupposed sets of features, one would think that the same account could be extended to other figures. All that would distinguish, say, metonymy or synchedoche from metaphor would be the particular contents of their respective presuppositions; in this respect different figures would differ no differently than different metaphors – all in virtue of the different contents of the relevant presuppositions. Furthermore, other figures like irony seem to be context-dependent as much as metaphor: although the ironic interpretation of an utterance is the "opposite" of its literal interpretation, what counts as "opposite" – the contradictory or a contrary (and which one) – is fixed in context. Nonetheless there seem to be semantically significant differences between two classes of figures: metaphor, metonymy, synechdoche, simile, on the one hand, irony, over and understatement, on the other. Although knowledge of each depends on knowledge of the literal, the first class (centered around metaphor) involves an operation that takes a literal meaning (character) and yields a figurative meaning (character) which, given its contextual parameter, then determines its truth conditions or content. The second class (centered around irony) involves an operation that takes propositions (content) to yield different proposi-tions (content) (Stern 2000).

Second, is metaphor a language-specific phenomenon? Are or could there be non-linguistic, say, pictorial metaphors? Since we have argued that grounds like resemblance are not essential to metaphor but aspects like context-dependence are, is there anything analogous to the semantic context-dependence of indexicals in non-linguistic mediums like pictures?[11] Indeed, on reflection it is not even clear what it is to be a pictorial or musical metaphor. Without question there are illustrated metaphors, i.e., illustrations in pictures of what are essentially linguistic metaphors; but could there be metaphors in the pictorial medium that are not parasitic off language? (On this question, see Goodman 1976; Carroll 1994; Stern 1997.)

Finally, what – in more precise terms than the working hypothesis we proposed at the beginning of this essay – is the literal on which the metaphor depends? Throughout this chapter, we have presupposed that there is *a* distinction between the literal and metaphorical, but that is not to say that it is always clear to which side of the divide a given interpretation of an expression belongs. If, as we have been arguing, context sensitivity to presuppositions is essential to metaphor, at least one notion of the literal may be characterized as context-*in*dependent inter-pretation. (See, however, Searle 1978; Recanati 1995; Stern 2000.) However, to make that case, we need finer distinctions between different kinds of context-in/ dependence and we need to take into account a continuum of metaphorical interpretations that range from the very live, productive, and highly context-specific, through various kinds and degrees of dead metaphors, metaphors that are not only less context-dependent but less so in various respects. Closer attention to this remarkable range of phenomena will increase our understanding not only of metaphor but of that literal language that was long thought to be the exclusive domain of semantics and the philosophy of language.[12]

Notes

1 By 'metaphor' or 'figurative language,' I always mean the metaphorical or figurative *use* or *interpretation* of language. It is widely acknowledged nowadays that expressions (types) are not themselves either literal or figurative, only interpretations or uses of their tokens or utterances (in context).

2 As a matter of fact, current semantic theory is not yet in a position to state with any authority *what* the semantic interpretation of a simple expression is, but it should also be noted that, from what we do know, it is nothing like a set of necessary and sufficient descriptive conditions. Minimally, it contains the extension or referent of the expression and the constraints and conditions that govern both its interaction with the syntax and with its extra-linguistic context. For proposals about the literal, see Alston 1964, Searle 1978, Davidson 1986, Stern 2000. We return to the literal at the end of the chapter.

3   A red herring is a fallacy of irrelevance, so-called because of the reputed practice of escaped convicts who used pickled herrings to throw bloodhounds off the scent. It is not difficult to imagine a current speaker who knows that a red herring is an irrelevant argument even if she has never learned that a herring is a fish or (much less plausibly) that 'red' is the name of a color.

4   It should be noted that Grice himself uses his conversational maxims only to explain how we recognize an utterance as a metaphor; when he turns to interpretation, he falls back on similarity or other traditional grounds.

5   Note that the feature R metaphorically expressed by P is itself expressed metaphorically as 'being the center of Romeo's world.' This is no problem unless one takes an analysis of metaphor to require that the contents of all metaphors be expressible in literal language. It is arguable, to the contrary, that what characterizes metaphors is that they are explicated and extended using additional metaphors; on this issue, see Tirrell 1989; Stern 2000; T. Cohen forthcoming.

6   In this respect, metaphors are closer to predicate demonstratives such as 'thus' or the predicative 'is that F'; see Stern 2000.

7   Here it is important to distinguish the question whether a given feature is appropriate content from the further question whether the content, once fixed, is an appropriate thing to assert or utter in the context.

8   In addition to his descriptive linguistic research, Lakoff makes a number of radical claims that challenge most of "Western philosophy" which he charges is based on a falsifying model of literal language; this critique has had little, if any, impact on philosophers. His work does, however, raise a number of important methodological questions. Should evidence consist primarily in one rather than another kind of metaphor – poetic or ordinary? Is metaphor a mapping of one conceptual domain onto another, or should metaphors be primarily understood as predicative, or class-inclusion, statements? Connected to this second question is the status of similarity or resemblance as a 'ground' for metaphorical interpretation. Since various critiques in the 1960s, the notion of similarity has been rehabilitated throughout the cognitive sciences, largely due to Amos Tversky 1977. At the same time, its application to metaphor has been challenged on the grounds that metaphors are not relational or comparative in form but rather devices for expressing novel, ad hoc categories. See Glucksberg 2001, Gibbs 1994, and Glucksberg and Keysar 1990, 1993.

9   Similarly, to report someone's metaphor, either the reporter can try to express only the content of the original utterance without replicating its metaphorical character or, if he wishes to preserve the metaphorical mode of expression, he must also recover the presuppositions of the original context in order to preserve the content. For additional constraints carried by metaphorical character, or meaning, see Stern 2000 and, for criticism, Bezuidenhout (2001).

10   In Stern (2000) I compare "essential metaphors" of this kind to John Perry's (1979) "essential indexicals," arguing that in both cases it is the meaning, or character of the respective indexical or metaphor that carries the additional information relevant to the explanation.

11   This question should be distinguished from whether, and how, linguistic metaphors are pictorial. On the pictorial dimension of metaphor, see Moran (1989); Stern (2000).

12   My deep thanks to Ted Cohen for critical comments on the penultimate draft of this essay.

Further Reading

Many of the primary sources on metaphor referred to in this chapter are included in two good anthologies: Johnson (1981) which includes most of the older classics (e.g., Beardsley, Black, T. Cohen, Davidson, and Lakoff and Johnson) and Ortony (1993) which focusses on more recent work (e.g., by Searle, Sadock, Boyd, Gibbs, Glucksberg and Keysar, and Lakoff), and illustrates the deep impact of the cognitive sciences on current research. For a philosophical introduction, I would recommend the excellent overviews by Moran (1996) and T. Cohen (forthcoming). Among books, a philosophically acute and very readable monograph is Fogelin (1988). Other useful book-length studies are Cooper (1986) which defends a Davidsonian approach and Kittay (1987) who employs semantic field theory to elaborate a Black-like approach to metaphor. White (1996) presents by far the best philosophical treatment of complex metaphors in literature and poetry as well as an original analysis of the structure of metaphorical interpretation. For a detailed presentation of the semantic context-dependent account sketched in this chapter, see Stern (2000).

Chapter 10

Propositional Attitude Ascription

Mark Richard

In the last quarter century, debate over propositional attitude ascriptions has centered on how, if at all, "modes of presentation" or "ways of thinking" of an object enter into the ascriptions' truth conditions. What follows critically surveys that debate.

1

Propositional attitude verbs – examples are 'believes,' 'says,' 'wonders,' and 'wants' – are certain verbs which take clausal complements (e.g., 'that it's sunny,' 'whether it's snowing') as arguments. Propositional attitude ascriptions – sentences such as 'Margaret believes that Tom is in Australia' – are ones whose main verb is a verb of propositional attitude. Common to such sentences is that they ascribe psychological states (such as belief and desire) or speech acts (assertions, suggestings, and so forth).[1]

Propositional attitude ascriptions (PAs) are paradigms of non-extensionality: replacing one sentence, predicate, or term following a propositional attitude verb with another with the same extension may change the ascription's truth value.[2] Someone may, for example, wish that the British Prime Minister would come without wishing that Mrs. Blair's husband come. Truth value may apparently change even on replacement of an expression by one with the same (possible worlds) intension. One might, it seems, guess that Twain wrote a book without guessing that Clemens did; 'Twain' and 'Clemens,' conventional wisdom tells us, have the same intension, being rigid designators of one individual.

Whence this non-extensionality? The standard answer flows from the syntax of PAs. To say that a PAs complement clause is an argument is to make a syntactic claim, mandated by syntactic facts. Verbs of propositional attitude (VPAs) *require* complementation: 'I believe' and 'I guess' are acceptable only if elliptical for something longer. VPAs accept a range of phrases as completions. You can doubt: that all men are created equal; the most famous claim in the Declaration of independence; Jefferson's Doctrine; everything Syd said.

The syntactic claim suggests a semantic claim, that VPAs pick out relations. And PAs are so called, of course, because they are taken to ascribe relations to what (declarative) sentence uses say, to propositions. To say that Mary believes that snow is white is apparently to say that Mary is related by belief to the proposition that snow is white. On this view, the clausal complement *that S* in *x believes that S* picks out a proposition – presumably the one expressed by S when it's not embedded under 'believes.'[3] But sentences which differ only in co-extensive expressions can say different things. So substitutions of co-extensive expressions in the complement of a VPA can change the truth value of a PA. Thus the non-extensionality of PAs.

If clausal complements name propositions, this comes to be the case composition-ally: the expressions in the clausal complement are associated with things – *contents*, let's call them – which determine (along with syntax) what proposition is named. If *that S* in *x says that S* names what's expressed by S unembedded, these contents are naturally taken to be what determines what is said by utterance of S. And there is presumably a rather intimate relation between what determines what a sentence's use says and the meaning of the sentence. The upshot is that there appears to be a close connection between propositional attitude ascription semantics and the specification of sentence meaning. No wonder there is so much interest in the semantics of verbs such as 'says' and 'believes.'[4]

2

What are propositions and contents? The two classical answers to this question come from Gottlob Frege and Bertrand Russell.

Frege 1892 answers the question with another: What accounts for the difference in epistemic properties of pairs of sentences, such as

Hesperus is Hesperus
Hesperus is Phosphorus,

which differ only by terms which pick out the same thing? Frege's answer is that associated with any significant expression is a "way of thinking" of what it picks out. ("mode of presentation" and "sense" are alternate names for ways of think-ing.) Frege's examples of ways of thinking are given using definite descriptions: The point of interesection of lines a, b, and c can be thought of as the point of intersection of lines a and b, or as the point of intersection of lines b and c. Given that the epistemic significance of a sentence is determined systematically by the senses of its parts and its syntax, and that for any object there are many different ways of thinking of it, we have the bare bones of an account of why, for example, 'Hesperus is Hesperus' is trivial, while 'Hesperus is Phosphorus' is not.

What does this have to do with propositional attitude ascription? According to Frege:

> In reported speech one talks about the sense, e.g., of another person's remarks. It is quite clear that in this way of speaking words do not have their customary reference, but designate what is usually their sense.   (Frege 1892, 59)

Likewsie for reports of other attitudes: in

(M)   Margaret believes that Tom is in Australia,

the clausal complement refers to what Frege called the *thought* that Tom is in Australia, the result of amalgamating the senses associated with 'Tom' and 'is in Australia.'

To think that Tom is in Australia is to think about Tom and Australia. But according to Frege, in using (M) we do not refer Tom or Australia, but to ways of thinking of them. The relation one has to Tom in virtue of thinking that he is in Australia is mediated. One is "directly related" only to a way of thinking. The most dramatic differences between Russell's and Frege's accounts of propositions and contents are here.

For Russell, propositional attitudes are individuated in terms of the objects, properties, and relations they are about. Russell holds that there are beliefs "directly involving" Tom, whose ascription requires reference to Tom, not a way of thinking of him. Early on (Russell 1903), Russell holds that in principle any one can think such thoughts. By Russell 1911, however, Russell holds that only someone "acquainted" with Tom can think such thoughts. Since one is acquainted only with sense data, universals, one's self and one's mental activities, only Tom can think these thoughts. Thus, our apparent reference to Tom in (M) is to be explained away. Most uses of proper names (as well as demonstratives and indexicals), Russell claims, are "truncations" of definite descriptions. The thought Margaret expresses with 'Tom is in Australia' turns out to be something like that expressed with a sentence such as 'My husband is in Australia,' where the name is replaced with a description she would use to identify Tom, one involving reference only to objects of her acquaintance.[5]

As an upshot, the truth conditions of (M) needn't differ at all on the accounts of Russell and Frege. For the sense of 'Tom' on Frege's view might be given by the very description which, on Russell's view, the name truncates.[6] That this is so doesn't undermine the rather dramatic difference between the views. In particular: If 'Hesperus' and 'Phosphorus' in

Ralph doubts that Hesperus is Phosphorus

function as 'genuine names,' and not truncations of descriptions, then for Russell the doubt ascribed to Ralph is the very doubt ascribed by

Ralph doubts that Hesperus is Hesperus.

Put otherwise: For Russell, there is a kind of term ("real" terms, not "disguised" definite descriptions) any two instances of which, when co-referential, are inter-substitutable within the clausal complement of a VPA. For Frege, since the reference of a term doesn't determine its sense, the idea that there could be such terms is absurd.

3

In the 1970s, telling criticisms of Frege and Russell were made by Donnellan 1972, Kaplan 1989, Kripke 1980, and others. These criticisms seem to many to show that a Russellian account of content is preferable to a Fregean one.

Frege seemed to think that typical uses of proper names had the same sense as definite descriptions which the user would offer in identification of the name's referent. Russell certainly thought that replacing a name with the description it 'truncates' didn't affect propositional identity. Thus each is committed to something like the thesis that a speaker who identifies Aristotle as the teacher of Alexander says the same thing with each of

> Aristotle taught Alexander
> The teacher of Alexander taught Alexander.

As Kripke 1980 notes, this assigns the wrong (possible worlds) truth conditions to the first sentence: That Aristotle taught Alexander is something that would have been false if Aristotle had never taught anyone; that Alexander's teacher taught Alexander is not something that would have then been false. Worse yet, the Frege/Russell view assigns the wrong truth *values* to a *lot* of sentences in which names are used, as many speakers will misdescribe the referents of their uses of proper names.[7]

These problems disappear if we assume that (1) the truth conditional properties of (uses of) sentences are determined by what they say; (2) what is said by a sentence in which a proper name is used is to be individuated in terms of what the name refers to, not in terms of a way of thinking the user associates with the name. Many impressed with Kripke's points about the modal properties of ordinary names and cognate points in David Kaplan 1989 about indexicals and demonstratives have assumed just this. One implementation of such assumptions adopts a broadly Russellian account of content, while jettisoning both Russell's requirement of an intimate epistemic relation to the constituents of our thoughts and his view that proper names are "truncated descriptions." According to such 'direct reference' (aka 'Millian' or 'Russellian') accounts of content, the content of a (use of a) name, indexical, or demonstrative is its bearer; of a verb, noun or adjective a property or relation.

On such views, sentences which differ only by co-referring singular terms – pairs such as

Mark Twain was a newspaperman
Sam Clemens was a newspaperman

– express the same proposition. These sentences clearly needn't have the same epistemic properties for someone who understands them. Such views thus abandon Frege's assumption, that what a sentence says determines its epistemic significance for the user.

4

These views are not without apparent problems. If the above sentences express the same proposition, and x *assumes that* S does nothing more than ascribe a relation between x and what S expresses when unembeded, then the ascriptions

(M)   Jane assumes that Mark Twain was a newspaperman
(S)   Jane assumes that Sam Clemens was a newspaperman

cannot diverge in truth value. But it seems obvious they could. Direct reference views require an enormous gap between the truth values of attitude ascriptions and speaker's intuitions about these values.[8]

A standard Millian response to this objection distinguishes between what a sentence use says as a matter of its semantics and what the use implies or conveys in virtue of extra-semantic factors (background assumptions, Gricean mechanisms, etc.).[9] If a local answers my question, 'Where's a gas station?' with 'There's a gas station down the road,' what he says, simply in virtue of the meaning of his words, is that there is a gas station down the road. Of course, he conveys to me that there's a gas station which hasn't been closed for ten years. But this is presumably an "extra-semantic" matter, as witnessed by the fact that if said gas station has been closed for ten years, his utterance is still true.

Now, speakers don't reliably distinguish the truth-conditional content of an utterance from "pragmatic accretions": I would call the local in the example a liar, for having told me that I could get gas down the road. Perhaps our intuitions about the truth conditions of attitude ascriptions are the result of failing to distinguish what the ascriptions strictly speaking say from what they merely imply. Perhaps our intuitions about the truth values of pairs like (M) and (S) are to be explained in terms of our focus on the differing information such sentences may (non-semantically) convey. For example, when we know that Jane uses 'Twain' to name Twain, (M) conveys that Jane's assumption is framed using 'Twain'; this is not true of (S). Since it is thus obvious that normal uses of the two ascriptions can convey different things, we take them to ("strictly") say different things. But this doesn't mean that the ascriptions *in fact* say different things, any more than my reaction to the local shows that his utterance was strictly speaking false.

This response has been discussed at length in the literature. (See, for example, Richard 1990 and Braun 1998) Among its problems is that speakers quickly pick up the distinction, between what's strictly speaking said and what's just pragmatically conveyed and can make what seem to be reliable judgments about whether something is semantic or pragmatic. But speakers don't seem at all inclined to judge that, for example, (M) and (S) "strictly speaking" come to the same thing. A different response is given in Soames 2002. He holds that (ignoring context sensitivity) the meaning of a sentence is the claim its use always asserts. Thus, the meaning of

(T)   Twain is wearing a red shirt

is the singular proposition the Russellian says it expresses. But this is not to say that uses of this sentence assert *only* this proposition. Background information and speaker intentions can bring it about that an utterance is an assertion, not only of what the sentence means, but of other claims as well. To adapt one of Soames' examples: Suppose A asks 'Where is Twain?' and B utters (T), gesturing towards a crowd. We surely speak truly if we say

B said that the man A was looking for was wearing a red shirt,

for B *did* say that the man A was looking for was wearing a red shirt.

Now, suppose I have heard A and B. You know that B seeks Twain; you ask me 'Did B tell A what the man he was looking for is wearing?' I may correctly answer

(R)   B said (to A) that Twain is wearing is red shirt.

I would not only thereby assert that B said that Twain was wearing a red shirt; according to Soames, I would thereby assert that B said that the man A was looking for was wearing a red shirt. I would also assert that B said that Twain, the man A was looking for, is wearing a red shirt. If the truth of an utterance requires the truth of what is asserted, this shows that the truth conditions of an attitude ascription needn't be "simply Russellian." My use of (R) ascribes an attitude involving a "descriptive conceptualization" of Twain. If this is right, then we can give a Russellian account of meaning and *still* allow that (M) and (S) can diverge in truth value.

There are problems. On Soames' view, one always asserts the meaning of a sentence one assertively utters. Suppose that Smith is a competent user of 'Twain' and 'Clemens,' but only just now realized (as we would normally put it) that Twain is Clemens. If so, my utterance of 'Smith just realized that Twain is Clemens' is surely true. Smith did not just now realize, of Twain and Twain, that the first is the second. But the meaning of 'Twain is Clemens,' on Soames' view, is the claim one realizes, iff one realizes, of Twain and Twain, that the first is the second. So either meaning is not compositionally determined (as the meanings of 'Smith just realized that Twain is Clemens' and 'Smith just realized that Twain is

Twain' differ, though the meanings of their components do not), or it is impossible, when Smith learns that Twain is Clemens, to (straightforwardly) say so without saying something false.

Soames (2005) acknowledges this problem and suggests that the meaning of a sentence is a "propositional matrix" – something like a proposition containing "gaps" waiting to filled by constituents. When a speaker assertively utters a sentence, her intentions and the context (typically) "enrich" the sentence's meaning with propositional constituents; the result is asserted. For example, the meaning of 'Twain is Clemens,' is something like the singular proposition involving the identity relation, Twain, Clemens, *and* two 'gaps' which can be filled with descriptive material "presenting" Twain and Clemens. When it is mutual knowledge that Twain wrote *Huck Finn* and that Clemens was a newspaperman, an utterance of 'Twain is Clemens' might be enriched with the properties *being Huck Finn's author, being a newspaper man*. If so, the utterance would express the proposition that the x such that x = Twain and wrote *Huck Finn* and the y such that y = Clemens and was a newspaperman are identical.[10] The meaning of 'Smith just realized that Twain is Clemens' is straightforwardly composed from that of 'Smith,' 'just realized' and 'Twain is Clemens.' But a typical utterance of this sentence will be "enriched" with descriptive material presenting Twain and Clemens. Thus, a typical use of the sentence ascribes to Smith a "partially descriptive belief" about Twain, and not a belief in a simple Millian identity. So we can truly say that Smith just realized that Twain is Clemens.

This is vulnerable to the sorts of objections Kripke and others originally made to Frege and Russell. Kripke's point was that whether what is said by 'Aristotle was a philosopher' is true at a world turns only on whether the person we in fact call 'Aristotle' is, at the world, a philosopher. But if I utter the sentence and "enrich" it with the property of being the *Metaphysics'* author, what I say is false at worlds at which Aristotle was a philosopher but died before he got to the *Metaphysics*. Indeed, if I enrich the sentence's meaning with the property of being the *Timeaus'* author – which I might if the background assumptions in my context are erroneous – what I say might not even be true. Because of this, the amended account does not even solve the problem it is supposed to solve.[11]

I take the moral to be that while "modes of presentation" may be relevant to the truth conditions of attitude ascriptions, modes of presentation do not contribute to truth conditions of the objects of those attitudes. If this is right, then an approach such as Soames,' which has these modes of presentation *truth conditionally* enriching what is said and ascriptions of its saying, cannot be correct.

5

A central use of attitude ascription is in the explanation, rationalization, and prediction of behavior. It is not clear that our explanatory practices make sense if these ascriptions have a Russellian semantics.

(J)   Jane wants to avoid Sam Clemens; she thinks that Sam Clemens is in Room 12.

(J')   Jane wants to avoid Mark Twain; she thinks that Sam Clemens is in Room 12

express the same Russellian claim. (J') in itself gives us no reason to think that Jane might avoid entering Room 12 and thus cannot explain why Jane avoids entering the room. So the Millian view seems committed to saying that (J) cannot explain Jane's avoiding Room 12.

One response (Braun 2000) is that explanations are often elliptical, as when we explain Max's illness by saying that he ate a wild mushroom. The explanation gives an aspect of an event which as a matter of contingent fact figured importantly in the causal etiology of the *explanandum*; simply to have eaten a wild mushroom is not in itself something which normally leads to illness. One might say the same of explanation by attitude ascription.

If explaining behavior via attitudes was by and large a one-off affair, this might be an adequate response. But our explanatory practice presupposes that *quite generally*, should someone want to avoid Twain and think that Twain is in Room 12, she will be inclined to avoid the room; analogously for instances of the schema *one who wants p and thinks that if q then p will have some inclination to try to make it the case that q*. This presupposition doesn't seem to make any sense on the Russellian account.

Or does it? Many Russellians accept a psychological picture along the following lines.[12] When an attitude ascription is true, this is because the subject is in a token mental state – a *belief state* – whose properties and environmental relations determine propositional content. Such states have aspects – call them *representations* – with a role reminiscent of Fregean modes of presentation. Representations "represent to the subject" what the attitude is about; they are shared by different states (so that a belief and desire may represent an individual "in the same way"). Believers are sensitive to their identity across states, so that when a belief and desire share a representation, it seems to the subject that they concern the same thing. A Russellian with this picture allows that something like a mode of presentation is involved in belief, but denies it a role in the semantics of 'believes.'

A Russellian with this picture might say that *all else being equal*, when (J) is true, it's made by states involving the same representation of Twain.[13] Thus, ceteris paribus, when someone wants to avoid Clemens and thinks that Clemens is in Room 12, they will be inclined to avoid the room. Explanation of behavior via attitude ascription does make sense on a Russellian view.

Whether this is tenable depends upon how we understand the ceteris paribus claim (CPC) *all else being equal, if A then B* is to be understood. Braun 2000, whose proposal this is, says context provides "suitable conditions" for evaluating a use of a CPC; situations outside such conditions in which the claim fails are "tolerable exceptions" to it. (For example, a vacuum is not suitable for 'struck matches light.' So a struck and unlit match in space is a tolerable exception to it.)

A CPC is true in context c provided that the closest A-world in which (relative to c) conditions are suitable is a B-world. Braun claims that for a normal use of

(W)   Ceteris paribus, when someone wants to attract Twain's attention and thinks they can do so by waving at Twain, they will be inclined to wave,

situations in which one's desire involves one representation of Twain and one's belief involves a disconnected one are *not* suitable situations; they are normally "tolerable exceptions."[14]

Braun gives three reasons to think this. (1) Given (W), ordinary speakers will first think of cases with a single representation of Twain. "So they tend to think of these cases (and only these cases) as "typical" or "normal." But their judgments about typicality... partly determine the suitable conditions ... So ... the suitable conditions for the generalizations in [these] contexts include the [condition that the same representation be involved in belief and desire]." (Braun 2000: sec. 8) In response: that we first think of such cases makes them typical. It doesn't follow that the other cases are atypical or exceptions. When Americans think about (W), cases involving Americans spring to mind; it doesn't follow that (W) would be true if it failed to apply to Russians.

(2) Speakers recognize cases involving demonstrative beliefs and "mismatched" representations as ones in which the antecedents of the relevant generalizations are satisfied, but not as counter-examples. For example, told that Smith accepts 'he [Twain is demonstrated] is sad' and 'if Twain is sad, then cheer him up!,' but isn't inclined to cheer the demonstrated man, a speaker will think the case is "a "funny" case, one that does not really count against the [relevant] generalization." In response: it's not clear whether we think here that all is not equal or that Smith just doesn't think that Twain is sad. Only if the latter is true is Braun's view supported.

(3) If I tell you that Jo said 'I want Twain's attention. If I wave I'll get Clemens's attention,' but she didn't wave, you wouldn't think that this falsified (W). We don't find cases in which beliefs and desires involve unconnected (non-demonstrative) representations to be counter-examples to things like (W). In response: again, is this because we think all else is not equal, or that (W)'s antecedent is not satisfied? I would say the latter. In this regard, consider

(W')   Ceteris paribus, if someone wants to attract Twain's attention but isn't inclined to wave, they don't think they can attract Twain's attention by waving.

A counter-example to (W') is also one to (W). Now, suppose Jo wants to attract Twain's attention, knows she can wave, but hasn't any inclination to wave at Twain. We don't think that all else is not equal, or that this is a "funny case"; we think Jo doesn't believe that she can attract Twain's attention by waving. Telling us that Jo accepts and understands 'I could get Clemens' attention with a wave' isn't going to dislodge this reaction; we think that *if* Jo believes she could get Twain's attention by waving, that's a counter-example to (W'). We *do* take "mismatch cases" to be normal in the relevant sense. A Russellian account of attitude ascriptions is inconsistent with the explanatoriness of common sense psychological explanation.

6

Kripke raises three problems for traditional Fregeanism: (1) its account of the 'modal profile' of sentences containing names is wrong; (2) it mistakenly requires that speakers be able to identify the referents of names they understand; (3) it mispredicts the epistemic properties of certain sentences. Fregeans have given a variety of responses.

One might divorce sense and reference (Recanati 1993): Names have sense, which enters into what's said, but sense doesn't determine reference or truth conditions. This makes what is said a bit like a marriage of a Russellian proposition and a Fregean thought: the latter accounts for epistemic properties; the former determines truth conditions.

One might introduce a novel story about how sense determines reference (Evans 1982): it needn't be in terms of "descriptive fit"; the relation between sense and reference might, for example, be broadly causal. As developed by Evans and McDowell 1984, this involves the claim that senses are "de re": whatever they in fact present they must present.

One might "rigidify" sense (Plantinga 1978; Stanley 1997). If 'actual' is an indexical, then an actual use of 'the actual teacher of Alexander' rigidly picks out Alexander's actual teacher, Aristotle. Perhaps the sense of a name for a speaker is that of the *the actual F*, where *the F* identifies the referent for the speaker.[15] This doesn't deal with the problem about mistaken identification, but one might combine this idea with a novel account of name sense. Perhaps each person who understands 'Aristotle' has a body of information (a "dossier") associated with the name; a user's sense of 'Aristotle' is captured by the description 'the actual source of *this* body of information.' (See Forbes 1989.)

The proposals address Kripke's complaints. Even if successful in this regard, there is a residual problem concerning attitude ascription. As the first Fregean observed, a name's sense can be expected to vary across speakers. I think of Artistotle as Alexander's (actual) teacher, or the source of information in *my* dossier; you think of him as the *Metaphysics'* (actual) author, or the source of information in *your* dossier. We thus express different thoughts with

(H)   Aristotle knew Herodotus.

So what exactly am I saying, when I utter

(Y)   You think that Aristotle knew Herodotus

– that you think the thought I express or the one you express with (H)? The first answer conflicts with the obvious fact that I can correctly report the belief you express with (H) by using (Y). And the second creates logical problems, rendering the argument *you think that S, she thinks that S, so there's something you both think* invalid; ditto for *it's necessary that S, you think that S, so you think something necessary.*[16]

There is a response. (Isn't there always?) One naturally thinks that if the verb 'believes' names a relation to a proposition, it is a fairly "direct" relation which involves having the proposition "in one's epistemic ken." Suppose this direct relation to be called *Belief*. Perhaps 'believes' actually doesn't name Belief, but the relation one bears to p when one bears Belief to a proposition similar to p. If so, then my echo of your 'Aristotle knew Herodotus' in 'You think that Aristotle knew Herodotus' may be true even if my clausal complement names a claim different from the one you expressed: all that is required is that your claim and mine are similar in the relevant respect. If in addition the reference of a clausal complement is determined by the speaker, we have no untoward logical results.

Given that we can usually report what is said by non-context sensitive utterances by echoing them is, the similarity invoked here must vary with the context. One might well wonder how. But no matter what the answer, there is a fatal problem.

Let R be the similarity relation invoked in an utterance of

Lionel wants [it] to be [the case that he is] photographed with Michael

by Jody. Since R is a *similarity* relation, for any p, pRp. So on the present suggestion, if Lionel Wants what Jody expresses with 'he [Lionel] is photographed with Michael,' then Jody's utterance is true. But now consider the following scenario. Room A is full of philosophers – Michael, Alex, Benjie, and so on. Room B is full of people – Lionel, Stephen, Kathrin, etc. – who want to have their pictures taken with a philosopher. Jody and I are orchestrating this: Jody takes a person from Room B, lets him look in Room A and point out who he'd like to be photographed with. I quiz Jody and decide on the basis of what I hear who gets photographed with whom. Jody shows Lionel Room B; Lionel (who has never seen any of these people) decides that he wants to be depicted with *him* (Alex) or *him* (Benji) but not with *him* (Michael). The following conversation ensues

Me: Who does Lionel want to be photographed with, Alex, Benjie, or Michael?
Jody: Alex or Benjie. He doesn't want to be photographed with Michael.

Jody has surely spoken truly here. He has spoken truly *even if* (1) his sense for 'Michael' is *the author of Consciousness and Cognition*, and (2), Lionel has always wanted to be photographed with the author of that book. But (1) and (2) entail that Jody's utterance is false, given the current account.[17]

7

Where does all this leave us?

When I see and recognize Marsha, my thought *Marsha is there* is integrated with the body of my beliefs and desires in a way in which it is not, when I see her without recognizing her and think *that woman is there*. It is natural to assume that something about the first thought, missing from the second, effects this integration. Call this something a *representation*. It is controversial but natural to assume that the mechanism underlying successful explanation of behavior via attitude ascription involves identity of representations across attitudes ascribed. Crudely put, beliefs and desires incline to action only if they share a representation. We are thus led to suppose that attitude ascription, explanatory of behavior as it is, invokes – via reference, quantification, or some more arcane method – the representations of those to whom attitudes are ascribed.

What are representations? Token mental states ('dossiers of information,' 'vivid names,' 'lexical entries')? Aspects of mental organization (functional roles of one sort or another)? Links between thinker and world? Something else? I duck this question, limping along with the functional characterization of section V: representations are aspects of attitudes which may be shared by different token mental states – so the states represent an individual "in the same way" – with believers sensitive to representational identity across states. I assume that representations contribute nothing to truth conditions beyond what is represented. For the unacceptable alternative is to allow the descriptive (mis)-information associated with a representation to contribute to truth conditions.

Thau 2002 denies that representations so conceived have much to do with the attitudes or their ascription.[18] If one is going to invoke representations in an account of the attitudes, he says, they should help explain how sentences with the same Russellian content can have different epistemic properties; they must, that is, aid in a solution to "Frege's Puzzle." If they do, Thau suggests, it is because information is individuated not just in terms of truth conditions, but in terms of representations: To come to accept 'Twain is dead' must be to get information one did not already have in virtue of accepting 'Clemens is dead.'

Thau is suspicious of such a view, for "whenever someone gets new information in virtue of accepting some sentence, he also gains a belief that differs from any of his old beliefs with respect to its" truth-conditional content. (Thau 2002: 127) Indeed, says Thau, "whatever the significance of the new information" one gets, one gets "information that is new with respect to its [truth conditional] content that is equally significant" (2002: 128). Why? Consider Nora, who accepts 'Twain wrote *Huck Finn*' and 'Clemens was a newspaperman,' but doesn't know that *Huck Finn*'s author was a newspaperman. If she accepts 'Twain was Clemens,' she gains new information, that she might express with 'Twain was a newspaper man.' Now the truth-conditional content of this is that Clemens was a newspaperman, something she already knew. But the significance of the new information for Nora is that of the truth-conditionally novel claim that Twain, who wrote *Huck Finn*, was a newspaper man.

Thau's hunch is that if we don't need to appeal to representations to individuate information, we don't need to appeal to them to explain behavior. And if we don't need to then we probably don't. I agree with the two conditionals. But I think Thau is wrong about individuating information.

Nora could have another way to refer to Twain – 'Bob,' say – unconnected with 'Twain' and 'Clemens.' She might, under this name, *already* have beliefs with the truth conditional content of the beliefs she acquires when she comes to accept 'Twain is Clemens.' She might have acquired these beliefs in a way in which it is not at all obvious that they are beliefs about the men she knows as 'Twain' or 'Clemens.' For example, she might have learned that *this novel* (*Huck Finn* is demonstrated) was written by Bob, and that Bob was a newspaperman. If so, then it is *not* news to Nora, at least not in terms of truth conditions, that Twain, who wrote *Huck Finn*, was a newspaperman: she already knew of him that he had both properties. With sufficient stage setting, we can give Nora other beliefs about Bob (e.g., that he has a name that is spelled m-a-r-k-space-t-w-a-i-n) in such a way that she need not see that the beliefs are ones which concern Mark Twain or Sam Clemens.[19]

It seems implausible to think that the new information Nora acquires in

Case I: Nora comes to accept 'Twain is Clemens' and does *not* have a store of disconnected information about Twain labeled 'Bob'

is different from that she acquires in

Case II: Nora comes to accept 'Twain is Clemens' and *does* have a store of disconnected information about Twain labeled 'Bob.'

But if the information in question is the same in both cases, then the new information acquired in Case I cannot be what Thau takes it to be. It cannot, for example, be identified with the Russellian claim that Twain, *Huck Finn's* author, was a newspaperman – for this is something Nora already believes in Case II. We do, after all, have to appeal to representations in individuating information.

8

How are representations involved in the semantics of attitude ascription? We don't overtly refer to or quantify over them. There is no evidence of syntactic but covert, unphoneticized reference or quantification to them. Could there be such reference or quantification simply in virtue of the intentions, dispositions, or other mental states of attitude ascribers? So say John Perry and Mark Crimmins (Crimmins and Perry 1989; Crimmins 1992). They claim that unembedded, 'Twain is younger than Clemens' expresses a Russellian proposition P whose constituents are Twain, the younger than relation, and Twain. But when one embeds the sentence in

(M)   Marsha believes that Twain is younger than Clemens,

one may "tacitly refer" to Marsha's representations of Twain and the relation, somewhat in the way in which one tacitly refers to a location in uttering 'it's snowing,' or to normal conditions when one says 'struck matches light.' (M) then says that Marsha believes P via a state involving the representations referred to. In some cases, one does not refer to particular representations, but to representational kinds, saying that Marsha believes P by being a state involving the relevant kind of representation.[20]

Stephen Schiffer 1992 objects: (1) One means p (or refers to x) only if one intends that one's audience recognize that fact. Thus on the Perry/Crimmins account, (2) when one utters (M) there must be representational kinds or particulars one means to say Marsha deploys in her belief. But (3) on any plausible story, there will be many representations involved in realizing a belief, and countless types of such. None will be consciously intended by the speaker to be recognized as meant or referred to, no one of them will be more salient than the others. So it's implausible that speakers have the intentions referred to in (2).

In thinking about this objection, we do well to consider gradable adjectives, such as 'red,' 'rich,' and 'round.' Almost all think these contextually sensitive, in that their proper interpretation – what property they express – varies across contexts. But that doesn't mean that whenever someone uses such a word there is a single property he intends the word to express, or expects the audience to recognize as meant. Our intentions, when we say 'that's red,' just aren't finely enough honed to determine one resolution of the vagueness of 'red' over another. Neither are our intentions determinate enough to fix a particular vague or fuzzy property. When a speaker calls something 'red,' her intentions determine a vague range of candidate interpretations for the adjective.[21] There is no particular proposition which the speaker means, since there is no particular property which the speaker means to ascribe.

Should we conclude that adjectives meanings are not (aptly represented as) rules mapping speaker intentions to properties? No! We should conclude that we can communicate while only imperfectly exploiting the semantics of our expressions. The point holds of other context sensitive expressions. For example, it is the exception, not the rule, that uses of 'here' pick out a determinate location.

This holds of 'believes' if it involves (tacit) quantification over representations or types thereof. Sometimes a speaker won't mean to restrict quantification over representations in any significant way; in that case something definite will be said. Sometimes the speaker will be focused on some aspect or aspects of the way the ascribee represents the world. Then there will be a range of candidates for the quantifier's restriction. It will usually be clear enough what sort – i.e., what vaguely delineated *range* of sorts – of representations a speaker (presupposes her audience will think she) has in mind. The mere choice of words ('Twain' instead of 'Clemens') can signal this.

Why should anything more need to be true? Whoever thought that it was always determinate, as to what is the restriction in a tacitly restricted quantification, anyway?

Of course, if 'believes' does involve quantification over representations, anyone who understands it must know that in intending to ascribe belief, one is trying to convey something about types of representations. To understand the term is to know (something which makes manifest) that in saying that someone believes so and such, one makes a claim whose explicit representation involves quantifying over representations. A speaker uttering (M) would typically have to intend to make a claim to the effect that there are certain types of representations T and T' such that (1) Marsha believes that Twain is older than Clemens, and (2) she uses instances of these to represent Twain in framing her belief. But there isn't evidence that speakers have any such intentions that I am aware of. As I observed above, there certainly isn't *syntactic* evidence, evidence of the sort which makes it well nigh indisputable that there is something in the logical form of 'Mary wants to go home' which plays the role of the subject of the infinitive phrase 'to go home.'[22] For this reason alone, I am inclined to think that Perry and Crimmins' account is unacceptable.[23]

9

If in attitude ascription we do not advert to representations by referring to or quantifying over them, how do we do it? Elsewhere (Richard 1990, 1993, 1995) I have defended the view that ascribing an attitude is a sort of translation: what makes my use of (M) true is that something which realizes one of Marsha's belief is well translated into my idiom with 'Twain is older than Clemens.' Representations are what realize attitudes; thus, it is they which are translated. It is because we are adequately translating such when we correctly ascribe attitudes that representations are involved in an account of the truth conditions of ascriptions. One can, of course, translate from one idiom to another without referring to or quantifying over the words or sentences of the idiom; if Mullet says to you 'tu es dégelasse,' and you ask me to translate, I do so by simply saying 'he said you disgust him.' In doing so I refer to him and you, but not to his words.

I will sketch how I think this idea ought to be fleshed out. Then I turn to some objections.[24] Suppose I am utter (M) because I hear Marsha say 'Twain is older than Clemens.' Focused on how she expresses what she thinks, my uses of names represent her mental tokenings thereof. For the purposes of ascribing beliefs to Marsha, I have adopted a partial "translation manual", which we might display so:

(T1) Marsha: 'Twain' → 'Twain'
       'Clemens' →'Clemens'

Translation requiring reference to remain the same, the first line of our manual abbreviates: In rendering Marsha's representations, my 'Twain' used as a name of Twain can translate only Marsha's uses of 'Twain' as a name of Twain.[25]

I may use different manuals for different people. If I know the woman in the corner sees Twain, I might use 'he,' referring to Twain, to render her perceptual representations or tokenings of 'that man over there.' I might render her tokenings of both 'Clemens' and 'Twain' indifferently with my uses of 'Twain' or 'Clemens.' (I might do so if, for example, I take her to accept 'Twain is Clemens.') If my task is to speak of Marsha and this other woman, my translation manual contains (T1) and

(T2)   the woman in the corner:
        'he' → 'that man over there,' the woman's perceptions of Twain
        'Clemens' →'Twain,' 'Clemens'
        'Twain' →'Twain,' 'Clemens'

(T2) indicates that in speaking of the woman in the corner, my 'he' (as name of Twain) may represent a representation r iff it is of one of the sorts indicated after the arrow, and that my uses of 'Clemens' or 'Twain' translate (only) her uses of (either of) those names.

My manual says nothing about translating Marsha's 'is older than,' or her uses of 'is cleverer than,' or the woman in the corner's perceptual representations of my nose, or … When no such rules are in effect, we can translate the idiom of another in any way we please – so long as we preserve reference (i.e., Russellian content).

Pretend, for simplicity, that representations are mental tokens of English sentences, so the representation that determines Marhsa's belief, that Twain is older than Clemens, is the English sentence 'Twain is older than Clemens.' Its (relevant) parts are 'Twain,' 'is older than,' and 'Clemens.' This sentence determines a Russellian content which, let us assume, is the tuple < the being older than relation, <Twain, Clemens>>. Focus on the fusion of this Russellian content and the parts of 'Twain is older than Clemens' which contribute the parts of the proposition – i.e., <<'being older than,' the being older than relation>, <<'Twain,' Twain>, <'Clemens,' Clemens>>>.) Call these sorts of things *sentential propositions*, their representation/value pairs *words*.[26]

Both mental representations and English sentences determine sentential propositions. The translation rules introduced above are rules which restrict what words in a believer's sentential propositions the words in a belief ascriber's sentential propositions can translate. Let a translation function be a mapping f from English words (i.e., expression / value pairs) to the words which may occur in X's sentential propositions. When p is a sentential proposition determined by an English sentence and q the result of replacing each word w in p with f(w), say that f(p) = q. Say f is acceptable for X in context c provided it preserves reference (f((<a,b>) = <a,' b'> only when b is b'), and it obeys all the translation rules in effect in c concerning X. An English sentence (properly: the sentential proposition p determined by) S is an acceptable translation in c of a representation R of X's (properly: the sentential proposition q determined by R) provided f(p) = q, for some translation function f acceptable for X in c. And a belief ascription X *believes that* S is true in a context provided (the sentential proposition determined in c by) S is an acceptable translation for X in c of some belief making representation of X's. Analogously, for other propositional attitude verbs.

An example. We are at Barnes and Noble, waiting for Clemens to show up for an autograph session. Everyone knows that Twain is Clemens, though not everyone knows what he looks like. Someone enters, and the person next to us whispers 'That's Clemens!.' People fall silent as they realize the great man has arrived. The woman in the corner, though obviously aware of the man (Twain) who has entered keeps talking. I might turn to you and say

(W1)   That woman doesn't realize that he (I gesture at Twain) is Clemens.

What I say seems true, though it seems it wouldn't be right, in this situation, to say that 'that woman doesn't realize that Twain is Clemens.' We may suppose that the representations which the woman "realizes-true" are

> that man is that man
> Twain is Twain
> Twain is Clemens.

Given (T2), my use of 'he is Clemens' cannot translate any of these, since 'he' only translates the woman's demonstrative references to Clemens, 'Clemens' only translates 'Clemens' and 'Twain.' Thus, 'that woman realizes that he is Clemens' is false, and thus what I say is true. But, of course, I would speak truly, if I were to say 'that woman realizes that Twain is Clemens,' since my use of 'Twain is Clemens' translates her use thereof.

10

Let us discuss some objections.

Soames (2001: 159–203) gives an extensive and helpful critical discussion of this view. According to Soames, the "most revealing ... problem" with the view is that it "misidentifies the basis of our reluctance to substitute coreferential names ... in belief ascriptions"; that basis, says, Soames, is that "the relevant ascriptions would naturally be taken to attribute descriptively different" beliefs. (171) The problem, as Soames sees it, is that the account explains our intuitions that (W1) and

(W2)   That woman doesn't realize that Twain is Clemens

differ in truth value in terms of a difference in how we are to "translate" the "words" of the woman. But the reason we feel that moving from (W1) to (W2) doesn't preserve truth is, Soames thinks, that we take the two ascriptions to come to something like

That woman doesn't realize that that man, the man over there, is Clemens, the author.

That woman doesn't realize that Twain, the author, is Clemens, the author.

Soames is just wrong on one straightforward interpretation of what it is to "attribute descriptively different beliefs." Suppose that my rules for rendering the woman's idiom are as follows:

(T3)   the woman:
'he' → representations which the woman associates with the property of being the man over there
'Twain,' 'Clemens' → representations which the woman associates with the property of being *Huck Finn*'s author.

Then to utter (W1) is to say something true only if the woman fails to represent Twain as a person over there who is an author. (W2) is true if and only if the woman fails to represent Twain (as author) as identical with Twain (as author). Surely the difference here is, *inter alia*, that descriptively different (collections of) beliefs are being ascribed to Smith.

Now, I have not been altogether fair to Soames. I have accurately conveyed Soames' official description of his worry, but not conveyed his real worry.[27] For he concedes that the response just made is possible. But he thinks the way in which the proposal captures the fact that pairs of ascriptions like (W1) and (W2) ascribe attitudes with different descriptive contents is

indirect, complicated, and theoretically contentious. Do ordinary speakers really intend to commit themselves to claims about the languages or internal mental representations used by agents to which they typically ascribe beliefs? Are the descriptive contents of the beliefs that ordinary speakers attribute to agents when assertively uttering ascriptions like ['Hammurabi believed that Phosphorus was not visible in the evening'] really mediated by complicated assumptions (sufficient to account for Pederweski-type cases) about the expressions or mental representations used by agents? (Soames 2001, 170)

The questions get their rhetorical force from their suggestion that on my view speakers *commit* themselves to claims about internal representations, that they make *assumptions* about such – that speakers have a heavy intentional commitment to a theory about representations.

Is it really that contentious that people discussing the ancient beliefs about the heavens mutually presuppose that the ancients had two ways of representing Venus, one associated with one celestial position and translated 'Hesperus,' the other associated with another position and translated 'Phosphorus'? Surely not. Speakers who know enough to use 'Hesperus' and 'Phosphorus' know these things. They know that others know them.[28] Does the idea – that our intuitions about the truth conditions of belief ascriptions track our beliefs about such representations, so that the words in such ascriptions are proxies for the presupposed representations – make attitude ascription an "indirect and complicated" affair? Frankly, the "complexity" here seems about on the order of what is involved in getting from Pierre's utterance of 'you drank domestic wine yesterday' to the content sentence of 'Pierre said that I drank French wine Thursday.' Humdrum interpretation of context sensitive speech obviously involves a "translation" of one idiom into another. Such translation is, of course, largely unconscious, but that doesn't mean that it doesn't occur.

It should be uncontroversial that we routinely make presuppositions about how others represent the world, keeping track of their representations by making our words proxies for them. It is, in my opinion, hardly more controversial that we routinely and correctly expect our audience to be cognizant of this, just as they are cognizant of presuppositions. We expect their recognition of this sort of thing to help them extract information about how the subjects of attitude ascriptions represent the world. These facts have considerable explanatory power for our intuitions about the truth conditions of attitude ascriptions, as well as for intuitions about explanation of behavior. Taking these facts as determining the truth conditions no more makes semantics baroque than, say, building facts about contextual common ground into the semantics of conditionals does.

Sider 1995 and Soames (1995, 2001) raise a more significant worry. A belief ascriber may be confused or ignorant about the identity of an ascribee. Suppose: I don't realize that Superman is Clark Kent; I wish to convey that Superman believes Twain (under a 'Twain' representation) boring, and that Clark believes Twain (under a demonstrative representation) tired. My context might contain the translation rules

(R1)   Superman: 'Twain' → 'Twain'
(R2)   Clark Kent: 'Twain' → 'that man over there.'

For each of

(S)   Superman believes that Twain is boring
(C)   Clark believes that Twain is tired,

to be true, its complement must translate some sentential proposition realizing one of Superman's (= Clark) beliefs. The translation cannot violate any of my context's translation rules. But these rules can't all be followed at once: (R1) mandates that 'Twain' translate Twain when we speak of Superman, the other that 'Twain' translate 'that man over there' when we speak of Superman – i.e., Clark Kent. So neither of (S) and (C) are true. This is so, even if what I am trying to covey – that Superman believes Twain boring, using a 'Twain' representation, and that Clark Kent believes Twain tired using a 'that man over there' representation – is completely accurate. If we are trying to capture the idea that the truth conditional point of attitude ascriptions is to convey just this sort of information, this is a genuine problem.

A translation manual is a contextual parameter determined (in good part) by speaker intentions and dispositions. So are many other contextual parameters, such as reference classes for adjectives such as 'tall.' When speakers are confused, the determination of such parameters may be defective. Suppose in uttering

(N)   Nancy is tall

I intend to compare Nancy Kerrigan's height with that of, as I put it to myself, 'that man's, Grandpa Kerrigan, grandchildren' Suppose the gentleman is her maternal, not her paternal, grandfather. Then there will be two candidates for the reference class for 'tall,' the maternal grandchildren and the paternal ones. There may be no non-arbitrary way to decide between these candidates. Thus, it seems that no reference class is associated with 'tall,' and thus – since the adjective needs such, if (N) has a truth value – my utterance will be without truth value, even if Nancy towers over all the grandchildren, maternal and paternal.

The right thing to say in this case, I think, is that when there are multiple "best candidates" for a required contextual parameter, truth value is determined by looking to see whether the choice among them makes any difference. If I utter (N) and context provides S1, S2, ... , and Sk as "best candidates" for the reference class of 'tall,' then my utterance is: true if true under any choice of S1, ... , Sk as reference class; false, if false under any such choice; truth valueless, otherwise.

The same holds for attitude ascriptions and translation manuals. I think Superman is not Clark. I try to use 'Twain' to represent Superman's tokenings of 'Twain,' while trying to use 'Twain' to represent Clark's tokenings of 'that man.' This can't be done; the context's translation manual is defective. What *can* be done is to correct the context's translation manual in various ways, by removing one or more of the manual's rules for translation until (and only until) we have a manual which can be used. Call such corrections *resolutions* of the manual. When a context's translation manual is defective, an attitude ascription's truth depends upon how it fares under resolutions of that manual: If it would be true under all resolutions, it is true; if false under all resolutions, it is false; otherwise, it is not determinately true or false.

As Soames 2002 observes, this response apparently makes (S) and (C) truth valueless if: I have no opinion whether Superman is Clark; my intentions put rules (R1) and (R2) into play; Superman has no opinion whether Twain is Clemens; he accepts both 'Twain is boring' and 'that man [referring to Twain] is tired,' but not 'Twain is tired' or 'that man is boring.' So it may seem that no headway has been made on the problem: after all, the *relevant* translation rule for (S) is (R1); (R2) is an unfortunate contextual hanger-on. (S)'s truth condition, if anything like a translational account is correct, should be that Superman believes that Twain is boring under a 'Twain' representation.

I think this objection is mistaken: a translational semantics *does* assign such truth conditions to (S) and (C). Here is why.

The contexts of semantics are abstractions from actual and possible "concrete speech situations." In constructing an utterance's context it is often possible to construct it in different ways; sometimes there won't be any (interest independent) reason to prefer one account of "the" context of an utterance to another.

For example: suppose we agree with Lewis (1979), that standards of application (and thus extension) of adjectives shift (within reason) so as to accommodate utterances. If, for example, Tom utters

(F)   France is not hexagonal

and conversants let him get away with it, the standards for something's being hexagonal shift so that his utterance is true.

Suppose Tom utters (F) but only several conversational moves later does Jerry take exception. Tom concedes to Jerry, saying 'You're right – France is hexagonal, and I shouldn't have said it wasn't.' What is the context of Tom's original utterance u of (F), or of his latter utterance, u'? It seems hard to say. Suppose u's context c has standards introduced by u, and u' occurs in context c' with standards reflecting Jerry's refusal to accommodate Tom. Then Tom should not say in c' that he (should not have) said that France was not hexagonal: because of the shift in standards from c to c,' 'France is hexagonal' in c' does not contradict 'France is not hexagonal' as uttered in c. Since what Tom says seems perfectly appropriate, it seems wrong to contextualize his utterances so that his latter remark is obviously false. On the other hand, the idea that u and u' occur in contexts such as c and c' is well motivated, simply because Lewis' account of vague adjectives in such terms is well motivated.

A natural – and I believe correct – conclusion to draw is that Tom's original utterance occurs in at least two contexts, one "local" (determined by what happens in the situation "immediately surrounding" u), the other "global" (determined by the overall history of the conversation). Interpreted locally, as one would naturally interpret it as it is uttered, u is a true utterance; interpreted globally, as one would interpret it after Jerry has had his say, it is not. u,' interpreted globally, is perfectly appropriate and true.

Now, suppose that I utter (S) and latter (C) with focus and dispositions which would bring rules (R1) and (R2) into play. It is not unreasonable to think that, just as Tom's utterance u occurs in two contexts, so these utterances occur in multiple contexts. Each utterance has its own "local" context – (S)'s contains only (R1), if my focus as I speak is "on Superman", (C)'s contains only (R2), if my focus as I speak is "on Clark Kent." And each utterance can be taken globally, taking into account all of the intentions and dispositions operative in my conversation. Interpreting each utterance locally – and such interpretation is natural – a translational semantics makes each utterance true. Thus, a translational semantics *does* validate our intuitions about (natural fleshings out of) the case under discussion: Interpreting (S) and (C) in natural ways assigns them truth values in accord with our intuitions.

Of course, a conjunctive utterance, of say

Superman thinks that Twain is boring and Clark thinks that that man is tired

or of

Superman, but not Clark, thinks that Twain is boring

will most naturally be interpreted against a background involving both (R1) and (R2). (Actually, the first sentence can be interpreted, not unnaturally, as involving a "context switch" somewhere around the 'and.') That a sentence such as the last will, given the facts we have been presupposing about my intentions and Superman's beliefs, come out truth valueless does not seem counter-intuitive.

It will, perhaps, be said that I have jettisoned logical intutions. Consider the argument

> Superman thinks that Twain is boring.
> Clark does not think that Twain is boring.
> So, Superman, but not Clark, thinks that Twain is boring.

Haven't I backed myself into the position of having to say that someone might utter the premises truly, the conclusion falsely? If so, then (absurdly) I must say that this argument is not valid.

The validity of the argument is a matter of the truth of its premises in a context guaranteeing the truth of its conclusion *in that context*. True utterances of *all* three of the argument's parts must occur in different contexts (given that 'Superman' and 'Clark' co-refer), if contexts are individuated in part in terms of the translation manual they provide. It is hardly surprising that uttering an valid argument containing context sensitive expressions may not be the giving of a valid argument, for contextual parameters can shift as one speaks.

There is much more to say about translational accounts of attitude ascription, but there is not space here to say it.[29] I close instead with a general comment.

It is beyond serious debate that information conveyed by attitude ascriptions is gleaned by using background assumptions about how the ascriber represents how the ascribee represents the world. What can be debated is whether this information is truth conditional or is "pragmatically conveyed" by implicature or some other (ill understood) communicative mechanism. But I sometimes feel that framing the debate in these terms (Is it a semantic or ("merely") pragmatic matter, that we convey such information?) is the wrong way to proceed.

When we speak we impart a lot of information and misinformation. There is a good deal of systematicity to the ways in which we do. Even information which by common consensus does not effect truth conditions may be conveyed by means systematic enough to be the subject of a theory. When a problem is as difficult as that of saying what we are doing in ascribing attitudes, perhaps the right approach is not to begin by worrying about which of our communicative strategies are best seen as semantic, which pragmatic. Let us see if we can understand "the total speech act in the total speech situation" performed in speaking of someone's attitudes, and worry about its truth conditions only once we have reached consensus on that.[30]

Notes

1 Some psychological verbs – 'be angry,' for example – take clausal complements as "adjuncts" which (unlike arguments) are syntactically optional. Some verbs which require a clausal complement – 'be necessary,' 'make it the case' – do not ascribe psychological relations or speech acts. Though such verbs have many of the properties of VPAs, they are not the focus of this chapter.

   Other verbs – 'seek,' 'worship,' 'portray' are examples – ascribe intentional states and actions, but differ from VPAs in apparently not accepting clausal complements. (One worships Zeus/a Greek god/money; one doesn't worship that so and such.) It is a matter of contemporary debate whether sentences such as 'I seek the Golden Fleece' involve "covert" clausal complementation. The interested reader can pursue this topic in Parsons 1997, Forbes 2000, Larson 2002, and Richard 2002.

2 The extension of a sentence is its truth value; of a predicate, the set of things it is true of; of a term, what it names or denotes.

3 This needs qualification because (for example) S may say different things in different contexts. For the most part I suppress such qualifications in this essay.

4 There is plenty of reason to be unhappy with the idea that the semantics of attitude ascriptions encapsulates that of natural language semantics. Cappelen and Lepore 1997, Richard 1998, and Cappelen and Lepore 1998 debate as to whether it is reasonable to think that they do.

5 Russell's views about propositional attitudes undergo various changes from 1900 to 1918. Russell 1903 takes them to be relations to singular propositions – propositions, expressed by sentences containing 'genuine names,' which are individuated in terms of individuals and not conceptualizations thereof. Russell 1903 lacks: Russell 1905's account of descriptions, the view of ordinary names as 'truncated descriptions,' and the view that entertaining a proposition requires (a restrictive form of) "acquaintance" with its constituents. By the time of Russell 1912, Russell has abandoned the view that propositional attitudes are relations to propositions (replacing it with the "multiple relation" account of the attitudes); the three elements missing from Russell 1903, however, are firmly in place.

   The view described in the text is what one gets from Russell 1912 if one replaces the multiple relation account with the view that attitudes are relations to propositions.

6 Complicating matters here is the issue of the relation between the Fregean sense of a predicate and the universal which, on Russell's view, is a predicate's contribution to a proposition. Both are 'Platonic' objects, but it is far from clear that they can be identified. The sense of a predicate for Frege is, roughly speaking, a way of thinking of the set of objects to which the predicate applies; the Russellian universal is something which, inter alia, solves the "one over many" problem. I doubt they

should be identified; I am frankly puzzled as to whether identifying them for the purposes of comparing Russell and Frege's semantics is harmless.

7   On these views, someone who "identifies" Einstein as the inventor of the atomic bomb apparently says that the inventor of the atomic bomb worked in Zurich in 1905, which is false, when they utter the true 'Einstein worked in Zurich in 1905.'

Kripke also objects that Frege and Russell's views mis-predict the epistemic properties of pairs of sentences like those displayed above, since even someone who thinks of Aristotle as Alexander's teacher will not know a priori that Aristotle taught Alexander (if just one person did), though they will know a priori that Alexander's teacher taught him (if just one person did).

8   Arguably, this problem is tied to the Millian's individuating the objects of propositional attitudes so coarsely that appeal to them cannot solve Frege's puzzle, as to how sentences differing only by co-referential terms can have differing epistemic properties. This issue is touched upon in sec. 7.

9   See Richard 1983, Salmon 1986, Soames 1987, Berg 1988.

10   Here 'Twain' and 'Clemens' are to be interpreted in a "Millian" way.

11   This is argued for at greater length in Richard 2005.

12   Braun 2000 and 2001, Salmon 1986 and Soames 1987 are examples. Richard 1990 also accepts such a picture. Thau 2002 criticizes it.

13   Think of it this way: all else being equal, the states will be instantiated by mental tokenings of things like 'I want to avoid Sam Clemens' and 'Sam Clemens is in Room 12.'

14   Fodor 1994 gives a somewhat similar response.

15   As Salmon 1981 observes, it is not clear that this gives names the correct modal properties. Names arguably pick out their referents at *every* world, even those at which the referent does not exist (this is needed, given standard treatments of necessity, for true identities to be necessary); standard treatments of descriptions (as quantifiers) would have *the actual F* pick out nothing at worlds at which its actual referent doesn't exist.

Soames 2001 argues that, given that denizens of other worlds have no de re beliefs about the actual world, this view implies that (for example), if Aristotle had not written exactly what he actually wrote, I would not have believed that Aristotle existed.

16   The latter becomes invalid, because in the first premiss S will express my thought, which may differ in modal status from yours.

One could propose that propositional quantification is substitutional. I don't think this is tenable. See Richard 1990, 1997, and the response in Azzouni 2001.

17   The reader may well find this puzzling. How can *x wants it to be true that S* be false, when x wants that very thought (i.e., that S)? The view developed in the last section of this essay is intended, among other things, to explain cases like this one.

18   David Lewis 1990 voices kindred complaints about kindred accounts of representation.

19   In saying this, I assume that Nora can, for example, acquire a belief, of a particular letter, to the effect that it has property P as follows: someone Nora trusts says to her, "Bob often goes by a name which is a four letter first name followed by a five letter surname. Call the letter which starts *his* first name (the speaker points at Marky Mark) 'L1'; L1 is the first letter in the name of Bob of which I speak. Call the letter which starts *her* first name (the speaker points at Annie Sprinkle) 'L2'; L2 is the second letter

in the name of Bob of which I speak … " If someone goes through all this with Nora and she has a very good memory, she will believe, of Twain and the letters

m,a,r,k,space,t,w,a,i,n

that the former has a name which the latter, in that order spell.

Unless we are going to say that one can have beliefs, of people, letters, and the like, only under certain modes of presentation, I do not see how one can avoid granting the points necessary for this argument.

20 In particular, one often quantifies over what Crimmins calls "normal representations." Crimmins 1992 develops these ideas in considerable detail, to which the interested reader is referred. I have simplified his view in various ways.

21 This idea informs a great deal of work on vagueness – an early development of it is in Lewis 1979.

22 For such evidence see, for example, Radford 1997, section 4.2.

23 There are other reasons to be nervous about the account. For example, the view makes invalid arguments such as *Marsha believes whatever Patty does, Patty believes that Twain is dead, so Marsha believes that Twain is dead* are valid. See Richard 1993, 1997.

24 This section borrows from Richard 1995. It incorporates improvements in the position sketched there due to Soames 1995 and 2001.

25 Think of a word, used with a particular semantic value, as a pairing of a linguistic item and that semantic value: 'Twain,' used as a name of Twain, is thought of as <'Twain,' Twain>. The form of the rules above is this: In speaking of X, translate <word, value> only via representations having property P. (In the first rule in (T1), P is something like: being associated by Marsha with <'Twain,' Twain>.) The rules in a translation manual can then be represented as triples <X, <w,v>, P>, which tell us that in rendering X, the word w (with value v) translates only representations with P.

This way of putting things is an improvement on how I put them in Richard 1990, where instead of a property P of representations, the third element of a translation rule was a set of representations. (For one thing, this yields a better account of the modal profile of attitude ascriptions.) The improvement is due to Soames 2001, Chapter 7. Soames also suggests – correctly – that for a fully general account, we should replace the first member of such trios with a property, so that rules will look something like <being identical with Marsha, <'Twain,' Twain>, being expressed by Marsha with <'Twain,' Twain>>, <being an ordinary citizen of Metropolis, <'Clark Kent,' Clark Kent>, representing Clark Kent as a mild mannered reporter>.

26 This is a terminological change from Richard 1990 (where these things were called Russellian annotated matrices, and what I am here calling words were called annotations) and Richard 1995 (where sentential propositions were called articulated propositions).

27 Indeed, the response is suggested by Soames, who notes that the way in which I originally formulated the view made it liable to such an objection, and offered the above response.

In a difficult passage, Soames worries (Soames 2001: 169) that the possibility of cases like that in Kripke 1979 of Peter (who mistakenly takes different tokens of 'Pederewski' to refer to different people) makes even Soames' suggested emendation inadequate. So far as I understand the passage, Soames' objection is that in such a case, ascriptions of the forms *X believes that Fa* and *X believes that Ga* might both be true (in virtue of there being two representations r and r' that *a* can translate) while *X believes that a is F and G* is not true (since beliefs which r and r' realize are not integrated in the appropriate way). Soames claims that this would mean that the proposal does not capture descriptive belief content.

If I understand the worry – and I fear I do not completely understand it – the response is to observe, as is observed in 4.3 of Richard 1990, that in normal conversation we use one of our words to translate one and only one word of another person. (In the jargon of Richard 1990, we employ a single correlation, or translation, function in interpreting several attitude ascriptions.)

28 Surely Soames must agree. For Soames holds that 'The ancients didn't realize that Hesperus is Phosphorus' typically conveys something like: the ancients didn't realize that Hesperus, which appeared in such and such a position, wasn't Phosphorus, which appeared in so and so a position. And the mechanism he takes to underlie this requires the sort of presuppositions just mentioned.

29 I have not responded here to all of the objections which Soames (and others) have lodged to translational accounts of attitude ascription; more is found in Richard, 2005.

30 The echo here is of Austin 1962: "The total speech act in the total speech situation is the *only actual* phenomenon which, in the last resort, we are engaged in elucidating" (148).

A brief essay cannot do justice to the rich and varied recent literature on propositional attitude ascription, and here I have been forced to ignore much more than I attended to. In particular, I have not discussed accounts which in one way or another seek to account for our intuitions about attitudes or their ascription without invoking modes or presentation or mental representations.

Two such accounts ought at least be mentioned. Robert Stalnaker has developed an interesting account of attitude ascription on which propositions are identified with sets of possible worlds. A well known problem for such accounts is that they seem to identify distinct propositions. (For example, if the proposition expressed by a sentence is the set of worlds in which it is true, then all necessarily true sentences express the same proposition.) Stalnaker suggests that in many cases, an ascription *A believes that S* ascribes belief, not in the proposition which "straightforward semantic rules" assign to (unembedded uses of S), but to what Stalnaker calls the *diagonal proposition* determined by S. Roughly, this is the set of those worlds w such that what S says *as used in w* is true in w. Stalnaker 1999 provides an introduction to this idea.

Recently, Mark Crimmins has suggested that attitude ascription involves a kind of pretense. *Very* roughly, in uttering *A believes that S*, one pretends that the world is as A thinks it is; one thereby conveys facts about the nature of A's beliefs. (Compare utterances in games of pretend: If I say 'the Indians are attacking' while playing cowboys and Indians, I pretend that we are cowboys fighting Indians and thereby convey that certain of the players are running towards us.) This idea is developed in Crimmins 1998. Some critical discussion of it can be found in Richard 2000 and Stanley 2001.

Chapter 11

Conditionals

Frank Jackson

Examples of conditionals are: 'If it rains, then the match will be canceled,' 'If Oswald did not shoot Kennedy, then someone else did,' and 'If Carter had been re-elected, the pundits would have been surprised.' It is no straightforward matter to give a precise delineation of the class of conditional sentences. Conditionals do not have to contain the word 'if.' 'No ticket, no start' is a conditional (provided it is thought of as directed to some particular person, not as a covert *universal* saying that anyone without a union ticket will not be allowed to start). Nevertheless, we all have a reasonable intuitive grasp of the intended class of sentences, and that will suffice for our purposes here.

Conditionals are typically formed by applying a dyadic sentential operator or connective. 'If Mary went to the party, it was a success' is the result of applying 'if—, (then)—' to the two sentences 'Mary went to the party' and 'It was a success.' The sentence that goes into the first place is the antecedent, and the one that goes into the second place is the consequent of the conditional. Other examples of dyadic sentential operators are '—or—' which operates on two sentences to form their *disjunction*, the component sentences being known as disjuncts; and '—and—' which operates on two sentences to form their *conjunction*, the component sentences being known as conjuncts. We will also have occasion to refer to the monadic sentential operator 'It is not the case that—' which operates on a sentence to form its *negation*. We will follow (reasonably) common practice and use '&' for 'and,' 'v' for 'or,' '~' for 'not,' and '→' for 'if, then.'

We will be concerned with various theories of the conditional and the interconnections between these theories and valid inference patterns for conditionals.

The Equivalence Theory

It is widely agreed that '~,' '&,' and 'v' are *truth functions*: the truth value of a compound sentence formed using them is fully determined by the truth value or values of the component sentences. (Sometimes this is made a matter of definition for the symbols, and then the wide but not universal agreement is that the meanings of the natural language operators are captured, near enough, by the relevant symbols.) This is reflected in the following simple rules for these operators: (A & B) is true if and only (iff) A is true and B is true; (A v B) is true iff at least one of A and B is true; and ~A is true iff A is false. The simplest and oldest theory of the conditional holds that '→' likewise is a truth function. For some history, see Sanford (1989) and Mackie (1973).

If '→' is a truth function, which truth function is it? Logical intuitions give us the answer.

First, the inference pattern

A
A → B
B

known as *modus ponens*, is intuitively valid. But then whenever A is true and B is false, A → B is false. Otherwise it would be possible to have the premises of an instance of modus ponens true together when the conclusion is false.

Secondly, (A → A) is a logical truth. It follows that some conditionals whose antecedents and consequents have the same truth value (are both true or both false) must be true. But if '→' is a truth function, what is true for some cases where the antecedent and consequent have the same truth value, is true for all such cases; hence, if '→' is a truth function, then whenever A and B are alike in truth value, (A → B) is true.

Finally, [(A & B) → A] is a logical truth. But there are substitution instances of it where A is true and B is false, and so (A & B) is false. But this tells us that some conditionals with a false antecedent and a true consequent are true, and so that if '→' is a truth function, then whenever A is false and B is true, (A → B) is true.

This covers all combinations of truth values for A and B – both true, both false, A true and B false, and A false and B true – and, on the assumption that the truth value of a conditional is a truth function of the truth values of its antecedent and consequent, gives the truth value of (A → B) for each. The result can be summarized in the rule: (A → B) is true except when A is true and B is false. Given the rules for '~,' '&,' and 'v' stated above, this amounts to treating (A → B) as equivalent to each of: (~A v B), [~A v (A & B)], and ~(A & ~B). This makes sense if we translate back into English. For instance, the sentence 'If it rains, then the match will be canceled' does seem equivalent to the sentence 'Either it will not rain, or it will and the match will be cancelled.'

It is common to use 'A ⊃ B' – read as 'A hook B' or as 'A materially implies B,' and known as the *material conditional* – as a definitional abbreviation of (~A v B), so the simplest theory of the conditional can be expressed as the theory that (A → B) is equivalent to (A ⊃ B). We will call this theory the equivalence theory.

The Paradoxes of Material Implication

If (A → B) is equivalent to the material conditional, the following two inference patterns, known as the paradoxes of material implication, are valid.

$$\frac{\sim A}{(A \rightarrow B)}$$

$$\frac{B}{(A \rightarrow B)}$$

This follows from the fact that a material implication is true whenever its antecedent is false, and whenever its consequent is true. The paradoxes are not so much paradoxes of material implication but paradoxical consequences of the view that the ordinary, natural language conditional is equivalent to the material conditional, for it is counter-intuitive that the falsity of 'Mary went to the party' is logically sufficient for the truth of 'If Mary went to the party, it was a success,' particularly because it would then also be sufficient for the truth of 'If Mary went to the party, it was *not* a success.' It is also counter-intuitive that the truth of 'The party was a success' is sufficient for the truth of 'If Mary went to the party, it was a success.'

The Possible Worlds Theory

It is widely agreed that the equivalence theory is right to this extent: a conditional with a true antecedent and a false consequent is false, and hence that a necessary condition for the truth of (A → B) is the truth of (A ⊃ B). The moral typically drawn from the paradoxes of material implication is that more than the truth of (A ⊃ B) is required for the truth of (A → B).

One addition sometimes suggested is that A be somehow relevant to B. However, sometimes we use conditionals to express a *lack* of relevance between A and B. One who says 'If Fred works he will fail, and if Fred does not work he will fail' is saying, sadly, that for Fred working is irrelevant to whether or not he passes. Similarly, it would not be plausible to require that A support B. Ozzie Bob's being in the UK may support his being in Wales in the sense of raising its chance of being true, but it may still be true that if he is in the UK, he is not in Wales.

A more promising approach, due to Stalnaker (1968) and Lewis (1973), draws on the resources of possible worlds semantics. It starts from the appealing idea that when we reflect on a conditional, we add 'in the imagination' the antecedent to the way things actually are, keeping everything else as much like the way they actually are as is possible consistent with the addition, and then ask whether in that case the consequent is true. Why, for instance, do we think that 'If there is an earthquake in five minutes time, we will have something to worry about' is true? Because we think that adding an earthquake in five minutes and keeping things otherwise as much as possible like the way they actually are – earthquakes are kept as nasty as they actually are, houses and bones as vulnerable as they actually are, what things we need to worry about the way they actually are, and so on – gives a situation, a possible, non-actual (we hope) situation, in which we have something to worry about.

We can make the idea more precise and amenable to evaluation by putting it in terms of truth conditions of the following general shape

(A → B) is true (is true at the actual world) iff the closest A-world (the possible world most like the actual world at which A is true) is a B-world.

This preserves the feature that a necessary condition for the truth of (A → B) is the truth of (A ⊃ B). For suppose that A is true and B is false at the actual world. The actual world is maximally similar to itself, so the closest A-world would not in that case be a B-world. It also respects the putative lesson of the paradoxes of material implication that the truth of (A ⊃ B) is not sufficient for the truth of (A → B). For suppose, to illustrate, that A is false. Then (A ⊃ B) is true, but nothing is implied one way or the other about whether the world most like the actual world except that A is true is a B-world or is a not-B-world.

Historically, the possible worlds theory of conditionals was preceded by a meta-linguistic view according to which (A → B) is true iff there is an X that meets some specified condition and is such that (A & X) entails B, or, equivalently, B is deducible from (A & X). See, e. g., Goodman (1947). The major issue for this view is getting the specified condition right. With the benefit of hindsight, we can see the meta-linguistic approach as a natural precursor of the possible worlds approach. (A & X) entails B iff every possible world where (A & X) is true is one where B is true. This in turn is true iff, for every world where A is true, any world where X is true is a world where B is true. So the problem of specifying the condition that X must meet parallels the problem in the possible worlds approach of deciding which worlds where A is true should be counted as closest, that is, as the worlds that need to be worlds where B is true in order for (A → B) to be true.

A major strength of the possible worlds account are the answers it delivers concerning the validity of inferences involving conditionals: it delivers the intuitively right answers – as we will now observe.

Some Famous Inference Patterns

Modus ponens

A
A → B
―――
B

is validated by the possible worlds account. If A is true then the closest A-world is the actual world, and so the closest A-world is a B-world just if the actual world is a B-world, that is, just if the conclusion, B, is true.

Modus tollens

~B

A → B
_____
~A

is validated by the possible worlds account. If B is false and the closest A-world is a B-world, then the closest A-world is not the actual world. But then the actual world is not an A-world, and so A is false.

Despite the appeal of modus ponens and modus tollens, they have occasionally been challenged. There are apparent counter-examples to modus ponens involving conditionals whose consequents are themselves conditionals. (A similar case can be mounted against modus tollens.)

Imagine, following McGee (1985), that we are talking before the presidential election in which the Republican challenger Reagan beat the Democrat incumbent Carter, as expected, and there was a maverick Republican candidate, Anderson, who had very little chance of winning. And consider the following (putative) instance of modus ponens.

A Republican will win.

If a Republican wins, then if Reagan does not win, Anderson will.
_____

If Reagan does not win, Anderson will.

The plausible claim is that in the case as described, the two premises are true but the conclusion is false. The conclusion is false because the right thing to say before hand is that if Reagan does not win, Carter and not Anderson will.

The best reply, in my view, to this argument points out that we sometimes need to do a certain amount of massaging of surface linguistic structure in order to display logical form. For instance, if I ask, Who knows where the body is buried? and am told that either Jones or Robinson could tell me, then despite the presence of the 'or,' what I am being told is that both Jones *and* Robinson could tell me. Now it is plausible that the second premise of the putative counter-example should strictly be written as 'If a Republican wins and Reagan does not win, then Anderson will.' The sentence whose surface form is [A → (B → C)] has logical form [(A & B) → C]. Hence, the alleged counter-example is not really an instance of modus ponens.

Strengthening the antecedent is the inference pattern

$$\frac{A \rightarrow B}{(A \;\&\; C) \;\rightarrow\; B}$$

If the equivalence thesis is true, Strengthening the antecedent is valid. For then $(A \rightarrow B)$ is true just if $(A \supset B)$ is true, that is, if it is not the case that A is true and B is false. But then it is not the case that A is true and B is false and, in addition, C is true. But that is just the case in which $[(A \;\&\; C) \supset B]$ is true. There are, however, intuitive counter-examples to strengthening the antecedent.

Take any conditional you confidently judge to be true, and yet falls short of being logically true. Its truth depends on contingent features of the situation. An example might be 'If I jump from the top of the Empire State Building, I will fall to my death.' There will always be *something* that added to the antecedent seems to turn the conditional into a false one, namely, something which (1) is known false, and (2) whose falsity is crucial to the truth of the original conditional. For instance, part of the reason that 'If I jump from the top of the Empire State Building, I will fall to my death' is true is that it is *false* that I am wearing an extremely effective, quick opening parachute. But then, surely, 'If I jump from the top of the Empire State Building wearing an extremely effective, quick opening parachute, I will fall to my death' is false. We have, that is, the following counter-example to strengthening the antecedent

If jump from the top of the Empire State Building, I will fall to my death.
If I jump from the top of the Empire State Building wearing an extremely effective, quick opening parachute, I will fall to my death.

The possible worlds theory has a simple explanation of why strengthening the antecedent fails. $(A \rightarrow B)$ is true on the theory iff the closest A-world is a B-world – that is, iff the closest A-world is an $(A \;\&\; B)$-world. This is consistent both with this world being an $(A \;\&\; B \;\&\; {\sim}C)$-world and with its being an $(A \;\&\; B \;\&\; C)$-world. But *only* in the latter case is the closest $(A \;\&\; B)$-world an $(A \;\&\; B \;\&\; C)$-world – that is, only in the latter case is $[(A \;\&\; B) \rightarrow C]$ true on the theory.

Hypothetical syllogism (sometimes known as *transitivity*) is the following inference pattern

$$\frac{\begin{array}{l} A \rightarrow B \\ B \rightarrow C \end{array}}{A \rightarrow C.}$$

It is intuitively appealing stated in symbols, and on the equivalence thesis it is valid. However, we can show that if hypothetical syllogism is valid, then so is strengthening the antecedent. Hence, the strong case against the latter is equally a strong case against the former. Consider the following instance of hypothetical syllogism

$$(A \& C) \rightarrow A$$
$$A \rightarrow B$$
$$(A \& C) \rightarrow B.$$

If hypothetical syllogism is valid, then necessarily whenever both premises are true, so is the conclusion. But the first premise is necessarily true, so necessarily whenever the second premise is true, both premises are. Hence, if hypothetical syllogism is valid, necessarily whenever the second premise is true, so is the conclusion. But the passage from the second premise to the conclusion precisely is strengthening the antecedent.

Here, to add to the just given case against hypothetical syllogism, is a direct counter-example. Suppose that it may rain but will not rain much, that is to say, if it rains, it is not the case that it will rain a lot. It is plausible that the following inference has true premises and a false conclusion.

> If it rains a lot, it will rain
> If it rains, it is not the case that it will rain a lot
> If it rains a lot, it is not the case that it will rain a lot.

Our final example is *contraposition*, the inference pattern

$$A \rightarrow B$$
$$\sim B \rightarrow \sim A$$

It is like strengthening the antecedent and hypothetical syllogism in being valid on the equivalence theory, invalid on the possible worlds theory, and intuitively invalid, i.e., there are intuitively appealing counter-examples to it. Here is a counter-example to contraposition, drawing on the kind of situation described when we gave the counter-example to hypothetical syllogism, and assuming the equivalence of $\sim\sim A$ with A.

> If it rains, it is not the case that will rain a lot
> If it rains a lot, it is not the case that it will rain

It is easy to explain why hypothetical syllogism and contraposition fail on the possible worlds theory. This is left as an exercise, or see Lewis (1973).

The No-truth Theory

The possible worlds theory is one response to the difficulties of the equivalence theory of conditionals. A different response is the no-truth theory. According to the no-truth theory, conditionals have justified assertion or acceptability conditions but not truth conditions. 'If I jump from the Empire State Building, I will fall to my death' is not strictly speaking true but is instead highly acceptable. One motivation for the theory is the view (1) that only assertions have truth values because only assertions make a claim about how things are and so get to be true just if how things are corresponds to how they are claimed to be, combined with the view (2) that to utter a conditional is not to make an assertion but rather to make a conditional assertion. We do not, strictly speaking, assert conditionals but rather assert their consequents *under* the condition given by their antecedents. Another motivation is the idea that conditionals are really condensed arguments (Mackie 1973). To assert $(A \rightarrow B)$ is to offer an argument from A to B via contextually given additional premises, rather than making a statement concerning how things are. A similar view sees the conditional as providing an 'inference ticket' to go from its antecedent to its consequent (Ryle 1950).

On the no-truth theory, there is no question of inference patterns like modus ponens and modus tollens being necessarily truth preserving. We need a different way of looking at questions of validity of inference involving conditionals. This was provided by Adams (1975).

What makes 'If I jump from the Empire State Building, then I will fall to my death' highly acceptable or assertable? Adams's plausible answer is the very high probability of falling to my death given that I jump, in the sense that the probability that I jump and die is a high fraction of the probability that I jump. According to Adams, the justified assertability of conditionals is governed by

$$\text{(Adams) Ass}(A \rightarrow B) = \Pr(B/A) = \Pr(A\&B)/\Pr(A)$$

where $\Pr(B/A)$ is read 'the conditional probability of B given A.' (This idea can be found in Ramsey 1931, but that paper also has suggestions akin to the metalinguistic and possible worlds theories.)

Validity of inference on the no-truth theory is now (what follows is a rough sketch) analyzed in terms of assertability preservation. We set the assertability of a non-conditional premise or conclusion identical to its (unconditional) probability, and the assertability of a conditional premise or conclusion equal to the conditional probability of its consequent given its antecedent. An inference is ass-valid iff making the assertability of each premise sufficiently close to one makes the assertability of its conclusion as close to one as we please.

If we use this test for validity, we get the following results applied to the inference patterns discussed earlier: modus ponens and modus tollens come out valid, and strengthening the antecedent, hypothetical syllogism, contraposition and the paradoxes of material implication come out invalid. We get, that is, the intuitively plausible answers when judged against examples. The no-truth theory and the possible worlds theory thus share this notable advantage over the equivalence theory.

The equation of the assertability of a conditional with the probability of its consequent given its antecedent leads to an influential argument for a no-truth theory. If conditionals have truth values, then how assertable or acceptable they are should plausibly be given by how likely they are to be true, and so if (Adams) is right, it should be the case that $Pr(A \rightarrow B) = Pr(B/A)$. However, conditional probabilities are not the probability *of* anything. They are *quotients* of probabilities: $Pr(B/A) = Pr(A \& B)/Pr(A)$. We can put the essential point in terms of the possible worlds way of thinking of probability. The probability of A is the sum of the probabilities of all the A-worlds; likewise, for B, (A & B), etc. The probability of B given A is the fraction of the probability of the A-worlds that goes to worlds where B is true, and that in turn is the sum of the probabilities of all the (A & B)-worlds divided by the sum of the probabilities of all the A-worlds.

It might be suggested that a quotient of probabilities is nevertheless the probability of something: perhaps the meaning of a conditional is such that for a suitably wide range of probability functions: $Pr(A \rightarrow B) = Pr(A \& B)/Pr(A)$. There are, however, a number of demonstrations that this assumption leads to unacceptable results. Here is a simple version of the best known (and first) proof due to Lewis (1976, expanded in 1986).

Suppose that the equality holds for all probability functions Pr and all A and B. Now $Pr(A \rightarrow B) = Pr(A \rightarrow B/B).Pr(B) + Pr(A \rightarrow B/\sim B).Pr(\sim B)$, by expansion by cases. But if $Pr(A \rightarrow B) = Pr(B/A)$ holds for all Pr, it holds for $Pr(-/B)$ and $Pr(-/\sim B)$, as the class of probability functions is closed under conditionalization. Hence, we have $Pr(A \rightarrow B) = Pr(B/A \& B).Pr(B) + Pr(B/A \& \sim B).Pr(\sim B) = 1.Pr(B) + 0.Pr(\sim B) = Pr(B)$. But then, by the claim under discussion, $Pr(B) = Pr(B/A)$. This is a *reductio*, for in general the probability of B is not independent of that of A.

Indicative versus Subjunctive Conditionals

If the possible worlds theory and the no-truth theory come out roughly equal in terms of validating and invalidating the inferences they ought to validate and invalidate, how do we choose between them? One answer is that we do not have to choose. The two theories should be seen as directed towards different kinds of conditionals (see e.g. Gibbard 1981). Conditionals like 'If it rained, the match was canceled' are sometimes called indicative conditionals. The contrast is with subjunctive conditionals like 'If it had rained then the match would have been canceled.' (Adams) is only plausible for indicative conditionals. A famous example to illustrate this is the subjunctive

If Oswald had not shot Kennedy, someone else would have.

If we assume general agreement with the Warren Commission, this subjunctive conditional is highly unassertable. But the conditional probability of someone other than Oswald shooting Kennedy given that Oswald did not is very high indeed, and the corresponding indicative conditional

If Oswald did not shoot Kennedy, someone else did

is highly assertable.

Thus, one major reason for holding a no-truth theory – namely, the appeal of (Adams) – only applies to indicative conditionals.

Moreover, there is an independent reason for giving truth conditions to subjunctive conditionals. Subjunctive conditionals are intimately connected with matters to do with dispositional properties and causation. A glass may be fragile even though its fragility is never manifested. Indeed those who own valuable fragile glasses hope that their fragility will never be manifested. What makes it true that a glass that is never dropped is fragile? The fact that, roughly, its nature is such that if it had been dropped it would have broken. But this means that if subjunctive conditionals cannot be true, we cannot say that it is true that a glass that is never dropped is fragile. Again, we frequently distinguish flukey successions from causal ones in terms of the obtaining or failing to obtain of subjunctive conditionals, that is, in terms of whether or not they are true. Thus, we address a question like, Did Fred's getting caught in a storm cause him to get a cold? by asking, Would Fred have got the cold if he had not been caught in the storm?

In consequence, a position some find attractive is that the possible worlds theory applies to subjunctive conditionals, whereas the no-truth theory applies to indicative conditionals.

However, others worry about offering very different accounts of indicative and subjunctive conditionals. They distrust assigning to a somewhat recondite grammatical difference a very substantial semantical difference. They typically prefer a possible worlds account for both kinds of conditionals, pointing out that it makes sense that the similarity metric by which closeness of possible worlds is settled should vary with context and mood, and explain the manifest difference between 'If Oswald had not shot Kennedy, someone else would have' and 'If Oswald did not shoot Kennedy, someone else did' in terms of a difference in the metric operative in the two cases.

However, there is a reason not to apply the possible worlds theory to indicative conditionals (Jackson 1981). The possible worlds theory in effect construes a conditional as being potentially about possible worlds other than the actual world. But whereas we can say in the subjunctive that had Oswald not shot Kennedy, then things would be very different from the way they actually are in American politics, it is nonsense to say in the indicative that if Oswald did not shoot Kennedy, things are very different from the way they actually are in American politics.

The Supplemented Equivalence Theory

We have seen the attractions of the no-truth theory for indicative conditionals but it faces problems. One is that it flies in the face of the strong intuition that indicative conditionals with true antecedents and false consequents are false. This objection can perhaps be blunted by insisting that the pre-analytic data is really that an indicative conditional with a known true antecedent and a known false consequent is about as unassertable as they come. A second problem is that it cannot offer the obvious account of the notion of (justified) assertability or acceptability that figures so centrally in it, namely, that it is tied to the likelihood of being true. It is, therefore, worth noting a variety of equivalence theory that explains (Adams) in terms of the view that indicative conditionals have the truth conditions of material conditionals.

The supplemented equivalence theory (Jackson 1979) argues that there is a convention governing the assertion of $(A \rightarrow B)$ to the effect that it should only be asserted when it would be right to infer B on learning A. This convention is like that governing the use of 'but.' 'A but B' has the same truth conditions as 'A and B,' but the use of former conventionally *implicates*, in the terminology of Grice (1989), a contrast. Likewise, runs the suggestion, $(A \rightarrow B)$ has the same truth conditions as $(A \supset B)$ but its use carries the implicature that the reasons for $(A \supset B)$ are such that it would be right, on learning A, to infer B (that is, to *use* modus ponens). Now that will be the case just if $(A \supset B)$'s probability would not be unduly diminished on learning that A is true – otherwise it would not *then* be available as a probably true premise to combine with A on the way to inferring B. It follows that it will be right to assert $(A \rightarrow B)$ to the extent that a) $(A \supset B)$ is probable, and b) $(A \supset B)$ is probable given A. But $Pr(A \supset B/A) = Pr(B/A)$, and $Pr(A \supset B) \geq Pr(B/A)$. Therefore, this two-fold condition is satisfied to the extent that $Pr(B/A)$ is high. The supplemented equivalence theory therefore explains (Adams) in the context of an account of indicative conditionals that gives them the truth conditions of hook.

This view is akin to an earlier view entertained in Grice (1989) (see also Lewis 1976) which gave indicative conditionals the same truth conditions as hook but sought to explain away the paradoxes of material implication in terms of violations of conversational propriety or implicature instead of the conventional implicature of the supplemented theory: the claim is that ' ~A, therefore $(A \rightarrow B)$' is valid precisely because arrow is hook but seems 'crook' because when you know ~A, you should come out and assert it rather than the pointlessly weaker $(A \rightarrow B)$. Among the difficulties for this suggestion is the fact that supporters of the Warren Commission *do* assert 'If Oswald did not shoot Kennedy, someone else did' despite being sure that it has false antecedent. The supplemented equivalence theory explains this in terms of the fact that the probability that someone else shot Kennedy given that Oswald did not is very high independently of the very low probability, according to Warrenites, of 'Oswald did not shoot Kennedy.'

Conditionals with Compound Constituents

It is hard enough to give a plausible account of conditionals with relatively simple antecedents and consequents. Indeed, it is a matter of note that a construction we all use with relative ease has proved so recalcitrant to theory. Matters do not get easier when we look at conditionals with compound components, including cases where one or more are themselves conditionals.

Some examples seem to be sentences whose grammatical form should be distinguished from their logical form. 'If Tom had voted for Dick or for Harry, then Fred would not have won' would appear to say that if Tom had voted for Dick, then Fred would not have won, and that if Tom had voted for Harry, then Fred would not have won. What is syntactically a narrow scope 'or' seems logically to be a wide scope 'and.'

Subjunctive conditionals within the scope of conditionals, both subjunctive and indicative, are reasonably common. Examples are: 'If it had rained, then I would have got wet had I gone to the game,' 'If Fred would have died had he not agreed to the operation, then he did the right thing in agreeing to the operation,' and 'If Fred would have died had he not agreed to the operation, then he would have caused his family great grief had he not agreed to the operation.'

The issue of indicative conditionals within the scope of conditionals is more difficult. An example like 'If the match was canceled if it rained, then the game was cricket' seems to make sense inasmuch as it is construed as 'If the match would have been cancelled had it rained, then the game was cricket'; i.e. with the indicative conditional within the scope of the conditional replaced by a subjunctive one. And we noted above that an example like 'If a Republican wins, then if Reagan does not win, Anderson will' is plausibly construed as 'If a Republican wins and Reagan does not win, Anderson will.' Incidentally, the situation is different for the corresponding subjunctive conditional. Suppose that Reagan did not win and we are having a postmortem. We would no doubt agree that if a Republican other than Reagan had won, it would have been Anderson. But we might well doubt that if a Republican had won, then if Reagan had not, it would have been Anderson, arguing that as the only way a Republican could have won would have been by Reagan winning, the right thing to say is that if a Republican had won, then if Reagan had not, a Republican would not have won.

Further Reading

Adams, Ernest (1975). *The logic of conditionals*. Dordrecht: Reidel. This is an extended defense of a no-truth theory of conditionals, focussed especially but not exclusively on indicative conditionals. It is noteworthy for its account of validity tailored for sentences that may or may not have truth values and exploiting the idea that the assertability of conditionals goes by the probability of their consequents given their antecedents.

Edgington, Dorothy (1995). On conditionals. *Mind* 104, 235–329. This is a good, detailed account of the state of play in the debate as at 1995 as well as being a contribution to the philosophy of conditionals in its own right

Grice, H.P. (1989). *Studies in the way of words*, Cambridge: Harvard University Press. This book contains a full scale treatment, building on earlier work of his, of the notion of implicature and its relevance to the theory of conditionals (and much else besides).

Harper, W.L., Stalnaker, R., and Pearce, C.T. (eds.) (1981). *Ifs*. Dordrecht: Reidel. This is a useful collection of papers on conditionals with a helpful introduction.

Jackson, Frank (1987). *Conditionals*. Oxford: Basil Blackwell. This book expounds and defends the supplemented equivalence theory with more discussion of surrounding issues than in Jackson (1979).

Jackson, Frank (ed.). (1991). *Conditionals*. Oxford: Oxford University Press. This is a useful collection of papers on conditionals covering the main theories with a (I trust) helpful introduction.

Lewis, David (1973). *Counterfactuals*. Oxford: Basil Blackwell. This is an exposition and defense of the possible worlds theory for subjunctive conditionals including a discussion of the virtues of various versions of the possible worlds theory. Lewis holds that indicative conditionals have the truth conditions of material conditionals.

Lewis, David (1976). Probabilities of conditionals and conditional probabilities. *Philosophical Review*, 85, 297–315.

Lewis, David (1986). Probabilities of conditionals and conditional probabilities II. *Philosophical Review*, 95, 581–9. This paper and the preceding one by Lewis give in detail the proof that $Pr(A \rightarrow B) = Pr(B/A)$ cannot hold with sufficient generality to explain (Adams).

Mackie, J.L. (1973). *Truth, probability and paradox*. Oxford: Clarendon Press. This book contains a long section which discusses many views of conditionals, coming down on the side of a version of a no truth view which sees conditionals as a kind of elliptical argument or assertion under a supposition.

Stalnaker, Robert (1968). A theory of conditionals. In Studies in Logical Theory, *American Philosophical Quarterly Monograph*, 2. Oxford: Basil Blackwell. This paper defends a possible worlds theory differing from Lewis's in a number of interesting ways; also the theory, unlike Lewis's version, is intended to apply to both indicative and subjunctive conditionals.

Chapter 12

Vagueness

Stephen Schiffer

I The Sorites Paradox

There is a philosophical problem of vagueness because of various conceptual puzzles to which vagueness gives rise. The most famous of these puzzles is the *sorites paradox*, and it very quickly leads to all the other semantical and logical puzzles associated with vagueness. 'Sorites' derives from the Greek word for heap, 'soros,' and the original paradox turned on the vagueness of that word, but paradoxes of the same kind can be generated for virtually any vague concept, and *sorites paradox* is now used as a label for any paradox of that kind. For example, a sorites paradox is generated by the following inference, which I'll call *SI*:

(1) A person with $50 million is rich.
(2) $\forall n$(a person with n is rich $\rightarrow$ a person with $n - 1$¢ is also rich) – i.e. you can't remove someone from the ranks of the rich by taking 1¢ away from her fortune.
(3) ∴A person with only 37¢ is rich.

This constitutes a paradox because it appears to be valid, each of its two premises appears to be true (at least when considered on its own), and its conclusion certainly appears to be false.

It's reasonable to assume (at least initially) that a solution to the sorites, as manifested in SI, would do two things. First, it would tell us which of the four appearances just cited was deceptive; and, second, it would explain away that deceptive appearance by explaining why that false proposition appeared to be true; it would strip from the masquerader its appearance of plausibility so that we were no longer duped by it. Most, if not virtually all, writers on vagueness assume that the sorites has such a solution, and the various theories of vagueness strain to provide it. Very well; what is that solution?

II   Some Attempts at a Solution

One may reasonably find it hard to question the validity of SI, as it turns just on modus ponens and universal instantiation, and we can remove the reliance on universal instantiation by replacing its *sorites premise*, (2), with its millions of instances (if a person with $50,000,000 is rich, then so is a person with $49,999,999.99; if a person with $49,999,999.99 is rich, then so is a person with $49,999,999.98 ...). Assuming the validity of SI, one's apt to suppose that, *faute de mieux*, the sorites premise is false. After all, it's plainly true that a person with $50,000,000 is rich and that a person with only 37¢ isn't rich, and if SI is valid, then, one is apt reasonably to suppose, so is

> A person with $50 million is rich.
> A person with only 37¢ isn't rich.
> ∴ ~∀n(a person with n is rich → a person with n − 1¢ is also rich).

But if this little argument is valid and its premises are true, then its conclusion, the negation of SI's sorites premise, is true, and thus the sorites premise is false.

Now, we don't solve the sorites merely by supposing that the sorites premise is false. We would still need to explain why, though it's false, we're so tempted to think it's true. We're tempted to think the sorites premise is true to the extent that we're tempted to think the following argument for it, which I'll call *SPA*, is sound:

> (i)   There is no 1¢ cutoff between those who are rich and those who aren't – i.e., there isn't some *particular number n* such that the proposition *that a person with n is rich but a person with n − 1¢ isn't* is true.[1] (In symbols, ~∃ n(the proposition that [a person with n is rich & a person with n − 1¢] is true).)
> (ii) ~∃ n(the proposition that [a person with n is rich & a person with n − 1¢] is true) → ∀n(a person with n is rich → a person with n − 1¢ is also rich).
> (iii) ∴∀n(a person with n is rich → a person with n − 1¢ is also rich).

SPA must be unsound if the sorites premise is false. But SPA generates its own paradox, since it appears to be valid, its conclusion seems unacceptable, and yet each of its premises appears plausible when viewed on its own.

SPA appears to be valid, since its validity depends only on modus ponens, and we've already noticed why its conclusion, SI's sorites premise, seems unacceptable (one pretty much has to say at least that if one deems the argument unsound).

Premise (i) *looks* right. Isn't it patently absurd to suppose that there is a precise 1¢ cutoff between what suffices for being rich and what suffices for not being rich? Is it that $495,946.47 is the cutoff point such that if you have that much, then you're rich, but if you have only $495,946.46, then you're not rich? This is hard to take seriously.

Premise (ii) also looks right. If there is no particular amount of money such that it is true that having *that amount* makes you rich but having 1¢ less than it doesn't, then, one might reasonably suppose, if any amount of money makes you rich, then so will 1¢ less than it.

One hasn't achieved a solution to the sorites of the kind typically sought by theorists of vagueness until one has both revealed what is wrong with SPA and explained why it's wrong in a way that allows us to see why we were wrongly tempted to think it was right. Familiar would-be solutions of the kind typically sought don't question the validity of SPA, which, as we've seen, relies only on modus ponens, and may be grouped according to which of the two premises they take not to be true. Here the contest has up to now mostly been played out in the literature between those who deny the truth of (i) and those who deny the truth of (ii).

Theorists who deny that (i) is true do so because they hold that there is a precise 1¢ cutoff between the rich and non-rich. These theorists hold that there is such a precise cutoff because they accept the principle of bivalence – the principle that every proposition, and thus every borderline proposition, is true or false. A theorist who is committed to bivalence is constrained to hold that there is a precise cutoff, that is, a particular number n such that the proposition *that a person with $n is rich but a person with $n − 1¢ isn't* is true, and no one who didn't think that borderline propositions were true or false would be tempted to suppose that there was such a precise 1¢ cutoff between the rich and the non-rich. A theorist who is committed to bivalence is constrained to hold that there is such a precise cutoff, because if she holds that every proposition of the form

A person with n is rich but a person with $n − 1¢ isn't

is false, then that would be tantamount to accepting the sorites premise, and that would force her either to accept that a person with only 37¢ is rich or else to deny that a person with $50 million is rich, and thus, accepting bivalence as she does, the theorist is committed to holding that some proposition of the displayed form is true.

The theorist who holds that even borderline vague propositions are true or false has a few serious debts. The first debt is epistemic. For consider borderline Harry, who isn't definitely bald and isn't definitely not bald. If, nevertheless, the proposition that Harry is bald is either true or false, then it's either a fact that Harry is bald or else a fact that he isn't bald. At the same time, no one can know which fact obtains; if borderline propositions have truth values, no one can know what they are. Presumably, there must be some explanation of this ineluctable ignorance. Thus, the first debt of the theorist who would deny (i) is to explain why we're necessarily ignorant of the truth values of borderline propositions.

The second debt is semantic. If there is a precise 1¢ cutoff between what suffices to make a person rich and what suffices to make a person not rich, then the property of being rich is a precisely bounded property, which, being precisely bounded, determines a precise extension for the term. Suppose that the cutoff is $495,946.47 in that if you have that much, then you're rich, but you're not rich if you have 1¢ less than that. In the event, the property of being rich would be identical to the property of having at least $495,946.47, and, by an obvious generalization, something analogous would hold for every vague term. For example, if we pretend that baldness supervenes just on the number of hairs on a person's scalp, then there would be some number – say, 3,343 – such that you're bald if, but only if, the number of hairs on your scalp isn't greater than that number, and in this case baldness would be identical to the property of having no more than 3,343 hairs on one's scalp. Now, the meaning of a predicate supervenes on its use, and the semantic question confronting the theorist in question would be to explain what it is about the use of our terms that makes the meaning of each general term such an absolutely precise property. What is it about the way we use 'rich' such that it expresses the property of having at least $495,946.47 and not the property of, say, having at least $495,946.48? What is it about our use of 'bald' such that it expresses the property of having no more than 3,343 hairs on one's scalp, rather than, say, 3,342 or 3,344? The situation is actually worse. The foregoing gloss of the semantic problem indulges in the fiction that words like 'rich' and 'bald' express context-independent properties, when, in fact, what property is expressed by a token of either word is very heavily dependent on contextual factors. What the epistemic theorist must say is that those factors determine an absolutely precise property for each token. For example, the epistemic theorist must hold that when I say that I worked for a little while this morning, there is some absolutely precise span of time such that my statement is true if, but only if, it falls within that span of time, and is false if the amount of time I worked was one attosecond longer than that span of time to which my utterance of 'a little while' referred. What kind of "factors" could with any degree of plausibility have that result? And, to add a third debt, the theorist who accepts bivalence must cash the two preceding debts in a way that makes clear why (i), which the theorist denies, strikes us as so very plausible.

There are theorists who embrace bivalence for borderline propositions and therefore deny (i). Such a theorist is said to hold an *epistemic theory of vagueness* if she defines the notion of a borderline proposition as a proposition of whose truth value we must be ignorant for such-and-such reason. For these theorists, vagueness is a form of ignorance. Recent interest in such theories was partly generated by Roy Sorensen (1988), but the view is most fully elaborated and defended in Timothy Williamson (1994). According to Williamson, the reason we can't know a true borderline proposition even if we believe it is that had things been ever-so-slightly and indiscernibly different, the proposition we believed would have been a slightly different and false proposition, even though it would have been produced in us by the same belief-forming mechanism. But we are precluded from knowing a proposition if the mechanism that produces belief in it might just as well have caused us to believe a false proposition. Thus, if we pretend that 'bald' in fact expresses the property of having fewer than 3,344 hairs on one's scalp, then we shall have a true belief if we believe that Harry is bald, given that he has exactly 3,343 hairs on his scalp. But we would have believed the proposition expressed by 'Harry is bald' even if our use of 'bald' had been indiscernibly different but different enough so that 'bald' expressed the property of having fewer than 3,343 hairs on one's scalp, and in that case our belief about Harry would have been false. Since the factors that produced in us the true belief about Harry might just as easily have produced in us a false belief about him, our true belief that he's bald can't constitute knowledge. But Williamson's account presupposes what to my mind is incredible – namely, that the use of every unambiguous vague predicate in every natural language always succeeds in picking out, as that predicate's meaning or reference, a single precisely bounded property, and that the factors which determine the contents of our thoughts determine those thoughts to have contents that are as exquisitely precise as can be. Moreover, Williamson offers no account of meaning or language use or content determination to make this bizarre claim credible; he accepts it because his theory of vagueness requires him to accept it, much as Leibniz accepted that this is the best of all possible worlds.[2]

Other theorists who accept bivalence for borderline propositions, and thus accept that we are ineluctably ignorant of the truth-values of borderline propositions, resist calling themselves epistemic theorists, presumably because their program isn't to *define* vagueness in terms of ignorance. For example, Hartry Field (2001a) suggested (nearly enough) that meaning was *not* a use-dependent property and that sentences such as

> 'Harry is bald' is true iff Harry is bald
> 'Bald' is true of a thing iff it's bald
> 'Bald' means baldness

are all conceptual truths – necessary, a priori truths that, being necessary, hold regardless of how anyone uses language. Field's commitment to bivalence derives from his acceptance of the truth and falsity schemas

> 'S' is true iff S
> 'S' is false iff not S

together with his acceptance of excluded middle (every instance proposition of the form p or not-p is true). But this is no more promising than Williamson's solution. There are three problems. First, meaning simply is *not* a use-independent property. What an expression means for someone is determined by how that expression is used, if the expression is semantically simple, or, if it's semantically complex, by how the expressions and structures composing it are used. If anything is a datum in these muddy waters, that is.[3] Second, Field still owes an account of why we can't know either the truth values of borderline propositions or the precise criteria for belonging to the extensions of vague terms (the two points of ignorance are connected, since one could in principle know the truth values of borderline propositions if one could know the precise extensions of vague terms, and vice versa). Third, in order to achieve the kind of solution he seeks, Field would still have to explain away our temptation to think that (i) was true.

Paul Horwich (1998, 2000) is another theorist whose commitment to bivalence and the truth and falsity schemas for propositions forces him to deny (i) and to accept the existence of sharp cutoffs. Thus, Horwich accepts that there is some precisely bounded property – say, the property of having at least $495,946.47 – such that 'rich' expresses that property. He also holds that the meaning of a term is determined by its use. How, then, does he avoid the complaint lodged against Williamson, that it's highly implausible that our use of predicates determines them to mean precisely bounded properties? And how does he explain the fact that no one can know the boundaries of the properties her words mean or the truth values of borderline propositions? In response to the first question, Horwich claims that we won't find it incredible that our use of 'rich' determines it to mean a precisely bounded property such as the property of having at least $495,946.47 once a certain false assumption is removed. The false assumption is that if use determines meaning and meaning determines extension, then it must be possible to explain the term's having the extension by deducing that it has that extension from the proposition that it has whatever use happens to constitute its meaning. Use, Horwich (2000) holds, does determine meaning, but no reductive definitions of semantic relations are possible, and, therefore, there can be no explanations of the kind involved in the false assumptions. In response to the second question, Horwich (2000) says that the conceptual role of a vague term leads to unimprovable partial belief because the explanatorily basic fact which governs the term's use and thereby constitutes its meaning is "gappy" in that, roughly, the predicate "is confidently applied to things whose value of underlying parameter # is greater than y, its negation is confidently applied to things whose value of # is less than x; and neither is confidently applied to things whose value of # is in between x and y" (p. 277).

I don't think Horwich makes denying (i) any more palatable than Williamson or Field did. In the first place, Horwich is wrong in suggesting that only someone with a commitment to a reductionist brand of explanation could be puzzled about how language use could determine precisely bounded meanings. The puzzle isn't about reductive accounts of meaning and reference; it's about there being any kind of coherent story to tell about how the facts about how we use a term could give it a meaning of the kind required. Second, this puzzle is exacerbated in Horwich's case by his explanation of the ineluctable ignorance to which he's committed: How could one's use of a term determine a precisely bounded property as its meaning or reference if the "explanatorily basic fact which governs the term's use" is "gappy" in the way he suggests?

I think the proper conclusion to draw isn't that we've yet to hit on the best way to defend sharp cutoffs; it's rather that no plausible case can be made for accepting sharp cutoffs. If there is a solution to the sorites, it doesn't entail the negation of (i). And if that is right, then it can't be right that the principle of bivalence is determinately true. More on this presently.

Just as there are theorists who deny (i) and accept (ii), so there are theorists who accept (i) and deny (ii). There is more than one way to challenge the truth of (ii), but by far the most prevalent way is that of those theorists who hold that the correct semantics for vague language is a *supervaluationist* semantics.[4] The supervaluationist on vagueness holds that (ii) is false: it has a true antecedent but a false consequent. The idea, roughly, is that a vague sentence is true just in case it's true under every admissible precisification of the language to which it belongs, false just in case it's false under every admissible precisification, and neither true nor false just in case it's true under some admissible precisification while false under another. A precisification is a model-theoretic interpretation of the language wherein the set assigned as extension to a vague term includes everything to which the term definitely applies, nothing to which it definitely doesn't apply, and may include none, some, or all of the term's borderline applications. A precisification is admissible just in case it respects all analytic connections among vague terms (e. g., if x is assigned to the extension of 'tall' and y is taller than x, then y must also be assigned to the extension of 'tall'). Truth under a precisification is defined in the standard model-theoretic way. Thus, truth under a precisification is bivalent: for any given precisification of the language, a sentence of the language is either true or false under that precisification. But truth *tout court* isn't truth-under-a-precisification. Since a sentence can be true under some admissible precisification while false under another, truth *tout court* isn't bivalent. So suppose Harry is borderline bald. Then 'Harry is bald' is neither true nor false, but 'Harry is bald or not bald' is true, since on every admissible precisification one of the disjuncts will be true, and 'Harry is bald and not bald' is false, since on every admissible precisification one of the conjuncts is false – although, since both the atoms of these molecular sentences are borderline, which one is true and which false will vary from one admissible precisification to another. In this way the supervaluationist hopes to retain classical logic while rejecting the semantic principle of bivalence.

Now, let's abbreviate the negation of (ii)'s consequent as

$$\sim\forall n(R(\$n) \rightarrow R(\$n - 1\text{¢})),$$

which for the supervaluationist is equivalent to

$$\exists n(R(\$n) \,\&\, \sim R(\$n - 1\text{¢})).$$

This sentence is true for the supervaluationist, since in every admissible precisification there is some number or other that satisfies

$$R(\$n) \,\&\, \sim R(\$n - 1\text{¢}).$$

But since there is no one number which satisfies that open sentence in every admissible precisification, there is no number n such that the proposition *that a person with \$n is rich but a person with \$n − 1¢ isn't rich* is true. It is in this way that the supervaluationist holds that (ii) has a true antecedent but a false consequent, and is therefore false.

But it's very hard to see how this can provide a solution to the sorites. There are several problems.

(a) Our concept of disjunction does seem to require that a disjunction can be true only if one of its disjuncts is true; our concept of conjunction does seem to require that a conjunction can be false only if one of its conjuncts is false; and our concept of the existential quantifier does seem to require that no existential generalization can be true without there being some particular thing of which the quantified open sentence is true. So, the supervaluationist is evidently just wrong if she is proposing an account of the meaning our connectives and quantifiers actually have, and if she is merely proposing a useful *revision*, then it's hard to see how that can be part of a *solution* to the sorites.

(b) Even if the supervaluationist's semantical claims were correct, she would still have done nothing yet to explain away (ii)'s appearance of being true, and so would again have failed to provide a solution to the sorites of the kind she seeks.

(c) The supervaluationist offers a semantics for vague language, but it's a - semantics that makes it hard to see how to explicate vagueness. This is because the semantics uses the notion of a precisification, which is itself defined in terms of vagueness. One would hope that a solution to the sorites would throw light on what vagueness is and on what it is to be a borderline proposition.[5]

(d) There are apparent counterexamples to the supervaluationist semantics.

Suppose that Alice says to Bob, 'Harry's biggest problem is baldness,' and Bob later says to Carla, 'Baldness, Alice said, is Harry's biggest problem,' which we may pedantically but usefully restate as

(1) Baldness is such that Alice said that it was Harry's biggest problem.

We may suppose that, notwithstanding the vagueness of 'baldness,' Bob's utterance (1) is determinately true. The problem for the supervaluationist is that he must say that (1) is determinately false.

There are two accounts of the semantics of (1) the supervaluationist might offer, but they come to the same thing. First, the supervaluationist might say that 'baldness' in (1) indeterminately refers to numerous precise properties, those that comprise the admissible precisifications of 'baldness' (I here ignore higher-order vagueness: borderline cases of borderline cases, borderline cases of borderline cases of borderline cases, and so on). Then (1) will be true iff it's true on each of those precisifications, false iff it's false on each of them, and neither true nor false iff it's true on some of the admissible precisifications, false on others. Since, even allowing for the vagueness of the rest of (1), Alice quite clearly didn't say of *any* precise property (e.g., the property of having fewer than 3,137 hairs on one's scalp) that *it* was Harry's biggest problem, the supervaluationist must hold that on this first way of doing the semantics for (1), (1) is determinately false. On the second way of doing the semantics of (1), the supervaluationist holds that 'baldness' determinately refers to a single vague property, baldness, and (1) will be true just in case Alice said of that vague property that it was Harry's biggest problem. At first glance this is apt to look promising as a way of getting (1) to come out true. But not really. For the supervaluationist has to provide truth conditions for propositions involving the vague property baldness, and the only way he has of doing that is to hold that a proposition involving the property is true only if it's true on every admissible precisification of baldness, and this will, again, have (1) come out, unacceptably, as determinately false. (More generally put, when we take propositions into account, the supervaluationist must say, nearly enough, either that a vague sentence token indeterminately expresses a bunch of precise propositions, in which case the sentence is true just in case each of those propositions is true, or else it expresses a single vague proposition, in which case the proposition, and hence the sentence, is true just in case every admissible precisification of the proposition is true. Precisifications of propositions are easily understood on analogy with the precisifications of sentences.)

David Lewis (1999), replying to remarks of Saul Kripke's which evidently raised the sort of problem (1) raises, concedes that such examples can't be accommodated by the supervaluationist but claims that this doesn't show supervaluationism to be mistaken:

> What's mistaken is a fanatical supervaluationism, which automatically applies the supervaluationist rule to any statement whatever, never mind that the statement makes no sense that way. The rule should instead be taken as a defeasible presumption. What defeats it, sometimes, is the cardinal principle of pragmatics: The right way to take what is said, if at all possible, is the way that makes sense of the message. Since the supervaluationist rule would have made hash of our statement of the problem, straightway the rule was suspended.   (173–4)

This may be a good reply to Kripke's objection, but it makes no sense as applied to (1). For if the correct semantical treatment of (1) is non-supervaluationist, then what is that alternative semantics, and who's to say that it isn't the correct semantics for vagueness generally?

(e) While supervaluationism is incapable of giving a positive account of what vagueness is, it nevertheless succeeds in implying a false account of it. The point has been very nicely made by Crispin Wright (2001). The main problem with supervaluationism, he would say, is that according to it "indeterminacy consists ... in some kind of status other than truth or falsity – a *lack* of a truth-value, perhaps, or the possession of some other truth-value," and to such "*third-possibility views of indeterminacy*" he objected that "it is quite unsatisfactory in general to represent *in*determinacy as any kind of determinate truth-status – any kind of middle situation, contrasting with both the poles (truth and falsity) – since one cannot thereby do justice to the absolutely basic datum that in general borderline cases come across as hard cases: as cases where we are baffled to choose between conflicting verdicts about which polar verdict applies, rather than as cases which we recognize as enjoying a status inconsistent with both" (pp. 69–70). In other words, when confronted with borderline Harry we have some temptation to say that he's bald and some temptation to say that he's not bald, but supervaluationism can't account for this. If supervaluationism were correct, we should recognize that the proposition that he's bald is neither true nor false and therefore have no temptation to say either that he's bald or that he's not bald.

So much for a supervaluationist solution to the sorites. Some theorists hope to resolve the sorites by appeal to a *degree-theoretic* notion of truth. On this way of reckoning truth, a borderline proposition and its negation will both be true to a degree greater than 0 and less than 1, given the convention typically adopted by degree-of-truth theorists that degrees of truth can be measured by real numbers in the interval $[0, 1]$. There is, however, more than one way of developing a degree-theoretic notion of truth, some of which comport with classical logic, some of which don't.

The degree-theoretic notion of truth that departs from classical logic is the one most commonly invoked in application to vagueness; it is a degree-functional account of the connectives due to Lukasiewicz (1956), which, following Dorothy Edgington (1996), we may restate as follows for negation, conjunction, disjunction, and implication:

$$[\sim] \ T(\sim p) \ = \ 1 \ - \ T(p)$$

$$[\&] \ T(p \,\&\, q) \ = \ Min[T(p), T(q)]$$

$$[v] \ T(p \,v\, q) \ = \ Max[T(p), T(q)]$$

$$[\supset] \ T(p \supset q) \ = \ 1 \ \text{if} \ T(p) \leq T(q), 1 \ - \ [T(p) \ - \ T(q)]$$
$$\text{otherwise}$$

This requires a departure from classical logic in that, for example, excluded middle and non-contradiction fail: if $T(p)$ and $T(\sim p)$ are both 0.5, then both $T(p \,v\, \sim p)$ and $T(p \,\&\, \sim p)$ are also 0.5.

There are a couple of problems, but here I'll mention just one (I state another one in Schiffer (2003: 193)). This problem is that the theory is a "third-possibility view of indeterminacy," and thus subject to Wright's trenchant objection to all such theories (2001). The theory is evidently constrained to hold that p is true just in case p is T to degree 1 (or – allowing for the vagueness of ordinary language 'true' – to a contextually relevant high degree); false just in case p is T to degree 0 (or to a contextually relevant low degree); and neither true nor false just in case p is T to some (contextually relevant) degree greater than 0 and less than 1. But suppose Harry is borderline bald. Then, since it would be definitely wrong to stay that 'Harry is bald' is T to degree 1 (or to some other contextually relevant high degree), the theory entails that it would also be definitely wrong to say it is true that Harry is bald. But if Harry is borderline bald, it would *not* be definitely wrong to say that he's bald, and thus not definitely wrong to say it's true that he's bald.

A degree-theoretic account of truth which comports with classical logic can be defined in terms of a supervaluational account of truth, for, on such an account, a proposition's degree of truth can be defined in terms of the proportion of admissible precisifications on which it is true.[6] And Dorothy Edgington (1996) shows how we can achieve the same effect by introducing a degree-theoretic construal of truth wherein T mimics the behavior of prob in classical probability theory. For example, in probability theory, $\text{prob}(p \vee q) = \text{prob}(p) + \text{prob}(q) - \text{prob}(p \& q)$; accordingly, the Edgington-inspired proposal holds that $T(p \vee q) = T(p) + T(q) - T(p \& q)$. Whereas the Lukasiewiczian account is degree-functional (the degree of truth of a compound is a function of the degrees of truth of its components), the Edgingtonian T, like prob, isn't. Thus, even when both $T(p)$ and $T(\sim p) = 0.5$, it will still be the case that $T(p \vee \sim p) = 1$ and $T(p \& \sim p) = 0$, and, in the same way, $\exists x Fx$ can be true to degree 1 even though no substitution instance of its quantified open sentence is true to degree 1. Since this theory is a form of supervaluationism, it has all the problems that theory has.

III Happy- and Unhappy-Face Solutions

A paradox can always be cast as a set of apparently mutually incompatible propositions each of which seems plausible when considered on its own, and I said that it's reasonable to suppose that a solution to a paradox would two things: first, identify the odd guy out, and second, explain why this false proposition appeared to be true. Let's say that such a solution to a paradox is a *happy-face* solution to that paradox. Well, it may be *reasonable* to suppose the sorites has a happy-face solution, but I doubt that it does. The "paradox" of the barber who shaves all and only those who don't shave themselves enjoys a happy-face solution (it's simply impossible for there to be such a barber), but I doubt that many, if any, of the real philosophical paradoxes do. The reason standard solutions to these problems never ultimately satisfy is that they are attempting to give happy-face solutions to problems that don't admit of them. Think of the libertarian, hard determinist, and compatibilist solutions to the problem of free will, or think of any of the familiar solutions to the skeptical problem of our knowledge of mundane propositions about the external world, such as the proposition that I have a hand.[7] The reason philosophers are still debating these problems after a couple of thousand years isn't that they haven't yet hit on the correct happy-face solutions; it's that the puzzles don't have happy-face solutions.

The sorites does, however, admit of an *un*happy-face solution. An unhappy-face solution of a paradox explains why the paradox doesn't have a happy-face solution.

Such explanations share a common form: they locate a crucial indeterminacy in the paradox set of propositions, or in closely related propositions, and they account for this indeterminacy in terms of a certain kind of glitch in the underived conceptual role of the concept generating the paradox (or in the underived conceptual roles of the concepts generating it).[8] For example, the problem of free will is a paradox because it's posed by the following three mutually incompatible propositions, each one of which looks plausible viewed on its own: we sometimes act freely; everything we do is caused by factors over which we had no control; and if everything we do is caused by factors over which we had no control, then we never act freely. This paradox doesn't admit of a happy-face solution because it's indeterminate which proposition in the paradox set is false, and this is so because of a glitch in our concept of free will. The underived conceptual role of that concept has two parts that don't cohere. On the one hand, we're disposed to judge that an act was done freely when it satisfies certain paradigm conditions, while on the other hand we're disposed to deny that an act was done freely when we learn that the propositional attitudes which led to it were caused by factors over which the agent had no control. Further, there is nothing in the concept to resolve the conflict. The conflicting aspects of conceptual role don't mean that the concept of free will is inconsistent (it isn't like the concept of a round square), for we don't take the aspects of conceptual role to provide necessary conditions for the concept's application when we learn of their conflict. The extent to which one experiences these conceptual pulls can vary from person to person, and even within a person over time, but for anyone who has our concept of free will, both pulls are inherent in the concept, and they remain there even if one decides to ignore them in applying the concept. This is why the paradox of free will can have no happy-face solution.

The sorites has an unhappy-face solution, and part of the explanation of why that is so, I submit, is that, even if we feel forced, *faute de mieux*, to deny the sorites premise, there is no determinate resolution of the argument, paradox-generating in its own right, for the sorites premise. More specifically, it's *indeterminate* whether (i) or (ii) is correct, hence indeterminate whether bivalence holds for borderline vague propositions.[9] To understand what this comes to, and to say more about why the sorites doesn't have a happy-face solution, we need to inquire into the nature of indeterminacy.

IV Vagueness, Indeterminacy, and Partial Belief

Harry is a borderline case of a bald man, and this means that he's neither determinately bald nor determinately not bald, but how are we to understand the 'determinately' operator and therewith the notion of a borderline case (and therewith the nature of vagueness)?[10]

Those who accept bivalence will either explicate indeterminacy as a certain kind of ignorance, or else hold that the notion admits of no reductive explication. Even if this theorist denies that indeterminacy can be explained in other terms, he ought to be able to explain why we can't know the truth-value of a borderline proposition. In any event, I have argued that it's not determinately true that bivalence holds for borderline propositions.

Those who reject bivalence will want to understand a proposition's being indeterminate at least partly in terms of its being neither true nor false, but I have argued that it's not determinately true that bivalence doesn't hold for borderline propositions.

Indeterminacy is neither an epistemic nor a semantic notion. But it is, as I shall now propose, a certain kind of *psychological* notion.

My account of indeterminacy turns on a distinction between two kinds of partial belief. Although we philosophers often suppress the point, we know that believing is a matter of degree having to do with how firmly – the degree to which – one accepts a proposition. One can believe a proposition more or less firmly, and to say that someone believes p *tout court* really means that she believes p to some contextually relevant high degree. What is less well known is that there are two distinct kinds of partial belief. One kind is what philosophers usually have in mind when they think about partial belief; I call this kind of partial belief *standard partial belief* (SPB). This is the kind of partial belief which can under suitable idealization be identified with subjective probability in that under suitable idealization SPBs satisfy the standard axioms of probability theory. Pretend that degrees of belief can be measured by real numbers from 0 (unqualified disbelief) to 1 (unqualified belief). Then examples of SPBs might be your believing to degree 0.7 that it will rain tonight and your believing to degree 0.16 that your nephew will pass his logic course. So, if you take these two partially believed propositions to be unrelated, then you, rational person that you are, will believe to degree 0.112 the conjunction that [it will rain tonight and your nephew will pass his logic course]. The following points also characterize SPB.

- SPB is the kind of partial belief we would have even if, *per impossibile*, there were no indeterminate propositions.
- SPB is a measure of *uncertainty*. If one s-believes p to a degree less than 1 and greater than 0, then one takes p to be uncertain and oneself to be in a state of partial *ignorance* in that one doesn't know for certain what truth value p determinately has (as we'll presently see, one can only s-believe propositions one takes to be determinately true or determinately false).
- SPBs generate corresponding likelihood beliefs. Thus, if Renata s-believes to degree 0.5 that she left her glasses in her office, then she thinks it's just as likely that she left them there as that she didn't. She's apt to say that she thinks that there's a fifty-fifty chance she left her glasses in her office. If she believes to degree 0.01 that England will win the World Cup, then she thinks it's extremely unlikely that England will win the World Cup.

- In every, or virtually every, case in which one s-believes p to some degree between 0 and 1, one doesn't take oneself to be in the best possible position to pronounce on the truth of p, even if one has complete confidence in the integrity of the evidence one has for or against p's being true. Sometimes one thinks there's a better epistemic position available to oneself, as, for example, Renata believes she can find out for certain whether her glasses are in her office by looking for them there. And even if one thinks one can't get into a better epistemic position oneself, one will think there's a better position others might occupy, or might have occupied. Thus, there's nothing I can do to improve my opinion about the color of Thales' eyes, but a contemporary of his could have satisfied herself on that score.

The other kind of partial belief is what I have elsewhere called *vagueness-related partial belief* (VPB).[11] VPBs are those partial beliefs that can't under any idealization be identified with subjective probability. Moreover, the just-displayed points that characterize SPB don't characterize VPB. Thus, as we'll presently see:

- We couldn't have VPBs if our language could express only determinate propositions. VPBs go hand-in-hand with indeterminacy. Our language couldn't express indeterminate propositions if we didn't have VPBs, and our having VPBs secures our ability to express indeterminate propositions.
- VPB is *not* a measure of uncertainty. VPB is the kind of partial belief we have when confronted with a proposition we take to be neither determinately true nor determinately false. In such a case, we have some temptation to judge p true and some temptation to judge p false, but we don't feel *uncertain* about the proposition's truth-value, as though we're in the dark about something hidden.
- VPBs don't give rise to corresponding likelihood beliefs. If, for example, you v-believe to degree 0.5 that borderline Harry is bald, then you *won't* think there's a fifty-fifty chance that he's bald.
- If one v-believes p to any degree between 0 and 1, and one's epistemic circumstances are known to be ideal in a certain way, then one won't think that one, or anyone else, can get into a better epistemic position with respect to p.

Now for an admittedly somewhat artificial example.

Sally is a rational speaker of English, and we're going to monitor her belief states throughout the following experiment. Tom Cruise has consented to have his hairs plucked from his scalp one by one until none are left. Sally is to witness this, and will judge Tom's baldness after each plucking. The conditions for making baldness judgments are ideal and known by Sally to be such. For simplicity of exposition I'll assume both that Sally's degrees of belief can be measured by real numbers from 0 to 1 and that Sally's partial beliefs are always of some determinate degree.

Sally starts out believing to degree 1 that Tom is not bald and to degree 0 that he is bald. This state of affairs persists through quite a few pluckings. At some point, however, Sally's judgment that Tom isn't bald will have an ever-so-slightly-diminished confidence, reflecting that she believes Tom not to be bald to some degree barely less than 1. The plucking continues and as it does the degree to which she believes Tom not to be bald diminishes while the degree to which she believes him to be bald increases. At some point, we may pretend, the degree to which Sally believes both that Tom is bald and that he isn't bald is 0.5, and Tom thereby represents for Sally a solid borderline case of baldness. Having reached 0.5, Sally's degrees of belief that Tom is bald will gradually increase as the plucking continues, until she believes to degree 1 that he is bald.

Although there's more to be said on the matter (see my 2003: 231–3), I believe, and will assume, that Sally's qualified judgments express partial beliefs. My claim is that Sally's partial beliefs that Tom is bald are VPBs. For consider her at the point in the plucking when she believes to degree 0.5 that Tom is bald:

- Sally *won't* believe that there's a fifty-fifty chance that Tom is bald. She won't wonder how the issue of Tom's baldness might turn out, or what the under-lying reality of it *really* is.
- If Sally's 0.5 partial belief that Tom is bald were a SPB, then she'd believe to degree 1 that he's bald or not-bald. But Sally won't believe to degree 1 that Tom is bald or not bald. Sally, a non-philosopher, has no views about excluded middle per se, and she's apt to react to the question whether Tom is bald or not bald the same way she reacts to the question whether he's bald.
- Suppose that in addition to having his hairs plucked one-by-one from his scalp, Tom has also suffered the indignity of being entirely nude throughout the process, and that he is a paradigm borderline case of a thin man. Suppose further that at the point in the plucking when Sally believes to degree 0.5 that Tom is bald, she also believes to degree 0.5 that he is thin, and that, pretheor-etically speaking, she takes the two propositions to be completely unrelated: the truth of neither proposition would give her any reason to believe or to disbelieve the other. Now, to what degree does Sally believe the conjunction that Tom is bald and thin? It's intuitively clear, I submit, that Sally, confronted with what she would say are "all the facts," will believe the conjunction to the same degree she believes each conjunct, viz., 0.5. If her partial beliefs were SPBs, she would s-believe the conjunction to degree 0.25.

Now, what is it for Tom to be a borderline case of baldness?

Certain VPBs are unimprovable and known to be such: there is nothing one can do or learn that would improve one's epistemic situation as regards the proposition one v-believes. These are VPBs formed under ideal epistemic conditions – condi-tions that yield unimprovable VPBs. In those cases where it belongs to the concept of a vague property that the property's application supervenes on some other property – in the way, for example, baldness supervenes on the hair situation on a person's scalp – then a VPB formed under ideal epistemic conditions is a VPB formed in circumstances in which one has certain knowledge of the facts on which the vague property in question supervenes, in the way illustrated by Sally's VPBs about Tom Cruise's baldness. Let's call those VPBs formed under ideal epistemic conditions VPB*s.

Now, to begin, we can say that, to a first approximation:

> x is to some extent a borderline case of being F *only if* someone could v*-believe that x is F

It's hard to see how this could fail to be true. To say that someone could v*-believe that x is F is to say that there is *some* possible world similar in relevant respects to the actual world in which someone v*-believes that x is F. The relevant respects are defined by the supervenience base for being F – e.g., the hair situation on Tom's scalp. Thus the ability to form a VPB* that x is F would fail to be a necessary condition for x's being a borderline case of being F only if there is a possible world in which x is a borderline case of being F but there is *no* possible world similar to that world in all F-relevant respects in which someone v*-believes that x is F.

We can, I submit, also say that, to a first approximation:

> p is to some extent indeterminate iff someone could v*-believe p

But we can't further conclude that

> x is to some extent a borderline case of being F *if* someone could v*-believe that x is F

unless we could say that vague borderline propositions were the only indeterminate propositions, and I don't think we can say that; there are sources of indeterminacy other than vagueness.[12] In order to say what it is for something to be a borderline case of a property, we must first say what it is for a concept to be vague.

It's a *primitive and underived* feature of the conceptual role of each canonical concept of a vague property (e.g., the concept of redness expressed by one's use of 'red') that under certain conditions we form VPBs involving that concept, and *it's in this that vagueness consists*. To use a metaphor, what makes a property vague is simply the fact that its predicate name has an underived conceptual role that determines the name to go into a person's VPB box under certain conditions. When the sentence 'Tom is bald' goes into Sally's VPB box, it's not as a response to her perception of the independently explicable fact that he's a borderline case of baldness. His being a borderline case consists in the conceptual fact, and it's *this* that accounts for the familiar "no-fact-of-the-matter" intuition many have about borderline cases. But since there is nothing more to the essence of a property than is determined for it by our property-hypostatizing linguistic and conceptual practices, there can be no further question of what is "really going on" at any non-conceptual level.[13] In this regard, notice how unlike the case of vagueness is from a case where we really may want to say there is no fact of the matter. For suppose we are told that the concept of a shmadult is exhausted by these two conditions: anyone who has reached his or her twenty-second birthday is a shmadult, and anyone who has not yet reached his or her seventeenth birthday is not a shmadult. Confronted with someone we know to be nineteen years old, we might well not v-believe that she is a shmadult but rather s-believe that it's not true that she is a shmadult and not true that she isn't a shmadult.

All this puts us in a position to explicate vagueness in terms of VPBs and, in the course of doing that, to clarify the notion of a VPB*, the notion of a VPB formed under "ideal epistemic conditions." There are two kinds of vague properties. If a vague property Φ belongs to the first kind, then there is some other property Ψ, however complex, such that Φ instantiations supervene on Ψ instantiations, and Φ judgments are based on Ψ judgments. Baldness is a property of this type, since baldness supervenes on the hair situation on a person's scalp and baldness judgments are based on hair-on-scalp-situation judgments. If a vague property Φ belongs to the second kind, then whether or not instantiations of that property supervene on instantiations of some other property Ψ, Φ judgments are not necessarily based on Ψ judgments. Pain, for example, is a vague property, but when we ascribe the property to ourselves, our judgments are not based on any of our other beliefs. When we ascribe pain to others, we do so on the basis of evidence, but the ascribed pain need not be thought by us to supervene on that evidence. Despite the disrepute of the "argument from analogy" as an attempted solution to the problem of other minds, it's not unreasonable to suppose that our ascriptions of pain to others is analogically based on our self-ascriptions of pain. I suspect that all vague properties of the second kind are like pain in these two respects.

If a vague property Φ is a property of the first kind, then to v*-believe that a thing has Φ is to have one's VPB that the thing is Φ based on certain knowledge of the thing's Ψ situation. In our Tom Cruise thought experiment, Sally's VPBs are VPB*s because all of her judgments about Tom's baldness are based on certain knowledge of the hair situation on his scalp. For vague properties of this type – and most vague properties are of this type – being in ideal epistemic circumstances for making a Φ judgment about a thing simply consists in having certain knowledge of the thing's Ψ situation. If a vague property Φ is of the second kind, then to v-believe oneself to have Φ is to v*-believe oneself to have Φ. For properties of this type, in other words, one is always in "ideal" epistemic circumstances for self-ascriptions of Φ. As regards ascriptions of vague properties of this type to others, one may never be in ideal epistemic circumstances, but one approximates to them to the extent that one has evidence that the other is in a state like one's own when one v*-believes oneself to have Φ. Of course, the person about whose having Φ one is judging can know that she is a borderline case of having Φ by way of her v*-believing herself to have Φ. In all of these cases, when one v*-believes a thing to have Φ, that judgment is dictated just by one's canonical concept of Φ if Φ is a vague property of the second type, and by one's canonical concept of Φ together with one's certain knowledge of the thing's Ψ situation, when Φ is a vague property of the first type. If we say that in each of these cases one's VPB* that x has Φ is Φ-concept driven, then we can say that

> x is a borderline case of being F iff someone could have an F-concept-driven VPB* that x is F.

In other words, a proposition is borderline when it's indeterminate, and its indeterminacy is owed to the possibility of someone's v*-believing it in the concept-driven way just sketched. Needless to say, the notion of someone's having an F-concept-driven VPB* that x is F is, like everything else, vague, and one can v*-believe to some solidly intermediate degree whether the condition is satisfied in a given case, thereby starting the escalation known as "higher-order vagueness" – borderline cases of borderline cases, borderline cases of borderline cases of borderline cases, and so on.

Anyway, there is a lot more to be said on these topics,[14] but I find, not for the first time, that I've exhausted my allotted number of pages before I've exhausted my subject.

Notes

1 Equivalently, there is no numeral n such that the sentence ⌈A person with $n is rich & a person with $n − 1¢ isn't⌉ is true.

2 Hartry Field (2001b) offers an especially telling objection against theorists, such as Williamson, who take there to be a determinate fact of the matter in borderline cases. It's a *conceptual truth* that a person who knows the complete hair situation on borderline Harry's scalp and has full command of the concept of baldness can't know that Harry is bald or that he's not bald, but the epistemic theorist can't hold this. He must hold that the fact that we have no means to detect the fact of the matter about Harry's baldness is "a medical limitation on our part, not a conceptual necessity" (ibid., p. 286).

3 Field may have intended his claims about the use-independent status of semantic statements to be a proposal for conceptual reform.

4 Supervaluationist semantics was first proposed by Bas van Fraassen (1966) as a way of accommodating truth-value gaps due to the sort of presupposition failure one finds in 'The present King of France is bald.' The classical supervaluationist treatment of vagueness is Kit Fine (1996).

5 Why can't the supervaluationist simply say that a borderline proposition is a proposition that is neither true nor false? Because this theorist will almost certainly want to say that there are propositions other than borderline propositions that are neither true nor false, such as, for example, the proposition that the present King of France is bald.

6　See Lewis (1970); Kamp (1975); McGee and McLaughlin (1994: 236–9).

7　See my (1995/6), where I first introduced the happy/unhappy-face distinction in connection with skeptical arguments about our knowledge of the external world.

8　By 'underived conceptual role' I mean, roughly speaking, the processing role your brain was programmed to follow as soon as you were plugged in.

9　Actually, I believe that the sorites premise is also indeterminate, but it's not possible to make the case for this, or to address its consequences, in this article. They are, however, addressed in Schiffer (2003: ch. 5).

10　In this context, I use 'determinately' and 'definitely' interchangeably and don't assume that being indeterminate means not having a truth value.

11　I first called it that in (1998) and discussed it further in (2000) and (2003), from which a fair amount of this paper is lifted.

12　See my (2003). I introduced the label 'vagueness-related partial belief' with an eye just on the application of VPBs to vagueness. If I were labeling VPBs now, I would probably do better to call them "indeterminacy-related partial beliefs."

13　Here I allude to my notion of "pleonastic" properties and propositions. See my (2003).

14　See Schiffer (2003: ch. 5).

Chapter 13

The Semantics of Non-factualism, Non-cognitivism, and Quasi-realism

Simon Blackburn

Introduction

A natural approach to semantics works in terms of what words and sentences represent: what things words stand for, and what truths or facts sentences represent there as being. In classical semantics the central concern is to individuate the 'truth condition' of a sentence, and the central role of words is their contribution to that truth condition.

The distinctive claim of non-factualism is that this is not the correct approach to take to some particular area of thought and speech. The claim is that words in the area do not function (purely) representatively, and sentences in the area are not simply representing the world as being one way or another. Instead, an account should be given in terms of what mental state the speaker is voicing. These mental states, according to the non-factualist, should not fundamentally be seen as beliefs, and at least at the beginning of the theory, need not be seen as apt for truth or falsity at all. They have some other functional identity. Standardly, when we voice them, we put them into public space with the intention that our hearers share them, and agreement consists in this sharing. They thus differ from expressions of belief about our own mental states, which would gain agreement from anyone who thought we were sincere (contra van Roojen 1996; Jackson and Pettit 1998; see Mautner 2000; Smith and Stoljar, forthcoming).

Philosophers may be motivated to give 'non-factualist' accounts of our thoughts, in various areas, and by a variety of considerations. First, the task of explaining or describing the kinds of fact that seem to be needed, in order to make our thoughts and beliefs about some area true, may prove difficult. These facts may themselves seem queer, or only queerly related to other more familiar facts. Second, we might find it difficult to give a satisfactory account of our awareness of any such facts, and allied with this we might fail to find any account of why we would want to be aware of them in any case. Third, we may find that what we are doing, when we voice our commitments in the area in question, is not exactly like voicing a belief. It may be better seen in terms of voicing a stance or plan, or an inferential disposition or other function of the mind, in which case the supposition that we are dealing with beliefs, needing to be made true or false by facts of a particular kind, will drop out of the picture.

These three families of reason, metaphysical, epistemological, and those concerning functional role, have found application in many areas, although ethics is probably the most familiar. Ethical or normative facts can seem metaphysically strange, epistemologically demanding, and of no use in explaining our interest in ethics, while the mental states we voice as we communicate values or moralize to each other seem to be attitudes or practical stances that orientate us towards the world rather than representing any part of it. In a familiar metaphor they have a different 'direction of fit' with the world, behaving more like desires, whose function is to effect changes in the world, rather than beliefs, whose function is to represent the world (Anscombe 1957; Smith 1987). Hence the attraction of expressivism, a non-factualist theory of moral thought and discourse (Ayer 1936; Stevenson 1963; Gibbard 1990).

Although non-factualist theories have been prominent only in the last century or so, the basic idea is visible much earlier. Berkeley (1710: introduction, sec. 20) highlights the importance of realizing that many words have a function other than that of presenting ideas of things. Hobbes and Hume, Kant, Schleiermacher, and Nietzsche can plausibly be interpreted exploiting the same separation, in areas as diverse as ethics, aesthetics, the philosophy of causation and natural necessity, philosophy of mind, and theology. Such an interpretation often rescues such writers from the fate of being branded implausible subjectivists, wrongly supposing that we are talking about our own minds (Blackburn 1990; Darwall 2000; Hopkins 2001; Ward, 2002). In the twentieth century the approach was a natural companion to logical atomism and logical positivism, with their insistence that genuine facts had to be of some specific nature. Thoughts that appear on the surface to be about facts of a different nature could be diagnosed as non-factual, and the threat they pose to the general theory disappears. Both F. P. Ramsey and Wittgenstein make widespread use of non-factualism, in areas as diverse as probability, conditionals, modality, natural law, self-ascription of mental states, as well as ethics, religion, and aesthetics (Ramsey 1931; Logue 1995; for Wittgenstein, see Blackburn 1990; Jacobsen 1997; Bar-On and Long 2001). Wittgenstein's insistence on the practicality of language also helped to prepare the ground for speech-act theory, as it developed in the work of Austin (1962) and Searle (1969).

However, the general approach of expressivism received a severe check at just this time (Geach 1962, 1965). It was Geach's argument that forced expressivists to become much more attentive to the semantic problems confronting their approach.

The Frege–Geach Problem

Drawing on a point of Frege's Geach challenged expressivist theories to give an account of 'indirect' contexts. These are contexts in which a sentence is used, but not itself asserted or put forward as true. The expressivist will have an account of what happens when a sentence is asserted. For instance, if he is treating of ethics, he may say that a sentence 'lying is wrong' expresses condemnation of lying. But then he needs an account of many other contexts in which the sentence may occur but in which no condemnation of lying is made.

This might point simply to an incompleteness in expressivism, and the need for further work. But Geach sharpened his point by showing how the different contexts produce sentences that work together in arguments:

(A)   Lying is wrong
(B)   If lying is wrong, then getting your little brother to lie is wrong
So: (C)   Getting your little brother to lie is wrong.

An expressivist account of the meaning of (A) is that an attitude to lying is expressed. But since no attitude to lying is expressed by (B), how can the two provide the premises for the valid deduction to (C)? The inference is clearly valid, yet the expressivist seems to say that there is a fallacy of equivocation.

Although Geach icily claimed that his argument showed expressivism to be 'hopeless,' and described it as refuting the prescriptive theory of ethics of R. M. Hare, it was usually taken as a challenge rather than a refutation. Early responses were given in Hare (1970) and Dummett (1973). Hare made the point that a parallel "equivocation" could be laid at the door of a classical semantic account. If (A) expresses a belief or assertion, as classically it appears to do, but the same sentence as it occurs in (B) expresses no belief or assertion, then equally there seems to be ground for the charge of equivocation. Classically this would be met by the distinction between the force with which a sentence is put forward and the sense of the sentence, which is the representation or content that it expresses. The first may shift, from (A) to (B), but the identity of content remains, and is sufficient to ensure the validity of the argument. However, the Geach objection runs, it is just this component of representational content that the expressivist wishes to abolish, so he must provide a substitute. In reply to this Hare also pointed out that the attitude expressed in (A) remains 'in the offing' in (B), and just as the classical notion of 'content' is designed precisely to provide something in common to occasions of assertion like (A) and others such as (B), so a notion of attitude or stance should be available to cover the same shift.

Hare's point is reinforced by Gibbard, who points out that the problem of moving from apprehendings (such as animals might be thought to make) to representations capable of negation, disjunction, or implication, has to be confronted by factualists and non-factualists alike. It is a common problem for everyone (Gibbard 1992a).

Dummett (1973) recognized that the expressivist will have his own explanation for the discursive practices which result in compounds such as (B). His own proposal for construing the conditional saw it as equivalent to 'were I to come to say that lying is wrong, I should also say that getting little brother to lie is wrong.' Yet this seems to substitute a different conditional for the original. Thus I would not hold 'if Hitler was a good thing, then I am corrupt,' but I might well hold that 'if I were to come to say that Hitler is a good thing, I would be corrupt.' In general, if we ask what is hypothesized in the conditional, it does not seem to be a proposition about my own possible doings.

Blackburn (1984a) proposed to exploit the Fregean view that in indirect contexts the proposition normally expressed by a sentence becomes the topic of reference. He viewed the conditional as itself expressing a higher order attitude to the interplay of two first-order attitudes: the disapproval of lying, and the disapproval of getting your little brother to do it for you. The conditional voices a disapproval of any moral system, or sensibility, that contains the first but not the second. Coupled with premise (A), construed as voicing disapproval of lying, a sensibility must then contain the second, on pain of being so badly 'fractured' that one would not know what to make of the overall combination. The vice seemed sufficiently parallel to classical inconsistency to deliver a satisfactory expressivist theory of the inference, since logically valid inference and avoidance of logical inconsistency are generally regarded as coming to the same thing.

Critics rapidly complained that rather than manifesting any logical flaw, a fractured sensibility would at worst deserve to be regarded as a moral nuisance (Wright 1988; Hale 1986; Schueler 1988; Hurley 1989; Brighouse 1990; Zangwill 1992b; Wedgwood, 1997). In response to early critics Blackburn (1988) modified the theory. Drawing on conceptual role semantics (Harman 1973) he proposed to view the conditional (B) as given its meaning simply by its role in forcing (A) to (C) (or not-C to not-A). One voicing the conditional is announcing himself as 'tied to a tree,' in which if one side is closed off, the other must be followed, and this tie can be construed the same way whether or not the limbs of the tree express attitudes or beliefs with truth conditions. This idea is independently plausible, or indeed mandatory if we take seriously the problem of understanding how modus ponens works in any event (Carroll 1895). A generalization leads to a somewhat Byzantine (Fine 1995) semantics based on the idea of joint realizability of a set of goals, an idea derived from deontic logics. The higher-order attitudes to attitudes of Blackburn 1984 remain in place only as motivations or justifications for conditionals, with their inferential role alone giving the meaning. The proposal has continued to be controversial (Wedgwood 1997, Kölbel 2002), and critics have doubted whether expressivism can even cope with the more elementary context of negation (Hale 1993a and Hale 2002; Unwin 2001; responses include Blackburn 1993a and 2002).

Gibbard (1990) provided an elegant related semantical development of expressivism. In Gibbard's accounts norms are treated rather like prescriptions. Accepting a normative directive is treated as basic and is assimilated to having a plan rather than having a belief. But only a limited number of statements express such acceptance directly. Others are explained by their inferential relations to this basic kind of state. The semantics proceeds by generalizing the classical view of inconsistency. What is especially wrong with an inconsistent set of statements is that it rules out all full possibilities. In the factual realm this means ruling out all possible worlds. When we include plans as well as factual statements, inconsistency is generalized: what is wrong with an inconsistent set of statements-plus-norms is that it rules out every 'factual normative world.' Its special defect in other words is that it logically rules out every combination of (1) a full way the world might be, and (2) a full contingency plan. Gibbard (1990) presented the view in terms of systems of norms, and critics queried whether the expressivist should be entitled to this much (implying, for example, the applicability of negation, disjunction, and so on) at the outset (Blackburn 1992; Gibbard 1992b takes up the point). However Gibbard's (1990) proposal and Blackburn's agree on their stress on inferential role semantics, the assimilation of logic to the avoidance of inconsistency, and their exploitation of the inconsistency of attitudes or plans directed onto the world in unsatisfiable ways.

Turning from ethical expressivism, another prominent non-factualism is the theory of indicative conditionals, such as 'if it rains, the match will be canceled.' In his 1965 Ernest Adams presented an elegant theory working in terms of the assertability conditions of such conditionals, summed up in the slogan that the probability of the conditional is the conditional probability. In other words, our assent to the conditional goes by the conditional probability of cancelation, given rain. This might seem to be consistent with thinking that our assent expresses belief in a special kind of conditional fact. But in his bombshell 1976 David Lewis showed that there cannot be a proposition whose assertibility obeys Adams's constraint. If Adams has the assertibility conditions correct, as is widely agreed, then non-factualism is forced upon us. As Edgington explicates it, the problem is to relate any such proposition to the material conditional of propositional logic (the truth function which is true except when A & – B). In some respects it looks as though nothing different from this will do as a truth-condition for the ordinary conditional. For example, certainty that – (A & – B) suffices for certainty that if A then B. On the other hand, it is not necessarily irrational to have a high degree of belief in -A, yet a low degree of belief that if A then B. The material conditional does not obey this last condition, and no other proposition can obey both. Informally, the problem is that any other candidate would have a probability that is partly a function of what goes on in -A worlds. But 'if A then B' expresses a commitment entirely to be judged on how things stand with respect to B in A worlds, and -A worlds do not enter in (Edgington 1997). Lewis's proof is a rare example of a purely formal motivation for a non-factualist approach to some part of discourse.

The Impact of Minimalism

Minimalism or deflationism in the theory of truth is the view that application of the truth predicate adds nothing to a statement: it makes no difference whether you say p, or 'p is true' and it makes no difference whether you say 'not-p' or 'p is false.' Deflationists add to this claim an account of the real function of the truth predicate in terms of its enabling us to make generalizations (as in 'everything John said in the meeting was true'). Some minimalists retain a 'normative' function of the notion of truth (Wright 1992), but even this residue is somewhat ethereal (Dodd 2000). Minimalism has been an increasingly popular, almost orthodox, position in the philosophy of truth, and its impact on non-factualism has been the topic of much debate. Holton 2000 divides the field into those who hold that minimalism is compatible with non-factualism and those who do not. The former include Stoljar 1993; Kraut 1993; Horwich 1994; Field 1994; Jackson, Oppy and Smith 1994; Smith 1994; O'Leary Hawthorn and Price 1996; Blackburn 1998. Those who hold that the pair are incompatible include Boghossian 1990, Wright 1992, Divers and Miller 1994. Unselfconscious compatibilists appear to include the older generation of Ramsey, Ayer, and Wittgenstein, all of whom advance both non-factualist treatments of various parts of language, and a minimalist theory of truth. Indeed Ayer 1936 was the target of Boghossian 1990, which initiated the recent debate (the problem had previously been noticed in Stevenson 1963). An irony of the debate is that minimalism appears itself to be an example of a non-factualism, since it denies that the truth predicate refers to a 'robust' or 'substantive' property, in just the way expressivists deny that 'good' refers to a robust or substantive moral property. If that is right, it is itself the very kind of position that according to incompatibilists it rules out.

The apparent incompatibility is easy to state. Non-factualists have no quarrel with our habit of communicating using the sentences they treat. Expressivists approve of sayings such as 'slavery is wrong,' or conditionals such as 'if it rains the match will be canceled.' But minimalism then allows us to cast these as 'it is true that slavery is wrong' and 'it is true that if it rains the match will be canceled.' So expressivists should have no quarrel with these, nor with equivalents put in terms of 'fact,' 'really,' and so on. The addition of such terms does not raise the theoretical temperature. But just because of this there can be no space for saying that 'slavery is wrong,' but then denying that there is a fact that slavery is wrong, or really slavery is wrong, or really truly it is wrong. So what remains of the 'non-factualism'? Minimalism takes away the terms within which the expressivist position can be formulated.

The example of conditionals suggests that there must be something wrong about the swift incompatibilist argument. For applied to conditionals it would reinstate the view that Lewis showed to be impossible, that 'if P then Q' is simply true or false, with truth conditions fixed by Adams's assertibility conditions.

Furthermore, the incompatibilist argument may be met in part by insisting on a distinction between truth-aptitude and truth itself. Even if the truth predicate is minimal, there may remain room for serious theory of how a sentence arrives in the business of putting forward a claim as true or false. Some sayings are not in this business: greetings, questions, fictions, commands and others seem to have a quite different function, and Lewis's argument shows the same to be true of conditionals. So we need a story about what this function may be, and how different classes of sentences are supposed to perform it. And it is here, the non-factualist can insist, that his distinctive view of the function of the part of language in question has a proper explanatory role to play. Perhaps in the light of minimalism it is unwise to call the position non-factualism, but the result is the same. Indeed, reformulated like this expressivism can benefit from minimalism. For it can now say, without blushing, that moral remarks, probability statements, or what it may be, are true, really true, in just the same sense as anything else. And that disarms the sense that such positions lose something, or fail to do justice to the seriousness with which we take the areas in question. This is the tack pursued by the figure Blackburn 1984a christened the quasi-realist. The quasi-realist regards the expressivist functional account of commitments in an area as primary, but explains and justifies the emergence of the 'propositional surface' on that basis. He attempts to provide a geology underlying the familiar landscape, or a genealogy explaining the emergence of a 'quasi proposition,' or object of thought. This may even be a thought known to be true, making the alternative label for expressivism, 'non-cognitivism,' inappropriate.

Reactions to this can divide according to the scope allowed to minimalism. If minimalism is allowed to embrace not only the truth predicate, but all semantic terms, including such notions as representation or reference, then the result will tend to quietism, or the renunciation of any attempt at articulate semantic theory. It will be permissible, but totally without interest, to announce that just as 'red' refers to the color, and 'x is red' represents x as being red, so 'probability' refers to probability, and 'x is probable' represents x as being probable, or 'good' refers to goodness, and 'x is good' represents x as being good. Semantics itself stops being substantive, and this means that no substantive distinctions can be made in its terms. But such quietism is not very comfortable, being close to saying that philosophical theory is always a dead duck. One ironic consequence would be that no notion of representational content or truth condition would remain to help keep the Frege–Geach argument in business, against Hare and Gibbard's queries, mentioned above. And to most theorists it seems premature to let the substantive notion of representation disappear into the minimalist ether (Horwich 1998 is the most prominent exception, although Wright 1992 comes close to minimalism, even about truth aptitude).

Conclusion

Factualism and representative semantics are often thought of as the default, in which case non-factualist theories need substantive arguments to motivate them, and to insist upon their distinctive claims. Since these arguments must derive from theses in metaphysics, or epistemology, or theories of functional role, they will be resisted by those who think they have adequate grip on the metaphysics or epistemology, or can stand fast on identifying the functional role of commitments in the area with simple beliefs, true or false. Non-factualism is then in general vulnerable to dead-duck quietism. However, it can well be argued that factualism is no kind of default and that a relaxed pluralism about functional roles played by different kinds of assertion provides a fairer perspective on our situation (Kraut 1993; Price 1994).

If quasi-realism mirrors everything a realist wanted to say, it may seem to be an unwitting ally of quietism, suggesting that there are no terms left in which to conduct semantic debate (de Gaynesford 1995). An interesting twist is given to this in Lewis (2003) which endorses quasi-realism's semantic program, but then identifies it with a fictionalism. Realists are interpreted as spinning a fiction; the quasi-realist is seen as accepting everything they say but only in a sense in which it is prefaced by an 'in the realist fiction' operator (Rosen 1990). Blackburn (2003) resists this interpretation of things, urging that it would be expressivism's distinctive account of what comes within the fictional operator that matters.

An important and positive result of the entire discussion is that non-factualism provides an interesting litmus test or laboratory for claims across the whole range of semantic theory. It puts pressure on notions of representation, truth, fact, as well as our understanding of the scope of theory and the nature of belief and inference.

Part III

Reference

Chapter 14

Names

William G. Lycan

In school we were taught that nouns are divided into common nouns and proper nouns, and that a *proper noun* is 'the name of a person, place or thing.' More generally, philosophers and logicians speak of *singular terms*, expressions which purport to denote or designate particular individuals – people, places, or physical objects, or other items–as opposed to *general terms* such as 'horse' or 'fat' that normally apply to more than one thing. Singular terms include proper names ('Franklin D. Roosevelt,' 'Marge,' 'Afghanistan,' 'Piccadilly,' '1,217'), definite descriptions ('the fat horse in the barn,' 'the prime minister of Israel,' 'the third cinder block from the end'), singular personal pronouns ('you,' 'she'), demonstrative pronouns ('this,' 'that'), and a few others.

This article will concentrate on proper names, and will address two main issues: (1) In virtue of what does a proper name (hereafter just 'name') designate or refer to its bearer? Call this 'the Referring Question.' (2) What and how does a name mean or signify? What does it contribute to the meaning of a sentence in which it occurs? That I label 'the Meaning Question.' (As Devitt (1989) argues, it is important to distinguish theories of the meanings of names from philosophical accounts of referring.)

How Does a Name Refer? The Description Theory

The Referring Question may seem strange; some readers may find themselves answering 'It just does. A person's name is that person's name; what else is there to it?' Of course when a person is born and given a name, the name becomes that person's name – normally, but not always, for life. But our question is more general: When a speaker utters a sentence containing a name, what determines who that name refers to? To see that there are difficulties here, consider *ambiguous* names, names that are common to more than one person: In my own university department there have been two philosophers each of whom is named 'John Roberts.' And more than one woman in the United States is named 'Mary

Lycan.' (In fact, a majority of names are ambiguous; a name is unambiguous only by historical accident.) If someone in a bar in Saskatoon, Saskatchewan, is heard to utter the sentence 'I'm told Mary Lycan is coming here next month,' to which person does her particular use of 'Mary Lycan' refer, and in virtue of what?

One way of answering the Referring Question more generally would be to appeal to our practice of asking and answering identificatory questions. Suppose I hear you use a name, say 'Robertson Davies,' and I ask, 'Who's that?' All you can say by way of reply is something like, 'The Canadian novelist who wrote all those trilogies.' In general, when asked 'Who [or what] do you mean?' after one has just used a name, one immediately and instinctively comes up with a **xxdefinite descriptionxx**, as an explanation of who or what one meant.

Russell (1905/1956, 1919/1971) proposed that names actually abbreviate definite descriptions that speakers at least tacitly have in mind. The facts just mentioned seem to confirm that proposal; when asked to explain my use of a name, I promptly and without thinking produce a description. This idea yields a clear answer to the Referring Question: A name as used on a particular occasion refers to the individual who uniquely fits the description that the speaker mentally associates with the name on that occasion. If what our Saskatoon protagonist associated with her use of 'Mary Lycan' was the description 'the music publisher and choral conductor in North Carolina,' the name designates that publisher and conductor. But if what the speaker had in mind was 'the porpoise trainer in Key Largo, Florida,' the name instead designates that person.

That surely is plausible. But there are problems. Here are a few.

First, John Searle (1958) pointed out that if proper names refer by being mentally associated with particular descriptions, then for each name, there must be some particular description with which that name is associated; and that consequence is disputable. For example, if I unreflectively say, 'Robertson Davies was a better novelist than he was a playwright,' and if I happen to know quite a few identifying facts about Davies, what is the associated description? 'The author of *The Rebel Angels*'? Or 'the former Old Vic actor turned playwright, whose wife was a stage manager,' or 'Canada's foremost writer of ghost stories'? I do not seem to have had any one of those descriptions in mind to the exclusion of the others.

As we have seen, it is still plausible to think that a speaker can normally spit out a fairly specific description when prodded. But it is far from obvious that this is always because the description was one the speaker had already had determinately in mind. If you ask me, 'Who is Davies?,' I might make any of a number of answers that come to mind, depending on what sort of information I think you may want about the man. It does not follow that the answer I do produce is the precise description that my use of 'Robertson Davies' expressed at the time. (The problem is not merely that it would be hard to *find out* which description a speaker had in mind in uttering a name. It is that in many cases *there is no* single determinate description that the speaker has in mind, either consciously or subconsciously. It is hard to believe that there is a fact of the matter as between the various descriptions of Davies aforementioned; I need have had no particular one of those in mind when I unreflectively said what I did.)

Searle offered an improved version of the Description theory, designed to meet the foregoing criticism and other objections to Russell's view. He suggested that a name is associated, not with any particular description, but with a vague cluster of descriptions. As he put it, the purport of 'This is N,' where 'N' is replaced by a name, is to assert that a sufficient but so far unspecified number of 'standard identifying statements' associated with the name are true of the object demonstrated by 'this.' That is, the name refers to whatever object satisfies a sufficient but vague and unspecified number (I shall say a 'preponderance') of the descriptions generally associated with it. Thus, Searle abandoned the commitment that for each name, there must be some one particular description that it expresses; the name is tied semantically just to a loose cluster of descriptions. In that way, his Cluster theory allowed Searle to avoid the objection. But the theory is still subject to the two further ones I shall now present. (We shall return to it below.)

Second problem (Kripke 1980: 80ff): If Russell's Description theory of referring is true, then every name is associated with a definite description that applies *uniquely* to the name's referent. But most people associate the name 'Cicero' only with 'a famous Roman orator' or some other *in*definite description, and, say, 'Richard Feynman' only with 'a leading [then] contemporary theoretical physicist'; yet these people succeed not only in using those names correctly but also in referring to Cicero and to Feynman respectively when they do so.

Third and more radically: It does not take much to succeed in referring to a person. Donnellan (1970) offers an example in which a child who has gone to bed is awakened briefly by his parents. They have with them Tom, an old friend of the family who is visiting and wanted just to see the child. They say, 'This is our friend Tom.' Tom says, 'Hello, kiddo.' The child has only barely woken. In the morning, the child wakes with a vague memory that Tom is a nice man, which he expresses by saying 'Tom is a nice man.' But the child associates no description at all with the name 'Tom'; he may not even remember that Tom was the person that he was half-awake to meet during the night. Yet, Donnellan argues, that does not prevent the boy from succeeding in referring to Tom. There is a person who is being said to be a nice man, and it is Tom.

How Does a Name Refer? The Causal-historical Theory

Kripke sketches a different answer to the Referring Question.

> [A baby's] parents call him by a certain name. They talk about him to their friends. Other people meet him. Through various sorts of talk the name is spread from link to link as if by a chain. A speaker who is on the far end of this chain, who has heard about, say Richard Feynman, in the market place or elsewhere, may be referring to

Richard Feynman even though he can't remember from whom he first heard of Feynman or from whom he ever heard of Feynman. He knows that Feynman was a famous physicist. A certain passage of communication reaching ultimately to the man himself does reach the speaker. He then is referring to Feynman even though he can't identify him uniquely. (p. 91)

The idea, then, is that your utterance of 'Feynman' is the most recent link in a causal-historical chain of reference-borrowings, whose first link is the event of the infant Feynman's being given that name. You got the name from somebody who got it from somebody else who got it from somebody else who got it from somebody else etc., all the way back to the naming ceremony. You do not have to have any particular description, or anything else, in mind. All that is required is that a chain of communication in fact have been established by virtue of your membership in a speech community that has passed the name on from person to person, which chain goes back to Feynman himself.

Admittedly, when a new user first learns a name from a predecessor in the historical chain, it can only be by the new user's sharing with the predecessor at least one identifying description. But it may be very shallow, as in 'the person she is talking about.'

Taken at face value, this Causal-historical view makes the right predictions about examples such as Donnellan's Tom. In each example, referring succeeds because the speaker is causally connected to the referent in an appropriate historical way.

Kripke (1980: 66–7) offers the further case of the biblical character Jonah. He argues that we should distinguish between stories that are complete legends and stories that are, rather, substantially false accounts of real people. Suppose historical scholars discover that in fact no prophet was ever swallowed by a big fish, or did anything else attributed by the Bible to Jonah. The question remains of whether the story is grounded ultimately in a real person, or the Jonah character was fictional in the first place. There are several possibilities. The story could originally have been a complete fabrication, made up by a parent as a bedtime story. Or someone could have made up and spread many false stories about a real person named Jonah immediately after his death. Or because the real Jonah was an exciting individual, all sorts of rumors and stories might have begun to circulate about him, and the rumors got out of hand. Or there might have been a very gradual loss of correct information and accretion of false attributions over the centuries. But in any of the last three cases, it would follow that today the Bible is saying false things about the real person, Jonah.

We saw that the Description theory handled the problem of ambiguous names with ease. (If anything, as we shall see, the Description theory makes proper names *too lavishly* ambiguous.) So that problem might be thought to pose an obstacle to the Causal-historical view. But in fact the Causal-historical theory has a straightforward solution to it: If a name is ambiguous, that is because more than one person has been given it. What disambiguates a particular use of such a name on a given occasion is, of course, that use's causal-historical grounding, specifically, the particular bearer whose naming ceremony eventually led to that use.

Kripke emphasizes that he has only sketched a picture; he does not claim to have an actual theory. (For the first worked-out version of the Causal-historical approach, see Devitt (1981).) But several objections already loom, the first two of which were anticipated by Kripke himself.

The Causal-historical view's central notion is that of the passing on of reference from one person to another. But not just any such transfer will do. First, we must rule out the 'naming after' phenomenon. If I acquire a mynah bird and name it 'Cicero' after the orator, having the historical Cicero explicitly in mind and wanting to commemorate him, I have added a link to a causal-historical chain: it is only because the orator was named 'Cicero' that my mynah bird is now named that. But it is the wrong kind of link. To rule it out, Kripke requires that '[w]hen the name is 'passed from link to link,' the receiver of the name must ... intend when he learns it to use it with the same reference as the man from whom he heard it' (p. 96). This requirement is clearly not met in the present case, for I deliberately changed the referent from the orator to the bird and I meant everyone to be aware of that.

Second, Kripke offers the example of 'Santa Claus.' There is thought to be a causal chain tracing our use of that name back to a certain actual person named some version of 'Nicklaus' who lived in eastern Europe centuries ago. But no one would say that when children use it they unwittingly refer to that person; clearly they refer to the fictional character who comes down chimneys on Christmas Eve. But then, how does the name 'Santa Claus' differ from 'Jonah'? Why should we not say that there was a real Santa Claus, but that all the mythology about him is false? Instead, of course, we say that there is no Santa Claus, period. We use the name 'Santa Claus' as though it abbreviates a description.

Probably the most obvious feature to note is that 'Santa Claus' as we use that name is associated with a powerful stereotype, an American cultural icon. Its social role is so prominent that it really has frozen into a fictional description, as the name 'Jonah' has not even among religious people. Jonah's iconic properties remain side by side with his historical properties in the Old Testament, but 'Santa Claus' is now purely iconic. For the average American, the ritual has entirely overcome the putative historical source.

Third: The Causal-historical theorist appeals to causal chains leading back in time from our present uses of names to ceremonies in which actual individuals are named. But how, then, can the theory accommodate *empty* names, names that have no actual bearers? (Notice that the Description theorist succeeds effortlessly here: An empty name, like 'Santa Claus' or 'Atlantis,' is just one whose associated description fits no actual individual.)

A promising response is to note the fact that even empty names are introduced to the linguistic community at particular points in time, either through deliberate fiction or through error of one kind or another. From such an introduction, as Devitt (1981a) and Donnellan (1974) point out, causal-historical chains begin spreading into the future just as if the name had been bestowed on an actual individual. So reference to fictional or otherwise nonexistent items is by causal-historical chain, but the chain's first link is the naming event itself rather than any putative properties of the nonexistent bearer. (This move would also help with two similar problems: the names of future individuals, as when we choose a name for the baby we plan to have, and the names of abstract objects, such as individual numbers, which have no causal powers.)

Fourth objection: Evans (1973) points out that names can quietly change their reference, through error or otherwise, but the Causal-historical theory as presented so far cannot allow for that. According to Evans, the name 'Madagascar' originally named, not the great African island, but a portion of the mainland. Or:

> Two babies are born, and their mothers bestow names upon them. A nurse inadvertently switches them and the error is never discovered. It will henceforth undeniably be the case that the man universally known as 'Jack' is so called because a woman dubbed some other baby with the name. (p. 196)

We do not want to be forced to say that our use of 'Madagascar' still designates part of the mainland rather than the island, or that 'Jack' continues to refer to the other character rather than to the man everyone calls 'Jack.'

To fix this, Devitt (1981a: 150) proposes *multiple grounding*. A naming ceremony, he says, is only one kind of occasion that can ground an appropriate historical chain; other perceptual encounters can serve also. Instead of there being just the one linear causal chain that goes back from one's utterance to the original naming ceremony, the utterance proceeds also out of further historical chains that are grounded in later stages of the bearer itself. Once our use of 'Madagascar' has a large majority of its multifarious groundings in the island rather than the mainland region, it thereby comes to designate the island; once our use of 'Jack' is heavily grounded in many people's perceptual encounters with the man called that, those groundings will overpower the chain that began with the naming ceremony. This is vague, of course, but probably not objectionably so.

Fifth objection: We can misidentify the object of a naming ceremony. Consider a variation on the 'Jack' example: I am the father. When I first visit the nursery, the nurse inadvertently shows me the wrong neonate. With great ceremony, I name the (wrong) baby 'Jack,' after the great J.J.C. Smart. But in this case the nurse's error is not perpetuated, even though it is never discovered; on the next visit I get the right infant and take him home. But *he* was never given the name 'Jack,' or any other name, in any ceremony. The other baby was given it, though (because I am not his father) the giving did not take. Yet surely my own son is the bearer of 'Jack,' not just after subsequent multiple groundings have been established, but even just after the naming ceremony I did perform. The multiple-grounding strategy does not help here. Rather, what matters is which child I *had in mind* and believed I was naming at the time. (Devitt 1981a speaks of 'abilities to designate,' construing these as mental states of a certain sophisticated type.) To fix the Causal-historical theory on this point, one will have to do some work in the philosophy of mind.

Sixth objection: People can be mistaken as to what *kind* of thing a name designates. Evans cites E.K. Chambers' *Arthur of Britain* as asserting that King Arthur had a son Anir 'whom legend has perhaps confused with his burial place.' A speaker thus confused might say 'Anir must be a green and lovely spot'; the Causal-historical theory would interpret that sentence as saying that a human being, Arthur's son, was a green and lovely spot.

Devitt and Sterelny (1987) call this the '*qua*-problem.' They specify that the person who presides over a naming ceremony or who is responsible for any of a name's groundings must not be categorically mistaken and must indeed intend to refer to something of the appropriate category. This is a small concession to the Description theory.

On the basis of the foregoing objections and others, it seems that Kripke initially overreacted to the Description picture of referring. He was right to insist that causal-historical chains of some kind are required for referring and that descriptions do not do nearly as much work as Russell or even Searle thought they did; but there still are some descriptive conditions as well. The trick is to move back in the direction of the Description view without going so far as even Searle's weaker Cluster doctrine. But that trick is a difficult one.

On to the Meaning Question: What does a name contribute to the meaning of a sentence in which it occurs?

The obvious and natural answer is that what a name does is *name*. That is, its function is simply to designate its bearer and, when used, to introduce that item into discourse. A name that does that and only that is called 'Millian' (after Mill (1843/1973), who held something like the view that names generally are merely labels for individual persons or objects and contribute no more than those individuals themselves to the meanings of sentences in which they occur).

But that natural answer, which I shall also call the 'Millian' view, faces very formidable objections based on some logical puzzles introduced by Russell (1905/1956), following Frege (1892/1952). First, there is again an objection from empty names. 'Atlantis' cannot contribute its bearer to the meaning of 'Atlantis lies under the ocean,' because it has no bearer at all. If its meaning is simply its referent, then 'Atlantis lies under the ocean' is precisely synonymous with the subsentential phrase 'lies under the ocean.'

Second, the objection from negative existential sentences: 'Atlantis never existed' seems to be true and seems to be about Atlantis, but if it is true, there is no Atlantis for it to be about; if the name 'Atlantis' is Millian, *what* never existed? Notice that there is a worse difficulty here than was raised by the problem of empty names alone: While 'Atlantis lies under the ocean' is indisputably meaningful despite the nonexistence of Atlantis, 'Atlantis never existed' is not only meaningful despite Atlantis' nonexistence but actually and importantly true.

Third, there is 'Frege's Puzzle': An identity statement such as 'C. L. Dodgson is Lewis Carroll' (where 'is' has the sense of numerical identity, as also expressed by '=') contains two names, both of which pick out or denote the same person or thing, and so, if the names are both Millian, it should be trivially true. Yet 'C. L. Dodgson is Lewis Carroll' seems both informative and contingent. Certainly many people are unaware that Dodgson was Carroll, and it further seems that he might not have been Carroll.

Fourth, when one name of a person is substituted for a different name of the same person in the same sentence, the sentence can change from true to false or vice versa: Suppose 'Edwina believes that C. L. Dodgson's middle initial was "L"' is true (since Edwina can read). 'Edwina believes that Lewis Carroll's middle initial was "L"' may still be false; Edwina may even never have heard of Lewis Carroll. But if names are Millian, this should not be possible. If the names contributed nothing to meaning besides the introduction of their referents into discourse, the substitution should make no difference at all.

How Does a Name Mean? The Description Theory

Russell (1905/1956, 1919/1971) offered an alternative. As we have seen, he thought that every use of a name is backed by a description associated in the speaker's mind with the name. Indeed, he contended that names are *semantically equivalent to* their associated descriptions. Thus, names express (normally) contingent properties of their bearers, and they have what Frege called 'senses,' that can differ despite sameness of referent.

In support of this Description theory of how names mean (hereafter just 'the Description theory of names'), Russell gave a direct argument, and a second is easily extracted from his writings. Then he pointed out how the theory sweeps aside all the nasty objections to the natural Millian view.

Russell's direct argument was that his theory captures the intuitive logic of sentences containing names. 'C.L. Dodgson is Lewis Carroll,' surely, does not pick out one man, pick him out a second time, and assert simply that he is him. Rather, it means something like 'C.L. Dodgson is the author of *Alice's Adventures in Wonderland* and *Through the Looking-Glass*.' (Actually, since 'C.L. Dodgson' is itself a name, the identity sentence means something more like 'The nineteenth-century Christ Church Oxford mathematician and photographer is the author of *Alice's Adventures in Wonderland* and *Through the Looking-Glass*.') Or take one of the toughest cases of all, a negative existential. 'Atlantis never existed' is actually true. What, then, could it mean? It does not pick out an existing thing and assert falsely that the thing is nonexistent; rather, it assures us that in fact there was no such island nation swallowed up by the sea. Similarly, 'Ebenezer Scrooge never existed' means that there never actually was a miserly old London financier who was visited by three spirits one Christmas Eve. That sounds right.

The second argument is based on the point made above regarding identificatory questions. When I ask you whom you mean by 'Robertson Davies,' and you instantly reply, 'The Canadian novelist . . .' as an explanation of what you meant, it sounds as though you are producing a synonym. I asked because, as it were, I did not understand the name I heard you utter; in order to come to understand it, I had to ask a 'who' question, and you granted my request for a meaning explanation. Notice that the answer had to be a description; merely giving a second proper name of Davies would not have enlightened me, unless I had previously associated *that* name with a description.

Searle (1958) made a similar appeal to learning and teaching: How does one teach a new proper name to someone who does not already know it? And how does one learn the referent of a particular name from someone else? In the first case, one produces one or more descriptions; in the second, one elicits them. Of course, sometimes we teach or learn names nonverbally, by pointing. But even if you had replied to my query by pointing Robertson Davies out to me on the street, what I would have learned is that the name means something like 'the elderly man who looks like such-and-such [to some degree of visual detail].'

These phenomena are very striking; the Description theory is not just a desperate swerve made in order to evade the various objections to the Millian view. But, just as there were objections to the Description theory of referring, there are objections to the Description theory of names. In fact, since the two Description theories are very closely allied, they are some of the same objections. It could be argued that the Description theory of names, taken together with the assumption that a description always refers to whatever uniquely fits it, entails the Description theory of referring. (However, for a critique of that entailment claim, see Donnellan 1966.) Thus, any objection to the Description theory of referring would automatically stand as an objection to the Description theory of names.

And that proves to be the case. We surveyed three criticisms of the Description theory of referring, and each of them carries over. First, if Searle was right in denying that for every use of a name, there must be some particular description associated with it in the speaker's mind, then the name cannot very well be *synonymous with* any particular description. Second, if Kripke was right to claim that some names ('Cicero,' 'Feynman') are associated only with indefinite descriptions, rather than with definite descriptions that apply uniquely to the names' referents, then it cannot be true that all names abbreviate definite descriptions. (Moreover, two names of the same person, such as 'Cicero' and 'Tully,' may well have the same indefinite description as backing, and when they do, no Russellian theory can explain their continuing failure to substitute in belief contexts (Kripke 1979: 246–7).) And, third, if the child in Donnellan's example can refer to Tom and express a truth in saying 'Tom is a nice man' without associating 'Tom' with any description (save being nice and a man), then obviously the name is not synonymous with one.

And there are additional problems for the Description theory of names. A fourth is that different people know different things about other people. In some cases my knowledge about person X and your knowledge about X may not even overlap.

The Description theory of names entails that the same name will have different senses for different people; every name is wildly ambiguous. For if names are equivalent to definite descriptions, they are equivalent to different definite descriptions in different people's mouths, and for that matter to different descriptions in the same person's mouth at different times, both because one's knowledge keeps fluctuating and because what is psychologically prominent about one person for another keeps fluctuating too.

It gets worse. To see how, we need a little Russellian background. Russell held the Description theory of names, but in turn he also held a particular theory of the meanings of definite descriptions themselves. Take a typical sentence of the form 'The F is G,' such as 'The author of *The Blind Assassin* is a poet as well.' It appears to be a simple subject–predicate sentence, referring to an individual (Margaret Atwood) and predicating something (the writing of poetry) of her. But Russell (1905/1956) maintained that that appearance is deceptive. Notice that our sentence implies each of two general propositions: that *The Blind Assassin* was authored, and that it does not have more than author. Guided by those logical facts, Russell proposed that the sentence as a whole is semantically equivalent to a conjunction of three general statements, none of which makes reference to Atwood in particular: '(i) At least one person authored *The Blind Assassin*, and (ii) at most one person authored *The Blind Assassin*, and (iii) whoever authored *The Blind Assassin* is a poet as well.' The original definite description 'The author of *The Blind Assassin*' is, Russell argued, *only superficially* a singular term at all; logically speaking it is entirely general.

Since according to Russell, names are synonymous with definite descriptions, names inherit the foregoing analysis. In particular, surprisingly, names too are only superficially singular terms; for Russell they 'disappear on analysis' in favor of entirely general statements.

And that exacerbates our fourth problem for the Description theory of names, as follows. Suppose I am thinking of Kingsley Amis as 'the food-hating curmudgeon who gave La Tante Claire a libelously bad review,' and you are thinking of Amis as 'the author of *Lucky Jim*.' Then we would be strangely unable to have disagreements regarding Amis. If I were to say, 'Amis disliked his son Martin's novels,' and you said 'No, no, Amis was very fond of them really; he just pretended not to like them,' we would, on Russell's view, not be contradicting one another. For the sentence I had uttered would be synonymous with 'The food-hating curmudgeon who gave La Tante Claire a libelously bad review disliked Martin Amis' novels,' while your sentence would be synonymous with 'The author of *Lucky Jim* disliked Martin Amis' novels.' From a purely logical point of view, those two statements are entirely compatible. They could both be true (provided that either someone other than Amis had reviewed La Tante Claire or someone other than he had written *Lucky Jim*). What looked like a promising dispute turns out to be no real dispute at all; you and I are merely talking past each another. But that seems quite wrong.

One might try to blame the problem on Russell's theory of descriptions themselves rather than on his Description theory of names. But work would have to be done to show why the latter is more credible than the former, and an alternate theory of descriptions would have to be suggested. I shall continue to presume Russell's theory of descriptions, bearing in mind that its rejection remains an option.

How Does a Name Mean? The Cluster Theory

Searle's Cluster theory of referring was also intended by him as a theory of how names mean. As before, he suggested that a name is associated with a vague cluster of descriptions rather than with any particular description. Turning to meaning, he said that the force of 'This is N,' where 'N' is replaced by a proper name, is to assert that a sufficient but so far unspecified number of 'standard identifying statements' associated with the name are true of the object demonstrated by 'this'; the name refers to whatever object satisfies what I earlier called a preponderance of the descriptions generally associated with it.

The vagueness is important. Searle says it is just what distinguishes names from definite descriptions. In fact, it is why we have and use names in the language, in addition to descriptions. Notice that if Russell's Description theory were correct, then names' only function would be as abbreviation or shorthand. Searle maintains that, rather than being equivalent to a single description, a name functions as a 'peg . . . on which to hang descriptions' (p. 172), and that is what enables us to make linguistic contact with the world in the first place.

Some refinements are needed. For example, we would have to require that a 'sufficient number' be at least *over half*; for otherwise, two obviously distinct individuals could both be the referent of a single name. Also, doubtless we would want to say that in determining a person's identity, some of that person's identifying properties would be more important than others; some way of *weighting* the identifying descriptions is involved.

This Cluster theory allows Searle to avoid several objections we have raised against Russell's Description theory of names. As we saw, the first criticism is blunted because Searle has abandoned the commitment that for each name, there must be some one particular description that it expresses. The name is tied semantically just to a loose cluster of descriptions. The fourth problem is solved (Searle believes) by the fact that different people can have different subclusters of descriptive material in mind, yet each have a preponderance of identifying descriptions and thereby succeed in referring to the same individual. (It is not clear whether Searle can solve the aggravated version of the fourth problem, regarding non-disagreement. On Searle's view, even though two speakers who have different particular descriptions in mind may succeed in picking out the same individual, the sentences they use may still have different meanings, and so far as has been shown, those meanings might be mutually compatible.)

Searle tried to soften the opening objections to Russell's theory of names by offering his looser Cluster version of the Description approach. Though it still falls foul of the second and third criticisms above, it seems to qualify as a sensible middle way between Russell's account and the Millian view of names apparently discredited by the four objections to the natural view. But, building on some important ideas of Ruth Barcan Marcus (1960, 1961), Saul Kripke (1980) went on to subject Russell's Description theory and Searle's Cluster theory together to a more sustained critique. He argued that Searle had not backed far enough away from Russell, for Searle's view inherits problems of much the same kinds.

Kripke's Critique of the Description and Cluster Theories of Names

First objection: Suppose the name 'Ted Hughes' is equivalent to 'the Poet Laureate of England from 1984 till 1998.' And now consider a question about possibility. Could Ted Hughes have failed to be Poet Laureate of England from 1984 till 1998? The answer seems to be *yes* without question, assuming that 'could' expresses merely theoretical, logical or metaphysical possibility rather than something about the state of our knowledge. But according to the Description theory, our question means the same as 'Is the following a possible state of affairs?: that the Poet Laureate of England from 1984 till 1998 was not Poet Laureate of England from 1984 till 1998?,' the answer to which is just as clearly *no*.

Searle's Cluster theory may seem to offer an improvement, because it is possible that a person who satisfies a preponderance of the cluster associated with 'Ted Hughes' nonetheless does not satisfy the particular description 'Poet Laureate of England from 1984 till 1998.' But, Kripke points out, human possibility extends further than that: Hughes the individual person might not have done *any* of the things generally associated with him. He might have run away at age ten and joined a circus for life, never writing a single poem and never once (apart from the circus) coming to the attention of the public. According to the Cluster theory, the character who joined the circus would not have been the referent of 'Ted Hughes,' and for that matter would not have *been Ted Hughes*. That seems just wrong. (But a strong rebuttal has been made to this argument by Michael Dummett 1973.)

Second objection: Kripke (1980: 83–7) offers an extravagantly fictional example involving Gödel's Incompleteness Theorem, a famous result in mathematical logic. In Kripke's outrageous story, the theorem was really proved in the 1920s by a man named Schmidt, who died mysteriously without publishing it. Kurt Gödel came along, swiped the manuscript, and dishonestly published it under his own name. Now, most people know Gödel, if at all, as the man who proved the Incompleteness Theorem; if 'Gödel' abbreviates a description, at least for philosophers and mathematicians the description would have to be 'the man who proved the Incompleteness Theorem.' So the sentence 'Gödel was named "Gödel," not

"Schmidt" ' would be synonymous with 'The man who proved the Incompleteness Theorem was named "Gödel," not "Schmidt," ' which in Kripke's scurrilous story would be false; yet 'Gödel was named "Gödel," not "Schmidt" ' would still be true, not false.

(Notice that this example goes against the Description theory of referring as well. It seems clear that when even those who know nothing else about Gödel utter the name 'Gödel,' their use of the name does refer to Gödel rather than to the entirely unknown Schmidt. After all, as in the real world, 'Gödel' is still Gödel's name and is used to denote him by those who know more about him.)

This objection too tells against the Cluster theory as well as against the classical Description view. Suppose no one in fact proved the Incompleteness Theorem; Schmidt's alleged proof was irreparably flawed. Or perhaps there was not even any Schmidt, but 'the proof simply materialized by a random scattering of atoms on a piece of paper' (p. 86). Here it is even more obvious that most people's uses of 'Gödel' refer to Gödel rather than to anyone else at all; yet those uses are not even backed by any cluster of descriptions.

Kripke has a third and more fundamental objection to the Description theory, but it requires some technical apparatus.

Rigid Designation

Here is the apparatus. Let us begin with the notion of a 'possible world,' which is widely appealed to in philosophy of language more generally (e.g., Lewis (1970)). Consider the whole universe we live in. Our talk about things in our universe is talk about what actually exists, what things there really are: Tony Blair the British prime minister, La Tante Claire, your right ear, my computer, etc., but not Hamlet, Santa Claus, or the perfectly honest politician. And what is true in this universe is of course actually true. But there are things that are in fact false, yet might have been true. Things might have gone otherwise; the world could have been different from the way it is. Someone else might have been elected prime minister, I might have gone into songwriting instead of philosophy, and (think of it) you could have been reading something about needlework instead of this article.

Thus, there are a number of ways the world might have been. A little more fancifully, there are *alternate worlds*–different worlds, worlds which could have been ours, but that are only possible and not actual. Think of an array of possible universes, corresponding to the infinitely many ways in which things, very broadly speaking, might have been. All the merely possible worlds represent non-actual global possibilities.

Now, plainly, a sentence's truth depends on which world we are considering. 'Blair is prime minister' is true at the actual world, but since Blair need not have been prime minister, there are countless worlds at which 'Blair is prime minister' is false: in those worlds, he lost the election or never ran for the office or never even existed. And in some other worlds, someone else is prime minister; Jeffrey Archer, Sir Peter Strawson, Jane Horrocks, you, me, or Bugs Bunny. In still others, there is no such office, or not even a Britain at all; and so on. So a given sentence or proposition varies its truth value from world to world.

Just as sentences change their truth values from world to world, a given singular term may vary its referent from world to world: In our actual world in 2005, 'The present British prime minister' designates Tony Blair. But as before, Blair might not have been elected or even run in the first place, or even existed at all. So in some other worlds the same description, meaning what it does here in our world, designates someone else, say Archer, or no one at all, since in some other possible worlds, Archer was elected, and in some no one was, etc. This is why the description's referent changes from world to world.

I shall call such a singular term, one that designates different things at different worlds, a *flaccid* designator. It contrasts specifically with what Kripke calls a *rigid* designator: a term that is not flaccid, that does not change its referent from world to world, but denotes the very same item at every world in which that item exists.

Now we are able to state Kripke's further objection to Description theories of names (1972/1980, pp. 74ff): A definite description of the sort Russell had in mind is flaccid, as has just been illustrated. Yet names, Kripke says, do not (usually) vary their reference across worlds or hypothetical situations in that way. If we imagine a world in which Richard Nixon does such-and-such, it is one in which *Nixon* does that thing and has some properties different from those he has here in the real world. Our name 'Nixon' denotes *him* there, not someone else. Names are (normally) in that sense rigid designators, keeping the same referent from world to world, while Russellian descriptions are flaccid. Thus, names are not equivalent to Russellian descriptions.

Kripke offers a further intuitive test for telling whether a term is rigid: Try the term in the sentence frame, 'N might not have been N.' If for 'N' we substitute a description like 'the Poet Laureate of England from 1984 till 1998,' we obtain 'The Poet Laureate of England from 1984 till 1998 might not have been the Poet Laureate of England from 1984 till 1998'; and the latter sentence is true, at least on its most natural reading: The person who was in fact Poet Laureate from 1984 till 1998 might, had things gone differently, have failed to be Poet Laureate then or at any other time. The truth of the foregoing sentence shows that the description refers to different people in different worlds.

But if we substitute the proper name 'Hughes,' we get 'Hughes might not have been Hughes,' at best a very strange sentence. It might mean that Hughes might not have existed at all, which is perhaps the most obvious way in which Hughes could have failed to be Hughes. But given that Hughes existed, how could he have failed to be Hughes? He could have failed to be *named* 'Hughes,' but that is not to have failed to *be Hughes*, himself (because, of course, Hughes need not have been named 'Hughes'). He could have failed to have the properties stereotypically associated with Hughes, hence failed to 'be Hughes' in the same sense in which

Bypass, North Carolina is no New York City, but such flaccid uses of names are unusual.

Kripke argues that when one uses the name 'Hughes' to refer a person in this world and then starts describing hypothetical scenarios or alternative possible worlds, continuing to use the name, one is talking about the same person. So if you ask, 'Might Hughes have run off with the circus rather than becoming Poet Laureate?,' the answer may be yes or may be no, but the scenario you are considering is one in which Hughes, that very person, has run off with the circus, not one in which whoever or whatever was Poet Laureate had (also) run off with the circus. You are not imagining a world in which a circus performer is also Poet Laureate.

But what of Russell's argument from identifying questions? In response to 'Whom do you mean by "Robertson Davies"?,' you promptly cough up a description or cluster of descriptions. Likewise Searle's appeal to teaching and learning. These facts seem both undeniable and insuperable.

In response, Kripke introduces an important distinction. Russell had assumed that if a name has a description associated with it in the way he pointed out, then the name must share the meaning of that description. But that assumption is unwarranted, because there is a weaker relation that the description might bear to the name and still explain the phenomena: Even though the description does not give the linguistic meaning of the name, it is what is used to determine the name's reference on an occasion. Although the name 'Robertson Davies' is not synonymous with 'the Canadian novelist who wrote all those trilogies,' the latter description can be used merely to indicate the person one is referring to when one uses 'Robertson Davies.' And it can be used as part of an explanation to a pupil, merely to identify the individual to which the name is attached.

So, even if a name someone uses on an occasion has a determinate and conscious association with a particular description in that person's mind, it does not follow that the name is synonymous with the description. For all that has been shown, when the person obligingly spits out the description in response to an identificatory question, the person is merely identifying the name's referent. Similarly, if I tell a small child who 'Tony Blair' is, identifying that name's referent by saying 'Tony Blair is the British prime minister,' it does not follow that the name 'Tony Blair' simply means 'the British prime minister.'

How Does a Name Mean? Direct Reference

Russell attacked the view that ordinary names are Millian, in favor of the Description theory of names. In turn, Kripke attacked the Description theory in favor of the claim that ordinary names are rigid designators. But the latter claim does not quite amount to Millianism, for not all rigid designators are Millian names.

A Millian name is one that has no meaning but its bearer or referent. Its sole function is to introduce that individual into discourse; it contributes nothing else to the meaning of a sentence in which it occurs. If we say 'Jack is brilliant,' 'Jack' being a Millian name, the meaning of that sentence consists simply of the person Jack himself concatenated with the property of being brilliant.

All Millian names are rigid. But the converse does not hold; rigidity does not entail being Millian. For definite descriptions can be rigid. For example: *Arithmetical* truths are all necessary truths, or so many people believe. So there are arithmetical descriptions, such as 'the positive square root of 49,' that are rigid, because they designate the same number in every possible world, but are certainly not Millian because in order to secure their reference they exploit their conceptual content. The only reason 'the positive square root of 49' designates 7 is that 7 is positive and yields 49 when multiplied by itself. So that description is not Millian even though it is rigid, because it does not simply introduce its bearer (the number 7) into the discourse; it also characterizes 7 as being something which when multiplied by itself yields 49. Thus, in defending the rigidity of names, Kripke did not thereby establish the stronger claim. (Nor did he intend to; Kripke (1979) argues that names are not Millian. Following an important idea of David Kaplan's (1978), Plantinga (1978) and Ackerman (1979) defend positive theories according to which names are rigid but not Millian.)

However, other philosophers have championed the Millian view, which has come to be called the 'Direct Reference' theory of names. The first of these in the past century was Ruth Barcan Marcus (1960, 1961). Subsequent Direct Reference (DR) theories of names have been built on Marcus' and Kripke's work (for example, Kaplan (1975) and Salmon (1986)).

Of course, DR must confront the four original objections to the natural Millian view. Let us begin with the fourth, regarding substitutivity, for it will be the easiest though it will not be easy. Recall that our sentence 'Edwina believes that C. L. Dodgson's middle initial was "L" ' is true, but 'Edwina believes that Lewis Carroll's middle initial was "L" ' is false. How can DR allow that fact, much less explain it, given that 'C. L. Dodgson' and 'Lewis Carroll' have the same bearer?

DR theorists pursue a double strategy, putting forward a positive thesis and a negative thesis (though these are not often explicitly distinguished). The positive DR thesis is that the names in question really do substitute without altering the containing sentence's truth value. On this view, 'Edwina believes that Lewis Carroll's middle initial was "L" ' is true, not false. At the very least, that sentence has a reading or understanding on which the two names really do just refer to what they refer to; certainly Edwina does believe *of Carroll* that his middle initial was 'L.'

We naturally think otherwise; the sentence does not seem true to us. That is because when we see a belief sentence, we usually take its complement clause to reproduce the way in which its subject would speak or think. If I assert 'Edwina believes that Lewis Carroll's middle initial was "L," ' I thereby somehow imply that Edwina would accept the *sentence* 'Lewis Carroll's middle initial was "L," ' or something fairly close to it. If I say, 'Edwina does not believe that Lewis Carroll's middle initial was "L," ' I thereby suggest that if confronted by the sentence

'Lewis Carroll's middle initial was "L," ' Edwina would say either 'No' or 'If you say so.'

But the DR theorists point out that such suggestions are not always true, perhaps not ever true. Suppose a good friend of mine at another university is involved in an academic scandal, say is accused (quite falsely) of plagiarism. I might say to a colleague, 'The Provost there believes that my good friend and old tennis partner is guilty.' Obviously what I would mean is that the Provost believes *that person* to be guilty, with no presumption that the Provost represents him as 'Lycan's good friend and old tennis partner'; the Provost (being somewhat backward) has never heard of me. In issuing a belief sentence, a *speaker* can make that kind of reference in the sentence's complement clause without at all assuming that the subject of the sentence would have referred to the individual in any parallel or analogous way. So it seems undeniable that there are singular-term positions inside belief sentences in which the referring expression does just refer to its bearer, without any further suggestion about the way in which the subject of the belief sentence would have represented the bearer.

Most of the DR literature has been devoted to establishing the positive thesis, that names do have Millian readings even in belief contexts. But the positive thesis is far from all that the DR theorist needs. For although we may accept it and agree that belief sentences have readings on which the speaker may substitute her/his own referring expression for the one the believer would have used, many philosophers also remain convinced that every belief sentence also has a *non*-substitutive reading. *In one sense* the Provost believes that my good friend and old tennis partner is guilty, but in another, he believes no such thing, for the obvious reason that he has never heard of me or possibly even of tennis. Yet it seems DR cannot allow *so much as* a sense in which belief contexts do not allow substitution of co-referring singular terms. That is DR's negative thesis: that names do not have nonMillian readings, even in belief contexts.

The problem gets worse: It is hard to deny that the non-substitutive readings are more readily heard than the substitutive ones. Indeed, that is implicitly conceded by the DR theorists, in that they know they have had to work to make us hear the substitutive readings, coming up with examples such as mine. The DR theorists must try to explain the fact away as a particularly dramatic illusion. That is, they must hold that in fact, ordinary belief sentences cannot literally mean what we usually would take them to mean, as after all implying that their complement clauses reproduce the ways in which their subjects would express the beliefs in question; there is some extraneous reason why we are seduced into hearing such sentences non-substitutively. A few such putative explanations have been sketched, using materials from the **theory of conversational coöperation** or elsewhere in **linguistic pragmatics** (Salmon (1986), Soames (1987, 2002), Wettstein (1991), and see Marcus (1981)). Here, in my opinion, the DR theorists have failed to come up with any very convincing account. Perhaps the most promising is Soames,' which appeals to the idea that in uttering a sentence one often *asserts* more than the semantic content of that sentence.

Frege's Puzzle is even worse for the Millian. According to DR, a sentence like 'C. L. Dodgson is Lewis Carroll' can mean only that the common referent, however designated, is himself. Yet such a sentence is virtually never understood as meaning that. And anyone might doubt that Dodgson is Carroll, without doubting anyone's self-identity. Here again, the DR theorist bears a great burden, of explaining away our intuitive judgments as illusory.

The problems of negative existentials and empty names are if anything worse yet. If a name's meaning is simply to refer to its bearer, then what about all those perfectly meaningful names that lack bearers entirely? (However, for an attempt, see Salmon 1998.)

We have come to what is nearly a paradox. On the one hand, we have seen compelling Kripkean reasons why names cannot be thought to abbreviate flaccid descriptions, or otherwise to have substantive senses or connotations. Intuitively, names are Millian. Yet because the original objections to the Millian view are as urgent as ever, it also seems that DR is untenable. This is a trilemma, because it has further seemed that we are stuck with one of these three possibilities: either the names are Millian, or they abbreviate descriptions outright, or in some looser way such as Searle's, they have some substantive 'sense' or content. But none of these views is acceptable.

A few theorists have claimed to find ways between the three horns. As remarked above, Plantinga (1978) and Ackerman (1979) have appealed to rigidified descriptions. Devitt (1989, 1996) has offered a radical revision of Frege's notion of sense. I myself (Lycan 1994) have offered a subtle, beautiful and fairly effective weakened version of DR, but it would be immodest to do more than mention it.

Further Reading

Almog, J., Perry, J., and Wettstein, H. (eds.). (1989) *Themes from Kaplan*. New York: Oxford University Press. Contains further representative papers on DR.

Berger, A. (2002). *Terms and truth*. Cambridge: Bradford Books/MIT Press. Defends a distinctive form of DR.

Burge, T. (1973). Reference and proper names. *Journal of Philosophy*, 70, 425–39. Defends a Description theory of names against Kripke.

Devitt, M. (1981a). *Designation*. New York: Columbia University Press. The first worked-out version of the Causal-historical theory of referring.

Devitt, M. (1989). Against direct reference. *Midwest Studies in Philosophy*, 14, 206–40. Offers a survey and a critique of DR.

Donnellan, K. (1970). Proper names and identifying descriptions. *Synthese*, 21, 335–58. Offers some further criticisms of the Description theory of names.

Erwin, E., Kleiman, L., and Zemach, E. (1976). The historical theory of reference. *Australasian Journal of Philosophy*, 54, 50–7. Offers further objections to the Causal-historical theory.

Evans, G. (1973). The causal theory of names. *Aristotelian Society Supplementary Volume 47*, 187–208. Offers further objections to Kripke's picture, and an interesting revision of it.

Evans, G. (1982). *The Varieties of Reference*. Oxford: Oxford University Press. Makes concessions to Kripke but insists that the idea of a 'name-using [social] practice' must be introduced as a further element.

Everett, A. and Hofweber, T. (eds.) (2000). *Empty names, fiction and the puzzles of non-existence*. Stanford: CSLI Publications. Contains articles on empty names and negative existentials.

Kvart, I. (1993). Mediated reference and proper names. *Mind*, 102, 611–28. Elaborates a version of the Causal-historical theory of referring.

Linsky, L (1977). *Names and descriptions*. Chicago: University of Chicago Press. Offers further objections to the Causal-historical theory.

Loar, B. (1976). The semantics of singular terms. *Philosophical Studies*, 30, 353–77. Defends a Description theory of names against Kripke.

Lycan, W.G. (1994). *Modality and meaning*. Dordrecht: Kluwer Academic Press. Defends a distinctive form of DR.

McKinsey, M. (1976). Divided reference in causal theories of names. *Philosophical Studies*, 30, 235–42. Pushes in the direction of a Description theory of referring. See also McKinsey, M. (1978). Names and intentionality. *Philosophical Review*, 87, 171–200.

Recanati, F. (1993). *Direct reference*. Oxford: Basil Blackwell. Defends a distinctive form of DR.

Russell, B. (1918/1956). The philosophy of logical atomism. In R. Marsh (Ed.). *Logic and knowledge*. London: Allen and Unwin. Defends Russell's Description theory of names most accessibly.

Searle, J. (1979). *Expression and meaning*. Cambridge: Cambridge University Press. Chapter 3 addresses the matter of empty names.

Searle, J. (1983). *Intentionality: An essay in the philosophy of mind*. New York: Cambridge University of Press. Chapter 9 replies to some of Kripke's objections.

Chapter 15

General Terms and Mass Terms

Stephen P. Schwartz

Gold should mean gold. In fact, what these distributors and retailers were selling was nothing more than fool's gold. Without expert training or testing equipment, there is no way for consumers to know whether gold jewelry is real or not.

Eliot Spitzer, Attorney General of New York State as quoted in *The Ithaca Journal* (Rochester jeweler fined for 'fool's gold') November 23, 2001

I Introduction

Issues about the semantics of general terms (including the count nouns such as 'tiger' and 'bachelor') and mass terms (e.g. 'water' and 'gold') have been the focus of intense interest among philosophers of language recently because ancient and hallowed theories have been dramatically overthrown and new and revolutionary ones have been formed. Alas these new theories also seem now to be beset on all sides by critics and skeptics. The situation can best be described as fluid. I will here set out the recent history of these upheavals and point to some future directions.

Among general terms and mass terms we usually distinguish natural kind terms such as 'tiger,' 'water,' and 'gold,' from artifact kind terms such as 'chair,' 'computer,' and 'cathedral,' and social kind terms such as 'bachelor,' 'grandmother,' and 'philosopher.' General terms and mass terms are to be distinguished from proper names and definite descriptions in that general terms and mass terms typically do not denote or pick out just one individual.[1] A general term (for ease of exposition I will use 'general term' rather than the more cumbrous 'general term and mass term' unless the distinction is relevant in the context) such as 'tiger' or 'bachelor' can be applied truly to a large number of different but similar individuals. This collection that contains all and only the individuals to which the general term is correctly applied is called the extension of the term. We can speak of the extension of a general term as its reference much as we would speak of the bearer of a proper name as its reference. The crucial question then is how do general terms get their references? What determines what the extension of a general term is?

Until about the 1970s there was little to contest about this issue. The answer seemed obvious and indisputable, and except for some fussy details, frankly, there was not much disagreement about it. Then due to the revolutionary and bold thinking of Saul Kripke and Hilary Putnam in the late 1960s and early 1970s philosophers realized that the obvious and indisputable answer was not correct for at least large numbers of general terms. (See especially Kripke, 1972, 1980 and Putnam, 1975.)

II The Traditional Description Theory

The traditional answer to the question of how a general term gathers its extension was simple, clear, and elegant. With every general term there is associated an intension and it is the intension that determines the extension. The intension of a term provides a necessary and sufficient condition for being in the extension of the term. The simplest and clearest version of the traditional theory holds that each speaker of the language associates with each general term in her or his vocabulary a concept. This concept is a list or combination of properties or features that represents the necessary and sufficient condition. In one very ordinary sense of the term 'meaning,' the intension of a term is its meaning, and knowing what a term means is knowing its intension. (The intension is also sometimes called the 'sense' or 'connotation' of the term.) Each candidate for membership in the extension is compared with the concept. If the candidate has all the features included in the concept, then it is in the extension of the term and thus is correctly called by the term. If it does not have all the features, then it is not in the extension.[2] Hilary Putnam on the way to attacking the traditional view describes it neatly and clarifies its provenance.

> [I]n spite of the variety of metaphysical theories about the nature of concepts, this much was not doubted: concepts were uniformly thought of as capable of being completely contained in or recollected by 'the mind' (which was itself conceived of as a private theater, isolated from other individuals and from the 'external world').
> It was also taken for granted by almost all philosophers in the tradition that the idea in the mind, or the possession or recollection of the idea by the mind, determines the extension of the 'name' associated with the idea or concept: a name, say, 'dog,' is *true of* a particular thing inasmuch as that particular thing falls under the concept in mind.   (Putnam 1996: xv)

Since the concept in mind is like a description, it is now common practice to call this view the 'traditional description theory.'

Virtually the only disagreement among philosophers was over the nature of the intension. Some, such as Carnap (1967) and his positivist allies, thought the intension must be a collection of observable features; others of a more platonic bent held that the intension was an abstract universal grasped or 'recollected' by the subjective concept in the mind of the speaker (Frege, 1892, 1949). Among the modern variants of the traditional description theory is the 'family resemblance' or 'cluster' theory of Wittgenstein (1953). The cluster theory is an attempt to accommodate vagueness and open-texture. According to the cluster theory the intensions of most terms do not provide neat necessary and sufficient conditions for falling into the extension. Rather the intension would require that an item have most or some subset of important features in the intension but not absolutely all.[3]

If the intension of a term is viewed simply as a subjective psychological state, then the traditional description theory fits nicely with empiricism, because it has a disarming way with necessity and a prioricity. Such truths as 'All tigers are animals,' 'No bachelors are married,' and 'All gold is yellow' are necessary and knowable a priori because they are analytic. That is, we as speakers of the language somewhat arbitrarily create a concept that contains features – yellow, metal, malleable, ductile, shiny – and associate with it a general term, say 'gold.' That all gold is yellow will be true, necessarily true and knowable a priori, not on the basis of some pure rational insight into the nature of reality, but just on the basis of how we have constructed the concept 'gold.' This analysis can be applied across the board to all general terms. We can even create new ones at will according to this pattern. I associate three features, red, round, and wooden with a term 'balluba.' That all ballubas are red is necessarily true and knowable a priori, and not at all informative except about how I have chosen to create and name a concept. Since a standard lexical definition is the linguistic correlate of the concept associated with a term, we can say then that these truths are necessarily true by definition. They are purely analytic. This approach completely demystifies the notions of necessity and a prioricity.

If we are concerned about ancient metaphysical notions, we are even justified in claiming that the concept associated with the general term is the essence of the kind; thus also demystifying the notion of essence. The concept in the mind is the essence of the kind because it is fitting the concept that makes something belong to the kind. The concept yellow, metal, malleable, ductile, shiny is the essence of gold because it is fitting this concept that makes something gold – according to this traditional view. Accordingly we learn the essences of things by examining our concepts. Ballubas are a kind of thing because I framed a concept to define them. We know the essence of ballubas – being red, round, and wooden. The essences of every kind of thing can be known in this way. The view that essence is linguistic in this way was central to the ordinary language philosophy of the 1950s and 1960s.

Due to the work of Kripke and Putnam and their followers the tide has turned so completely that the traditional description theory has gone from being assumed and obvious (at least in some version or other) to almost universal rejection. True, there have been attempts to offer complex revisions of the traditional description theory (see e.g. Searle 1996 and for a more sophisticated attempt McKinsey 1991), but in view of the progress made by Kripke and Putnam this seems to be a futile and unrewarding path. (E.g. see Putnam 1996: xviii–xx; for a convincing dissection of Searle 1996.)

Although saving the traditional description theory is a forlorn endeavor, we should not leave it unappreciated. It is the very ideal of a philosophical theory. As noted, it is simple, clear, and elegant. It offers a unified theory of the meaning and reference of general terms that ties together all the loose ends: meaning, reference, essence, definition, and concept, a prioricity, etc.. It offers the resolution of philosophical problems and demystifies notions such as necessity and a prioricity that are liable to lead us far astray if left to their own devices. It can be used to support empiricism – a noble and worthy tradition itself. Furthermore it is not internally inconsistent or incorrect. General terms *could* function the way the traditional theory says they do – my term 'balluba' demonstrates that – and some terms of natural language, for example, kinship and social terms such as 'grandmother' and 'bachelor' probably do. The traditional description theory seems to be too good to give up. Unfortunately it is also too good to be true.

III   Kripke and Putnam

The main arguments of Kripke's and Putnam's attack on the traditional description theory are found in a series of articles from the 1970s (Kripke 1971, 1972, 1980; Putnam, 1971, 1973, 1975). The focus of Kripke and Putnam was on natural kind terms but was not by any means restricted to them. The attack was coupled with and deeply informed by Kripke's work on proper names. Both Kripke and Putnam argued that natural kind terms are, like names, rigid designators whose extensions are not gathered by concepts that represent necessary and sufficient conditions. A rigid designator is a term that has the same reference when talking about other possible worlds as it does when talking about the actual world, if it has a reference at all in those worlds. Thus the rigid designator 'Benjamin Franklin' refers to the same man when talking about counterfactual situations, but 'the inventor of bifocals' need not. In some other counterfactual situations, i.e. possible worlds, someone besides Franklin invented bifocals. Since natural kind terms are rigid designators, their reference is not determined by descriptions, not even loose 'cluster' descriptions. Descriptions of the sort supposed by the traditional description theory are typically non-rigid – like 'the inventor of bifocals.' Although according to this new theory, descriptive concepts have a role to play, the reference of natural kind terms and many other general terms is not mediated by concepts. For this reason the revolutionary theory of Kripke and Putnam is usually called the 'direct reference theory.'

To appreciate the failure of the traditional theory consider, from the perspective of Kripke and Putnam, the functioning of a natural kind term such as 'gold.' The features in the concept of gold such as being yellow, and being shiny are superficial observable features, but a moment's reflection is sufficient to remind us that these are not what makes some substance gold – not even the combination of all of them, otherwise fool's gold would be gold. Gold is an element that has an atomic structure and according to the direct reference theory this atomic structure, represented by the atomic number, is what makes some stuff gold. Gold is the element with atomic number 79. The superficial features that the traditional description theory included in the concept, far from being necessary and sufficient conditions for membership in the extension, play no role whatsoever in determining whether some stuff is gold. Nor is the deeper description 'being the element with atomic number 79' a part of a traditionally conceived intension of the term 'gold.' True, being the element with atomic number 79 is a necessary and sufficient condition for being gold so it could serve admirably as the defining feature of the term 'gold' but it doesn't. For one thing, most people who know what gold is, in the sense of understanding the term 'gold,' having it in their vocabularies, and so on have no idea that it is the element with atomic number 79. Most of us who have never studied chemistry or physics have only the vaguest idea anyway what atomic number is. Furthermore, that gold is the element with atomic number 79 was an empirical discovery. Nobody who was not in the grip of a theory would imagine that the word 'gold' changed its meaning when chemists discovered the atomic structure of gold. Since it is an empirical discovery that gold is the element with atomic number 79, it is not analytic or a priori as propositions that follow from definitions are supposed to be. And since the fact that gold is the element with atomic number 79 was a discovery we could, in some sense, discover that this 'fact' is not a fact after all. Nothing guarantees that our current physical and chemical theories are absolutely true and unrevisable.

Consider a claim such as 'All tigers are animals.' Kripke and Putnam, against traditional thinking, hold that 'All tigers are animals' is not analytic or a priori, but that it is necessarily true. 'All tigers are animals' is not analytic but it is not like an ordinary contingent empirical generalization either. It has a certain stability that e.g. 'No tigers are found in Iceland' lacks. Presumably this stability comes from the rigidity of 'tiger.' To see this, consider that the proposition 'All tigers are animals' is not refutable by counterexample. A proposed 'tiger' that was not an animal, given that all the other tigers are animals, would just not be a tiger even if it is striped, cat-like, etc. It would be a fake tiger, or a tiger-mimic. The fact that 'All tigers are animals' is not refutable by counterexample fooled traditional theorists into thinking that this claim was analytic. They did not consider that we can imagine discovering that none of the tigers were animals but actually elaborate robots sent by aliens to spy on us. In other words, traditional thinkers did not consider the possibility that our entire theory of tigers could be in error. In such a case Kripke plausibly claims we would say that we have discovered that tigers are not animals. "All tigers are animals" is in this sense empirically revisable, thus not analytic – not true by definition.

Since being an animal is necessary, i.e. essential, for being a tiger (assuming that our tiger theory is not in error), we discover essence empirically. Essence is not uncovered by pure rational insight nor is it merely linguistic. Gold is the element with atomic number 79, water is H_2O, and tigers are animals with a certain genetic makeup. Chemical composition in the case of water and genetic makeup in the case of tigers play the same role as atomic structure in the case of gold. With natural kinds there is an underlying trait that makes things be of the kind. According to Kripke and especially Putnam these are not unique features of the term 'gold' and 'tiger' but apply to all natural kind terms and most other terms as well. Putnam (1975: 164) claims that all general and mass terms tend to be like natural kind terms, with the possible exception of what he calls 'one criterion terms' such as 'bachelor' and 'hunter' (one who hunts).

The upshot is that the features supposed by the traditional description theory to be included in the concept of gold play no role in determining the extension of gold, and the scientifically discovered necessary and sufficient condition for being gold does not figure in the concept of gold in anything like the way the traditional theory would suppose – it does not generate a priori analytic truths. On the other hand it does seem to be the essence of gold, but not one that empiricists have to balk at since it is empirically discovered. So the traditional view has gotten everything wrong. Even the very terms of the theory are misleading. If we mean by 'intension' whatever it is that determines the extension, then obviously every general term that has an extension also must have an intension. Nevertheless, the cleanest way to express the view of the direct reference theory is to say that natural kind terms and terms that function like them have no intension at all. This claim is not as outrageous as it seems, since the very use of the term 'intension' suggests something in the mind, psychological, subjective, or at least conventional – not 'out there.'

What then about the superficial properties that most people have in mind when they think of gold? Obviously we have such concepts associated with many natural kind terms. Putnam calls these concepts 'stereotypes' (Putnam 1975: 166–73). Stereotypes are like the clusters that Wittgenstein discussed, but they play a different role. My concept of gold does not determine what gold is or what the term 'gold' means even for me. I do not want my wedding ring just to match my concept of gold. I want it to *be* gold. Furthermore as Putnam (1975) so effectively pointed out, many of the concepts that we associate with natural kind terms are not uniquely identifying, even when treated as clusters, and are partly or entirely erroneous. I could not distinguish leopards from cheetahs, my concepts of them are indistinguishable. I have a vague idea that leopards live in trees and eat only at night – or is that cheetahs? I know that leopards have spots. Do all leopards have spots? Don't cheetahs have spots too? Anyway, the idea that my concept of leopard or cheetah determines whether something is or is not a leopard, even for me, is preposterous. I leave to zoologists the task of discovering the differences between cheetahs and leopards, if there are any. In fact for most natural kind terms, experts have established ways of learning whether something is in the extension of the term that are far more reliable than any concept that the standard speaker has in mind. Speakers will defer to the experts on matters of classification. This is what Putnam (1975: 144–6) calls the 'linguistic division of labor.'

> I can refer to gold, talk about gold, purchase gold, etc., perfectly well without being able reliably to distinguish gold from non-gold because there are others in the community – experts – upon whom I can rely. In short, there is a *linguistic division of labor.* (Putnam 1996: xvi)

If natural kind terms and other general terms that are like natural kind terms do not get their extensions via intensions, then how do they get them? There is no crisp, clear answer to this question. The idea however is something like this: Speakers pick out a paradigm example of what they take to be a kind. In a 'baptism' of sorts they determine to call anything of the same kind by the term being 'defined.' Usually the speakers have only the vaguest notion of what makes something to be of the kind of thing baptized. When they do discover what it is – the underlying trait of the kind – they may discover that some of the things they thought belonged to the kind do not and that other things which are superficially quite different from the paradigm actually are members of the kind. The underlying trait determines whether or not a candidate is a member of the kind and thus in the extension of the term. According to the direct reference theory natural kind terms are very much like proper names in the way that they function. Like names, the general terms are directly 'pinned' to the things in the extension via the baptism and then the term is handed on from one speaker to another in a causal chain much as with proper names. This part of the direct theory is called the 'causal theory of reference.' Proper names, according to the direct reference theory, do not function by means of uniquely identifying descriptions or even clusters and neither do natural kind terms. And like names, natural kind terms are rigid designators. Kripke says:

> [C]ertain general terms, those for natural kinds, have a greater kinship with proper names than is generally realized. This conclusion holds for certain for various species names, whether they are count nouns, such as 'cat,' 'tiger,' 'chunk of gold,' or mass terms such as 'gold,' 'water,' 'iron pyrites.' It also applies to certain terms for natural phenomena, such as 'heat,' 'light,' 'sound,' 'lightning,' and, presumably, suitably elaborated to corresponding adjectives – 'hot,' 'loud,' 'red.' (Kripke 1980: 134)

As already noted Putnam claims that almost all general terms have a 'natural kind sense' and thus are like names. Kripke says that ' "Heat" like "gold" is a rigid designator.' (Kripke 1980: 136).

IV Criticisms of the Direct Theory

The direct theory of reference for general terms as formulated by Kripke and Putnam has itself been in for its share of criticism recently. The arguments against the Kripke/Putnam account of general terms have focused primarily on four areas: (1) The direct theory is not unified. Even its proponents claim that it applies to only many or most general terms. (2) The difficulty in understanding how terms could get directly attached to extensions without using descriptions in a way reminiscent of the traditional theory. This is the *Qua* problem. (3) The difficulty of clarifying what the notion of rigid designation is when applied to general terms. (4) The fact that most natural kind terms do not refer to a kind with a unique underlying trait. These objections have not for the most part been offered by thinkers who are unsympathetic to the direct theory. On the contrary, most have emerged during the attempt to defend, refine, and elaborate it. Although the situation is not as decisive as the collapse of the traditional theory, the direct theory of Kripke and Putnam also seems to be doomed. The formulation of satisfactory alternatives is the work of the future (e.g. see Devitt and Sterelny 1999: especially 96–100, for suggestions about a hybrid theory.)

Let us take a look at each of the areas of criticism in somewhat more detail.

(1) Putnam admits that some terms do not fit the direct theory, but the more we focus on close examination of different general terms the more exceptions we find. Kinds of artifacts do not have underlying traits and it is hard to see how they could function like natural kind terms. Putnam claimed that the general term 'pencil' is indexical (his way of saying that it is a rigid designator) (Putnam 1975: 162) but his arguments are weak. He claimed that the proposition 'All pencils are artifacts' is not analytic and not a priori, and thus that 'pencil' functions here like 'tiger' in 'All tigers are animals.' 'All pencils are artifacts' is not analytic, but not much follows from this except that being an artifact is not part of the defining concept of pencil. Direct theorists attacking the traditional description theory weaken their case by attributing crude and incorrect definitions to terms. Often the first things that spring to mind are not part of the intension of a term. What is the definition of 'lake'? Is 'lake' a natural kind term? Many lakes are artifacts, others are natural. With careful reflection we realize that lakes need not contain water – there could be lakes of mercury or other liquids; they need not even be filled with liquids. There are frozen lakes, perhaps lakes of dust on other planets, ships that sail across them to harbors on them and so on. Does this demonstrate that 'lake' is a rigid designator and a natural kind term? Hardly. It only demonstrates that we have not taken care to properly formulate the concept of 'lake.' Likewise with 'pencil.' Being an artifact is not part of the intension of 'pencil.' 'Pencil' is defined by certain features of form and function and these could conceivably occur naturally (Schwartz 1978).

What about our standard examples of natural kind terms? Many natural kind terms have what appear to be large amounts of conventionality and to have something like traditional definitions. At least they do not work by being directly 'pinned' to objects. For example, 'vixen' means female fox, 'carnivore' means meat-eating, and so on. That vixens are female foxes does not seem to be an empirical discovery. 'Diamond' does not just refer to carbon, but only carbon in a certain form that must have a certain superficial appearance. Descriptions seem to play an important and indispensable role in the functioning of many, perhaps most, natural kind terms.

Kripke and Putnam and their followers would not be happy with the result that their view only applies to a few central examples of natural kind terms, if to any at all. They fashioned arguments based on the wide application of the direct theory to general terms. For example Kripke (1972: 334–42; 1980 144–55) offered a famous argument against the mind/brain identity theory that relies on the terms of mind/brain process identities being rigid designators. But if it is unclear whether, which, and how many such terms are really natural kind terms that fit the direct theory mold, then his argument is seriously undermined.

(2) Descriptions enter essentially in the very grounding of a term in a baptism. This is the *Qua* problem. A person cannot simply baptize an object and say solemnly 'Any object of the same kind as this ... ' etc. Each object is a member of many kinds. Tigers are cats, mammals, animals, physical objects, and so on. The individual tiger that figures in the baptism must also be located somewhere, be either male or female, young or old, etc. The baptizer must think that he is baptizing the object *qua* one of these features. As Devitt and Sterelny point out in their original discussion of the problem: " ... [T]he grounder of a natural kind term associates, consciously or unconsciously, with that term first some description that in effect classifies the term as a natural kind term; second, some descriptions that determine which nature of the sample is relevant to the reference of the term" (Devitt and Sterelny 1999: 92). These descriptions then play an essential role in fixing the reference of the term. This means that the direct theory is in error when it relegates descriptions to an inessential subsidiary role.

Stanford and Kitcher examine what they call the 'Simple Real Essence Theory' (SRE). SRE is basically the direct reference theory of natural kind terms. " ... (SRE) suggests that a natural kind term is associated with a sample of some substance, and that the term refers to the set of things that share the same inner constitution [i.e. underlying trait] as the sample" (Stanford and Kitcher 2000: 99). According to Stanford and Kitcher:

> As Michael Devitt and Kim Sterelny point out, a theory like SRE is *too* simple ...
> Because it is utterly mysterious how, without something more than our causal relation
> to the sample, we can pick out one, rather than another, of the many kinds the sample
> instantiates. (Stanford and Kitcher 2000: 100–1)

After a searching investigation, Stanford and Kitcher conclude: "The upshot of our story is that there is no simple account of the reference of natural kind terms" (Stanford and Kitcher 2000:126).

(3) There are technical problems with the direct theory as well. As we have seen both Kripke and Putnam hold that natural kind terms and other general terms that work like them are rigid designators. But the technical notion of rigid designator does not seem to fit general terms. (Recall that a rigid designator has the same

reference, i.e. extension, in every possible world in which it refers at all.) If we consider other possible worlds, then some of our actual tigers would not exist in some of those other worlds and other tigers that were never born in our world would exist. The extension of 'tiger' can vary from possible world to possible world. With only a few exceptions, the extensions of all general and mass terms can vary in this way. Thus unlike a proper name, a general term typically does not have the same reference, i.e. extension, in every possible world in which it refers at all. If the extension of a natural kind term changes from world to world, then natural kind terms cannot be rigid designators. The notion of rigid designation as applied to singular terms can be formally explained with the technical apparatus of set theory and possible worlds. A singular term that is a rigid designator is a constant function from possible worlds to the set of possible individuals. It is a function that takes the same value at every world where it has a value. No such definition is possible for general terms, since they have different extensions in different possible worlds. E.g. the set of tigers is different in different possible worlds. The problem in a nutshell is that the notion of a rigid designator grew out of Kripke's work in formal semantics but there is no correct way for formal semantics to represent rigid designation of general terms (Schwartz 1980).

Several philosophers have suggested solutions for this problem but none seem satisfactory. For example, Donnellan (1983) and others (LaPorte 2000; 2004: ch. 2) have suggested that a rigid general term, such as a natural kind term, does not designate its extension in each world but that it designates a kind, and this stays the same from world to world. Thus 'tiger' will designate the same kind of animal in every possible world in which it designates at all, and 'gold' will designate the same element, etc. The problem with this idea is that every general term will turn out to be a rigid designator – even terms that Kripke and Putnam do not want to be rigid designators. For example, 'bachelor' will designate the same marital status in every possible world, 'hunter' the same occupation, etc. Donnellan's move seems to trivialize the notion of rigid designation when applied to general terms.[4] Other technical solutions that have been suggested are not sensitive to the actual uses of natural kind terms. For example, Deutsch's (1993) formal semantics for natural kind terms requires that they be nested whereas in fact many natural kind terms are cross-cutting.

Kripke started from the insight that natural kind terms are analogous to names in the way their reference-gathering works. On closer scrutiny we see that the analogy with proper names is oversimplified and misleading and cannot be formalized. If natural kind terms are not like proper names in the way they function, the direct theory loses much of its motivation and appeal. Kripke's claim that natural kind terms are like proper names seemed at first to clear the air and point in the right direction. Now it appears to be a wrong turn.

(4) The direct theory and SRE also must confront the fact that very few of the natural kind terms of our language refer to basic kinds that have unitary underlying traits. This is most clear with biological kinds but also applies to chemical and physical kinds (LaPorte 1996). The philosopher who has been most persistent in

pointing out the failings of the direct theory to capture the actual functioning of biological natural kind terms has been John Dupré (1981, 1993). Dupré notes that "it is far from universally the case that the preanalytic extension of a [natural kind] term of ordinary language corresponds to *any* recognized biological taxon" (Dupré 1981: 73). Some biological terms such as 'tiger,' 'horse,' and 'dog' do refer to animals of a species or narrow group of related species. Others however refer to much higher taxa. For example, 'duck' refers to a family, 'bird' to an even higher taxa and so on. Some natural kind terms such as 'monkey'[5] and 'bug' are used loosely to refer to similar looking animals that may not be closely related biologically or form a distinct group. Many common biological terms, e.g. 'vegetable,' 'shrub,' are based on uses and commercial value rather than underlying trait. Dupré claims "The various cedars ... are not closely related. It is reasonable to suppose that the term 'cedar' has more to do with a kind of timber than with a biological kind" (Dupré 1981: 77). LaPorte (1996) in his insightful treatment points to other similar examples from chemistry and physics. Many of our natural kind terms in these areas do not refer to kinds with underlying traits and indeed according to LaPorte there is a great deal of conventionality in defining these terms. "That 'topaz' refers to all of one chemical compound and 'ruby' to only the red of another seems to represent decision, not discovery" (LaPorte 1996: 123). Obviously this issue is highly technical and requires close scrutiny, but I think that Dupré and LaPorte and others (e.g. Mellor 1977; Wilkerson 1995) have demonstrated that whereas some natural kind terms refer to scientifically recognized kinds with unitary underlying traits this is far from the norm.

Even with biological terms such as 'elephant' and 'honeybee' that do refer to the members of a single species we cannot simply assume that there is an underlying trait or underlying trait of the sort assumed by the direct theorists and proponents of SRE. Biological taxonomy is itself in a state of confusion. There are several different conceptions among biologists of what a species is and what makes a group of organisms a species. Even if we insist contrary to much biological practice that species' differentiation rests solely in genetics, there is tremendous genetic variation among the members of a species and genetic similarity across species. Genetics is unlikely to provide the underlying traits for biological kinds. " ... [I]f an essential property is essential for a natural kind, then species are not natural kinds" (Dupré 1993: 53).

V Legacy of the Direct Theory

Despite the fact that the direct reference theory of Kripke and Putnam is beset by fatal problems it has fundamentally changed the philosophy of language. Most dramatically, the traditional description theory has been deposed and is no longer a live option. With the demise of both the direct theory of Kripke and Putnam and the traditional description theory the hope for a single, clear, unified theory of the functioning of general terms dies as well. The future direction of work in this area is far from clear, but we have learned several important things from the work of Kripke and Putnam. No one can now ignore the fact that there is a strong social element to the meanings and functioning of general terms. Their meanings and reference-gathering are embedded as it were in the very social fabric of our lives. As Putnam has so dramatically put it: "Cut the pie any way you like, 'meanings,' just ain't in the *head*" (Putnam 1975: 144). The recognition of this feature of language is called 'semantic externalism' and is a permanent and valuable philosophical insight. "[K]nowledge of meanings is not something that is possible for a thinker in isolation, and ... it presupposes both interactions with the world and inter-actions with other language users" (Putnam 1996: xvi). "[T]hat a speaker means what she does by 'water' must be constituted at least in part by her physical and social environment"(McDowell 1992: 305). Along with semantic externalism, the linguistic division of labor is now a permanent part of our understanding of the functioning of general terms. "Language ... is not a tool like a hammer, that anyone can use by him- or herself. It is a tool like a large ship, which it takes many people working together to operate" (Putnam 1996: xvi).[6]

Work in the philosophy of language is having an impact on philosophy of mind in that the arguments for semantic externalism are being extended to mental contents. Inspired by the work of Kripke and Putnam, philosophers such as Tyler Burge (1979) and John McDowell (1992) have demonstrated that extern-alism not only features in the meanings of all general terms but applies to the supposed internal and private contents of our minds as well. Not only are linguistic meanings not in the head, but our thoughts and their contents aren't in the head either – externalism applies to thoughts and their contents. "[T]he moral of Putnam's basic thought for the nature of the mental might be,..., that the mind – the locus of our manipulations of meanings – is not in the head either"(McDowell 1992; cited from 1996: 306).

Lastly, our understanding of empirical generalizations about natural kinds is deeper now, thanks to Kripke and Putnam. We cannot go back to viewing "All tigers are animals" as a priori and analytic, nor is it merely a contingent empirical generalization. It is necessarily true and expresses something essential to tigers, but not something that can be discovered by linguistic analysis. Likewise with the claim that gold is the element with atomic number 79. Nathan Salmon (1981) has demonstrated that rigid designation is not the source of the necessity of these propositions, so their necessity can ride free of the dubious claim that "tiger" and "gold" are rigid designators. Precisely how far essentialism about natural kinds can be pressed and what connection it has to the philosophy of language is unclear, especially considering the work of Dupré and LaPorte. This is an important area for further work in the future.

Notes

1   A general term can occur in a definite description or as an adjective, and in other
    constructions – e.g. 'A tiger is in my office.' But not every use of a general term that

seems to be a definite description is one. Even though a sentence such as 'The tiger is a carnivore' seems to treat 'tiger' as the name of an individual or of a kind of animal, we should usually understand this sentence as a way of saying 'All tigers are carnivores.'

2 Among world-historical philosophers John Locke comes the closest to expressing this view just this baldly. See Locke (1690, 1961) Book III, especially parts i–iii.

3 'The main problem [of this work] concerns the possibility of the rational reconstruction of the concepts of all fields of knowledge on the basis of concepts that refer to the immediately given.' (Carnap 1928; 1967: v)

'A painter, a rider, a zoologist probably connect very different images with the name "Bucephalus." The image thereby differs essentially from the connotation of a sign, which latter may well be common property of many and is therefore not a part or mode of the single person's mind.' (Frege 1892; 1949: 88)

'I am saying that these phenomena have no one thing in common which makes us use the same word for all, – but that they are *related* to one another in many different ways.' (Wittgenstein 1953: 31)

4 But on this see LaPorte (2000). LaPorte attempts to provide a clear non-trivial distinction between rigid general terms and non-rigid ones. See Schwartz (2002) for a criticism of LaPorte's position. See also LaPorte (2004) for a further discussion of many of these issues.

5 'Monkeys comprise all the tailed members of the Anthropoidea ... It might be supposed that the monkeys would form a unified natural group; but such is not the case. The American or New World monkeys and the Old World forms constitute two separate groups, with many significant differences ... The Old World monkeys are actually closer zoologically to the great apes and even to man, than they are to the American monkeys.' *The Encyclopedia Americana* article on monkeys.

6 Although Kripke (1986) has expressed qualms about the linguistic division of labor as it has been misunderstood by some, he does not reject outright Putnam's description of it. Kripke emphasizes that experts do not determine or decide the extensions of general terms except in very special circumstances (although these circumstances may not be as rare as Kripke supposes, if LaPorte (1996) is correct). All the experts, and everyone else as well, could be wrong about the actual extension of a natural kind term.

Further Reading

A good place to start is with the now 'classic' works of Kripke (1972, 1980) and Putnam (1975). Schwartz (1977) and Pessin and Goldberg (1996) are two useful anthologies that contain much that is relevant. Even though they are not focused just on general terms, they include many of the essential articles in this area. A great deal of work has been done recently on natural kinds and natural kind terms. Wilkerson (1998) has a very good summary and discussion of the most important aspects of this work and many references. Dupré (1993) is an excellent analysis of the actual practice of using natural kind terms in science and ordinary life. The Dupré should be supplemented by LaPorte (1996) which is also very well researched and extremely interesting. Devitt and Sterelny (1999: ch. 5) is an indispensable survey of many of the issues concerning general terms. Devitt and Sterelny are excellent on the contrast between the description theory and the views of Kripke and Putnam as well as the difficulties with the Kripke/Putnam view of general terms, especially the *Qua* problem. Both Schwartz (2002) and Soames (2002: chs. 9–11) argue (independently) that natural kind terms are not rigid designators, contrary to the claims of Kripke. Soames, although sympathetic to Kripke's semantic program, offers especially detailed and searching arguments against the claim that natural kind terms are rigid designators, at least in their most common uses. But also see LaPorte (2004: ch. 2) for an argument that common natural kind terms are rigid. LaPorte (2004) has detailed discussions of many of the issues concerning the meanings of natural kind terms.

Chapter 16

Descriptions

Peter Ludlow and Stephen Neale

1   Introduction

When philosophers talk about descriptions, usually they have in mind singular *definite* descriptions such as 'the finest Greek poet,' phrases formed with the definite article 'the.' English also contains *indefinite* descriptions such as 'a fine Greek poet,' phrases formed with the indefinite article 'a' (or 'an'); and *demonstrative* descriptions (also known as *complex demonstratives*) such as 'this Greek poet,' formed with the demonstrative articles 'this' and 'that.' In this chapter often we use 'description' as short for 'definite description'; and 'definite,' 'indefinite,' and 'demonstrative' as shorthand nouns. For the most part we focus on definites and indefinites.

At the centre of debates about descriptions is the matter of whether they are devices of reference or of predication (simple or higher-order), and much discussion focusses on how various proposals are to be incorporated into broader theories of the semantics of natural language. But philosophical interest goes beyond the confines of linguistics, logic, and the philosophy of language because choices made about the semantics of descriptions have repercussions elsewhere, particularly in epistemology and metaphysics.

A simple match of form and meaning appears to fail.[1] First, many occurrences of expressions of both forms 'the φ' and 'a φ' appear to be used to talk about particular individuals. Consider (1):

(1)   the whale rammed the boat.

Here the subject expression would be used to talk about an individual whale; similarly if 'the' were replaced by 'a.' So the first question concerns the precise difference in meaning between 'the' and 'a'; and it is natural to say, with traditional grammars, that 'the' indicates some sort of *familiarity, definiteness, specificity,* or *uniqueness* not indicated by 'a.' Second, expressions of both forms may be used in other ways. Consider (2):

(2)   the whale is a mammal.

Here the subject expression might be used to talk about a *species*; similarly if 'the' were replaced by 'a.' Third, in many cases where a description follows the copula, the resulting VP (verb phrase) seems to function as a simple predicate:

(3)   Keiko is a whale
(4)   Keiko is the whale.

Fourth, there are expressions with surface forms distinct from 'a φ' that seem to function as indefinite descriptions: many (but not all) occurrences of the indefinite article 'a' can be replaced without gain or loss by 'some.' Fifth, possessives like 'Paul's mother' seem to function just like definites, whilst 'Paul's finger' seems to function more like an indefinite. Sixth, many pronouns appear to be interpreted as if they are definites or indefinites. In (5), 'it' is naturally interpreted as 'the song' or 'the song John wrote':[2]

(5)   John wrote a song, and Paul sang it.

And in (6), 'one' is naturally interpreted as 'a song':

(6)   John wrote a song, and Paul sang one.

Seventh, it has been argued that some occurrences of ordinary proper names should be analysed as definite descriptions. Some occurrences of 'Neptune' for example, might be analysed as short for something like 'the planet causing perturbations in the orbit of 'Uranus.'[3] Eighth, once we take into account languages other than English, we find complications: Russian does not have anything resembling English definite and indefinite articles; Greek routinely uses a definite article with proper names and demonstrative descriptions.

One might despair of finding much order here, but order there is, and understanding it has proved essential to clear-headed philosophy. Frege sketched a theory of descriptions before Russell, but it makes sense to discuss Fregean theories once we have Russell's theory clear. Following philosophical custom, we use 'Russell's Theory of Descriptions' and 'The Theory of Descriptions' as labels for Russell's account of definites. And we use 'The Theory of Indefinites' for his theory of indefinites.

2   The Theory of Descriptions

2.1   Overview

On Russell's account of an utterance of a referring expression (e.g. a proper name), the expression's *referent* is its meaning. An utterance of a sentence 'β is G,' where β is a referring expression that refers to b and '—is G' is a one-place predicate, expresses an *object-dependent* proposition, one whose identity depends upon the identity of b, one that simply would not exist if b did not exist.[4] This proposition is *true* iff b has the property expressed by '— is G.' When someone utters (7), for example,

(7)   Pierre Dupont has brown eyes.

the subject expression 'Pierre Dupont' is used to refer to a particular person, Pierre Dupont, and the predicate 'has brown eyes' to attribute some property to him. If Pierre Dupont has brown eyes, the proposition expressed by the utterance is true; if not, it is false. The proposition is *object-dependent*: if Pierre Dupont did not exist, the proposition that he has brown eyes would not exist either.

If a description 'the ϕ' were a referring expression, it would be natural to take its reference to be whatever is uniquely ϕ. But according to Russell, 'the ϕ' is *not* a referring expression; the proposition expressed by an utterance of 'the ϕ is ψ' is *object-independent*; the identity of this proposition does not depend on the identity of whatever is uniquely ϕ, for the *same* proposition would be expressed by an utterance of the 'the ϕ is ψ' if *something else* happened to be uniquely ϕ, indeed if nothing turned out to be uniquely ϕ; 'the ϕ' is no more a referring expression than 'a ϕ,' 'some ϕ,' 'no ϕ,' or 'every ϕ'; indeed, 'the ϕ' amounts to a useful compound formed from 'some ϕ' and 'every ϕ': the proposition that the ϕ is ψ is just the proposition that there exists just one ϕ and every ϕ is ψ. Consider,

(8)   the richest person in France has brown eyes.

Suppose 'the richest person in France' is a referring expression that refers to whoever is richest amongst people in France. And suppose Pierre Dupont is the richest man in France. Then 'the richest person in France' refers to Pierre Dupont. One important Russellian observation is that the proposition expressed by an utterance of (8) is *not* object-dependent – of course it depends upon the existence of *France*, but when we talk of object-dependent propositions, we are focusing on propositions that are object-dependent with respect to the *subject* position of the sentences used to express them. If Pierre Dupont had never been born, somebody else would have been the richest person in France, and the proposition expressed by an utterance of (8) could still be true. Thus a major difference between (7) and (8). There is a particular individual (Pierre Dupont) upon whose existence the existence of the proposition expressed by an utterance of (7) depends; there is no such individual upon whose existence the existence of the proposition expressed by an utterance of (8) depends. The proposition expressed by an utterance of (8) appears to depend only upon the existence of certain *properties*: the property of being richer than any other person in France and the property of having brown eyes.

The object-independence of the proposition can be stressed, as it is by Russell, by considering an example containing a description to which nothing answers:

(9)   the French king has brown eyes.

What about the proposition expressed by an utterance made today of (9)? France is no longer a monarchy, it has no king or queen. Is the proposition expressed *false*? Or is it *neither true nor false*? Or is *no* proposition expressed at all? Russell's answer is that the proposition expressed has determinate truth conditions, that those conditions are not satisfied if there is no French king, and that in such circumstances the proposition is therefore straightforwardly false. In effect, he claims that the proposition expressed by an utterance of (9) shares crucial features of the proposition expressed by an utterance of (10):

(10)   some French prince has brown eyes.

In a familiar idiom, we might represent the truth conditions of an utterance of (10) as follows:

(10′) $\exists x((\textit{French } x \wedge \textit{prince } x) \wedge x \textit{ has brown eyes})$.

The fact that there are no French princes appears to be no barrier to understanding how (10) works. It involves existential quantification, so an utterance of (10) is straightforwardly false.

According to Russell's Theory of Descriptions, (9) is also an existential quantification, albeit one of some complexity. We can lead up to the details via Russell's Theory of Indefinites, according to which the truth conditions of an utterance of (11) are given by (11′):

(11)   a French prince I know has brown eyes
(11′) $\exists x(((\textit{French } x \wedge \textit{prince } x) \wedge I \textit{ know } x) \wedge x \textit{ has brown eyes})$.

The proposition expressed by an utterance of (11) made today is false. We can make one last stop before getting to Russell's Theory of Descriptions. The truth conditions of (12) are given by (12′):

(12)   exactly one French prince has brown eyes
(12′) $\exists x(((\textit{French } x \wedge \textit{prince } x) \wedge x \textit{ has brown eyes}) \wedge$
            $\forall y(((\textit{French } y \wedge \textit{prince } y) \wedge y \textit{ has brown eyes}) \supset y = x))$.

We can now state Russell's analysis of (9):

(9)   the French king has brown eyes.
(9′) $\exists x(((\textit{French } x \wedge \textit{king } x) \wedge x \textit{ has brown eyes}) \wedge \forall y((\textit{French } y \wedge \textit{king } y)$
           $\supset y = x))$.
(9′)   amounts to the conjunction of the following:

(a) there is a French king with brown eyes
(b) there is exactly one French king.

Without the uniqueness given by (b) we would have an analysis of (13), which is not what we want:

(13) a French king has brown eyes.

We see here the precise relation between Russell's theories of definite and indefinite descriptions, which we may summarize for the moment as follows (where '$=_{df}$' is read as 'is definitionally equivalent to'):

(INDEF) a ϕ is ψ $=_{df}$ $\exists x(\phi x \wedge \psi x)$
(DEF) the ϕ is ψ $=_{df}$ $\exists x((\phi x \wedge \psi x) \wedge \forall y(\phi y \supset y = x))$.

There is a clear sense, then, in which definite descriptions are complex devices of existential quantification.

Just as clearly, they are complex devices of *universal* quantification, for (9') also amounts to the conjunction of (a') and (b):

(a') every French king has brown eyes.

Truth conditionally, there is nothing to choose between conjoining (a) and (b), or (a') and (b); but a change in perspective can be illuminating, as we shall see later. For the moment, the important point is that Russell's account of indefinites involves an *existence* implication; and his account of definites involves both *existence* and *uniqueness* implications.

Perhaps the most common way of informally setting out Russell's analysis of 'the ϕ is ψ' is as the conjunction of the following:[5]

(i)   there is at least one ϕ
(ii)   there is at most one ϕ
(iii) every ϕ is ψ.

The logician's favourite rendering of this is the one Russell uses, which is structured perfectly for proofs involving rules of instantiation and generalization.:

(14) $\exists x(\forall y(\phi y \supset y = x) \wedge \psi x))$.

The apparent complexity of the Theory of Descriptions may invite some skepticism. But the theory must be judged on the basis of its predictive power, and it is important not to be overly concerned with the particular formalism used to state it, for there turn out to be more general and more natural methods, as we shall see.

3 Motivating the Theory of Descriptions

Why was Russell so interested in the word 'the'? His motivations were ontological, semantical, and epistemological.[6]

3.1 Ontological concerns

The general question of how to treat sentences containing so-called *empty* terms is an old one. The following sentences are interesting because each contains such a term yet is usable to express a truth:

(15) The present king of France does not exist.
(16) Smith thinks the present king of France is bald.
(17) Smith thinks the largest prime number is smaller than 10^{99}.

Russell thought it important to explain these facts. At one time he entertained the idea of a realm of non-existent entities containing a largest prime, a present king of France, etc. to serve as the referents of 'the largest prime number,' 'the present King of France' etc.[7] But by 1905 he felt this idea conflicted with a 'robust sense of reality,' and his Theory of Descriptions came about, in part, as an attempt to purify his ontology. Utterances of (15)–(17) express determinate propositions with determinate truth conditions with no unsavoury metaphysical commitments.

Negative existentials

As we saw earlier, Russell does not regard 'exists' as a genuine predicate, and the existence claim in (15) really flows from the meaning of 'the.' Since the verb phrase supplies no genuine predicate, there is no possibility of a genuine scope ambiguity here, and (15) is understood as (15'):

(15') $\sim \exists x \forall y (presently\ king\ of\ France\ x \equiv y = x)$.

Empty descriptions

If you utter (16), you are claiming that Smith believes an object-independent proposition to the effect that exactly one person is presently king of France and that whoever is king of France is bald. That is, according to the Theory of Descriptions you report Smith's belief without referring to any particular individual or even supposing that some individual answers to the description used.

The possibility of accounting for *de re-de dicto* ambiguities in terms of scope permutations emerges naturally. For example, (17) may be analysed as either (17') or (17″), according as the description 'the largest prime number' is given large or small scope with respect to 'John thinks that':

(17′) $\exists x(\forall y(\textit{largest-prime } y \equiv y = x) \wedge \textit{John thinks that } x < 10^{99})$
(17″)   *John thinks that* $\exists x(\forall y(\textit{largest-prime } y \equiv y = x) \wedge x < 10^{99}).$

(17′) is false; but (17″) may be true. Thus Russell is able to explain the intuitive ambiguity in (17), avoid positing an ontology that includes a largest prime.

3.2   *Logico-semantical concerns*

Sir Walter Scott was the author of the *Waverley* novels. But someone who uttered (18) would not be expressing the proposition that a certain object is self-identical:

(18)   Scott is the author of *Waverley.*

And someone uttering (18) would most likely not be saying that George IV was curious about an example of the law of identity:

(19)   King George IV wondered whether Scott was the author of *Waverley.*

Russell appears to have an explanation. 'Scott is Sir Walter' is an identity statement of the form $s = t$, involving two names. But (18) is not: one of the expressions is a description, and when its logical form is spelled out in accordance with the Theory of Descriptions, all is revealed:

(18′) $\exists x(\forall y(x \textit{ authored Waverley} \equiv y = x) \wedge x = \textit{Scott}).$

To wonder whether (18′) is true is not to be curious about an instance of the law of identity. And someone uttering (19) would most be likely be saying the following:

(19′)   King George IV wondered whether $\exists x(\forall y(x \textit{ authored Waverley} \equiv y = x) \wedge x = \textit{Scott}).$

The fact that, on Russell's Theory of Descriptions, a definite description is not a genuine singular term, and the fact that statements like (18) are not therefore genuine identities (but abbreviations of quantified formulae) has profound repercussions. *The Principle of Substitutivity for Singular Terms* (PSST) is an inference principle that validates the following:

(A)   Scott snored
      Scott = Sir Walter
      _____
      Sir Walter snored

If descriptions are not singular terms, then PSST cannot be used in logical deductions that do not involve genuine identities. So the following inference must be validated in some other way:

(B) Scott snored
     Scott = the author of *Waverley*
     ────────────────────────────
     the author of *Waverley* snored

Whitehead and Russell prove two 'derived' rules of inference for truth-functional contexts which enable them, for purposes of proof, to treat definite descriptions *as if* they were singular terms. These theorems about contextually defined definite descriptions occurring in truth-functional contexts should not obscure the quantificational character of the Theory of Descriptions, which comes through clearly in Russell's talk of *object-independent* propositions.

Logicians have recognized the importance of distinguishing PSST from Whitehead and Russell's derived inference principles for descriptions occurring in truth-functional contexts. Smullyan (1948), for example, recognized that if descriptions are not singular terms then the following inference involving non-truth-functional contexts poses no threat to PSST:

(C) necessarily 9 is odd
     9 = the number of planets
     ────────────────────────────
     necessarily the number of planets is odd

Quine (1943, 1947) had worried that in (C) we appear to move from two true premises to a false conclusion, putting the blame squarely on the vagaries of the non-truth-functional, modal operator 'necessarily' which, he claimed, does not permit the substitution of identicals within its scope. Quine (1953, 1960) went on to argue that since modal operators do not permit substitution, it makes no sense to quantify into their scopes. He claimed (20) was incoherent, for example:

(20) $\exists x$ necessarily (x is odd).

The truth of 'necessarily 9 is odd' suggests that 9 satisfies 'necessarily x is odd.' But 9 = the number of planets, and 'necessarily the number of planets is odd' is false.

Smullyan (1948) recognized that on Russell's Theory of Descriptions (C) cannot be viewed as a unique inference involving PSST. Indeed, it is ambiguous according as the description 'the number of planets' in the conclusion has small or large scope with respect to non-truth-functional material:

(21) $\exists x(\forall y(y$ *numbers the planets* $\equiv y = x) \wedge$ *necessarily*$(x$ *is odd*$))$
(22) *necessarily* $\exists x(\forall y(y$ *numbers the planets* $\equiv y = x) \wedge x$ *is odd*$)$.

(22) is false – there might have been, say, six planets – but (21) is true, on the assumption that nine is necessarily odd.[8] When Quine read (C) as an invalid

argument, he was implicitly taking the description to have small scope. But that reading is not derivable from the argument's premises using standard rules of inference, so its existence poses no threat to the soundness of those rules. By contrast, the reading upon which the description has large scope (and hence occurs in a truth-functional context) is readily derived.

3.3   *Epistemological motivations*

Russell distinguishes objects that we are directly acquainted with from those that we only know under description. So, for example, you might know yourself by acquaintance, but very likely you know the richest man in France or the first person to recite the Lord's Prayer whilst crossing the Atlantic only under a description.

Of course, there are a number of individuals to talk about besides yourself and the richest man in France, and that is where matters get interesting. It is at least conceivable that some person or thing you think exists does not, that "he" or "it" is the result of an elaborate hoax or a hologram or something created in our minds by an evil demon with the power to create collective hallucinations. But our own existence and our own individual experiences (or sense data) do not appear to be subject to such doubt, as Descartes argued. It might be tempting, then, to draw the acquaintance-description distinction along skeptical or Cartesian lines, the objects of knowledge by acquaintance restricted to those entities whose existence cannot be doubted. This was the position Russell had reached by the time of 'Knowledge by Acquaintance and Knowledge by Description' (1911), although this was not his original position in 'On Denoting' (1905), where there are, at most, hints of the road he would take. Under the spell of a Cartesian epistemology, the Theory of Descriptions now assumed a correspondingly broader role in characterizing the contents of thoughts that purported to be about entities with which we are not acquainted. A seemingly object-dependent thought about Cicero, for example, was analyzed as an object-dependent thought "about," say, being the greatest roman orator. Thus the origins of the ideas that led to Russell sometimes expressing the view that ordinary proper names are, in fact, truncated definite descriptions.[9]

The Theory of Descriptions has encountered its fair share of criticism. For expository purposes, criticisms may be put into one of two groups. Those in the first revolve around quite general points made by Strawson in a series of works published between 1950 and 1986, but these have at best struck glancing blows. Those in the second group take off from one of Strawson's specific points and aim not to undermine the theory but to show that it is at best only *half* of an acceptable theory because of a common and important use of descriptions that Russell's theory misses.

According to Strawson (1950), someone who uses a description 'the φ' typically intends to *refer* to some object or other and say something about it; there is no question of the speaker saying that something is uniquely ф. Someone who says 'the table is covered with books.' for instance, does not say something that entails the existence of exactly one table, as Russell's analysis appears to suggest.

This issue had, in fact, been addressed some years earlier by Quine (1940) and Reichenbach (1947); and the basic point was reiterated by Sellars (1954): an utterance of a description like 'the table' will be understood in the context as elliptical for an utterance of a fuller description such as 'the table over here,' or 'the table of which we are speaking.' Again the phenomenon is not confined to descriptions, but is found with 'no table,' 'every table' and so on. This idea has not met with universal acceptance, however, and criticisms and implementations have raised issues at the heart of the matter of linguistic interpretation and, in consequence, spawned an impressive literature which we examine later.

6 Attributive and Referential

Consideration of the behavior of descriptions in non-extensional contexts and the possibility of misdescribing an individual, but successfully communicating something about it, have led some philosophers to suggest that definite descriptions are systematically ambiguous between Russellian and referential interpretations.[10] When 'the ф' is used in the Russellian way, the proposition expressed is object-independent; when it is used referentially the proposition expressed is object-dependent.

6.1   Donnellan's considerations

Drawing upon familiar facts about ordinary speech, Keith Donnellan (1966, 1968) argued that Russell and Strawson were both right because descriptions can be used in (at least) two different ways, which he calls *attributive* and *referential*. Donnellan considers examples like the following: (i) A detective discovers Smith's mutilated body but has no idea who killed him. Looking at the body, he exclaims, 'The murderer is insane.' (ii) Jones is on trial for Smith's murder; we are convinced of his guilt; hearing Jones ranting in court, you say to us, 'The murderer is insane.' In case (i), says Donnellan, you are using the description *attributively*, and a Russellian treatment seems adequate. In case (ii), by contrast, you are using it *referentially*, and a Russellian interpretation seems quite inappropriate: a separate referential interpretation is required.

The position Donnellan advocates has been reconstructed as the position that the speaker expresses an object-independent proposition when 'the ф' is used attributively and an object-dependent proposition when it is used referentially.[11] The word 'the' has two distinct *uses*, Donnellan claims, a suggestion that appears to involves postulating a systematic ambiguity.[12]

6.2   Pragmatic responses

A good number of philosophers have argued that (i) so-called referential uses of descriptions can be accommodated within Russell's theory by invoking an antecedently motivated Gricean distinction between what a speaker *says* and what he *means*. One useful way of drawing such a distinction is in terms of the proposition the speaker *expresses* by (an utterance of) a sentence on a given occasion and the proposition he *primarily intends to communicate* on that occasion (the latter being of relevance to the theory of communication but not to the more limited discipline of semantics); (ii) that the phenomenon of referential usage is not specific to definite descriptions (it arises with quantified DPs quite generally); (iii) that the referential-attributive distinction is neither exclusive nor exhaustive; and (iv) that no binary distinction of this sort can mimic the work done by Russell's notion of the scope of a description.[13]

The assumption underlying this 'pragmatic' response to the suggestion of ambiguity is this: We know from Grice's work that we must distinguish what a speaker *says* and what he *means* by uttering a sentence on a given occasion.[14] If a professor writes a letter of recommendation for a student which reads, 'Smith is very punctual and has excellent handwriting,' he may not have *said* that Smith is no good, but he may well have *meant* just that, intending his addressee to recognize that this is his opinion. Similarly, Grice and those he has influenced have said that when you use the description 'the murderer' in Donnellan's courtroom case, you say that someone uniquely murdered Smith and that whoever murdered Smith is insane, but also, in the circumstances, *mean* that Jones is insane.[15]

Several reasons have been given for favouring the pragmatic approach to the phenomenon of referential usage.[16] (1) A general methodological reason is summed up in what Grice calls Modified Occam's Razor: Do not multiply meanings beyond necessity. If some phenomenon can be explained without positing an ambiguity, other things being equal that explanation is to be preferred. (2) Since no natural language appears to make an explicit lexical distinction between attributive and referential descriptions, talk of a simple lexical ambiguity of the sort found in 'bank' cannot be right; if 'the' really is ambiguous, the type of ambiguity involve must be cross-linguistic, and this suggests strongly that the phenomenon of note is a *speech act* notion rather than a semantic one. (3) We could easily imagine a community that spoke a surface form of a what Kripke calls 'Russell' English in which the word 'the' does not occur; when speakers wish to say what we say using 'the ϕ is ψ,' they use 'there is exactly one ϕ and every ϕ is ψ'; it is hard to believe that such sentences would not be used to communicate object-dependent propositions, thus replicating our referential uses of 'the ϕ.'[17]

It is all well and good to say that a Gricean-pragmatic explanation of referential usage is preferable to the postulation of an ambiguity. But if such explanation is to be taken seriously it must be set out and justified in Gricean terms. It is surprising that most advocates of the pragmatic explanation have provided next to nothing here. One exception is Neale (1990), who attempts to explicate the way in which a genuine Gricean will need to appeal to the notion of (generalized) conversational implicature to explain how a speaker might mean an object-dependent proposition using 'the φ.'[18]

However, as Neale notes, his derivation inherits a problem stressed by Sperber and Wilson (1986): it provides no explanation of how or why a hearer infers the speaker's full intentions; at best it constitutes an *ex post facto* justification of the existence of a particular implicature.[19]

7   Three Ambiguity Arguments

Having looked at the sorts of considerations that have been cited in support of a pragmatic explanation of referential usage, we turn now to six common arguments for a semantically referential interpretation.[20]

7.1   *The argument from opacity and transparency*

One of the earliest argument used for a semantic ambiguity in the definite article is one based on the ambiguity in sentences like the following:[21]

(23)   necessarily the number of planets is odd
(24)   the president has always been a republican.

The thought is that the true readings of (23) and (24) (given that George W. Bush is currently president) are attributable to the fact that they contain *referential* descriptions. Support for this position is supposed to come from the fact that the readings are transparent (non-opaque): co-referential terms are intersubstitutable *salva veritate* on these readings. Replacing the purportedly referential term 'the number of planets' in (23) by a co-referential term such as 'nine,' 'the square of three,' or 'the length in months of a typical human pregnancy' preserves truth; similarly, replacing 'the president' in (24) by 'George W. Bush' or 'the Governor of Texas in 1999.' By contrast, on the readings of (23) and (24) upon which the descriptions contain Russellian descriptions, analogous substitutions do not preserve truth. In short, the modally qualified (23) and the temporally qualified (24) appear to have opaque readings, explicable on assumption that their descriptions have Russellian readings; and they appear to have transparent readings, explicable on the assumption that descriptions have genuinely referential, name-like readings.

But the alleged ambiguities in (23) and (24) do not, in fact, support the existence of a non-Russellian reading of 'the,' for the Russellian can already explain the transparent readings by appeal to *scope*, as noted earlier. Moreover, the

Russellian can explain the existence of *more than two* readings of sentences containing two operators with which descriptions interact:

(25)   John thinks the president has always been a republican.

No binary distinction can supply what is needed here. And once the ambiguity theorist appeals to scope to capture the readings upon which the descriptions take intermediate scope, he has already availed himself of what is needed to explain the alleged referential readings in (23) and (24).

7.2   *The argument from misdescription*

Suppose you use 'Smith's murderer' referentially in the courtroom, intending to refer to Jones, who is ranting in the dock. And suppose Smith was not murdered but died of natural causes. On Russell's account, the proposition expressed will be false (it is not the case that there exists someone who murdered Smith). According to Donnellan (1966), if the man you *meant*, viz., Jones, is insane then you have said something true. In general, when using a description referentially, the speaker may say something true even though the description he uses to say it is not true of the individual the speaker is referring to, indeed even if the description itself is true of *nothing*. And the conclusion Donnellan urges upon us is that this is explicable if the proposition expressed is object-dependent: it is the individual the speaker is seeking to communicate information about rather than any descriptive condition that is of semantical relevance.

The main problem with this argument is that it relies on the presence of a clear judgment that the proposition expressed is still true despite the fact that neither Jones nor anyone else is Smith's murderer. In fact, we find an uneasy tension is our phenomenology: we want to say the speaker did something right but *also* that he did something *wrong*. After all, the description he used *failed to fit* the person he wanted to 'talk about,' and to that extent the speech act was defective. We are ambivalent about the truth of what was said, and the distinction between the proposition literally expressed and the proposition meant sheds light on this fact: the former is false, the latter true.[22]

There is a residual issue here, dubbed the *residue of the problem of misdescription*.[23] It does not actually involve misdescription and it is no part of any argument for a semantically referential reading of description, but it is convenient to mention it here because of a phenomenological similarity. Let us return to the detective looking down at Smith's body. Suppose Smith has been murdered not by one person but by an insane gang of several people. When the detective says, 'the murderer is insane,' has he said something true or false? On Russell's account, he has said something false, but we feel pulled in two directions here, much as we did in the case of misdescription, but this time no appeal to the distinction between the what is literally said and what is meant helps explain the phenomenology. We will return to this matter.

7.3 The argument from incompleteness

Strawson attempted to get some mileage out of the incomplete description 'the table' in his critique of Russell's Theory of Descriptions. Incomplete descriptions are interesting because of a *question* they force the Russellian to answer: How are we to explain the incontrovertible fact that a speaker can use a description 'the φ' in an utterance of the simple form 'the φ is ψ' (e.g. 'the table is brown') and thereby perform a perfectly felicitous speech act, indeed *say something true*, even though he and his addressee both know that φ is true of more than one thing?

According to the ambiguity theorist, a speaker who uses the incomplete description 'the table' referentially in an utterance of 'the table is brown' is not expressing a Russellian object-independent proposition; he is, rather, expressing an object-dependent proposition referring to a particular object. Moreover, the ambiguity theorist argues that it is not possible for the Russellian to capture what is going on in such a case.

Russellians have tended to dismiss the Argument from Incompleteness as doomed to failure because it makes no serious attempt to appreciate the location of particular semantic theses within an overall theory of utterance interpretation.[24] Incompleteness, as the Russellian sees it, is far bigger than Russell's Theory of Descriptions, it is indicative of the quite general phenomenon of the under-determination of the proposition expressed by the linguistic form of the sentence used to express it. An utterance of 'the φ is ψ' may be *elliptical*, it is usually claimed, for an utterance of something along the lines of 'the φ that ζ is ψ.' where 'that ζ' is something the speaker *could have* made explicit but didn't.' Alternatively, some Russellians have explored the idea that if 'the' is a quantifier, as Russell's Theory of Descriptions claims, then there will always be an *implicit background restriction* on the domain over which an utterance of it ranges, as with an utterance of any other quantifier.[25] Call these the *explicit* and *implicit* replies, respectively.[26]

The Russellian's confidence in one or other of these replies has several sources. For one thing, incompleteness arises with descriptions used *attributively*, indeed with quantified DPs more generally. At the scene of a grisly crime, the detective, who has no idea who murdered Smith, says 'the murderer is insane.' Here it is natural to say the detective wishes to be understood as saying that the murderer *of Smith* is insane (or, in case he does not know the dead man is Smith, that the murderer *of this man* is insane; or, in case he cannot discern the gender of the deceased, that the murderer *of this person* is insane). By hypothesis we have here a canonical example of an *attributive* use of a definite description. No appeal to the expression of an object-dependent proposition about whoever it is was that murdered Smith solves the incompleteness problem. This point is reinforced by the fact that the problem of specifying what the speaker said is still with us even if, in fact, Smith was not murdered but died of a disease that results in corpses looking as if they have been mutilated.

Furthermore, it is not just DPs of the form 'the φ' that may be incomplete. Yogi Bera once quipped about a restaurant, 'nobody goes there anymore, it's too crowded.' The truth in Bera's seemingly inconsistent claim emerges once the hearer realizes that 'nobody' is an incomplete DP understood, in this particular context, as something like 'nobody in the know' or 'nobody cool' or 'nobody who likes crowded restaurants.' Part of the beauty of Bera's comment is the indeterminacy and range of possible completions, and this is very often the case when people use incomplete DPs, particularly where humour is involved. Occasionally, however, a single completion will stand out, although others could certainly be constructed. If you had a dinner last night for six guests and all six arrived late because of traffic, you might say 'everyone was late,' intending your audience to understand your remark as 'everyone invited to my dinner last night.' Incompleteness is ubiquitous because hearers can be expected to work out what we mean without us having to spell things out in a tedious and time-consuming manner. It would seem, then, what incompleteness forces us to accept is not the existence of a semantically referential reading of descriptions but the need for a general explanation of how speakers manage to get away with so much incompleteness and how hearers manage to deal with it apparently so effortlessly (and how, in certain cases, indeterminacy and effort interact to produce humour). That is, we want an explanation, as part of a cognitive account of utterance interpretation, of the fact that (roughly) for a range of determiners, D, a speaker can use 'D φ' in an utterance of the simple form 'D φ is ψ' and thereby perform a perfectly felicitous speech act, indeed *say something true*, even though speaker and hearer both know that φ is true of some things that are not relevant to the truth or falsity of what the speaker said.

The difference between the explicit and implicit replies corresponds to a difference in focus and in the attitude taken to the two major parts of 'the φ.' Where we have incompleteness we have *slippage* between language and the world. There are only two things we can do about this slippage: tinker with language, or tinker with the world. When we tinker with *language*: we do something about the *matrix* φ, availing ourselves of the *explicit* reply. When we tinker with the *world*, we do something about the *objects* that (potentially) satisfy the matrix, and hence restrict the range of either the unrestricted quantifier 'the' or the restricted quantifier 'the φ,' availing ourselves of the *implicit* reply.

Some philosophers have objected to the explicit approach on the grounds that there fails to be a *principled basis* for determining the content of completions.[27] Is it to be a completion that the speaker has in mind? Is the resulting description really sufficient to uniquely identify the object in question? Is it always clear that the speaker has a particular description in mind? If there is a genuine complaint here it is one that carries over to the interpretation of incomplete descriptions used attributively and, indeed, to quantified DPs quite generally, which suggests very strongly that the requirement of a principled basis is too strong a condition to impose on any account of interpretation.

On a related note, it is difficult to imagine anyone sympathetic to the explicit response seeing it as subject to the following strange and quite ad hoc constraint:

two superficially identical descriptions occurring in a single sentence must be completed in precisely the same way. At the end of boxing match between a Russian and a Swede you might say, upon hearing that the panel of eleven international judges has declared the Swede the winner by ten votes to one, 'I know why it wasn't unanimous.' 'Why?' your companion asks, and you reply by uttering (26):

(26)   the Russian voted for the Russian.'[28]

Obviously you would be saying that the Russian judge (in this contest) voted for the Russian boxer (in this contest), and this fact is easily statable on the explicit approach.

Notice that (26) creates a serious problem for the implicit account of incompleteness. There can be no domain of discourse containing exactly one Russian with respect to which (26) can be evaluated and come out true (unless the Russian boxer *is* the Russian judge, of course). If the implicit approach is to be saved, it will have to mirror what the explicit approach does by allowing different completions for superficially identical descriptions, and this means allowing the domain over which quantifiers range to shift *within* a sentence. This may seem ad hoc, but the sting of such a charge would, perhaps, be lessened if it could be shown in some independent way that every quantified DP contains a silent, indexical, domain variable in its syntax, an aphonic item of LF, construed as a level of syntactic representation.[29]

8   Synthesis

Before looking at the next three arguments for an ambiguity, we want to outline a theory that is, in effect, a synthesis of the Russellian and ambiguity theories.[30] If the matrix of a description may contain a referential expression ('the king of *France*.' 'the person who murdered *Smith*.' '*Smith*'s murderer'), and if, as the explicit theorist maintains, an incomplete description may be understood as going proxy for some readily constructible, more complex description, then there is no reason in principle why an incomplete description (e.g. 'the king') may not go proxy for a fuller description ('the king of France') containing a referential expression ('France') not contained in the original matrix. And, at least in principle, there is no reason why the fuller description should not contain a referential device that stands for the individual the speaker intends the description to pick out. For example, an utterance of 'the table' might go proxy for 'the table that's *that*.' understood as $[the\ x:\ table\ x \wedge x = that]$.[31] In which case, an incomplete description used referentially is both Russellian and referential.[32] This preserves the basic Russellian insight that the descriptive material in the matrix of a description contributes to the proposition expressed and at the same time preserves the intuition that the proposition expressed is object-dependent. If this is correct, then arguments for or against an ambiguity in the definite article lose much of their initial interest.[33]

9   Three More Ambiguity Arguments

9.1   The argument from convention

Devitt (1997, 2004) and Reimer (1998*a*) have presented an intuitive argument for an ambiguity in definite descriptions: referential uses are common, standard, regular, systematic, and cross-linguistic; indeed so much so that it would be absurd to deny that such uses are *conventional*, a direct function of linguistic meaning in a way that referential uses of other quantified DPs are not. This point seems to demonstrate an inherent weakness in the simplest unitary Russellian analyses, such as those proposed by Grice (1969), Kripke (1977), and Neale (1990), which amount to generalized conversational implicature stories. But the synthesis sketched in the section 8 is not really touched by the Argument from Convention; indeed, the synthesis seems to *explain* the purported convention as a *systematic regularity* in referential usage.

9.2   The argument from anaphora

Consider the following argument, due in its essentials to Strawson (1952): (i) The occurrence of 'he' in (27) can be understood as anaphoric on the occurrence of 'the man in the gabardine suit':

(27)   The man in the gabardine suit is a spy. He tried to bribe me.

(ii) If an occurrence of a pronoun β is anaphoric on an occurrence of another expression α, then β is either a variable bound by α or a device that inherits its reference from α. (iii) The occurrence of the pronoun 'he' in (27) is *not* a bound variable. (iv) Therefore, it inherits its reference from the occurrence of 'the man in the gabardine suit.' (iv) Therefore, this occurrence of 'the man in the gabardine suit' is a referring expression.

Before addressing the Argument from Anaphora directly, we should note the following: pronouns that do not refer may appear perfectly felicitously in negative existentials and belief reports:

(28)   The present king of France doesn't clean my pool. In fact, he doesn't exist.
(29)   Mary believes that the present king of France is wise and that he lives in Arles.

If the occurrences of 'he' in (28) and (29) are referring expressions, then the unwelcome metaphysical commitments that were defeated by treating the descriptive phrases in these sentences in accordance with Russell's Theory of Descriptions would re-enter via the back door with the anaphoric pronouns. Thus the interpretation of anaphoric pronouns has implications for the Theory of Descriptions that extend well beyond the Argument from Anaphora for a semantically referential reading of descriptive devices: it threatens to pull the rug out from under the entire theory. But if we treat anaphors as standing proxy for descriptions, the back door is blocked as well.

But as it turns out, both the Argument from Anaphora and the more general worry are easily dealt with, for it is plausible to suppose that a pronoun lying outside the scope of a quantified DP upon which it is nonetheless anaphoric is basically an incomplete description.[34] The details are spelled out in chapter 18 of the present volume; for immediate purposes it will suffice to note that on this independently motivated and fully general account of 'unbound anaphora,' the occurrences of 'he' in (28) and (29) are treated as if they were occurrences of 'the present king of France' with small scope.[35] The belief attributed to Mary by someone uttering (29) may have little going for it, but it is object-independent for all that, so we can report it without being committed to the existence of a present king of France.

9.3   The argument from binding

A number of philosophers and linguists have argued that some occurrences of definite descriptions function as bound variables and hence as referential expressions.[36] Consider the following example, used by Wilson (1991):

(30) [every scientist who was fired from the observatory at Sofia]^1 was consoled by [someone who knew [*the fired scientist*]$_1$ as a youth].

(31) [every scientist who was fired from the observatory at Sofia]^1 was consoled by someone who knew [*him*]$_1$ as a youth.

The italicised description in (30), like the pronoun 'him' in (31) that could replace it, Wilson claims, is a variable bound by the subject expression. The truth conditions of what is said by utterances of (30) and (31) are both given by (32), the underlined variable x inside the second quantifier doing the work of the italicised pronoun in (31) and the italicised description in (30):

(32) [*every$_x$: scientist x · x was fired from the observatory at Sofia*]
[*some$_y$: y knew x as a youth*] (*x was consoled by y*).

There are several things to note here.

(a) For some speakers, there is an important difference between (30) and (31): what someone says by uttering the latter, but not by uttering the former, can entail that every scientist fired from the observatory at Sofia was male.

(b) Demonstrative descriptions (phrases of the form 'that ϕ') can be used to signify an anaphoric link in much the same way as definite descriptions. In (30), for example, 'the scientist' could just as well have been 'that scientist.'

(c) A simple Russellian treatment of the description 'the fired scientist' in an utterance of (30) would yield (33), which fails to capture the intended interpretation of the utterance:

(33) [$every_x$: scientist x · x was fired from the observatory at Sofia]
[the_z: fired scientist z] [$some_y$: y knew z as a youth] (x was consoled by y).

(33) fails to relativize values of z to values of x in the way the bound variable treatment (in effect) does by treating 'the fired scientist' as an occurrence of x.

(d) On a more subtle Russellian treatment, 'the fired scientist' as it occurs in an utterance of (30) is an incomplete description that is meant to be interpreted as if it were an utterance of richer description that is bound-into, a Gödelian description containing variables on *both* sides of the identity sign:

(30') [$every_x$: scientist x · x was fired from the observatory at Sofia]
[the_z: fired scientist z · z = x] [$some_y$: y knew z as a youth]
(x was consoled by y).

The matrix of [the_z: fired scientist z · z = x] is understood as uniquely satisfied relative to values of x. In short, the Russellian says that the incomplete description in (30) is not a bound variable, but just another incomplete description – one for which the speaker could provide a fuller description that is bound-*into* – a description *containing* a bound pronoun. It is an incomplete, relativized description whose natural completion contains an expression understood as a variable bound by the subject expression.

(e) The Russellian account explains the semantic difference between (30), which contains 'the fired scientist,' and (34), which contains 'the gifted astronomer': the respective analyses (30') and (34') are not equivalent:

(34') [$every_x$: scientist x · x was fired from the observatory at Sofia]
[the_z: gifted astronomer z · z = x] [$some_y$: y knew z as a youth]
(x was consoled by y).

It would appear, then, that the Russellian has a perfectly good account of why sentences can contain descriptions that *appear* to be functioning as bound variables – they are bound-*into*. Far from presenting problems for a unitary Russellian theory of descriptions, the examples discussed serve only to emphasize the elegance and extraordinary range of Russell's Theory of Descriptions.

10 Indefinite Descriptions

10.1 Predication

To say that definite and indefinite descriptions are quantified DPs is to focus on their *predicational* powers in at least two senses. First, a DP such as [$_{DP}$ a [$_{NP}$ soldier]] is composed of a determiner and a nominal, the latter functioning as a first-level predicate. Second, as Frege made clear, a function-argument approach to composition that treats a name like 'Napoleon' as referring to an object and a first-level predicate like 'snores' as referring to a function from objects to truth-values, leads naturally to the idea that a quantifier is a second-level predicate that refers to a function from the referents of first-level predicates to truth values. Putting these two ideas together we have the basis of generalized quantifier theory. A DP like 'every soldier' or 'a soldier' is a second-level predicate (containing a first-level predicate 'soldier') that refers to a function from the referents of first-level predicates to truth values.[37]

On a Russellian theory of indefinites, 'a ϕ is ψ' is a quantified sentence whose logical form may be represented as [*an x*: ϕx]ψx. But cases of negation suggest that where an indefinite appears inside a predicate 'is a ϕ,' a simple first-level predication provides a more natural interpretation than a second-level predication introduced by quantificational structure:[38]

(35)   John is not a soldier

On Russell's account, (35) is predicted to be ambiguous between (35') and (35''):

(35') $\sim$([*an x*: *soldier x*] John = x)
(35'')   [*an x*: *soldier x*] $\sim$ (John = x).

But there appears to be no reading of (35) upon which it is understood as (35''). There are some scope ambiguities involving indefinites:[39]

(36)   John wants to marry a woman his mother loathes.

That such ambiguities do not arise when indefinites combine with the copula might suggest that an explanation of what is going on will emerge from an understanding of copula constructions *per se*, regardless of whether they involve adjectival or indefinite complements. In many languages no overt counterpart of the English copula appears in equivalent constructions, and it is arguable that where it does appear this is largely for purposes of indicating tense or conveying other information typically indicated by inflection; this suggests the copula serves only to indicate a predication whose content is supplied by its complement. One question that will be taken up later is whether, on such an account, the presence of the indefinite article before a nominal in copula constructions is likewise semantically inert or whether we are dealing with a first-level predication involving indefinites that in such constructions derives from their standard role as second-level predicates (quantifiers) elsewhere.

10.2   Referential usage

Are indefinite descriptions ambiguous between quantificational and referential and quantificational interpretations, as a number of people have argued?[40] The issues here are virtually identical to those discussed earlier in connection with definites, although novel syntactic and interpretive considerations have been brought to bear in the realm of indefinites. The most interesting of these involve seemingly general syntactic constraints (so called *island* constraints) on quantifier scope, which apparently preclude straightforward scope-based explanations of ambiguity involving indefinites and apparently admit of explanation if a (systematic) lexical ambiguity is assumed.[41]

However, as is the case in discussions of definites used referentially, various distinct notions appear to have been run together in the literature purporting to demonstrate the existence of a referential semantics for indefinites, and again the major conflation involves using a description to communicate an object-dependent thought and merely using a description with a particular individual in mind. With a view to imposing some order on claims made by referentialists, we can distinguish at least *referential, specific, definite,* and *purely existential* uses (although they see the taxonomy as carrying no theoretical weight).[42]

- *Referential use*: A lone red-haired student is sitting in the front row of a class. The teacher, who believes this particular student cheated on yesterday's examination, announces to the class, 'I'm not going to name names, but I have good reason to believe that a red-haired student in the front row cheated on yesterday's exam.' We have a *referential* use iff the teacher is attempting to communicate to his audience an object-dependent proposition about the red-haired student sitting in the front row, identifying him as the cheat, this individual being the one about whom the teacher has the object-dependent belief that furnishes the grounds for his utterance.
- *Specific use*: A teacher sees someone in his class cheating on an examination. The following day he makes an announcement to the class: 'I'm sorry to say that yesterday I witnessed a student in this class cheating on the examination.' The grounds for the teacher's utterance are furnished by an object-dependent belief about a particular student. If the teacher does not seek to communicate to the class an object-dependent proposition identifying the cheat, then he is not using the indefinite referentially. But since he wishes to communicate that the grounds for his utterance are nonetheless furnished by an object-dependent belief, we can say he is making a *specific* use of the indefinite.

- *Definite use*: Suppose a teacher has deduced in some complex statistical way that exactly one person cheated on yesterday's examination, and that he is utterly baffled as to who it was. He announces to the class, 'I have deduced from statistical data that a student cheated on the exam. Fortunately there only appears to be one cheat, and I intend to find out who it is.'
- *Purely quantificational use*: In this instance not only does the teacher fail to know the identity of the cheater, but also fails to know whether or not there was a unique cheater (perhaps there were several). 'The fact that everyone scored 100 on yesterday's examination suggests a student broke into my office and stole a copy the night before.'

It is implausible to think that all of these uses can be chalked up to semantic facts. In each case, the proposition expressed is that which would be expressed if the indefinite determiner were replaced by the existential quantifier. The different uses of descriptions then stem from the application of Gricean principles of conversational implicature to what was literally said.

11   Indefinites as Logically Basic?

Having laid bare a plausible semantic connection between definite and indefinite descriptions – a closer one will be examined in a moment – it is natural to ask how the demonstrative description 'that φ' fits into the nexus.[43] Although many philosophers and linguists have assumed that demonstrative descriptions are referential, it is sometimes suggested they are *quantificational* by virtue of being definite descriptions with certain special properties.[44] But a demonstrative description might be seen as an indefinite description used referentially and involving an implicit Gödelian completion signaled by the use of the determiner 'that' rather than 'a.'[45] On this account, an utterance of 'that φ is ψ' is interpreted with the truth conditions of $[an\ x:\ \phi x \wedge x = that]$.[46]

Given that Gricean or other pragmatic principles can explain definite uses of indefinite descriptions, one might well wonder whether the distinction between definite and indefinite descriptions might be collapsed, at least truth condition-ally. For example, 'the' and 'a' might make the same contribution to the truth conditions of utterances containing them, and differ only in their suggestive power, in much the same way that those influenced by Frege and Grice see the difference between 'but' and 'and.'[47] Very few natural languages have what we would recognize as definite and indefinite descriptions. In most Slavic languages, for example, 'the man' and 'a man' would both be expressed in the same way. Perhaps it is just an obsession with surface grammatical form that leads us to think that English or German or French have two different truth-conditional elements at LF correspond-ing to surface forms 'the' and 'a.' Perhaps there is a single logical element whose surface forms are associated with different discourse conditions. That is, perhaps utterances of both 'a ϕ is ψ' and 'the ϕ is ψ' have the truth-conditional content given by $[\exists x\colon \phi x](\psi x)$.

By employing a Gricean account of conventional implicature, a unified semantical treatment of definite and indefinite descriptions may well allow one to avoid uniqueness implications in some cases, and still account for uniqueness implications in other cases. The problem of incompleteness does not disappear, however. Incompleteness is a quite general phenomenon affecting quantified DPs, and with indefinites it shows up clearly if the indefinite is embedded within negation:

(37)   the table is not dirty.

If incompleteness did not arise, then assuming the existence of at least one table that is not dirty, every utterance of (37) would be true, and this is clearly wrong. On a unified theory that assumes the explicit approach to incompleteness, someone who utters (37) will be saying something like 'a table over here is not dirty' or 'a table I have selected is not dirty,' which seem perfectly fine.

The unified indefinite treatment may also make it possible to explain the phenomenology of the residue of the problem of misdescription noted earlier.[48] Recall we want to explain the phenomenology in the following sort of case: The detective says, 'the murderer is insane,' when he sees the state of Smiths's body; but Smith was actually killed by several insane members of a gang. We feel pulled in both directions when asked if the detective said something true or false. On the unified indefinite treatment, we seem to have a possible explanation of this: what the detective literally says does not entail that there is a unique murderer of Smith. He literally expresses the proposition that there is at least one murderer of Smith who is insane, and this is true. But general Gricean reasoning leads us to believe that the detective means that there is a *unique* murderer of Smith and that he is insane, and this is false.

12   Conclusion

Debates about descriptions have been framed by the considerations Russell set out a century ago, and work on the theory of descriptions has demonstrated the tremendous insights that Russell had. Equally impressive is the fact that the theory has been extended in so many interesting and provocative ways – for example to pronominal anaphora, temporal and modal anaphora, plural descriptions, mass terms, and generics. The allure of the Theory of Descriptions remains its promise of metaphysical austerity, its ability to untangle numerous semantical puzzles in the theory of meaning, and its role in making sense of the epistemic status of our knowledge claims. Even where philosophers have departed from the stock Russellian theory (for example by rejecting his formalism or the uniqueness clause) they have usually done so with the goal of servicing the more central insight of the theory – that many English DPs, despite appearances, are not referring expressions but are in some way or other predicational.

Notes

1   Evans (1982), Geach (1962), Mitchell (1962), Moore (1944), Neale (1990), Rundle (1965) Strawson (1950), Wiggins (1965).
2   See ch. 18.
3   See ch. 14.
4   Russell sometimes cashes out object-dependence in terms of propositions *containing* objects as constituents, an idea revived by Kaplan (1978).
5   Moore (1944), Strawson (1950), Neale (1990).
6   Russell himself said the discovery of the Theory of Descriptions played a key role in his development of the Theory of Types. Some scholars have disputed this. See (e.g.) Cartwright (1990, 2004), Ostertag (1998).
7   Russell (1904), Meinong (1904), Parsons (1980), Zalta (1983, 1988).
8   Neale (1990) argues that the threat to quantified modal logic vanishes once Smull-yan's Russellian points about descriptions, substitution and scope are appreciated. Neale (2000) argues that this is incorrect.
9   See ch. 14.
10   Barwise and Perry (1983), Devitt (1978, 2004), Donnellan (1966, 1977), Hornsby (1976), Kaplan (1972), Rundle (1965), Wettstein (1981).
11   See Barwise and Perry (1983), Hornsby (1976), Kaplan (1972), Peacocke (1975), Wettstein (1981), Schiffer (1995, 2005).
12   See also Mitchell (1962), Rundle (1965).
13   Davies (1981), Grice (1968), Kripke (1977), Neale (1990), Sainsbury (1979), Searle (1979).
14   Grice (1961, 1989).
15   Davies (1981), Grice (1968), Kripke (1977), Neale (1990), Sainsbury (1977).
16   Grice (1968, 1989), Kripke (1977), Neale (1990), Sennett (2002). For counter-arguments, see Reimer (1998) and Devitt (1998, 2004).
17   A more controversial consideration is sometimes invoked in support of the pragmatic approach. According to Kripke (1977), the distinction between attributive and referential uses of definite descriptions is a reflex of, or at least mirrors, a general distinction between *semantic reference* and *speaker's reference.*
18   Neale's explanation avoids appealing to Kripke's distinction between *semantic reference* and *speaker's reference* (it draws only upon the notion of speaker's reference). Appealing to Kripke's distinction in defending Russell's theory would be somewhat self-defeating as Russell's theory holds that a description does not have a semantic reference. See Neale (1997).
19   All conversational implicatures must be calculable in Grice's sense, even those he takes to be generalized. The conversational implicatures associated with uses of the words 'and,' 'or,' 'if,' 'every,' 'a,' 'the' etc. – i.e. those words corresponding to formal devices in logical theory – are *generalized* implicatures for Grice, the ones of philosophical importance, the ones that really bothered him (unlike the particularized ones which have no real philosophical significance). It is equally clear that 'generalized' has

no *theoretical* import for Grice in the context of his account of the properties an implicature must have if it is to count as conversational (hence the calculability requirement) and that generalized conversational implicatures are quite different from conventional implicatures.

20 The labels for the arguments are taken from Neale (1990, 2004a).

21 Rundle (1965).

22 Neale (1990).

23 Ludlow and Segal (2004).

24 Bach (1987), Davies (1981), Evans (1982), Neale (1990), Quine (1940), Reichenbach (1947), Sainsbury (1979), Sellars (1954).

25 Davies (1981), Neale (1990).

26 These labels derive from Neale (1990). The concepts behind them are elaborated and clarified by Neale (2004a).

27 Devitt (2004), Wettstein (1983).

28 Lewis (1979), Ludlow and Segal (2004), Neale (2004a), Soames (1986), Stanley and Szabó (2000).

29 On LF and aphonic expressions, see Chapter 18.

30 For more detail, see Neale (2004a).

31 The use of such descriptions goes back at least to an argument reconstructible from Gödel's (1944) discussion of Russell's Theory of Facts.

32 It will be referential but not *directly* referential in Kaplan's (1989) sense, because the contribution to the proposition expressed made by the utterance of the description is not exhausted by the object referred to.

33 Neale (2004a).

34 Ludlow and Neale (1991), Neale (1990, 2004b).

35 This would make them equivalent to what are sometimes called 'pronouns of laziness.' devices which go proxy for repetitions of their antecedents. But the theory of anaphora alluded to here is not a laziness theory in this strict sense because it applies equally to quantified DPs beginning with determiners other than 'the.' In (i), for example, the pronoun 'he' goes proxy for something like 'the man who drank rum last night at Mary's party':

(i) Just one man drank rum last night at Mary's party. He was very ill afterwards.

36 See (e.g.) Kempson (1986), Wilson (1991), Larson and Segal (1995).

37 Equivalently (if everything is done correctly), a determiner like 'every' or 'a' is a second-level predicate referring to a function from pairs of first-level predicate referents to truth values.

38 Graff (2000), Heim (1982/1988), Williams (1983).

39 King (1988), Kripke (1977), Ludlow and Neale (1991).

40 Chastain (1975), Donnellan (1978), Fodor and Sag (1982), Wilson (1978).

41 See Fodor and Sag (1982).

42 Ludlow and Neale (1991).

43 Demonstratives are discussed in detail in ch. 17.

44 King (2001), Neale (1993b).

45 Neale (2001, 2004a).

46 Lepore and Ludwig (2000) arrive at virtually the same analysis by a different route.

47 Heim (1982), Kamp and Reyle (1993), Kempson (1975), Ludlow and Segal (2004), Szabo (2000), Zvolensky (1997). Unfortunately, the suggestion is sometimes put very incautiously, that 'the' and 'a' have the same *literal* meaning but differ *pragmatically*. This is a very bad way of putting things, for the whole point is that 'the' and 'a' do differ in meaning but not in a way that is truth-conditionally significant. (To claim that literal meaning just *is* truth-conditional meaning is either to say something counter-intuitive or else to make a pointless stipulation.)

48 Ludlow and Segal (2004).

Chapter 17

Using Indexicals

John Perry

1 Introduction

In this essay I examine how we use indexicals. The key function of indexicals, I claim, is to help the audience find supplementary, utterance-independent, channels of information about the object to which or to whom the speaker refers.

This exploration of the use of indexicals is based on the reflexive-referential theory of the meaning and content of indexicals and other referring expressions (Perry 2001).

I review the reflexive and referential aspects of indexicals in sections 2 and 3. In section 4 I explore the way we use indexicals and then, in section 5 try to use the lessons learned to think about some problems cases, suggested by Stephano Predelli and Varol Akman, that suggest that the standard semantic rules for indexicals may be too simple.

2 Indexicals

Icon, index, and symbol

The term 'indexical' comes into the philosophy of language from Charles Sanders Peirce. Here is an explanation of Peirce's threefold division of signs: icon, index, and symbol:

> Signs are icons, indices (also called "semes"), or symbols ... accordingly as they derive their significance from resemblance to their objects, a real relation (for example, of causation) with their objects, or are connected only by convention to their objects, respectively. (Burch 2001)

Suppose I am talking to Mr. Fritchey. I may use his first name, and refer to him as 'Elwood.'[1] Here, at first pass, it seems that the story goes as follows. There is a completely arbitrary convention that allows me to refer to a certain individual, standing before me, as 'Elwood.' Although in this case he is standing before me—a "real" relation—that has nothing to do with the fact that I refer to *him* when I say "Elwood."[2] I will be able to refer him by using 'Elwood' after he has gone. The work of securing reference is done by the convention, and does not depend on any further connection between the speaker and Elwood. So 'Elwood,' it seems, is a symbol, connected to Mr. Fritchey only by convention.

One of Peirce's central examples of indexicals was smoke, which is a sign of fire. Here the real relation is causation: fire causes smoke. No convention is involved, and no language. Smoke is a natural sign of fire, not a conventional one. The term "indexicality" is not much used for natural signs in contemporary philosophy of language, however.

Since I am talking to Elwood, I can refer to him with the word 'you.' The word 'you' has a conventional meaning in English. We use it to refer to the person to whom we are talking. However, this conventional meaning does not determine reference all by itself. 'You' refers to Elwood, *given* its conventional meaning, because Elwood is *the person I am talking to*. This is a real relation between Elwood and I, involving causation and perception. This conventional species of indexicality is our topic, and it is the phenomenon for which "indexicality" is used in contemporary philosophy of language. Words like 'here,' 'now,' 'you' and 'I,' with their partly conventional, partly relational, links to their referents, are paradigms.

Utterances and tokens

The term 'token' is also due to Peirce. Tokens are distinguished from types; tokens are particular bursts of sound or bits of ink. Consider the list: cow, dog, cow. It contains *two* tokens of the type *cow*, one token of the type *dog*.

Hans Reichenbach developed his token-reflexive account of indexicals in *Elements of Symbolic Logic* (Reichenbach 1947). The expressions in the formal languages studied by symbolic logic up to that time were taken to be non-ambiguous and also had a property Reichenbach called *equisignificance*. This means that two tokens of the same type have the same semantic value. The symbol '2' always stands for the number two; the description 'The first president of the United States' always stands for George Washington. If the expression is a declarative sentence, all tokens of it have the same truth-value. If '$2+2=4$' or 'All ravens are black' are true when I say them, they will be true when you say them, as long as we are using the same words with the same meaning.

In contrast, indexicals and larger expressions containing them are not equisignificant. Different tokens of the same type, with the same meaning, can stand for different things. The type gives us a relation between tokens and semantic values.

Hence, different tokens of the same type can have different semantic values. Different tokens of 'I' stand for different people; different tokens of 'here' stand for different places, and so forth. Elwood might say truly

(1)   I have been to Paris

while Elwood Jr. when he repeats his father's remark,

(2)   I have been to Paris

says something false. They both use the same English sentence, with the same meaning, but their statements have different truth conditions and different truth values.

Reichenbach sees that we could get at what (1) and (2) have in common and how they differ, by stating the truth-conditions in terms of the two different tokens:

(3)   (1) is true IFF the speaker of (1) has been to Paris.
(4)   (2) is true IFF the speaker of (2) has been to Paris.

The type gives us a formula, the same for every instance; the token gives us the thing to which the formula applies. I call this *reflexive* because the token *itself* is mentioned in giving the truth conditions.[3]

I emphasize the distinction between *tokens* and *utterances*. By 'utterance' I mean an intentional act of speaking, signing, typing, writing, etc. By 'token' I mean an effect of such acts, a burst of sound or a mark that is intended to be perceived, recognized, and interpreted by a hearer or reader. In *Elements* Reichenbach confuses or conflates utterances and tokens. He announces that he means an *act* by 'token,' but soon is talking about the *ink marks* on a page as tokens.

Utterances are *semantically* basic. The intentionality of linguistic acts is a special case of the intentionality of purposeful action. The language to which a token belongs, the identity of the words and their meanings, the syntax, the reference of terms, all derive from the minds of the speakers, and connections between those minds, other minds, things, and properties. On the other hand, tokens are often *epistemically* basic. When you read this essay, for example, you see tokens produced by me (not directly by me, of course, but by a complex process I initiated). You take these to be the result of utterances by me—purposeful acts of typing, in this case. When the utterance itself cannot be observed, tokens are what the reader or listener has as evidence. Skilled speakers take into account the extent to which the token will be the main source of information. One speaks louder when the audience is distant, and less loud when they are close. When speaking on the telephone, or writing a note, one should not rely on contextual clues that the hearer or reader cannot perceive.

Tokens can be re-used, and when they are, the new utterances may have different semantic and syntactic properties than the originals. An expensive name-tag that said 'George Bush' may have been put in the White House Museum when George I left office; it may now be recycled for George II. A veteran protestor might use a sign, 'You are a scumbag' time after time, referring to different politicians. Eros Corazza imagines (or remembers) a philosophy department, faced with steadily diminishing budgets, using a Post-it note, 'I'll miss my office hours today,' for different faculty members on different, days, thriftily getting years of use from the same piece of paper (Corazza 2004).

Wilfred Sellars and others have called utterances "tokenings." I prefer 'utter-ance,' perhaps because 'tokenings' suggests that tokens are semantically basic.

The importance of the utterance/token distinction grows with changes in the technology of language. In face-to-face communication, the token is the burst of sound that travels to one's ears; there is typically not much difference between perceiving the utterance and perceiving the token. (There is even less in face to face signing, as with American Sign Language.) Writing makes a dramatic difference; tokens remain long after the utterance. Publishing permits the reproduction of tokens; telephony the distant perception of tokens at the time the utterance occurs. Each change in technology makes new patterns of production and percep-tion of tokens possible, and so new expectations and intentions based on these possibilities. We will return to this theme below.

This picture of language use suggests the importance of theories of utterances and tokens. Communicating involves causing physical events that have predictable effects that we can exploit. As noted above, we plan our utterances paying atten-tion to the circumstances under which the tokens we produce will be perceived. An adequate theory of these plans requires representation of the myriad of relations into which utterances and tokens can stand to other concrete objects, people, purposes, projects, and other factors. These factors will figure in the process of reaching a reasonable interpretation of what the speaker is trying to communicate. The most natural way to approach meaning and content would seem to be, then, as properties of utterances.

In David Kaplan's system (Kaplan 1989) pairs of sentence types and contexts model utterances. Although his theory is in the token-reflexive tradition, it has neither tokens nor utterances. Nevertheless, utterances are implicit in the theory. Kaplan's contexts model properties of utterances. The quadruple of speaker, time, location, and world are made up of the person, time, place, and world that play the appropriate roles in relation to an utterance.

Kaplan abstracts these properties from the utterance, and combines them with the character of the expression uttered to give us a sentence in context, a pair of context and character. Context and character suffice to determine content, and it is the interplay between context and content on which Kaplan bases his logic. This approach has provided considerable insight about the meaning (character), content, and logic of indexicals and demonstratives. But to understand how indexicals work in communication, why they are useful, and how we develop communication plans using them, we need the utterances and tokens with all of the properties that are involved when one produces them and sees or hears them. The meaning of the sentence used is important, but so may be the volume with which it is spoken, the direction from which it comes, the visibility of the speaker to the hearer, the differences between synonymous expressions, and many other things.

Indexicals and demonstratives

By *indexicals*, then, I mean expressions that have conventional meanings that associate them with certain relations objects may have to utterances of them, or, in somewhat more convenient terms, with *roles* objects occupy *relative to* utterances of them. For example, 'I' is associated with the utterance-relative role of *being the speaker*. A given utterance *u* of 'I' refers to the speaker of *u*.

Here are some plausible utterance-relative roles for familiar indexicals:

An utterance *u* of 'today' refers to the day on which *u* occurs
An utterance *u* of 'you' refers to the person to whom the speaker of *u* is speaking.
An utterance *u* of 'yesterday' refers to the day before the day on which *u* occurs

'This,' and 'That,' are demonstrative pronouns when used alone, and demonstrative adjectives in phrases like 'this pencil' and 'that pencil sharpener.' Given our working definition of indexicals, demonstratives are a species of indexicals. In the paradigm case, the referent of 'this' or 'that' will be an object that the speaker is attending to and to which he is directing the attention of his audience. This is not a matter of convention, but involves a real relation between the utterance and the object entails the perceptions and intentions of the speaker. The fact that in English 'this' is the word that has been assigned that role is, however, a matter of convention.

'This,' 'that,' I,' and 'you' are all pronouns. But not all pronouns are indexicals, and not all indexicals are pronouns. 'Today,' 'tomorrow,' and 'yesterday,' for example, are adverbs. The pronouns 'he' and 'she' can be used indexically, as demonstratives, or they can also be used in ways that do not clearly fall under the definition of indexicals. In,

Elwood is a man so he is mortal

the word 'he' is used with 'Elwood' as antecedent, and refers to Elwood because its antecedent does. In

Every young man thinks he is immortal

the 'he' does not refer to anything, but functions more or less as a bound variable. Now consider this statement,

(5)   Harry likes to drink at the local bar

The word 'local' is connected with the relation *x is near y*. Here the description 'the local bar' identifies the bar Harry likes to drink at as one that is near something. But what?

Contrast this with

(6)   Harry likes to drink at the bar that is near his house

In (6), the parameter of being the thing the bar is near is represented by an explicit argument place, filled with the noun phrase, 'his house.' In (5) there is no explicit argument place for that parameter. I call expression like 'local,' which leaves an essential parameter of the relation that they express unarticulated, *role* expressions. Suppose by 'the local bar' in (5) we mean the bar near Harry's house, and that bar is McGinty's. Then McGinty's bar is the occupant of the role, and Harry's house is the anchor for the role, the thing relative to which the occupant has the associated relation.

Mandatory indexicals are role expressions, where the anchor is fixed by the rules of language to be the utterance of the expression itself. The referent of an utterance of 'I' is the speaker of that utterance, but there is no argument role in 'I' to indicate which utterance is in question. The fact that it is the very utterance whose reference is in question is fixed by the rules of language, so it need not be articulated. There is no option.

In the case of 'local,' there is an option. (5) can be read as saying that Harry likes to drink at the bar that is near the place of the utterance. If we were driving through a neighborhood in which there is just one bar, and Harry, although he lives miles away, is very fond of that bar, (5) would be appropriate. Or it could be the bar that is local to the neighborhood about which we are seeing a television documentary. Or it could be the bar that is near Harry's house. The rules of language do not fix which location is the anchor for the role.

Such *optional* indexicals are role-expressions that can have anchors mediated by previous parts of the discourse (or later parts, in some cases). So, we can say

(7)   Harry wants to move to a town on the beach. He likes the local bar

and mean the bar that is local relative to the town on the beach to which Harry wants to move. We can also bind the anchor, as in

(8)   Everywhere that Harry lives, he likes the local bar

These things are not possible with indexicals where the anchor is fixed as the utterance. For example,

(9)   Harry made an important utterance. He said I am getting old

cannot be read as saying that Harry said that the speaker of the utterance that Harry made is getting old. It means that Harry said that the speaker of (9) is getting old.

(10)   All the senior citizens said I am getting old

means they all of the senior citizens said that a certain person, the speaker of (10), is getting old, not that each one said the she (herself) or he (himself) was getting old.
   Demonstrative pronouns, such as 'that man,' are more flexible. We can say

(11)   Elwood was upset by a cabinet member. He's very suspicious of that man.

The pronouns 'he' and 'she' can be used demonstratively, anaphorically or as bound variables:

(12)   Harry thinks she [pointing] is intelligent
(13)   Harry has a new neighbor. He thinks she is intelligent.
(14)   Whenever Harry has a new boss, he thinks she is intelligent

These phenomena suggest that a proper understanding of role words should help provide a unified treatment of indexicality, anaphora, and quantification.[4] In this essay, however, we will focus on the mandatory indexicals and on the indexical uses of optional indexicals.
   Indexicality, then, is not a syntactic category. Indexicality is a semantic category, having to do with meaning, reference, and truth. It is also a pragmatic phenomenon, in both senses of the term. In one sense of 'pragmatics,' it means aspects of meaning that depend on the properties of particular users; this is how Montague used the word in his essay "Pragmatics" (Montague 1968). Pragmatics is now usually conceived as the study of how speakers use their utterances to achieve goals of communication. Although what makes an expression an indexical is a semantic issue, the ways we use indexicals and the reasons they are important can only be understood within a pragmatic account. Pragmatics is also needed to help us understand how our use of indexicals adapts to changes in the basic communicative situation brought about by technologies of various sorts.
   In *Reference and reflexivity*, I classified indexicals with a two-fold distinction:

- Does designation depend on narrow or wide context? Narrow indexicals depend only on the constitutive facts of an utterance: speaker, time, and place. Wide indexicals depend on other facts.
- Is designation 'automatic' given meaning and public contextual facts, or does it depend in part on the intentions of the speaker? (I called these indexicals "intentional" in *Reference and Reflexivity*, but here I call them "discretionary.")

Of course, with all expressions the intention to use them with their ordinary meanings is relevant. However, it seems that with a word like 'I,' no further intention is relevant to determining the referent. If I am speaking English, 'I' refers to me when I use it (although we will consider a possible counterexample below in section 5).

The indexicals 'now' and 'here' seem at first glance as automatic as 'I.' But with 'now' there is a question of how long an interval of time as counted as the present moment; with 'here' the is a question of how much of the surrounding territory is counted as the place of utterance. It seems there is a bit of additional intention that is at least possibly relevant to the determination of reference. Hence, these two are demoted to Discretionary/Narrow.

The ordinary demonstratives and third-person pronouns are clustered in the wide/discretionary cell. The reference of a use of 'that man,' for example, is not determined *merely* by the meaning of the expression, and the speaker, time and place of utterance. Wider facts are relevant. I see the determination of reference coming in two stages. First, which objects of the appropriate sort are *salient?* This is not a matter of the speaker's intention. Second, given the set of salient objects, the speaker's *directing intention* chooses among them.

Suppose I say "that man takes the money," to you, pointing at the man behind the cash register. I do this in order to get you to believe that that man is the one to pay, so that you will pay him, so that we can leave the restaurant. What links my speech to the rest of my plan is the belief that the man I am attending to and directing your attention toward is the cashier. My plan of reference is that I intend to refer to the fellow I see behind the counter, and *thereby* refer to the cashier, for I believe that man behind the counter is the cashier. It is the lower level intention, to refer to the man behind the counter, and not the higher level intention, to refer to the cashier, that is the directing intention, the one determinative in fixing the reference of my utterance. If my belief is wrong, I will succeed in referring to the man behind the counter, but I will *not* succeed in referring to the cashier. If the man behind the counter is cleaning the cash register, while the cashier stands outside having a smoke, I will have said something false about the man behind the cash register, not something true about the cashier. It is such directing intentions that are relevant in determining reference, not the various higher level intentions to refer that we hope to fulfill by carrying out the directing intention. The idea and the term "directing intention" are due to Kaplan (1989).

Let us now turn to the words in the Automatic/Wide cell. One might say, holding one's hands a foot apart, "The bass was yea big," or holding one's hand a couple of feet off the ground, "Her dog was yea big." 'Yea' is wide, because its

Table 17.1 Types of indexicals

	Narrow	Wide
Automatic	I	yea, dthat(α)
Discretionary	Now, here	That, this man, there, he, she, it

reference depends on how one holds one's hands as one says it. It is automatic, because the distance between one's outstretched hands is the distance to which one refers with 'yea,' whether one manages to match the distance one has in mind or not. One may have intended to hold one's hands a foot apart but have actually held them fourteen inches apart. Then the statement is false if the fish in question was exactly twelve inches long. It is not one's intention, but the distance one holds one's hands apart, that determines the semantic value of 'yea.'

On this account, then, the demonstration that accompanies a use of 'yea' differs in significance somewhat from one that accompanies of use of 'that man.' The demonstration is essential to the use of 'yea'; an aspect of the demonstration itself, the distance between the hands, is referred to. The speaker's intention is relevant in his decision to exhibit the length to which he intends to refer, but once he had done that, there is no discretion left. In the case of 'that man,' however, the demonstration is not essential. The demonstration helps to direct our attention to the object referred to, rather than determining which object is referred to.

Kaplan's invented demonstrative 'dthat(α)' *automatically* refers to the object which *in fact* fits the description α. It is *wide* because any sort of fact at all, and not just facts about who is speaking, where, and when, can be incorporated into α. It is automatic, because one refers to the person or thing that fits the description, whatever or whomever one might have wanted to refer to. For example, if you think Jefferson was the first President, and intended to refer to Jefferson by uttering "Dthat (the first President of the U.S.)," you would have failed. You would have referred to Washington instead.

Later on, we will amend this table.

3   Reflexivity and Direct Reference

The reflexive-referential theory treats *meaning* as a property of expression types, and *content* as a property of utterances. Meanings are basically rules that determine the content for specific utterances. The contents of statements are propositions that capture their truth-conditions; the contents of subsentential expressions are the semantic values an utterance of them contributes to the contents of the statements of which they are parts. The English sentence 'I am happy' has the same meaning each time it is used (setting ambiguities, subtleties and odd uses aside). Different utterances of it have different contents, however, since the truth of those utterances depends on different people being happy at different times.

On the reflexive-referential theory, utterances have a variety of contents, the most important of which are *reflexive contents* and *referential contents*. The referential contents of utterances of sentences containing names, indexicals, and demonstratives will be just those assigned by standard referential theories.[5] The referential content of

(15)   I am happy,

uttered by me, is the proposition

(16)   that **John Perry** is happy.

I use bold face to identify the particular constituents of the proposition. The constituents are the subject matter, the things the proposition is about. (16) is what Kaplan calls a "singular proposition" true in worlds in which I am happy—a proposition with me as a constituent, rather than any identifying condition or "mode of presentation" of me.

I use italics to indicate that an identifying property, rather than the object that fits it, is the constituent of a proposition. So the proposition

(17)   That *the speaker of* (**15**) is happy

has an identifying condition as constituent; it is what Kaplan calls a "general proposition" and is true in worlds in which whoever uttered (15) in the world is happy there. (18), on the other hand, is the same proposition as (16), a singular proposition with me as constituent:

(18)   That **the speaker of (15)** is happy.

Kaplan and others use various arguments to show that (16) and not (17) is the proposition expressed by my utterance of (15); (16) is *what I said* (Kaplan 1977). I agree with this. I call (16) the *referential content* or *subject matter content* or *official content* of (15). (16) captures what are sometimes called the *counterfactual truth conditions*. These are the worlds in which the official content is true; worlds such, if they were actual, the proposition would be true. It is also crucial to recognize (17) as the *reflexive* content of (15). I call it "reflexive" simply because it is a condition on (15) *itself.* (15) is not what (15) is *about*; it is not part of the subject matter of (15). (17) is not the counterfactual truth condition of (15); the proposition expressed by (15) can be true in worlds in which (15) itself does not occur. Still, (15) will be true if (17) is true, and vice versa. I claim that the reflexive content helps us understand the reasoning that motivates the production of utterances, and the reasoning that is involved in their interpretation.

4   Using Indexicals

Epistemic and pragmatic roles

When an object plays an *epistemic role* in our lives we have ways of finding out about it. If I am holding something in my hand, I can look at it, feel it, smell it, and so forth to get information about it. If I am standing in front of someone, I can open my eyes and look, ask questions, walk forward and touch, and so forth. Some epistemic roles are utterance-mediated. If you are telling me about your mother, I can ask you questions to find out more about her. I am in an utterance-mediated epistemic relation to your mother. Objects which are playing epistemic roles in our lives, or could easily do so if our attention were suitably directed, are *salient.*

If something plays a *pragmatic role* in our lives, then we can affect it, or use it to affect other things. We can do things with it and to it. Some pragmatic roles are utterance-mediated. I can thank your mother by asking you to convey my thanks to her next time you see her. Some of our examples of epistemic relations were also pragmatic relations. If I am holding something I can squeeze it, throw it, give it to you, and so forth. If I am standing in front of you, I can shove you, annoy you, or startle you. These are *epistemic-pragmatic* relations. However, not all epistemic relations are pragmatic relations. If am looking through binoculars pointed at a bird on a distant tree, I can find out about it, but cannot do much to have an effect on it. If I control big guns on a battleship I can have a devastating effect on the distant countryside, but having a big gun doesn't give me a way of knowing about the countryside I plan to shell.

Being at is also an epistemic-pragmatic relation. I can typically find out about the place I am at by looking around, and can effect it in countless ways. *Being at* may not be a causal relation, but it makes possible many sorts of causal interactions. I can plow the field I am in, paint the room I am in, and so forth.

We live in a world in which technology has created epistemic-pragmatic relations of all kinds. You and I are on opposite sides of the world, sitting at computers that are in turn hooked into the internet. We can exchange email; I can use the relation of *being on computers hooked to the internet* to find out about you and to affect you. I can also stand in an epistemic relation to objects around you, if you are telling me about them via email or your webcam. In addition, I may stand in a pragmatic relation to them, if you are willing to follow my instructions about what to do with them. I will return to this theme below. But for now, let us bracket technology. Let us think about the relatively simple and direct epistemic and pragmatic relations, as they were at the time our basic set of indexicals were developed—long before the internet. My hypothesis is that these indexicals are associated with roles that serve conversational purposes by directing the hearer to a second channel of information about their referent.

These epistemic and pragmatic roles are occupied by objects (including times, places, and other people) relative to knower/agents. Among these objects are tokens. When I speak, I typically create the token I use, and directly affect its salient properties. I can also hear it as I speak it. I have an epistemic-pragmatic relation with the token. My listeners have an epistemic relation to it; by hearing it or seeing it, they can determine several of its properties. By standing in this epistemic relation to the token they stand in epistemic relations to other things: the utterance that produced it, the mind behind that utterance, and the object the mind is referring to. Being in a conversation puts us in a variety of epistemic-pragmatic relations with one another by putting us in an epistemic-pragmatic relation to our own tokens and an epistemic relation to the tokens produced by other conversants. If I am using the tokens I produce to tell you about things, then I have opened an *utterance-mediated* epistemic route to those objects for you, a way for you to get information about them.

Suppose you are looking across the room, where there is a man. You are in an epistemic relation to the man; you can find out more about him by looking, walking over to him and asking him questions, and so forth. You are also in a pragmatic relation to him. For example, you could ask him to give you a cigar, or play the cello for you. You do not do these things, although you like cigars and listening to the cello, since you have no idea whether the man smokes cigars or plays the cello. This is not something you can find out by looking closely—at least, not unless you are Sherlock Holmes.

Now I point to the man and say to you, "That man plays the cello." You hear the token I produce. If you know English, you will know:

> The utterance that produced this token is true IFF the person the speaker attends to and seeks to draw my attention to, plays the cello.

Note that you are at this point in a utterance-mediated epistemic relation to the man. This is a rather complicated relation:

- You are in an epistemic relation to the token I produce, which you can hear.
- You are thereby in an epistemic relation to my utterance, since you can infer its properties from the properties of the token you hear; you know the utterance is true iff the person the speaker refers to plays the cello.
- You are thereby in an epistemic relation to my beliefs about the referent, as expressed by the rest of the sentence or clause.
- You are thereby in an epistemic relation to the man I am talking about, since you can infer properties of his from my beliefs, assuming they are accurate.

This utterance-mediated channel is the *first* channel my utterance opens. It would have been opened, even if I had used 'he' unhelpfully rather than 'that man' demonstratively. My use of the demonstrative and my demonstration open up a *second* channel of information about the man I am talking about. It tells you that by finding the man to whom I am attending, directing your attention towards him, and looking at him, you can find out *more* stuff about the very same person you are learning about by listening to me. When you combine the information from both channels, you learn that there is someone you can easily walk over to (knowledge obtained by looking at him), who does in fact play the cello (knowledge obtained by listening to me). So you do this.

My sentence, then, opens up for you an utterance-mediated channel of information about an individual for whom you have, or easily can have, another channel of information that is *not* mediated by the utterance. *The indexical indicates what that other channel is*—or at least provides a first step that makes it easy to find.

Suppose you are looking for the teacher of philosophy 10. I say, "JP is the teacher of philosophy 10." This opens up a channel of information. The person you want to know more about is the person the speaker is referring to. You can ask me more about "JP." If instead I say "I am the teacher of philosophy 10," I open up this channel. You can ask me about the person I am talking about. But I also open up a different channel. The person in question is not only the person the speaker is talking about, but also the speaker himself. You can hear what I have to say about myself, but in addition you can look at me and draw some of your own conclusions.

Honoring roles

Which roles do we assign to indexicals? There are countless relations that objects stand to us, that are relevant to our thought and action. It is clear that only a small portion of these is honored by having an indexical assigned to express it. For example, the movements required to pick up a coffee mug that is fifteen inches from me are quite different than those required to pick up a coffee mug twenty inches from me. I need to stretch my arm in a different way, and perhaps lean forward for the one that is further away. I know what to do because the situations will look slightly differently to me. Here are two roles that coffee mugs can play, then, that are cognitively different, typically connected to somewhat different perceptions and somewhat different actions. However, we have no indexicals to capture the difference. Our ways of talking are more coarse-grained than our ways of thinking. I would call either of the cups "that cup" if I was just looking at it, and "this cup" once I reached for it and picked it up.

The roles that we have honored by having indexicals and demonstratives assigned to convey them are those that are useful in opening useful supplementary channels of information a variety of recurring conversational situations. Let us look at some examples.

Suppose that Elwood is sitting on the sofa. Mel, in the kitchen, looking out at the people in the living room, asks if anyone would like a beer. Elwood says, "I'd like a beer." This utterance is well designed to achieve his goal in uttering it, to get a beer from Mel. It puts only a modest cognitive burden on Mel. He just needs to see who is speaking, and he will know to whom he should give the beer. He does not need to know much about Elwood, and in particular he does not need to know Elwood's name. Here the utterance-mediated channel gives Mel the information that a certain man, the one Elwood is referring to, wants a beer. The 'I' constrains the referent to be the speaker. This is useful because Mel can see the speaker. He visually learns where the speaker is sitting and what he looks like. Combining the information from the two channels, Mel knows that the person who looks a certain way and is sitting in a certain place wants a beer.

Suppose Elwood had said, "Elwood would like a beer." If Mel had not known who Elwood was, he would not know to bring the speaker a beer. The name would be as useless as 'he' used unhelpfully. Mel might naturally ask, "Who is Elwood?" and, when Elwood says, "I am," feel somewhat put upon. The word 'I' is perfectly suited in this case to link Mel's ideas of *is a person who wants a drink* and his perceptual ideas of *people in the living room*. It would be irritating if Elwood used his name rather than this ready-made device. It would probably be taken to suggest self-importance, as if everyone was expected to know who Elwood was. In both cases,

(19) I'd like a beer
(20) Elwood would like a beer

Mel learns that the person the speaker refers to would like a beer. In both cases, Mel sees where the speaker is located. With the first utterance, Elwood uses the indexical 'I' to *coordinate* these two sources of information. Consequently, Mel knows where to bring the beer. In the second case, Elwood does not coordinate. He leaves Mel in the dark as to whom he is referring, and so leaves Mel in the dark as to whom he should bring the beer. Elwood is not giving enough information.

If we assume Elwood is being helpful, this generates the implicature that we already have the missing information; that Mel knows who Elwood refers to with 'Elwood.' That is why if Elwood says the second thing it sounds pretentious; it implicates that everyone can be expected to know his name. Even when Charles DeGaulle used to refer to himself as "DeGaulle," it sounded pretentious, although he was probably correct, that virtually everyone knew who he was.

Now suppose that Elwood is not seated where Mel can see him, but is down the hall and around the corner. He shouts, "I'd like a beer." In this case, the second channel of information may not be very helpful. It will depend on how much Mel can get out of the sound of Elwood's voice. Maybe he knows Elwood and will recognize his voice; then it is helpful. Maybe the acoustics of the house are such that Mel can pinpoint the beer-needer's location just from the perceived direction of the request. In many cases, it will not be helpful. The point is that it isn't simply the knowledge that *the speaker* is the referent that is crucial, it is the nature of the additional channels, such as *being the person I'm looking at*, that this knowledge will allow the hearer to open that is important. In cases where the hearer can take no step beyond *the speaker*, the use of 'I' will usually be inappropriate.

Later, Mel has delivered the beers and the party starts in earnest. Mel and Elwood are talking. Elwood introduces himself, "I'm Elwood," and extends his hand. As a result, Mel learns Elwood's name. Notice that this simple transaction would not work without the indexical. "Elwood is Elwood" would not do the job. It provides no way for Mel to connect the person occupying one epistemic role (the person in front of him he is talking to) with the occupant of the other (the person that the person he is talking to is talking about). When he hears "I'm Elwood," Mel knows that for the statement to be true the speaker must be named Elwood. He knows that the speaker is the person talking to him, whose lips he sees move in cadence with the sounds. He learns that the person speaking to him, whose looks he can focus on and associate with the name, has the name 'Elwood.'

Other indexicals: *this, that, he, she, here, today,* etc. all are useful in common conversational situations. In each case, their utility consists in linking the object talked about with the occupant of another epistemic and/or pragmatic relation relative to the hearer or reader.

The skilled user of language keeps in mind the goal of getting ideas appropriately linked to one another in a listener's or reader's head, so she will have the desired thoughts. One wants the listener to think of the object one is talking about in a certain way, that will connect with what one wants them to know and to do with this knowledge. To do this, one must put some thought into the cognitive burden one is assuming, and whether it is likely to be met. The skilled leaver of messages on answering machines, for example, will think about whether it will be obvious to the person playing the machine when the call was made; if not, he will not express important information in terms that presuppose this knowledge, like 'today' and 'tomorrow.'

5   Tokens and Technology

Primordial conversation was face to face. This meant the time of utterance and the time of perception of the uttered token were, for all practical purposes, the same. The location of the speaker and the location of the hearer, on the other hand, could be significantly different. There was a natural dichotomy between 'here' and 'there,' one for the speaker's position, the other for the hearer's. Not so with 'now.' The contrast between 'now' and 'then' would not be between speaker's time and hearer's time, but time of utterance and some other salient time. Speakers and hearers share their nows, but not always their heres. Shouting and smoke signals allow communication at considerable distance, and the telephone takes that further—but the time of utterance and time of perception remain the same. With written language, however, the times of utterance and token-perception can be distant from one another. Copying allows multiple listeners at different times and places to perceive the same token; printing magnifies this effect. Email and the rest of the internet push the envelope in all of these directions.

Must I be here now?

The way we use indexicals has adapted to the situations technology makes possible. As we observed above, Kaplan argued in the late 1970s that 'I am not here now' could not be used truly, in any context. Given the rules,

(21)   An utterance *u* of 'I' refers to the speaker of *u*

(22) An utterance *u* of 'here' refers to the position of *u*

(23) An utterance *u* of 'now' refers to the time at which *u* occurs.

it seems that Kaplan has a strong case. Leave aside the issue whether the certainty is a matter of logic, or a matter of a necessary truth about utterances, or simply a very well entrenched truth about utterances. Whatever the exact reason, it seems that if these rules are correct, no utterance of 'I am not here now' will be true.[6]

By the 1980s, answering machines had proliferated, and "I am not here now" became an oft-heard and easily understood and believed message. Is there something wrong with (21), (22), or (23)? Or something wrong with the 1980s?

One might suppose that it has become conventional to refer to the time of listening to the recording with 'now.' However, messages like

(24) I've got to leave now. I won't be here when you hear this recording. I'll try to call you back later.

in which the use of 'now' refers to the time of utterance, are permissible and intelligible. It seems to be the speaker's choice, whether to use 'now' for the time the recording is made or the time it is heard.

Stephano Predelli (1998a) argues that the phenomenon in question predates answering machines. Only the technology of leaving notes is required. Predelli's character Jones has to flee unexpectedly; he leaves his wife a note:

[P] As you can see, I am not at home now. If you hurry, you'll catch the evening flight Los Cabos. Meet me in six hours at the Hotel Cabo Real.

The token produced in this case is the note. Jones has a plan, that his wife see the note when she returns at 5 p.m. He uses 'now' to refer to that time, not to the time when he writes the note.

Again, we cannot simply suppose that there is a convention with notes to use 'now' for the time of token-perception. Jones could have written:

[P'] I'm leaving now for Los Cabos. I'll have been gone for a long time by the time you read this when you get home. If you hurry, you'll catch the evening flight to Los Cabos, and can meet me by 11.

If Jones had written P,' the use of 'now' would have referred to the time he left the note. It would be his intention to have his wife understand it as so referring that would be crucial.

Predelli advocates adding parameters for the intended place and time, which are the values for 'here' and 'now,' to Kaplan's contexts. The values may be the same as the time and place of utterance, but need not be. Jones intends to refer with 'now' to 5 p.m., the time he expects his wife to see the note. According to Predelli, this intention rules; had Jones' wife arrived home early or late, that wouldn't have made the 'now' refer to her time of arrival; it would have still referred to 5 p.m., when Jones expected her to read it. I am not so sure about this.[7]

Here is a somewhat different approach. In cases in which there is a separation between the time of utterance and time of token-perception, both times may be relevant and/or salient, and directing intentions may have a role. The note-writer or voice-recorder may have a directing intention that determines to which of two or more salient times he refers to with 'now,' as and ordinary speaker might with 'that man.'

The function of 'now' is to help the listener establish a separate information channel for the time the speaker refers to. In the face to face case the listener simply looks and listens at what is going on around him. If we are in a face to face conversation, and you say, "It's time for the meeting now," I do not need to examine your demonstrations or eye-gaze to see to which time you refer. I do not even need to make sure it is me to whom you are talking, as I might with 'you' or 'there.' The time to which you refer is the time that is present for both of us, and all within earshot, the time of utterance and the time of perception.

Writing changes this. You write me a postcard,

(25)   Made it to Tokyo. I'm now very tired. Call you when I get back.

The simple techniques appropriate in face to face communication won't work. I need to know when you wrote the card. Perhaps I infer from the postmark that you probably wrote it last Tuesday; then I can find out about last Tuesday in all the usual ways—checking Wednesday's newspaper, for example. If I do not know when you wrote the postcard, 'now' is a pretty unhelpful indexical.

When the time of utterance is separated from the time of token-perception, the usual epistemic techniques associated with 'now'—listening and looking to what is going on—are techniques for the audience to find out more about the time of perception, but not more about the time of utterance. If the time of token-perception is relevant, it will be a live candidate for the referent of 'now.'

From this point of view, the Jones case goes as follows. Jones expects his wife to read the note, and assumes that the time at which she reads it will be salient to her: it will be a live candidate to be the time he is referring to with his use of 'now.' It is relevant to what he wants to tell her, for it is the time relative to which the plane is leaving soon. He has a directing intention to refer to that time. He thinks she will see it at 5 p.m., so he thinks *by* referring the time when she reads the note, he will refer to 5 p.m. If his belief is wrong, and she reads it at 3:30 p.m., then he refers to 3:30 p.m.

Suppose the note contains the sentence

[P″]   You must leave right now to catch the plane

This what actually happens. His wife sees the note at 3:30. She hurries to catch the evening flight, but finds she has to wait at the airport, having arrived an hour and a half before Jones thought she would. After they meet, she criticizes him, for saying something false, that she had to leave at 3:30 to catch the plane. According to the present approach, she is right, he did say that. On Predelli's analysis, he did not say that; he said that she had to leave at 5 p.m. to catch the plane, and she misunderstood.

Suppose Jones' expectation that his wife would return at 5 and see the note then was based on her usual schedule. Then she should have known when he expected her to read it, and he could reply that she should have figured out what he *meant* to say. It does not seem to me, however, that he could claim to have actually *said* it. The term 'said' is to a certain extent a *forensic* term; it has to do with what message people can be held responsible for conveying. At the same time, the hearer is responsible for using a bit of common sense, in figuring out what the speaker is trying to say especially when the speaker is obviously confused. Jones' wife has a legitimate complaint against Jones, but he has a legitimate comeback. A normal married couple.

On Varol Akman's view the word 'I' has the speaker as a *default* reference, but in certain circumstances 'I' can refer to others. I'll express some doubts about his case for the word 'I' below, but here I want to adapt his suggestion to the word 'now.' The default value for a use of 'now' is the time of utterance, in the sense that the speaker can always use 'now' to refer to the time of utterance. He can use 'now' to refer to the time of token-perception when it is salient and relevant.

Where is here, anyway?

Let us think a bit about "here." Suppose Jones's situation was more dangerous than Predelli suggests. He called his wife and told her not to go home at all but to look through a telescope from a neighbor's house at a note he would leave on the refrigerator with instructions about what she should do. The note begins

I am not here now . . .

In the situation, the 'here' seems to refer to the house where the note is, the 'now' to the expected time of perception of it. It does not seem possible to read 'here' as referring to the neighbor's house, the place of perception. If the note continued:

I am hiding there, in the front-hall closet . . .

Mrs. Jones would look for her husband in the neighbor's front-hall closet. She would take 'here' to refer to the place where the note was, 'there' to the place where she was.[8]

These considerations seem to me to weigh in favor of my account. Both the place of the note and the place from which Mrs. Jones perceives the note are salient. However, it seems Jones should refer to the first as "here" and the second as "there." The reason is that the contrast between 'here' as the place of the speaker and 'there' as the place of the listener is well established, as is the difference in epistemic techniques. If I say, "look over there" without any further indication of a place, you will take me to have told you to look around the part of the world you are at. If I say, "it's over here" you would look for the desired object close to me.

When we return to the telephone answering machine, things get rather murky, however. Sometimes answering machines are located near the telephones, calls to which they pick up after a few rings. Sometimes, however, the answering machines are at a central location, perhaps a telephone company office, or the communications department of a corporation. When the message says, "I am not here now" the "here" seems to refer to the place where the telephone is, whether or not the answering machine is there.

The use of 'here,' 'there,' 'now,' and 'then' as contrastive demonstratives is also confusing. This is most clear when there is some sort of representation we are using to discuss events. With appropriate demonstrations to a map of an intersection in a courtroom, I can say, "I was stopped here. He backed out of his garage there and ... " I can use 'now' and 'then' similarly with a chronology of events. What, if anything, do these uses have to do with the time and place of utterance? 'Now' and 'then,' seem to amount to 'this time' and 'that time,''here' and 'there' to 'this place' and 'that place.' I'll, reluctantly treat these uses as separate senses, subscripted with 'D' for 'demonstrative,' until a clearer vision allows a unifying account.

Here then is a revised table.

Table 17.2 Types of indexicals

	Narrow (speaker and time and place of utterance are only relevant facts)	Less narrow (time and place of token-perception are also relevant)	Wide
Automatic	I		Yea, dthat(α)
Discretionary		Now, then, here there	That, this man, he, she, it, now$_D$, then$_D$, here$_D$, there$_D$

There seems to be a steady drift away from the upper left corner. Only 'I' is left as automatic and narrow. Can it hold that ground?

Must I be me?

Varol Akman suggests that 'I' is more flexible than its lonely position in the narrow and automatic cell indicates.[9] Akman imagines an ill Yeltsin, looking at the man who has been serving as his double asking "How am I doing today?" If we take the "I" to refer to the double, then we seem to have a case where 'I' does not refer to the speaker. Taken this way, Yeltsin would be asking the double how the double was doing; was he hot? tired? bored with pretending to be Yeltsin? and so forth.

Suppose Yeltsin was at a conference with some other big shots, all of who had doubles. Stopping by the double buffet for a drink, Yeltsin asks a series of questions, addressing each to the appropriate double: How is Bill Clinton today? How is François Mitterrand today? How is John Major today? How am I today? It seems to me that to understand what is going on we don't need defeasible interpretations for the names, but rather what W. V. Quine called "deferred ostension" (1969). There is a "proxy-function" ρ. By referring to X one identifies, and talks about, the ρ of X. One car park attendant says to another, "Here comes the Porsche," meaning the owner of the Porsche is coming to get his car. Thus, Yeltsin asks about Bill Clinton's double, the person in front of him, when he says, "How is Bill Clinton today." Yeltsin can pretend to be taken in, by referring to the doubles the way the deceived commoners are expected to refer to them. The joke comes when he uses 'I,' when the deferred ostension still works, but the pretense runs aground; he cannot refer to his double as 'I' without betraying that he realizes that it is a double, and not the real Yeltsin. The case is interesting, and the default/defeasible is plausible in the case of deferred ostension. However, the default is that the person referred to is the person talked about or asked about, the propositional constituent of the what is said or what is asked. If we approach Akman's example this way, we can leave 'I' its honored place in the chart.

Notes

1 I use double quotes for quoting language and thought, and as scare-quotes; I use single quotes for mentioning expressions.

2 As I mentioned above, I use "real relation" for one not mediated by utterances. As a matter of convenience, not scholarship, I'll take Peirce to mean something by "real relation" that implies my sense.

3 Reichenbach's own approach was a bit different, as was what he meant by "reflexivity." I am stating the truth-conditions of (1) and (2), not trying to produce synonymous translations for them. Reichenbach wanted to produce a synonymous symbolic formula. For this purpose he introduced one all-purpose indexical, τ, which means roughly "this very token." For (1) this would have been something like

   (1R) $\exists x$ x is the speaker of τ & x has been to Paris

   (1R), like (1) and (2), is token sensitive. The difference is that Reichenbach has isolated the token-sensitivity to a single word, his invented token-reflexive τ.

4 See ch. 18.

5 I use the term "referential" for theories that take names and/or indexicals to be "rigid designators" (Kripke), or to be "directly referential" (Kaplan) or to take statements containing such expressions to "say something about" the object referred to (Wettstein, Donnellan). The idea is that sentences using these terms will be about

the objects referred to, rather than any mode of presentation or identifying description of them.

6   For discussion of the status of "I am here now," see Predelli 1998b and Perry forthcoming.

7   I agreed with Predelli on this point in Perry, forthcoming.

8   Note also that in the case of the answering machine's message "I am not here now," it is the place where the telephone is or is expected to be, not the place where the answering machine is. Some answering machines are provided by telephone service providers, and are located miles from the phones they answer. I may use such an answering machine, and in addition, for some reason or other, disconnect my telephone and bring it with me when I take a short trip. So there is no telephone at my home, and the answering machine you hear is not there either. Still, it seems that "here" refers to my home, the location where the telephone you were trying to call was expected to be. If you called my office, where I had also removed the telephone, and received a message from the same central location for answering machines, the 'here' would refer to my office. The application of all of this to cell telephones is left to the reader.

9   V. Akman, "Context and the indexical 'I'," paper read at NASSLLI'02 Workshop on Cognition: Formal Models and Experimental Results, CSLI, Stanford, CA (30 June 2002).

Chapter 18

Pronouns and Anaphora

Stephen Neale

1 Introduction

Many of the philosophical problems raised by names, descriptions, and demonstratives discussed in other chapters recur with pronouns and intersect with problems raised in linguistics involving *anaphora* (from the Greek, "carry back"), which concerns *interpretive dependencies* among expressions.

A traditional taxonomy of English pronouns might be this. Demonstrative pronouns ('that,' 'this') are used to refer to things that are *salient* (or being made so). Personal pronouns are used to refer to persons: first-person pronouns ('I,' 'me') are used to refer to oneself; second-person pronouns ('you') are used to refer to one's audience; and third-person pronouns ('he,' 'she') are, used in place of 'fuller' phrases ('John Lennon,' 'Beatlemania') to refer to persons, places or things speakers could have referred to using those fuller phrases. Personal pronouns also have possessive ('his') and reflexive ('himself') forms; the third-person has an interrogative/relative ('who') form; and some differ in form according as they are subjects ('I,' 'he,' 'who') or objects ('me,' 'him,' 'whom'). Possessives indicate possession (construed broadly), reflexives signal anaphoric connections to expressions (of the same number and gender) in the same clause, and the interrogative/relative form is used in asking questions ('who has met a Beatle?') and in forming relative clauses ('everyone who has met a Beatle').

Philosophy shares with linguistics the desire to understand how pronouns fit into a general account of the semantics of natural language, but their roles in puzzles about self-knowledge, substitutivity, existence, identity, modality, indexicality and attitude ascriptions has tended to drive philosophical investigations. In the present chapter, attention will be restricted to third-person pronouns in so far as they may be devices of anaphora.[1]

2 Pronouns and Variables

Philosophical interest in pronouns has tended to centre on distinguishing their use as something akin to the *bound variables* of quantification theory, their *deictic* (*indexical, demonstrative*) use to refer to salient individuals ('Look at him!'), and their use as devices that finesse repetition ('John orders lobster if he's in Maine').[2] The quantifier-variable combination is still part of philosophy's *lingua franca* (although the dictum 'to be is to be the value of a bound variable' exerts less influence than it once did). Variables are often said to be the formal counterparts of third-person pronouns, but the relationship is not straightforward.

(a) Unlike variables in logic, pronouns may be marked for such things as *gender, number,* and *case*: 'she' is nominative, feminine, and singular; 'them' is accusative and plural. And it is arguable that such features impinge upon the truth or falsity of our statements.

(b) Unlike variables in logic, natural language pronouns may be subject to *locality* conditions on binding.[3] For example, 'him' *cannot* function as a variable bound by 'every man' in (1), whereas 'himself' *must* so function in (2):

(1) every man loves him
(2) every man loves himself.

That is, (1) *cannot*, but (2) *must*, be understood as expressing what (2') expresses:[4]

(2') [*every x: man x*] *x loves x.*

The non-reflexive 'him' is *too close* (in some sense to be elucidated) to 'every man' in (1), but not in (3), for example:

(3) every man loves the woman who married him.

And the reflexive 'himself' is *too far* from 'every man' in (4):

(4) every man loves the woman who married himself.

So, where (3) *can* be used to express what (3') expresses, (4) *cannot*:

(3') [*every x: man x*] *x loves the woman who married x.*

Since there is no condition on variables in first-order logic corresponding to this locality difference, its existence in natural language is something that needs to be described exactly and explained. For it *appears* that natural language is making things more complicated than it might.

(c)   Wherever we find a pronoun bound by a quantifier, we can replace the quantifier by a singular term. For example, we get the following quantified-singular pair:

(5)   every man loves himself
(5′) John loves himself

It is often said that 'himself' is co-referential with 'John' in (5′), that its reference is determined by 'John.' If this is right, pronouns can function in a way that traditional variables in logic cannot. It might seem that 'himself' is a device for avoiding repetition, that an underlying form 'John loves John' surfaces as (5′) in ordinary English. But are we not missing something? Surely 'himself' functions *identically* in (5) and (5′), these sentences being used to make claims involving the following condition:

(5″)   *x loves x.*

(5) is used to say that this condition is true of every man, and (5′) is used to say that it is true of John. As it is sometimes put, (5) and (5′) contain the same predicate, 'loves himself,' understood as $\lambda x\,(x\ loves\ x)$.[5] So if 'himself' is really functioning as a bound variable in the quantified case (5), shouldn't we explore the idea that it functions in the same way in the singular case (5′)? And if that is right, in order to preserve as much compositionality as possible, shouldn't we see all predicates as ultimately devices of abstraction, 'snores' expressing $\lambda x(x\ snores)$, 'loves' expressing $\lambda y\,(\lambda x\,(x\ loves\ y))$, and so on? Since we have to start somewhere, let us assume until further notice that 'himself' is, in fact, bound by 'John' in (5′) in whatever way it is bound by 'every man' in (5), details to be provided.

(d)   Variable-binding will not supply everything needed to understand pronouns. Take (6) and (6′):

(6)   every man loves his wife
(6′) John loves his wife

On one use of 'his' it appears to be a device of anaphora in both (6) and (6′), the respective sentences used to make claims involving the following condition:

(6″)   *x loves x's wife.*

(6) is used to say the condition is true of every man; and (6′) to say it is true of John, the common predication being $(\lambda x\,(x\ loves\ x's\ wife))$. In line with what was said about reflexives, let us call this the *bound* use of 'his.'
    On a second use of 'his,' it is *free*: it is used to make independent, indexical reference to some particular male. Suppose we have been talking about Paul, who

is known to be married to a woman who is utterly captivating. We might use 'his' in (6) and (6') to refer to Paul, to make claims involving not condition (6″) but condition (6‴):

(6‴)   *x loves Paul's wife.*

We might say that on this use of 'his' it functions as a *free* variable, an expression to which some specific value must be assigned for interpretation to take place. A question now arises concerning the precise relationship between these two uses of 'his.'

(v) Related to the matter of ambiguity is the matter of the interpretation of expressions pared down by rule-governed ellipsis.[6] We need to explain the contrast between (7) and (8), for example:

(7)   John loves himself. So does Paul.
(8)   John loves his wife. So does Paul.

There is a single reading of (7). But there are two distinct readings of (8), one upon which Paul is being said to satisfy (8'), another on which he is being said to satisfy (8″):

(8')   *x loves x's wife*
(8″)   *x loves John's wife*

This might suggest we need to distinguish a reading of (8) upon which 'his' is bound by 'John' and another upon which it is an indexical used to refer to John, the same person 'John' is being used to refer to. This would comport with the idea that the ellipted structure is understood as the ungainly 'so does Paul love his wife' with 'his' preserving its interpretation either as a variable to be bound by the subject expression or as an indexical used to refer to John. It would also explain why (7) has only one reading: reflexives permit only bound readings.

(vi) A pronoun may be used in such a way that it seems to be interpreted neither as a variable bound by some antecedent phrase nor as an indexical.[7] For anaphoric dependencies seem to exist that do not involve binding. Consider (9) and (9'):

(9)   Just one man drank rum. He was ill afterwards.
(9')   John drank rum. He was ill afterwards

Treating 'he' as a variable bound by 'just one man' in (9) yields the wrong result:

(10)   [*just one x: man x*] (*x drank rum* ∧ *x was ill afterwards*).

(10) can be true if two men drank rum but only one of them was ill afterwards, i.e. its truth is consistent with the *falsity* of the first conjunct of (9).[8] Thus (10) appears to capture the meaning not of (9), but of (10'):

(10′)   Just one man drank rum and was ill afterwards.

So we still need an account of the pronoun in (9). But the fact that (9) and the ungainly (9″) below appear to be equivalent suggests we explore the view that the pronoun in the former functions as a disguised definite description:[9]

(9″)   Just one man drank rum. The man who drank rum was ill afterwards.

But the desire to preserve a uniform treatment of pronouns as variables might suggest exploring a rather different idea: that the occurrence of 'he' in (9) is a variable bound by *something other than* 'just one man,' something not revealed until we have an account of the underlying *logical form* of the sentence and a general theory of the *pragmatics of discourse.*[10]

Now what of the singular case (9′)? If the quantifier 'just one man' cannot bind the pronoun 'he' in (9), there is no good reason to think 'John' can bind it in (9′). We would appear to have three options for dealing with the pronoun in (9′): we could view it (a) as an indexical being used to refer to John, this being licensed in some way by John's salience; (b) as a pronoun of laziness, interpreted as if it were just another occurrence of 'John'; (c) as a device of co-reference – the difference between positions (b) and (c) would need to be articulated clearly.

The issue raised by the pronoun in (9) recurs with more interesting examples. Consider the so-called 'donkey' sentence (11):

(11)   every man who bought just one donkey paid cash for it.

If the quantifier 'just one donkey' is to bind 'it,' it will have to be given large scope:

(12)   [*just one y: donkey y*] [*every x: man x* ∧ *x bought y*] (*x paid cash for y*).

But again this yields the wrong result. The fact that (11) appears to be equivalent to the ungainly (11′) below suggests we may profit again by exploring the view that the pronoun functions as a disguised definite description:

(11′)   every man who bought just one donkey paid cash for the donkey he bought.

On such an account, the description the pronoun 'it' abbreviates itself contains a pronoun 'he' bound by the subject expression 'every man who bought a donkey.' This raises questions about the nature of the mechanisms involved in interpreting a pronoun that appears to be anaphoric but not bound by the expression upon which it appears to be anaphoric; and it might suggest sweeping up all anaphoric pronouns within a theory of the pragmatics of discourse.[11] Alternatively, it might suggest sweeping them up with a description-based approach.[12]

3 Anaphoric Pronouns in Generative Grammar

One of the central ideas in generative linguistics in the 1960s was a distinction between a sentence's *surface* structure and its *deep* structure.[13] Deep structures were generated by phrase structure rules such as

$$S \rightarrow NP + VP$$
$$VP \rightarrow V + NP.$$

Transformational rules would then map deep structures into surface structures by processes that might delete, add, re-order or substitute constituents. For example, a surface structure of roughly the form of (1) might be derived by a *passivization* transformation from something of roughly the form of (1′):

(13)   Mary was kissed by John
(13′) John kissed Mary.

The surface structure (14) might be derived from the deep structure (14′)

(14)   John wishes to leave
(14′) John$_1$ wishes John$_1$ to leave.

by a *deletion* transformation on the basis of an *identity* in the latter, the presence of two distinct occurrences of the same noun phrase, 'John,' marked in some way in grammar as co-referential, perhaps using integers as indices.[14] That identity of form was required seemed clear from the fact that the deletion transformation could not apply to, say, 'John wants Mary to leave'; that identity of interpretation was required seemed evident from the fact that (14) cannot be used to say that John Lennon wants John Kennedy to leave.[15]

It seemed natural within this framework to explore the idea that anaphoric pronouns were the superficial manifestations of fuller noun phrases, derived by *pronominalization* and *reflexivization* transformations.[16] For example, the surface structures (15), (16), and (17) (the last two only on their anaphoric readings), were taken by some linguists to be derived transformationally from the deep structures (15′), (16′), and (17′) respectively (on the basis of noun phrase identity in those deep structures):

(15)   John shaves himself
(15′) John shaves John
(16)   John$_1$ loves his$_1$ wife
(16′) John$_1$ loves John$_1$'s wife
(17)   John$_1$ thinks he$_1$ is smart
(17′) John$_1$ thinks John$_1$ is smart

But pronominalization could not provide an explanation of *all* anaphoric pronouns.[17] First, anaphora on quantifiers was a problem. Transformational rules were supposed to be meaning-preserving.[18] Thus (18) (on its anaphoric reading) could not be derived from (18′), as they clearly differ in meaning:

(18) [every man]₁ loves his wife.
(18′) [every man]₁ loves [every man]₁'s wife.

Second, infinite regresses were discovered in so-called "crossing co-reference" structures like (19):[19]

(19) [the pilot who shot at it₂]₁ hit [the MiG that was chasing him₁]₂.

(19) contains two anaphoric pronouns, 'it' and 'he,' each of which appears to be anaphoric on an expression containing the other. If these pronouns are the products of pronominalizing 'the MiG that was chasing him' and 'the pilot who shot at it' respectively, then (19) derives from (19′):

(19′) [the pilot who shot at [the MiG that was chasing him₁]₂]₁ hit
        [the MiG that was chasing [the pilot who shot at it₂]₁]₂.

But (19′) contains occurrences of 'him' and 'it' that need to be derived. If they are derived by pronominalization too, we have an infinite regress on our hands.

By the mid-1970s it was generally accepted that at least some anaphoric pronouns were 'base-generated,' i.e. present at deep structure rather than derived by a pronominalization transformation. Around the same time, the idea that there were general constraints (or conditions) restricting the nature of transformations was being explored.[20] Soon enough, pronominalization was abandoned in favour of the idea all pronouns were base-generated.[21] And soon enough, the original idea that anaphoric relations were marked in syntax was itself called into question: the reading of a sentence upon which a (non-reflexive) pronoun β is seemingly anaphoric on some expression α is nothing more, it was suggested, than a reading upon which nothing in the grammar *precludes* α and β from being co-referential.[22] The interesting task was seen to be that of specifying precisely the syntactic conditions that precluded co-reference in examples such as those marked with an asterisk below:

(20) John₁ realized he₁ was ill
(21) * he₁ realized John₁ was ill
(22) his₁ mother thought John₁ was ill
(23) although he₁ was ill, John₁ went to work
(24) * Anne asked him₁ about John₁
(25) * Mary asked John₁ about him₁

The wisdom of giving up the idea that anaphoric relations were marked in syntax was called into question by certain philosophers.[23] To talk of conditions on *co-reference*, it was pointed out, was to talk of conditions on a *symmetric* relation. But the anaphoric relations at issue are inherently *asymmetric*. Talk of *de facto* co-reference, and even talk of intentional co-reference, needed to be replaced, it was argued, by talk of *referential dependence*, a species of *de jure* co-reference. Co-reference is *not* actually precluded in the examples marked with asterisks above; what is precluded is *referential dependence*.

A good case can be made that talk of *de jure* co-reference and referential dependence is ultimately misplaced in a theory of anaphora. In accordance with where we began in our discussion of pronouns, let us say that what is precluded in the relevant examples above is *binding*, leaving it open for now whether binding is a primitive notion or one that can be analysed in terms of some form of *de jure* co-reference (as, for example, Evans (1977, 1980) holds). Thus we can talk of both quantifiers and names binding pronouns, deferring until later precisely how a unified theory is to be elaborated.

4   Phonetic Form and Logical Form

By the early 1980s, the emphasis in linguistics shifted from rules for generating (and interpreting) particular linguistic structures to constraints on possible structures and interpretations.[24] Diverse linguistic phenomena, seemingly governed by intricate rules that differed from language to language, were now viewed as consequences of the interaction of general principles of the human language faculty, principles that were meant to be invariant across typologically distinct languages, superficial differences between particular languages reflecting only the setting of different values to each of a batch of structural parameters as part of the process of language acquisition, and the peripheral effects of relatively unimportant, learned idiosyncrasies. The interpretation of pronouns was prominent in this work because of the importance within the emerging theory of a sub-theory that concerned itself with the *binding* of one expression by another.[25] Before presenting the Binding Theory, however, we need to understand how the general syntactic framework has developed recently.

In the 1990s, syntactic theory further evolved in the light of *minimalist assumptions*, the net effect of which was to restrict the posits of grammatical theory – whether categories, processes, constraints, or levels of representation – to those that are conceptually necessary or empirically unavoidable.[26] A motif that runs through this work is an argument from 'virtual conceptual necessity': complexity and stipulation are to be avoided as, all else being equal, language will employ only those devices needed to link sound and meaning. One consequence of this outlook is that all properties of sentences relevant to sound and meaning – and this includes *binding* properties – should be derivable from quite general considerations about the way the language faculty must engage with two other cognitive systems, one dealing with the articulation of sounds and their perception (henceforth *the sound system*), the other trading in intentional/conceptual representations (henceforth *the intentional system*). A particular language, on this account, is an instantiation of the language faculty (with certain options specified) that provides 'instructions' to be interpreted by the sound system, on the one hand, and the intentional system, on the other. More specifically, a language generates *pairs* of representations, a PF (or 'Phonetic Form') to be read by the sound system, and an LF (or 'Logical Form') to be read by the intentional system.[27]

For Chomsky, the basic idea behind the concept of LF representations has remained robust since its inception: An LF incorporates, 'whatever features of sentence structure (1) enter into the semantic interpretation of sentences and (2) are strictly determined by properties of sentence grammar' (Chomsky, 1976b: 305). The only difference today is what is meant by 'strictly determined by properties of sentence grammar.' With the emergence of the minimalist outlook, this phrase may be usefully understood as 'strictly determined by the exigencies of connecting sound and meaning.'

Expressions such as 'some student,' 'a student,' 'the student,' 'every student,' and so on are usually called DPs (determiner phrases) today to reflect the idea that they are projected from the Ds (determiners) 'some,' 'a,' 'the,' 'every' and so on (rather than from the N (noun) 'student' as earlier theory suggested).[28] On this usage, which we shall follow, the label NP is reserved for the nominal expression, simple or complex, with which the determiner merges to form a DP, as in the following tree and labelled bracketing:

(26)
```
                    S
        DP               VP
     D      NP           V
            N

    some  student     groaned.
```
$[_{DP}[_{D}some]$ $[_{NP}[_{N}student]]]$ $[_{VP}[_{V}groaned]]]$

The LF corresponding to (26) will look something like (27):[29]

(27)
```
                    S
        DP¹                   S
     D      NP       DP           VP
            N                     V

    some  student    x₁        groaned
```
$[_{S}[_{DP}[_{D}some]$ $[_{NP}[_{N}student]]]^{1}$ $[_{S}x_{1}[_{VP}[_{V}groaned]]]]]$

In (27) the quantifier expression 'some student' has been extracted – indeed forced by general principles of morphosyntax – from its original position (discernible in (26)) and has merged with the original S node to form another. From this 'new' position it binds the variable x that has been left as a sort of 'trace' in its 'original' position, that position being within the scope of its new position. The numerical *sub*script on x indicates that it is to be interpreted as bound by the quantifier expression 'some student,' which bears the same index as *super*script.[30] This talk of variables and binding amounts to a description of an important part of the *interpretive* information, precisely the sort of thing Chomsky ascribes to LFs. Variables are expressions *interpreted* in a certain way. One question that will have to be addressed is whether quantifier expressions are the *only* DPs that are raised at LF in this way or whether the phenomenon is fully general, involving names and pronouns for example

Within the minimalist framework, the Binding Theory is now just a set of constraints imposed by virtually unavoidable facts about an interpretive system, a set of principles operative at the interface of the language faculty and the system of conceptual-intentional representations, i.e. it holds at LF.

5 Binding and Scope

It would be incorrect to say the conception of binding involved in the Binding Theory is *purely* syntactic because it has a clear interpretive dimension. (The nature of this interpretation, via the notion of abstraction, will be examined later.) The usual Binding Theory definition of binding is as follows:

> α binds β iff (a) α and β are *co-indexed*, and
> (b) β is within the *scope* of α.

Much turns on what is meant by 'scope' here. In the first-order predicate calculus, a variable β may be bound by a quantifier α (in a formula X) only if β resides in *the smallest sentence (open or closed) (in X) that contains* α. Following Russell, this is what we mean when we say that a variable may be bound by a quantifier only if it lies within the quantifier's *scope*. The only non-atomic expressions in the calculus are whole sentences (open or closed) and the only expressions whose scopes we care about are the sentence operators $(\forall x)$, $(\exists x)$, $\neg$, $\wedge$, $\vee$, $\supset$, and $\equiv$. So we say, with seeming generality, that an expression β is within the scope of an expression α iff β resides in the smallest *sentence* containing α.[31] The full generalization is not hard to find:

> For any *expression* α, α's scope = the smallest *constituent* properly containing α.[32]

Consider (28) and (29):

(28)   John told Paul's mother a lot about himself

(29)   * John's mother told Paul's mother a lot about himself.

What prevents 'himself' being bound by 'John' in (29)? The lay answer is that 'John' is not the *subject* of (29), 'John's mother' is.[33] However, while there are, in fact, languages in which a reflexive must be bound by a subject expression (e.g. German), English appears not to be such a language:

(30)   John^1 told Paul^2 a lot about himself$_{1'2}$.

Here, 'himself' can be bound by 'John' or 'Paul.' Although the lay answer to our question appears to be technically incorrect, it is *right in spirit*. The *subject* of a sentence S is the DP that combines with a VP to form S (the DP 'immediately dominated' by the S node). This simple fact gives us *everything we need* to understand scope. We can characterize scope 'inclusively' (in the manner familiar to philosophers and logicians), or 'exclusively' (in a manner more familiar to linguists:

Inclusive: If α and β merge to form {αβ}, then {αβ} = the scope of α = the scope of β.

Exclusive: If α and β merge to form {αβ}, then α = the scope of β, and β = the scope of α.

Scope is something you get when you merge expressions. And from a combinatorial or computational point of view, this makes the notion virtually trivial, something that arises once we accept the possibility (as we must) of expressions merging to form larger expressions. In a sense, then, it is hard to imagine anything more trivial than scope.[34]

It is now easy to see what is going on in (28)–(30). In (28), 'himself' lies within the scope of 'John' but not within the scope of 'Paul'; in (29) it lies within the scope of neither; and in (30) it lies within the scopes of both.

To say that α and β are *co-indexed* is to say something of syntactic import that may or may not have interpretive consequences, depending upon how indexing is elaborated. Let us suppose each DP is assigned some index, which we might indicate with a subscript.[35] What prevents co-indexing being of 'merely syntactic' interest (if this even makes sense) is its *interpretation*. The whole point of indices would disappear if co-indexing were not meant to indicate something of *interpretive* significance. When 'himself' takes the same index as 'John' in (30) we think of the two expressions as linked for purposes of interpretation. One option is to say that the linking involves *co-reference*, the reflexive being *referentially dependent* upon the name. But let us continue with the idea that the linking actually involves *binding* in the sense familiar from quantification theory, with the aim of providing a uniform treatment of (30) and (31)

(31)   [every bishop]^1 told [some prince]^2 a lot about himself$_{1'2}$.

When 'himself' takes the same index as 'John' in (30), it is being used to say something that is true iff the following condition is true of (is satisfied by) some person John:

(32)   *x told Paul a lot about x.*

When 'himself' takes the same index as 'Paul,' it is being use to say something that is true iff the following condition is true of (is satisfied by) some person Paul:

(33)   *John told x a lot about x.*

If we did not have distinct interpretations in mind, we could never have even reached the point of bringing indices into the picture. And to this extent it would be misleading to say that binding and co-indexing are *purely syntactic* notions. The principal phenomenon we are investigating is an *interpretive* one with a *syntactic* dimension. (*Any discussion* of the syntactic conditions governing anaphora is up to its neck in matters of *interpretation*, for tautologically that is *precisely* what the facts that are being accounted for involve.)

6   The Binding Theory

Chomsky's Binding Theory comprises three principles meant to characterize the syntactic constraints on interpretation. It aims to capture the fact that, roughly, (A) a reflexive pronoun (e.g. 'himself') must not be 'too far' from its binder; that (B) a non-reflexive (e.g. 'him') must not be 'too close'; and that (C) a name (broadly construed) must not have a binder at all. In the 1980s and 1990s, great effort was expended on defining 'too far' and 'too close.' To a first, rough approximation the first of the three principles that make up the Binding Theory is this:

> *Principle A*: a reflexive is to be interpreted as bound in within the smallest clause containing it.

We can indicate binding by placing a numerical superscript on the binder and a corresponding subscript on the bound, asterisks before subscripts signalling impossible bindings. Consider (34) and (35):

(34) $[_s \text{John}^1$ says that $[_s[\text{no barber}]^2$ shaves $\text{himself}_{*1/2}]]$
(35) $[_s \text{John}^1$ says that $[_s\text{Paul}^1$ shaves $\text{himself}_{*1/2}]].$

The reflexive 'himself' in utterances of these sentences is bound by the subject of the embedded clause ('no barber' in (34), and 'Paul' in (35)) not by the subject of the larger clause ('John,' in both examples). It is common in linguistics to say that pronouns satisfying Principle A are "locally bound."[36]

By contrast, the non-reflexive 'him' in utterances of (34′) and (35′) below *cannot* be bound by the subject of the embedded clause, but *may* be bound by the subject of the larger clause:

(34′) [$_S$ John^1 says that [$_S$[no barber]^2 shaves him$_{1'*2}$]]
(35′) [$_S$ John^1 says that [$_S$ Paul^2 shaves him$_{1'*2}$]].

These data are in accordance with the second principle of the Binding Theory:

Principle B: a non-reflexive is not to be interpreted as bound by an expression within the smallest clause containing it.

The third and final principle concerns names (broadly speaking):

Principle C: a name is not to be interpreted as bound.

Thus, an utterance of (36) cannot be understood in such a way that 'Tully' is bound by either 'Cicero' or 'a barber':

(36) [$_S$ Cicero^1 says that [$_S$ [a barber]^2 shaves Tully$_{*1'*2}$]].

To say this is not to say that 'Cicero; and 'Tully' may not be *de facto* co-referential.[37] On the assumption that the concept of binding involves interpretive as well as syntactic notions, it is unclear why the issue of binding a name should come up in the first place, and this might cast doubt on the need for Principle C.

Despite all sorts of counterexamples, the Binding Theory is still at the core of discussions of pronouns and anaphora, a fixed point from which to explore. Providing a clear and precise specification of the (seemingly) complementary distribution of reflexives and non-reflexives with respect to their binding possibilities, one that holds across a multitude of languages would be a phenomenal accomplishment, of course. But even if a version of the Binding Theory were to emerge that everyone found acceptable, it might still fall short of where Chomsky want, for what he wants (and surely we should agree with him) is not just a *description* of the facts, but an *explanation* of *why* the Binding Theory holds. The theory would certainly not be 'necessary' in any sense of this word usually employed by philosophers; but this does not mean it may not be 'conceptually' or 'empirically' necessary in Chomsky's (1995, 2002) sense: if a grammar is the optimal solution to the problem of relating form and meaning for a system as expressively rich as the ones we do, as a matter of empirical fact, possess, it may turn out the interpretive difference between 'himself' and 'him' (or, rather more plausibly, between two more general classes of expressions) is pretty much unavoidable. As Chomsky might put it, it is a matter of 'virtual conceptual necessity.'[38] Since there is no condition on variables in first-order logic corresponding to the locality difference described by the Binding Theory, its existence in natural language is something that needs an empirical explanation, as it *appears* natural language is making things more complicated than it might.

7　Aphonic Pronouns

Expressions that are both *asemantic* (semantically empty) *and aphonic* (phonologically empty) are straightforwardly excluded in Chomsky's minimalist framework. However, the postulation of an expression that is semantic but aphonic is no less problematic than the postulation of an expression such as the 'it' in 'it's raining,' which is phonic but asemantic. The discovery or postulation of *any* expression constitutes a contribution to syntax, but its existence is justified only if it is doing something at either PF or LF. Consequently, the discovery or postulation of an *aphonic* expression must be justified by its role at LF.

Compare (37) and (38):

(37)　John persuaded Paul^2 to shave himself$_2$.
(38)　John^1 promised Paul to shave himself$_1$.

At first blush, (37) seems to satisfy Principle A of the Binding Theory, while (38) seems to violates it. 'Paul' seems to be the subject of the embedded infinitival clause, which explains why it can bind 'himself' in (37). But (38) seems problematic. The 'understood subject' of 'shave' in (38) is surely 'John'; but 'John' does not lie in the smallest clause containing 'himself,' so Principle A declares it incapable of being the reflexive's binder. In fact, the problem is illusory: in both (37) and (38) the subject of the embedded infinitival clause is an aphonic pronoun usually called PRO:

(37')　[$_S$John persuaded Paul^2 [$_S$PRO$_2$ to shave himself$_2$]].
(38')　[$_S$John^1 promised Paul [$_S$PRO$_1$ to shave himself$_1$]].

In (37'), the syntax and meaning of the verb 'persuade' require PRO to be bound by the object expression 'Paul' ('persuade' is an *object*-control verb). In (38'), by contrast, the syntax and the meaning of the verb 'promise' require PRO to be bound by the subject expression 'John' ('promise' is a *subject*-control verb). In both sentences, 'himself' is bound by PRO, in accordance with Principle A. And PRO is bound by 'Paul' in (37) and by 'John' in (38). So the *real* question to be faced is how PRO can be simultaneously bound and a binder. This question has to be answered in any case, for it is not only PRO which must be able to behave in this way. On natural readings of (39) and (40), the phonic pronoun 'he' must also be bound and yet a binder if Principle A is to be respected:

(39)   John^1 says that [$_S$she$_1$ shaves himself$_1$]
(40)   [every man]^1 says that [$_S$she$_1$ shaves himself$_1$].

So there is a general question to be answered here – one taken up later – that has nothing to do with aphonicity.

Gerundive sentences may also contain aphonic subjects. Contrast the following, discussed by Fodor (1975: 133–41):

(41)   Only Churchill remembers [$_S$ himself giving the speech about blood, sweat, toil, and tears].
(42)   Only Churchill remembers [$_S$Churchill giving that speech about blood, sweat, toil, and tears].
(43)   Only Churchill^1 remembers [$_S$PRO$_1$ giving the speech about blood, sweat, toil, and tears].

Any adequate account of (43) must reflect the fact that an utterance of it cannot be true unless (roughly) Churchill conceives of the experiencer of the memory and the agent of the remembered event as identical.[39]

8   Pronouns as Determiners

An idea from 1960s linguistics that has been resuscitated recently is Postal's (1966), that pronouns are determiners.[40] Traditional grammars distinguish sharply between the possessive (or genitive) determiners in (44) and their absolute possessive (or genitive) counterparts in (44′):

(44)   *our/your/his/her/John's/their* dog is the black one
(44′)   *ours/yours/his/hers/John's/theirs* is the black one.

But linguistics suggests a single possessive determiner the superficial form of which depends upon whether it occurs with a *phonic* (phonologically non-null) or *aphonic* (phonologically null) NP complement:

(45)   [$_{DP}$[$_D$his][$_{NP}$[$_N$car]]] dog is the black one
(45′)   [$_{DP}$[$_D$his][$_{NP}$*e*]] is the black one.

[$_{NP}$[$_N$car]] is phonic, [$_{NP}$[$_N$*e*]] is aphonic. There are two ways to think about [$_{NP}$*e*] here. (i) It might be construed as the result of a process of *NP deletion* at PF.[41] With (46) and (46′), this seems fine:

(46)   John prefers my painting to [$_{DP}$[$_D$hers] [$_{NP}$*e*]]
(46′)   John prefers my painting to [$_{DP}$[$_D$her] [$_{NP}$[$_N$painting]]].

But if (45) and (45′) derive from a single LF, we lose the recoverability of deletion.[42] (ii) Alternatively, [$_{NP}e$] might be construed as an NP that itself appears in the LF of (45′) and as such is in need of pragmatic interpretation just like an occurrence of a pronoun, but at least recoverability would not be violated.

Possessives are not the only determiners that have both reliant and absolute occurrences:

(47) *many* (people) applied but *few* (people/of them) were suitably qualified

(48) *both* (senators) spoke in favour but *neither* (senator/of them) was convincing

(49) *some* (guests) arrived late but *some/others/most* (guests/of them) did not

(50) *that* (piece) is geometric; *this* (piece) is Mycenaean.

The determiners 'no,' 'a,' 'the,' and 'every' seem always to be reliant:

(51) no/a/the/every guard fell asleep.
(51′) *no/ *a/ *the/*every fell asleep.

But we must not overlook the possibility, found with possessives, of morphological variation depending upon the phonicity of the complement.[43] For example, it is plausible that 'none' is the absolute form of the reliant 'no,' and that 'one' is the absolute form of the reliant 'a' (as well as of the reliant 'one'):

(52) many people had dessert but *none* (of them) ordered coffee.
(53) many people had dessert; indeed *one* (of them) had two portions.

Is there an absolute form of 'the'? Postal's hypothesis is that there is, and that it comes in three gender variants: 'he,' 'she,' and 'it.'[44] Third person pronouns are actually forms of the definite article taking aphonic complements:

(54) [$_{DP}$[$_D$the][$_{NP}$[$_N$president]]] is asleep
(55) [$_{DP}$[$_D$he][$_{NP}e$]] is asleep
(56) Don't wake [$_{DP}$[$_D$him][$_{NP}e$]].

In the first instance, the reflexive 'himself' might be viewed as a fusion of the determiner 'him' (or, perhaps (see below), the possessive determiner 'his') and the nominal 'self':

(57) every man loves [$_{DP}$[$_D$him][$_{NP}$self]].

If this is adequate, and if we wish to maintain that reflexives and some occurrences of third person pronouns are understood as bound, it might seem we will have to say that some occurrences of *determiners* are bound variables. But we can obtain the desired result with something interestingly weaker: a purportedly bound occurrence of a third person pronoun is just the head of a DP that *contains* (or is at least interpreted *as if* it contains) a bound variable. Take a bound occurrence of 'he' in (58):

(58) [every man]^1 thinks that he$_1$ snores.

On the hypothesis in question the occurrence of 'he' in (58) has the form [$_{DP}$[he][$_{NP}e$]]. Our task is to make sense of the idea that this DP is interpreted as if it contains a variable bound by 'every man.' Suppose we add to our formal language RQ a new quantificational determiner *he*. And suppose, mirroring the pronominal hypothesis we are considering, that *he* is a special form of *the* (forget about gender for a moment). Then the following trivial modification of the familiar Russellian axiom for *the* is what we want for *he*:

(HE) [*he* x_k: ϕ]ψ is true of a sequence s iff ψ is true of every sequence that ϕ is true of differing from s at most in the k-th position, and there is exactly one such sequence.

(If we want gender to affect truth conditions, we just insist that ϕ contain *male x* as a conjunct.) The truth conditions of (58), on one of its readings, are captured by *either* of the following sentences of RQ:

(59) [*every* x_1: *man* x_1] (x_1 *thinks that* ([*he* x_2: $x_2=x_1$] (x_2 *snores*)))
(59′) [*every* x_1: *man* x_1] (x_1 *thinks that*([*he* x_2: *man* x_2 $\wedge$ $x_2=x_1$] (x_2 *snores*))).

If we see [$_{NP}e$] as the product of NP-deletion, then we will see (58) as derived from something like (58′):

(58′) [every man] realizes that [he man] snores.

And on such account, there is a natural inclination to use (59′) in characterizing the logical form of (58). By contrast, if we see [$_{NP}e$] as base-generated, so to speak, then (59) seems more natural. Either way, the unrestricted quantifier *he* binds the occurrence(s) of x_2 in the open sentence with which it combines to form a restricted quantifier; and either way the restricted quantifier – [*he* x_2:$x_2=x_1$] in (59), [*he* x_2: *man* x_2 $\wedge$ $x_2=x_1$] in (59′) – binds the occurrence of x_2 in x_2 *snores*; so either way, we get a variable inside the matrix of a restricted quantifier that the other restricted quantifier [*every* x_1: *man* x_1] binds.

We need to tie all this up with the English syntax of course; and in order to keep our options open, we need to do it for both (58) and (58′). If the structure of the DP 'he' in (58) is [$_{DP}$[he [$_{NP}e$]], we get what we want if this DP is understood as equivalent to $[he\ x_2 : x_2 = x_1]$ in (59), which we get if the D 'he' – which is only *part of the DP* 'he' – is understood as equivalent to the RQ determiner $he\ x_2$ and if the NP $[_{NP}e]$ is understood as equivalent to the RQ formula $x_2 = x_1$. The morphosyntax of English will, in fact, insist upon the complement of 'he' always being $[_{NP}e]$. So we might schematically specify the semantics of $[_{NP}e]$ as given by $x_k = x_j$ (for $j \neq k$) when such a device functions as the complement of the determiner 'he' (thus the aphonic NP in $[_{DP}[_Dhe][_{NP}e]]$ has a definite semantic role here – made transparent by (59) – which would justify its existence in Chomsky's minimalist framework). When we have a suitably placed co-indexed binder as in (58), we have what will amount to a *bound* occurrence of 'he.' If there is no such binder, we have what amounts to *free* occurrence of 'he,' used to make indexical reference to some individual.[45]

Talk of *bound* pronouns is still perfectly intelligible on this account. The D 'he' is not bound; indeed it is a binder. And the DP 'he' is not *wholly-bound* the way a bound variable is; rather it is just *bound-into* (just as the formula Rx_2x_1 is bound into in $(\exists x_1(Rx_2x_1))$.) The subscript on 'he' in (58) must now be understood as indicating that $[_{DP}[_Dhe][_{NP}e]]$ is *bound-into* rather than wholly bound.

Two questions of largely notational import now arise: (i) Where should we place the subscript '1' in the spelled out DP? (ii) Will we ever need a subscript '2' corresponding to the '2' in the RQ rendering (59)?

(59) $[every\ x_1: man\ x_1]\ (x_1\ realizes\ that\ ([he\ x_2: x_2 = x_1]\ (x_2\ snores)))$.

In order to have something fixed, let us adopt the conventions implicit in (58″):

(58″) $[_{DP}\ every^1\ [_{NP}[_Nman]]]^1$ realizes that $[_{DP}[_Dhe^2]\ [_{NP}e]_1]^2$ snores.

The index '1' is placed on the empty NP (or at least on its node); and just as the index '1' on the D 'every' projects to the DP 'every man' it heads, so the index '2' on the D 'he' projects to the DP 'he' it heads.

On this account, the RQ sentences (60′) and (57′) might explicate the logical forms of (60) (on one of its readings) and (57), respectively:

(60) every man thinks Mary loves him
(60′) $[every\ x_1: man\ x_1]\ (x_1\ thinks\ that([him\ x_2: x_2 = x_1]\ (Mary\ loves\ x_2)))$
(57) every man loves himself
(57′) $[every\ x_1: man\ x_1]\ ([him\ x_2: x_2 = x_1]\ (x_1\ loves\ x_2))$.

(The axiom (HIM) for the RQ determiner *him* is just (HE) with $[he\ x_k: \phi]$ replaced by $[him\ x_k: \phi]$.)

We can probably improve upon (16′) once we have dealt with the possessive 'his.' There is a long tradition in philosophy of treating possessive DPs as definite descriptions, motivated in part by the apparent equivalence of 'Smith's murderer' and 'the murderer of Smith,' and so on. (See chapter 16.) So, in the first instance we might explicate the logical form of (61), on its bound reading, by treating it as superficial variant of (62), the logical form of which we can sketch using (62′):

(61) every man loves his wife
(62) every man loves the wife of him
(62′) $[every\ x_1:\ man\ x_1]\ ([the\ x_2:\ x_2\ wife\ x_1]\ (x_1\ loves\ x_2))$.

Now (62′) is only a sketch because it contains a (mere) variable corresponding to the occurrence of the DP 'him' in (62), a view we have already gone beyond. What we need is (62″):

(62′) $[every\ x_1:\ man\ x_1]\ ([the\ x_2:\ [him\ x_3:\ x_3 = x_1]\ (x_2\ wife\ x_3)]\ (x_1\ loves\ x_2))$.

Now what of (61)? A desire for a sentence of RQ more closely resembling the English sentence whose semantic structure it is meant to explicate might lead one to add another determiner, *his*, to RQ:

(61′) $[every\ x_1:\ man\ x_1]\ ([his\ x_2:\ x_2\ wife\ x_1]\ (x_1\ loves\ x_2))$.

The relevant axiom will be an interesting modification of the one for *he*, to be given in a moment. To bring out another feature of possessives, let us switch examples: Consider a particular utterance of (63)

(63) $[every\ man]^1$ groomed his$_1$ horse.

The DP 'his horse' might be understood as (e.g.) 'the horse he owned' or 'the horse he rode' or 'the horse he trained.' In RQ we might represent the DP as $[his\ x_k:\ (horse\ x_k \wedge R(x_k, x_j))]$ where R is *owned* or *rode* or *trained*, as the case may be. The following axiom would appear to yield what we want:

(HIS) $[his\ x_k:\ \phi]\psi$ is true of a sequence s iff ψ is true of every sequence that $(\phi \wedge R(x_k, x_j))$ is true of differing from s at most in the k-th position, and there is exactly one such sequence.

Of course this does actually throw any light on the syntactic relation (if there is one) between the English sentences (61) and (62).

Finally, the reflexive 'himself.' We might see this as the result of combining a pronominal determiner with 'self,' construed as a genuine nominal like 'wife.' If this determiner is just a phonetic variant of 'his,' we can think of 'himself' as a possessive just like 'his wife' and use (57″) rather than (57′) to explicate the logical form of (57):

(57) every man loves himself

(57′) $[every\ x_1:\ man\ x_1]\ ([him\ x_2:\ x_2 = x_1]\ (x_1\ loves\ x_2))$
(57″) $[every\ x_1:\ man\ x_1]\ ([his\ x_2:\ x_2\ self\ x_1]\ (x_1\ loves\ x_2))$.

On this account, no new axiom is needed as 'himself' is just a special case of 'his NP' where the relation R is identity.[46] Alternatively we could introduce a new determiner *himself* whose complement is always understood as an identity:

(57‴) $[every\ x_1:\ man\ x_1]\ ([himself\ x_2:\ x_1 = x_2]\ (x_1\ loves\ x_2))$.

The axiom (HIMSELF) for *himself* will involve a trivial modification of (HIM). (Of course, it does not provide an explanation of what is *special* about reflexives; that is something we still need to provide.)

The upshot of all this is that even if pronouns are determiners, there is no barrier to making sense of the idea that some occurrences (indeed, all occurrences of reflexive pronouns, for reasons that ought to emerge) are *bound*. To say that an occurrence of, say, 'him' is bound by a quantifier α is to say that the determiner 'him' is the head of a DP $[_{DP}[_{D}him]\ [_{NP}e]]$ whose aphonic complement is understood as containing a variable bound by α.

A problem raised in section 7 in connection with examples (64) and (65) has been silently solved:

(64) John[1] says that $[_{S}she_1\ shaves\ himself_1]$
(65) $[every\ man]^1$ says that $[_{S}she_1\ shaves\ himself_1]$.

Recall that on the readings of interest we need 'John'/'every man' to bind 'he,' and 'he' in turn to bind 'himself.' If 'he' were a mere variable a *transitive* conception of binding might be required, the semantics of which might involve some rather fancy footwork. But on the proposal sketched here, what is needed drops out automatically, with Principles A and B respected. Qua *binder* the DP 'he' bears a superscript; qua device that is *bound-into*, its NP bears a subscript:

(65′) $[every\ man]^1$ says that $[_{DP}he\ [_{NP}e]_1]^2$ shaves himself$_{*1,2}$.

We can usefully abbreviate this:

(65″) $[every\ man]^1$ says that he$_1{}^2$ shaves himself$_{*1,2}$.

Putting everything together, the sentence comes out as equivalent to the following, confirming that the Binding Theory has not been violated:

(65‴) $[every\ x_1:\ man\ x_1]\ (x_1\ says\ that$
       $([he\ \ x_2:\ x_2 = x_1]\ ([his\ x_3:\ x_3\ self\ x_2]\ (x_2\ shaves\ x_3))))$.

A final word about the free or indexical use of pronouns. There is no obvious reason to think they differ syntactically from those that are bound (in English, at any rate). Either way, the general form is $[_{DP}he\ [_{NP}e]]$. But what of the interpretation of an indexical occurrence? Since the D 'he' is not indexical on the current proposal, the indexicality of the DP 'he' must lie in $[_{NP}e]$. The right thing to say is that whereas a bound use of 'he' is understood as $[he\ x_j:\ x_j = x_k]$ with x_k bound by some other DP, on an indexical use it is understood as $[he\ x_j:\ x_j = x_k]$ with x_k free to refer indexically. Thus, what amounts to a unitary theory.

10   A Unified Account of Binding

The working assumption up to this point has been that an anaphoric pronoun is one occurring within the scope of some other expression α that binds it. However, many linguists and philosophers hold that the pronoun in (66) functions as a device of *co-reference* because its antecedent is a name not a quantifier:

(66)   John^1 loves his$_1$ wife.

This may be a harmless assumption for many philosophical purposes, but it is incorrect. One reasonable desideratum is a uniform account of how 'his' (and derivatively 'his wife' and 'loves his wife') function in (66) and (67):

(67)   [every man]^1 loves his$_1$ wife.

And it is not immediately obvious how a co-reference account of 'his' in (66) and a bound variable account of 'his' in (67) can constitute a unified account.

Contrary to what is assumed by (e.g.) Evans (1977, 1980), it seems binding cannot be reduced to coreference.[47] Consider the following quantified-singular pair:

(68)   Mary thinks that John^1 loves his$_1$ wife
(69)   Mary thinks that [every man]^1 loves his$_1$ wife.

The bound variable treatment of the pronoun in (69) delivers (69'):

(69')   *Mary thinks that* $([every\ x:\ man\ x]\ (x\ loves\ x's\ wife))$.[48]

This captures the fact that (69) is true (on one reading) if and only if Mary thinks that every man is an own-wife's lover. Of course (69') is quite schematic as we are treating 'his' as a determiner. (69'') is closer to what we want:

(69'')   *Mary thinks that* $([every\ x:\ man\ x]\ ([his\ y:\ y\ wife\ x]\ (x\ loves\ y)))$.

The analogous reading of (68) is true iff Mary thinks that John is an own-wife's lover, but that reading is *not* captured by saying that 'John' and 'his' are co-referential. For on such an account an utterance of (68) could be true if Mary believes that John loves the wife of some man she sees but does not realize is John.[49] So even if 'his' can be used as a device of *de jure* co-reference – which has not yet been established – we still need to take into account its use as a device that can be bound by names. We are left with three remaining questions, then: (a) Can we provide a plausible unification in the reverse direction? (ii) If so, can we do it without treating names as quantifiers; and (b) Can we then dispense altogether with appeals to a use of 'his' as a device of *de jure* co-reference?

(a) To explain what is going on in (68), we seem to need the *abstraction* introduced by the quantification in (69'). That is, we appear to need a formula in which the name 'John' binds a variable. Schematically, (68'), with more detail (68''):

(68')   *Mary thinks that* ([*John x*] (*x loves x's wife*))
(68'')   *Mary thinks that* ([*John x*] ([*his y: y wife x*] (*x loves y*))).

This might suggest we unify the treatment of pronouns bound by quantifiers and those bound by names, by treating names as quantifiers.[50]

So as to avoid the rather general complications raised by attitude ascriptions for a moment, let us go back to example (66), the logical form of which, on the present account, may be sketched using (66'):

(66')   [*John x*] ([*his y: y wife x*] (*x loves y*)).

The following Tarskian axiom would appear to suffice for a quantifier *John*:

(JOHN)   [*John*]$_k\psi$ is true of a sequence s iff ψ is true of every sequence with John in the k-th place differing from s at most in what it assigns to x_k and there is exactly onesuch sequence.[51]

We now have a complete theory of bound pronouns: quantifiers, names, and pronouns can all bind pronouns. Furthermore, we have made semantic sense of the seemingly transitive binding in a sentence like (70) and at the same time respected the Binding Theory:

(70)   John says that he loves his wife.
(70')   [*John x*] (*x says that* ([*he y: y = x*] ([*his z: z wife y*] (*y loves z*))).

(b) We don't *have* to treat names as quantifiers, however, for here are reasons for thinking that the relevant abstraction emerges in another way. On an independently motivated account of predication, an intransitive V, say 'snores' amounts to a one-place predicate λx (*x snores*). An intransitive verb, say, 'loves,' amounts to a two-place predicate λy (λx(*x loves y*)). On this account, α's binding β amounts to α's merging with a λ-predicate whose operator binds β.[52] Schematic logical forms of (66) and (67) are given by (66″) and (67″):

(66)   John loves his wife.
(66″) *John(λx(x loves x's wife))*
(67)   every man loves his wife
(67″) *[every y: man y](y(λx(x loves x's wife))).*

These are schematic as the treatment of 'his' is suppressed and I have finessed the abstraction (λy) involving the object of 'loves' in a manner to be elaborated. Spelling out 'his' we get (1‴) and (2‴)

(66‴) *John(λx([his z: z wife x](x loves z))*
(67‴) *[every y: man y](y (λx ([his z: z wife x](x loves z))).*

We are now in a position to say something about locality. The VPs 'loves him' and 'loves himself' are formed by merging the verb 'loves' with a DP. Assuming economy drives languages to contain devices whose job is to register mandatory binding, there will surely be pressure on such devices to be locally bound. The V 'loves' is understood as λy (λx (x loves y)), and it is implicitly asking the DP with which it combines to form a VP how y stands with respect to x. A reflexive replies, 'y = x,' thus terminating discussion – the question cannot arise again for *that* reflexive later in the building process – meaning that the reflexive is locally bound. By contrast, a non-reflexive such as 'him' replies, 'y ≠ x,' leaving the matter open.

On this view, 'himself' is the reflexive form of the accusative 'him.' The absence of a reflexive form of the nominative 'he' would now be explained: the subject of S is outside the scope of the λ-operator introducing the VP of S. This leaves us with 'his,' which will be discussed later.

(c) Can we now dispense with talk of *de jure* co-reference in an account of pronominal anaphora? Examples like (71) might suggest not:

(71)   John loves his wife. Yesterday I saw him buying her roses again. He spends a lot of money on flowers. His wife is lucky.

On the proposed unification we have no account of the apparently cross-sentential, unbound anaphora exemplified here. We can say that the first occurrence of 'his' is bound by 'John'; but then we appear to be stuck. The occurrences of 'him' and 'he,' and the second occurrence of 'his' are not within the scope of 'John' so they are not bound. They can certainly be used to refer to John, but does this mean they are *anaphoric* on 'John' in any sense relevant to grammatical theory? Is there anything problematic involved in saying that John has been raised to sufficient salience by the use of 'John' in the first sentence of (71), that he is a reasonable target for indexical uses of 'he,' 'him,' and 'his' in the subsequent sentences? If not, then it seems we have not yet found a reason for thinking that co-reference plays a role in a theory of anaphora.

Syntactic ellipsis is illuminating here. The literature on this is vast and consensus is not easy to find, but traditionally syntactic ellipsis is subject to a stringent parallelism condition on form and interpretation.[53] A constituent may be deleted at PF only if it is a copy of another constituent at LF, as Heim and Kratzer (1998) put it, moreover a copy *interpreted in the same way*. This is basically today's analogue of what used to be known as the *recoverability of deletion* (see Chomsky (1964)), itself basically a consequence of Katz and Postal's (1964) hypothesis that transformational rules do not affect meaning. Compare (72) and (73):

(72)   John loves himself, and Paul does too
(73)   John loves his wife, and Paul does too.

There is a single reading of (72). But there are two distinct readings of (73):

(73′) $Paul(\lambda x([\text{his } z: z \text{ wife-of } x](x \text{ loves } z)))$
(73″) $Paul(\lambda x([\text{his } z: z \text{ wife-of John}](x \text{ loves } z)))$.

The former is usually called the *sloppy* reading, the latter the *strict* reading. The sloppy reading is explained assuming 'his' is bound by 'John' in the first clause of (72). On that assumption, the first clause predicates $\lambda x([\text{his } z: z \text{ wife-of } x]$ $(x \text{ loves } z))$ of John, the second predicates it of Paul.[54]

But what of the strict reading? There are two ways to go here. The first involves abandoning the dream of dispensing with *de jure* co-reference altogether: 'John loves his wife' is ambiguous between two distinct anaphoric readings, one on which 'John' binds 'his,' yielding the sloppy reading of (73) as before, the other on which 'his' is a device of *de jure* co-reference, yielding the strict reading. However, this proposal might be thought to be undermined by the absence of a strict reading of (72), which demonstrates that 'John loves himself' has only a bound reading (if 'himself' could be used as a device of *de jure* co-reference, referentially dependent upon 'John,' a strict reading of (72) should be available). On the other hand, the contrast might be construed as merely illustrating an important difference between reflexives and non-reflexives: the former permit only bound readings.

The alternative proposal involves saying there is only one anaphoric use of 'his,' the bound use, and then explicating the strict reading of (73) in terms of an indexical use of 'his,' one upon which it is used to refer to John, who has been made salient by the use of 'John.' This may well be the correct analysis, but it raises an interesting issue. Principle B prevents 'him' being *bound* by 'John' in (74):

(74)   John loves him.

That is, Principle B prevents (74) being read as (74′):

(74′) *John*(λ*x*(*x loves x*)).

But aren't we now forced to posit a principle that prevents a speaker from using 'him' indexically in an utterance of (74) to refer to John, to block the reading whose truth conditions we might represent using (74″)?

(74′) *John*(λ*x*(*x loves John*)).

Unclear. First, I might utter (74) whilst pointing at a man I do *not* take to be John but *do* take to be someone John loves, unaware that it is actually John. At most it would seem we need a principle that prevents a speaker from using 'him' indexically in (74) to refer to someone he takes to be the referent of his use of 'John.' But even this seems too strong. Suppose you and I are sitting at a sidewalk café discussing John. You say to me, 'He loves no-one.' I am about to reply, 'Untrue. John loves himself,' when I notice John across the street and instead utter, 'Untrue. John loves him,' pointing at John, knowing that you will recognize him immediately.[55]

On this account, only indexical readings of the pronouns are possible in (74)–(76), as they do not lie within the scope of 'John':

(74) his wife loves John
(75) the woman he married loves John
(76) the woman who married him loves John.

This seems to me a good result. First, only indexical readings of the pronouns are available in the quantified counterparts of (74)–(76):

(74′) his wife loves every man
(75′) the woman he married loves every man
(76′) the woman who married him loves every man.

If we are serious about giving a unified account of what is going on in quantified-singular pairs like (66) and (67), we should be just as serious about giving a unified account of what is going on in the quantified-singular pairs (74′)/(74), (75′)/(75), and (76′)/(76).

For each of (74)–(76) there is certainly a reading upon which the pronoun and 'John' are co-referential. But that is no threat to the theory at hand: the occurrences of 'his,' 'he,' and 'him' in (74)–(76) can be used indexically to refer to whoever 'John' is being used to refer to, John being as salient as any other potential target of an indexical occurrence of a masculine pronoun (at least by the time the name 'John' is uttered). With utterances of the quantified examples, by contrast, there is no corresponding individual to target. i.e. no individual who is also the intended referent of the relevant DP, which is quantificational, except perhaps when the DP is a definite description used referentially.[56]

Does the fact that 'his' admits of distinct bound and indexical uses mean that it is *ambiguous*, and that (66) and (67) are correspondingly ambiguous? The fear of being assailed for postulating ambiguities has driven philosophers to heroic lengths in preserving unitary semantic analyses.[57] But ambiguity is a tricky notion: some forms (by whatever fancy name) are seemingly less expensive than others; some may result in theoretical simplification elsewhere; and some may make more sense if seen from the perspective of more than one language, as we shall see.

11 Bound and Free

Suppose we found languages with no unique translation of either (66) or (67) because quite unrelated pronouns – rather than mere morphological variants – were used depending upon whether a bound or indexical use of 'his' is intended:

(66)   John loves his wife

(67)   every man loves his wife.

And suppose these languages contained only one translation of (77), containing the indexical pronoun where English has 'his':

(77)   his wife loves John.

An English speaker might say these languages make a pointless lexical distinction. But a speaker of a Scandinavian language (Danish, Faroese, Icelandic, Norwegian, or Swedish), where there appears to be a *lexical* distinction between genitive and possessive pronouns (the latter being reflexive), might say that the English 'his' is ambiguous, albeit in a systematic way. Translating (66) or (67) into Icelandic, for example, requires fixing whether or not 'his' is bound by the subject expression:

(78)   *Jón*[1] / [*sérhver maður*][1] *elskar konuna sína*₁
John [every man] loves wife-the self's-FEM+ACC+SG
('John[1] / [every man][1] loves his₁ wife').

The word *sína* is a reflexive possessive (or possessive reflexive), feminine, accusative, and singular to agree with *konuna*, the noun it qualifies (which is why it is rendered as *self's* above, rather than *his*).

But if the English pronoun is understood indexically, indicated here with a subscripted arrow, (66) and (67) must be translated as follows:

(79)   *Jón / sérhver maður elskar konuna hans*
every man loves wife-the he-(MASC+GEN+SG).
('John / every man loves his ↓ wife').

Here *hans* is the simple genitive, which (unlike *sína*) occurs in the masculine and enters into no agreement relations whatsoever with *konuna*. The important *interpretive* point, is that *sína* must be bound and hence within the scope of its antecedent.

12   Discourse Anaphora

There are sentences in which a pronoun β appears to be anaphoric on an expression α (singular or quantified) yet does not lie within α's scope and hence cannot, on our assumptions, be bound by α. We can use subscripts in parentheses if the (purportedly) anaphoric connection is not one of binding:

(80)   John^1 has come alone. His$_{(1)}$ wife is unwell

(81)   If John^1 is late again, he$_{(1)}$ will be fired.

It would seem sufficient to say that the use of the name 'John' in utterances of (80) and (81) renders some individual salient enough to be a natural target for indexical uses of the pronouns 'his' and 'he.' If we insist on using 'anaphora' and 'anaphoric' here, let's preface them with a qualifier like 'unbound' or 'discourse' or 'pragmatic.' Continuing with Postal's idea that 'his wife' and 'him' are descriptions, the idea would be that $[_{DP}he\,[_{NP}e]]$ in (81) is understood as $[he\,x_1: x_1{=}x_2]$ with x_2 free to refer indexically to John.

What about cases in which a pronoun is seemingly anaphoric on a *quantified* DP outside whose scope it lies, for example (82) and (83)?

(82)   John bought [only one donkey]^1 and Paul vaccinated it$_{(1)}$

(83)   If John buys [just one donkey]^1 then he pays cash for it$_{(1)}$

Construing the pronouns in these examples as variables bound by the quantified DPs upon which they appear to be anaphoric, by giving the quantifiers large scope, yields the wrong results.[58] Someone who utters (82), for example, would not be claiming that only one donkey satisfies *John bought x and Paul vaccinated x*. For that claim is consistent with John buying two donkeys, while the claim made by uttering (82) is not.

If genuine grammatical anaphora involves binding, what are we to say about discourse anaphors? We have construed a pronoun seemingly anaphoric on but not bound by a *name* as an indexical co-referential with the name. What is the analogue of this where the discourse antecedent is a quantified DP? A number of philosophers and linguists have argued that that the pronouns in question *go proxy for descriptions*.[59] On such an account, the occurrence of 'it' in (80) is understood as if it were an occurrence of the description 'the donkey John bought'; in (81) it is understood as if it were an occurrence of 'the donkey John buys.' Pronouns that go proxy for descriptions in are called *D-type* or pronouns. Since descriptions may enter into scope relations with other expressions, the D-type proposal predicts certain ambiguities. For example, (84) has two readings according as 'he,' understood as a proxy for 'the man who assaulted the queen last night,' is read with small or large scope in the second sentence:

(84)   A man assaulted the queen last night. The police think he's an escaped convict.[60]

The D-type proposal appears to be successful with examples like (85) and (86) involving what is known variously as 'relativization,' 'covariation,' or 'implicit binding':

(85)   every villager owns [a donkey]^1 and feeds it$_{(1)}$ at night
(86)   every villager who bought [a donkey]^1 vaccinated it$_{(1)}$

The pronoun 'it' is naturally understood as going proxy for 'the donkey he bought,' read with smaller scope than the subject quantifier, capturing the implicit binding of the pronoun 'he' in the description for which 'it' goes proxy. Obviously the D-type proposal harmonizes with the general idea that third person pronouns are descriptions. There is no explicit commitment here to the view that whereas the PFs of (85) and (86) contain 'it,' their LFs contain the fleshed out definite description 'the donkey he owns'; but that is certainly one option that could be explored.[61]

With the distinction between bound and 'pragmatic' anaphora in mind, let us reflect for a moment on the nature of the distinction between, on the one hand 'his$_k$' and the Icelandic *sína* (etc.), and on the other 'his↓' and the Icelandic *hans*. A donkey sentence containing a relative clause can be used as a diagnostic:

(87)   [every man who has [a son]^2]^1 admires his$_{1'(2)}$ wife.

The important feature of (8) is that 'his' is *within* the scope of the subject DP 'every man who has a son' but *outside* the scope of the DP 'a son.' When 'his' is anaphoric on the subject DP it is bound; but when it is seemingly anaphoric on 'a son' it is unbound (plausibly going proxy for the relativized description 'his son's'). Since Icelandic reflexives are always bound, it is not surprising that the translation of (87) depends upon whether 'his' is to be read as bound by 'every man who has a son' or as an unbound pronoun seemingly anaphoric on 'a son':

(87′)   [*sérhver madur sem á son*]^1 *elskar konuna sína*$_1$
        every man who has son loves wife-the self's-FEM+ACC+SG
        ('[every man who has [a son]^2]^1 loves his$_{1'*2}$ wife')
(87′)   [*sérhver madur sem á son*] *elskar konuna hans*$_{(2)}$
        every man who has son loves wife-the his-(MASC+GEN+SG)
        ('[every man who has [a son]^2] loves his$_{(2)}$ wife').

On the bound, reading, 'his wife' will be rendered as *konuna sína*; on the unbound ('donkey') reading it will be rendered as *konuna hans*.

As one might now expect, the only Icelandic translation of (88) is (88') because the pronoun is not within the scope of the name:

(88) his wife loves John
(88') *konan hans elskar Jón*

As in English, intended co-reference is not excluded, but *konan hans* would almost always cede to *konan hans Jóns* in actual speech if co-reference were intended.

Using the distinction between bound and discourse pronouns, we can explain facets of an old chestnut mentioned earlier:[62]

(89) [the pilot who shot at it$_{(2)}$]^1 hit [the MiG that was chasing him$_1$]^2

If the subject DP has larger scope, 'him' is bound and 'it' is D-type pronoun understood as 'the MiG that was chasing him.' Suppressing some details (in particular, the structure of 'him'), (10) will be read as follows:

(89') [*the x: pilot x* $\wedge$ [*the y: MiG y* $\wedge$ *y chased x*](*x shot at y*)]
　　　　([*the y: MiG y* $\wedge$ *y chased x*](*x hit y*)).

(If the object DP has larger scope the situation is reversed: 'it' is bound and 'him' is D-type, understood as 'the pilot who shot at it.')

13   Unselective Binding and Donkey Problems

We have assumed a traditional account of binding throughout, but we have rejected the idea that pronouns may function *as* bound variables in favour of the idea that they *contain* variables that may be bound. And this has formed part of a general picture according to which definite pronouns are, in fact, all definite descriptions.

A rather different approach to anaphoric pronouns attracted a good deal of attention in the 1980s, and teasing out its virtue and vices will help sharpen problems that *any* adequate theory must solve. Consider (90) and (91):

(90) If [$_S$[a man]^1 buys [a donkey]^2] [$_S$he$_{(1)}$ vaccinates it$_{(2)}$]
(91) [Every man who [$_S$e buys [a donkey]^2]] vaccinates it$_{(2)}$.

The simple D-type theory seems to fail here. If the pronoun 'it' in (91) were analysed in terms of the singular description 'the donkey he buys' (with 'he' bound by 'every man who buys a donkey') an utterance of (91) would be true just in case every man who buys a donkey vaccinates the unique donkey he buys. Consequently, it would be false if any man buys more than one donkey. But this is incorrect; the truth of (91) is quite compatible with some men buying more than one donkey, as long as every man who buys a donkey vaccinates *each* donkey he buys. That is, *universality* or *maximality* attaches to something in the sentence. One thing is certain: the universality cannot be due to the indefinite description 'a donkey' – normally an *existentially* quantified phrase – being understood as a *universally* quantified phrase with large scope that binds 'it,' for (91) does not mean that there is a donkey such that everyone who buys it vaccinates it. If one is determined to locate the universality in the indefinite, one will have to break up the subject DP to get something like (91′):

(91′) $(\forall x)(\forall y)((man\ x \wedge donkey\ y \wedge x\ buys\ y) \supset x\ vaccinates\ y)$.

Whilst (91′) does, in fact, have the right truth conditions, it does not flow from any known systematic theory of indefinite descriptions, relative clauses, and pronouns. It is simply a brute statement of those conditions in a familiar idiom.

Examples like these motivate Kamp (1981/1984) and Heim (1982/1988) to propose a radical departure from existing frameworks.[63] Kamp and Heim reject Russell's analyses of definite and indefinite descriptions as well as D-type theories, and they propose a common explanation of the apparent "universalization" of the indefinites in (90) and (91). The idea (roughly) is that definites and indefinites are not quantificational; rather, they introduce variables to which common nouns and predicates supply "conditions" within a "discourse representation" or DR. Various other expressions may bind these variables, and variables that are still free when the construction of a DR is completed are mopped up by a closure device, essentially an existential quantifier taking scope over the entire DR.

A good entry to the basic idea is Lewis's (1975) account of adverbs of quantification (AQs) such as 'always' 'sometimes,' 'usually,' 'often,' 'seldom,' and 'never.' According to Lewis, an AQ functions as a binary quantifier that combines with an if-clause *if-ϕ* and a matrix clause ψ to form a sentence [AQ](*if-ϕ*, ψ). An AQ *unselectively* (*indiscriminately*) binds all free variables inside ϕ and ψ, and in this sense it is an *unselective* quantifier. For 'always,' Lewis posits the following:

(ALWAYS)   [*always*](*if-ϕ*, ψ) is true iff *every* assignment of values to variables free in ϕ that satisfies ϕ also satisfies ψ.

Assuming indefinite descriptions and pronouns introduce variables that the unselective quantifier captures, (92) is assigned the semantic structure given by (92′), ripe for interpretation by Lewis's rule:

(92)   always if a man own a donkey he vaccinates it.
(92′)   [*always*]((*if-(man x* $\wedge$ *donkey y* $\wedge$ *x buys y*)), (*x vaccinates y*)).

So (92) is true just in case every assignment of values to x and y that satisfies (93) also satisfies (94):

(93) *man $x \wedge$ donkey $y \wedge x$ buys y*
(94) *x vaccinates y.*

Naturally enough, analogous rules can be constructed for other adverbs: For 'sometimes' we want 'some assignment' of values to free variables; for 'usually,' we want *most* assignments; for 'never,' we want *none*, and so on. When there is no overt adverb of quantification, as in (95), Lewis suggests the sentence is understood as though there were an implicit 'always':

(95) If a man buys a donkey he vaccinates it.

Lewis's theory was not originally intended to form the basis of a general theory of the semantics of anaphora, the semantics of indefinites, or the semantics of conditionals; it was intended to explicate the semantical structure of a certain class of conditional sentences containing adverbs of quantification. But the theory can be generalized with a view to producing more comprehensive theories of anaphora and indefinite descriptions. Indeed, as Heim (1982) makes clear, DR theory is, in certain respects, an attempt to do just that.

On Kamp's account, the DR for (90) might be represented as:

(90′) [man(x) $\wedge$ *donkey*(y) $\wedge$ *buys*(x, y)] IF-THEN [*vaccinates*(x, y)].

Because of the presence of IF-THEN, (90′) is true if and only if *every* assignment of values to x and y that makes (93) (the antecedent of (90′)) true also makes (94) (the consequent of (90′)) true. The apparent universalization of the indefinite descriptions 'a man' and 'a donkey' is thus explained as a consequence of a general analysis of conditionals.

Kamp suggests that although (91) is not actually a conditional, the fact that the subject expression is universally quantified means we get a DR with universal force:

(91″) [*man*(x) $\wedge$ *donkey*(y) $\wedge$ *buys* (x, y)] EVERY [*vaccinates*(x, y)].

Generalized, the idea is this: a quantified sentence [Dx: ϕ]ψ is true if and only if D assignments of values to variables free in ϕ that satisfy ϕ also satisfy ψ.

DR theory faces a number of challenges. One emerges when we look at sentences with proportional quantifiers like 'most.'[64] Consider,

(96) Most men who bought a donkey vaccinated it.

By analogy with (91″), the DR for (96) will be

(96′) [*man*(x) $\wedge$ *donkey*(y) $\wedge$ *buys* (x, y)] MOST [*vaccinates*(x, y)]

which is true just in case *most* assignments of values to x and y that make (93) true, also make (94) true. But as Richards points out, on its most natural reading (96) is true if and only if most men who buy a donkey vaccinate *each* of the donkeys he buys, whereas (96′) will be true as long as most donkeys bought by men are vaccinated by the their respective buyers. If Alan buys five donkeys, Bill buys one donkey, Clive buys one, and no other man buys any, then (96′) will be true if Alan vaccinates at least four of the donkeys he buys, even if neither Bill nor Clive vaccinates the donkey he buys. But in such a situation the original English sentence (96) would be false.[65] The problem here is that whereas 'most' in the original English sentence is quantifying over donkey-buying men, MOST in (96′) is quantifying over *pairs* of donkeys and donkey-buying men, This suggests that the success DR theory had in capturing the implication of universality in (91) was actually due to an artefact of the example: its first-order nature. (Similarly for examples involving 'some' and 'no.')

It also suggests that the implication of universality in (91) is not generated by the determiner 'every.' So where does it originate? Not in a special universal reading of the indefinite article in 'a donkey,' as we see the same implication when we use other determiners:[66]

(97)   Every man who buys two or more donkeys vaccinates them.

An utterance of (97) is true just in case every man who buys two or more donkeys vaccinates *each* of the donkeys he buys. Thus (97) is not equivalent to (91), and it simply false that all determiners D in 'D donkey(s)' take on a common universal reading when embedded in relative clauses (an idea which would in any case have no syntactic or semantic appeal).

These considerations strongly suggest that if we are to understand the systematic universality in the quantified examples (91), (96), and (97) we will have to see it as generated elsewhere than the subject DP. And since there is nothing universal in the verb 'vaccinate,' that means we must look to the *object* DP, i.e. to the anaphoric pronoun itself. In short, we have run out of options and are pushed back to our original D-type theory, which has been shown to require fine-tuning rather abandoning. (97) presents no problem for our original version: the plural pronoun 'them' is interpreted as if it were an occurrence of the plural description 'the donkeys he buys.' The problem is the *singular* 'it' in (91) and (96), and one obvious question to ask is whether it is genuinely singular *semantically* speaking. DPs headed by 'a' or 'every' or 'each,' although *syntactically* singular, are not semantically singular; so the question naturally arises whether it is not a little presumptuous to treat pronouns anaphoric on such DPs (which are *syntactically* singular for the purposes of number agreement) as semantically singular. Like their discourse antecedents, perhaps such pronouns have syntactic number (because that is a feature DPs must have) but are *semantically* numberless.[67] There are two ways of thinking about number neutrality, *disjunctively* or *selectively.* On the disjunctive approach, the occurrences of 'it' in (91) and (96) are interpreted as if they were occurrences of the 'the donkey or donkeys he buys.' On the selective approach, it is interpreted either as 'the donkey the buys' or as 'the donkeys he buys,' the selection being a context-sensitive matter. Disjunctive neutrality yields the right result in these cases, but it is not difficult to find cases where it goes astray.

Consider (98):

(98)   every Apple employee who owned a car drove it to work on July 12, 2003

Surely the truth of an utterance of (98) requires only that every Apple employee who owned a a car drove *some* car he owned to work to July 12, 2003, not *each* car he owned. This might suggest that at least some D-type pronouns go proxy for *in* definite descriptions.[68] If this idea is to be pursued, a story would be needed to explain why in some cases an indefinite description better captures the pronoun's force. It cannot be discounted, of course, that general pragmatic considerations at work, indefinite readings being forced in certain circumstances due to the implausibility (in comparison) of the definite reading – normally one can drives only one car at a time, and if one drives to work normally one drives there only once a day.

A further problem is raised by (99):

(99)   No man who buys a donkey vaccinates it.

DR theory correctly predicts that an utterance of (99) is true just in case no man who buys a donkey vaccinates *any* of the donkeys he bought. On the singular D-type proposal, however, the pronoun goes proxy for 'the donkey he bought,' and we get a less plausible reading with an implication of relative uniqueness. If we appeal to the disjunctively numberless idea, 'it' goes proxy for 'the donkey or donkeys he bought,' and we appear to get the right result: 'No man who buys a donkey vaccinates the donkey or donkeys he buys.' But this only brings into sharp relief a problem for the standard Russellian account of non-singular descriptions occurring within the scope of monotone decreasing quantifiers like 'no':

(100)   No man vaccinates the donkeys he buys

The plural description here is naturally interpreted as '*any* of the donkeys he (they) buys' rather than '*each* of the donkeys he (they) buys.' Which just reinforces the point that we are unlikely to come up with a plausible theory of anaphoric pronouns without a plausible account of definite descriptions.

A further problem: suppose *Larry's Liquors* sells beer only in six-packs and permits people to buy at most one six-pack at a time. The following might be used to say something true:[69]

(101)   If a man buys a bottle of beer from *Larry's Liquors* he buys five others along with it.

If 'it' goes proxy for a singular description, patently we get the wrong result for there is no unique bottle of beer bought when a man buys a six-pack:

> (101′)   If a man buys a bottle beer from *Larry's Liquors* he buys five others along with the bottle of beer he buys from *Larry's Liquors*.

And if 'it' goes proxy for the numberless 'the bottle or bottles of beer he buys from *Larry's Liquours*,' the result is no less unimpressive, for it is untrue that a man who buys a bottle of beer from *Larry's* buys five bottles of beer along with those in his six pack. But if 'it' goes proxy for 'each of the beers he buys,' the result seems better, for it is quite true that a man buys five bottles of beer along with *each* of the bottles in the six-pack. This suggests the real issue here has to do with partitives and groupings, and that the full story about (99) and (100) involves the switch to the negative polarity determiner 'any' in downward entailing contexts.

Now suppose Larry relaxes the rules a little, allowing people buy up to two six-packs at a time. Can (101) still be used to say something true (assuming some men do, in fact, take advantage of Larry's liberalization)? Judgments are murky here, and it is not hard to construct scenarios and examples where robust judgments disappear altogether. Clearly all sorts of unresolved complexities about the way we speak and expect to be understood are lurking here.

A further problem arises with examples such as (102) and (103), clearly related to one version of the problem of incomplete descriptions discussed in chapter 16:[70]

> (102)   If a bishop meets another bishop, he blesses him.
> (103)   A woman and her sister came to my office today.
>   She sat down calmly, but her sister stood there nervously.

Since 'meet' expresses a symmetric relation, there cannot be a unique bishop who meets another. So 'he' cannot go proxy for 'the bishop who meets another bishop' understood in the Russellian way.[71] But none of the numberless options appears to yield the correct result either. (The truth of (102) does not require, for example, that a bishop who meets another bishop bless each bishop who has been met by any old bishop.)

The final problem to be mentioned here involves so-called D-type contradiction.[72] Consider the following exchange:

> A: A man fell in front of the train.
> B: He didn't fall, he was pushed.

If 'he' goes proxy for 'the man who fell in front of the train,' *B*'s statement is self-contradictory. One natural response to such cases is to say that *B*'s beliefs push him into a form of pretense or a form of quotation in replying to *A*'s statement, his reply having the force of something like 'The man who "fell" in front of the train didn't fall, he was pushed.'[73] In some case, *B*'s statement might be viewed as more abstract: 'The person of whom you spoke didn't fall, he was pushed.'

It should be noted finally that virtually all theories of anaphoric pronouns can be made more discriminating by taking into account implicit reference to, or quantification over, times, events, or situations.[74] But the issues raised by such manoeuvres take us into territory that cannot be covered here.

Notes

1 Expressions other than pronouns may be devices of anaphora, broadly construed, for example 'there' and 'then':

(i) John and Mary are in Paris. They are getting married there.

(ii) In 1963, Jane paid £600 for her house. That was a lot of money then.

2 Quine (1960), Geach (1962).

3 Chomsky (1981, 1986, 1995).

4 The formalism of a system of restricted quantification (see Chapter 16) will be assumed throughout in illuminating the "logical forms" of sentences. On a Tarskian account of quantification, the relevant axiom could be (ii):

(i) $[every\ x_k\colon \phi(x_k)]\psi(x_k)$ is true of a sequence s (of objects) iff $\psi(x_k)$ is true of every sequence that $\phi(x_k)$ is true of differing from s at most in the k-th position.

5 Geach (1962, 1972), Heim (1982), Heim and Kratzer (1998), Kamp (1981), Partee (1975), Reinhart (1983), Salmon (1986, 1992), Soames (1990, 1994), Wiggins (1976). λ is the *lambda* (or *abstraction*) operator. On the usage adopted here, $\lambda x\,(x\ snores)$ and $\lambda x(x\ loves\ x)$ are one-place predicates. Thus $John(\lambda x(x\ loves\ x)\,)$ is a sentence.

6 Heim and Kratzer (1998), May (2002), Partee (1975), Sag (1976), Williams (1977).

7 Cooper (1979), Evans (1977), Heim (1982), Kamp (1981), Partee (1972).

8 Evans (1977).

9 Cooper (1979), Davies (1981), Elbourne (2001), Evans (1977, 1980), Neale (1988, 1990, 2004b).

10 Heim (1982), Kamp (1981).

11 Heim (1982), Kamp (1981).

12 Elbourne (2001), Neale (2004b).

13 Chomsky (1964, 1965).

14 Chomsky (1965), Postal (1966). The non-synonymy of (14) and (14'), and related pairs, was not appreciated by linguists at the time. Consider,

(i) Mary thinks John wishes to leave.

For an utterance of this to be true Mary must believe that John satisfies *x wants x to leave*. It is not enough that Mary believe he satisfies *x wants John to leave*. Furthermore, any adequate account of the original sentence (14) must reflect the fact that an utterance of it cannot be true unless (roughly) John conceives of the experiencer of his wish and the agent of the wished-for event (or at least the agent of an event of the wished-for type) as identical. This is not so for every utterance of (14').

15 Chomsky (1965), Postal (1966).

16 Langacker (1969), Lees and Klima (1963), Postal (1966), Ross (1967).

17 Bach (1970), Fodor (1975), Jacobson (1977), Jackendoff (1972), Lasnik (1976), McCawley (1976), Partee (1975), Wasow (1972). That pronouns anaphoric on quantified phrases could not be interpreted as repetitions of their antecedents was already recognized by Geach (1962).

18 Katz and Postal (1964), Chomsky (1964, 1965).

19 Bach (1970).

20 Ross (1967), Chomsky (1973).

21 Jackendoff (1972), Wasow (1972).

22 Lasnik (1976), Chomsky (1976), Reinhart (1976).

23 Evans (1977, 1980), Higginbotham (1980).

24 Chomsky (1977, 1981).

25 Chomsky (1981, 1986).

26 Chomsky (1995, 2002).

27 Where early generative grammar distinguished the Deep Structure and Surface Structure of a sentence, and later versions distinguished its D-Structure, S-Structure, PF, and LF, minimalism allows for just PF and LF.

28 For discussion, see Abney (1987), Cardinaletti (1994), Chomsky (1995), Elbourne (2001), Neale (2004b), Szabolcsi (1994).

29 Higginbotham (1980), Higginbotham and May (1981), May (1977, 1985).

30 Using only subscripts to co-index would obscure the fact that binding is an asymmetric relation. I am deliberately simplifying here. For example, I have ignored the fact that the superscripted index on the DP 'every man' has been projected upwards from the index on D 'every.'

31 In syntactic terminology, β's being within the scope of α amounts to α's *commanding* β in Langacker's (1966) sense: α commands β iff the minimal S node dominating α also dominates β.

32 In syntactic terminology again, β's being within the scope of α now amounts to α's *c-commanding* β in Reinhart's (1976, 1978) sense: α *c-commands* β iff the first branching node (of whatever category) dominating α also dominates β. (α and β are assumed to be non-overlapping).

33 Since mothers are female, there is no acceptable reading of (29). By contrast, brothers are male, so there is an acceptable reading of (i), despite the fact that 'himself' still cannot be bound by 'John':

>   (i)   John's brother told Paul's mother a lot about himself.

34 See Reinhart (1983, 2000), Reuland (2001b), Neale (2004b).

35 As Chomsky (1995) points out, such a use of indices is not obviously consistent with his minimalist assumptions.

36 It is not difficult to find apparent problems of Principle A. Consider the contrast between (i) and (ii):

>   (i) John^1 bought a picture of himself_1
>   (ii) John^1 bought my picture of himself_{*1}

'John' cannot bind 'himself' in (ii) even though the former is a constituent of the smallest clause containing the latter. This suggests Principle A is too weak as stated.

Examples from other languages suggest it is too strong. In the Icelandic (iii), for example, either *Jón* or *Páll* may bind the reflexive *sig*:

(iii) *Jón¹ segir að* [*s Páll² raki sig₁·₂*]
John says that Paul shaves-SUBJ self-ACC
('John¹ says that Paul² shaves him₁ 'himself₂').

The interesting question here is whether this and related cases (in Chinese for example) undermine the core concepts of the Binding Theory, or merely push in the direction of explicable revisions, or indicate a lexical division between two different types of reflexive, only one of which satisfies Principle A. (The general issue is discussed in a way that philosophers should find congenial by Baker (2001) and Neale (2004*b*).)

The word 'pronoun' is used in a special technical way by Chomsky and many other linguists so as to exclude what we have been calling 'reflexive pronouns'; along with reciprocals ('each other'), reflexives fall under the label 'anaphor.' Principle A concerns 'anaphors,' so a more general formulation would contain 'anaphor' where 'reflexive pronoun' occurs above. The non-reflexive 'him,' by contrast is a 'pronoun' (or 'pronominal') for Chomsky. Since Principle B of the Binding Theory concerns 'pronouns,' a proper formulation would contain just 'pronoun' where 'non-reflexive pronoun' occurs above. This usage will not be adopted here as we want to ensure continuity with the philosophy literature (and, indeed, a good portion of the linguistics literature, where there is frequent talk of 'unbound anaphors'), so we shall continue to use 'pronoun' in the broad way, distinguishing reflexive and non-reflexive forms.

37 Evans (1980).
38 See Reuland (2001*b*).
39 See Castañeda (1966, 1967, 1968), Cherchia (1990), Fodor (1975), Higginbotham (1990), Lewis (1979), Partee (1975), Perry (1979, 2000), Salmon (1986, 1992), and Soames (1990, 1994). The combined force of these works establishes two incontrovertible results. First, not all pronouns are the product of transformations; second, anaphora cannot be reduced to *de jure* co-reference.
40 Abney (1987), Elbourne (2001), Neale (2004b), Postal (1966), Stockwell et al. (1973).
41 Elbourne (2001).
42 It is arguable that (46)/(46′) does not satisfy it either, at least if 'painting' is stressed.
43 Elbourne (2001).
44 Elbourne (2001), Neale (2004b), Postal (1966), Stockwell et al. (1973).
45 We will need the usual constraints on indexing to prevent a DP binding into a pronoun that is meant to be free, as in (i):

(i) [every man]¹ thinks he [free] likes him₁.

46 In examples like (i) and (ii), R would be some other relation only *involving* identity:

(i) At the waxwork museum, John Lennon took a photograph of himself.
(ii) Yeats hated hearing himself read in an English accent.

47 Versions of the problem I discuss have been raised by Castañeda (1966, 1967, 1968), Heim and Kratzer (1998), Partee (1975), and Soames (1989, 1990, 1994).

48 Henceforth, I often use x, y, etc. in place of x_1, x_2, etc. where possible.

49 Various assumption are made here, some non-trivial. See Soames (1990, 1994).

50 On names as quantifiers, Montague (1973), Barwise and Cooper (1981).

51 If Montague's approach is taken, the quantifier would be regarded as standing for a higher-order property: 'every man' would stand for that property true of just those properties every man has; 'John' would stand for that property true of just those properties John has.

52 Heim and Kratzer (1998), Neale (2004*b*), Reuland (2001*a,b*), Reinhart (2000), Salmon (1986, 1992), Soames (1990, 1994).

53 For user-friendly discussions of linguistic ellipsis, see Heim and Kratzer (1998) and May (2002).

54 Keenan (1971), Sag (1976), Williams (1977), Heim and Kratzer (1998), Reinhart (1983), Reinhart and Grodzinsky (1993).

55 Reinhart (1983, 2000), Reinhart and Grodzinsky (1993), Reinhart and Reuland (1997), and Reuland (2001b) have explored various formulations of some sort of interpretive condition on (roughly) intrasentential co-reference. The underlying thought is if a given message can be conveyed by two LFs differing only in whether a particular pronoun β is construed as bound by α or as co-referential with α, the former is to be strongly preferred. An alternative has been explored by Heim (1993).

56 See Neale (2004a, 2004b).

57 See, for example, the discussion of the referential-attributive debate in ch. 16.

58 Evans (1977).

59 Cooper (1979), Davies (1981), Heim (1990), Ludlow and Neale (1991), Neale (1988, 1990, 1994, 2004*b*). In a similar vein, see also Elbourne (2001). Such theories have their origins in Evans's (1977) theory of *E-type* pronouns, according to which, the pronouns in (82) and (83) *have their references fixed rigidly by descriptions*. Many D-type theorists hold that there are no E-type pronouns in natural language.

60 In the same vein, consider (i):

(i) [Mary[1] wants [$_s$PRO$_1$ to marry [a wealthy man]^2]]. He$_{(2)}$ must be a millionaire.

The first sentence in (i) may be read *de dicto* ('a wealthy man' read with small scope). Moreover, the pronoun 'he' in the second clause can be discourse-anaphoric on 'a wealthy man.' But as Karttunen (1976) notes, on this *de dicto* reading the modal expression 'must' must be present for the discourse anaphora to work. Compare (i) with (ii):

(ii) [Mary[1] wants [$_s$PRO$_1$ to marry [a wealthy man]^2]]. He$_{(2)}$'s a millionaire.

In (ii) it is not possible to get the *de dicto* reading for the antecedent clause if 'he' is discourse-anaphoric on 'a wealthy man.' The contrast between (i) and (ii) is explicable on the assumption that 'he' is interpreted as if it were the description 'the man Mary marries,' which may take small scope with respect to the modal 'must' in (i) (an infelicitous existence implication results if it is interpreted with large scope). In (ii) on the other hand, since there is no modal operator with respect to which the pronoun can be understood with small scope, the sentence has no felicitous reading when the antecedent clause is read *de dicto*.

61 On the matter of whether descriptive material not present at PF is nonetheless in the LF, See Elbourne (2001).

62 For the details of such proposals, see Jacobson (1977), Higginbotham and May (1981), and Neale (1988, 1990).

63 There are some differences between Kamp's theory and Heim's, but we can, I think, put these aside for present concerns.

64 Richards (1984).

65 It is sometimes suggested that there is another reading of (97), which requires that most men who buy at least one donkey vaccinate most of the donkeys they buy; but (97') does not capture this alleged reading either.

66 Harman (1972), Neale, (1988, 1990).

67 Davies (1981), Lappin (1989), Neale (1988, 1990). For evaluation, see Kanazawa (2001).

68 Chierchia (1996), Groenendijk and Stokhof (1991), Neale (1994), van der Does (1994). For evaluation, see van Rooy (2001).

69 Heim (1982, 1990), Kadmon (1990), Neale (1988, 1990).

70 Heim (1990).

71 Similarly 'him' in (102). And similarly 'she' in (103) cannot go proxy for the woman who came to my office today since sisters are women. Hans Kamp and David Kaplan presented me with this example.

72 Davies (1981), Neale (1988, 1990), Ludlow and Neale (1991), Strawson (1952), van Rooy (2001).

73 Davies (1981), Neale (1988, 1990), Ludlow and Neale (1991).

74 Evans (1977), Elbourne (2001), Ludlow (1994), Ludow and Neale (1991), Neale (1990).

Chapter 19

Naturalistic Theories of Reference

Karen Neander

Introduction

"Bill Clinton" refers to the man, Bill Clinton, and "Paris" refers to the city, Paris. In philosophy of language, the term "reference" is sometimes used only for naming relations like these, but sometimes it is used more broadly to include other relations, such as the relation that holds between a kind term (e.g., "cats") and its extension (all cats) or between a predicate ("red") and a property (redness). In philosophy of mind, the term "reference" is usually used in the broader sense. On a representational theory of thought, my thought that cats are excellent hunters, or my thought that cats make me sneeze, involves a mental representation of cats, and cats are said to be its reference (or its referential or extensional content). Most broadly, a theory of reference is an attempt to describe the relation between a representation and what it represents. That is, it aims to describe what it is about the former in virtue of which it represents the latter.

Naturalism is an approach to philosophy that involves using science, ultimately physics, as our guide to the fundamental ontology of the universe. In practice, with respect to theories of reference, this amounts to not admitting such things as moral norms, mental states or semantic properties as fundamental, so that any appeal to them in an analysis of the reference relation must eventually be accounted for in other terms. Three alternatives to a naturalistic theory of reference are (1) to maintain that reference is not real (e.g., talk of reference is merely instrumental), (2) to maintain that reference can be analyzed in terms of fundamental but non-natural phenomena (e.g., Platonic concepts and propositions) and (3) to maintain that reference itself is fundamental (so that physicalism is false). As the title suggests, this entry looks only at naturalistic theories of reference.

Original and Derived Meaning

Naturalistic theories of reference tend to focus on mental representations because those who offer them tend to believe that the semantic properties of linguistic utterances ultimately derive from the semantic properties of mental representations. This is consistent with the derivation going to some extent in both directions; so social factors, including a community's linguistic conventions, might determine the reference of some mental representations, but it is generally thought that this presupposes certain psychological capacities (perception, memory, learning, and so on) that are themselves representational.

Furthermore, naturalistic theories of reference focus on the most basic (or simple) mental representations. Here, a basic representation is one that does not derive its referential content from that of other representations. The controversial classical view of concepts (e.g., Katz 1972) illustrates the distinction between basic and non-basic representations. On one version of this view, lexical entries in the semantic component of our linguistic system provide definitions for linguistic terms and their corresponding mental representations. For example, the lexical entry for "spinster" and for the corresponding mental representation (here denoted by the English term all in capitals) SPINSTER, might be ADULT, FEMALE PERSON WHO HAS NEVER MARRIED. On this view, the reference of SPINSTER is the intersection of the references of ADULT, FEMALE, PERSON, and NEVER MARRIED, so that the reference of the first is allegedly determined by the references of the last four. The representations used in the definition may in turn be defined but at some point this process must bottom out. On this view, some mental representations are basic; they are not defined and they do not derive their referential content from that of other representations. These mental representations must, according to the classical theory, derive their referential content in some other way.

Philosophers disagree as to which mental representations are the basic ones, the simples. They also disagree about the nature of the relation between the simples and other mental representations. As already remarked, the classical theory of concepts is controversial. However, most who offer naturalistic theories of content agree that some mental representations are basic, and that some of them must therefore possess their content without deriving it from the contents of other mental representations. Some have argued that virtually all mental representations corresponding to the morphemes of a natural language are simple (e.g., Fodor and Lepore 1992). Whereas others have supported the idea that there is a restricted set of simples which form the constitutive base for the references of other representations (e.g., Devitt 1996; Prinz 2002).

The fewer simples there are, the easier it is to give a first-stage naturalistic theory that accounts only for the referential content of the simples. There are, however, serious objections to a two-stage approach, which first explains how the simples refer and then explains how complex concepts derive their referential powers from the simples. One is based on Quine's (1953) claim that we lack a principled analytic-synthetic distinction; the idea being that the second-stage requires a distinction between meaning constitutive relations and other relations among representations. There are a number of replies to Quine, but those who think that complex concepts can be constructed out of simpler concepts must also face Kripke's (1980) critique of description theories of reference.

Kripke's argument from ignorance and error is most relevant here. Kripke argued that we could be mistaken in almost everything we think we know about Aristotle and yet succeed in referring to Aristotle, and that even when no one knew the chemical analysis of water, our term "water" (or its cognate) referred to H_2O and only to H_2O. If so, not even implicit knowledge of some true definite description of Aristotle is needed to refer to Aristotle, and not even implicit knowledge of the essential properties of water is needed to refer specifically and exclusively to water. While Kripke's argument was directed at description theories of meaning for linguistic terms, his point generalizes. First, it seems to generalize to mental representations: a thinker, as well as a speaker, need have no mental description that accurately and exclusively characterizes (e.g.) water in order to use WATER to think exclusively and specifically about water. And second, the point seems to raise difficulties for more than description theories. It seems that *no* inner characterization of water, which accurately and exclusively characterizes water, is required for WATER to refer to water. Thus, whether the structure of the concept takes the form of a definition, a prototype, an exemplar, or a theory, it would seem that the content of component concepts could not be what determines the reference of WATER.

Some conclude that reference is always or almost always "atomistic." "Atomism" is variously defined, but here the reference of a mental representation is atomistic if it is determined independently of the references of other mental representations. Thus, to claim that reference is always or almost always atomistic is to claim that all or almost all concepts are simples. However, it would be too quick to come to this conclusion on the basis of the foregoing. For one thing, we need to consider what range of concepts the Kripkean point applies to, and for those within the range, we need to consider whether their reference might be partly determined by the references of other representations without being wholly so determined.

This issue complicates the assessment of naturalistic theories of reference. Different philosophers have alleged, against one or another such theory, that it cannot account for our reference to, say, non-existent objects (e.g., Santa and Satan), entities that cannot affect us or have not yet affected us (e.g., spatially very distant or future events), or entities that have diffuse impacts on us (e.g., the Big Bang or electrons). Such objections can succeed only if the corresponding representations (SANTA, SATAN, etc.) are simples, or are at least alleged to be simples by the target theory. If they are not simples, then accounting for their reference is a joint venture involving a naturalistic theory of simples plus an account of reference derivation for complex concepts.

The Causal-Historical Theory

What natural properties can serve to ground reference? Kripke's critique, along with Putnam's (1975) Twin-Earth thought experiment, have suggested to some that reference must involve causal relations between thinkers and what they think about. Twin-Earth is an imaginary planet somewhere in the universe that is as like Earth as possible, except that wherever there is H_2O on Earth there is an alien stuff on Twin-Earth, designated 'XYZ.' Liquid consisting of XYZ is indistinguishable from liquid consisting of H_2O, short of chemical analysis: it tastes the same, looks the same, quenches thirst, falls from the sky, etc. Everyone on Earth has a Twin-Earth doppleganger, including Oscar, whose Twin-Earth counterpart is Twin-Oscar. Neither knows about the chemical composition of the liquids on their planets, and nor do their respective communities, and Putnam claims that, none-theless, Oscar's English term "water" refers to H_2O and not XYZ and that Twin-Oscar's Twin-English term "water" refers to XYZ and not H_2O.

One implication, says Putnam, is that meaning has two components: an internal one, which is the same for both "twins," and an external one – referential content – that is different. Since the twins are doppelgangers they possess the same internal characterization of what they call "water," and the environment must be responsible for the difference in referential content. But the mere fact that there is H_2O in Oscar's environment whereas there is XYZ in his "twin's" is not enough to account for the difference. This claim is supported by the intuition that if Oscar and Twin-Oscar were exchanged without their knowledge (e.g., by teletransportation during sleep) they would still have thoughts about water (H_2O) and Twin-water (XYZ) respectively. If so, this suggests that a history of causal interaction between a thinker and what the thinker thinks about may be required to fix reference.

Neither Putnam (1995) nor Kripke (1982) support the naturalism project but, with Donnellan (1970), they are responsible for sketching a causal-historical theory of referential content. The main idea of a causal-historical theory is that reference begins with an act of dubbing that involves a perception of or a descrip-tion of the referent, which establishes a chain of reference as the name of the item is passed from one person to another in communication. For example, an infant, Richard Feynman (to use one of Kripke's examples) is named at birth, and his parents talk about him and introduce him to others and, as he matures and becomes known, word of him spreads. Someone might hear of him and later refer to him without remembering anything that is both true and distinctive about him. What is required, on this theory, is that we partake in a "... certain passage of communication reaching ultimately to the man himself" (Kripke 1980: 91). This passage of communication involves a causal chain, from speaker to speaker, and thinker to thinker.

A causal-historical theory seems to presuppose intentional psychological states that remain in need of analysis, as Kripke recognized. For example, the dubbing ceremony seems to require an intention to name something, and what is named seems to depend on the content of the dubbing intention: e.g., on whether Feynman's parents intended to name him, a time-slice of him, or his crib, or babies in general. In addition, not just any passing on of a name will do. Reference borrowing needs to be distinguished from 'naming after' (as in the case of naming a pet after a famous person). Reference borrowing seems to require certain intentions, such as the intention to use the name to refer to the same individual as the one referred to by the person from whom the name was received.

Devitt (1981) has argued that a causal-historical theory can be naturalized if it is articulated in terms of causal relations of the right kind, although it will then be incomplete. Among other things, it will lack a solution to the "qua-problem" (whether what was named was Feynman, time-slices of Feynman, and so on). Devitt argues that it might nonetheless be part of an overall naturalistic theory.

The Crude Causal Theory

The causal-historical theory is not a complete fundamental theory, but perhaps further appeal to causal relations between representations and their represented can ground reference (Stampe 1977). The crude causal theory (too crude to have been held by anyone) often serves as a starting point in thinking about how to further naturalize reference. The crude causal theory says that representations of a given type refer to the causes of its tokens: e.g., tokens of the type SKUNK refer to skunks if skunks and only skunks cause SKUNKs.

This theory has many problems, and as a further preliminary it will be useful to mention some of them. First is the *problem of error*. If I see a long tailed weasel striped from walking under a newly painted fence, I might think, "there goes a skunk." I'd be mistaken, but the crude causal theory does not give that result. Instead, it entails that once a non-skunk has caused a SKUNK, SKUNKs refer to skunks *and* some non-skunks (e.g., some painted long-tailed weasels). Error is impossible on the crude causal theory. Second is the *problem of distal content*. When a skunk causes me to token SKUNK, so do light rays reflected from the skunk, as well as neural firings en route to my visual cortex. There is a causal chain involved in the causing of SKUNKs, not a single cause, and the crude theory does not identify the part of the chain that is referred to. Third is *the problem of intentional inexistence*: the represented may not be the kind of thing that can cause a representation because it might not exist. No unicorn has ever caused a UNICORN because there are no unicorns. Fourth is *the problem of the absent represented*. Even in cases of correct representation, the represented may not be among the causes – or at least, not the immediate causes – of the representation. Your talk of your pet dog might remind me of my long-dead pet cat, in which case your talk is the more immediate cause of my representation. But my FLUFF represents my pet cat and not your talk of your pet dog for all that. Fifth is the qua-problem again: when a skunk causes a token of SKUNK, so might an unde-tached part of it (e.g. its tail or its face), or a spatio-temporal slice of it.

There will not be space to discuss how each theory, outlined below, aims to deal with each of these problems. The following sections focus mainly on their re-sponses to the problem of error, the problem of distal content, and the problem of intentional inexistence, but this should not be taken to suggest that the other problems are less important.

Another problem that gets mentioned in this context is *the fine-grainedness problem*. The issue is that content seems to be more fine-grained than causation is. Our thoughts can distinguish between metaphysically co-extensive properties such as being triangular and trilateral or being a rabbit and being a collection of undetached rabbit parts but, it is alleged, causation cannot. However, it is not clear that this is a problem for a naturalistic theory of *reference*. On some views, if 'X' and 'Y' refer to properties that have identical causal powers, then X and Y are one and the same property. On this view, if we cannot discriminate between the causal powers of triangularity and trilaterality, TRIANGULAR and TRILATERAL refer to the same property. So, if they differ in meaning, the difference must be else-where, such as in Putnam's internal component, in their inferential role perhaps.

The Asymmetric Dependency Theory

Fodor (1990b) aims to solve the above-mentioned problems. He starts with the problem of error. We solve this problem, he suggests, when we distinguish the *right* from the *wrong* causes, and he adds that the wrong causings are dependent on the right causings and not *vice versa*. More carefully, representations of a type, R, refer to Xs and not non-Xs if non-Xs can cause Rs only because Xs can, and not vice versa. It's because skunks can cause SKUNKs that non-skunks can too, and not vice versa, and that's why SKUNKs refer to skunks. According to Fodor, there's one ceteris paribus causal law to the effect that skunks can cause SKUNKs, another to the effect that (e.g.) some long-tailed weasels can too, and a depend-ence between the two that is synchronic, not diachronic, such that the second law depends on the first.

Some philosophers have found this theory hard to test. The theory requires that one-kind-of-event' s-causing-R (where "R" stands for a representation) depends on another-kind-of-event's-causing-R and these higher-order dependencies are somewhat mysterious. On occasion, Fodor explains them in terms of counter-factuals: in the nearest possible world where skunks cannot cause SKUNKs, painted long-tailed weasels cannot either, but in the nearest possible world where painted long-tailed weasels cannot cause SKUNKs, skunks still can. As Fodor puts it, the link between SKUNKs and skunks is more *resilient* than the link between SKUNKs and non-skunks. Some have proposed counter-examples based on possible world scenarios, but Fodor argues that they are mistaken about which content is correct or about the direction of dependency (see e.g., the papers by Baker, Block and Boghossian, as well as Fodor's replies, in Loewer and Rey 1991). This debate might show that our intuitions in these cases are too malleable to be useful, and/or that the theory needs to be more fully specified.

Another problem for the asymmetric dependency (ASD) theory is the problem of systematic error and ignorance. The problem arises because the theory requires that thinkers have certain synchronic dispositions such that the relevant asymmetric dependencies hold true of them. It is neutral as to how they hold, but hold they must. ASD requires that, if we think of skunks, we must be disposed to have skunks cause SKUNKs in us – otherwise, non-skunks could not cause SKUNKs in us only because skunks can. The problem is that we can think about skunks even if we lack the ability to recognize them – even if we are not disposed to have skunks cause SKUNKs in us. Further, ASD seems to entail that, if I misconceive the nature of skunks, my mental representation of skunks will not refer to skunks but to the kind that best matches my conception (i.e., my misconception of what a skunk is like).

Fodor maintains that the ASD theory allows reference to unicorns, since the relevant counterfactuals hold in nearby possible worlds: if there were unicorns, they would cause UNICORNs, and non-unicorns could only cause UNICORNs because unicorns would. But this move, which might be essential for accommodating reference to non-existent entities, has a high price. For now suppose that Tom believes that skunks have a sweet scent and pink polka dots. Were there such a creature – call it a squunk – it would cause him to token SKUNK. Worse, a skunk would cause him to token SKUNK only if he mistakenly thought it had squunky features. In other words, skunks could cause SKUNKs in Tom only because squunks could. So the squunk-to-SKUNK connection seems more resilient for Tom than the skunk-to-SKUNK connection.

One could invoke Fodor's ceteris paribus clause to maintain that the asymmetric dependencies pertain to suitably well-informed people, but this invokes something intentional, which undermines the naturalistic aims of the theory. It might also be circular, for we must ask what is it to be suitably well informed. Is being suitably well informed about skunks a matter of having the capacity to recognize skunks as skunks? If so, it seems we must peek at the content of SKUNK to apply the ceteris paribus condition. One might also claim that the skunk-to-SKUNK connection is more resilient than the squunk-to-SKUNK connection, even for someone as benighted as Tom, because Tom would respond to appropriate instruction by revising in favor of the skunk to SKUNK connection. But this also invokes something intentional and apparently circular. Instruction is an intentional notion, and Tom will only revise appropriately if he is instructed correctly. A better response might be to suggest that SKUNK is not an apt subject for a fundamental theory of reference, on the grounds that it is not plausibly a simple. While Fodor's atomism may not allow that response, others may want to consider its merits.

Fodor thinks his ASD theory has a good shot at dealing with the absentee problem (Fodor 1990). Basically, the claim is that cases of absentee representation depend asymmetrically on cases where the represented is present. He also offers a solution to the problem of distal content. Consider a case where a SKUNK has a proximal cause that is a certain pattern of retinal firings, *RF*. Fodor claims that *RF* can cause SKUNKs to be tokened only because skunks can too. On the face of it, this seems wrong, since skunks cannot cause SKUNKS except through the mediation of more proximal causes, including *RF*. However, Fodor points out that skunks can cause SKUNKs without the assistance of *RF* in particular, since any number of patterns of retinal firings could mediate between a skunk and a SKUNK. Under the right circumstances, a mere sniff, or glimpse of brown fur, or rustle in the grass, could cause us to token SKUNK. Indeed, says Fodor, there is no closed disjunct of retinal impressions or sensory inputs – RF or RF^1 or RF^2 or $RF^3 \dots RF^n$ – that could satisfy the ASD theory's requirements for referential content. While this might be true, we might still ask if it goes to the heart of the matter. Suppose we discover that a certain neural process immediately prior to SKUNK tokening *is* required for SKUNK tokening. This seems possible, but we would not then conclude that SKUNK referred to this more immediate neural process (Loar 1991).

Teleosemantics

The naturalistic theories on which there has been most work done of late are the teleosemantic theories. These are a diverse class of theories that share the claim that the contents of mental representations are determined (somehow) by the functions of the systems that (it depends on the version) produce or use the representation.

The relevant notion of function is given an etiological analysis (following Wright, 1976). According to such an analysis (e.g., Neander 1991) items of a type have the function of doing what that type of item was selected for doing. For example, our pineal glands have the function of secreting melatonin at nightfall because their doing so in the past contributed to their past selection. In the case of innate representational capacities, the relevant selection process is neo-Darwinian natural selection, so that the function of a system is to do whatever ancestral systems did which caused systems of that type to be preserved and/or proliferated in the population. These functions are referred to as "normal functions" or "proper functions," following biological talk of the proper functioning or normal functioning of a system.

Theories that appeal to this notion of function are known as "teleological theories" because the notion has a teleological flavor. To say that hearts have the function of pumping blood seems equivalent to saying that they are *for* pumping blood or even (metaphorically) that their *purpose* is blood pumping. On an etiological analysis, they *are* literally *for* pumping blood in so far as this is what they were selected for. However, the relevant notion is not literally purposive, and if mental content is to derive from past selection, it must ultimately derive from non-intentional processes of selection, such as neo-Darwinian natural selection.

However, according to some proponents of teleosemantics, other forms of selection can also serve to ground appropriate (content determining) functions: for example, there is also talk of meme selection, cultural selection, and learning or conditioning doing so.

The relevant notion of function is also said to be normative in the sense that it permits the possibility of malfunction: a token trait can have a function that it lacks the ability to perform. For example, my pineal gland can have the function of secreting melatonin at nightfall even if it is unable to do so. If it cannot secrete melatonin because it is malfunctioning, we might say that it is "supposed to" secrete melatonin, nonetheless. However this is cashed out in descriptive rather than prescriptive terms on an etiological theory, for all it means on such a theory is that pineal glands were selected for doing so. Even if my pineal gland cannot secrete melatonin, it belongs to a homologous type that was selected for secreting melatonin, and thus secreting melatonin is its function. Some prefer to reserve the term "normative" for prescriptive contexts only. According to this more restrictive use of the term, only statements that entail ought-claims without the addition of further premises count as normative statements. Function ascriptions are not claimed to be normative in this sense by those who advocate teleological theories of content. On an etiological analysis of proper function, no ought-claims follow from function ascriptions alone. (Consider that some HIV genes are adapted for disabling our immune system, but it doesn't follow that they should do so, or that we should help them to.) Content ascriptions might also be normative in only the more liberal, descriptive sense. Indeed, those who try to naturalize content usually assume that this is so. Representations can misrepresent, beliefs can be true or false, and so on, but content ascriptions might not entail ought claims without the addition of further premises. If so, the attempt to naturalize semantic norms is not an attempt to derive ought-statements from is-statements.

Teleosemantic theories are offered by among others: Dennett (1969: ch.9; 1987: ch.8; 1995: ch.14); Dretske (1986, 1988, 1991); Fodor (1990a), although he repudiated his offering long before it was published; Israel (1987); Jacob (1997); Matthen (1984); McGinn (1989: ch. 2); Millikan (1984, 1989, 1991, 2000); Neander (1995, forthcoming); Papineau (1984; 1987; 1993: ch. 3); Price (2001) and Sterelny (1990). The theories of Papineau and Millikan were the earliest detailed versions of teleosemantics and these are outlined in this section. Some of the above theories are very different to these and are discussed in the last section.

Millikan maintains that the content of a representation is determined, not by *its* function, but by the functions of its consumers – the systems that used the representation to perform their proper function. These consuming systems may or may not be cognitive systems. A much discussed example is the frog's response to anything appropriately small, dark, and moving past its retina by flicking out its tongue and attempting to catch and swallow it (Lettvin et al.: 1959). One consumer of its perceptual representation is its digestive system, another is the neural components of the frog's brain that control its tongue snapping. Contents,

Millikan claims, concern the conditions required for the consumers to perform their function in the historically normal way. That is, it concerns the conditions required for them to do what traits of the type did in the past when they contributed to their own selection on those occasions when the representation was used in doing so. Specifically, Millikan maintains that the frog's perceptual representation represents frog-food (and not, say, something small, dark, and moving) because it was only when frog-food corresponded to the representation that the frog's digestive system or its tongue snapping mechanism succeeded in feeding the frog and hence succeeded in contributing to the preservation and/or proliferation of such systems in frogs. On this account, misrepresentation therefore occurs when the stimulus is not frog food (e.g., when the frog snaps at a BB, a small plastic pellet).

Like Millikan, Papineau maintains that content is determined by the past use of representational states and by the environmental conditions that obtained when their use contributed to fitness. For Papineau, a desire's satisfaction condition is "... that effect which it is the desire's biological purpose to produce" (1993:58–9). By that he means that "[s]ome past selection mechanism has favored that desire – or, more precisely, the ability to form that type of desire – in virtue of that desire producing that effect' (1993: 59). The main function of beliefs, he maintains, is to collaborate with desires to cause behavior that bring about their satisfaction conditions. The truth condition of a belief, he tells us, is the condition that must obtain if the desire with which it collaborates in producing an action is to be satisfied by the condition brought about by that action. A desire that has the function of bringing it about that we have food has the content that we have food, since it was selected for bringing it about that we have food. If this desire collaborates with a belief to cause us to go to the fridge, the content of the belief is that there is food in the fridge if our desire for food would only be satisfied by our doing so if it is true that there is food in the fridge.

As Fodor (1990b) has argued, it is a problem for this formulation that some desires do not or cannot contribute to their own satisfaction (e.g., the desire for rain tomorrow and the desire to be immortal) and that others would not have been selected for any such contribution (e.g., novel desires, or an adolescent's desire to kill himself or herself).

Of course, Papineau and Millikan know that some mental representations are not "innate," or the direct result of ordinary natural selection. Papineau claims that learning (he seems to have conditioning in mind) is a process that is sufficiently similar to ordinary natural selection (Papineau 1993: 59–67) to ground content. But it is not plausible that we learn all of our new beliefs by something akin to natural selection (e.g., I might acquire a new belief by reading a sentence in a book). Millikan appeals to what she calls "derived" proper functions and to mapping rules that, when applied in new contexts, furnish novel representations (Millikan 1984: 41–3). To illustrate the notion of a derived proper function, Millikan mentions a mechanism in a chameleon, which she says has the proper function of matching the color of the chameleon to the color of the surface on which it sits (within a certain range of colors). Millikan says that if a particular chameleon is sitting on a particular shade of green, the mechanism has the derived proper function of matching that particular chameleon to that particular shade of green, even if no chameleon has happened to sit on that particular shade of green before. Millikan claims that, along similar lines, belief-producing mechanisms (and belief-consuming mechanisms) can have the derived proper function to produce (or consume) particular beliefs, including novel beliefs never believed before.

Exactly how, or whether, this idea could determine contents for sophisticated representational states (e.g., beliefs in humans) remains obscure. But perhaps an analogy with literal mapping might help. Suppose we (intentionally) select a system for mapping terrain. This involves our selecting certain mapping rules. However, once we have done so, we can apply these rules to generate indefinitely many maps that represent indefinitely many terrains. We do not need to select a fresh set of mapping rules for each new map. Along similar lines, the idea might be that natural selection can select certain mapping rules (or respects of isomorphism), which a cognitive system can then exploit to produce indefinitely many novel representations. Millikan's response to the problem of novel concepts (e.g., the concept of an electron, when the concept was first proposed) is along the same lines. (Readers should also see Millikan's newer treatment of these issues, in Millikan 2000.)

Another option, to return to points made earlier, is to claim that teleosemantics only determines the reference of representational simples, and that no novel concept is a simple. This approach at any rate seems unavoidable for non-existent objects, which cannot be the reference of simples on a teleological theory. Those who support teleological theories of mental content can also opt for a combinatorial semantics, thus avoiding the problem of novel, impotent and destructive desires, mentioned above.

On the surface, Papineau and Millikan have a solution to the problem of distal content – i.e., of determining what is represented from among the items involved in the chain of more proximal and distal causes of a representation. In the case mentioned above, neither light rays nor neural firings, in the absence of frog food, feed the frog or contribute to fitness. Nor do they satisfy our desire for food when we walk to the fridge. However, on closer inspection, it is not clear whether the problem is solved. The question to ask, according to Millikan, is not "What feeds the frog?" but rather, "What condition was required for the consumers of the representation to perform their function in the historically normal way?" The problem is that not just food was required. Food that goes undetected is of no use to a frog and its detection requires that light hit the frog's retina. A similar problem arises for Papineau. The mere presence of food does not satisfy our desire for food, since the food must be perceived and eaten, and so it must stimulate our retinas or our olfactory nerves and pass into our gut. We return to this in (2) below.

Two main objections to teleosemantics are (1) the Swampman objection and (2) the so-called functional indeterminacy problem. (For discussion of lack of epistemic access to selection histories and the theory's alleged commitments to adaptationism, see Fodor 1996, Peacocke 1992, and Neander 1999).

(1) Swampman-style examples have been around for a while (see Boorse 1976). But Swampman, in particular, is a creature of Donald Davidson's imagination. Swampman begins his existence as a molecule-for-molecule synchronic doppelganger of Davidson at time *t*. He comes about as a result of a purely random collision of elementary particles. Crucially, he is not a copy of Davidson in any causal sense; the resemblance between them is just a stupendous coincidence. Moreover, Swampman lacks any selection history whatsoever: he has no evolutionary history and at the start at least no learning history. The troublesome intuition is that when Swampman first pops into existence, he has thoughts, perceptions, and so on, just like Davidson's at *t*, whereas according to teleosemantics, he lacks all such intentional or representational states, since his systems lack the appropriate function-conferring histories.

In defense of teleosemantics, a number of points have been made. One is that teleosemantics is usually meant as an account of what referential content *really is*, not what we conceive of it as being. Were he to exist, Swampman's states would superficially resemble states with referential content. Everyone can agree on that. But it can be argued that a deeper analysis can show that Swampman would not have the same kind of states as we have. A deeper analysis could show that content requires a selection history. Just so, were XYZ to exist, it would superficially resemble water. But a deeper analysis of water has shown that the XYZ liquid would not be the same kind of thing as water.

Some respond to this by maintaining that what is of most interest, in the case of referential content, is the larger category that includes our referrings as well as Swampman's analogous call-them-what-you-will. However, this shifts the subject, since we have been interested in the norms of reference, and according to teleosemantics the norms of reference depend on history. So, unless Swampman really has referential content, Swampman is beside the point. In support of the intuition that Swampman really has referential content, the most difficult intuition to resist is that it will *seem* to Swampman that he is thinking about all sorts of things. And if things seem a certain way to Swampman, it would appear that he has contentful states – if it seems to him that he is thinking about cats, then presumably he at least has a representation that refers to his thought, or at any rate to his Swampish equivalent. Again, however, proponents of teleosemantics can claim that appearances could be deceptive, and that Swampman's seemings would not be the same kind of thing as our seemings.

Most proponents of teleosemantics reject the idea that we should care about Swampman intuitions. It would be enough, they claim, if we could find a theory of referential content that was successful for real creatures. While this would certainly be an achievement, some argue that we should still care about Swampman, on the grounds that scientific classifications should be based on similarities and differences in causal powers (e.g., see Antony 1996). If we classify mental states according to their content, and content depends on history, then we do not classify mental states on the basis of their causal powers, since two states can have the same causal powers but different histories or the same histories but different causal powers. This introduces a debate called the "Methodological Individualism debate." One problem with Methodological Individualism is that it is radically revisionist. Biology has many historically based classifications (e.g., species, clades, and physiological kinds, which are often based on function or homology or both). If, for instance, one were to classify Swampman's "kidney" with Davidson's, on the basis of their having the same causal powers, one would do so at the expense of excluding the (malfunctioning) kidneys of many real people. (For further discussion of Swampman, see the essays in the issue listed under Antony 1996, plus Braddon-Mitchell and Jackson 1997, and Papineau 2001.)

(2) The second objection to teleological theories of content that will be considered here is the objection that function ascriptions are too indeterminate to determine content. Consider the toad, similar to the aforementioned frogs (Ewert 1983). Motivated toads will hunt and try to eat anything with a suitably worm-like configuration: i.e., they will hunt and try to eat anything that's, roughly, small, elongated and moving parallel to its longest axis. They cannot discriminate between toad food and cardboard cutout rectangles with the right configuration, but in their ancestral environment, things with that configuration were often enough toad food, so a device that responded to these features sufficed for the job. We can describe the function of the relevant part of the toad's perceptual system in different ways: e.g., as detecting toad food and as detecting things with the right configuration of features. What does the toad's perceptual representation represent then? Does it misrepresent the cardboard cutout as a toad food? Or does it correctly represent the cardboard cutout as an item in worm-like motion?

As Fodor (1990b) sees it, the problem is that natural selection cannot discriminate between co-extensive features. If it's adaptive to snap at Fs and Fs are co-extensive with Gs, then it's equally adaptive to snap at Gs. This leaves it up to us how we choose to describe the function of the toad's systems. We can equally well describe them as having the function of snapping at Fs or at Gs. And if function ascriptions are indeterminate, they cannot determine content. We have not naturalized content if the content depends on our choice of description. The standard reply to this version of the problem is that something *can* be selected *for* occurring in the presence of Fs and not for occurring in the presence of Gs if it was Fs and not Gs that played a causal role in the selection. Selection *for* is a causal notion. A type of item is selected for doing that which caused the type of item to be preserved and proliferated in the population. (See Fodor 1996, for his updated version of the problem, and Neander 1999, for a reply.)

Nonetheless, a problem remains because traits are selected for complex causal roles, and so more than one property can be causally efficacious in selection (Neander 1995). Components of the toad's perceptual system were selected for helping to feed the toad *by* detecting a certain configuration of visible features, and so both properties of the stimulus – both its being nutritious and its having a certain configuration of visible features – played a causal role in this case of selection. A problem remains for teleosemantics because we can obtain different function ascriptions by focusing on different aspects of the complex causal roles for which traits were selected. And so it remains true that if we must choose among different descriptions of the relevant function, we have not naturalized content by appealing to functions.

Some think that teleosemantics must isolate a unique correct function ascription if teleosemantics is to work (Enc 2002). And some have tried to do so by adding further conditions to an etiological analysis of functions (e.g., Price 2001). However, proponents of teleological theories of content need not insist that function ascriptions are determinate. That is to say, they can allow that traits are selected for complex causal roles, and that the functions of traits can be described in different ways by focussing on different aspects of these complex causal roles. They can do this because they can appeal to other things in addition to functions that can make content more determinate.

Millikan claims that her focus on the consumers of representations helps. Only if the toad gets fed do the consumers of the prey-representation perform their proper function in the historically normal way, she maintains. However, the appeal to consumers is no help since the functions of consumers are just as complex (and hence "indeterminate") as the functions of producers are. The function of the frog's tongue-snapping mechanism, for example, can be described as snapping at frog food, or as snapping where and when the frog's brain tells it to snap.

What might be doing more real work for Millikan is an implicit reliance on what was *most* crucial for a contribution to fitness (see Millikan 1991). In the past, for a contribution to fitness to occur, it was Normally (in the teleological sense) required that the stimulus have the right configuration of features, for otherwise it would not have been detected, *and* that it be nutritious, otherwise it would not have fed the frog. But the latter was more crucial than the former in the following sense. If the toad could have had the toad food minus the right configuration of features, it would have been perfectly fine, whereas if it could have had the right configuration of features minus the toad food it would have starved to death.

Both Millikan and Papineau might also try to appeal to what was, in this sense, most crucial for fitness, to try to handle the problem of distal content. What was most important for fitness: food or the light reflected from it? By the same reasoning, the answer is food, for if we could have had the food without the light all would have been well, whereas if we had only the light without the food, we would have starved to death. The difficulty here is that if we press the point we can go too far. If we could have had digested nutrients in the gut, without the food outside, all would have been well also, but if we had only the food outside, without the digested nutrients in the gut, we would have died. Digested nutrients are distal, but not appropriately distal.

Hall (1990) argues that Millikan's theory leads to overly specific content: a contribution to fitness didn't just require food. The food must have contained no deadly toxins, no viruses, bacteria, or parasites that tipped the balance between costs and benefits. In the toad's case, it also required that no fishing line be attached and no crow lurking nearby, and so on and so forth. All this, it seems, must be included in the content. Pietroski (1992) also argues that the content generated is the wrong content. He asks us to imagine creatures, called "kimu," that are initially color blind. Due to a mutation, one kimu is able to see red and is attracted to the red glow of sunrise. It ascends the top of the nearest hill each morning to see the rising sun. By doing so, it happens to avoid the dawn-marauding predators below. The trait would be selected because it guided the creature and its descendents to predator-free spaces. Pietroski argues that, in this case, Millikan's theory gives the wrong perceptual content because it would not allow him to tell the story this way. Intuitively, the creatures see red and love to see red. But according to Millikan, they do not see and love to see red. They instead see and love to see predator-free spaces, even if they have never in their lives seen these predators (for Millikan's response, see Millikan 2000: appendix B). Neander (forthcoming) also argues that standard teleological theories of content generate the wrong content ascriptions. Her argument is based on an analysis of the kind of content needed to play a role in mainstream cognitive science. A careful look at neuroethological explanations of frog and toad perceptual systems, she argues, supports the view that standard teleosemantics cannot serve the purposes of information processing explanations of cognitive capacities.

Informational semantics

A different style of teleological theory is a theory that links contents less directly to contributions to fitness. On such theories content concerns the information that representations are supposed to carry, where the "supposed to" is teleological, or a matter of what something was selected for.

Dretske's theory (1981, 1986, 1988, and 1991) is the best known of these. He defines an informational relation, called "indication." Events of one kind, R, *indicate* events of another kind, C, just in case (within the relevant environment) if there is an instance of R then there is an instance of C. Dretske tells us that C need not be a cause of R; C and R might have a common cause, for instance. Nor need C's connection with R be nomological. To use one of Dretske's examples, if there is someone ringing the doorbell whenever the doorbell rings, its ringing indicates that someone is at the door, even though there's no law that doorbells ring only if someone rings them. If squirrels start to ring doorbells because people start making them out of nuts, it would no longer be the case that doorbell ringings indicate that someone is at the door.

Mere indication is not sufficient for representation. There can be no error if representation is equivalent to indication, as Dretske explains, because "R indicates C" is incompatible with "R and not-C." So Dretske suggests, at a first pass, that representations are items that have the function of indicating. Since items don't always perform their function, misrepresentation would then be possible.

The initial proposal is that *R represents C* only if *R*s were recruited for indicating *C*s and for bringing about some behavior, *M*. It follows that *R* need only indicate *C* during recruitment and error is possible after that time and in other environments.

Dretske (1986) maintains that content is determinately distal in creatures with a capacity to acquire an indefinite number of epistemic routes to the same representation, thus ensuring that there is no time-invariant closed disjunct of proximal features that the representation was recruited to indicate. This is similar to Fodor's response, and it suffers from the same problem (see also Loewer 1987). In addition, it denies distal content to representations based on innate representational capacities.

Another problem stems from Dretske's stringent definition of "indication," according to which *R*s indicate *C*s only if "'if *R* then *C'* (in the relevant environment) has a probability of one. This seems to force Dretske's theory to rely on an unrealistic distinction between recruitment and post-recruitment phases and places. To see this, note that nothing can be selected by a natural (as opposed to an intentional) process of selection for doing something that it does not do. So if *R*s are selected for indicating *C*s, they must actually indicate *C*s during this selection. It follows that during recruitment there can be no misrepresentation of *C*s by *R*s, or more neutrally, no *R*s in the absence of *C*s. Thus, during this period, which Dretske early on refers to as the learning period, there can be no representation of *C*s by *R*s either, since (Dretske says) representation requires the possibility of misrepresentation. It is only once recruitment of *R*s for indicating *C*s ceases that an *R* in the absence of a *C*, and hence mis/representation of *C*s by *R*s, becomes possible. This seems quite unrealistic because, if *R*s can occur without *C*s after the learning or recruitment period, *R*s could surely occur without *C*s during the learning or recruitment period (Fodor 1991a).

In places, Dretske talks as though he is using a less strict notion of indication, one that permits talk of the "maximally indicated state." He does not elaborate much on this, but it is an interesting consequence that the content ascriptions he supports are different from those supported by a theory like Millikan's or Papineau's. Consider again the frog or toad. The maximally indicated (distal) state is presumably not frog or toad food but instead the presence of a stimulus with a certain configuration of visible features. The more maximally indicated state, at least, is something small, dark and moving (in the case of the frog) or something elongated and moving parallel to its longest axis (in the case of the toad).

Neander (1995) and Jacob (1997) have defended accounts that generate similar contents for simple systems. Neander (forthcoming) offers an informational teleosemantics that uses a more lenient notion than Dretskean indication. She stipulates that a mechanism *informs* a state or event of type *R* about something, *C*, to the extent that it does something to enhance the correlation between *R*s and *C*s by causally mediating between them. Neural components can causally connect *R*s and *C*s by being caused by *C*s to produce *R*s (as happens in perception) or by being caused by *R*s to produce *C*s (as happens in motor output). Neander claims that the referential content of a representational simple at the sensory/motor periphery is what it is "supposed" to be informed about. That is, its content is what the systems that were adapted for informing it were adapted for informing it about. This proposal extends the scope of Dretske's theory, which only applies to perception, and it avoids the need for a distinct learning or recruitment period, in which if there is an R there must also be a C. The correlation between representations and their representeds need never have been perfect on this version of informational semantics.

It is an intended implication of both Dretske's and Neander's proposals that the toad's perceptual representation has the content (roughly) *elongated thing moving parallel to its longest axis (at such and such a location)* and that the frog's representation has the content (roughly) *small, dark, moving thing*. As Dretske puts it, these are the more maximally indicated states, which the representation was selected for indicating. And, as Neander puts it, these are what the relevant perceptual systems were selected for informing the representations about. They were not selected for informing them about packets of nutrients, as Neander defines "informing," because they were causally insensitive to the presence or absence of nutrients. Neander (forthcoming) argues that this is the right result for an information-processing account of the toad's perceptual capacity, on the grounds that such content ascriptions, unlike those generated by more standard teleological theories of content, can play a role in information-processing accounts of the relevant cognitive or perceptual capacity.

Toads are not in error, on this account, if they snap at a suitably sized cardboard rectangle moved parallel to its longest axis, but they are in error if they snap at a stunned worm, a cricket, or a millipede that is dangled by its tail and moved perpendicular to its longest axis, which can happen in cases of severe neurological damage to the toad (e.g., ablation of parts of or all of its thalamus). This is the inverse of the results that the teleological theories of Millikan and Papineau aim to deliver.

Like the others before her, Neander also offers a solution to the problem of distal content. To say that (e.g.) the frog represents something small, dark and moving is not the same as saying that the content of its representation is proximal, since (after all) some small, dark, moving things are insects and insects are appropriately distal. However, there is a prima facie problem for her theory, regarding distal content. If a mechanism was selected for informing a representation about a distal item, it was also selected for informing it about the proximal items that carry the information about the distal item to the representation. It was *by* being informed about these that it was informed about the more distal item. Neander proposes that appropriately distal content is found at the end of the causal chain that the representation is supposed to be informed about. Take it as given that neural components were adapted for informing Rs about Cs. If so, she says, they were also selected for informing Rs about more proximal items (Ps) that carry information about Cs to Rs. But, she maintains, there is a difference: the neural components were adapted for informing Rs about Ps because they were adapted for informing Rs about Cs, but they were not adapted for informing Rs about Cs because they were adapted for informing Rs about Ps.

Some (even in the face of Pietroski's argument) will find the kinds of contents ascribed by theories like Millikan's and Papineau's more intuitive than those ascribed by theories like Dretske's and Neander's. Millikan also argues that theories of the latter kind preclude the possibility of representing kinds with hidden natures or essences (Millikan, 2000, appendix B). However, Dretske's and Neander's theories are offered as theories for representational simples, and it is questionable whether kinds with hidden natures are plausibly represented by simples. On an account of this sort, kinds with hidden essences, as well as non-existent kinds, must be represented by complex concepts.

The main problem with this kind of approach is the modesty of its scope. This is a bottom-up approach – one that seeks to account for the contents of representational simples and one that leaves the bulk of the work for the second-stage theory, which aims to explain how complex concepts can be derived from simpler ones. While this might turn out to be the correct approach, it is certainly a long way to the top and it is far from clear that we can get from here to there. (A somewhat more detailed introduction to different kinds of teoleological theories is given in Neander 2004.)

Along with consciousness, intentionality has been thought to be the mark of the mental. Both have been traditional philosophical puzzles. Many philosophers are inclined to think that consciousness is the less tractable of the two, and that we have some idea, at least, of how to proceed toward an understanding of mental representation. As we have seen, a number of ideas have been put forward. There are, however, serious difficulties with all of the presently available naturalistic theories of content and, to say the least, much work remains to be done. Some think that what is needed is more work on the same basic ideas, whereas others think that a radically novel idea, unlike anything proposed so far, is still needed.

Chapter 20

Truth

Vann McGee

I Plato's Theory

In the *Sophist* 263, Plato gives a rudimentary theory of truth. Although the account applies only to the very simplest sentences, it is a good place to start a discussion of truth, for it leads directly to the so-called *semantic conception* of truth, developed by Alfred Tarski in the 1930s, which is at the center of contemporary discussions of the notion of truth.

The simplest sentences, says Plato, consist of two parts, a *verb*, which designates an action, and a *name*, which denotes an individual, and the sentence is true just in case the individual designated by the name performs the action designated by the verb. "Theaetetus flies," for example, is not true, because the boy Theaetetus, who is denoted by the name, does not perform the action designated by the verb "flies." "Theaetetus sits," by contrast, is true.

What Plato provides is a modest beginning to a task of the first philosophical importance, for understanding what makes a true sentence true is likely to be central to any attempt to understand how human language and human thought are connected to the world around us. We are not going to understand much of human history until we recognize that human beings communicate with one another by meaningful speech, and knowing what speech means is largely a matter of recognizing the truth conditions of assertions. We use language for purposes other than making assertions, like wishing and promising, but we can explain the fulfillment conditions of wishes and promises in terms of the truth conditions of corresponding assertions. (In what follows, I shall follow the logicians' sloppy custom of using "sentence" as if assertion were sentences' only role.)

We need the notion of truth in a public language if we want to understand group behavior, and we need truth in the language of thought if we want to understand individual behavior, for we explain a person's actions in terms of the truth conditions of her beliefs and the fulfillment conditions of her desires. That, at least, is the situation if Jerry Fodor (1975) is correct in postulating a language of thought. If Fodor is mistaken, then the relation between the truth of thoughts and the truth of sentences will be one of analogy rather than inclusion, but the truth of sentences will still be a crucial theoretical notion.

Plato's account can be extended beyond the very simplest sentences without great effort. Instead of an intransitive verb, a sentence might contain a verb phrase consisting of the copula and an adjective or common noun, like "is brave" or "is a mathematician." Such a verb phrase designates a property, and the sentence is true if and only if the individual named by the name has the property. We can use a transitive verb instead, getting a sentence like "Socrates loves Theaetetus," which is true just in case the individual denoted by the subject performs the action denoted by the verb on the individual denoted by the direct object. A similar treatment works for relational statements, like "Socrates is older than Theaetetus."

Truth conditions for compound sentences are derived from those for their components. "Theaetetus sits or Theaetetus flies," for example, is a compound sentence that is true iff (if and only if) one or the other of its component sentences is true. "Theaetetus does not fly" is true iff "Theaetetus flies" is not true.

A merit of this account is that it provides compositional truth conditions. The truth conditions of a compound sentence are determined by the truth conditions of its simple components, and the truth conditions of the simple sentences, like "Theaetetus sits," are fixed by the meanings of their constituent words. The fact that we are able to express and understand sentences that we have never heard before – indeed, that speakers are able to grasp the meanings of the infinitely many sentences of a language on the basis of exposure to a small finite sample – shows that, somehow or other, the meanings of sentences have to be compositionally determined.

The Platonic account loses its footing when we get to complex sentences that are not composed of simple sentences. For example, we can think of "Theaetetus is wise and brave" as an abbreviated version of "Theaetetus is wise and Theaetetus is brave." We cannot analogously regard "Someone is wise and brave" as short for "Someone is wise and someone is brave," since the two sentences mean different things. To get a compositional theory that takes account of sentences that have a complex structure even though they are not constructed out of simpler sentences, a new idea is needed.

The new idea was Gottlob Frege's understanding of the quantifiers. According to Frege, quantifiers – words like "someone," "something," "everything," and "anything" – represent properties of properties. Phrases like "is wise," "is brave," and "is wise and brave" represent first-level properties, properties that are had by individuals. Quantifiers represent second-level properties, properties of first-level properties. "Someone" represents the property that a first-level property has if it is possessed by at least one person.

II   Convention T

Semantics, according to Tarski (1936: 401), studies "connections between expressions of a language and the objects or states of affairs that those expressions refer to." Tarski's semantic conception of truth employs the methods of modern logic to consolidate the insights we get from Plato and from Frege in order to obtain an explicit definition of truth. That is, it provides a characterization of the form,

$$x \text{ is a true sentence of the language } \mathcal{L} \text{ iff } \underline{\hspace{1cm}},$$

where no semantic terms are utilized in filling in the blank. Syntactic notions – notions concerned merely with the internal structure of language, like "is a grammatical sentence of $\mathcal{L}$" – can appear, but no semantic notions, or, rather, no semantic notions that have not already been explicitly defined in nonsemantic terms.

The qualifying phrase "of the language $\mathcal{L}$" is often left tacit, but it is important to keep it in mind. A sentence is not either true or false; a sentence is true or false in a language in a context. An utterance of "It is snowing," for example, is true in English at some times and places, and false at others. Even if we restrict our attention to context-independent sentences – what Quine (1960: 193ff), calls "eternal sentences" – we still have to acknowledge that the same sentence can occur in different languages with different meanings. Propositions (the things "that" clauses refer to, assuming "that" clauses refer) are either true or false absolutely, but the truth or falsity of a sentence is relative to a language. One approach to understanding sentential truth is to divide the problem into two parts, first recognizing what proposition a given sentence expresses (in a given language), and second understanding what makes a proposition true or false. Because propositions are intangible and not well understood, the more direct approach of defining a restricted notion of truth-in-a-language for one or another particular language is likely to prove more fruitful, at least in the short run, even though its results are limited in scope.

Tarski's results have a severely limited range of application – he restricted his attention almost entirely to formalizations of various branches of mathematics – but they are admirably precise. His theory doesn't specify which sentences are true. To do that, we'd have to have a complete theory of whatever it is the language talks about. His theory gives us the truth *conditions* of every sentence, enabling us to determine which sentences are true on the basis of nonsemantic facts. Morever, if the language is fully precise, the truth conditions will be fully precise.

For a restricted but substantial class of formal languages $\mathcal{L}$, Tarski is able to provide a definition of "true sentence of $\mathcal{L}$," then he is able to prove as a mathematical theorem that the proposed definition is correct. It is amazing that such a theorem is even possible. If we already had a precise understanding of truth in $\mathcal{L}$, we would not require a definition. Lacking such a precise understanding, how are we able to recognize – much less prove as a theorem – that a proposed definition is correct?

Tarski's response focuses on what he calls "(T)-sentences," sentences that follow the paradigm:

"Snow is white" is true in English iff snow is white.

If $\mathcal{L}$ is our object language – the language whose theory of truth is under construction – the (T)-sentences for $\mathcal{L}$ are obtained from the following schema by filling in the blanks appropriately:

_____ is true in $\mathcal{L}$ iff _____.

The first blank is filled in with a "structural-descriptive name" of a sentence of the object language. A structural-descriptive name of a sentence might be a quotation name, or it might be a Gödel number. It is part of a system of names with the property that there is an algorithm by which, if I give you a structural-descriptive name of a sentence, you will be able to write down the sentence. The second blank is filled in with a sentence of the metalanguage – our own language, the language we employ while constructing the semantic theory – that is the transla-tion of the sentence named in the first blank. In case the object language is part of the metalanguage, the natural translation will be the homophonic one, the one that translates "Snow is white" from English to English as "Snow is white." The general question of what makes a translation correct is, regrettably, one that Tarski does not address.

Convention T declares a proposed definition of truth to be *adequate* if it is possible to derive all the (T)-sentences from it. (In the derivation, we are permitted to make use of the laws of syntax and of basic mathematics, as well as pure logic.) Convention T appeals to deeply held intuitions about truth. Ordinary English speakers who understand the meaning of the word "true" and who accept the proposed translation of the object language into English regard the (T)-sentences as entirely obvious. The convention uses these intuitions to full advantage. Given the syntax, the requirement that a definition of truth has to yield the (T)-sentences uniquely determines the extension of "true in $\mathcal{L}$."

On behalf of definitions that meet his criterion, Tarski makes only the rather modest claim that they are "materially" adequate. The notion of material ad-equacy adverts to a medieval distinction between real and nominal definitions. A real definition gives the essence of the thing defined, whereas a nominal defin-ition picks the thing out by some accidental property. The inevitable example is "rational animal" and "featherless biped" as real and nominal definitions of "human being." A materially adequate definition has to pick out the right thing, but it might be a mere nominal definition.

Perhaps Tarski is being too modest. If a proposed definition is adequate in the sense of Convention T, then the (T)-sentences are derivable from the definition, together with the laws of syntax and the laws of mathematics. The latter are widely thought to be necessary. It is, of course, contingent that we speak a language in which every sentence has a verb, but it doesn't follow from this that it is contingent that in English every sentence has a verb, since it is contingent that we speak English. If, indeed, the laws of syntax and of mathematics are necessary, it follows that a definition that is adequate in the sense of Convention T entails the (T)-sentences, in the technical sense of entailment, according to which φ entails ψ just in case the conjunction of φ with the negation of ψ is impossible. Thus a T-adequate definition does not merely pick out the right extension for "true in $\mathcal{L}$" in the actual world; it picks out the right extension in every possible world. In other words, it doesn't merely get the correct extension; it gets the right intension.

Under plausible metaphysical hypotheses, acceptance of Convention T requires regarding the T-sentences as necessary. It is, of course, contingent that we use words as we do, and if we had used words differently, our sentences would have had different truth conditions. If we had used "white" to refer to the things that are warm, "Snow is white" wouldn't have been true, even though snow would have still been white. This appears to conflict with the necessity of the (T)-sentences, but the appearance comes from neglecting the language-relativity of sentential truth. If English[*] is the variant of English in which "white" refers to things that are warm, then "Snow is white" translates from English[*] to English as "Snow is warm." Consequently, " 'Snow is white' is true in (actual) English iff snow is white, but "Snow is white" is true in English[*] iff snow is warm.

By emphasizing that he claimed nothing more than material adequacy for the theory he developed, Tarski perhaps invited the criticism that, while his account picks out the correct extension for "true," it doesn't give us the essence of truth. We now see that this complaint is a little misleading. If giving the essence of a concept means determining what things satisfy the concept in every possible situation, then a definition of truth in $\mathcal{L}$ that is adequate in the sense of Convention T does give the essence of truth in $\mathcal{L}$. What Tarski has failed to do is to give a theory of truth that reaches beyond one or another specific language. He has defined truth in $\mathcal{L}_1$ and truth in $\mathcal{L}_2$, but he hasn't said what truth in $\mathcal{L}_1$ and truth in $\mathcal{L}_2$ have in common. He has given a real definition of truth in this or that particular language, but he hasn't given a definition of truth.

III   Tarski's Theory of Truth

We illustrate Tarski's method with a simple example, examining a language $\mathcal{L}_0$, whose individual constants are "t" (which stands for "Theaetetus"), "s" (which stands for "Socrates"), and "p" (which stands for "Plato"); whose predicates are "B" (which stands for "is brave") and "W" (which stands for "is wise"); and whose logical operators are "∧" (which stands for "and"), "~" (which stands for "not"), and "∃" (which stands for "for some person"). The *terms* of the language are "*t*," "*s*," "*p*," and the variables "v_0," "v_1," "v_2," … The *atomic formulas* take the forms "*B*τ" and "*W*τ," where τ is a term. The *formulas* constitute the smallest class that contains the atomic formulas and contains ~φ, (φ ∧ ψ), and $(\exists v_i)$φ, for each i, whenever it contains φ and ψ. An occurrence of the variable v_i is *bound* if it occurs within some subformula that begins with $(\exists v_i)$, and free otherwise. A formula with no free variables is a *sentence*; it is sentences that are either true or false. Examples are "(*Bt* ∧ *Wt*)" ("Theaetetus is both brave and wise"), "$(\exists v_0)(Bv_0 \land Wv_0)$" ("Someone is both brave and wise"), and "$((\exists v_0)Bv_0 \land (\exists v_0)Wv_0)$" ("Someone is brave and someone is wise"). Other logical symbols, like "∀" ("for all"), "∨" ("or"), "→" ("if …, then"), and "↔" ("iff"), can defined in the usual way. $(\forall v_i)$φ $=_{Def}$ ~$(\exists v_i)$ ~ φ;(φ ∨ ψ) $=_{Def}$ ~ (~ φ∧ ~ ψ); (φ → ψ) $=_{Def}$ ~ (φ∧ ~ ψ);(φ ↔ ψ) $=_{Def}$ ((φ → ψ) ∧ (ψ → φ)).

A *variable assignment* for $\mathcal{L}_θ$ is a function that associates a person with each variable. We say that a term τ *denotes* a person P with respect to a variable assignment σ iff either τ = "*s*" and P = Socrates, or τ = "*t*" and P = Theaetetus, or τ = "*p*" and P = Plato, or τ is a variable and P = σ(τ). ("Denotes" here really means "denotes in $\mathcal{L}_θ$," and similarly "true," when we define it below, will mean "true in $\mathcal{L}_θ$"; I hope the ellipsis causes no confusion.) Now that we have explicitly defined this notion of denotation with respect to a variable assignment, we are free to utilize the notion in defining truth. Before doing so, we introduce one further auxiliary notion, *satisfaction*, which meets the following conditions:

(S1) If x satisfies y, x is a variable assignment and y is a formula.

(S2) A variable assignment σ satisfies Bτ iff, for some person P, τ denotes P with respect to σ and P is brave.

(S3) A variable assignment σ satisfies Wτ iff, for some person P, τ denotes P with respect to σ and P is wise.

(S4) A variable assignment satisfies a formula of the form (φ ∧ ψ) iff it satisfies both φ and ψ.

(S5) A variable assignment satisfies a formula of the form ~φ iff it does not satisfy φ.

(S6) A variable assignment σ satisfies a formula of the form $(\exists v_i)$φ iff there is a variable assignment that agrees with σ except possible in the value it assigns to v_i and that satisfies φ.

The motive for introducing satisfaction is compositionality. If, within our language, every person had a name, then we could give the truth conditions for sentences that begin with "$(\exists v_i)$" by stipulating that $(\exists v_i)$φ(v_i) is true iff there is a name η such that φ(η) is true. Since not every person has a name, however, we have no way of giving the truth conditions of a complex sentence in terms of the truth conditions of simpler sentences. We can, however, give the satisfaction conditions for complex formulas in terms of the satisfaction conditions of simpler formulas, so defining truth in terms of satisfaction gives us a compositional account of truth indirectly.

So far, what we have is an *implicit definition* of satisfaction. Assuming that the defining notions – "sentence," "ordered pair," "Theaetetus," "brave," and so on – are well-understood, our system of axioms uniquely determines the extension of "satisfies." We do not yet have an explicit definition, but Frege (1879) devised a technique for converting implicit to explicit definitions. It yields this:

> **Definition.** *y satisfies z* iff there there is a binary relation *S* satisfying conditions (S1) to (S6) such that <*y, z*> ∈ *S*.

If this were written out in full, the conditions (S1) to (S6) would need to be cashed out explicitly, clause by clause. For (S2), for example, we would have, "For any variable assignment σ and term τ, < σ,Bτ > ∈S iff, for some person P, τ denotes P with respect to σ and P is brave."

Frege's technique is general, but it can only be applied when the implicit definition is given by an finite system of axioms. If we were only looking for an implicit definition of truth, we could simply take the (T)-sentences as axioms, but this infinite axiom system could not be converted to an explicit definition. The compositionality of satisfaction permits a finite axiomatization that can be converted to an explicit definition.

Once we have satisfaction, we can define truth:

> **Definition.** *x is true* iff *x* is a sentence satisfied by every variable assignment.

Equivalently, we could have said "at least one variable assignment." Either way, the definition will be adequate in the sense of Convention T.

IV   The Liar Paradox

As an advance in the semantics of formalized languages, Tarski's theory was an undoubted triumph. When we attempt to apply the same methods toward the understanding of natural languages, things become much more difficult.

One source of difficulty is that the natural languages are vastly more complicated than languages purposefully designed for explicit clarity. It is hardly surprising that the techniques that succeed for simple languages will not work without modification for more complex languages. One modification that has proven especially useful is, rather than assigning to each predicate an *extension* consisting of all the individuals that (actually) satisfy the predicate, to assign each predicate an *intension*, a function that associates each possible world with the set of individuals that satisfy the predicate in that world. The resulting *possible world semantics* has proven extremely fruitful in helping us understand modal and counterfactual statements, and it shows promise as a way of understanding propositional attitude attributions. We can be sure that further modifications will be required as semantic theory advances, but there is no reason to fear that the variety and complexity of natural-language constructions pose a fundamental obstacle.

Something that does pose a fundamental obstacle is the *Liar Paradox*, which first appeared in the sixth century BC, when the Cretan poet Epimenides said that Cretans always lie. Pretending, for argument, that every other statement made by a Cretan is a bald-faced lie, we see that both the assumption that Epimenides' statement is true and the statement that Epimenides' statement is false lead to an absurd conclusion. Epimenides' version of the paradox is needlessly complicated, not only because of the pretense that no Cretan has ever told a simple truth, but also because it presumes that any statement that is not true is a lie. A clean and simple version of the paradox is obtained by considering the following *Liar Sentence*:

The Liar Sentence is not true in English.

The (T)-sentence for the Liar Sentence is this:

"The Liar Sentence is not true in English" is true in English iff the Liar Sentence is not true in English

Since, by the way we defined "the Liar Sentence":

(L=) "The Liar Sentence is not true in English" = the Liar Sentence,

we can substitute to obtain an outright contradiction:

The Liar Sentence is true in English iff the Liar Sentence is not true in English.

Consequently, the (T)-sentences for English are inconsistent with manifest fact, in particular, the fact noted by (L=).

Presenting the Liar Paradox for English involved changing English slightly, by introducing a new name. This feature of the puzzle is inessential, as we can see by observing that the sentence printed in red on page 65 of the June 1969 issue of *Scientific American* (a page of Tarski's article "Truth and Proof") is "The sentence printed in red on page 65 of the June 1969 issue of *Scientific American* is false." We would get a crisper version of the paradox if Tarski had written "not true" in place of "false," since that would thwart any attempt to evade the paradox by supposing that the sentence in red is neither true nor false. This paradox still depends on the accident that a certain sentence is printed in ink of a particular color in a particular magazine, but we can obtain a similar paradox that only depends on permanent laws of syntax, if we follow Quine (1962) (slightly modified) in considering the (T)-sentence for the following sentence:

> "Does not yield a true English sentence when appended to its own quotation" does not yield a true English sentence when appended to its own quotation.

There is no getting around it. The (T)-sentences for English cannot be consistently maintained.

Severe problems call for drastic solutions. Tarski proposes radical surgery, demanding that the semantic theory for a given object language must never be developed within the language itself, but always within a richer metalanguage. He developed this idea in the context of his work on formalized languages. It is obvious that the metalanguage in which we develop the semantic theory of $\mathcal{L}_\theta$ has to be richer in expressive power than $\mathcal{L}_\theta$, since the object language doesn't talk about sentences at all; it only talks about people, and the semantic theory has to talk about people and about sentences. One can, however, construct formal languages that can give perfectly satisfactory accounts of their own syntax. Such languages cannot, however, give accounts of their own semantics, if giving such an account includes providing a consistent theory of truth that entails all the (T)-sentences. Indeed, an object language that can describe its own syntax cannot even express an account of truth that is *consistent* with the (T)-sentences. This was proved by Tarski (1935: 247ff), applying techniques devised by Gödel (1931).

The name "English" does not have a fully determinate referent, because English usage varies somewhat from time to time and locality to locality. In particular, as science develops, it introduces new theoretical vocabulary that is not a part of present-day English. Even apart from the Liar Paradox, it would not be surprising if the semantic theory of present-day English could not be presented within present-day English, because developing the theory would require the introduction of theoretical concepts we do not currently employ. One can imagine the following scenario: The development of a theory of truth for present-day English requires the theoretical resources of an extension of present-day English that will be developed in the future, called "Future English-1." Although Future English-1 has the resources to develop the semantics of present-day English, it does not have the theoretical vocabulary required to develop the semantics of Future English-1; that ability will await a language that will evolve in the still more distant future, Future English-2. The semantics of Future English-2 cannot be formulated in Future English-2, but it can be formulated within Future English-3, and so on, until the linguistic community loses interest or is wiped out by an errant asteroid. Such an account will not give us everything we might ask for – it won't give us an account of truth in English as it is spoken in year n, for variable n – but it will give us reason to hope that the language we speak today will eventually submit itself to scientific understanding.

Unfortunately, the envisaged scenario is overly optimistic. Let me ask you to use the capitalized expression "Present-Day English" as an abbreviation for the expression you get from "English as it is spoken by residents of _____ on _____" by filling in the blanks with the name of your community and the date you are reading this. Then "true in Present-Day English" is an abbreviation of an expression of Present-Day English. If Future English-1 contains a consistent theory Γ of truth for Present-Day English that is consistent and adequate in the sense of Convention T, then the set of consequences in Present-Day English of Γ will be a consistent set of sentences of Present-Day English that includes all the (T)-sentences for Present-Day English. But such a set of sentences in impossible, because of the Liar Paradox. Not only do we not now have a consistent T-adequate theory of truth for Present-Day English, we shall never have such a theory. We shall never even have a theory of truth for Present-Day English that is consistent with the (T)-sentences for Present-Day English. If our naive conception of truth, which is governed by the (T)-schema, is at all on target, our problem is not that our future theory of truth for of Present-Day English will be vague or sketchy; we shall never have a theory of truth for Present-Day English at all. That is the thorny situation in which the Liar Paradox snares us.

The conclusion Tarski draws it that it will never be possible to develop a satisfactory theory of truth for a natural language. The best we can hope for is a semantic theory that takes account of one or another restricted fragment of a natural language. I cannot emphasize too strongly what a disappointment this conclusion is for those of us who have held out the hope that human society and human history can be taken into the fold of scientific understanding. Much of what people do will be simply unintelligible unless it is recognized that people are able to communicate with one another by meaningful speech. Now it is by no means obligatory that the meanings of human utterances be understood in terms of truth conditions, but, in the present state of our understanding, no other approach to a theory of meaning looks at all promising. Thus, to accept Tarski's restriction prohibition against applying semantic notions to natural languages is to admit that substantial aspects of human life lie forever beyond the reach of our scientific understanding.

In spite of its bitter taste, Tarski's prohibition against attempting to obtain a comprehensive semantic theory for a natural language has been nearly universally accepted. Attention has focused on trying to select the fragment of English to which semantic notions are applicable in such a way that sentences that do not appear to be implicated in the paradoxes are allowed to go about their business. The simplest policy would be to forbid semantic notions to be applied to sentences that contain the word "true" or any other semantic terms that are implicated in Liar-type paradoxes. Such a policy seems excessively restrictive, since it rules out sentences, like " " "$5 + 7 = 12$" is true' is true," that are intuitively harmlessly and unequivocally true.

Developing an idea of Whitehead and Russell (1927: ch. 2), Tarski suggested partitioning the naive notion of truth into an infinite sequence of notions. Let

English$_0$ be the fragment of English obtained by removing "true" and the other semantic terms. Let "true$_0$" be a predicate true of all and only the true sentences of English$_0$; they can be identified by taking as axioms all sentences obtained from

$$\text{``}\varphi\text{'' is true}_0 \text{ iff } \varphi$$

by replacing "φ" by a sentence of English$_0$. Let English$_1$ be English$_0$ with "true$_0$" as an added predicate, and let "true$_1$" be a predicate true of all and only the true sentences of English$_1$, identified by taking appropriate (T)-sentences as axioms. And so on. English$_{n+1}$ is obtained from English$_n$ by adding the new predicate "true$_n$," which applies to all and only the true sentence of English$_n$. If we let English$_\omega$ be the language obtained from English$_0$ by adding all the "true$_n$"'s as extra predicates, we see that English$_\omega$ is, in a certain sense, semantically closed. Every sentence is evaluated at some level, although there is no level at which every sentence is evaluated.

A language like English except that occurrences of "true" are explicitly subscripted would be, as Tarski notes, only distantly related to English. Charles Parsons (1974) and Tyler Burge (1979) have developed the idea that the indexing is tacit, the English word "true" being highly ambiguous. Contextual features resolve the ambiguity in such a way that, when we ascribe truth to an utterance of a sentence, our ascription receives a higher index than any of the occurrences of "true" within the utterance. The specifics of how to supply the indices are delicate. No syntactic rule is going to tell us what subscript to supply to "Some of the statements written on the walls of the men's room in Penn Station are true." To supply the subscript, we have to physically examine the walls of the men's room. Investigation of these specifics has led to subtle and illuminating investigations of how the content of an utterance is connected to the context in which it is produced or evaluated.

The simplest way to assign language levels, and the method closest to Tarski's original idea, would be to employ the following rather imprecise principles: A nonsemantic sentence gets level 0. An attribution of truth to an utterance is a assigned a level greater than the level assigned to the utterance. A compound sentence is assigned a level greater than or equal to the levels assigned to its components. Looking at the hierarchy from the outside, we can see that an utterance is really true or false – we identify the falsity of a sentence with the truth of its negation – if it is assigned a truth value at some level. We shouldn't regard those sentences, like the Liar Sentence, that aren't assigned a value at any level, as either true or false.

The simple method is overly timid. We can be assured that the conjunction of the Liar Sentence with "$5 + 7 = 57$" is false, because its second conjunct is false, not matter what truth value, if any, we decide to ascribe to its first conjunct. Thus, in order for a conjunction to be true$_n$, both its conjuncts have to be true$_n$ (assuming that truth is cumulative, so that anything that is true$_n$ is true$_{n+1}$), but for a conjunction to be false$_n$, it's enough that one or the other conjunct be false$_n$.

To make this idea precise, let us examine a formal language $\mathscr{L}$, with the following properties: Each of the atomic nonsemantic sentences already has a well-defined truth value, gotten in the usual way. The only semantic term in the language is the predicate "Tr." Each member of the universe of discourse is named by some term; this permits us to just talk about truth, without bringing in satisfaction. The syntax of $\mathscr{L}$ can be described within $\mathscr{L}$ itself, so that each sentence φ is named by a term $\ulcorner\varphi\urcorner$. The primitive logical symbols of $\mathscr{L}$ are "∃," "∧" and "∼."

A true atomic nonsemantic sentence is true$_\alpha$, for every α, whereas a false atomic nonsemantic sentence is false$_\alpha$, for every α (we allow infinite ordinal numbers as indices). A sentence of the form $\mathrm{Tr}(\tau)$ is true$_\alpha$ iff for some sentence φ and some $\beta < \alpha$, τ denotes φ and φ is true$_\beta$; $\mathrm{Tr}(\tau)$ is false$_\alpha$ iff either τ denotes something that isn't a sentence or, for some sentence φ and some $\beta < \alpha, \tau$ denotes φ and φ is false$_\beta$. A conjunction is true$_\alpha$ iff both its conjuncts are true$_\alpha$, and it is false$_\alpha$ iff either conjunct is false$_\alpha$. A negation is true$_\alpha$ iff its negatum is false$_\alpha$, and false$_\alpha$ iff its negatum is true$_\alpha$. An existential sentence is true$_\alpha$ iff at least one of its instances is true$_\alpha$, and it is false$_\alpha$ iff each of its instances is false$_\alpha$. If we say a sentence is *eventually true* if it is true$_\alpha$ for some α (and hence for every $\gamma > \alpha$), and *eventually false* if it is false$_\alpha$ for some α, we see that a sentence φ is eventually true iff $\mathrm{Tr}(\ulcorner\varphi\urcorner)$ is eventually true, and φ is eventually false iff $\mathrm{Tr}(\ulcorner\varphi\urcorner)$ is eventually false.

We can describe the same construction without bringing in the idea that "true" is ambiguous, by thinking of the construction as building the interpretation of a language that has a single, univocal truth predicate and that has truth-value gaps. Maintaining our assumption that every symbol of the language $\mathscr{L}$ other than "Tr" has an ordinary interpretation, we can think of an interpretation of $\mathscr{L}$ as gotten by giving a pair (E,A), where E, the *extension*, consists of those things that are definitely true, and A, the *antiextension*, consists of those things that are definitely not true. E and A cannot overlap, but they need not exhaust the universe, since there may be sentences for which there is no fact of the matter whether the sentence is true.

We specify what it is for a sentence to be true or false with respect to (E,A) by induction, following Kleene (1952: sec.54). An atomic nonsemantic sentence is true with respect to (E,A) iff it's true, and false with respect to (E,A) iff it's false; truth and falsity conditions for atomic nonsemantic sentences are presumed given. $\mathrm{Tr}(\tau)$ is true with respect to (E,A) iff τ denotes an element of E, and $\mathrm{Tr}(\tau)$ is false with respect to (E,A) iff τ denotes an element of A. A conjunction is true with respect to (E,A) iff both conjuncts are true with respect to (E,A), and it's false with respect to (E,A) iff one or both conjuncts are false with respect to (E,A). A negation is true with respect to (E,A) iff its negatum is false with respect to (E,A), and false with respect to (E,A) iff its negatum is true with respect to (E,A). An existential sentence is true with respect to (E,A) iff at least one of its instances is true with respect to (E,A), and an existential sentence is false with respect to (E,A) iff all its instances are false with respect to (E,A). These are just the ordinary truth and falsity conditions from classical semantics.

An ordinary classical model is what we get in case E and A together to exhaust the universe. With respect to such models, every sentence is either true or false. If E and A do not exhaust the universe, there will be sentences that are neither true nor false, although there will be no sentences that are both true and false. There is no way to find a classical model (E,A) with E equal to the set of sentences true with respect to (E,A) and A equal to the union of the set of nonsentences with the set of sentences false with respect to (E,A). This is because of the Liar Sentence, which was constructed in such a way that it is true with respect to (E,A) iff it is not an element of E.

Once we allow truth-value gaps, the situation changes drastically. If we let E equal the set of sentences that are eventually true and A equal the set consisting of the nonsentences together with the set of sentences that are eventually false, we find that $E =$ the set of sentences true with respect to (E,A) and $A = \{\text{nonsentences}\} \bigcup \{\text{sentences false with respect to } (E,A)\}$. A pair (E,A) with this property is called a *fixed point*, and the fundamental theorem of Kripke (1975) (which was obtained independently by Martin and Woodruff (1975)) is that there are fixed points.

Kripke's construction does a remarkably good job at assigning intuitively satisfying truth values to sentences with convoluted self-reference, sentences that just skirt the edge of paradox. However, our method for handling truth-value gaps yields a pathologically weak logic that has a hard time dealing with even very simple generalizations, so that even such an apparently harmless generalization as "Every true sentence is a true sentence" – in symbols, $(\forall \nu_0)(\text{Tr}(\nu_0) \rightarrow \text{Tr}(\nu_0))$ – is exiled to the gap between truth and falsity.

There are versions of Kripke's construction that avoid this defect by upholding classical logic. Thus, we can take the sentences true with respect to (E,A) to be those true in every classical model obtained by taking the extension of "Tr" to be a set that includes E and is disjoint from A. The price we pay is compositionality; $(\varphi \vee \psi)$ can be true without either φ or ψ being true.

The basic idea that motivates the Kripke construction, in whichever version, is that there are sentences that are neither true nor false, and, in particular, the Liar Sentence is neither true nor false. These are claims that can be stated within the language $\mathscr{L}$. There are not, however, statements that can be recognized as true within the language $\mathscr{L}$. The language $\mathscr{L}$ leaves them in the gap between truth and falsity. That there are truth-valueless sentences, the Liar Sentence among them, is something that can only be seen from the outside, from the perspective of a richer metalanguage. Tarski's fundamental prescription, always to develop the semantics of a language from within a richer metalanguage, is dutifully obeyed.

A great many other programs for capturing linguistic intuitions while observing Tarski's fundamental prescription have been explored. The *revision theory* of Herzberger (1982), Gupta (1982), and Gupta and Belnap (1993) is particularly prominent. According to it, the semantic value of the predicate "true" is not given by a classificatory principle that divides sentences into true and untrue, but rather by a principle that shows us how to take a given candidate for the extension of "true" and improve upon it. Namely, if E is our given candidate, the improved candidate is {sentences true in the classical model in which the extension of "Tr" is taken to be E}. The characteristic feature of the paradoxical sentences is that they ensure that we never settle upon an ideal candidate. The search for the perfect extension continues endlessly – there is provision for extending the construction into the transfinite – with each iteration yielding a candidate that is in some ways superior to the candidate that came before. An elegant mathematical development yields an illuminating classification of sentences into those that are eventually true, whatever the starting point; those that are eventually true from some starting points and eventually false from other starting points; those that are eventually true from some starting points and eventually unsettled from other starting points; and so on. But this classification can only be seen from the vantage point of a richer metalanguage.

A hardy minority have advocated resisting the prohibition against development of the semantics for a language within that very language, and avoiding inconsistency by restricting schema (T). Such a program is threatened by the prospect that the (T)-schema is so deeply entrenched in our understanding of the notion of truth as to be constitutive of the meaning of the word "true," so that any theory that restricted the (T)-schema wouldn't be a theory of truth at all, merely a misuse of the word "true." To respond to this objection, it is necessary systematically to maintain enough (T)-sentences to ensure that we still are working with a recognizable notion of truth. One version of this response has it that, while φ and $\ulcorner\ulcorner\varphi\urcorner$ is true$\urcorner$ are not intersubstitutable, they are equi-assertible and equi-deniable. That is, we have rules of inference that permit us to infer $\ulcorner\ulcorner\varphi\urcorner$ is true$\urcorner$ from φ, and *vice versa*, and to infer $\ulcorner\ulcorner\varphi\urcorner$ is not true$\urcorner$ from $\sim\varphi$, and *vice versa*. These rules can be legitimately applied within direct proofs, but they cannot be employed within conditional proofs or proofs by *reductio ad absurdum*. If they could, we could assume φ, infer $\ulcorner\ulcorner\varphi\urcorner$ is true$\urcorner$, then discharge to derive $\ulcorner\varphi \rightarrow \ulcorner\varphi\urcorner$ is true$\urcorner$, then do the same thing in the other direction to derive the (T)-sentence. That the rules don't yield a contradiction when they are allowed to operate only within direct proofs can be demonstrated using the classical-logic version of Kripke's fixed-point theorem; see McGee (1991).

To complete the program, it is not enough to show that a there is a way to utilize the phrase "true in English" in English in a manner that is consistent. We must show that the phrase can be utilized in a manner that is consistent and useful. We must demonstrate that the restrictions needed to avoid antinomy are not so severe as to prevent the notion of truth from fulfilling our legitimate practical and theoretical needs. This hasn't been done yet.

V   Disquotation and Correspondence

Before Tarski's work, the notion of truth was regarded with grave suspicion, particularly by the logical positivists, who regarded the supposed connection between language and the world that makes true sentences true as the sort of quasi-mystical association that a scientific philosophy ought to eschew. Legend has it that Otto Neurath, the dean of the Vienna Circle, put "truth" on an index of forbidden words. Syntactically defined notions, like derivability in a formal system, were scientifically respectable, but semantic notions, like truth and denotation, were outlawed.

After Tarski, such complaints disappeared. Tarski explicitly defined truth and denotation in terms of syntactic and mathematical notions, and anything defined in terms of scientifically reputable notions is scientifically reputable.

Hartry Field (1972) revived the positivist complaints, arguing that Tarski had not done enough to put semantics on a scientifically secure footing. Field's objection focussed on the structure of Tarski's definition. The language $\mathcal{L}_\theta$ contains three individual constants, and the definition of denotation contains a separate clause for each of them. Had there been more constants, there would have been more clauses. Basically, the denotation conditions for constants are given by providing a list that associates a person with each name, without giving any reason why "p" is associated with Plato rather than Pythagoras. Similarly, the satisfaction conditions for atomic formulas are given by a list, with one item for each predicate. The situation would be the same if, in place of the formal language, we used Tarski's methods to obtain a semantic theory for a fragment of English that has been regimented so as to avoid the Liar Paradox.

Merely supplying a list is inadequate, Field argues, for reducing a specialized science to a more fundamental one. The example he uses is valence. We wouldn't pride ourselves on having successfully reduced chemistry to physics if all we had to say about the valences of elements was to give a list that associated a number with each element. A satisfactory reduction wasn't available until valence was explained in terms of the structure of electron shells.

There aren't irreducible, brute facts about meaning that obtain independently of human thought and action. The semantic facts are somehow or other reducible to the nonsemantic facts. Tarski's theory does not provide a satisfactory reduction, Field argues, because the semantic values of the simple terms are given merely by supplying a list. It's not that enumerative definitions are never acceptable; an alphabetical listing is an unexceptionable method of specifying the function taking a person to her telephone number. For key theoretical concepts, however, one wants more than an apparently arbitrary roster. Field suggests supplementing Tarski's account with a causal theory of reference, explaining how simple terms get their semantic values by describing the causal connection between the terms and the things they refer to, as a way of putting the theory of truth on a physicalistically secure footing.

Field argues that, unsupplemented, Tarski's theory is inadequate to the needs of physicalism, but his basic point doesn't require a physicalist premiss. The basic point will hold even for someone who thinks that there are irreducible mental facts or who is suspicious of reductions altogether. The premiss Field really needs was already expressed by Aristotle (*Metaphysics* A). The mark of scientific knowledge is that it allows one not merely to say how things are, but to explain why things are as they are. Tarski hasn't given us an explanation.

The crucial presupposition here is that truth plays a role as a key theoretical concept. An alternative view treats the notion of truth as a mere logical device for simulating infinitary logical operators. If I tell you "Everything the Pope says is true," I have, in effect conveyed the conjunction of infinitely many sentences of the form "If the Pope says that φ, then φ." Quine (1986: 10ff), calls this way of thinking the "disquotational" conception of truth. Appending the words "is true" to a quotation name of an English sentence cancels the effect of the quotation marks.

Disquotational truth is useful not only for communicative needs, as a way of endorsing other people's judgments *en masse*, but also for deliberative purposes. To illustrate, consider Peano Arithmetic, a powerful axiomatic system for number theory consisting of a small collection of familiar facts from elementary school and infinitely many *induction axioms*, obtained by substituting arithmetical formulas into the *induction axiom schema*:

$$(\varphi(0) \vee .(\forall \nu_0)(\varphi(\nu_0) \to \varphi(\nu_0 + 1))) \to .(\forall \nu_0)\varphi(\nu_0).$$

PA contains infinitely many axioms. For each finitely axiomatized subsystem of PA, one can prove in PA that the subsystem is consistent, but we cannot prove in PA that all of PA is consistent; this is Gödel's (1931) second incompleteness theorem. We can add a new predicate "Tr" to the language of arithmetic, and we can use this predicate to construct a finitely axiomatized theory of truth for the language of arithmetic that is adequate in the sense of Convention T. (Because every number is named by a numeral, we don't need to bring in satisfaction.) Introducing the truth theory is a cognitive free lunch, inasmuch as Volker Halbach (1999) has shown that it is provable in PA that every purely arithmetical sentence that we can prove with the aid of the truth predicate can already be proved without it. Once we have the truth predicate, we can write down a single sentence that says that all the axioms of (original) PA are true; in effect, we form the conjunction of infinitely many axioms. Not only can we write such a sentence, we can prove it, though we can't prove it in PA. Our reason for accepting the induction axioms is that we think they are ensured by the nature of the natural numbers. Our willingness to accept them does not depend on limitations of the expressive power of the language of arithmetic. Indeed, anyone who understands how the natural numbers work will be willing to accept any instance of the induction axiom schema formulated within any language she understands (once we make it explicit that quantification in the schema is over numbers). In particular, we are willing to extend PA by allowing the predicate "Tr" to appear within induction axioms. In this expanded theory, we can prove that all the axioms of PA are true, from which we can immediately derive that PA is consistent; and we can derive lots of other useful arithmetical facts as well.

The disquotational conception of truth, which thinks of the notion of truth as a logical device, is contrasted with the view that notion of truth values and truth conditions play a vital theoretical role in causal historical explanations of human communications; see Field (1986) and David (1994). The latter way of thinking has come to be called the "correspondence conception," in recollection of the doctrine that truth is correspondence to a fact. This doctrine has not proved terribly successful. Even if one is willing to agree that, in addition to the person Theaetetus and the act of flying, there is a third thing, the fact that Theaetetus does not fly, in virtue of which "Theaetetus does not fly" is true, the correspondence relation between sentences and facts has resisted successful illumination.

The name "correspondence conception" is well entrenched, but it is misleading. Field's program of supplementing Tarski's account with a causal theory of reference counts as a correspondence theory – it postulates a robust, causally explanatory connection between the activities of a community of speakers and the truth conditions of sentences – yet it says nothing about a semantics of correspondence or an ontology of facts. On the other hand, a disquotationalist could accept the slogan "Truth is correspondence to the facts" because she takes the same deflationary attitude toward facts as toward truth, regarding "Snow is white," " 'Snow is white' is true," and "It is a fact that snow is white" as three ways of saying the same thing.

The central battleground of the conflict between the two conceptions of truth is semantically defective sentences, such as borderline attributions of vague terms. English usage of the word "bald" does not determine a sharp partition between those who satisfy "bald" and those who satisfy "not bald" (or so it is natural to suppose, although Williamson (1994) disputes this). According to the inaptly named correspondence conception, in order for "Harry is bald" to be true, English usage, together with the configuration of hairs on Harry's head, has to make it true. Similarly, for the sentence to be false, English usage and the configuration of hairs have to make it false. If Harry is right on the border, then the relevant facts don't settle the issue whether Harry is bald, and so, according to the correspondence conception, "Harry is bald" is neither true nor false.

The disquotationalist sees things differently. For her, the meaning of the word "true" (or "true in English," really, but we're suppressing the "in English") guarantees the truth of this:

"Harry is bald" is true iff Harry is bald.

The definition of falsity as truth of the negation gives us this:

"Harry is bald" is false iff Harry is not bald.

These two biconditionals imply (not only in classical logic, but in the very weak logic of truth-value gaps we discussed when we talked about Kripke):

"Harry is bald" is either true or false.

Thus, whereas the correspondence theorist will want to say that vague terms sometimes yield meaningful sentences that lack truth values, the disquotationalist is resolutely committed to bivalence, the principle that every meaningful statement is either true or false.

Other purported examples of semantically defective sentences include moral and aesthetic judgments, for emotivists, who think that such judgments merely report the speaker's emotional responses, rather than report moral facts; conditionals with false antecedents, on some theories of conditionals (English conditionals, that is, not the formal-language "→"); and sentences implicated in Liar-type paradoxes.

The two conceptions of truth have different attitudes toward the Liar Paradox. For the disquotationalist, the constraint that the notion of truth can only be applied to a restricted fragment of English means that we cannot form infinitary conjunctions and disjunctions quite as freely as we would have hoped. An inconvenience, no doubt, but hardly a cause for bewilderment.

The correspondence theorist depends on the notions of truth values and truth conditions to understand how human language works, so that accepting the object-language/metalanguage restriction means leaving parts of human language beyond the reach of human understanding. It is not immediately obvious, however, that the pressure to accept the restriction is as severe for the correspondence theorist as for the disquotationalist. The motivation for the restriction is that, if we ignore the restriction, we can no longer uphold the (T)-sentences. But the correspondence theorist doesn't want to uphold the (T)-sentences, since the (T)-sentences imply bivalence, which the correspondence theorist repudiates. Relieved of the pressure of the (T)-schema, can the correspondence theorist live comfortably with the Liar Paradox?

Unfortunately, no, on account of Montague's (1963) Paradox. The right-to-left direction of schema (T) yields unwanted bivalence, but the correspondence theorist still wants to uphold the left-to-right direction. Putting the Liar Sentence into the schema yields:

If "The Liar Sentence is not true" is true, then the Liar Sentence is not true. Applying (L=), we obtain

If the Liar Sentence is true, then the Liar Sentence is not true.

Consequently

The Liar Sentence is not true.

Now we recognize that we have derived this conclusion from true premisses, and things we derive from true premisses are, presumably, true. Consequently,

"The Liar Sentence is not true" is true

Using (L=) again, we derive

The Liar Sentence is true.

A contradiction, alas. I don't know of any truly adequate response to this paradox, and without such a response, it is hard to envisage how a satisfactory theory of communication by natural language is possible.

Bibliography

Abney, S. (1987). The English noun phrase in its sentential aspect. Ph.D. dissertation: MIT.

Ackerman, D. (1979). Proper names, propositional attitudes and non-descriptive connotations. *Philosophical Studies*, 35, 55–69.

Adams, E. (1965). On the logic of conditionals. *Inquiry*, 8, 166–97.

Adams, E. (1975). *The logic of conditionals*, Dordrecht: Reidel.

Almog, J., Perry, J., and Wettstein, H. (eds.) (1989). *Themes from Kaplan*. New York: Oxford University Press.

Alston, W. (1964). *Philosophy of language*. Englewood Cliffs, N.J.: Prentice-Hall.

Anscombe, G.E. (1957). *Intention*. Oxford: Blackwell.

Anscombe, G.E. (1975). The first person. In S. Guttenplan (ed.), *Mind and language*. Oxford: Clarendon Press.

Aristotle (1984). *The complete works of Aristotle* (2 vols). J. Barnes (ed.), Princeton, New Jersey: Princeton University Press.

Austin, J. (1962). *How to do things with words*. Oxford: Oxford University Press.

Ayer, A. (1936). *Language, truth and logic*. London: Gollancz.

Azzouni, J. (2001). Truth via anaphorically unrestricted quantifiers. *Journal of Philosophical Logic*, 30, 329–54.

Bach, E. (1970). Problominalization. *Linguistic Inquiry*, 1, 121–2.

Bach, E. (1989). *Informal lectures on formal semantics*. Albany: State University of New York Press.

Bach, K. (1987). On communicative intentions: A reply to Recanati. *Mind and Language*, 2, 141–54.

Bach, K. (1987). *Thought and reference*. Oxford: Clarendon Press.

Bach, K. (1994). Conversational impliciture. *Mind and Language*, 9, 124–62.

Bach, K. (1995). Standardization vs. conventionalization. *Linguistics and Philosophy*, 18, 677–86.

Bach, K. (1999a). The semantics–pragmatics distinction: What it is and why it matters. In K. Turner (ed.), *The semantics–pragmatics interface from different points of view*. Oxford: Elsevier, 65–84.

Bach, K. (1999b). The myth of conventional implicature. *Linguistics and Philosophy*, 22, 327–66.

Bach, K. (2000). Quantification, qualification, and context: A reply to Stanley and Szabo. *Mind and Language*, 15, 262–83.

Bach, K. (2001). You don't say?. *Synthese*, 125, 11–31.

Bach, K. (2004). Descriptions: Points of reference. In A. Bezuidenhout and M. Reimer (eds.), *Descriptions and beyond*. Oxford: Clarendon Press, 189–229.

Bach, K. and Harnish, R. (1979). *Linguistic communication and speech acts*. Cambridge, Mass.: MIT Press.

Bach, K. and Harnish, R. (1992). How performatives really work: A reply to Searle. *Linguistics and Philosophy*, 15, 93–110.

Bach, K. and Perry, J. (1983). *Situations and attitudes*. Cambridge, Mass.: MIT Press.

Baker, L. (1991). Has content been naturalized.? In B. Loewer and G. Rey (eds.), *Meaning in mind: Fodor and his critics*. Oxford: Blackwell, 17–32.

Baker, M. (2001). *The atoms of language*. Oxford: Oxford University Press.

Barker, S. (2000). Is value content a component of conventional implicature. *Analysis*, 60, 268–79.

Bar-On, D. and Long, D. (2001). Avowals and first person privilege. *Philosophy and Phenomenological Research*, 62, 311–35.

Barwise, J. and Cooper, R. (1981). Generalized quantifiers and natural language. *Linguistics and Philosophy*, 4, 159–219.

Barwise, J. and Perry, J. (1983). *Situations and attitudes*. Cambridge, Mass.: MIT Press.

Beardsley, M. (1962). Metaphorical twist. *Philosophy and Phenomenological Research*, 22, 293–307.

Beardsley, M. (1978). Metaphorical senses. *Noûs*, 12, 3–16.

Benthem, J. and ter Meulen, A. (eds.) (1997). *Handbook of logic and language*. Amsterdam: Elsevier/MIT Press.

Berg, J. (1988). Metaphor, meaning, and interpretation. *Journal of Pragmatics*, 12, 695–709.

Bergmann, M. (1982). Metaphorical assertions. *Philosophical Review*, 91, 229–42.

Berkeley, G. (1710). *A treatise concerning the principles of human knowledge*.

Bezuidenhout, A. (2001). Metaphor and what is said: A defense of a direct expression view of metaphor. In P.A. French and H.K. Wettstein (eds.), *Midwest studies in philosophy*, vol. 25: *Figurative language*. Boston, Mass. and Oxford, UK: Blackwell, 156–86.

Binkley, T. (1976). On the truth and probity of metaphor. *Journal of Aesthetics and Art Criticism*, 33, 171–80.

Black, M. (1962). Metaphor. In M. Black, *Models and metaphors*. Ithaca, N.Y.: Cornell University Press, 25–47.

Black, M. (1993). More about metaphor. In A. Ortony (ed.), *Metaphor and thought*. Second edition. Cambridge: Cambridge University Press, 19–41.

Bjornsson, G. (2001). Why emotivists love inconsistency. *Philosophical Studies*, 104, 81–108.

Blackburn, S. (1984a). *Spreading the word*. Oxford: Oxford University Press.

Blackburn, S. (1984b). The individual strikes back. *Synthese*, 58, 281–301.

Blackburn, S. (1988). Attitudes and contents. *Ethics*, 98, 501–17.

Blackburn, S. (1990). Hume and thick connection. *Essays in quasi realism*. New York: Oxford University Press.

Blackburn, S. (1992). Gibbard on normative logic. *Philosophy and Phenomenological Research*, 52, 947–52.

Blackburn, S. (1993a). Realism, quasi or queasy. In J. Haldane and C. Wright (eds.), *Reality, representation, and projection*. Oxford: Oxford University Press.

Blackburn, S. (1993b). *Essays in quasi realism*. New York: Oxford University Press.

Blackburn, S. (1998). Realism and truth: Wittgenstein, Wright, Rorty, and minimalism. *Mind*, 107, 157–81.

Blackburn, S. (2002). Replies. *Philosophy and Phenomenological Research*, 65, 165–77.

Blackburn, S. (2003). Expressivism not fictionalism. In M. Kalderon (ed.), *Fictionalist approaches to metaphysics*. Oxford: Oxford University Press.

Block, N. (1986). Advertisement for a semantics for psychology. In S.P. Stich and E.A. Warfield (eds.), *Mental representation: A reader*. Oxford: Blackwell.

Block, N. (1994–5). An argument for holism. *Proceedings of the Aristotelian Society*, 95, 151–69.

Boër, S. and Lycan, W. (1976). *The myth of semantic presupposition*. Bloomington, Ind.: Indiana Linguistics Club.

Boghossian, P. (1989). The rule following considerations. *Mind*, 98, 392, 507–50.

Boghossian, P. (1990). The status of content. *Philosophical Review*, 99, 157–84.

Boghossian, P. (1991). Naturalizing Content. In B. Loewer and G. Rey (eds.), *Meaning in mind: Fodor and his critics*. Oxford: Blackwell, 65–86.

Boghossian, P. (1994). The transparency of mental content. *Philosophical Perspectives*, 8, 33–50.

Boghossian, P. (1996). Analyticity reconsidered. *Noûs*, 30(3), 360–91.

Boghossian, P. (1997). Analyticity. In B. Hale and C. Wright (eds.), *A companion to the philosophy of language*. Oxford: Basil Blackwell, 331–68.

Boorse, C. (1976). Wright on functions. *Philosophical Review*, 85, 70–86.

Boyd, R. (1993). Metaphor and theory change: What is "metaphor" a metaphor for? In A. Ortony (ed.), *Metaphor and thought*. Second edition. Cambridge: Cambridge University Press, 481–532.

Braddon-Mitchell, D. and Jackson, F. (1997). The teleological theory of content. *Australasian Journal of Philosophy*, 75, 474–89.

Brandom, R. (1994). *Making it explicit*. Cambridge, Mass.: Harvard University Press.

Brandom, R. (1996). The significance of complex numbers for Frege's philosophy of mathematics. *Proceedings of the Aristotelian Society*, 293–315.

Brandom, R. (2000). *Articulating reasons*. Cambridge, Mass.: Harvard University Press.

Braun, D. (2000). Russellianism and psychological generalizations. *Noûs*, 34, 203–36.

Braun, D. (2001). Russellianism and explanation. *Philosophical Perspectives*, 15, 253–89.

Brighouse, M. (1990). Blackburn's projectivism: An objection. *Philosophical Studies*, 59, 225–33.

Brown, M. (1992). On denoting updated. *Acta Analytica*, 8, 7–32.

Burch, Robert W. (2001). Charles Sanders Peirce. *The Stanford Encyclopedia of Philosophy*. http://plato.stanford.ed.u/archives/fall2001/entries/peirce/.

Burge, T. (1979a). Individualism and the mental. In P.A. French, T.E. Ueling, and H.K. Wettstein (eds.), *Midwest studies in philosophy*, vol. 4. Minneapolis: University of Minnesota Press, 73–122.

Burge, T. (1979b). Sinning against Frege. *Philosophical Review*, 88, 3, 398–432.

Burge, T. (1979c). Semantical paradox. *Journal of Philosophy*, 76, 169–98.

Burge, T. (1980). Truth and singular terms. In M. Platts (ed.), *Reference, truth and reality: Essays on the philosophy of language*. London: Routledge & Keegan Paul, 167–81.

Buzkowski, W., Marciszewski, W., and van Benthem, J. (eds.) (1988). *Categorial grammar*. Amsterdam: John Benjamins.

Cann, R. (1993). *Formal semantics*. Cambridge: Cambridge University Press.

Cappellen, H. and Lepore, E. (1997). On an alleged connection between indirect speech and the theory of meaning. *Mind and Language*, 12, 278–96.

Cappellen, H. and Lepore, E. (1998). Reply to Richard and Reimer. *Mind and Language*, 13, 617–21.

Cardinaletti, A. (1994). On the internal structure of pronominal DPs. *Linguistic Review*, 11, 195–219.

Carnap, R. (1947). *Meaning and necessity*. Chicago: University of Chicago Press.

Carnap, R. (1952). Meaning postulates. *Philosophical Studies*. Reprinted in *Meaning and necessity: A study in semantics and modal logic*. Chicago: University of Chicago Press.

Carnap, R. (1956). *Meaning and necessity: A study in semantics and modal logic*. Chicago and London: University of Chicago Press.

Carnap, R. [1928] (1967). *The logical structure of the world*. Trans. R.A. George. Berkeley: University of California Press.

Carroll, L. (1895). What the tortoise said to Achilles. *Mind*, 4, 278–80.

Carroll, N. (1994). Visual metaphor. In J. Hintikka (ed.), *Aspects of metaphor*. Dordrecht: Kluwer Academic Publishers, 189–218.

Carston, R. (1988). Implicature, explicature, and truth-theoretic semantics. In Ruth Kempson (ed.), *Mental representations: The interface between language and reality*. Cambridge: Cambridge University Press, 155–81

Carston, R. (2002). *Thoughts and utterances*. Oxford: Blackwell.

Cartwright, R. (1987). The origins of Russell's Theory of Descriptions. In *Philosophical essays*. Cambridge, Mass.: MIT Press, 95–133.

Cartwright, R. (2005). Propositional functions. *Mind* (Centenary issue on Russell's theory of descriptions, Stephen Neale (ed.). forthcoming.)

Castañeda, H.-N. (1966). He*: A study in the logic of self-consciousness. *Ratio*, 8, 130–57.

Castañeda, H.-N. (1967). Indicators and quasi-indicators. *American Philosophical Quarterly*, 4, 85–100.

Castañeda, H.-N. (1968). On the logic of attributions of self-knowledge to others. *Journal of Philosophy*, 65, 439–56.

Cavell, S. (1967). Aesthetic problems of modern philosophy. In M. Black (ed.), *Philosophy in America*. Ithaca: Cornell University Press, 74–97.

Chalmers, D. (2002). The components of content. *Philosophy of mind: Classical and contemporary readings*. Oxford: Oxford University Press.

Chastain, C. (1975). Reference and context. In K. Gunderson (ed.), *Minnesota studies in the philosophy of science*, vol. 7: *Language, mind and knowledge*. Minneapolis: University of Minnesota Press.

Chierchia, G. (1990). Anaphora and attitudes de se. In R. Bartsch et al. (eds.), *Language in action*. Dordrecht: Foris, 1–31.

Chierchia, G. (1996). *Dynamics of meaning, anaphora, presuppositions, and the theory of grammar*. Chicago: University of Chicago Press.

Chierchia, G. and McConnell-Ginet, S. (1990). *Meaning and grammar: An introduction to semantics*. Cambridge, Mass. and London: MIT Press.

Chomsky, N. (1964). *Current issues in linguistic theory*. The Hague: Mouton.

Chomsky, N. (1965). *Aspects of the theory of syntax*. Cambridge, Mass.: MIT Press.

Chomsky, N. (1969). Quine's empirical assumptions. In D. Davidson and J. Hintikka (eds.), *Words and objections*. Dordrecht: Reidel.

Chomsky, N. (1973). Conditions on transformations. In S. Anderson and P. Kiparsky (eds.), *A Festschrift for Morris Halle*. New York: Holt, Rinehart & Winston, 232–86.

Chomsky, N. (1975). *Reflections on language*. New York: Pantheon.

Chomsky, N. (1976). Conditions on rules of grammar. *Linguistic Analysis*, 2, 303–51.

Chomsky, N. (1977). On WH-movement. In P. Culicover, T. Wasow, and A. Akmajian (eds.), *Formal syntax*. New York: Academic Press, 71–132.

Chomsky, N. (1980). *Rules and representations*. New York: Columbia University Press.

Chomsky, N. (1981). *Lectures on government and binding*. Dordrecht: Foris.

Chomsky, N. (1986). *Knowledge of language: Its nature, origin, and use*. New York: Praeger.

Chomsky, N. (1987). Reply to review discussion of *Knowledge of language*. *Mind and language*, 2, 178–97.

Chomsky, N. (1995). *The minimalist program*. Cambridge, Mass.: MIT Press.

Chomsky, N. (2000). *New horizons in the study of language and mind*. Cambridge: Cambridge University Press.

Chomsky, N. (2002). *On nature and language*. Cambridge: Cambridge University Press.

Church, A. (1956). *Introduction to mathematical logic*, vol. 1. Princeton: Princeton University Press.

Churchland, P. (1981). Eliminativist materialism and the propositional attitudes. *Journal of Philosophy*, 78, 67–90.

Clements, G. (1975). The logophoric pronoun in Ewe. *Journal of West African Languages*, 10, 141–77.

Cohen, L. (1971). Some remarks on Grice's views about the logical particles of natural language. In Y. Bar-Hillel (ed.), *Pragmatics of natural language*. Dordrecht: Reidel, 50–68.

Cohen, L. (1993). The semantics of metaphor. In A. Ortony (ed.), *Metaphor and thought*. Second edition. Cambridge: Cambridge University Press, 58–70.

Cohen, L. and Margalit, A. (1972). The role of inductive reasoning in the interpretation of metaphor. In D. Davidson and G. Harman (eds.), *Semantics of natural language*. Dordrecht: Reidel, 721–62

Cohen, T. (1975). Figurative language and figurative acts. *Journal of Philosophy*, 72, 669–90.

Cohen, T. (1976). Notes on metaphor. *Journal of Aesthetics and Art Criticism*, 34, 249–59.

Cohen, T. (1978). Metaphor and the cultivation of intimacy. *Critical Inquiry*, 5, 3–12.

Cohen, T. (1990). Figurative incompetence. *Raritan*, 10, 30–44.

Cohen, T. (forthcoming). Metaphor. In J. Levinson (ed.), *Oxford handbook of aesthetics*. Oxford: Oxford University Press.

Cole, P., Hermon, G., Huang, G., and Huang, C. (eds.) (2000). *Syntax and semantics*, vol. 33: *Long-distance reflexives*. San Diego, Calif.: Academic Press.

Cooper, D. (1986). *Metaphor*. Oxford: Oxford University Press.

Cooper, R. (1979). The interpretation of pronouns. In F. Heny and H. Schnelle (eds.), *Syntax and semantics*, vol. 10: *Selections from the third Gröningen Round Table*. New York: Academic Press, 61–92.

Crane, T. (1991). All the difference in the world. *Philosophical Quarterly*, 41, 1–25.

Cresswell, M. (1973). *Logics and languages*. London: Methuen.

Cresswell, M. (1976). The semantics of degree. In B.H. Partee (ed.), *Montague grammar*. New York: Academic Press, 261–92.

Cresswell, M. (1978). Semantic competence. In F. Guenthner and M. Guenthner-Reutter (eds.), *Meaning and translation*. London: Duckworth, 9–43.

Cresswell, M. (1985). *Adverbial modification*. Dordrecht, Reidel.

Cresswell, M. (1994). *Language in the world*. Cambridge: Cambridge University Press.

Cresswell, M. (1996). *Semantic indexicality*. Dordrecht: Kluwer.

Cresswell, M. (2002a). Why propositions have no structure. *Noûs*, 36, 643–62.

Cresswell, M. (2002b). Static semantics for dynamic discourse. *Linguistics and Philosophy*, 25, 545–71.

Crimmins, M. (1992). *Talk about beliefs*. Cambridge, Mass.: MIT Press.

Crimmins, M. (1998). Hesperus and Phosphorus: Sense, pretense, and reference. *Philosophical Review*, 107, 1–47.

Crimmins, M. and Perry, J. (1989). The prince and the phone booth: reporting puzzling beliefs. *Journal of Philosophy*, 86, 685–711.

Culicover, P. (1976). A constraint on co-referentiality. *Foundations of Language*, 14, 109–18.

D'Arms, J. and Jacobson, D. (1994). Expressivism, morality and the emotions. *Ethics*, 104, 739–65.

Danto, A. (1978). Freudian explanations and the language of the unconscious. In J.H. Smith (ed.), *Psychoanalysis and language*. New Haven, Conn.: Yale University Press, 325–53.

Darwall, S. (2000). Naturalism and projection in Hobbes's *Leviathan*. *Philosophical Review*, 109, 313–47.

Darwall, S., Gibbard, A., and Railton, P. (1997). *Moral discourse and practice*. New York: Oxford University Press.

David, M. (1994). *Correspondence and disquotation*. New York: Oxford University Press.

Davidson, D. (1967a). Truth and meaning. *Synthese*, 17, 304–23.

Davidson, D. (1967b). The logical form of action sentences. In N. Rescher (ed.), *The logic of decision and action*. Pittsburgh: University of Pittsburgh Press, 81–95.

Davidson, D. (1976). Reply to Foster. In G. Evans and J. McDowell (eds.), *Truth and meaning: Essays in semantics*. Oxford: Clarendon Press, 33–41.

Davidson, D. (1978). What metaphors mean. *Critical Inquiry*, 5, 31–48.

Davidson, D. (1984). *Inquiries into truth and interpretation*. Oxford: Clarendon Press.

Davidson, D. (1986). A nice derangement of epitaphs. In E. LePore (ed.), *Truth and interpretation: Perspectives on the philosophy of Donald Davidson*. Oxford: Blackwell, 433–46.

Davidson, D. (1999). Reply to Gabriel Segal. In U.M. Zeglen (ed.), *Donald Davidson: Truth, meaning and knowledge*. London and New York: Routledge, 57–8.

Davies, M. (1981). *Meaning, quantification, necessity: Themes in philosophical logic*. London: Routledge & Kegan Paul.

Davies, M. (1982). Idiom and metaphor. *Proceedings of the Aristotelian Society*, 83, 67–85.

Davies, M. (1987). Tacit knowledge and semantic theory: Can a five percent difference matter? *Mind*, 96, 441–62.

Davis, S. (ed.) (1991). *Pragmatics: A reader*. Oxford: Oxford University Press.

De Gaynesford, M. (1995). Shades of realism. *Philosophical Books*, 36, 1–9.

Denham, A. (1998). Metaphor and judgments of experience. In R. Casati and C. Tappolet (eds.), *European Review of Philosophy*, vol. 3. Stanford: CSLI Publications, 225–53.

Dennett, D. (1969). *Content and consciousness*. London: Routledge & Kegan Paul.

Dennett, D. (1987). *The intentional stance*. Cambridge, Mass.: MIT Press.

Dennett, D. (1995). *Darwin's dangerous idea*. New York: Simon & Schuster.

Deutsch, H. (1993). Semantics for natural kind terms. *Canadian Journal of Philosophy*, 23, 389–412.

Devitt, M. (1981a). *Designation*. New York: Columbia University Press.

Devitt, M. (1981b). Donnellan's distinction. *Midwest studies in philosophy*, 6, 511–24.

Devitt, M. (1989). Against direct reference. *Midwest studies in philosophy*, 14, 206–40.

Devitt, M. (1996). *Coming to our senses*. Cambridge: Cambridge University Press.

Devitt, M. (1997). Responses to the Maribor papers. In D. Jutronic (ed.), *The Maribor papers in naturalized semantics*. Maribor: Pedagoska Fakulteta, 353–411.

Devitt, M. (2004). The case for referential descriptions. In A. Bezuidenhout and M. Reimer (eds.), *Descriptions and beyond*. Oxford: Oxford University Press, 280–305.

Devitt, M. and Sterelny, K. (1987). *Language and reality: An introduction to the philosophy of language*. Cambridge, Mass.: MIT Press.

Devitt, M. and Sterelny, K. (1999). *Language and reality: An introduction to the philosophy of language*. Second edition. Cambridge, Mass.: MIT Press.

Devlin, K. (1991). *Logic and information*. Cambridge, Mass.: Cambridge University Press.

Diesing, M. (1992). *Indefinites*. Cambridge: MIT Press.

Divers, J. and Miller, A. (1994). Why expressivists about value should not love minimalism about truth. *Analysis*, 54, 12–19.

Dodd, J. (2000). There is no norm of truth: A minimalist reply to Wright. *Analysis*, 59. 291–9.

Does, J. van der (1994). Formalising E-type logic. In P. Dekker and M. Stokhof (eds.), *Proceedings of the Ninth Amsterdam Colloquium*. Amsterdam, 229–48.

Donnellan, K. (1966). Reference and definite descriptions. *Philosophical Review*, 75, 281–304.

Donnellan, K. (1968). Putting Humpty Dumpty together again. *Philosophical Review*, 77, 203–15.

Donnellan, K. (1970). Proper names and identifying descriptions. *Synthese*, 21, 335–58. Reprinted in D. Davidson and G. Harman (eds.), *Semantics for natural language*. Dordrecht: Reidel, 1972, 356–79.

Donnellan, K. (1974). Speaking of nothing. *Philosophical Review*, 83, 3–31.

Donnellan, K. (1978). Speaker reference, descriptions, and anaphora. In P. Cole (ed.), *Syntax and semantics*, vol. 9: *Pragmatics*. New York: Academic Press, 47–68.

Donnellan, K. (1983). Kripke and Putnam on natural kind terms. In C. Ginet (ed.), *Knowledge and mind: Philosophical essays*. New York: Oxford University Press, 88–104.

Donnellan, K. (1989). Belief and the identity of reference. In P.A. French, T.E. Uehling, and H.K. Wettstein (eds.), *Midwest studies in philosophy*, vol. 13: *Contemporary perspectives in the philosophy of language II*. Notre Dame: University of Notre Dame Press, 275–88.

Dowty, D. (1977). Toward a semantic analysis of verb aspect and the English "imperfective" progressive. *Linguistics and philosophy*, vol. 1, 45–57.

Dowty, D., Wall, R., and Peters, P. (1981). *Introduction to Montague semantics*. Dordrecht: Reidel.

Dreier, J. (1996). Expressivist embeddings and minimalist truth. *Philosophical Studies*, 83, 29–51.

Dreier, J. (2002). The expressivist circle: invoking norms in the explanation of judgement. *Philosophy and Phenomenological Research*, 65, 136–42.

Dretske, F. (1981). *Knowledge and the flow of information*. Cambridge, Mass.: MIT Press.

Dretske, F. (1986). Misrepresentation. In R. Bogdan (ed.), *Belief: Form, content, and function*. New York: Oxford University Press, 17–36.

Dretske, F. (1988). *Explaining behavior: Reasons in a world of causes*. Cambridge, Mass.: MIT Press.

Dretske, F. (1991). Dretske's replies. In B. McLaughlin (ed.), *Dretske and his critics*. Oxford: Blackwell, 180–21.

Dummett, M. (1973). *Frege: Philosophy of language*. New York: Harper & Row.

Dummett, M. (1975). What is a theory of meaning? In S. Guttenplan (ed.), *Mind and language*. Oxford: Clarendon Press, 97–138.

Dummett, M. (1977). *Elements of intuitionism*. Oxford: Oxford University Press.

Dummett, M. (1978). *Truth and other enigmas*. Cambridge, Mass.: Harvard University Press.

Dummett, M. (1991). *The logical basis of metaphysics*. Cambridge, Mass.: Harvard University Press.

Dummett, M. (1993). *The seas of language*. Oxford: Oxford University Press.

Dummett, M. (1996). *Origins of analytical philosophy*. Cambridge, Mass.: Harvard University Press.

Dupré, J. (1981). Natural kinds and biological taxa. *Philosophical Review*, 90, 66–90.

Dupré, J. (1993). *The disorder of things: Metaphysical foundations of the disunity of science*. Cambridge, Mass.: Harvard University Press.

Edgington, D. (1996). Vagueness by degrees. In R. Keefe and P. Smith (eds.), *Vagueness: A reader*. Cambridge, Mass.: MIT Press.

Edgington, D. (1997). Commentary. In M. Woods (ed.), *Conditionals*. Oxford: Oxford University Press, 95–137.

Elbourne, P. (2001). E-type anaphora as NP-deletion. *Natural Language Semantics*, 9, 241–88.

Elbourne, P. (2002). Situations and individuals. Ph.D. dissertation: MIT.

Elgin, C. and Scheffler, I. (1987). Mainsprings of metaphor. *Journal of Philosophy*, 84, 331–5.

Enc, B., (2002). Indeterminacy of function attributions. In A. Ariew, R. Cummins, and M. Perlman (eds.), *Functions: New readings in the philosophy of biology and psychology*. Oxford: Oxford University Press.

Evans, G. (1972). *Logic matters*. Oxford: Blackwell.

Evans, G. (1973). The causal theory of names. *Proceedings of the Aristotelian Society*, supplementary volume, 47, 187–208.

Evans, G. (1975). Identity and predication. Reprinted in *Collected papers*. Oxford: Oxford University Press.

Evans, G. (1977). Pronouns, quantifiers and relative clauses (I). *Canadian Journal of Philosophy*, 7, 467–536.

Evans, G. (1980). Pronouns. *Linguistic Inquiry*, 11, 337–62.

Evans, G. (1981). Semantic theory and tacit knowledge. In S. Holtzman and C. Leich (eds.), *Wittgenstein: To follow a rule*. London: Routledge & Kegan Paul, 118–37. Reprinted in *Collected papers*. Oxford: Oxford University Press, 322–42.

Evans, G. (1982). *The varieties of reference*. Oxford: Clarendon Press.

Evans, G. (1985). *Collected papers*. Oxford: Clarendon Press.

Ewert, J., Burghagen, H., and Schurg-Pfeiffer, E. (1983). Neuroethological analysis of the innate releasing mechanism for prey-catching in toads. In J. Ewert, R. Capranica, and D. Ingle (eds.), *Advances in vertebrate neuroethology.* New York: Plenum Press, 413–75.

Field, H. (1972). Tarski's theory of truth. *Journal of Philosophy,* 69, 347–75. Reprinted in *Truth and the absence of fact.* Oxford: Oxford University Press, 3–29.

Field, H. (1977). Logic, meaning and conceptual role. *Journal of Philosophy,* 69, 379–409.

Field, H. (1978). Mental representation. *Erkentnnis,* 13, 9–16.

Field, H. (1981). Some thoughts on radical indeterminacy. *The Monist,* 81, 253–73.

Field, H. (1986). The deflationary conception of truth. In G. MacDonald and C. Wright (eds.), *Fact, science, and morality.* Oxford: Blackwell, 55–117.

Field, H. (1994). Disquotational truth and factually defective discourse. *Philosophical Review,* 103, 405–52.

Field, H. (1998). Some thoughts on radical indeterminacy. *The Monist,* 81, 253–73.

Field, H. (2001a). Deflationist views of meaning and content. In *Truth and the absence of fact.* Oxford: Oxford University Press, 104–56.

Field, H. (2001b). Indeterminacy, degree of belief, and excluded middle. In *Truth and the absence of fact.* Oxford: Oxford University Press, 278–314.

Fine, A. (1995). Review. *Ethics,* 106, 646–8.

Fine, K. (1996). Vagueness, truth and logic. In R. Keefe and P. Smith (eds.), *Vagueness: A reader.* Cambridge, Mass.: MIT Press.

firáinsson, H. (1976). Reflexives and subjunctives in Icelandic. *Proceedings of NELS,* 6. Amherst: University of Massachusetts, 225–39.

firáinsson, H. (1991). Long-distance reflexives and the typology of Nps. In J. Koster, J. Reuland, and E. Reuland (eds.), *Long-distance anaphora.* Cambridge: Cambridge University.

Fodor, J.A. (1975). *The language of thought.* New York: Crowell.

Fodor, J.A. (1980). Methodological solipsism considered as a research strategy in cognitive psychology. *Behavioral and Brain Sciences,* 3, 63–109. Reprinted in *Representations: Philosophical essays on the foundations of cognitive science.* Brighton: Harvester Press.

Fodor, J.A. (1981). *Representations.* Cambridge, Mass.: MIT Press.

Fodor, J.A. (1982). Cognitive science and the twin-earth problem. *Notre Dame Journal of Formal Logic,* 23, 98–118.

Fodor, J.A. (1984). Semantics Wisconsin style. *Synthese,* 59, 231–50.

Fodor, J.A. (1987). *Psychosemantics.* Cambridge, Mass.: MIT Press.

Fodor, J.A. (1990a). *A theory of content and other essays.* Cambridge, Mass.: MIT Press.

Fodor, J.A. (1990b). A theory of content. In *A theory of content and other essays.* Cambridge, Mass.: MIT Press, 51–136.

Fodor, J.A. (1990c). Information and representation. In P. Hanson (ed.), *Information, language and cognition.* Vancouver: University of British Columbia Press.

Fodor, J.A. (1991). Replies. In B. Loewer and G. Rey (eds.), *Meaning in mind: Fodor and his critics.* Oxford: Blackwell.

Fodor, J.A. (1994). *The elm and the expert.* Cambridge, Mass.: MIT Press.

Fodor, J.A. (1996). Deconstructing Dennett's Darwin. *Mind and Language,* 11, 246–62.

Fodor, J.A. (1998). Do we think in mentalese? In *In critical condition.* Cambridge, Mass.: MIT Press.

Fodor, J.A. (2001). Language, thought, and compositionality. *Mind and Language,* 1–15.

Fodor, J.A. (2004). Having concepts. *Language and Mind,* 19, 1, 29–48.

Fodor, J.A. and Lepore, E. (1991). Why meaning (probably) isn't conceptual role. *Mind and Language*, 6(4), 329–43.

Fodor, J.A. and Lepore, E. (1992). *Holism: A shopper's guide*. Oxford: Basil Blackwell.

Fodor, J.A. and Lepore, E. (1996). The pet fish and the red herring: Why concepts aren't prototypes. *Cognition*, 58(2), 243–76.

Fodor, J.A. and Lepore, E. (2002). *The compositionality papers*. Oxford: Oxford University Press.

Fodor, J.D. and Sag, I. (1982). Referential and quantificational indefinites. *Linguistics and Philosophy*, 5, 355–98.

Fogelin, R. (1988). *Figuratively speaking*. New Haven: Yale University Press.

Forbes, G. (1989). *Languages of possibility*. Cambridge: Basil Blackwell.

Forbes, G. (2000). Objectual attitudes. *Linguistics and Philosophy*, 23, 141–83.

Foster, J. (1976). Meaning and truth theory. In G. Evans and J. McDowell (eds.), *Truth and meaning: Essays in semantics*. Oxford: Clarendon Press, 1–32.

Fraser, H. (1975). Hedged performatives. In P. Cole and J. Morgan (eds.), *Syntax and semantics*, vol. 3. New York: Academic Press, 187–210.

Frege, G. (1918). The thought: A logical investigation. *Beiträge zur philosophie des Deutschen idealismus*, 1, 58–77.

Frege, G. (1952). On sense and reference. In M. Black and P. Geach (eds. and trans.), *Translations from the philosophical writings of Gottlob Frege*. Oxford: Blackwell, 56–78. Translation of Frege 1892, Uber Sinn und Bedeutung, *Zeitschrift fur Philosophie und philosophische Kritik*, 100, 25–50.

Frege, G. (1964). *The basic laws of arithmetic*. M. Furth, ed. and trans. Berkeley and Los Angeles: University of California Press. Partial translation of Frege 1893, *Grundgesetze der Arithmetik*. Jena: Verlag Hermann Pohl.

Frege, G. (1967). Concept script. In J. van Heijenoort (ed.), *From Frege to Gödel: A source book of mathematical logic, 1879–1931*. Cambridge, Mass.: Harvard University Press, 1–82. Translation by S. Bauer-Mengelberg of Frege 1879, *Begriffschrift*. Halle a. S. Louis Nevert.

Gamut, L. (1991). *Logic, language and meaning*. Chicago: University of Chicago Press.

Garner, R. (1993). Are convenient fictions harmful to your health? *Philosophy East and West*, 43, 87–106.

Geach, P. (1958). Imperative and deontic logic. *Analysis*, 18, 49–56.

Geach, P. (1960). Ascriptivism. *Philosophical Review*, 69, 221–5.

Geach, P. (1962). *Reference and generality*. Ithaca: Cornell University Press.

Geach, P. (1965). Assertion. *Philosophical Review*, 74, 449–65.

Geach, P. (1972). *Logic matters*. Oxford: Blackwell.

Gibbard, A. (1981). Two recent theories of conditionals. In W.L. Harper, C.T. Pearce, and R. Stalnaker (eds.), *Ifs*. Dordrecht: Reidel, 211–47

Gibbard, A. (1990). *Wise choices, apt feelings*. Cambridge, Mass.: Harvard University Press.

Gibbard, A. (1992a). Thick concepts and warrants for feelings. *Proceedings of the Aristotelian Society*, supplementary volume, 66, 267–83.

Gibbard, A. (1992b). Reply to Blackburn, Carson, Hill and Railton. *Philosophy and Phenomenological Research*, 52, 969–80.

Gibbard, A. (1993). Reply to Sinnott-Armstrong. *Philosophical Studies*, 69, 315–26.

Gibbard, A. (1994). Meaning and normativity. In E. Villanueva (ed.), *Philosophical issues*, vol. 5: *Truth and rationality*. Atascadero, Calif.: Ridgeview Publishing Company, 95–115.

Gibbs, R. (1994). *The poetics of mind*. New York: Cambridge University Press.

Gibson, R. (1988). *Enlightened. empiricism: An examination of W.V. Quine's theory of knowledge*. Gainesville: University Press of Florida.

Gibson, R. (1998). Quine's philosophy: A brief sketch. In L.E. Hahn and P.A. Schilpp (eds.), *Library of living philosophers*, vol. 18: *The philosophy of W.V. Quine*. Carbondale: Southern Illinois University, 667–83.

Glucksberg, S. (2001). *Understanding figurative language: From metaphors to idioms*. Oxford: Oxford University Press.

Glucksberg, S. and Keysar, B. (1990). Understanding metaphorical comparisons: Beyond similarity. *Psychological Review*, 97, 3–18.

Glucksberg, S. and Keysar, B. (1993). How metaphors work. In A. Ortony (ed.), *Metaphor and thought*. Second edition. Cambridge: Cambridge University Press, 401–24.

Gödel, K. (1931). Über formal unentscheidbare Sätze der Principia Mathematica und verwandter Systeme I. *Monatshefte für mathematik und physik*, 38, 173–98. Trans. J. van Heijenoort. Reprinted in *Collected works*, vol. 1. New York: Oxford University Press, 144–95.

Gödel, K. (1944). Russell's mathematical logic. In P. Schilpp (ed.), *The philosophy of Bertrand Russell*. Evanston, Ill.: Northwestern University Press, 125–53.

Goodman, N. (1947). The problem of counterfactual conditionals. *Journal of Philosophy*, 44, 113–28.

Goodman, N. (1976). *Languages of art*. Second edition. Indianapolis: Hackett.

Goodman, N. (1979). Metaphor as moonlighting. *Critical Inquiry*, 6, 125–30.

Graff, D. (2001). Descriptions as predicates. *Philosophical Studies*, 102, 1–42.

Grandy, R. (1972). A definition of truth for theories with intensional definite description operators. *Journal of Philosophical Logic*, 1, 137–55.

Grice, H.P. (1957). Meaning. *Philosophical Review*, 66, 377–88.

Grice, H.P. (1961). The causal theory of perception. *Proceedings of the Aristotelian Society*, supplementary volume, 35, 121–52.

Grice, H.P. (1967). Logic and conversation (William James Lectures). In H.P. Grice (1989), *Studies in the way of words*. Cambridge, Mass.: Harvard University Press, 3–143.

Grice, H.P. (1968). Utterer's meaning, sentence meaning, and word meaning. *Foundations of Language*, 4, 225–42.

Grice, H.P. (1969a). Utterer's meaning and intentions. *Philosophical Review*, 78, 147–77.

Grice, H.P. (1969b). Vacuous names. In D. Davidson and J. Hintikka (eds.), *Words and objections*. Dordrecht: Reidel, 118–45.

Grice, H.P. (1975). Logic and conversation. In D. Davidson and G. Harman (eds.), *The logic of grammar*. Encino: Dickenson.

Grice, H.P. (1989). *Studies in the way of words*. Cambridge, Mass.: Harvard University Press.

Grodzinsky, Y. and Reinhart, T. (1993). The innateness of binding and coreference. *Linguistic Inquiry*, 24, 69–101.

Groenendijk, J. and Stokhof, M. (1991). Dynamic predicate logic. *Linguistics and Philosophy*, 14, 39–100.

Gupta, A. (1980). *The logic of common nouns: An investigation in quantified modal logic*. New Haven and London: Yale University Press.

Gupta, A. (1982). Truth and paradox. *Journal of Philosophical Logic*, 11, 1–60.

Gupta, A. and Belnap, N. (1993). *The revision theory of truth*. Cambridge, Mass.: MIT Press.

Hagege, C. (1974). Les pronoms logophoriques. *Bulletin de la Société de Linguistique de Paris*, 69, 287–310.

Halbach, V. (1999). Conservative theories of classical truth. *Studia Logica*, 62, 353–7.

Haldane, J. and Wright, C. (eds.) (1993). *Reality, representation, and projection*. Oxford: Oxford University Press.

Hale, B. (1986). The compleat projectivist. *Philosophical Quarterly*, 36, 65–84.

Hale, B. (1993). Can there be a logic of attitudes. In J. Haldane and C. Wright (eds.), *Reality, representation, and projection*. Oxford: Oxford University Press.

Hale, B. (1993). Postscript. In J. Haldane and C. Wright (eds.), *Reality, representation, and projection*. Oxford: Oxford University Press.

Hale, B. (2002). Can arboreal knotwork help Blackburn out of Frege's abyss? *Philosophy and Phenomenological Research*, 65, 144–8.

Hale, B. and Wright, C. (eds.) (1997) *A companion to the philosophy of language*. Oxford: Blackwell.

Hall, R. (1990). Does representational content arise from biological function? In A. Fine, M. Forbes, and L. Wessels (eds.), *Proceedings of the 1990 Biennial Meeting of the Philosophy of Science Association*, 1, 193–9. East Lansing: Michigan State University.

Halliday, R. (1993). Cheshire Cat supervenience. *Journal of Value Inquiry*, 27, 417–30.

Hare, R. (1970). Meaning and speech acts. *Philosophical Review*, 79, 3–24.

Harman, G. (1972). Deep structure as logical form. In D. Davidson and G. Harman (eds.), *Semantics of natural language*. Dordrecht: Reidel, 25–47.

Harman, G. (1973). *Thought*. Princeton: Princeton University Press.

Harman, G. (1975). Language, thought and communication. In K. Gunderson (ed.), *Language, mind and knowledge*. Minneapolis: University of Minnesota Press.

Harman, G. (1982). Conceptual role semantics. *Notre Dame Journal of Formal Logic*, 28, 252–6.

Harman, G. (1986). The meanings of logical constants. In E. Lepore (ed.), *Truth and interpretation: Perspectives on the philosophy of Donald Davidson*. Oxford, Blackwell, 125–34.

Harman, G. (1987). (Non-solipsistic) conceptual role semantics. In E. Lepore (ed.), *New directions in semantics*. London: Academic Press.

Harman, G. (1993). Meaning holism defended. In J.A. Fodor and E. Lepore (eds.), *Holism: A consumer update*. Amsterdam: Grazer Philosophische Studien, 163–71.

Harman, G. (1996). Analyticity regained. *Noûs*. Reprinted in *Reasoning, meaning, and mind*. Oxford: Clarendon Press (1999), 144–52.

Harman, G. (1999). The death of meaning. *Reasoning, meaning, and mind*. Oxford: Clarendon Press, 119–37.

Harnish, R. (1976). Logical form and implicature. In T. Bever, J. Katz, and T. Langendoen (eds.), *An integrated theory of linguistic ability*. New York: Crowell, 313–92.

Hattiangadi, A. (forthcoming). *The normativity of meaning*.

Heal, J. (1997). Radical interpretation. In B. Hale and C. Wright (eds.), *A companion to the philosophy of language*. Oxford: Blackwell.

Heim, I. (1983). File change semantics and the familiarity theory of definiteness. In R. Bäuerle et al. (eds.), *Meaning, use and interpretation of language*. Berlin: de Gruyter, 164–89.

Heim, I. (1988). *The semantics of definite and indefinite noun phrases*. New York: Garland.

Heim, I. (1990). E-type pronouns and donkey anaphora. *Linguistics and Philosophy*, 13, 137–78.

Heim, I. (1993). Anaphora and semantic interpretation: A reinterpretation of Reinhart's approach. *MIT Working Papers in Linguistics*, 25, 205–46.

Heim, I. and Kratzer, A. (1998). *Semantics in generative grammar*. Malden, Mass.: Blackwell.

Herzberger, H. (1982). Notes on naive semantics. *Journal of Philosophical Logic*, 11, 61–102.

Higginbotham, J. (1980). Pronouns and bound variables. *Linguistic Inquiry*, 11, 679–708.

Higginbotham, J. (1983) Logical form, binding, and nominals. *Linguistic Inquiry*, 14, 395–420.

Higginbotham, J. (1986). Linguistic theory and Davidson's program in semantics. In E. LePore (ed.), *Truth and interpretation: Perspectives on the philosophy of Donald Davidson*. Oxford: Blackwell, 29–48.

Higginbotham, J. (1987). Indefiniteness and predication. In E. Reuland and A. ter Meulen (eds.), *The representation of (in)definiteness*. Cambridge, Mass.: MIT Press, 43–70.

Higginbotham, J. (1988). Contexts, models, and meaning: A note on the data of semantics. In R. Kempson (ed.), *Mental representations: The interface between language and reality*. Cambridge: Cambridge University Press, 29–48.

Higginbotham, J. (1989). Knowledge of reference. In A. George (ed.), *Reflections on Chomsky*. Oxford: Blackwell, 153–74.

Higginbotham, J. (1990). Reference and control. In R. Larson, S. Iatridou, U. Lahiri, and J. Higginbotham (eds.), *Control and grammar*. Dordrecht: Kluwer, 79–108.

Higginbotham, J. (1991). Truth and understanding. *Iyyun*, 40, 271–88.

Higginbotham, J. (1993). Grammatical form and logical form. In J. Tomberlin (ed.), *Philosophical perspectives*, vol. 7: *Language and logic*. Atascadero, Calif.: Ridgeview Publishing Company.

Higginbotham, J. (1999). Tense, indexicality, and consequence. In J. Butterfield (ed.), *The arguments of time*. Oxford: Oxford University Press, 197–215.

Higginbotham, J. and May, R. (1981). Questions, quantifiers, and crossing. *Linguistic Review*, 1, 41–80.

Hilbert, D. and Bernays, P. (1934). *Grundlagen der mathematic*, vol. 1. Berlin.

Hills, D. (1997). Aptness and truth in verbal metaphor. *Philosophical Topics*, 25(1), 117–54.

Hintikka, K.J. (1969). Deontic logic and its philosophical morals. *Models for modalities*. Dordrecht: Reidel, 184–214.

Hintikka, K.J. and Kulas, J. (1983). *The game of language*. Dordrecht: Reidel.

Hintikka, K.J. and Kulas, J. (1985). *Anaphora and definite descriptions: Two applications of game-theoretical semantics*. Dordrecht: Reidel.

Holton, R. (2000). Minimalism and truth-value gaps. *Philosophical Studies*, 97, 137–68.

Hookway, C. (1988). *Quine*. Cambridge: Polity Press.

Hopkins, R. (2001). Kant, quasi-realism, and the autonomy of aesthetic judgement. *European Journal of Philosophy*, 9, 166–89.

Hornsby, J. (1977). Singular terms in contexts of propositional attitude. *Mind*, 86, 31–48.

Horwich, P. (1993). Gibbard's theory of norms. *Philosophy and Phenomenological Research*, 22, 67–8.

Horwich, P. (1994). The essence of expressivism. *Analysis*, 54, 19–20.

Horwich, P. (1995). Meaning, use and truth. *Mind*, 104, 355–68.

Horwich, P. (1998a). *Meaning*. Oxford: Oxford University Press.

Horwich, P. (1998b). *Truth*. Second edition. Oxford: Oxford University Press.

Horwich, P. (2000). Stephen Schiffer's theory of vagueness. *Philosophical Issues*, 10, 271–81.

Horwich, P. (2005). *Reflections on meaning*. Oxford: Oxford University Press.

Hume, D. (1969). *A treatise of human nature*. Harmondsworth: Penguin Books.

Hungerland, I. (1960). Contextual implication. *Inquiry*, 3, 211–58.

Hurley, S. L. (1989). *Natural reasons*. Oxford: Oxford University Press.

Israel, D. and Perry, J. (1990). What is information?. In P. Hanson (ed.), *Information, language and cognition*. Vancouver: University of British Columbia Press.

Israel, D. and Perry, J. (1991). Information and architecture. In J. Barwise, J. M. Gawron, G. Plotkin, and S. Tutiya (eds.), *Situation theory and its applications*, vol. 2. Stanford: CSLI Publications, 147–60.

Jackendoff, R. (1972). *Semantic interpretation in generative grammar*. Cambridge, Mass.: MIT Press.

Jackson, F. (1979). On assertion and indicative conditionals. *Philosophical Review*, 88, 565–89.

Jackson, F. (1981). Conditionals and possibilia. *Proceedings of the Aristotelian Society*, 81, 125–37.

Jackson, F., Oppy, G., and Smith, M. (1994). Minimalism and truth aptness. *Mind*, 103, 287–302.

Jackson, F. and Pettit, P. (1993). Some content is narrow. In J. Heil and A. Mele (eds.), *Mental causation*. Oxford: Oxford University Press.

Jackson, F. and Pettit, P. (1998). A problem for expressivism. *Analysis*, 58, 239–51.

Jacob, P. (1997). *What minds can do: Intentionality in a non-intentional world*. Cambridge: Cambridge University Press.

Jacobsen, R. (1997). Semantic character and expressive content. *Philosophical Papers*, 26, 129–46.

Jacobson, P. (1977). The syntax of crossing coreference sentences. Ph.D. dissertation: University of California, Berkeley.

Jacobson, P. (1999). Towards a variable-free semantics. *Linguistics and Philosophy*, 22, 117–84.

Johnson, M. (ed.) (1981). *Philosophical perspectives on metaphor*. Minneapolis: University of Minnesota Press.

Kadmon, N. (1990). Uniqueness. *Linguistics and Philosophy*, 13, 273–324.

Kalderon, M. (ed.) (2003). *Fictionalist approaches to metaphysics*. Oxford: Oxford University Press.

Kamp, J. ("Hans") (1975). Two theories about adjectives. In E. Keenan (ed.), *Formal semantics of natural language*. Cambridge: Cambridge University Press.

Kamp, J. ("Hans") (1971). Formal properties of "now." *Theoria*, 37, 227–73.

Kamp, J. ("Hans") (1981). A theory of truth and semantic representation. In J. Groenendijk et al. (eds.), *Formal methods in the study of grammar*. Amsterdam: Mathematische Centrum, 277–322.

Kamp, J. ("Hans") (1984). Context, thought and communication. *Proceedings of the Aristotelian Society*, 239–261.

Kamp, J. ("Hans") and Reyle, U. (1993). *From discourse to logic: Introduction to the semantics of natural language, formal logic and discourse representation theory*. Dordrecht: Kluwer.

Kanazawa, M. (2001). Singular donkey pronouns are semantically singular. *Linguistics and Philosophy*, 24, 383–403.

Kant, I. (1781). *Critique of pure reason*. Trans. N.K. Smith.

Kaplan, D. (1975). How to Russell a Frege–Church. *Journal of Philosophy*, 72, 716–29.

Kaplan, D. (1978). Dthat. In P. Cole (ed.), *Syntax and semantics*, vol. 9: *Pragmatics*. New York: Academic Press.

Kaplan, D. (1989). Demonstratives, and afterthoughts. In J. Almog, J. Perry, and H. Wettstein (eds.), *Themes from Kaplan*. Oxford: Oxford University Press, 481–614.

Karttunen, L. (1976). Discourse referents. In J. McCawley (ed.), *Syntax and semantics*, vol. 7: *Notes from the linguistic underground*. New York: Academic Press, 363–85.

Katz, J. and Postal, P. (1964). *An integrated theory of linguistic descriptions*. Cambridge, Mass.: MIT Press.

Katz, J. (1972). *Semantic theory*. New York: Harper & Row.

Katz, J. (1984). An outline of Platonist grammar. In T. Bever, J.M. Carroll, and L.A. Miller (eds.), *Talking minds: The study of language in cognitive science*. Cambridge, Mass.: MIT Press, 1–33. Reprinted in J.J. Katz (ed.), *The philosophy of linguistics*. Oxford: Oxford University Press, 172–203.

Kayne, R. (2002). Pronouns and their antecedents. In S. Epstein and T. Seely (eds.), *Derivation and explanation in the minimalist program*. Oxford: Blackwell, 133–66.

Keefe, R. and Smith, P. (eds.) (1996). *Vagueness: A reader*. Cambridge, Mass.: MIT Press.

Keenan, E. (1971). Names, quantifiers, and the sloppy identity problem. *Papers in Linguistics*, 4(2), 1–22.

Keenan, E. (ed.) (1975). *Formal semantics of natural language*. Cambridge: Cambridge University Press.

Keenan, E. and Stavi, Y. (1986). A semantic characterization of natural language determiners. *Linguistics and Philosophy*, 9, 253–326.

Kempson, R. (1975). *Presupposition and the delimitation of semantics*. Cambridge: Cambridge University Press.

Kempson, R. (1986). Definite NPs and context-dependence: A unified theory of anaphora. In C. Travis (ed.), *Meaning and interpretation*. Oxford: Blackwell, 209–39.

King, J. (1988). Are indefinite descriptions ambiguous? *Philosophical Studies*, 53, 417–40.

King, J. (2001). *Complex demonstratives: A quantificational account*. Cambridge, Mass.: MIT Press.

Kirk, R. (1986). *Translation determined*. Oxford: Oxford University Press.

Kittay, E.F. (1987). *Metaphor: Its cognitive force and linguistic structure*. Oxford: Oxford University Press.

Kleene, S.C. (1952). *Introduction to metamathematics*. New York: American Elsevier.

Kolbel, M. (2002). *Truth without objectivity*. London: Routledge.

Kraut, R. (1993). Robust deflationism. *Philosophical Review*, 102, 247–63.

Kripke, S. (1963). Semantical considerations on modal logic. *Acta Philosophica Fennica*, 16, 83–94. Reprinted in L. Linsky (ed.), *Reference and modality*. Oxford: Oxford University Press, 63–72.

Kripke, S. (1971). Identity and necessity. In M.K. Munitz (ed.), *Identity and individuation*. New York: New York University Press, 135–64.

Kripke, S. (1975). Outline of a theory of truth. *Journal of Philosophy*, 72, 690–716.

Kripke, S. (1977). Speaker reference and semantic reference. In P.A. French, T.E. Uehling, Jr., and H.K. Wettstein (eds.), *Contemporary perspectives in the philosophy of language*. Minneapolis: University of Minnesota Press, 6–27.

Kripke, S. (1979). A puzzle about belief. In A. Margalit (ed.), *Meaning and use*. Dordrecht: Reidel, 239–83.

Kripke, S. (1980). *Naming and necessity.* Cambridge, Mass.: Harvard University Press. Previously published. in D. Davidson and G. Harman (eds.), *Semantics of natural language.* Dordrecht: Reidel (1972), 253–355.

Kripke, S. (1982). *Wittgenstein on rules and private language: An elementary exposition.* Cambridge, Mass.: Harvard University Press.

Kripke, S. (1986). A problem in the theory of reference: The linguistic division of labor and the social character of naming. In *Philosophy and culture: Proceedings of the 17th World Congress of Philosophy.* Montreal: Éditions du Beffroi.

Kripke, S. (2005). Hydras. *Mind* (Centenary issue on Russell's Theory of Descriptions, Stephen Neale (ed.), forthcoming.)

Kusch, M. (forthcoming). *A defence of Kripke's Wittgenstein.* Chesham: Acumen.

Lakoff, G. (1972). Linguistics and natural logic. In D. Davidson and G. Harman (eds.), *Semantics of natural language.* Dordrecht: Reidel, 545–665.

Lakoff, G. (1993). The contemporary theory of metaphor. In A. Ortony (ed.), *Metaphor and thought.* Second edition. Cambridge: Cambridge University Press, 202–51.

Lakoff, G. and Johnson, M. (1980). *Metaphors we live by.* Chicago: University of Chicago Press.

Lakoff, G. and Turner, M. (1989). *More than cool reason: A field guide to poetic metaphor.* Chicago: University of Chicago Press.

Lance, M. and Hawthorne, J. (1997). *The grammar of meaning.* Cambridge: Cambridge University Press.

Langacker, R. (1969). On pronominalization and the chain of command. In D. Reibel and S. Schane (eds.), *Modern studies in English.* Englewood Cliffs, N.J.: Prentice-Hall, 160–86.

LaPorte, J. (1996). Chemical kind term reference and the discovery of essence. *Noûs,* 30, 112–32.

LaPorte, J. (2000). Rigidity and kind. *Philosophical Studies,* 97, 293–316.

LaPorte, J. (2004). *Natural kinds and conceptual change.* Cambridge: Cambridge University Press.

Lappin, S. (1989). Donkey pronouns unbound. *Theoretical Linguistics,* 15, 263–86.

Lappin, S. (ed.) (1996). *The handbook of contemporary semantic theory.* Oxford: Blackwell.

Larson, R. (2002). The grammar of intensionality. In G. Preyer and G. Peter (eds.), *Logical form and language.* Oxford: Oxford University Press.

Larson, R. and Segal, G. (1995). *Knowledge of meaning.* Cambridge, Mass.: MIT Press.

Lasersohn, P. (1993). Existence presuppositions and background knowledge. *Journal of Semantics,* 10, 112–22.

Lasnik, H. (1976). Remarks on coreference. *Linguistic Analysis,* 2, 1–22.

Lees, R. and Klima, E. (1963). Rule for English pronominalization. *Language,* 39, 17–28.

Leezenberg, M. (2001). *Contexts of metaphor.* Amsterdam: Elsevier Science.

Lepore, E. (1995). Two dogmas of empiricism and the generality requirement. *Noûs,* 24, 468–80.

Lepore, E. (2004). An abuse of context in semantics: The case of incomplete definite descriptions. In A. Bezuidenhout and M. Reimer (eds.), *Descriptions and beyond.* Oxford: Clarendon Press, 41–67.

Lepore, E. and Ludwig, K. (2000). The semantics and pragmatics of complex demonstratives. *Mind,* 109, 199–240.

Leslie, A. (2000). How to acquire a representational theory of mind. *Metarepresentations: A multidisciplinary perspective.* Oxford: Oxford University Press, 197–223.

Lettvin, J., Maturana, H., McCulloch, W., and Pitts, W., (1959). What the frog's eye tells the frog's brain. *Proceedings of the Institute of Radio Engineers*, 47, 1940–51.

Levin, S. (1977). *The semantics of metaphor*. Baltimore: Johns Hopkins University Press.

Levinson, J. (2001). Who's afraid of a paraphrase? *Theoria*, 67, 7–23.

Levinson, S. (2000). *Presumptive meanings: The theory of generalized conversational implicature*. Cambridge, Mass.: MIT Press.

Lewis, D. (1969). *Convention: A philosophical study*. Cambridge, Mass.: Harvard University Press.

Lewis, D. (1970). General semantics. *Synthese*, 22, 18–67.

Lewis, D. (1972). Psychological and theoretical identifications. *Australian Journal of Philosophy*, 50, 249–58.

Lewis, D. (1973a). *Counterfactuals*. Oxford: Basil Blackwell.

Lewis, D. (1973b). Causation. *Journal of Philosophy*, 70, 556–67.

Lewis, D. (1974). Radical interpretation. *Synthèse*, 23, 331–44.

Lewis, D. (1975). Languages and language. In K Gunderson (ed.), *Language mind and knowledge*. Minneapolis: University of Minnesota Press, 3–35.

Lewis, D. (1976). Probabilities of conditionals and conditional probabilities. *Philosophical Review*, 85, 297–315.

Lewis, D. (1979). Scorekeeping in a language game. *Journal of Philosophical Logic*, 8, 339–59.

Lewis, D. (1986). Probabilities of conditionals and conditional probabilities II. *Philosophical Review*, 95, 581–9.

Lewis, D. (1990). What experience teaches. In W. Lycan (ed.), *Mind and cognition*. Oxford: Blackwell.

Lewis, D. (1999). Many, but almost one. In D. Lewis, *Papers in metaphysics and epistemology*. Cambridge: Cambridge University Press, 164–82.

Lewis, D. (2003). Quasi realism is fictionalism. In M. Kalderon (ed.), *Fictionalist approaches to metaphysics*. Oxford: Oxford University Press.

Linsky, B. (2002). Russell's logical form, LF, and truth conditions. In G. Preyer and G. Peter (eds.), *Logical form and language*. Oxford: Oxford University Press, 391–408.

Loar, B. (1976). The semantics of singular terms. *Philosophical Studies*, 30, 353–77.

Loar, B. (1981). *Mind and meaning*. Cambridge: Cambridge University Press.

Loar, B. (1991). Can we explain intentionality? In B. Loewer and G. Rey (eds.), *Meaning in Mind: Fodor and his critics*. Oxford: Blackwell, 119–96.

Locke, J. [1690] (1961). *An essay concerning human understanding*. London: J.M. Dent and Sons Ltd.

Loewer, B. (1987). From information to intentionality. *Synthese*, 70, 287–317.

Loewer, B. (1997). A guide to naturalizing semantics. In B. Hale and C. Wright (eds.), *A companion to the philosophy of language*. Oxford: Blackwell.

Loewer, B. and Rey, G. (eds.) (1991). *Meaning in mind: Fodor and his critics*. Oxford: Blackwell.

Logue, J. (1995). *Projective probability*. Oxford: Oxford University Press.

Ludlow, P. (1991). Review of ter Meulen and Reuland (eds.), *The representation of (in)definiteness*. Cambridge, Mass.: MIT Press. *Journal of Semantics*, 8, 277–86.

Ludlow, P. (1994). Conditionals, events, and unbound pronouns. *Lingua e Stile*, 29, 3–20.

Ludlow, P. (1999). *Semantics, tense, and time: An essay in the metaphysics of natural language*. Cambridge, Mass.: MIT Press.

Ludlow, P. (2001). Metaphysical austerity and the problems of temporal and modal anaphora. In J. Tomberlin (ed.), *Philosophical perspectives*, vol. 15: *Metaphysics*. Atascadero, Calif.: Ridgeview Publishing Company.

Ludlow, P. and Neale, S. (1991). Indefinite descriptions: In defence of Russell. *Linguistics and Philosophy*, 14, 171–202.

Ludlow, P. and Segal, G. (2004). On a unitary semantical analysis for definite and indefinite descriptions. In A. Bezuidenhout and M. Reimer (eds.), *Descriptions and beyond*. Oxford: Clarendon Press, 420–36.

Lukasiewicz, J. and Tarski, A. (1956). Investigations into the sentential calculus. *Logic, semantics, metamathematics*. Oxford: Oxford University Press.

Lycan, W. (1984). A syntactically motivated theory of conditionals. In P.A. French, T.E. Euhling, and H.K. Wettstein (eds.), *Midwest studies in philosophy*, vol. 9. Minneapolis: University of Minnesota Press.

Lycan, W. (1990). On respecting puzzles about belief ascriptions. *Pacific Philosophical Quarterly*, 71, 182–8.

Lycan, W. (1994). *Modality and meaning*. Dordrecht: Kluwer Academic Press.

Mackie, J. (1973). *Truth, probability and paradox*. Oxford: Clarendon Press.

Maling, J. (1984). Non-clause bounded reflexives in modern Icelandic. *Linguistics and Philosophy*, 7, 211–41.

Maling, J. (1986). Clause bounded. reflexives in modern Icelandic. In L. Hellan and K.K. Christensen (eds.), *Topics in Scandinavian syntax*. Dordrecht: Reidel.

Mandelbaum, D. (1994). Syntactic conditions on saturation. Ph.D. thesis: Graduate Faculty in Linguistis, CUNY Graduate Center.

Marcus, R.B. (1960). Extensionality. *Mind*, 69, 55–62.

Marcus, R.B. (1961). Modalities and intensional languages. *Synthese*, 13, 303–22.

Marcus, R.B. (1981). A proposed. solution to a puzzle about belief. *Midwest Studies in Philosophy*, 6, 501–10.

Margalit A. and Goldblum, N. (1994). Metaphors in an open-class test. In J. Hintikka (ed.), *Aspects of metaphor*. Dordrecht: Kluwer, 219–41.

Margalit, A. and Goldblum, N. (1995). A metaphor game. *Synthese*, 104, 299–323.

Martin, R. and Woodruff, P. (1975). On representing "true-in-*L*" in *L. Philosophia*, 5, 213–17.

Martin, R. (1984). *Recent essays on truth and the liar paradox*. Oxford and New York: Oxford University Press.

Matthews, R. (1971). Concerning a "linguistic theory" of metaphor. *Foundations of Language*, 7, 413–25.

Mautner, T. (2000). Problems for anti-expressivism. *Analysis*, 60, 196–201.

May, R. (1977). The grammar of quantification. Ph.D. dissertation: MIT.

May, R. (1985). *Logical form: Its structure and derivation*. Cambridge, Mass.: MIT Press.

May, R. (2002). Ellipsis. *Macmillan enclyclopaedia of cognitive science*, 1094–1102.

McCawley, J. (1976). *Grammar and meaning*. New York: Academic Press.

McDowell, J. (1984). Wittgenstein on following a rule. *Synthese*, 58(3), 325–63.

McDowell, J. (1987). Projection and truth in ethics. Reprinted in S. Darwall, A. Gibbard, and P. Railton (eds.), *Moral discourse and practice*. New York: Oxford University Press.

McDowell, J. (1992). Putnam on mind and meaning. *Philosophical Topics*, 20, 35–48. Reprinted in Pessin and Goldberg 1996: 305–17.

McDowell, J. (1994). *Mind and world*. Cambridge, Mass.: Harvard University Press.

McGee, V. (1985). A counterexample to modus ponens. *Journal of Philosophy*, 82, 462–71.

McGee, V. (1991). *Truth, vagueness, and paradox*. Indianapolis: Hackett.

McGee, V. and McLaughlin, B. (1994). Distinctions without a difference. *Southern Journal of Philosophy*, 33, 203–51.

McGinn, C. (1984). *Wittgenstein on meaning*. Oxford: Blackwell.

McGinn, C. (1989). *Mental content*. Oxford: Blackwell.

McLaughlin, B. (ed.) (1991). *Dretske and his critics*. Oxford: Blackwell.

McKinsey, M. (1991). The internal basis of meaning. *Pacific Philosophical Quarterly*, 72, 143–69.

Meinong, A. (1904). The theory of objects. In R. Chisolm (ed.), *Realism and the background of phenomenology*. New York: Free Press.

Mellor, D.H. (1977). Natural kinds. *British Journal for the Philosophy of Science*, 28, 299–312. Reprinted in Pessin and Goldberg 1996: 69–80.

Mill, J.S. [1843](1973). *A system of logic*. London: Longmans.

Miller, A. (2003). *An introduction to contemporary metaethics*. Cambridge: Polity Press.

Miller, A. (2003). Objective content. *Proceedings of the Aristotelian Society*, supplementary volume, 77.

Miller, A. and Wright, C. (eds.) (2002). *Rule-following and meaning*. Chesham: Acumen.

Millikan, R. (1984). *Language, thought and other biological categories*. Cambridge, Mass.: MIT Press.

Millikan, R. (1989). Biosemantics. *Journal of Philosophy*, 86, 281–97.

Millikan, R. (1990). Truth, rules, hoverflies and the Kripke–Wittgenstein Paradox. *Philosophical Review*, 99, 232–53.

Millikan, R. (1991). Speaking up for Darwin. In B. Loewer and G. Rey (eds.), *Meaning in mind: Fodor and his critics*. Oxford: Blackwell, 151–65.

Millikan, R. (1993). *White Queen psychology and other essays for Alice*. Cambridge, Mass.: MIT Press.

Millikan, R. (1996). On Swampkinds. *Mind and Language*, 11, 70–130.

Millikan, R. (2000). *On clear and confused ideas: An essay about substance concepts*. Cambridge: Cambridge University Press.

Mitchell, D. (1962). *An introduction to logic*. London: Hutchison.

Montague, R. (1963). Syntactic treatments of modality, with corollaries on reflexion principles and finite axiomatizability. *Acta Philosophical Fennica*, 16, 153–67.

Montague, R. (1968). Pragmatics. In R. Kiblanski (ed.), *Contemporary philosophy*. Florence: La Nuova Italia editrice, 102–21. Reprinted in R. Thomason (ed.), *Formal philosophy: Selected. papers of Richard Montague*. New Haven: Yale University Press, 95–118.

Montague, R. (1970). Pragmatics and intensional logic. *Synthèse*, 22, 68–94.

Montague, R. (1973). The proper treatment of quantification in ordinary English. In J. Hintikka, J. Moravcsik, and P. Suppes (eds.), *Approaches to natural language: Proceedings of the 1970 Stanford Workshop on Grammar and Semantics*. Dordrecht: Reidel, 221–42. Reprinted in R. Thomason (ed.)., *Formal philosophy: Selected papers of Richard Montague*. New Haven: Yale University Press, 247–70.

Montague, R. (1974). *Formal philosophy: Selected papers of Richard Montague*. R. Thomason (ed.), New Haven: Yale University Press.

Moore, A. (2002). Quasi-realism and relativism. *Philosophy and Phenomenological Research*, 65, 150–6.

Moore, G.E. (1942). A reply to my critics. In P.A. Schilpp (ed.), *The philosophy of G. E. Moore*. Evanston and Chicago: Northwestern University Press, 535–677.

Moore, G.E. (1944). Russell's theory of descriptions. In P.A. Schilpp (ed.), *The philosophy of Bertrand Russell*. New York: Tudor, 177–225.

Moran, R. (1989). Seeing and believing: metaphor, image, and force. *Critical Inquiry*, 16, 87–112.

Moran, R. (1996). Metaphor. In B. Hale and C. Wright (eds.), *A companion to the philosophy of language*. Oxford: Blackwell, 248–68.

Neale, S. (1988). Description and descriptive thought. Ph.D. dissertation: Stanford University.

Neale, S. (1990). *Descriptions*. Cambridge, Mass.: MIT Press.

Neale, S. (1992). Paul Grice and the philosophy of language. *Linguistics and Philosophy*, 15, 509–59.

Neale, S. (1993a). Grammatical form, logical form, and incomplete symbols. In A.D. Irvine and G.A. Wedeking (eds.), *Russell and analytic philosophy*. Toronto: University of Toronto Press, 97–139.

Neale, S. (1993b). Term limits. In J. Tomberlin (ed.), *Philosophical perspectives*, vol. 7: *The philosophy of language and logic*, 89–124.

Neale, S. (1994). Logical form and LF. In C. Otero (ed.), *Noam Chomsky: Critical assessments*. London: Routledge, 788–838.

Neale, S. (1997). Speakers reference and anaphora. In D. Jutronic (ed.), *The Maribor papers in naturalized semantics*. Maribor: Pedagoska Fakulteta, 202–14.

Neale, S. (1999). Coloring and composition. In R. Stainton (ed.), *Philosophy and Linguistics*. Boulder, Colo.: Westview Press, 35–82.

Neale, S. (2000). On a milestone of empiricism. In P. Kotatko and A. Orenstein (eds.), *Knowledge, language and logic: Questions for Quine*. Dordrecht: Kluwer, 237–346.

Neale, S. (2001). *Facing facts*. Oxford: Oxford University Press.

Neale, S. (2003). *Descriptions*. Second edition. Oxford: Oxford University Press.

Neale, S. (2004a). This, that and the other. In A. Bezuidenhout and M. Reimer (eds.), *Descriptions and beyond*. Oxford: Clarendon Press, 68–182.

Neale, S. (2004b). Pragmatism and binding. In Z. Szabó (ed.), *Semantics and pragmatics*. Oxford: Oxford University Press.

Neander, K. (1995). Misrepresenting and malfunctioning. *Philosophical Studies*, 79, 109–41.

Neander, K. (1996). Swampman meets swampcow. *Mind and Language*, 11, 118–29.

Neander, K. (1999). Fitness and the Fate of Unicorns. In V. Hardcastle (ed.), *Biology meets psychology: Philosophical essays*. Cambridge, Mass.: MIT Press, 3–26.

Neander, K. (forthcoming) *Mental representation*. Cambridge, Mass.: MIT Press.

Nelson, M. (2002). Descriptivism defended. *Noûs*, 36, 408–35.

Nogales, P. (1999). *Metaphorically speaking*. Stanford, Calif.: CSLI/Cambridge University Press.

Oehrle, R.T., Bach, E., and Wheeler, D. (eds.) (1988). *Categorial grammar and natural language structures*. Dordrecht: Reidel.

O'Leary-Hawthorn, J. and Price, H. (1996). How to stand up for non-cognitivists. *Australasian Journal of Philosophy*, 74, 275–92.

Orenstein, A. (2002). *W.V.O. Quine*. Chesham: Acumen.

Ortony, A. (ed.) (1993). *Metaphor and thought*, Second edition. Cambridge: Cambridge University Press.

Ostertag, G. (1998). Introduction to *Definite descriptions: A reader*. Cambridge, Mass.: MIT Press, 1–34.

Papineau, D. (1984). Representation and explanation. *Philosophy of Science*, 51, 500–72.

Papineau, D. (1987). *Reality and representation*. Oxford: Blackwell.

Papineau, D. (1993). *Philosophical naturalism*. Oxford: Blackwell.

Papineau, D. (1997). Teleosemantics and indeterminacy. *Australasian Journal of Philosophy*, 76, 1–14.

Papineau, D. (2001). The status of teleosemantics, or how to stop worrying about swamp-man. *Australasian Journal of Philosophy*, 79, 279–89.

Parsons, C. (1974). The liar paradox. *Journal of philosophical logic*, 3, 381–412.

Parsons, T. (1978). Pronouns as paraphrases. University of Massachusetts at Amherst.

Parsons, T. (1980). *Nonexistent objects*. New Haven: Yale University Press.

Parsons, T. (1990). *Events in the semantics of English*. Cambridge, Mass.: MIT Press.

Parsons, T. (1997). Meaning sensitivity and grammatical structure. In M. Dalla Chiara et al. (eds.), *Structures and norms in science*. Dordrecht: Kluwer, 369–83.

Partee, B. (1972). Opacity, coreference and pronouns. In D. Davidson and G. Harman (eds.), *Semantics of natural language*. Dordrecht: Reidel, 415–41.

Partee, B. (1975). Deletion and variable binding. In E. Keenan (ed.), *Formal semantics of natural languages*. Cambridge: Cambridge University Press, 16–34.

Partee, B. (1989). Binding implicit variables in quantified contexts. *Papers of the Chicago Linguistic Society*, 25.

Peacocke, C. (1975). Proper names, reference, and rigid designation. In S. Blackburn (ed.), *Meaning, reference, and necessity*. Cambridge: Cambridge University Press, 109–32.

Peacocke, C. (1992). *A study of concepts*. Cambridge, Mass.: MIT Press.

Perry, J. (1979). The problem of the essential indexical. *Noûs*, 13, 3–21.

Perry, J. (2001). *Reference and reflexivity*. Stanford: CSLI Publications.

Perry, J. (2003). Predelli's threatening note: contexts, utterances, and tokens in the philosophy of language. *Pragmatics*, 35, 373–87.

Pessin, A. and Goldberg, S. (eds.) (1996). *The twin earth chronicles: Twenty years of reflection on Hilary Putnam's "The meaning of 'meaning.'"* Armonk and London: M.E. Sharpe, Inc.

Pica, P. (1991). On the interaction between antecedent-government and binding: The case of long-distance reflexivization. In J. Koster, J. Reuland, and E. Reuland (eds.), *Long-distance anaphora*. Cambridge: Cambridge University Press, 119–35.

Pietrosky, P. (1992). Intentionality and teleological error. *Pacific Philosophical Quarterly*, 73, 267–82.

Plantinga, A. (1978). The Boethian compromise. *American Philosophical Quarterly*, 15, 129–38.

Postal, P. (1966). On so-called pronouns in English. In F. Dineen (ed.), *Report on the seventeenth annual round table meeting in Washington on linguistics and language studies*. Washington, D.C.: Georgetown University Press, 177–206.

Predelli, S. (1998a). Utterance, interpretation and the logic of indexicals. *Mind and Language*, 13, 400–14.

Predelli, S. (1998b). I am not here now. *Analysis*, 58, 107–15.

Price, A. (1986). Doubts about projectivism. *Philosophy*, 61, 215–28.

Price, C. (2001). *Functions in mind: A theory of intentional content*. Oxford: Clarendon Press.

Price, H. (1994). Semantic minimalism and the Frege point. In S. Tzohadzidis (ed.), *Foundations of speech act theory*. London: Routledge, 132–55.

Prinz, J. (2002). *Furnishing the mind: Concepts and their perceptual basis*. Cambridge, Mass.: Bradford, MIT.

Prior, A.N. (1957). *Time and modality*. Oxford: Clarendon Press.

Prior, A.N. (1967). *Past, present and future*. Oxford: Clarendon Press.

Putnam, H. (1971). Is semantics possible? In H. E. Kiefer and M. K. Munitz (eds.), *Language, belief, and metaphysics*. Albany: State University of New York Press, 50–63.

Putnam, H. (1973). Meaning and reference. *Journal of Philosophy*, 70, 699–711.

Putnam, H. (1975). The meaning of "meaning." In *Mind, language and reality: Philosophical papers*, vol. 2. Cambridge: Cambridge University Press, 215–71. Also in K. Gunderson (ed.), *Minnesota studies in the philosophy of science*, vol. 8: *Language mind and knowledge*. Minneapolis: University of Minnesota Press, 131–93.

Putnam, H. (1992). *Renewing philosophy*. Cambridge, Mass.: Harvard University Press.

Putnam, H. (1996). Introduction. In A. Pessin and S. Goldberg (eds.), *The twin earth chronicles: Twenty years of reflection on Hilary Putnam's "The meaning of 'meaning.' "* Armonk and London: M.E. Sharpe, Inc., xv–xii.

Quine, W.V.O. (1940). *Mathematical logic*. Cambridge, Mass.: Harvard University Press.

Quine, W.V.O. (1943). Notes on existence and necessity. *Journal of Philosophy*, 40, 113–27.

Quine, W.V.O. (1947). On the problem of interpreting modal logic. *Journal of Symbolic Logic*, 12, 43–8.

Quine, W.V.O. (1951). Two dogmas of empiricism. *Philosophical Review*, 60, 20–43. Commonly cited is the 1953 reprint in *From a logical point of view*. Cambridge, Mass.: Harvard University Press, 20–46.

Quine, W.V.O. (1953). *From a logical point of view*. Cambridge, Mass.: Harvard University Press.

Quine, W.V.O. (1960). *Word and object*. Cambridge, Mass.: MIT Press.

Quine, W.V.O. (1962). Paradox. *Scientific American*, 206, 4, 84–96. Reprinted as The ways of paradox. In *The ways of paradox and other essays*. Cambridge, Mass.: Harvard University Press, 3–20. (Cited from second edition.)

Quine, W.V.O. (1969). *Ontological relativity and other essays*. New York: Columbia University Press.

Quine, W.V.O. (1970). On the reasons for the indeterminacy of translation. *Journal of Philosophy*, 67, 178–83.

Quine, W. V. O. (1978). A postscript on metaphor, *Critical Inquiry*, 5, 161–2.

Quine, W.V.O. (1981). *Theories and things*. Cambridge, Mass.: Harvard University Press.

Quine, W.V.O. (1986). *Philosophy of logic*. Cambridge, Mass., London: Harvard University Press. (Cited from second edition).

Quine, W.V.O. (1990). *Pursuit of truth*. Cambridge, Mass.: Harvard University Press.

Quine, W.V.O. (1991). Two dogmas in retrospect. In R. Creath (ed.), *Dear Carnap, dear Van: The Quine Carnap correspondence and related work*. Berkeley, Calif.: University of California Press.

Quine, W.V.O. (1998). Reply to Roger F. Gibson, Jr. In L.E. Hahn and P.A. Schilpp (eds.), *Library of living philosophers*, vol. 18: *The philosophy of W.V. Quine*. Carbondale: Southern Illinois University, 684–5.

Radford, A. (1997). *Syntactic theory and the structure of English*. Cambridge: Cambridge University Press.

Ramsey, F.P. (1931). General propositions and causality. In R.B. Braithwaite (ed.), *The foundations of mathematics*. London: Routledge & Kegan Paul, 237–55.

Ramsey, F.P. (1931). Truth and probability. *The foundations of mathematics and other logical essays*. London: Routledge & Kegan Paul.

Recanati, F. (1986). Contextual dependence and definite descriptions. *Proceedings of the Aristotelean Society*, 87, 57–73.

Recanati, F. (1987). On defining communicative intentions. *Mind and Language*, 1, 213–42.

Recanati, F. (1989). The pragmatics of what is said. *Mind and Language*, 4, 295–329.

Recanati, F. (1993). *Direct reference*. Cambridge: Basil Blackwell.

Recanati, F. (1995). The alleged priority of literal interpretation. *Cognitive Science*, 19, 207–32.

Recanati, F. (2000). *Oratio obliqua, oratio recta*. Cambridge, Mass.: MIT Press.

Recanati, F. (2001). What is said. *Synthese*, 125, 62–79.

Recanati, F. (2004). *Literal meaning*. Cambridge: Cambridge University Press.

Reddy, M. (1969). A semantic approach to metaphor. *Papers from the Fifth Regional Meeting of the Chicago Linguistics Society*. Chicago: University of Chicago, Linguistics Dept., 240–51.

Reichenbach, H. (1947). *Elements of symbolic logic*. London: Macmillan.

Reichenbach, H. (1947). Token-reflexive words. *Elements of symbolic logic*. New York: Free Press.

Reimer, M. (1992). Incomplete descriptions. *Erkenntnis*, 37, 347–63.

Reimer, M. (1998a). Quantification and context. *Linguistics and Philosophy*, 21, 95–115.

Reimer, M. (1998b). Donnellan's distinction/Kripke's test. *Analysis*, 58, 89–100.

Reimer, M. (2001). Davidson on metaphor. In P.A. French and H.K. Wettstein (eds.), *Midwest studies in philosophy*, vol. 25: *Figurative language*. Boston, Mass. and Oxford, UK: Blackwell, 142–55.

Reinhart, T. (1970). On understanding poetic metaphor. *Poetics*, 5, 383–402.

Reinhart, T. and Reuland, E. (1993). Reflexivity. *Linguistic Inquiry*, 24, 657–720.

Reinhart, T. (1976). The syntactic domain of anaphora. Ph.D. dissertation: MIT.

Reinhart, T. (1978). Syntactic domains for semantic rules. In F. Guenthner and S.J. Schmidt (eds.), *Formal semantics and pragmatics for natural languages*. Dordrecht: Reidel, 107–30.

Reinhart, T. (1983). *Anaphora and semantic interpretation*. London: Croom Helm.

Reinhart, T. (2000). Strategies of anaphora resolution. In H. Bennis et al. (eds.), *Interface strategies*. Amsterdam: Royal Academy of Arts and Sciences, 295–325.

Reuland, E. and Sigurjónsdóttir, S. (1997). Long distance binding in Icelandic: Syntax or discourse. In H.J. Bennis, P. Pica, and J. Rooryck (eds.), *Atomism and binding*. Dordrecht: Foris, 323–41.

Reuland, E. (2001a). Anaphors, logophors and binding. In P. Cole, G. Hermon, and C.-T. J. Huang (eds.), *Syntax and semantics*, vol. 33: *Long-distance reflexives*. San Diego, Calif.: Academic Press, 343–70.

Reuland, E. (2001b). Primitives of binding. *Linguistic Inquiry*, 32, 439–92.

Richard, M. (1983). Direct reference and ascriptions of belief. *Journal of Philosophical Logic*, 12, 425–52.

Richard, M. (1990). *Propositional attitudes*. Cambridge: Cambridge University Press.

Richard, M. (1993). Attitudes in context. *Linguistics and Philosophy*, 16, 123–48.

Richard, M. (1995). Defective contexts, accommodation, and normalization. *Canadian Journal of Philosophy*, 25, 551–70.

Richard, M. (1997). Propositional quantification. In J. Copeland (ed.), *Logic and reality.* Oxford: Oxford University Press, 437–60.

Richard, M. (1998). Semantic theory and indirect speech. *Mind and Language*, 13, 605–16.

Richard, M. (2000). Semantic pretense. In A. Everett and T. Hofweber (eds.), *Empty names, fiction, and the puzzles of non-existence*. Stanford: CSLI Publications, 205–32.

Richard, M. (2001). Seeing a centaur, adoring Adonis: Intensional transitives and empty terms. In P.A. French and H.K. Wettstein (eds.), *Midwest studies in philosophy*, vol.25: *Figurative language*. Boston, Mass. and Oxford, UK: Blackwell, 103–27.

Richard, M. (2005). Meaning and propositional attitudes. *Philosophical Studies*, 126, 1–27.

Richards, B. (1984). On interpreting pronouns. *Linguistics and Philosophy*, 7, 287–324.

Rorty, R. (1987). Unfamiliar noises I: Hesse and Davidson on metaphor. *Proceedings of the Aristotelian Society*, supplementary volume, 61, 283–96.

Rosen, G. (1990). Modal fictionalism. *Mind*, 99, 327–54.

Ross, J.R. (1967). Constraints on variables in syntax. Ph.D. dissertation: MIT.

Rundle, B. (1965). Modality and quantification. In R.J. Butler (ed.), *Analytical philosophy*, second series. Oxford: Blackwell, 27–39.

Russell, B. (1903). *The principles of mathematics*. London: Allen and Unwin.

Russell, B. [1904] (1980). Letter to Frege. In G. Frege, *Philosophical and mathematical correspondence*. Chicago: University of Chicago Press, 166–70.

Russell, B. (1905). On denoting, *Mind*, 14, 479–93.

Russell, B. (1911). Knowledge by acquaintance and knowledge by description. *Proceedings of the Aristotelean Society*. Reprinted in his *Mysticism and logic*. London: George Allen & Unwin.

Russell, B. (1912). *The problems of philosophy*. Oxford: Oxford University Press.

Russell, B. (1919). *Introduction to mathematical philosophy*. London: George Allen & Unwin.

Russell, B. (1957). Mr. Strawson on referring. *Mind*, 66, 385–9.

Russell, B. (1985). *The philosophy of logical atomism*. LaSalle, Ill.: Open Court.

Russell, B. (1989). *The analysis of mind*. London and New York: Routledge.

Ryle, G. (1950). "If," "so" and "because." In M. Black (ed.), *Philosophical Analysis*. Englewood Cliffs: Prentice-Hall.

Sadock, J. M. (1993). Figurative speech and linguistics. In A. Ortony (ed.), *Metaphor and thought*. Second edition. Cambridge: Cambridge University Press, 42–57.

Sag, I. (1976). Deletion and logical form. Ph.D. dissertation: MIT.

Sainsbury, R.M. (1979). *Russell*. London: Routledge & Kegan Paul.

Sainsbury, R.M. (2004). Referring descriptions. In A. Bezuidenhout and M. Reimer (eds.), *Descriptions and beyond*. Oxford: Clarendon Press, 369–89.

Salmon, N. (1981). *Reference and essence*. Princeton: Princeton University Press.

Salmon, N. (1982). Assertion and incomplete descriptions. *Philosophical Studies*, 42, 37–45.

Salmon, N. (1986). *Frege's puzzle*. Cambridge, Mass.: MIT Press.

Salmon, N. (1986). Reflexivity. *Notre Dame Journal of Formal Logic*, 27, 401–29.

Salmon, N. (1992). Reflections of reflexivity. *Linguistics and Philosophy*, 15, 53–63.

Salmon, N. (1998). Nonexistence. *Noûs*, 32, 277–319.

Sanford, D. H. (1989). *If p, then q: Conditionals and the foundations of reasoning*. London: Routledge.

Scheffler, I. (1979). *Beyond the letter*. London: Routledge & Kegan Paul.

Scheindlin, R. (1986). Trans. *Wine, women, and death: Medieval Hebrew poems on the good life*. Philadelphia: Jewish Publication Society.

Schelling, T. (1960). *The strategy of conflict*. Oxford: Oxford University Press.

Schiffer, S. (1972). *Meaning*. Oxford: Oxford University Press.

Schiffer, S. (1987). *Remnants of meaning*. Cambridge, Mass.: MIT Press.

Schiffer, S. (1992). Belief ascription. *Journal of Philosophy*, 89, 499–521.

Schiffer, S. (1993). Actual-language relations. In J.E. Tomberlin (ed.), *Philosophical perspectives*, vol. 7: *Language and logic*. Atascadero, Calif.: Ridgeview Publishing Company, 231–58.

Schiffer, S. (1995). Descriptions, indexicals, and belief reports: Some dilemmas but not the ones you expect. *Mind*, 104, 107–31.

Schiffer, S. (1995–6). Contextualist solutions to skepticism. *Proceedings of the Aristotelian Society*, 317–33.

Schiffer, S. (1998). Two issues of vagueness. *The Monist*, 81, 193–214.

Schiffer, S. (2000). Vagueness and partial belief. *Philosophical Issues*, 10, 220–57.

Schiffer, S. (2003). *The things we mean*. Oxford: Oxford University Press.

Schiffer, S. (2005), Russell's theory of descriptions. *Mind*. (Centenary issue on *On denoting*, S. Neale (ed.), forthcoming.)

Schlick, M. (1959). Positivism and realism. In A.J. Ayer (ed.), *Logical positivism*. Glencoe, Ill.: Free Press.

Schueler, G. (1988). Modus ponens and moral realism. *Ethics*, 98, 492–500.

Schwartz, S. (1978). Putnam on artifacts. *Philosophical Review*, 87, 566–74. Reprinted in Pessin and Goldberg 1996: 81–8.

Schwartz, S. (1980). Formal semantics and natural kind terms. *Philosophical Studies*, 38, 189–98.

Schwartz, S. (ed.). (1977). *Naming, necessity, and natural kinds*. Ithaca: Cornell University Press.

Schwartz, S. (2002). Kinds, general terms, and rigidity: A reply to LaPorte. *Philosophical Studies*, 109, 265–77.

Scott, D. (1967). Existence and description in formal logic. In R. Schoenman (ed.), *Bertrand Russell: Philosopher of the century*. London: Allen & Unwin, 181–200.

Searle, J. (1958). Proper names. *Mind*, 67, 166–73.

Searle, J. (1962). Meaning and speech acts. *Philosophical Review*, 71, 423–32.

Searle, J. (1968). Austin on locutionary and illocutionary acts. *Philosophical Review*, 77, 405–24.

Searle, J. (1969). *Speech acts: An essay in the philosophy of language*. Cambridge: Cambridge University Press.

Searle, J. (1975). Indirect speech acts. In P. Cole and J. Morgan (eds.), *Syntax and semantics*, vol. 3. New York: Academic Press, 59–82.

Searle, J. (1978). Literal Meaning. *Erkenntnis*, 13, 207–24.

Searle, J. (1979). Referential and attributive. In *Expression and meaning*. Cambridge: Cambridge University Press, 137–61.

Searle, J. (1989). How performatives work. *Linguistics and Philosophy*, 15, 535–58.

Searle, J. (1993). Metaphor. In A. Ortony (ed.), *Metaphor and thought*. Second edition. Cambridge: Cambridge University Press, 83–111.

Searle, J. (1996). From intentionality: Are meanings in the head? In A. Pessin and S. Goldberg 1996: 89–97.

Segal, G. (2000). *A slim book about narrow content*. Cambridge, Mass.: MIT Press.

Sellars, W. (1954a). Presupposing. *Philosophical Review*, 63, 197–215.

Sellars, W. (1954b). Some reflections on language games. *Philosophy of Science*, 21, 204–28.

Sellars, W. (1969). Language as thought and as communication. *Philosophy and Phenomenological Research*, 29, 506–27.

Sennet, A. (2002). An ambiguity test for definite descriptions. *Philosophical Studies*, 111, 81–95.

Sharvy, R. (1980). A more general theory of definite descriptions. *Philosophical Review*, 89, 607–23.

Sider, E. (1995). Three problems for Richard's theory of belief ascription. *Canadian Journal of Philosophy*, 25, 487–513.

Sigursson, H.A. (1990). Long distance reflexives and moods in Icelandic. In J. Maling and A. Zaenen (eds.), *Modern Icelandic syntax*. New York: Academic Press, 309–46.

Sinnott-Armstrong, W. (1993). Some problems for Gibbard's norm expressivism. *Philosophical Studies*, 69, 297–313.

Sinnott-Armstrong, W. (2000). Expressivism and embedding. *Philosophy and Phenomenological Research*, 63, 677–93.

Smiley, T.J. (1981). The theory of descriptions. *Proceedings of the British Academy*, 67, 331–7.

Smith, M. (1987). The Humean theory of motivation. *Mind*, 96, 36–61.

Smith, M. (1994a). Why expressivists about value should love minimalism about truth. *Analysis*, 54, 1–12.

Smith, M. (1994b). Minimalism, truth-aptitude, and belief. *Analysis*, 54, 21–6.

Smith, M. (2002). Which passions rule? *Philosophy and phenomenological research*, 65, 157–63.

Smith, M. and Stoljar, D. (2003). Is there a Lockean argument against expressivism? *Analysis* 65, 76–85.

Smith, Q. (1989). The multiple uses of indexicals. *Synthese*, 78, 167–91.

Smith. N.V. (1999). *Chomsky: Ideas and ideals*. Cambridge: Cambridge University Press.

Smullyan, A. (1947). Review of Quine's the problem of interpreting modal logic. *Journal of Symbolic Logic*, 12, 139–41.

Smullyan, A. (1948). Modality and description. *Journal of Symbolic Logic*, 13, 483–545.

Soames, S. (1976). A critical examination of Frege's theory of presupposition and contemporary alternatives. Ph.D. thesis: MIT, Dept. of Linguistics and Philosophy.

Soames, S. (1986). Incomplete definite descriptions. *Notre Dame Journal of Fomal Logic*, 27, 349–75.

Soames, S. (1987). Direct reference, propositional attitudes, and semantic content. *Philosophical Topics*, 15, 47–87.

Soames, S. (1989a). Semantics and semantic competence. In J. Tomberlin (ed.) *Philosophical perspectives*, vol. 3: *Philosophy of mind and action theory*. Altascadero, Calif.: Ridgeview Publishing Company, 575–96.

Soames, S. (1989b). Review of Gareth Evans: *Collected papers*, *Journal of Philosophy*, 89, 141–56.

Soames, S. (1990). Pronouns and propositional attitudes. *Proceedings of the Aristotelian Society*, 191–212.

Soames, S. (1994). Attitudes and anaphora. *Philosophical Perspectives*, 9, 251–72.

Soames, S. (1995). Beyond singular propositions? *Canadian Journal of Philosophy*, 25, 515–49.

Soames, S. (2002). *Beyond rigidity: The unfinished. agenda of naming and necessity.* Oxford University Press.

Soames, S. (2005). Naming and asserting. In Z. Szabo (ed.), *Semantics versus pragmatics.* Oxford: Clarendon Press, 356–82.

Sorensen, R. (1988). *Blindspots.* Oxford: Oxford University Press.

Sperber, D. and Wilson, D. (1981). Irony and the use-mention distinction. In P. Cole (ed.), *Radical pragmatics.* New York: Academic Press, 295–318.

Sperber, D. and Wilson, D. (1986). *Relevance: Communication and cognition.* Cambridge, Mass.: Harvard University Press.

Sperber, D. and Wilson, D. (1985–6). Loose talk. *Proceedings of the Aristotelian Society,* 86, 153–71.

Sperber, D. and Wilson, D. (1995). *Relevance: Communication and cognition.* Second edition. Oxford: Basil Blackwell.

Stalnaker, R. (1968). A theory of conditionals. In N. Rescher (ed.), *Studies in logical theory.* Oxford, Basil Blackwell, 98–112.

Stalnaker, R. (1972). Pragmatics. In D. Davidson and G. Harman (eds.), *Semantics of natural language.* Dordrecht: Reidel, 380–97.

Stalnaker, R. (1973). Presuppositions. *Journal of Philosophical Logic,* 2, 447–57.

Stalnaker, R. (1974). Pragmatic presuppositions. In M. Munitz and P. Unger (eds.), *Semantics and Philosophy.* New York: New York University Press, 197–213.

Stalnaker, R. (1984). *Inquiry.* Cambridge, Mass.: MIT Press, Bradford Books.

Stalnaker, R. (1999). *Context and content.* Oxford: Oxford University Press.

Stampe, D. (1977). Toward a causal theory of linguistic representation. In P.A French, T.E. Uehling, and H.K. Wettstein (eds.), *Midwest studies in philosophy,* vol. 2. Minneapolis: University of Minnesota Press, 42–63. Reprinted in P.A. French, T.E. Uehling, and H.K. Wettstein (eds.), *Contemporary perspectives in the philosophy of language.* Minneapolis: University of Minnesota Press (1979), 81–102.

Stanford, P.K. and Kitcher, P. (2000). Refining the causal theory of reference for natural kind terms. *Philosophical Studies,* 97, 99–129.

Stanley, J. (1997). Names and rigid designation. In C. Wright and B. Hale (eds.), *A companion to the philosophy of language.* Oxford: Blackwell.

Stanley, J. (2000). Context and logical form. *Linguistics and Philosophy,* 23, 391–434.

Stanley, J. and Szabo, Z. (2000). On quantifier domain restriction. *Mind and Language,* 15, 219–61.

Stechow, A. von (1983). Comparing semantic theories of comparison. *Journal of Semantics,* 3, 1–77.

Steedman, M. (1988). Combinators and grammars. In R.T. Oehrle, E.W. Bach, and D. Wheeler (eds.), *Categorial grammar and natural language structures.* Dordrecht: Reidel, 417–42.

Steinberg D. and Jakobovits, L. (1971). *Semantics: An interdisciplinary reader in philosophy, linguistics and psychology.* Cambridge: Cambridge University Press.

Sterelny, K. (1990). *The representational theory of mind: An introduction.* Oxford: Blackwell.

Stern, J. (1983). Metaphor and grammatical deviance. *Noûs,* 17, 577–99.

Stern, J. (1997). Metaphors in pictures. *Philosophical Topics,* 25, 255–94.

Stern, J. (1998). Metaphor and philosophy of language. In M. Kelly (ed.), *Oxford encyclopedia of aesthetics,* 4 vols. Oxford: Oxford University Press, vol. 3, 212–15.

Stern, J. (2000). *Metaphor in context.* Cambridge, Mass.: MIT Press.

Stevenson, C. (1963). *Facts and values*. New Haven: Yale University Press.

Stockwell, R., Schachter, P., and Partee, B. (1973). *The major syntactic structures of English*. New York: Holt, Rinehart & Winston.

Stoljar, D. (1993). Emotivism and truth conditions. *Philosophical Studies*, 70, 81–101.

Stratton-Lake, P. (2000). Expressivism, description and normativity. *Res Publica*, 6, 117–25.

Strawson, P. (1950). On referring, *Mind*, 59, 320–34.

Strawson, P. (1952). *Introduction to logical theory*. London: Methuen.

Strawson, P. (1954). Reply to Mr. Sellars. *Philosophical Review*, 63, 216–31.

Strawson, P. (1964). Identifying reference and truth-values. *Theoria*, 30, 96–118.

Strawson, P. (1964). Intention and convention in speech acts. *Philosophical Review*, 73, 439–60.

Strawson, P. (1972). *Subject and predicate in logic and grammar*. London: Methuen.

Szabo, Z. (2000). Descriptions and uniqueness. *Philosophical Studies*, 101, 29–57.

Szabolcsi, A. (1987). Bound variables in syntax (are there any?). *Proceedings of the 6th Amsterdam Colloquium*. University of Amsterdam, Institute for Language, Logic and Information, 331–51.

Szabolcsi, A. (1994). The noun phrase. In F. Kiefer and K. Kiss (eds.), *Syntax and semantics*, vol. 27: *The syntactic structure of Hungarian*. New York: Academic Press, 179–275.

Szabolcsi, A. (2003). Binding on the fly: Cross-sentential anaphora in variable-free semantics. In G.-J.M. Kruijff and R.T. Oehrle (eds.), *Resource-sensitivity in binding and anaphora*. Dordrecht: Kluwer, 215–29.

Tarski, A. (1935). Der Wahrheitsbegriff in den formalisierten Sprachen. *Studia Philosophica*, 1, 261–405. Translated as The concept of truth in formalized languages by J. Woodger, in Tarski 1956 and 1983: 152–278.

Tarski, A. (1936). Grundlegung der wissenschaftlichen Semantik. *Actes du Congrès International de Philosophie Scientifique*, 3, 1–8. Translated as The establishment of scientific semantics by J. Woodger, in Tarski 1956 and 1983: 401–8.

Tarski, A. (1944). The semantic conception of truth and the foundations of semantics. *Philosophy and Phenomenological Research*, 4, 341–75.

Tarski, A. (1956). *Logic, semantics, metamathematics*. Trans. J. Woodger. Oxford: Oxford University Press.

Tarski, A. (1969). Truth and proof. *Scientific American*, 220, 6, 63–77.

Tarski, A. (1983). *Logic, semantics, metamathematics*. Second edition. Trans. J. Woodger. J. Corcoran (ed.). Indianapolis: Hackett.

Taylor, B. (1977). Tense and continuity. *Linguistics and Philosophy*, 1, 199–220.

Thau, M. (2002). *Consciousness and cognition*. Oxford: Oxford University Press.

Thomason, R. (1990). Accommodation, meaning, and implicature: Interdisciplinary foundations for pragmatics. In P. Cohen, J. Morgan, and M. Pollack (eds.), *Intentions in communication*. Cambridge, Mass.: MIT Press, 325–63.

Thompson, A. and Thompson, J. (1987). *Shakespeare, meaning, and metaphor*. Iowa City: University of Iowa Press.

Tirrell, L. (1989). Extending: The structure of metaphor. *Noûs*, 23, 17–34.

Tirrell, L. (1991). Reductive and nonreductive simile theories of metaphor. *Journal of Philosophy*, 88, 337–58.

Travis, C. (2000). *Unshadowed thought: Representation in thought and language*. Cambridge, Mass.: Harvard University Press.

Tversky, A. (1977). Features of similarity. *Psychological Review*, 84, 322–52.

Unwin, N. (1999). Quasi-realism and the Frege–Geach problem. *Philosophical Quarterly*, 49, 337–52.

Unwin, N. (2001). Norms and negation. *Philosophical Quarterly*, 51, 60–75.

Van Fraassen, B. (1966). Singular terms, truth-value gaps, and free logic. *Journal of Philosophy*, 63, 481–95.

Van Heijenoort, J. (1967). *From Frege to Gödel*. Cambridge, Mass.: Harvard University Press.

Van Roojen, M. (1996). Expressivism and irrationality. *Philosophical Review*, 105, 311–35.

Van Rooy, J. (2001). Exhaustivity in dynamic semantics: Referential and descriptive pronouns. *Linguistics and Philosophy*, 24, 621–57.

Von Fintel, K. (2004). Would you believe it? The king of France is back! (Presupposition and truth-value intuitions). In A. Bezuidenhout and M. Reimer (eds.), *Descriptions and beyond*. Oxford: Clarendon Press, 315–41.

Walton, K. (1993). Metaphor and prop-oriented make-belief, *European Journal of Philosophy*, 1, 39–57.

Ward, B. (2002). Humeanism without Humean supervenience: A projectivist account of laws and possibilities. *Philosophical Studies*, 107, 191–218.

Wasow, T. (1972). Anaphoric relations in English. Ph.D. dissertation: MIT.

Wedgwood, R. (1997). Non-cognitivism, truth and logic. *Philosophical Studies*, 86, 73–91.

Wedgwood, R. (2001). Conceptual role semantics for moral terms. *Philosophical Review*, 110, 1–30.

Wettstein, H.K. (1981). Demonstrative reference and definite descriptions. *Philosophical Studies*, 40, 241–57.

Wettstein, H.K. (1991). *Has semantics rested on a mistake?* Stanford: Stanford University Press.

White, R. (1996). *The structure of metaphor: The way the language of metaphor works*. Oxford: Basil Blackwell.

White, R. (2001). Literal meaning and "figurative meaning." *Theoria*, 67, 24–59.

White, S. (1991). Narrow content and narrow interpretation. In S. White, *The unity of the self*. Cambridge, Mass.: Bradford/MIT Press.

Whitehead, A. and Russell, B. (1927). *Principia mathematica*. Cambridge: Cambridge University Press. (Cited from second edition.)

Wiggins, D. (1965). Identity statements. In R.J. Butler (ed.), *Analytical philosophy*. Oxford: Basil Blackwell. (Cited from second edition.)

Wiggins, D. (1976). Identity, necessity, and physicalism. In S. Körner (ed.), *Philosophy of logic*. Berkeley, Calif.: University of California Press, 159–82.

Wiggins, D. (1997). Languages as social objects. *Philosophy*, 72, 499–524.

Wilkerson, T. (1995). *Natural kinds*. Brookfield: Ashgate Publishing Company.

Wilkerson, T. (1998). Recent work on natural kinds. *Philosophical Books*, 39, 225–33.

Williams, E. (1977). Discourse and logical form. *Linguistic Inquiry*, 8, 101–39.

Williams, E. (1983). Semantic vs. syntactic categories. *Linguistics and Philosophy*, 6, 423–46.

Williamson, T. (1994). *Vagueness*. London, New York: Routledge.

Wilson, G. (1978). On definite and indefinite descriptions. *Philosophical Review*, 87, 48–76.

Wilson, G. (1991). Reference and pronominal descriptions. *Journal of Philosophy*, 88, 359–87.

Wilson, N. (1959). Substances without substrata. *Review of Metaphysics*, 12, 521–39.

Wittgenstein, L. (1921). *Tractatus logico-philosophicus.* Trans. D.F. Pears and B.F. McGinness. London, Routledge & Kegan Paul.

Wittgenstein, L. (1953). *Philosophical investigations.* Oxford: Blackwell.

Wollheim, R. (1993). Metaphor and Painting. In F.R. Ankersmit and J.J. A. Mooij (eds.), *Knowledge and language,* vol. 3: *Metaphor and knowledge.* Dordrecht, Boston, and London: Kluwer Academic Publishers, 113–25.

Wright, C. (1986). *Realism, meaning, and truth.* Oxford: Blackwell.

Wright, C. (1987). Theories of meaning and speakers' knowledge. In *Realism, meaning and truth.* Oxford: Blackwell, 204–38. (Cited from second edition.)

Wright, C. (1988). Moral values, projection, and secondary qualities. *Proceedings of the Aristotelian Society,* supplementary volume, 62, 1–26.

Wright, C. (1992). *Truth and objectivity.* Cambridge, Mass.: Harvard University Press.

Wright, C. (1997). The indeterminacy of translation. In B. Hale and C. Wright (eds.), *A companion to the philosophy of language.* Oxford: Blackwell.

Wright, C. (2001a). *Rails to infinity.* Cambridge, Mass.: Harvard University Press.

Wright, C. (2001b). On being in a quandary: Relativism, vagueness, logical revisionism. *Mind,* 110, 45–98.

Wright, L. (1976). *Teleological explanations.* Berkeley: University of California Press.

Zalabardo, J. (1997). Kripke's normativity argument. Reprinted in A. Miller and C. Wright (eds.), *Rule-following and meaning.* Chesham: Acumen.

Zalta, E. (1983). *Abstract objects: An introduction to axiomatic metaphysics.* Dordrecht: D. Reidel.

Zalta, E. (1988). *Intensional logic and the metaphysics of intensionality.* Cambridge, Mass.: MIT Press.

Zangwill, N. (1992a). Quietism. *Midwest Studies in Philosophy,* 17, 160–76.

Zangwill, N. (1992b). Moral modus ponens. *Ratio,* 5, 177–193.

Zangwill, N. (1993). Quasi-realist explanation. *Synthèse,* 97, 287–96.

Zvolensky, Z. (1997). Definite descriptions: What Frege got right and Russell didn't. *Aporia,* 7, 1–16.

Index